ETHICAL ISSUES IN BUSINESS

ETHICAL ISSUES

INQUIRIES, CASES, AND READINGS

edited by Peg Tittle

IN BUSINESS

SECOND EDITION

broadview press

BROADVIEW PRESS – www.broadviewpress.com
Peterborough, Ontario, Canada

Founded in 1985, Broadview Press remains a wholly independent publishing house. Broadview's focus is on academic publishing; our titles are accessible to university and college students as well as scholars and general readers. With over 600 titles in print, Broadview has become a leading international publisher in the humanities, with world-wide distribution. Broadview is committed to environmentally responsible publishing and fair business practices.

The interior of this book is printed on 100% recycled paper.

© 2017 Peg Tittle

All rights reserved. No part of this book may be reproduced, kept in an information storage and retrieval system, or transmitted in any form or by any means, electronic or mechanical, including photocopying, recording, or otherwise, except as expressly permitted by the applicable copyright laws or through written permission from the publisher.

Library and Archives Canada Cataloguing in Publication

Ethical issues in business : inquiries, cases, and readings / edited by Peg Tittle.—Second edition.

Includes bibliographical references.
ISBN 978-1-55481-240-0 (paperback)

1. Business ethics. 2. Business ethics—Case studies. 3. Business ethics—Canada.
I. Tittle, Peg, 1957-, editor

HF5387.E78 2016   174'.4   C2016-907051-4

Broadview Press handles its own distribution in North America
PO Box 1243, Peterborough, Ontario K9J 7H5, Canada
555 Riverwalk Parkway, Tonawanda, NY 14150, USA
Tel: (705) 743-8990; Fax: (705) 743-8353
email: customerservice@broadviewpress.com

Distribution is handled by Eurospan Group in the UK, Europe, Central Asia, Middle East, Africa, India, Southeast Asia, Central America, South America, and the Caribbean. Distribution is handled by Footprint Books in Australia and New Zealand.

Broadview Press acknowledges the financial support of the Government of Canada through the Canada Book Fund for our publishing activities.

Copy-edited by Martin R. Boyne

Book design by Chris Rowat Design

PRINTED IN CANADA

Contents

Note to the Reader 9

PART I   Introduction to Ethics in Business 11
Making Ethical Decisions 11
The Role of Ethics in Business 13
A Few Words about Terminology 18
How to Think about Ethics 21
How to Discuss Ethics 29
Closing Comments 34

PART II   Introduction to Ethical Theory 39
Introductory Note 39
Egoism 40
Utilitarianism 42
Kantian Ethics 47
Virtue Ethics 48
Intuitionism 50
Rights Theories 51
Justice Theories 53
Religionism 55
Relativism 57
Closing Note 60

PART III Ethical Issues in Business 63
Introductory Note 63

CHAPTER ONE **Whistleblowing** 67
What to Do?—Rivertree's Grocery 67
Introduction 68
Whistle Blowers: Saints of Secular Culture *Colin Grant* 75
Whistleblowing and Employee Loyalty *Ronald Duska* 86
Case Study: Dr. Olivieri vs. Apotex 92

CHAPTER TWO **Advertising** 97
What to Do?—In-Your-Face Advertising, Inc. 97
Introduction 98
The Inconclusive Ethical Case against Manipulative Advertising *Michael J. Phillips* 107
It's All on Sale: Marketing Ethics and the Perpetually Fooled *Andy Wible* 130
Pop-Ups, Cookies, and Spam: Toward a Deeper Analysis of the Ethical Significance of Internet Marketing Practices *Daniel E. Palmer* 137
Case Study: Adbusters 149

CHAPTER THREE **Product Quality** 153
What to Do?—An Ungodly Insurance Policy 153
Introduction 154
Creative Destruction and Destructive Creations: Environmental Ethics and Planned Obsolescence *Joseph Guiltinan* 165
On the Ethics of the Use of Animals in Science *Dale Jamieson and Tom Regan* 177
Trans Fat Bans and Human Freedom *David Resnik* 186
Case Study: Personal Watercraft (PWCs) 196

CHAPTER FOUR **Employee Rights** 199
What to Do?—IT Tech and/or Hall Monitor? 199
Introduction 199
Affirmative Action and Employment Equity in Canada *Susan Dimock and Christopher Tucker* 226
Ethics and Genetics: Susceptibility Testing in the Workplace *Chris MacDonald and Bryn Williams-Jones* 243
Case Study: The Westray Mine Disaster 251

CONTENTS

CHAPTER FIVE	**Management, Corporate Governance, and CSR** 253
	What to Do?—Union's in the Air 253
	Introduction 254
	The Discourse of Control *Stephen Maguire* 279
	In Defense of the Right to Strike *Charlotte A.B. Yates* 286
	Why Corporations Should Not Abandon Social Responsibility *Moses L. Pava* 295
	Case Study: The Mountain Equipment Co-op 305
CHAPTER SIX	**International Business** 307
	What to Do?—The Processing Fee 307
	Introduction 307
	Ethics and Multinational Corporations vis–à–vis Developing Nations *James R. Simpson* 320
	Ethical Value-Added: Fair Trade and the Case of Café Femenino *J.J. McMurtry* 332
	Case Study: Scotiabank's Microfinance Services: A Good Thing? 360
CHAPTER SEVEN	**Profit and Capitalism** 363
	What to Do?—No Limits, Ltd. 363
	Introduction 364
	Economic Efficiency and the Quality of Life *Rockney Jacobsen* 378
	Capitalism and Its Regulation: A Dialogue on Business and Ethics *Martin Parker and Gordon Pearson* 389
	Case Study: Tembec: Losses to Profits to?? 403
CHAPTER EIGHT	**The Medical Business** 405
	What to Do?—The Fetal Tissue Transplant Business 405
	Introduction 406
	Ethics, Economics, and Public Financing of Health Care *Jeremiah Hurley* 412
	Ethics, Pricing and the Pharmaceutical Industry *Richard A. Spinello* 422
	Case Study: The St. Michael's-Wellesley Hospital Merger 434
CHAPTER NINE	**Information and Communications Technology (ICT) Issues** 437
	What to Do?—The IC 437
	Introduction 438
	Employer's Use of Social Networking Sites: A Socially Irresponsible Practice *Leigh A. Clark and Sherry J. Roberts* 445
	Online Multiplayer Games: A Virtual Space for Intellectual Property Debates? *Sara M. Grimes* 466
	Case Study: Canipre: Hero or Villain? 484

CHAPTER TEN **Business and Our Environment** 487
What to Do?—Canadian Natural Resources, Inc. 487
Introduction 488
Business Ethics and the International Trade in Hazardous Wastes   *Jang B. Singh and V.C. Lakhan* 513
If a Tree Falls…   *John Palmer, Eugene Tan, and Kent A. Peacock*   524
Ethics and Climate Change: An Introduction   *Stephen M. Gardiner*   531
Case Study: Neil Young's Tour   548

Part IV Institutionalizing Ethics 551

Introductory Note 551
Ethics Offices/Officers/Committees 551
Ethics Consultants 552
Ethics Programs 553
Codes of Ethics 554
Ethics Audits 556
Closing Note 557

Permissions Acknowledgements 559

Note to the Reader

I happened to read a comment expressing the view that most textbooks seem to be written for other professors rather than for students, and I suddenly realized why I had been procrastinating over the actual writing of this book. The thing is this: I love being in the classroom—I really enjoy talking to students, discussing stuff with them, getting into arguments with them. I can do the other—I can research and write a respectable academic essay that my peers, other professors, will consider publishable (or not)—but to be honest, I don't really like speaking in that rather formal, academic voice. So I decided to use my more informal, classroom voice for this book. Because this is, after all, a book *for students*, not a book for other professors.

But not *just* for students: my hope is that anyone in business who is new to philosophy will find this an exciting book, and that those in philosophy who don't know much about business will find something of value here as well.

A few bits of advice: do go through Part I all at once and do this before you do anything else. (No, actually, before you do anything else, figure out your answer to the question "Why should you be concerned about doing the right thing?" Consider that a prerequisite for the course.) *Don't* go through Part II all at once. It's heavy-going, and you don't need to know *all* the theory before you get into the issues. In fact, feel free to tread lightly the first time through this section, but then come back often as you work through the chapters and come across references to the theories. The chapters in Part III are meant to be done more or less in the order in which they're presented (there's some carefully planned, pedagogically minded progression there). As you read through the introductions, *do* take a look at the footnotes; they often add points or references that are well worth your attention!

At one point, I thought of including for each chapter an essay from an academic journal and an article from a business magazine (rather than, as it usually turned out, two essays from academic journals). However, the business magazine articles didn't seem rigorous enough: they seemed to start with assumptions that were not defended (but then that's why we call them assumptions, isn't it?), let alone identified. And they seemed more prescriptive ("Do this!") than analytic ("What if we do this?"). Even so, I urge you to check out the business magazines. See if you can identify the assumptions, then assess them, and figure out if the prescription (the code or best practice) being advocated in the article is soundly based on theory. If it is, great; follow that prescription! If it's not, figure out what the problem is and see if you can fix it with some modifications. The more of this book you read, the better equipped you'll be to do this.

A note of caution: Don't expect a singular view to be presented here—my intent is to make you aware of the possibilities, to get you to ask the right questions rather than to come up with the (single) right answer. Having said that, don't get discouraged and give up because of all the ifs, ands, and buts—this is complicated stuff, and getting to *better* answers (yes, some answers are better than others) is quite an achievement.

And one final note. Please take this text, this course (if you're taking one right now), and by extension all of your decisions, seriously. As I say later in the text, with great power comes great responsibility, and it should be clear to you even now that business does indeed have great power (consider, as just one bit of evidence, the voice given to business at current, and past, negotiations between governments regarding free-trade agreements).

PART I

INTRODUCTION TO ETHICS IN BUSINESS

Making Ethical Decisions

Suppose someone asks you to help them with their homework. Do you? What about helping with an assignment? What about an exam? Or a résumé? Okay now, how did you decide? That is—and this is **the** question of this whole book—*how do you decide whether something is right or wrong?*

Consider the following principles. Circle or check the ones that apply to you. Go ahead—this book is interactive!

1. If it feels right, I do it.
2. I follow my conscience.
3. I do what (my) God says is right.
4. If it's illegal, I don't do it.
5. If it's good for me, I do it.
6. If it's what I'd want others to do, I do it.
7. If someone, anyone, will get hurt, I don't do it.
8. If it's unfair, I don't do it.
9. It depends on the circumstances.
10. It depends on the consequences.
11. I follow a set of absolute values such as honesty, justice, and goodness.
12. I toss a coin.
13. I don't know, I just do it, okay?

Now consider the following comments and questions. (Don't put that pen down yet—get ready to talk back to me here!)

1. *If you follow your feelings....* So if in anger you feel like hitting someone, is it okay, morally acceptable, to do so?
2. *If you follow your conscience....* What exactly is your conscience? Is it just a collection of moral habits, "the way you were raised"? Is it just a more respectable, sort of religious, name for feelings? Is it something you're born with? (Is everyone born with one? Is it the same for everyone?) Can your conscience ever be wrong? How would you know?
3. *If you do what (your) God says is right....* Why your god and not someone else's? And how do you know that what your God says is right—does he or she talk to you? If you follow *The Holy Bible*, are you sure that what is in that book is God's word—every single (translated) word? Why are you so sure? What about contradictions ("Do not kill." But "Hey, Abraham...")? What about omissions? (I can't find a commandment about patenting DNA, for example.)
4. *If you do only what's legal....* So when the law changes, what was right yesterday is wrong today? Are there no bad laws? Does the law cover everything? (In Canada, it's not illegal to lie to your friend, so is it okay, is it right, to do so?) And anyway, why should you do what's legal? Why is it right to obey the law?
5. *If you do whatever's good for you....* No matter what the consequences are for everyone else? Okay, so where do you draw the line—with certain consequences and/or certain people? Why there?
6. *If you do to others what you'd like them to do to you....* What if you like pain?
7. *If you don't do something that will hurt someone....* No exceptions? What if they consented to that hurt? (Consider surgery and sports.) What if hurting one person will save a hundred? And how exactly do you define "hurt"?
8. *If you don't do something that's unfair....* How do you define "fair"? If fair is getting what one deserves, how do you determine what someone deserves? According to what they've earned? According to what they need?
9. *If it depends on the circumstances....* Exactly what aspects of the circumstances are relevant to whether something is the right thing to do? Is time of day relevant? Is who's involved relevant?
10. *If it depends on the consequences....* So the ends justify the means? Always? And what if you aren't sure about the consequences?
11. *If you follow a set of absolutes....* How did you come up with those absolutes? Why those and not others? And what do you do when they conflict (suppose you can't be both loyal and honest)? Which takes priority, and why?
12. *If you toss a coin....* Good luck! Or is there a higher power you're trusting with your decision?
13. *If you just do it...* kinda like Nike? With no reason whatsoever?

My guess (or maybe my hope) is that you found a lot of these questions not so easy to answer. And if your somewhat hostile response was "Look, everyone can sit here and ask 'what if' questions. I can ask 'what if' to everything, but what's the point?"—well, you wouldn't be the first student to respond that way. The point, the reason, for these "what if" questions is that they help us uncover (or construct, as the case may be) the foundations of our thought; they help us make distinctions—very important distinctions, in fact.

The thing is this: ethically speaking, most of us are quite undeveloped; we haven't updated our childhood. Most of our moral training stopped when we were somewhere around 13 or 14 years of age, but as adults we have to deal with a lot of ethical issues that our childhood morality simply can't handle very well. That primitive morality doesn't have much in the way of conceptual complexity and subtlety: it doesn't make the fine distinctions that are necessary; it's not as precise as it needs to be. For example, "Do what your parents tell you" is fine—until you realize that parents make mistakes, too. "Don't steal" is adequate as long as you're not starving. Even "Do unto others as you would have them do unto you" must eventually bite the dust: *you* may say "tell me the truth," but some people really may prefer not to know.

Just as someone who is educated about forestry can tell the difference between a sick, five-year-old white pine and a healthy, ten-year-old red pine (to me, they're all trees), and someone educated about colour can distinguish between magenta, scarlet, and burgundy (to you, they might all be red), someone educated about ethics will be able to distinguish between justified discrimination and unjustified discrimination or between morally acceptable profit and morally unacceptable profit. The educated person can make fine distinctions and use those distinctions to make decisions. To get to that point, we ask "what if" questions—relentlessly. There are several other questions we're relentless about asking as well, and I'll get to them later in this section, but first we have to discuss....

The Role of Ethics in Business

Some of you may be taking a business ethics course because it's mandatory, but you really don't see the need for it. After all, the whole point of business is to make a profit, and as long as you stay within the law, you won't end up doing anything really bad, so why worry about it?

First, consider the questions raised earlier in Item 4 ("do only what's legal"). Then consider this question: *is* the whole point of business to make a profit? What about non-profit businesses? And even those who think profit making *is* the main purpose of business (and there are some who don't—see Chapter Seven) usually attach a few strings: the activity has to be profitable, but it can't be illegal; it has to be profitable, but it also has to be fair; it has to be profitable, but it also has to be reasonably safe, or at least it can't kill (too many) people; and so on. So what ethical strings will you attach to your business or your employment with a business?

Some of you may recognize the importance of ethics for those in marketing or management, but say you're in accounting: there's nothing ethical about 2+2=4. Well true enough, but you *know* you do more than add and subtract numbers; you decide where to put those numbers, and when to put them there. And *that* can be a matter of ethics. But let's not just pick on accountants; I suggest that everyone in business—just like everyone in life—has to deal with decisions that involve ethics. Unfortunately, we often don't recognize the ethical element even when we trip over it; we make ethical decisions every day without even knowing it. Indeed, Carl Skoogland, at the time vice-president and ethics director at Texas Instruments, observed that "New hires have often stated that they couldn't see that their day-to-day work had *any* ethical content at all" (my emphasis, as reported by Dalla Costa, p. 95). And that's a two-part problem: one, unconscious "decisions" may well be worse than those we think about; two, if we don't even know we're doing something (let alone doing something badly), we won't recognize the need to learn how to do it better. I list a number of decisions below—which do you think involve ethics?

Management
1. What salary figures should we put into which places on the grid?
2. What benefit package should we offer to our employees?
3. What objectives should we put on the negotiating table?

Human Resources
4. Which applicant should we hire?
5. Should we offer a job to the spouse of our first choice as an added incentive?

Finance
6. What should our interest rate to creditors be?

Accounting
7. Should we take advantage of a particular tax shelter?
8. Should we adopt generally accepted accounting principles?

Operations
9. Where should we locate our next plant?
10. Is our predicted environmental impact acceptable?
11. What paper should we buy for photocopying?

Information Systems
12. Which e-mail messages should have a privacy screen and which should not?
13. Which company should we buy our software from?

Marketing
14. What content should go into our next advertising campaign?
15. Should we use emotional images to (try to) manipulate people?

Research and Development
16. Should we honour the company's trade secrets policy?
17. Should we use animals for our research?

Which of these are ethical questions? *All of them.* Consider the questions again, this time with a few more questions that expose *some* of the ethical issues, and *some* of the implicit assumptions involved:

1. *What salary figures should we put into which places on the grid? Should* there even *be* different wages for different positions? Why? Should people who have been with the company longer get paid more? Why? Should people doing the same job get paid the same, even if one person has special needs and requires more money than the other?
2. *What benefit package should we offer to our employees? Why* should a company *offer* a benefit plan to its employees? Why is employee health the company's responsibility? Should it offer such a plan only to its full-time employees? Is there something magical about the number 35 such that those who work 35 hours per week are entitled to medical and pension benefits, but those who work 34 or 24 or 14 hours per week are not?
3. *What objectives should we put on the negotiating table? Why* wouldn't you just put *all* your objectives on the table? Is it morally acceptable to bluff? Isn't that the same as lying? Do management–union negotiations have to be adversarial?
4. *Which applicant should we hire?* Should you consider race when you hire? Should you consider gender? Should you consider need? Should you consider only merit?
5. *Should we offer a job to the spouse of our first choice as an added incentive?* Isn't that unfair? Shouldn't the spouse have to apply, and compete, for the job? Even if s/he is well qualified, isn't s/he getting the job because of who s/he lives with? Or is the offer of a job to the candidate's spouse a justifiable enticement, no different from the offer of a company car?
6. *What should our interest rate to creditors be?* Should you accept the "going" market rate? Should the interest rate be the same for everyone? On what basis could you justify different interest rates? Is interest fair? (Why, as Michalos points out, do we call it "Third World debt" instead of "First World usury"?)
7. *Should we take advantage of a particular tax shelter?* Should tax shelters be used only because they're tax shelters? Or should the shelter just be a nice consequence to a choice motivated by other reasons?
8. *Should we adopt generally accepted accounting principles?* Are such principles sufficient to keep important stakeholders informed about the firm? What do you do if higher management requests a slight departure from accounting practices in order to exaggerate the actual performance of the company? What if they want you to hide certain damaging information by burying it in the financial statements? Is "creative accounting" really as harmless as it sounds?

9. *Where should we locate our next plant?* Should you set up your plant where it's most wanted by those living in the area or where it's cheapest? Why should you even set up another plant? (Is more/bigger always better?)
10. *Is our predicted environmental impact acceptable?* Is *any* environmental damage morally acceptable? Does the nature of the product or service matter?
11. *What paper should we buy for photocopying?* Should you buy the recycled stuff, even though it's more expensive? (Is it? What are you counting as expense: just the current dollar price?)
12. *Which e-mail messages should have a privacy screen and which should not?* Should supervisors be able to read any of their subordinates' e-mail messages? (Should there even be supervisors and subordinates?) Do employees have a right to any "personal" use of company-owned computers, printers, copiers, etc.?
13. *Which company should we buy our software from?* The one *not* exploiting its workers? And how do you tell if a company *is* exploiting its workers—ask the workers? Is that any of your business? (Get it? "Your *business*"?)
14. *What content should go into our next advertising campaign?* How do you determine what product information to withhold? Is it okay to advertise any product/service?
15. *Should we use emotional images to (try to) manipulate people?* Is it morally acceptable to manipulate people? Is it less acceptable if a business tries to do it than if it is done in other contexts?
16. *Should we honour the company's trade secrets policy?* Or should you share your knowledge with anyone who could benefit from it? And what if they (those with whom you shared your information) use what they have received from you to earn (more) profit rather than "just" to improve quality of life?
17. *Should we use animals for our research*? Does it depend on what you're researching? Does it depend on whether you hurt them?

Some of you might recognize the importance of ethics but think it's the responsibility of the executive directors or the Board—or the ethics officer; in any case, it probably won't be *your* responsibility (you figure you'll be happy just to climb the corporate ladder to an office with a window). There are two separate questions here: (1) *Is* ethics the responsibility of only the higher-ups? (2) *Should* it be?

I would say the answer to both questions is "no." Suppose you've got a run-of-the-mill factory job and you're required to provide a weekly urine sample to confirm that you're not pregnant because your work environment is hazardous to fetal development. That could be considered an unwarranted invasion of privacy (or it could be considered a warranted invasion—we're talking about the possibility of creating a severely "compromised" life); as such, it's an ethical matter that concerns *you*, and perhaps on that basis alone it's *your* responsibility to become involved. Or suppose you're the company's health officer, the one whose job it is to collect and analyze the samples. Are you prepared to agree to do such a thing (anything?) in return for a good (or maybe not so good) wage?

To ask the questions from the other side, does that arrangement make for the best business? Are employees who are coerced to act against their own ethical principles going to be good employees? Happy employees? Productive employees? Profitable employees? (Choose whichever is important to you as one of those executive directors or Board members.)

Another danger with this view is the potential for creating a chain of passing the buck in which *no one* ends up taking the moral responsibility: the low-level workers figure it's out of their hands; the middle management defers to the executives; the executives say they're obligated to their stockholders; and the stockholders just endorse the view of those involved in the company on a day-to-day basis.

In an excellent article titled "The Moral Muteness of Managers," Frederick B. Bird and James A. Waters observe that "many managers exhibit a reluctance to describe their actions in moral terms even when they are acting for moral reasons. They talk as if their actions were guided exclusively by organization interests, practicality, and economic good sense even when in practice they honour morally defined standards…" (237). They do this, Bird and Waters claim, because moral talk is perceived to be a threat to harmony, efficiency, and effectiveness.

I think there's yet another reason for not talking about whether something is right or wrong: the separation of our personal and work lives. It seems to be a workplace convention that one should leave one's personal "baggage" at home, and many are urged at home to leave their work at the office. Does that foster split selves? And are split selves happy and healthy? (To those who insist I demonstrate the value or importance of ethics to business, let me ask how you justify an ethical dimension at home, in your personal life. Shouldn't that be sufficient justification for ethics in business—that is, are you not "yourself" at work?)

But would the alternative lead to the following scenario? Your supervisor has several crucifixes on his office walls, and whenever he meets with you, whether to discuss policy and procedure or routine work matters, he tells you about the relevant teachings of Jesus. You might say, wait a minute, what about the separation of church and state? Okay, but what if it's a private business, not a public business (e.g., not a school, hospital, or government office)? Still, you may counter, I'm entitled to freedom of (and, equally, freedom from) religion: who is he to impose his religion on me like that? It's not like I can avoid his office. Okay, while his office is not necessarily a public place, you make a good point about not being able to avoid it—meeting with him in his office is part of your job. But you didn't have to accept the job, did you? Were you made aware that it was a Christian business? Were you asked if you were Christian? But, you ask, wouldn't that be discrimination? Good question, but let's back up: even if it *were* a government business, if that supervisor's ethics reside with his religion, and if we're saying ethics should be in business, then isn't it okay?

So maybe bringing ethics into the workplace would be a bad thing. But wait a minute: as we've seen above, *ethics are already in the workplace*; they're part of life. It seems to me that if we fail to recognize that, if we fail to recognize the moral dimension that, whether we like it or not, is present in so many business decisions, then any moral goodness (or badness) we end up with will be merely accidental. Is that what we want? Further, not only must we *recognize* that moral dimension; we must *talk* about it as well: failure to do so is a good way to ensure "moral totalitarianism" (the absence of plurality and diversity of opinion)—and is *that* what we want? Lastly, although managers, presidents, and directors have no right to impose their morality on others, their decisions affect a lot of people in a big way. So one could argue that not only do they have a *right* to become involved with the moral dimensions of their decisions, but they also have a *responsibility* to do so. So perhaps if the teachings of Jesus are relevant to the matter at hand, and your supervisor is presenting rationale rather than proselytizing, *and* that rationale is open to discussion (and disagreement), then maybe it's okay. And you might begin that discussion by pointing out that ethics can, and perhaps should, occur without reference to religion. (See the examination of religionism in Part II.)

A Few Words about Terminology

Often the way we use words in everyday speech is a little sloppy, not as precise as the way we use them in academic discussion. This is especially so with ethics. Strictly speaking, *ethics* means "matters of moral right and wrong"—it is a branch of philosophy inquiring into issues that are subject to judgements of right and wrong. So whether or not to cheat is properly called an ethical issue—it involves right and wrong. However, whether to dry your dishes with a teatowel or let them "air dry" is not an ethical issue (despite the impression your mother might have given you)—while it may involve effective and ineffective, it does not involve moral right and wrong.

To say, then, as we do all the time, that a certain person "has ethics" isn't quite right. The word that's wanted in this case is *morality*, which means "a particular system of ethical beliefs or principles," and no judgement is made about the system (you're not saying the person is good or bad; you're just saying that they have some rules about good and bad).

Strictly speaking, *moral* is a synonym for *ethical*; it simply means that the issue has to do with right or wrong. Still, no judgement is being made one way or another. So to say "That's a moral thing to do" isn't quite right. The phrase that is wanted in this case, when you *do* want to make a judgement, is *morally right* or *ethically right*—or, simply, *right* (in ethics discussions, *right* is usually understood as a short form of *morally right*—as opposed to, say, factually right or strategically right).

Now *immoral* means "morally wrong"; to say someone is immoral is to say they do wrong. This is probably why people think that *moral* means "morally right"—from a semantic point of view, one would think that *moral* is the opposite of *immoral*, but strictly speaking, it's not.

Rather, *moral* is the opposite of *amoral*—which means the issue does *not* concern matters of right and wrong. The issue of drying one's dishes is an amoral issue. An amoral person would be someone who doesn't have a morality, who doesn't have any morals at all (which is different from saying they're immoral: those people *have* morals; they just have *bad* ones!).

Which brings us to *moral* as a noun instead of as an adjective: "a moral" is a short form for "a moral belief or principle."

The following chart should clearly summarize things:

Ethics	= the study of right and wrong = the study of morality
Morality	= a system of ethical principles or beliefs = a system of morals
Issues can be	*moral* (ones that involve right/wrong) *amoral* (ones that do not involve right/wrong)
Actions can be	*right* (= ethically right = morally right) *wrong* (= ethically wrong = morally wrong = immoral)
People can be	*good* (= ethically good = morally good) *bad* (= ethically bad = morally bad = immoral)

By the way, I'm ignoring a great debate about the relation between "right" and "good." I'm suggesting they are the same, but this is not necessarily the case. A lot depends on how you define "right" and "good." Something could be right but bad, or wrong but good. For example, pushing someone away from a full lifeboat would surely be bad because you are essentially ensuring that person's death, but it may well be the right thing to do because otherwise the boat would capsize and everyone in it would die.

So, moving on, ethics is the study of right and wrong. Clear as that definition may seem, some business students, and even some business professionals, have trouble with ethics courses. Indeed, it's been my experience that for some students, it takes half a semester just to get to an understanding of what the course is all about. Some students will very thoroughly trace a decision-making scenario through several good ifs, ands, and buts, and then say, "Well, it depends on what you think is right and wrong" and stop there. As if there's a stone wall at that point, as if that's the end of it. But that's the *beginning* of it: that's exactly where a course in business ethics *starts*: What *do* you think is right and wrong? And why? *That's* what such a course, and this book, is all about. What you think is right and wrong is not written in stone: it is, like all of your ideas, open to discussion: it is subject to examination, justification, and modification.

Sometimes persistently distinguishing between (descriptive) "is" questions (What *do* companies do about trade secrets?) and (prescriptive) "ought" questions (What *should* companies do about trade secrets?) helps—it's the "ought" questions that ethics tries to answer. But sometimes even this is not enough because "ought" questions can be understood, especially by business students, as questions of effective strategy (What should companies do about trade secrets to maintain a competitive edge?) rather than as questions of ethics (What should companies do about trade secrets if they are to be morally good companies?). Ethics is not about instrumental value; it's about moral value.

To get a little advance practice at distinguishing moral questions from empirical and strategic questions, let's go back to a few of the decisions listed earlier, all of which I identified as involving ethics. Which of the subquestions listed below get us to the ethical aspects? (Keep that pen in hand.)

1. What salary figures should we put into which places on the salary grid?
    (a) How much can we afford to expend on salaries?
    (b) What figures are needed to attract top performers?
    (c) Is it fair to pay our clerical workers less than our maintenance workers?
    (d) Shall we start with equal pay for equal work, and then give bonuses for work well done?
    (e) Those with families to support need more money, so should we give them bonuses as well?

2. Where should we locate our next plant?
    (a) Does the area under consideration have a sufficient labour pool?
    (b) Is the area depressed, allowing us to pay lower wages and offer fewer benefits than at our current location?
    (c) Is there sufficient road access?
    (d) Are there environmental bylaws we have to worry about?
    (e) Will the proposed location benefit very many people?
    (f) Will the proposed location require residents to relocate or cause property devaluation because of the nature of our operation?

3. What content should go into our next advertising campaign?
    (a) Do we know what our competitor's next campaign is?
    (b) Can we find out?
    (c) Should we do so covertly?
    (d) What kind of budget do we have?
    (e) Should we withhold information about our product's potential danger?
    (f) Should we use a pop or rock music theme?
    (g) Could we exaggerate the product's merits?
    (h) Should we exaggerate the product's merits?

Okay, let's see how you did. For question 1, (c), (d), and (e) all address the ethical aspect because they all address the question of justice—what's fair? Subquestion (a) is an empirical question in that it inquires about fact; (b) is also an empirical question, directed toward strategy. However, if you scratch the surface of these two questions, you can get to an ethical issue: deciding how much to spend on salaries (whether to attract top performers or not) involves deciding how much to spend on other stuff—it's a question of allocation. And if the other stuff includes, for example, compensating victims of an earlier unsafe product of yours, then by deciding to put more money into salaries than injury compensation, you are making a decision of value, an ethical decision.

For question 2, (b) as it is worded is merely an empirical question: is the area depressed or not? However, there is a strong suggestion that if it *is* depressed, the company will engage in what might be considered exploitation, and this is an ethical issue (addressing rights and fairness). Subquestion (d) is similar in that as worded, it's just an empirical question; but as soon as environmental damage is contemplated, a question of ethics is involved. Subquestions (e) and (f) consider consequences of benefit and harm and thus also address ethical aspects. Subquestions (a) and (c) are empirical questions, asking about the facts of the matter.

For question 3, (a), (b), (d), and (g) are empirical questions, asking about what *is* or *could be* the case; (c), however, goes one step further, asking about what *ought to be* the case, and, because it suggests deception, it involves a moral "ought." Likewise, (e) and (h), both suggesting deception (and implying some "right to know"), address the ethical aspect. Note that (f), although it also asks a "should" question, it's referring to some strategic "should," not a moral "should."

How to Think about Ethics

Taking an ethics course is a little like taking a math course in that how you get the answer is, in many respects, more important than the answer itself. In fact, my aim throughout this text is not so much to have you arrive at a particular moral judgement (i.e., a particular answer), but to have you develop the skills necessary to do that.

And developing those skills is very much a matter of appreciating both the depth and the breadth of the issues involved. What answer you get depends a lot on what questions you ask (or don't ask). As Mark Twain said, if all you have is a hammer, an awful lot of things are going to look like nails. I want you to have a full toolbox.

Though I am not advocating any particular answer (well, I'm *trying* not to), I *am* advocating a particular way of getting to an answer: one that is conscious, reasoned, and informed by the complexities of the issue, rather than one that is instinctive, intuitive, conditioned, and/or superficial.

When I'm in class trying to facilitate a discussion about ethical issues, I find myself asking the same four questions, over and over, in different versions. So I'll put them here, upfront; if you can, try to get into the habit of asking yourself these questions (and not just when you're examining ethical issues—they're good for almost any situation).

(1) What Are Your Reasons?
You may be surprised at how often answering this question takes more than a little work. Consider yourself forewarned!

Once you have your reasons, make sure they're good ones. Good reasons are, first, *relevant*. For example, thinking that it's wrong to sell unsafe products because people can get hurt is good thinking in that the reason is relevant. Thinking that it's wrong to do so because your company doesn't make unsafe products is not good thinking: whether your company makes unsafe products is irrelevant to the point of whether it's wrong to *sell* unsafe products.

Sometimes what seems irrelevant can be made relevant by filling in a few missing steps. For example, suppose I said that selling unsafe products was wrong because it hurt people (and hurting people is wrong), and you responded by saying that everyone does it. That statement alone is irrelevant because whether everyone does it doesn't affect whether it's wrong: everyone could be wrong for doing it. However, you may have meant that right is determined according to what everyone does. So, since everyone does it, it's right. In that case, "everyone does it" is relevant, but you'd have to provide those missing steps.

There are several fallacies—errors in reasoning—that indicate lack of relevance:

i. To the person (*ad hominem*). When you're making a claim, whether positive or negative, about the person putting forth the position rather than about the position itself (and implying that your claim is a judgement about the position), you are committing the *ad hominem* error. For example, suppose the owner of a funeral parlour refuses to advertise her services, claiming that it's wrong to cash in on people's grief that way. If you dismissed her argument because she's an atheist, a cold-hearted pagan who has no understanding of the religious importance of rituals, you'd be making an *ad hominem* error—you'd be attacking the person instead of the argument. She may well be cold-hearted (though, of course, not all atheists are) and she may well not understand the religious importance of rituals (though, of course, most atheists do), but still, her *argument* that such advertising is wrong may indeed be a good one; what she is (or is not) isn't relevant to the strength of the argument.

ii. Paper tiger. When someone responds to someone else's argument but has turned it into something different (often something far simpler) than it was (perhaps because it's far easier to attack that way), that person is committing the paper tiger fallacy. For example, consider this exchange:

Union representative: We'd like a 5% wage increase effective September 1 of this year, and hereafter, annual increases equal to the cost of living increase.
Management representative: Hey, I'd like a lot more money too; everyone would like to be rich. Gee, it'd be nice to afford dinner out every night, and a new car every year, but this is the real world. We can't afford to give everyone everything they want.

In this case, the management rep has committed the paper tiger fallacy by responding to an exaggerated version of the union rep's argument: the union didn't ask to be rich; they didn't ask management to give *everyone everything* they wanted. The rebuttal may be a very good response to the argument responded to, but it's irrelevant to the argument that was actually presented.

iii. Red herring. A red herring is a distraction, and as such it's irrelevant. For example, consider this exchange:

A: I can't accept the plan; we'd be causing too much environmental damage. And given that our product is, in truth, not that essential, such damage is not ethically justified.
B: But if we don't cut down those trees, someone else will, you know that.

It may well be that someone else will, but that is irrelevant to whether it's morally acceptable for *you* to do it. (Unless you're defining "morally right" as "that which someone else will do," but that's unlikely.)

iv. Appeal to inappropriate authority. While it is usually acceptable to appeal to experts for support, be careful that you choose not only an expert, but an expert in the relevant field. Certain celebrities may be great actors, but why should their opinion that you should eat vegetables carry any weight? Also, mere appeal to authority involves a lot of trust, and although that may not be a problem for you, the person you're trying to convince may need more—so try to understand the expert's rationale for the support you claim (and cite the *rationale*, not just the expert's *opinion*).

v. Appeal to popularity. In a way, the appeal to popularity (sometimes called the *bandwagon fallacy*) is a version of the appeal to inappropriate authority: when you support your claim by saying something like "everyone does it" or "everyone agrees," you're implying that the opinion of the majority carries weight. Well, the majority has been known to be wrong, and I'm sure you can think of half a dozen examples. But even if they're right, the fact that they *are* right isn't a *reason* in support of your point; it's merely an observation that others agree with your point. You're better off to find out *why* the majority agrees and then use that reason to support your point.

vi. Appeal to tradition. "The company has always done it this way." So? Maybe we've always taxed food and water, but that's no reason to keep on doing it. As with the appeal to popularity, try to find out *why* the company has always done it that way. And if there is a good reason, use that *reason*, and not the mere *tradition*, to support your point.

As well as being relevant, good reasons are *adequate*. This means that they are strong enough to support your claim(s). For instance, to go back to a previous example, suppose that using a certain unsafe product will cause only a very little bit of harm, or suppose that using it will cause harm in only one in a million cases. If that's the case, one might say the reason (it hurts people) is inadequate; it's relevant, yes, but it's not strong enough to support the conclusion that selling the product is therefore wrong. Or maybe it's strong enough for that claim, but not for the next claim, which might be that we should take it completely off the market. Perhaps the product can be sold under restricted circumstances, such as only to adults. Perhaps the manufacture can be slightly modified, such as to incorporate a childproof mechanism. As you can see, adequacy is a matter of degree, and it's sometimes difficult to determine how strong is strong enough.

There are several fallacies—errors in reasoning—that indicate lack of adequacy:

vii. Slippery slope arguments. Arguing that one thing will lead to another which will lead to another—a slippery slope argument—can be a poor argument. For example, suppose the Human Resources Director says, "First we called Christmas a holiday, we give days off if people are sick, and we even allow a day off for them to get married; pretty soon they're going to want Earth Day declared a holiday, then they'll ask for a holiday in memory of Louis Riel, and eventually they'll ask for a day off to celebrate their dog's birthday." Although the individual links in the chain may be probable (or not), the connection between the first and the last, which is often the only part of the argument that is made, may not be as probable.

viii. *Post hoc.* This error is a case of assuming that because something happens *before* something else, it was the *cause* of that something else. For example, consider this argument: "Last January, we implemented random after-lunch breathalyzer tests for middle management personnel; since then, reports of excessively long lunches and afternoon aggressiveness toward subordinates have decreased. It seems to have worked quite well, and I say we include upper management starting next month." The speaker has assumed that the breathalyzer testing was the cause of fewer "liquid lunches" (actually, if you read closely, the only thing that can be assumed is that the breathalyzer testing was the cause of fewer *reports* of a certain activity *presumed to indicate* liquid lunches). But perhaps the only restaurant in town had its liquor licence revoked. Just because X precedes Y, don't assume X caused Y.

ix. Mistaking correlation for causation. The *post hoc* error is actually an instance of a broader category of mistaken reasoning in which one mistakes correlation for causation: just because two things, A and B, occur in association with each other (whether one occurs before the other, as in the *post hoc* case, or at the same time), that doesn't mean the one thing, A, necessarily *causes* the other thing, B. Perhaps the causal relationship is the other way around: perhaps B causes A. Or perhaps some third thing, C, causes *both* A and B. Or perhaps their association is total coincidence. For example, suppose your profits suddenly decrease at about the same time that people start using their cars less often. It would be a mistake to assume that the decrease in automobile use is causing the profit decrease. Perhaps a recession is causing both.

x. Confusing necessity with sufficiency. Flour may be necessary to bake a cake, but it's not sufficient; it's not *all* you need. You also need milk, sugar, eggs, and so on. A child's stuffed gorilla may be sufficient to stop its crying, but it might not be necessary; the child's stuffed crocodile might also do the trick. And legs are both necessary *and* sufficient for running; you definitely need them (so they're necessary), and really, they're all you need—you don't need fancy shoes, for example (so they're also sufficient). People commonly mistake one for the other. Think of your own examples of mistaking necessity for sufficiency, and then of mistaking sufficiency for necessity.

In addition to being relevant and adequate, the claims in your reasons, if they involve empirical claims, must be true. An empirical claim is one that can be tested, one that is subject to correspondence (or lack thereof) with reality: the "is" questions ask about empirical claims. While philosophers typically leave the establishment of truth to others, our arguments are, nevertheless, not good if our premises are false. For example, we might argue that, because affirmative action programs that require the hiring of members of a certain group just to fill a quota result in feelings of low self-worth on the part of those hired and feelings of resentment on the part of those not, such programs should not be implemented—they cause harm, they do not contribute to the good of society. Whether they *do*, in fact, result in feelings of low self-worth on the part of those hired and feelings of resentment on the part of those not is important to our argument (indeed, the truth of that premise is essential to the soundness of the argument), but it's not *our* job to figure that out—we leave that to the social scientists, the psychologists, to establish (or not). If that claim is true, then our argument may well be sound.

However, you should know about

xi. Appeal to ignorance. The fact that we can't prove something is false is no reason to suppose that it's true. For example, suppose the president of a company is considering whether to extend surveillance from e-mail communications to phone communications, and suppose someone points out that since they had no way of knowing before how many messages were gossip messages, they can't say that the surveillance decreased the number of gossip messages. If the president responds to that claim with "Yes, well, we don't know that it *doesn't* work," and so assumes that it does (and orders the extension of surveillance), s/he'd be making the "appeal to ignorance" mistake.

It's worth drawing your attention to a few other common errors of reasoning so that you can be on the alert for them:

xii. Circular reasoning. When your reasons assume or require the point they are supposed to support, then your argument is a case of circular reasoning. A classic example is "God exists—because the Bible says so"; since the Bible is supposedly written by God, by accepting it as evidence, you have *assumed* to be true the very thing you were trying to *prove was* true (God's existence). An example from the world of business would be arguing that unjustified discrimination is wrong because it's making judgements unfairly;

insofar as "unjustified discrimination" is *defined* as "making judgements unfairly," the argument is "X is wrong because it's X"—in which case you have assumed ahead of time the very point you were supposed to be proving.

xiii. Equivocation. When you use the same word but with different meanings, you are equivocating. For example, consider this argument: "Your supervisor is your superior, and someone who's superior is someone who's better than others, so your supervisor is better than you." "Superior" is used first to mean "organizational superior" or "superior in the hierarchy," but the second time, it's used in a different, general way to mean "better"; because the word "superior" has been equivocated, the argument is not a good one. Paying close attention to your definitions (see below) will keep you safe from this error.

xiv. False dichotomy. Be careful not to assume that a situation is an either/or (dichotomous) situation; often there will be more than two, especially opposing, options. For example, consider this argument: "If we don't lay off one hundred employees, we will go bankrupt and then everyone will be out of a job." The speaker has falsely assumed that there are only two options: laying off a hundred employees or going out of business. There is, in fact, a third option: all employees could accept a wage decrease, thus reducing payroll expenses and enabling all employees to be retained. No doubt there are more than three options: the profit margin could be reduced (or even eliminated), the stockholders' returns could be decreased, expansion plans could be postponed, etc. However, attending to alternatives (see below) will keep you safe from this error. (Note that in the red herring example above, B commits the false dichotomy error!)

Entire books are written about this field, which is variously called critical thinking, critical reasoning, informal logic, etc. See the list of references at the back of the book if you want to check out a few.

(2) What Are Your Assumptions?

This is the second question I find myself asking over and over when I'm trying to facilitate a discussion about ethical issues. Reconsider the previous argument about it being wrong to sell unsafe products because people can be hurt; the person *assumed* that causing harm is wrong. You may say, "Well, of course." But the value in identifying assumptions is that one can then assess them: one might just as well have *not* agreed that causing harm is wrong; *if you don't know what the assumptions are, you can't figure out if you agree with them or not*. And if it turns out that you *don't* agree with or accept an assumption that was being made, then maybe (if that was the only line of supportive reasoning) you don't have to agree with or accept the conclusion.

Let's consider a few other examples. Suppose that selling your product at cost means that you won't make any profit, so you implement a 10-per-cent mark-up. Sounds good. But what have you assumed? You have assumed that it's necessary, or at least important, or perhaps good, to make a profit. But what about not-for-profit business enterprises? Suppose that if you raise wages, you'll go out of business. So? Why is that a problem? What are you assuming? Maybe going out of business would be a good thing. (Do you make nuclear or biological weapons?)

(3) What Do You Mean by _____?
In other words, *define your terms*. To continue with the previous example, one may well ask, "What do you mean by 'harm'?", "What do you mean by 'unsafe'?", "How 'likely' are you calling 'likely'?", and, of course, "What do you mean by 'wrong'?"

(4) What Are the Alternatives?
Often the ethical decision seems to be X or not-X, or X or Y. But often there are alternatives: try to find a Z. Returning to our example, selling the product under restricted circumstances might be a good alternative (to selling it or not selling it): it might allow you to keep selling it and at the same time reduce or eliminate the harm caused.

Okay, practice time again! Each of the following, except one, illustrates an error in reasoning. See if you can identify and label them. The answers are below, but don't look until you've tried to respond to the questions.

1. Martens: Either our company refuses to hire people with AIDS or we put everyone here at risk.
2. MacNabb asks her supervisor for a day off to celebrate her divorce, claiming that since it's company policy to allow wedding leave, it should also be policy to allow divorce leave. MacNamara denies her request, saying that the company can't afford to give employees a day off whenever they request one.
3. Lariviere criticizes Marsh's argument that maximizing profit should be the least important goal of a company by pointing out that Marsh knows absolutely nothing about economics.
4. When Milburn suggests that the company should offer pro-rated benefits to all part-time workers regardless of the number of hours worked per week, Madden tells him that it's standard practice across the province to offer benefits only to employees who work 25 hours or more per week.
5. Thom claims that since she has been hired, sales have doubled; she therefore asks for a raise.
6. Cole claims that failing to advertise steel-toed construction boots to a female target audience is not only unjustified discrimination to women currently working on construction sites, but it is also harmful to all the little girls who see in the ads only men working in manual trades: their future job prospects will be limited by their narrowed imaginations. Shortt responds by saying he knows lots of women who work in construction.

7. In response to accusations about cruelty to animals, Purdon's firm's PR person, Charles, visits one of their research labs and then prepares a press release (either denying or affirming the accusation).
8. Roy argues that if we allow people to sell their organs, we'll end up with a murder epidemic: people will go on killing sprees, hoping to sell their victims' organs.
9. Didine is an asset to this firm. All assets can be liquidated. Therefore, Didine can be liquidated.
10. Warner and Ducharme question the strip-search policy at the detention centre they work at because they think that automatically assigning a same-sex worker to check a resident unjustifiably assumes that everyone is heterosexual. They wonder if homosexual residents and workers might prefer cross-sex arrangements, and suggest that henceforth the resident be asked whether she or he would prefer a male or female worker to conduct the search. The Director of the centre responds with incredulity, and a snicker, and simply says, "Our search policy has been in effect since the centre was opened, and I'm not about to change it!"
11. Gonzalez suggests that the company institute flex-time, saying that it doesn't really matter when people put in their 35 hours, as long as they get the job done; being able to miss rush hour, being at home when the kids get there—these things make for happier employees, and happier employees are more productive. Besides, people have a right to a certain amount of autonomy.
12. Eaton, Richmond, and Moulding: We should accept more students because then our tuition revenue would increase. And if we had more money, we could expand. And if we were bigger, we could accept more students.

And the answers are...

1. False dichotomy. An obvious third possibility is that you hire the person with AIDS but restrict his/her duties to those not involving the exchange of bodily fluids. Or perhaps a condition of employment could be disclosure to colleagues so they'll know to glove up before (or refrain from) administering first aid should the occasion arise.
2. Paper tiger. MacNamara responds to what was *not* MacNabb's argument: MacNabb didn't just request a day off; she asked for a *particular* day off, suggesting consistency with current company policy. Had MacNamara responded to her suggestion of consistency, arguing that divorces were somehow different from weddings with respect to needing or deserving a day off, he would have been okay.
3. *Ad hominem*. Lariviere has argued to the person instead of to the position. Marsh may well know nothing about economics (then again, he may be an economics expert), but that's irrelevant to whether maximizing profit should be the least important goal of a company.

4. Appeal to popularity. Madden's response suggests that "everyone does it this way" (i.e., offers benefits only after 25 hours per week). That may be true, but it's irrelevant to whether it's right, and that was Milbum's point (presumably).
5. *Post hoc.* Thom has assumed that she is the cause of the increased sales; perhaps the competition shut down.
6. Red herring. Shortt may well know lots of women who work in construction, but what does that have to do with whether or not the proposed advertising campaign would be discriminatory and harmful?
7. Appeal to inappropriate authority. By handling the issue in this way, Purdon's firm has made an erroneous appeal to authority: generally speaking, PR people are not experts about animal welfare and are therefore unqualified to make a judgement on this matter.
8. Slippery slope. Selling one's own organs, probably through carefully regulated channels, *may* lead to selling someone else's organs (though even this step is a leap); but for it to lead to murdering to do so, let alone to an epidemic of such murders, is not that likely.
9. Equivocation. The first *asset* refers to "benefit," but the second one refers to "physical and financial properties"—the meaning of the term has changed throughout the argument. Furthermore, the first *liquidated* refers to "conversion to cash," but the second one refers to "killed"—this term has also had its meaning equivocated.
10. Appeal to tradition. The Director may well be right in saying that the policy has been in place since the centre opened, but that's irrelevant to whether it should continue to be in place; the search policy may have been wrong for all those years. (Furthermore, I'd say the snicker is an inappropriate appeal to humour—and an embarrassing display of immaturity.)
11. This is an instance of good reasoning.
12. Circular reasoning. They have assumed to be good (accepting more students) exactly what they were supposed to be proving was good (accepting more students).

How to Discuss Ethics

One of my biggest challenges when I teach ethics is to shift the classroom discussion from sounding like a bad Jerry Springer show to sounding like a PBS or CBC radio discussion. It's not easy, and students have good reason to be frustrated with a discussion that doesn't go anywhere.

First, yes, everyone's entitled to their opinion. But, *some opinions are better than others.* You can express your opinion that Santa Claus exists until you're blue in the face, but until you present some reasons for your opinion, the rest of the class is justified in ignoring you (politely, of course). And until you present *good* reasons, the rest of the class is justified in not changing their minds (assuming they disagreed with you).

Second, being rational doesn't preclude being passionate. Indeed, I hope you get excited, I hope you care very deeply about ethical discussions. But in order to avoid hurting each other (which will just lead to people holding back from speaking, which eventually leads to non-discussion), think of yourself and everyone else as putting forth positions. The position you put forth at any given time doesn't necessarily have to be the position you personally subscribe to at the moment. In fact, we don't have to know whether you agree with the position or not. That way, people can disagree *with the position*, not *with you*. You should feel free to consider, to present in class, all sorts of positions. It's a great way to help refine and evaluate your own opinions.

Of course, we all try to run our lives according to our ethical principles. So when someone criticizes your ethical principles, they are criticizing the way you run your life. And that criticism can be hard to take. (Actually, they're probably just defending the way they run theirs; the fact that you run yours differently suggests they might be wrong. This of course is not necessarily the case: don't forget the false dichotomy fallacy—it could be that *both* ways are right. Then again, it could be that both ways are wrong.) But you can deal with that criticism on your own. You don't have to defend your *self* in class; just try to defend the *position*. Again, no one has to know which position you most support. In fact, *you* don't even have to know; and anyway, you may change your position, several times, as you think of or become aware of various arguments.

Or you may not change your position. But what's the point of discussion if people don't change? That's the value of disagreement! When someone disagrees with you, they're shining a spotlight on something, and it's to your advantage to take a good look: maybe that particular reason *is* a bad one, maybe you can strengthen it, maybe you should find another reason, or maybe you should reject the claim that reason was supposed to have supported. (That's called becoming wise.)

Now, having set the tone for *mature* discussion, there's a method you can follow (until you get the hang of it) that will lead you to *coherent* discussion: noodling. I came up with this one day in class, utterly exhausted by trying to keep the discussion moving, and moving in one direction. That day, I finally articulated what I was valiantly trying to do, and this ad lib response has now become a premeditated component.

Whenever someone said something, I explained, it was as if they just plopped a pile of spaghetti into the middle of the room and expected me to do the hard work of trying to make some order out of their mess—trying to figure out what, if anything, was relevant and how exactly it fit in with what was just said. I want you to try to do some of that work yourself, I said to my students: try to straighten out your noodles before you put them on the table. I then elaborated on the board, encouraging them to take note of what I was doing. Like this, I said: this is my point (and I drew a horizontal line/noodle) and this is my reason for it (another noodle below it, somewhat indented) and this is another reason for it (another noodle in line with the previous one).

_____
    _____
    _____

For example, perhaps I had argued that

My membership to the golf club should be considered a business expense.
(because)
    Sometimes when I play golf, I play with business partners.
(and)
    Sometimes when I play golf, I meet people who become clients.

Now when the next person says something, they should try to connect their noodles to the previous person's noodles. You can make a connection in several ways, I continued:

- **you can disagree with the point (I draw an X beside that noodle)**

    _____ ✗

That is, you don't think that the person's membership to the golf club should be considered a business expense.

- **because you disagree with one or more reasons (I draw an X beside the relevant noodle/s below)**

    _____ ✗
    _____ ✗
    _____

That is, you don't think that the person's membership to the golf club should be considered a business expense because you don't think it's true that the person sometimes plays with business partners.

- **because you don't think the point follows from the reasons, even though you agree with the reasons (I draw a line connecting the point with the reason/s and put an ✗ through it)**

    _____
    _____
    _____

That is, you agree that sometimes the person plays golf with business partners but you don't think it follows that the golf club membership should be considered a business expense.

- **because you have your own reason/s (I draw a separate set of horizontal lines) for your own counter point**

    For example, maybe you want to argue that only expenses incurred for activities during which one is 100% engaged in business (not "sometimes") should be considered business expenses because it is both impossible and too time-consuming to calculate a partial claim. (A pathetic argument, agreed.)

    > Only expenses incurred for activities during which one is 100% engaged in business should be considered a business expense.
    > (because)
    >   It's impossible to calculate a partial claim.
    > (and)
    >   It's too time-consuming to calculate a partial claim.

- **you can agree with the point (a check beside the noodle)**

    _____ ✓
    _____
    _____

    That is, you agree that the golf club membership should be considered a business expense.

- **but disagree with one or more reasons (Xs wherever)**

    _____ ✓
    _____ ✗
    _____

    That is, you agree that the golf club membership should be considered a business expense, but not that, or not because, the person sometimes plays with business partners.

- **or agree with the reasons (checks beside them)**

    _____ ✓
    _____ ✓
    _____ ✓

That is, you agree that the golf club membership should be considered a business expense, and you agree that this is so because the person sometimes plays with business partners and because the person sometimes meets people who become clients.

- **and add another reason (another noodle under the original column)**

  _____ ✓
  _____ ✓
  _____
  -

  That is, you agree that the golf club membership should be considered a business expense, and you agree that this is so because the person sometimes plays with business partners and because the person sometimes meets people who become clients, *and also* because golf is a high-status game and the business is elevated by association.

- **you can make an individual noodle thicker (I thicken the line) by adding an example, adding detail, elaborating on the explanation**

  _____ ✓
  _____ ✓
  _____ ✓

  Perhaps you add that when someone plays golf with business partners, plans, policies, and procedures are often discussed, which leads to improvements in the business…

- **you can ask for clarification about a specific noodle (a question mark beside a line)**

  _____
  _____
  _____?

  You can ask how it is it that while playing golf one can meet people who become clients.

- **you can question a noodle's truth, its relevance, or its adequacy**

And so on.

However, if you have something to say but can't figure out if, or how, it fits in, you should say it anyway and the rest of the class can help with the noodling; this method shouldn't become an inhibitor.

Also, it helps if there's a noodle emergency person: someone who doesn't try to participate *per se* in the discussion, but rather who listens very carefully and jumps in, as necessary, to untangle or straighten out the noodles in order to prevent a real mess from developing. At first, I act as the noodle emergency person, but after a while, I assign the role to individual students. The results are amazing: you'll see for yourself just how challenging it is to facilitate a coherent discussion, but more importantly, by consciously trying to keep the discussion on track, merely by trying to assess every comment for relevance, your own critical skills will really take off.

Lastly, there are a couple of discussion issues you should know about, whether you discuss out loud or in writing:

1. Try not to use loaded language. Consider the difference between "incentive" and "bribe," between "employment opportunity" and "job," between "affirmative action" and "reverse discrimination," between "downsizing" and "mass firing," and so on.
2. Be careful with statistics. Consider "80% of the workers in our Third World plant said they were happy with their wages"—if you asked only a handful, your statistic was not representative and is therefore misleading; if the workers thought they'd be fired if they said they weren't happy, your statistic is not reliable and is therefore misleading.

Closing Comments

Many business students are frustrated with philosophical discussion in general because it doesn't appear to go anywhere. Philosophy must be one of the few disciplines that's still dealing with ideas put forth centuries ago. Law has gotten past lynch mobs, physics has gone beyond Newton, and even the relatively new field of psychology has outgrown many of its early views. But philosophers are still discussing Plato. Why does philosophy go nowhere? Well, it doesn't go nowhere. Yes, it's still dealing with the same old issues in many cases, but our dealings are far more complicated; we are making much finer distinctions than we used to. (As an example, now philosophers write entire books on the single concept of voluntariness; centuries ago, that issue was exhausted by a mere page or two.)

Also, try not to be overwhelmed by the questions in this chapter (indeed, in this text). "Moral paralysis" can be avoided if you remember that all you need to do is make *better* ethical decisions, *more carefully considered* decisions—you don't have to figure out the single absolutely right answer. (Especially not by the end of just one course or text!) The theories covered in the next chapter will be of value; you can use them to answer those questions and to make those decisions.

And, as I have suggested, asking the right questions is a large part of the way toward getting the right answers. If all you can do at the end of what might be your first attempt to study ethics is know what questions to ask, that's a lot—don't underestimate your achievement.

Remember that ethics is a branch of philosophy and, contrary to popular opinion, philosophy is *not* a bird course—it's not easier than other disciplines; it's harder. That's why top scorers on the GRE tend to be philosophy majors or physics majors; they are the ones most adept at critical, abstract reasoning. To use Bloom's taxonomy of cognitive skills, most courses deal with knowledge, comprehension, and application; philosophy deals very much with the three higher levels—analysis, synthesis, and evaluation.

Lastly, in your struggle to do the right thing, it might be helpful to know what you're up against—to know why people *don't* typically do the right thing. I think there are a number of reasons:

- the belief that profit is supposed to come first: the belief that the CEO, the Board, and the shareholders want to maximize profit no matter what, and the belief that it's your job, your *primary* duty, to do what they want;
- herd behaviour: Asch[1] and many, many others have proven that people tend to follow the crowd;
- self-deception: we tell ourselves it's not our call or it doesn't really matter;
- greed: we want the bonus, the promotion, the job;
- simple immaturity: we don't care about the effects of our actions (or non-actions) on others;
- laziness: ethics is complicated, and even when it's not, we just don't bother to think, and perhaps especially we don't bother to think *ahead*, about the consequences of our behaviour;
- our discomfort with grey areas: we like black and white because it's so much easier—there are only two options and they're easy to tell apart;
- the belief that ethics is a sign of weakness, and that those who sacrifice profit in order to do the right thing are not as strong-minded as those who focus solely on the numbers (for men, this may also be related to a misguided belief that numbers, quantifiables, are masculine and ethical reasoning is somehow effeminate);
- the business suit—seriously: I suggest that the business suit confers a veneer of respectability (why else do lawyers insist that their clients wear a suit and tie in court?) and authority (ask any man *not* to wear suit and tie to an important event, and see what his response is) that enables "business" to proceed "as usual"—unchallenged. And when no one challenges you, when you have the right of way for whatever you do, it's all too easy to just go with the flow.

Okay, here's one final exercise. In groups of three, discuss the following situations:

1. The three of you work at an online gaming company. Your supervisor has asked you to add tracking cookies that will record for marketing purposes all the choices made by the players. At the moment, you're not sure what that information could be used for, but you can make a few educated guesses. What do you do?

---

1 Despite the clarity of the correct answer about as simple a matter as "Which line is the same length as this line?", 75 per cent gave the wrong answer *because everyone before them did*.

2. You are the team responsible for marketing, including promotion and distribution, of a product. The product is legal; it is also safe if used correctly, but you suspect that some potential buyers may use it incorrectly. What do you do?
3. The three of you would like to start an ethical investment firm, and you are now meeting to decide which stocks to include in your various ethical investment-fund portfolios. Proceed.

As you discuss each situation, try to get comfortable with the terminology covered in this opening section. Try noodling. And don't forget:

- What are your reasons? (And are they relevant and adequate?)
- What are your assumptions?
- Define your terms.
- Consider alternatives.

References and Further Reading

Arnold, Denis G., Tom L. Beauchamp, and Norman E. Bowie, eds. *Ethical Theory and Business*. 9th ed. New York: Pearson, 2012. (text/ anthology)

Bird, Frederick B., and James A. Waters. "The Moral Muteness of Managers." *California Management Review* 32.1 (1989). Rpt. in *Ethical Issues in Business: A Philosophical Approach*. Ed. Thomas Donaldson and Patricia H. Werhane. 5th ed. Upper Saddle River, NJ: Prentice Hall, 1996. 237–50.

Boatright, John R. *Ethics and the Conduct of Business*. 7th ed. New York: Pearson, 2013. (good introductions)

Dalla Costa, John. *The Ethical Imperative*. Toronto: HarperCollins, 1998.

De George, Richard T. *Business Ethics*. 7th ed. New York: Pearson, 2009. (very thorough, comprehensive)

Desjardins, Joseph R., and John J. McCall. *Contemporary Issues in Business Ethics*. 6th ed. Boston, MA: Cengage Learning, 2014. (text/anthology)

Di Norcia, Vincent. *Hard Like Water: Ethics in Business*. Toronto: Oxford, 1998. (text, Canadian)

Kehoe, William, ed. *Annual Editions: Business Ethics 13/14*. Guilford, CT: McGraw-Hill/Dushkin, 2013. (anthology of magazine articles; others listed as anthologies contain journal articles)

Michalos, Alex C. "Issues for Business Ethics in the Nineties and Beyond." *Journal of Business Ethics* 16.3 (1997): 219–30.

Newton, Lisa H., and Elaine Englehardt, eds. *Taking Sides: Clashing Views on Controversial Issues in Business Ethics and Society*. 13th ed. Guilford, CT: McGraw-Hill/Dushkin, 2013. (pro/con anthology)

Poff, Deborah C., ed. *Business Ethics in Canada*. 4th ed. Don Mills, ON: Pearson Education Canada, 2005. (text/anthology, Canadian, philosophical emphasis)

Shaw, William H., and Vincent Barry. *Moral Issues in Business*. 13th ed. Boston: Cengage Learning, 2015. (text/anthology)
Stewart, David. *Business Ethics*. New York: McGraw Hill, 1995. (lots of positive role models in case studies)
Trevino, Linda Klebe, and Katherine A. Nelson. *Managing Business Ethics: Straight Talk about How to Do It Right*. 6th ed. New York: John Wiley & Sons, 2014. (very practical, very applied, business emphasis)
Velasquez, Manuel G. *Business Ethics: Concepts and Cases*. 7th ed. New York: Pearson, 2011. (very thorough, comprehensive)

Critical Thinking References

Bickenbach, Jerome E., and Jacqueline M. Davies. *Good Reasons for Better Arguments: An Introduction to the Skills and Values of Critical Thinking*. Peterborough, ON: Broadview Press, 1997.
Browne, M. Neil. *Asking the Right Questions: A Guide to Critical Thinking*. 11th ed. New York: Longman, 2014.
Chaffee, John. *Thinking Critically*. 11th ed. Boston: Cengage Learning, 2014.
Darner, T. Edward. *Attacking Faulty Reasoning: A Practical Guide to Fallacy-Free Arguments*. 7th ed. Boston: Cengage Learning, 2012.
Diestler, Sherry. *Becoming a Critical Thinker: A User-Friendly Manual*. 6th ed. New York: Pearson, 2011.
Dowden, Bradley H. *Logical Reasoning*. Belmont, CA: Wadsworth, 1993.
Engel, S. Morris. *With Good Reason: An Introduction to Informal Fallacies*. 6th ed. New York: St. Martin's Press, 2014.
Feldman, Richard. *Reason and Argument*. 2nd ed. Upper Saddle River, NJ: Prentice Hall, 1999.
Groarke, Leo A. *Good Reasoning Matters!* 5th ed. Toronto: Oxford University Press, 2013.
Hughes, William, and Jonathan Lavery. *Critical Thinking: An Introduction to the Basic Skills*. 7th Can. ed. Peterborough, ON: Broadview Press, 2015.
Missimer, C.A. *Good Arguments: An Introduction to Critical Thinking*. 4th ed. New York: Pearson, 2004.
Ruggiero, Vincent Ryan. *Beyond Feelings: A Guide to Critical Thinking*. Mountain View, CA: Mayfield, 1995.
Seech, Zachary. *Open Minds and Everyday Reasoning*. Belmont, CA: Wadsworth, 1993.
Thomson, Anne. *Critical Reasoning: A Practical Introduction*. London: Routledge, 1996.

PART II
INTRODUCTION TO ETHICAL THEORY

Introductory Note

The big question is this: "How should we determine whether something is right or wrong?" Some people have given this question a lot of thought and have come up with rather coherent and complete answers. These have come to be known as ethical theories, and in this section I'll take you on a brief tour of these theories. For each theory, I'll describe the main principles and suggest some of its strengths and weaknesses; I'll also show that theory in action.

But first, a few comments. One important distinction to make is between descriptive and prescriptive theories. Simply put, as explained in the previous section, "descriptive" refers to what *is* the case, whereas "prescriptive" refers to what *should be* the case. So descriptive theories describe what, in fact, we do; prescriptive theories describe what we *should* do. Ethics, and this text, is interested in the latter; science is interested in the former. For example, to say that human beings are selfish and do only what's in their own interest is to be descriptive (and this particular theory is called psychological egoism). To say, however, that we *should* do whatever is in our own interest, to say that we should define "right" according to what's in our own interest—that's prescriptive (and that particular theory is called ethical egoism). The distinction is crucial, and failure to grasp it will definitely mess you up with ethical theories (especially egoism and relativism), and with ethical discussion in general.

And that takes us to my second point: understand that in this text we're concerned with "should," not "is." Science—whether physical or social—deals with empirical questions: it seeks to discover what is; it seeks to describe. Philosophy—including ethics—deals with conceptual questions. Now that's not to say that the sciences don't deal with concepts; on the contrary, they can be *very* conceptual, very abstract, and very theoretical. But they are so in order to explain, to describe what *is*. Ethics, by contrast, uses concepts to explain what *should* be. On the one hand, philosophers don't care about what *is*; we don't care whether something is true. But on the other hand, we do care (in fact, as explained in Part I, our carefully constructed arguments are worthless unless our premises are true)—but we leave the job of establishing truth to others, to science.

Third, be on the alert for the "is/ought" fallacy (a.k.a. the fact-value fallacy, Hume's law, and the naturalistic fallacy): when one *derives* ought from is, when one says that we *should* do X *because* we *do* do X, one is committing the "is/ought" fallacy. Why is it a fallacy? Because just because we do something, it doesn't follow that we *should* do it. For example, an angry person may lose his/her temper and hit someone, but surely we wouldn't conclude that they therefore *should* lose their temper and hit someone. Humans often attempt to settle conflicts with force; that doesn't mean we *should* attempt to settle conflicts with force. And one more example: if CEOs and managers concern themselves only with profit, that doesn't mean that they *should* concern themselves only with profit.

There are a number of ways to categorize ethical theories: one can divide them into objective and subjective theories, universal and relative, absolute and non-absolute, principle-based and consequence-based, cognitive and non-cognitive, and so on. Each of these labels looks at a different aspect, so a theory could be objective and consequence-based; or it could be subjective and non-cognitive. You get the picture. I'm going to steer a little away from categorizing; it's an important and useful skill, to be sure, but it can be confusing unless you spend a lot of time with it. And since this is not a text or a course in ethical theories, we're *not* going to spend that much time on it. But if you're interested, by all means check out some of the books on ethical theory (see the list at the end of this section) and know that most universities have entire courses on the subject.

On the same note, please realize that every one of the ethical theories presented here has a lot more breadth and depth than I will indicate. In a way, my superficial descriptions are quite unfair to the theories, and indeed many of the questions I will raise, often as weaknesses, already have extensive answers. However, my purpose here is to give you an introductory tour of the possibilities and to alert you to the important questions.

Lastly, insofar as theories are understood to explain reality, to explain what *is*, perhaps the prescriptive theories shouldn't be called theories at all, but rather approaches to ethical decision making.

Egoism

Egoism holds that "X is (morally) right if it's in my own interests"—if some action is good for me, it's right. As such, egoism is a consequentialist theory: it determines right and wrong according to the consequences, according to what happens (and, in this case, something is right when what happens is in your own interests).

So let's say you have to decide whether to create a daycare centre in your company. If you're an egoist, your thinking might go something like this: hey, I'm paying half my salary for private daycare, so a company daycare would probably be cheaper; it would cut out the hassle and expense of dropping the kids off and picking them up; I could go and spend time with them—we could have lunch together every day; I might be criticized for endorsing such a "soft" program—but then again, I might be commended as a progressive and innovative manager; it might attract some top performers and that would be to my credit. Yeah. I think I will go ahead with it, as it appears to be the right thing to do.

Notice how all his (let's assume a "he" for this one) thoughts focus on the benefits to himself. He mentions others—his kids and potential "top performers"—but he does so only insofar as *he* is affected. And he almost gets to "happier employees are better employees," but he really doesn't take that step—he stops at the implication that *he'll* be happier (to be able to spend time with his kids).

Thomas Hobbes, a seventeenth-century thinker and author of *Leviathan*, is often associated with egoism: he argues that our natural condition leads us to a morality of self-interest; he's the one known for the delightful phrase "Life is nasty, brutish, and short" (an attitude revived in the late twentieth century by t-shirts that proclaim "Life's a bitch, then you die"). But actually he went on to say that in the state of nature in which life is that way, there is no right and wrong; morality itself doesn't come to be until we become civilized.

Lest you dismiss the selfishness of egoism quickly and easily, consider Ayn Rand's critical but perhaps accurate definition of altruism: "Any action taken for the benefit of others is good, and any action taken for one's own benefit is evil. Thus, the *beneficiary* of an action is the only criterion of moral value—and so long as the beneficiary is anybody other than oneself, anything goes" (viii; italics in original). And indeed, why should any other person count more than me?

Perhaps the key is to distinguish selfishness from self-interest: the former is self-interest even at the other's expense, to the other's detriment. Thus, while egoists may be self-interested, they might not necessarily be selfish. (Also, don't confuse egoist with egotist: the latter has nothing to do with ethical theory; it merely describes someone who is conceited and brags a lot.)

In addition, it may be in our best interests to attend to the interests of others; in this regard, some distinguish between narrow self-interest and wide self-interest. But note that the egoist considers others only if it's in his/her interests to do so; considering others independent of one's own interests is utilitarian (see the next subsection).

Perhaps a strength of egoism is that we'd all be better off because, after all, who knows better what's good for us than our own selves? Altruism requires people to figure out, or second guess, what other people would like to happen. (And perhaps altruism is just another word for paternalism, that is, the belief that one knows what's good for other people.) But *knowing* what's in our own interests is far different from always *acting in* or *satisfying* our own interests.

Another of egoism's strengths is that it seems to work well. People do seem to be motivated by self-interest (perhaps we are, by nature or nurture, egoists). Certainly Adam Smith, the eighteenth-century thinker and author of *The Wealth of Nations*, used egoism as a starting point for what has become modern economic theory: he believed that individuals who were free to pursue their own interests would be led, as if by an "invisible hand," to achieve the common good. But so what if egoism works well? Torture works well, too. The point is that the fact of something working well doesn't make it right. And what about people who *can't* look out for their own interests, for example, children and the elderly? So maybe egoism works well only under certain conditions.

Also, unlike utilitarianism (the next approach we'll consider), egoism provides no help with moral conflicts. What if being honest and being dishonest are *both* in your own interest—how do you decide between the two? For example, suppose that reporting a conflict of interest will make your supervisor think very highly of you, and it might lead to a promotion; not reporting the conflict of interest will enable you to get that deal on the side. How do you determine the *greater* self-interest?

Even more problematic, what's in our self-interest isn't always apparent even in the absence of conflict. Sometimes we don't know what we want; sometimes we don't know what's in our own best interest. Is it in our best interest to maximize our own pleasure, to be hedonistic egoists? Or is it in our best interest to do for others, to be altruistic egoists?

In every business ethics class, there will be at least one student who insists that all of us always act out of self-interest anyway (supporting the theory I introduced earlier as psychological egoism, a *descriptive* theory); even altruists do what they do because it makes them feel good. See? They did it for themselves. Such students appeal to psychology, saying that we always act on our strongest desire.

Well, that may indeed be true. (Then again, it may not; I'm not sure science has established fact in this regard.) So what's the point of having a theory that tells you that you *should* do what you do anyway? Remember the is/ought fallacy: just because we *do* do it that way doesn't mean we *should*. So just because we *are* egoists doesn't mean we *should* be. But what if we can't help it? What if we have no choice? If you believe we don't have any free will at all, then I guess *all* of ethics, not just egoism, is irrelevant (But I don't believe science has established fact with regard to free will either, and most of us seem to think we have at least *some* free will.) (So I *am* going to continue writing this book....)

Before you go on to the next theory, make a few notes: In point form, outline (1) the elements, (2) the strengths, and (3) the weaknesses of this theory. Also, (4) write a short paragraph describing an egoist approach to an ethical decision in a business context (go back and reread the daycare decision example if you need to).

Utilitarianism

Utilitarianism, like egoism, is a consequence-based theory: it doesn't matter why you did something (intent), nor does it matter exactly what you did (action); only the end result counts (consequence). In fact, the name *utilitarianism* comes from "utility," the notion that actions have utility—they are useful because of the consequences they bring about. But whereas egoism considers only the one person, the agent (the one performing the action), utilitarianism considers everyone involved. And that is the first important element of utilitarianism, this attention to "all concerned" (the phrase comes from John Stuart Mill, a nineteenth-century thinker and author of the aptly named book *Utilitarianism*).

The second important element of utilitarianism is hedonism, the idea that pleasure is good and pain is bad: "Nature has placed mankind under the governance of two sovereign masters, *pain* and *pleasure*. It is for them alone to point out what we ought to do..." (from Jeremy Bentham, an eighteenth-century thinker and author of *Introduction to the Principles of Morals and Legislation* [p. 1]). More specifically, we ought to maximize good and minimize bad, what's known as "the greatest happiness principle" (Mill). Thus, putting the two elements together, utilitarianism is "the greatest good (happiness/pleasure) for the greatest number."

So far so good (excuse the pun), but how do you determine which of several possibilities will produce the *greatest* good? The method Bentham suggests is known as the "hedonistic calculus." He identified seven aspects of pleasure and pain and claimed that the results of each action should be measured according to these seven aspects; the action with the highest total (of hedons, or units) would be the one resulting in the greatest pleasure—it would be the (morally) right one. These seven aspects are as follows:

Imp *Intensity*: How strong will the pain or pleasure be?
Duration: How long will the pain or pleasure last?
Certainty: How likely is it that the anticipated pain or pleasure will occur?
Propinquity (nearness in time): How soon will the pain or pleasure be experienced?
Fecundity (fruitfulness): Will the pleasure sort of go forth and multiply? Will one be more able to experience other pleasures, having experienced this one?
Purity: How much pain is mixed in with the pleasure (or vice versa)?
Extent: How many sentient beings will be affected by the pain or pleasure?

One does the calculus, subtracting the pain from the pleasure for a net total, and voilà, you have the right answer!

Go ahead and try to apply Bentham's hedonistic calculus to a simple ethical decision: What is the right thing to do: read that great sci-fi novel or do your business ethics homework? Using an arbitrary scale of one to ten, assign numeric values into each of the boxes in the table below. Don't forget to consider everyone who would be affected by your decision.

Table II.1

	Sci-fi novel		Business ethics homework	
	Pleasure	Pain	Pleasure	Pain
1. Intensity				
2. Duration				
3. Certainty				
4. Propinquity				
5. Fecundity				
6. Purity				
7. Extent				
Subtotals	minus		minus	
Totals (in hedons)				

Which action resulted in the greatest total (the greatest pleasure for the greatest number)? *That's* the (morally) right thing to do!

Now, if one of the main weaknesses of this theory didn't become evident, try it with a more complicated decision: Should you hire the more qualified woman, knowing that men won't want to take orders from her, or should you hire the less qualified man? And again, for each measure, be sure to consider the consequences for everyone affected.

Table II.2

	More qualified woman		Less qualified man	
	Pleasure	Pain	Pleasure	Pain
1. Intensity				
2. Duration				
3. Certainty				
4. Propinquity				
5. Fecundity				
6. Purity				
7. Extent				
Subtotals		minus		minus
Totals (in hedons)				

Although the method promises a high degree of precision, it's almost impossible to make good on that promise: how do you quantify the qualities of pleasure? (How many hedons is a chocolate bar worth? And is a chocolate bar worth the same number of hedons to you as it is to me?) Even *identifying* the pleasures (and pains) is problematic, especially if they're not immediately evident.

And not only is "the greatest good" difficult to determine, but "the greatest number" is equally problematic: How can we determine, exactly who will be affected by the proposed action? How do we identify "all concerned"? In some cases, surely that would be society as a whole, perhaps even every person on Earth. (Why stop at people? Why not every *thing* on Earth? As Bentham says, "The question is not, Can they *reason?* nor Can they *talk?*, but Can they *suffer?*" [chap. XVIII, sec. I]. So where do we draw the line? Well, we can't foresee the future, but surely we can make educated predictions. Perhaps that's sufficient, or perhaps not.)

Another criticism of Bentham's utilitarianism is directed toward its hedonism: many think pleasure is too shallow a measure of morality. "Correcting" this "flaw," Mill expanded the definition of pleasure to include not just the so-called base, physical pleasures, but also the so-called higher, aesthetic, and intellectual pleasures. Furthermore, Mill distinguished between various pleasures, not just in quantity, but also in quality: he argued, for example, that intellectual pleasures are *better than* physical pleasures: "It is better to be a human being dissatisfied than a pig satisfied; better to be a Socrates dissatisfied than a fool satisfied. And if the fool, or the pig, are of a different opinion, it is because they know only their side of the question" (10). Mill's version is known as qualitative hedonism, Bentham's as quantitative hedonism. But with purity, fruitfulness, and intensity in Bentham's calculus, I'm not sure this is a fair description (or criticism). Most people equate hedonism with a sort of selfish self-indulgence, but it certainly can be more refined than that.

There are two kinds of utilitarianism: *act utilitarianism* and *rule utilitarianism*. Act utilitarianism judges just a single, one-time act: for example, is this lie in this advertisement morally acceptable? Rule utilitarianism judges the rule, the action in general: for example, is lying morally acceptable? (To this extent, however, rule utilitarianism may be more properly considered a separate principle-based theory than a species of utilitarianism, yet it does consider consequences.) Although rule utilitarianism may seem easier (you have to figure it out just once and for all), act utilitarianism allows fine differences in context to be taken into account: for example, maybe lying, generally speaking, is immoral, but in advertisements, for some reason, it's okay. (Hmm.... And the reason is?)

Some people consider one of utilitarianism's strengths to be the fact that it takes everyone into account. Not only that, it considers everyone equally; you can't play favourites. However, this is exactly what others see as a weakness: if you, as an organ peddler, have only one liver to sell, you can't choose your daughter over some stranger (well, you can, but not because she's your daughter: you can if and only if it works out that choosing her results in the greatest good for the greatest number; maybe she's on the edge of discovering a cure for cancer, for example, and the stranger is not).

Somewhat related to this "no favourites" aspect of utilitarianism is the criticism that it doesn't take into account any rights. Suppose the stranger had a greater right to the liver for some reason (you'd have to be clear about what right that was and how it was determined; maybe your daughter, an alcoholic, already used up two livers). That doesn't matter, says utilitarianism. And so, in addition, the decision may be called unfair. This is another criticism of utilitarianism: it ignores the matter of justice.

Now of course you could consider relationships, rights, and justice in your calculation: maybe not selling it to your daughter (Wait a minute—it's your *daughter*, so wouldn't you just *give* it to her? Hey, this is a *business* example—we don't just give stuff away!) would cause great pain to you, so much so that it outweighs the good created by selling it to the stranger; maybe violating rights, maybe doing an injustice, is not for the good of society at large. But these concerns (of relationships, rights, and justice) are relevant only insofar as they're relevant to "the greatest good for the greatest number."

Another strength of utilitarianism might be that because it involves comparison of potential actions, it encourages the consideration of alternatives. Many other theories involve consideration of just a single action: is *this* action right? Utilitarianism, on the other hand, involves a sort of competition between actions: *which* action is *most* right? One might, then, become more innovative with utilitarianism.

Cost–benefit analysis is sometimes considered an example of utilitarianism. It does, after all, involve a calculation of net good (benefits minus costs). However, it seems a little more like egoism in that often the issue is not the greatest good *for the greatest number* but the greatest good *for our company* (there's that self-interest characteristic of egoism). Second, it measures in dollars, not hedons; attaching *monetary* (market) value is different than just attaching value (see the Kelman article referenced in chapter 10). Third, it usually emphasizes short-term consequences. Fourth, cost–benefit analysts don't usually claim to be seeking the *morally* right answer as much as the *strategically* right answer.

Perhaps the greatest strength of utilitarianism is that, unlike most other ethical theories, it does provide—at least in theory—a solution to moral conflicts. You just do your calculus for whatever options are in conflict, and the one that wins, wins. (Though I suppose you could end up with a tie.)

Let's go back now to the decision about whether to create a daycare centre in your company. The utilitarian would certainly consider the benefits to oneself that the egoist considered, but she would also consider the benefits to the kids involved (they could see their parents at lunch every day), the benefits to other (current and potential) employees who are parents (they'd also save money and time, and get to see their kids), probably the benefits to society as a whole (the improved parent–child relationships might decrease a number of social ills). Then the utilitarian would figure in the negative side: the daycare would cost the company, so something (profits? wages?) would have to be cut, and how much of a "pain" this would be would probably depend on the size of the company; perhaps a local daycare would be put out of business (though maybe it would just be able to take more of the kids on its waiting list); employees without kids might resent the special program, so would they—could they—call it discrimination? If the good stuff outweighs, by hedons, the bad stuff, then the greatest good for the greatest number results if the daycare is, rather than is not, created, so that would be the (morally) right thing to do. (But did you consider alternatives to is/is not? Maybe you need to add a few more options to your tally chart.)

That would be an act-utilitarian analysis of the situation. A rule-utilitarian might generalize the question "Should I create a daycare centre in this company?" to "Should companies establish programs to meet employees' external needs?"—and then similarly, systematically, work through the pleasures and pains for all concerned. (And, conceptualized in this broader fashion, one might then consider also the impact of the decision on the role of government, and its need to tax, should companies take on the responsibility for such programs.)

Before you go on, again do your short summary: what are (1) the elements, (2) the strengths, and (3) the weaknesses of utilitarianism? And (4) try using this theory to make an ethical decision in a business context.

Kantian Ethics

Unlike consequence-based theories, the end cannot justify the means in principle-based theories. Principle-based theories consider not the consequences, but the intent. And intents are guided by certain principles (or, perhaps, virtues—see the next subsection on virtue ethics). However, don't assume that the principles in a principle-based ethical theory are necessarily absolutes; exceptions may be permissible.

The ethical theory of Immanuel Kant, an eighteenth-century thinker and author of *Grounding for the Metaphysics of Morals*, is perhaps the most famous (the most lionized?) principle-based ethical theory. Acts done with the right intent (the "good will") are right acts. So what's the right intent? Kant's answer is "that which accords with duty." And what's our duty? "That which is rational"—rationality is what makes us human. (It's interesting to note that Kant is not the first, or the last, to suggest that reason—rationality—plays a central role in morality; see Aristotle and Rawls.)

So how do we know what's rational? Enter Kant's categorical imperative: "Act only according to that maxim whereby you can at the same time will that it should become a universal law" (30). Now be careful that you understand him not to be appealing to bad consequences as the test, but to non-contradictoriness as the test; Kant considers rationality to be the essence of being human, and rationality is intolerant of contradictions. So his imperative is not just a "do unto others as you would have them do unto you" thing; rather, he's saying that whatever principle we can imagine everyone following *without ending up with some sort of logical impossibility or inconsistency* is a principle we should follow.

For example, if everyone cheated on tests, tests would lose their value and their meaning, and then so too would cheating: if everyone cheated, what would be the point of cheating? Actually, if everyone cheated, it couldn't even be called cheating: you're cheating in order to gain some sort of unfair advantage over other test takers, but if everyone's allowed to cheat, then no longer is what you're doing unfair, nor will it give you any special advantage. So in future when you cheated, you'd be acting for a purpose that would not, could not, be achieved; one couldn't "cheat" if everyone did. So cheating is *not* something you can make into a universal law (without it logically falling apart), so it's not rational. And therefore it's not (morally) right.

The other important element of Kantian ethics is respect for persons, which is expressed by Kant through his practical imperative: "Act in such a way that you treat humanity, whether in your own person or in the person of another, always at the same time as an end and never simply as a means" (36). And, since Kant understands persons to be essentially rational beings with free will, respect for persons means respect for their autonomy.

As with all principle-based theories, one must ask why these principles and not others? What's the justification for these principles? Do we agree that rationality is the essence of being human? And even if we do, why should that also be the essence of being moral?

One strength of Kant's theory is the attention to motive, the attention to one's reason for behaviour, regardless of the consequences. So if you meant well, if you intended to do good, but unfortunately injury still occurred, your action would still be judged favourably as having been the right thing to do. Like all non-consequentialists, Kant recognizes that consequences are not necessarily within our control.

Another strength of this theory is its universality: there is no "it depends" involved in Kant's theory. However, there is a bit of grey area here similar to the rule/act distinction in utilitarianism: when we ask about universalizing the act, does Kant mean us, for example, to consider cheating in general or cheating in this situation, by a person in these specific circumstances?

Yet another strength is its impartiality: everyone is considered equally, there's no playing favourites. One must apply both imperatives, the categorical and the practical, consistently; this would seem to lead to fairness. Of course, this could also be considered a weakness; recall the earlier example of the organ peddler with only one liver—and a daughter who needs exactly that.

What are its weaknesses? Well, it's certainly not as precise as, say, utilitarianism. What exactly does it mean to say one should respect another's autonomy? How far must we go to ensure that one can choose, that one can act freely and rationally?

Also, Kant is an absolutist: he allows no exceptions. For example, if a psychopath with a gun comes to your door and asks if anyone else is in the house, you must not lie; you must say, "Yes, my kids are asleep upstairs. (Would you like to meet them?)" For many, that's a problem, and one might argue, as Mill does, that a rational person would *not universalize* a moral rule that would result in harm (they *would lie* to the psychopath).

Lastly, as in many ethical theories, conflicts are a problem. What if actions X and Y both respect the other's autonomy and are both universalizable, what do you do?

Let's see how this theory can be applied to ethical decision making in a business context. Suppose you've got Kant on your marketing team, what do you do? Prepare yourself for some major changes in the advertising industry, that's what. Because there can be no deception, there must be full disclosure; that will enable the rational consumer, who is not a means to your end, to make his/her own free choices. (You say Kant's on your negotiating team as well?)

Don't forget to do your summary: elements, strengths, and weaknesses. And, for application practice, how would a Kantian ethicist handle this one: should you send your openly gay employee on an international mission to a country that considers homosexuality abnormal and sinful?

Virtue Ethics

Although most of the other ethical theories ask, "What is the right thing to do?", virtue ethics asks, "What is the right kind of person to be?" The answer is "a virtuous person." So far, so good. But you must define your terms: what's virtuous? You'll need to make a list of virtues (those things a virtuous person has). Then you'll have to justify that list.

Aristotle, a thinker who lived around 350 BCE and wrote *The Nicomachean Ethics*, is considered a virtue ethicist. His list of virtues includes the standard four of the ancient Greeks—justice, temperance, courage, and wisdom—and adds a few others such as pride, magnanimity, proper ambition, veracity, modesty, gentleness, sincerity, and frankness. The big thing for Aristotle is that all virtues are at the midpoint between two extremes: the extreme of deficiency and the extreme of excess; this is his theory of "the golden mean." For example, be courageous, not cowardly (the extreme at one end), nor foolhardy (the extreme at the other end). Also, the virtues are context-dependent; for example, courage might imply willingness to risk death for a soldier in combat, but for a modern businessperson it might mean something like willingness to speak up to one's employer about an injustice in the workplace or willingness to risk public backlash by recalling a dangerous product. Aristotle justifies his list of virtues by saying that these are the qualities that enable us to experience *eudaimonia* (loosely translated as happiness, but a broad, well-being kind of happiness rather than a narrow, pleasure kind of happiness), which is achieved by developing our unique human function, that of rationality. However, he also emphasizes that moral virtue is the result of habit and training: one is taught to become a virtuous person. This notion of habit seems, at least to me, to contradict his emphasis on rationality.

William David Ross, a twentieth-century thinker and author of *The Right and the Good*, suggests the following list, phrased in terms of obligations rather than virtues (and therefore his theory is perhaps more an example of principle-based ethics than of virtue ethics; however, one can simply regard virtues as deriving from principles): fidelity, reparation, gratitude, justice, beneficence, self-improvement, and non-maleficence. As for justification for this list, Ross says we intuitively know that these are our duties. But there's one problem: if these virtues are indeed intuitively known, or self-evident, then there would be no disagreement about them. And, of course, there is. So if my intuition is different from yours, where does that leave us? (Check out the subsection on intuitionism.)

Alasdair Macintyre, another contemporary virtue ethicist and author of *After Virtue*, says that virtues are dependent on the culture involved, and more specifically on the practice involved: virtues are whatever traits are needed to do whatever it is one is doing with excellence, according to the tradition of the endeavour. For example, a virtuous soldier has the virtues of loyalty, physical courage, and physical resilience. And perhaps a virtuous businessperson would have the virtues of innovativeness and persistence?

Whatever your list, and whatever your justification, eventually you'll have to decide on priorities: for example, what do you do when honesty and loyalty collide? That is one of the weaknesses of virtue ethics: it doesn't help us with moral conflict.

Many textbooks cover feminist ethics as a separate ethical theory, but I'm not sure this is warranted. It seems to me that what's called feminist ethics by some is a kind of virtue ethics in which the virtue of caring is most important, along with things like compassion and sensitivity—that is, those qualities *stereotypically* associated with women (note my emphasis!). For example, Alison Jaggar, a contemporary thinker and feminist, argues that for something to be called feminist ethics, it must in some way correct male bias and subvert women's subordination, it must address both public and private domains, and it must take women's experiences seriously.

Nel Noddings, author of *Caring: A Feminine Approach to Ethics and Moral Education*, advocates such an ethics of care: actions done out of care for others are (morally) right actions. This theory emphasizes responsibility, especially responsibility arising from relationships. However, reciprocity is also important: Noddings claims that caring-for is morally right when cared-for is also in the picture.

This ethic of care developed, perhaps, as a reaction to the Kantian ethic of duty; to some, and perhaps more often to women than to men, duty seemed too bereft of emotion. Further, the emphasis on relationships is thought to be a reaction to the Kantian ethic which emphasizes autonomy, often as if people existed completely independent of any social context.

Indeed, this rejection of the autonomous person, as either possible or preferable, is the basis of communitarianism (see Michael Walzer and Amitai Etzioni) which, like communism or Marxism (see Karl Marx, co-author of *The Communist Manifesto*), rejects this primacy of the individual: both claim that we are, and should be, presumably, *social* beings. African and Native ethical systems also give a dominant position to the community over the individual.

Let's try virtue ethics with the situation I left with you for Kantian ethics: should you send your openly gay employee on that mission to a country that considers homosexuality abnormal and sinful? An Aristotelian virtue ethicist would ask if doing so would be just and wise. (These seem to be the most applicable virtues from Aristotle's list; the question doesn't seem to be a matter of temperance, pride, magnanimity, etc.) And it seems to me that if that employee was indeed competent and deserving, sending him would indeed be just—but would it be wise? The employee might well be injured, and the company might lose the deal and possibly the client. Ross would encounter a similar conflict: sending him would be just, but it would surely do some harm (so it violates the virtue of non-maleficence). Perhaps Macintyre, who might identify as a necessary trait for a businessperson that of catering to the client, would say don't send that particular employee, as it could be an offense to the client. But *would* Macintyre identify that as a necessary trait, a virtue? And would—should—a virtue be adopted at any expense, possibly at the expense of other virtues? (I could just as easily suggest that Macintyre would identify competence as a virtue.)

Okay, you know the summary routine: elements, strengths, weaknesses, application. (I know this is getting boring, but it will help you learn about how the theories differ from one another.)

Intuitionism

Intuitionism as an ethical theory holds that you should act according to your intuition. I have seen some business ethics accounts refer to this as the "gut test." Another quick ethical check touted in business ethics circles, the "media test," is also basically intuitionism: you are asked to imagine that the media got wind of your contemplated action—how would that make you feel?

I am also going to put into the intuitionism category the "follow your conscience" theory. It seems to me that what we call our conscience is often no more than our feelings: "conscience" seems to refer to what we "deep down" (whatever that means) think is right. Yet despite the word "think," there doesn't seem to be any rational element involved: we never suggest that one critically examine one's conscience, develop it, or reconsider it. Some people may believe that conscience is something we're born with, but there's no scientific evidence of this. Rather, conscience seems to be nothing more than the moral habits we're conditioned to follow as we are raised, and as with many childhood acquisitions, it simply feels wrong to violate any of them.

There are a few problems with intuitionism. The most significant, I think, is the unreliability of our feelings. Emotion often seems to be a less evolved aspect of our existence: many times you feel a certain way because of some information, but after you realize the information is incorrect, it takes a while for your feelings to "catch up": you still feel angry or sad or whatever, even though you know you have no reason to.

Second, one might do well to ask whether we should always act on our feelings. Certainly anger is one feeling it is best not to act on—at least not right away. Sometimes even feelings of love (no, wait, maybe I'm thinking about lust) are better not acted upon.

A third problem with intuitionism is that it offers no solution for moral conflicts: what if your feelings tell you to do two mutually exclusive things—say, save employees' jobs and save shareholders' returns. How do you decide between the two?

Lastly, what if you don't know? What if your intuition doesn't give you a strong nudge one way or the other?

So how would an intuitionist decide what to do about creating a company daycare? If it feels right, do it! And sending the gay employee on that international mission? If it feels wrong, don't do it! Okay, you try one. Is it right for your company to sell weapons to those countries involved in human-rights violations? How about selling mediation services?

When you've completed your summary for intuitionism, take a few moments to do a bit of comparison among the five ethical theories we've covered so far. Are there any similarities? What are the main differences? Which theory is the best so far? (Define your terms: what do you mean by "best"?)

Rights Theories

There are many different rights theories, but all of them say it's wrong to violate someone's rights. So the big questions for rights theorists are the following: (1) What rights do we have? (2) Why those and not others? (i.e., what's the basis for those rights?) and (3) In the event of conflict, which rights can override which others?

Natural rights theorists argue that we have certain rights just because we are human; we don't have to do anything in particular to earn them. Such theorists would have to define *human*. For example, does a fetus have those "human rights"?

Natural rights are usually considered inalienable; that means that they can't be given or taken away (neither forfeited, nor waived, nor traded). Certainly proponents of capital punishment would disagree in this regard: they would claim that one forfeits one's own right to life when one violates another's.

Social contract theorists, on the other hand, argue that certain rights are ours because we *have* done something to acquire those rights; when we accept living in society, we enter into a tacit social contract, an agreement to respect each other's rights—and indeed, the purpose of government is to protect those rights.

Kant seems to be in both groups: he speaks of innate rights, those we have by nature, as well as acquired rights, those that depend on human society. However—no surprise—all rights must be universalizable and respectful of autonomy.

Since we've covered utilitarianism, you might be interested in the views of Ronald Dworkin, a contemporary advocate of rights theories and author of *Taking Rights Seriously*. He argues that rights, when they are applicable, should count more than social well-being. Violating people's rights is always an injustice. Unlike the utilitarian view, which holds the social good supreme, Dworkin's view is that it would be wrong to violate people's rights in order to achieve a social good.

It is important to distinguish rights from obligations: having a right to property doesn't mean someone (perhaps the state) is obligated to provide you with property; it just means they can't take away any property you have. At least so say natural rights theorists. Duty-based rights theorists, however, would disagree; they would say that a right *does* imply a corresponding duty or obligation: if I have a right to something, you have a duty to honour that right. Such rights are identified as "claim rights" by Wesley Hohfeld and Joel Feinberg, two contemporary rights theorists. This view would answer to some extent questions about why there are so many "rights" theories, but no "responsibilities" theories.

Let's consider a new ethical decision using a rights-based approach: you would like to conduct your business in the language of your choice—should you? Now remember, we're asking about the morally right thing to do, not the legally right thing—so it doesn't necessarily matter if we're talking about French or Cree or Japanese. I say "not necessarily"—if you define moral right by legal right, then it *would* matter (see the subsection on relativism): since French is one of Canada's official languages, you would have more of a legal right to conduct business in French than in Japanese. *As* for conducting business in Cree, well, depending who and where you are, you may argue that Canada's laws aren't binding on First Nations' business.

But as for *moral* rightness, independent of legal rightness, which rights and whose rights are you exercising or violating by conducting business in the language of your choice? Do you have language rights? Do you have a right to freedom of speech? Does that include language of speech or just, as is the usual interpretation, content of speech? Do you have a right to preserve your culture? Is using your language, in business, a way of doing that? A necessary way? Do your customers or clients have the same rights that may be supported or violated by your decision (depending on what *their* language of choice is)? What about your employees, current and potential—do you have a right to require them to speak (and learn?) the language you choose? Would it matter whether or not your customers and employees were unilingual? These are some of the questions that would need to be asked, from a rights-based point of view, before making a decision.

Don't forget to do your summary, and then try using the rights-based approach with an ethical decision in a business context of your choice.

Justice Theories

Generally speaking, justice theories say that whatever's fair is right. But what's fair? Well, there are a number of possibilities. One is egalitarianism: everyone gets an equal portion of whatever, and that's that.

However, another possibility considers desert: everyone gets what they deserve. But how do you determine what people deserve? Usually, it's what they've earned. But what if you can't do much? What if you'd *like* to earn your paycheque, but you just can't and part of it turns out to be *un*earned? Even if you *can* do whatever it takes, how do we connect doing with deserving? By time? So an hour's work is worth so much, no matter what you do in that hour? By effort? So the more you sweat in that hour, the more you deserve? (And what if you're unlucky enough to find most things easy, what if you never sweat?) By skill? So the better nurse gets paid more than the other one? By contribution? So an hour of literacy teaching is worth more than an hour of playing hockey? By risk to self? So an hour of playing hockey is worth more than an hour of literacy teaching? By "finder's keepers"? By inheritance?

Perhaps fair is getting what one needs rather than what one deserves. Then how shall we define "need"? Food, water, shelter? So when people say they need at least $50,000 per year, what are *they* calling "need"? Maybe the truth is that they *want* $50,000 per year.

Note that in both of these cases, determining by desert and determining by need, treating everyone justly would *not* mean treating everyone the same. To look only at the last example, people with greater needs would receive a greater share of the goods.

For a more specific consideration of justice theories, we can look at Aristotle, John Rawls, and Robert Nozick.

Aristotle divided justice into three kinds: distributive justice (how the goods are divided up), retributive justice (punishing transgressors), and compensatory justice (compensating those transgressed). He also distinguished between just procedures and just outcomes.

With respect to distributive justice, with which business is perhaps most concerned, Aristotle said to treat like cases alike; one has to identify relevant similarities and differences in order to determine whether cases *are* alike. For example, with respect to the opening discussion, A gets more X (for example, pay) than B if A has more Y (effort, value, need, etc.) than B, and the "more" is exactly proportionate: twice the pay for twice the effort, for example.

Of course, one might wonder whether one can calculate X and Y with as much precision as is necessary. And of course, Aristotle never says what the X, or especially what the Y, should be (though Aristotelians tend toward contribution); he simply identifies the procedures to be used. It's all form, then, and no content, but it does seem to many to be a very fair form(ula).

The utilitarian version of justice is simply that whatever provides the greatest utility is the most just; so it doesn't really matter who gets how much of what, just that the final total is as high as possible. So two societies with equal income per capita might be considered equally fair, despite the fact that in Society A, the wealth is spread out among everyone, and in Society B, there are a few very, very rich people and everyone else is poor.

It may well be, however, that those few rich people, through judicious use of their wealth, achieve a higher level of happiness for everyone than would result if everyone had the same amount of money. Or it may be that such unequal distribution has not violated anyone's rights: Mill argues that justice involves respect for rights, especially the right to equal treatment, *unless* utility says otherwise. However, it may also be that distribution among individuals that is perceived to be unfair causes unhappiness within the society, thus decreasing the overall utility.

John Rawls, a contemporary thinker and author of *A Theory of Justice*, emphasizes, like Kant, human rationality. And like Aristotle, Rawls takes a procedural justice approach: if the procedure is fair, the result of the procedure will be fair. The decision-making procedure that best ensures social justice and fairness is described with a thought experiment: imagine, Rawls says, a group of self-interested and rational people whose responsibility is to divide up the social goods—and they don't know their race, sex, socioeconomic status, abilities, etc. A group in this "original position" under that "veil of ignorance" would, says Rawls, establish the following two principles: (1) "Each person is to have an equal right to the most extensive total system of basic liberties compatible with a similar system of liberty for all," and (2) "Social and economic inequalities are to be arranged so that they are both: (a) to the greatest benefit of the least advantaged..., and (b) attached to offices and positions open to all under conditions of fair equality of opportunity" (302)—in other words, equal shares unless in a certain arrangement of unequal shares, where even the worst off is better off than in another arrangement. Rawls believes that this approach makes sure that certain biases do not taint the decision-making process: since no one knows whether they'll turn out to be wealthy or poor, able-bodied or disabled, or even elderly or young, Rawls argues that the rational person will always choose to divide up goods in a way that always benefits the least advantaged—unless he or she is a risk-taker, which is one of the criticisms of Rawls's theory.

Another criticism is that he doesn't rank the basic liberties—so what happens if they come into conflict? And his list of primary goods—the things any rational person is supposed to want—has been criticized *as* incomplete and not satisfactorily justified.

Robert Nozick, another contemporary thinker and author of *Anarchy, State, and Utopia*, presents a view of justice that incorporates very strongly a right to liberty, but he seems to assume that everyone is equally able to exercise that right. His view also incorporates an entitlement theory: things are just if what we have is what we're entitled to; and we're entitled to whatever is ours by history—by transfer, purchase, gift—as long as each step in the history is fair. And it is this phrase "as long as" that is a little problematic: what exactly *is* a "fair" transfer?

Imagine you've just opened up your very own business and you need to decide how much to charge for your service. What price is (morally) right? Well, you may have been taught some handy formula, for example, total expenses divided by anticipated sales plus 10-per-cent profit margin. But why is that morally right? Is it fair? Are you entitled to 10-per-cent profit? Why not 5 per cent? Why not 15? What do you deserve? Do you deserve *any* profit? So are not-for-profit businesses *un*fair?

And when you say expenses, are you including everything it took to make your service available, for example, long-term environmental degradation? Who pays for that if not your customers? Who *should* pay for that? For example, your heating bill, besides being heavily subsidized, doesn't reflect the real cost of the energy; I suspect your garbage disposal is also very much underpriced. Will you incorporate these less obvious costs?

And are you going to charge everyone the same or will you have a sliding scale? What if someone can't afford your standard fee? Okay, but what if they can't afford it because they just bought a new car (and they could have used public transit)? Is that different from not being able to afford it because their job pays only minimum wage?

So, once again.... Main elements? Strengths? Weaknesses? An application?

Religionism

Religionism isn't typically considered an ethical theory, but since many people connect religion with morality, it deserves some examination. (Also, it seems increasingly to be used as justification for political and military actions worldwide.) And although reference to religionism isn't very standard, reference to the divine command theory is; however, although I will deal with that, it's just part of what I want to address.

Some people connect religion with morality so much so that atheists are automatically considered immoral. There are a few errors and a few difficulties with this position. First, one can have moral beliefs, beliefs about what's right and wrong, without a religion, so one could be a morally good person without adhering to a religion. Keep in mind that religion involves much more than morality: mainly, it involves belief in a god (or gods); it also, usually, involves the practice of specific rituals. Not believing in a god and not practicing certain rituals, however, doesn't mean you can't establish some list of values or ethical principles. And in fact we've just covered several ways to do just that, to establish right and wrong, and none of them involved gods or rituals.

Religionists may counter by asking what those values or principles would be based on. Their assumption is that their values and principles are based on belief in a god, so without that god, there can be no values. And that's the error. One can say honesty is good because God says so (the divine command theory), but one could also say that honesty is good because that makes for a happy society (utilitarianism) or because that shows respect for others (Kantian ethics).

Indeed, my guess is that many religionists adhere to their value system not so much because God says so but because of those other reasons, which tend to be espoused by many, if not most, world religions. While this eliminates the difficulties of establishing the existence and moral expertise of God (see below), it invites the difficulties of principle-based theories: what is the basis (if not "because God says so") for that value system or for those principles? That is to ask, why those principles (for example, the Ten Commandments) and not others? Further, what do you do when principles conflict? Some religions may provide answers to these questions, but some may not, and you would need to do further work.

However, let's grant that religious people *do* consider what their God says to be the basis of ethics. This is what's called the "divine command" theory, and there are actually two versions of it. One argues that God, being the all-loving and benevolent being that he is, will command us to do only what is good and right. The problem with this version is that it suggests some standard of good and right (the "standard" on which God bases his commands) that is independent of, and presumably prior to, or higher than, God—so suddenly God is not the Creator of All, God is not "always was and always will be."

The other version of the divine command theory argues that whatever God says to do is what's right—his command *defines* (rather than is based on) right. Incidentally, from here we get to natural-law morality, according to which whatever is natural is right (because God made it so) and whatever is unnatural is wrong. (So if it's natural for me to feel a murderous rage any time a man dismisses a woman as unimportant, it's morally right for me to kill?) This version of divine command theory is essentially ethical relativism (see the next subsection): right/wrong is relative to one's God. But basically, it's an appeal to authority: the authority of God. And although appeals to authority can be valid, recall that they aren't necessarily so. There are actually two problems with appealing to God as an authority on moral matters. First, one needs to establish that he does, in fact, exist. And there are a considerable number of very good arguments *against* his existence (not the least of which is simply the absence of sufficient evidence), especially against his existence as a *god*. (See, for example, Johnson's *The Atheist Debater's Handbook*.)

Second, even if we did have proof of his existence, we would need to establish his moral authority. For example, the facts that the Judaeo-Christian God killed almost everyone on earth (see the story of Noah's ark) and that he condones animal torture (see the story about Samson and what he did to a few hundred foxes) seem to suggest that he may not be the one to consult about right and wrong.

There are also problems with the appeal itself. If one appeals by prayer, how can you be sure it's *God* who's telling you what to do and not just your own mind? And how can you convince others that it's God's voice you heard? (And without proof, how can you expect others to believe you?) Another question: what if two people claim that God spoke to them and, apparently, he told each of them a different thing, which person do you believe? How do you prove which one is telling the truth?

Well, religionists might counter, you could use the Bible (or the Torah or the Qur'an) instead of personal divine revelation. After all, it's the word of God. But appeals through some record of God's word are similarly problematic. First, there is the matter of validity: one would need to be sure that the Bible is indeed God's word. And even biblical scholars are in disagreement about that. For example, the story of Jesus' birth is very similar to many pre-Christian tales, suggesting that the Bible may be a book of myths instead of the word of a god.

Second, there is the matter of reliability: which version is the authoritative one? And then, what about errors of translation and errors of editing? Consider the Apocrypha, a collection of books edited out of the Bible by various popes and scholars. And what about the contradictions, even within the chosen version; for example, God said do *not* kill (Exodus 20:13), but he also said *do* kill (Exodus 22:18–20).

Third, there is the matter of adequacy: many moral issues are not dealt with in the Bible; quite simply, there are a lot of ethical issues that the Judaeo-Christian God hasn't said anything about. For example, is it morally acceptable to patent DNA? For the answer to questions like this, religionists often depend on biblical scholars to pull the answer from relevant values and principles, but what if the scholars disagree?

I have put Judaeo-Christianity front and centre in my discussion, because that's the dominant religion in Canada at the time of writing, but other religions argue in similar fashion and have similar difficulties. For example, Islamic ethics are also very much an instance of the divine command theory. During the Iran–Iraq war, many Shiite Muslims went willingly to their deaths, believing they were doing the (morally) right thing, acting according to their god's will.

On the other hand, Hindu ethics, while religionist, do not exemplify the divine command theory. Rather, "right" is defined as that which fulfils your particular role or *dharma*—your duty, according to the cosmic scheme of things. The questionable premise is that each person *has* a particular role, that people are born with a certain nature, fitting to certain responsibilities. Indeed, it's questionable that there *is* a "cosmic scheme of things."

Now of course many religionists would dismiss this whole discussion as irrelevant because, they would argue, religion is not a matter of reason but a matter of faith: one must simply *believe*, without reasons or evidence. Well, if that's the case, then I can simply believe in the Great Big Purple Platypus, who tells me to kidnap and eat your kids, and that's that (I don't need to tell you why; I don't need to give you any proof).

Let's reconsider the pricing decision: how would a religionist decide what price to charge? Given Jesus' treatment of the money-changers in the temple, maybe you shouldn't be in business in the first place! Or maybe—charity being a Christian virtue—you should just give it away.

Main elements? Strengths? Weaknesses? Application?

Relativism

I've left relativism for last because it's the most slippery, but if you keep clearly in mind the descriptive/prescriptive distinction, you should be okay. Many people think moral relativism means "all people have their own opinions about right and wrong" or "right and wrong depend on the person." Well, first, those two statements are not quite saying the same thing, and second, neither is quite right as an expression of ethical relativism.

The first, "all people have their own opinions about right and wrong," is just descriptive: it's simply expressing an observation. And the observation is implying that there are different ways to determine right and wrong. And this is certainly true. (As you are now, perhaps painfully, aware.)

The second statement, that "right and wrong depend on the person," verges on prescription, and recall that's what we're interested in. But "depend" needs a little clarification. If by "depend" we mean that different people will give different answers—the answer depends on the person giving it—then, again, we're just being descriptive, we're just recognizing moral plurality or moral diversity.

But if by "depend" we mean "is determined by" or "is defined by," then we have what we're after: individual relativism—X is right if I think it's right.

This may seem to be an almost useless theory, however, because it says nothing about *how* you should come to think X is right (in fact, it verges on being descriptive when you look at it closely). Any answer to that question ("How do you come to think X is right?") is bound to simply take you to another theory: X is right if I think it's right, and I think it's right if it's good for me (egoism); or X is right if I think it's right, and I think it's right if it's fair (justice theory). And so on. You get the picture.

More interesting is social/cultural relativism: X is right if my society or culture thinks it's right. A longer definition is provided by John Ladd: "Ethical relativism is the doctrine that the moral rightness and wrongness of actions varies from society to society and that there are no absolute universal moral standards binding on all men at all times. Accordingly, it holds that whether it is right for an individual to act in a certain way depends on or is relative to the society to which he belongs." Now you still have to respond, "Okay, but on what basis does the society/culture make *its* decisions?"—which, as was the case for individual relativism, may just take you to another ethical theory. But at least the question is answered for the individual: if the society I live in thinks it's right, then okay, I'll accept its terms and definitions—it's right. (Remember to make the descriptive/prescriptive distinction, though: it's not merely that what people *think* is right/wrong that varies according to the society in which they live, but that what actually *is* right/wrong varies according to the society in which a person lives.)

However, there are a number of problems even with this point. First, what group do you choose? There are cultures coexisting with other cultures, and cultures existing within cultures. The Canadian culture? The black subculture? (And what *is* the Canadian culture? Or the black subculture, for that matter?)

Second, what do you do when the answers from the various groups conflict? As you surely can imagine, there are ethical issues over which the Canadian cultural group (assuming there *is* such a thing) and the American cultural group disagree. How do you decide which group is morally right?

Third, and this goes back to my "assuming there *is* such a thing," how do you determine what the morality of the group is? By its customs? By its laws? So are there no bad customs? No bad laws? Apparently a lot of people thought it was wrong to deny women the vote even though it was legal; and a lot of people today don't think it's wrong to smoke marijuana, but it is illegal (at least it is at the time of writing). And when laws change, does that mean that yesterday X was wrong but today it's okay? On such and such a date it was not wrong to hire children for fourteen-hour shifts, but the next day it was? What about ethical matters not covered by law? It's not illegal to make fun of your roommate—so is it morally okay? (See, for example, *It's Legal but It Ain't Right*, listed below.)

Speaking of the law, I find it interesting (distressing, actually) that many business ethics texts give the law a fairly prominent place (it's often right next to economics—another distressing observation about many business ethics texts). Doing so seems to presume an ethical relativist stance, one sometimes called "legal moralism" or "legalism." In addition to the problems mentioned above, legalism would be very problematic for international business: which society's laws does one follow? Those of the society in which the investors/owners live? Those of the society in which the workers live? Those of the society in which the consumers live? (But for those who want to consider legal moralism as their ethical guide, Canadian law is helpfully indexed at The Canadian Legal Information Institute's website: http://www.canlii.org/en/index.html.)

But back to moral relativism in general. One might suggest that one of its strengths is that it accords with reality, and theories that fit reality are good theories; after all, it is a poor theory that says sunny skies cause rain because that's just not what happens. However, ethical theories are different from scientific theories—we're back again to the prescriptive/descriptive distinction. Ethical theories say not what *does* occur but what *should* occur, so correspondence with reality is not as crucial. To remind you of the example at the beginning of this section, it may be the case that angry men get violent, but that's not necessarily what we want to say *should* be the case. We may say that angry men should control their tempers, that although they may indeed get violent, doing so is morally *wrong*.

Perhaps the most interesting thing about relativism is the implications: if what is right is relative to one's group, then there is no objective or universal right or wrong. This caution might be laudable, but if there is no objective right or wrong, then all views are equally "correct," because how could one judge the various views? That is, by what measure, what standard, would one judge?

It seems to me that many people who subscribe to relativism believe they're being tolerant and open-minded. Indeed, that may be *why* they subscribe to it: they think being tolerant and open-minded is good. But first, if you are an individual relativist, there'd be no reason to discuss morality with anyone because there's no way disagreement can be reconciled: A thinks X is right and B thinks Y is right and that's the end of it—there are no reasons to examine and assess, no discussion, and no resolution of conflicts. Doesn't sound very open-minded to me.

And second, be careful: while open-minded is good at the consideration stage, it may not be at the acceptance stage. What I mean is, it may be good to have an open mind when you're considering things; in fact, consider everything. But when it comes to accepting things, do you want to accept everything? Do you want to accept—do you want to tolerate—torture? Just because "it's their way"? Child sacrifice, too? And yet as soon as you draw a line, any line, then you're not really a relativist—you're saying there *are* some things that are wrong, anywhere, anytime, for anyone (which makes you a universalist, but not necessarily an absolutist, since you could allow exceptions to your universals).

Furthermore, let's back up a bit: why do you think tolerance is good? If you *are* a (social) relativist, then you think tolerance is good because your society thinks it's good. And that gets you into circular reasoning: you value tolerance and therefore you're a relativist, and because you're a relativist, you value tolerance—something can't be both the cause and effect, both the reason for and the result of.

Lastly, the relativist assumes that the majority is right; s/he is uncritically conforming to social customs. But surely just because most people (or even a lot of people, or even just one person) think X is right, it isn't necessarily wise to agree. You should want to know *why* they think X is right (consider the reasons, identify the assumptions, define the terms, explore the alternatives).

So how would a relativist approach this ethical decision: you are part of an interviewing team for your company's new recruitment officer, and at the end of the interviews, discussion seems to focus less on the applicants' expertise and experience than on their appearance: it seems a given that lean and male bodies are preferable to large and female bodies. What do you do? Well, you might notice that there are very few large people in the company, and the few there are do not hold frontline positions. So the company culture seems clear. Then you might note that there are laws against sex discrimination, but not against size discrimination. And despite the realities of our bodies, our social culture seems to prefer those who are small (or at least not large); indeed, we seem to condemn, even in moral terms, those who are large (they're not very ambitious or industrious, they're certainly not hard-working, they have no self-control, etc.). And we do seem to attend more to the authority of men than to that of women, of male bodies than of female bodies. So choosing the lean male would be the right thing to do.

Summary time (one last time): Consider the main elements, strengths, and weaknesses of this theory, and use ethical relativism to reach a decision about an ethical issue of your choice in a business context.

Closing Note

A really good review assignment for this whole section would be to list the questions one would ask, for each theoretical approach, in order to make an ethical decision. (I know, that's a big task. But trust me—you'll be glad you did it!)

Some parting comments. Sometimes ethical theories will be mutually exclusive: two different theories will lead you to two different answers, so you obviously can't use them both; you'll have to choose. But sometimes, as R.M. Hare argues, the theories operate at different levels of moral thinking (rather like Newtonian and Einsteinian theories of physics), and sometimes, as W.D. Ross and others have suggested, it may be the case that different theories apply better in different situations.

One important point is that you *use* the theories to *get to* your answer—your decision about what to do—rather than use them "after the fact" merely to justify what you've already decided to do. Another important point is that you critically examine not only your decisions (what is right and wrong), but also your approaches to your decisions (how you determine what is right and wrong): both should be open to evaluation and perhaps modification or rejection. The rest of the book, I hope, gives you practice doing this.

References and Further Reading

Ethical Theories: Primary Sources

Aristotle. *The Nicomachean Ethics*. (There are many translations around; I used the one by J.E.C. Welldon, New York: Prometheus, 1987.)

Bentham, Jeremy. *Introduction to the Principles of Morals and Legislation*. 1789. London: Clarendon Press, 1907.

Dworkin, Ronald. *Taking Rights Seriously*. Cambridge, MA: Harvard University Press, 1977.

Epicurus. See Diogenes Laertius. *Lives of Eminent Philosophers*. Trans. R.D. Hicks. Cambridge, MA: Harvard University Press, 1972.

Etzioni, Amitai. *The Moral Dimension: Towards a New Economics*. New York: Free Press, 1988.

Feinberg, Joel. *Rights, Justice, and the Bounds of Liberty*. Princeton, NJ: Princeton University Press, 1980.

Hobbes, Thomas. *Leviathan*. 1651. New York: The Liberal Arts Press, 1958.

Hohfeld, Wesley. *Fundamental Legal Concepts*. New Haven, CT: Yale University Press, 1964.

Hume, David. *An Enquiry Concerning the Principles of Morals*. 1751. New York: Oxford University Press, 1976.

Jaggar, Alison. "Feminist Ethics: Some Issues for the Nineties." *Journal of Social Philosophy* 20.1–2 (1989): 91–107.

Johnson, B.C. *The Atheist Debater's Handbook*. New York: Prometheus, 1983.

Kant, Immanuel. *Grounding for the Metaphysics of Morals*. 1785. Trans. James W. Ellington. Indianapolis: Hackett, 1993.

Ladd, John, ed. *Ethical Relativism*. Belmont, CA: Wadsworth, 1973.

Locke, John. *Second Treatise on Civil Government*. 1690. Cambridge: Cambridge University Press, 1960.

Macintyre, Alasdair. *After Virtue*. Notre Dame, IN: Notre Dame University Press, 1981.

Marx, Karl, and Friedrich Engels. *The Communist Manifesto*. 1848. New York: Washington Square Press, 1965.

Mill, John Stuart. *Utilitarianism*. 1861. Indianapolis: Hackett, 1979.

Mill, John Stuart, and Harriet Taylor. *On Liberty*. London: J.W. Parker, 1859.

Nielsen, Kai. *Ethics Without God*. London: Pemberton, 1973.

Noddings, Nel. *Caring: A Feminine Approach to Ethics and Moral Education*. Berkeley: University of California Press, 1984.

Nozick, Robert. *Anarchy, State, and Utopia*. New York: Basic Books, 1974.

Passas, Nikos, and Neva Goodwin. *It's Legal but It Ain't Right: Harmful Social Consequences of Legal Industries*. Ann Arbor: University of Michigan Press, 2004.

Rand, Ayn. *The Virtue of Selfishness*. New York: New American Library, 1964.

Rawls, John. *A Theory of Justice*. Cambridge, MA: Harvard University Press, 1971.

Ross, William David. *The Right and the Good*. Oxford: Clarendon, 1930.

Smith, Adam. *An Inquiry into the Nature and Causes of the Wealth of Nations*. 1776. New York: Modern Library, 1937.

Spencer, Herbert. *The Principles of Ethics*. London: Williams & Norgate, 1892. (This is about evolutionary ethics. See Anthony Flew, *Evolutionary Ethics*. New York: Macmillan, 1967, for a critique.)

Tong, Rosemarie. *Feminine and Feminist Ethics*. Belmont, CA: Wadsworth, 1995.

Walzer, Michael. "The Communitarian Critique of Liberalism." *Political Theory* 18.1 (February 1990): 6–23.

Ethical Theories: Good Secondary Material

Art, Brad. *Ethics and the Good Life: A Text with Readings*. Belmont, CA: Wadsworth, 1994. (This book is delightful; Brad Art has an attitude I love!)

Beck, Clive. *Ethics: An Introduction*. Toronto: McGraw-Hill Ryerson, 1972.

Boss, Judith A. *Ethics for Life: An Interdisciplinary and Multicultural Introduction*. Mountain View, CA: Mayfield, 1998.

Ellin, Joseph. *Morality and the Meaning of Life: An Introduction to Ethical Theory*. Fort Worth, TX: Harcourt Brace, 1995. (Includes a very thorough discussion of egoism, and a sophisticated discussion of religion and naturalism.)

Holmes, Robert L. *Basic Moral Philosophy*. Belmont, CA: Wadsworth, 1993. (Includes a good discussion of the divine command theory.)

MacKinnon, Barbara. *Ethics: Theory and Contemporary Issues*. Belmont, CA: Wadsworth, 1995. (Includes clear, careful, and brief explanations of many of the ethical theories.)

Pojman, Louis P. *Ethics: Discovering Right and Wrong*. Belmont, CA: Wadsworth, 1995.

PART III

ETHICAL ISSUES IN BUSINESS

Introductory Note

Part III is divided into 10 chapters, each devoted to one important ethical issue in business. Each of these chapters will have four components.

First, you'll be presented with a hypothetical decision-making scenario (called a "What to Do?"), created to get you thinking about that particular issue. You may be tempted to just read these and then carry on, but I urge you to stop and really think about what you would do and why. One, you'll get good practice in critical thinking about ethical issues—and that *is* the point of this book: to develop the ability to think deeply and clearly about such issues. Two, you might surprise yourself and discover on your own some of the major problems, and solutions, regarding these issues.

Second, you will be presented with an introduction outlining those major problems and (some of) the solutions. To get the (morally) right answer, you need to know which questions to ask; I hope these introductions will lead you to that knowledge.

Third, you will find two or three essays, each with a set of questions. Paragraphs are numbered for ease of reference. Some of the essays are comprehensive, seeming to repeat the introductory material; some take one single aspect of the issue and examine it in detail; and some argue for one particular view or aspect of the issue.

For many of you, this will be your first experience reading essays of this nature that make an argument of some kind. *Merely reading the essays will not be enough.* You are advised also to do the following:

1. Write an outline of the claims made in the essay, along with the support (reason, evidence) given for each claim. (That is, what values, principles, and/or concepts does the author argue for?) Do not make the mistake of writing a paragraph-by-paragraph summary: authors don't always present one claim per paragraph—several paragraphs may

be background, there may be a claim made in one paragraph while its support may be found in another, or perhaps a claim and its support may be in the same paragraph, or maybe the support is quite extensive and spread over several paragraphs, and so on. You will need to *pick out* the author's claims (sometimes the author may not be as explicit as you'd like) and then recognize what supports those claims. (And if you're really up for it, you can try to distinguish between major and minor claims, and try to understand which claims, if any, depend on other claims.) However, many authors do summarize their argument in one of the introductory paragraphs (and/or a concluding paragraph), so look for that!
2. Think about those arguments (the claims with their support) and decide whether you agree: if you do, make sure you know why; if you don't, figure out why not. (That is, are the reasons that are given *good* ones? Why or why not? Are there any unacceptable assumptions? Has the author neglected to consider anything? Are there exceptions or distinctions the author has failed to make? Reread the subsection "How to Think about Ethics" in Part I.) You might even want to prepare a "reading guide"—a list in point form of things to do, to look for, or to ask, as you read. Then, if you follow your list, consciously and systematically, for each of the essays you'll read, you will become a better reader/thinker by the end of the book, or of your course—the training you will have put yourself through will, I promise, make such a difference not only in your studies, but in your life more generally!
3. Prepare a list of questions raised by the essay that you're interested in discussing (and, I hope, writing about: how can you add to the academic discourse? how can you solve the remaining problems?).

Nor will merely reading the essays once be enough. In fact, you will probably spend more time per page with philosophical material than with readings in other disciplines. This is (one would hope) not because such material is poorly written, but rather, as mentioned above, because (1) it deals with concepts, rather than with facts (to use Bloom's taxonomy, it deals with the higher cognitive skills of analysis, synthesis, and evaluation, rather than knowledge, comprehension, and application: you're not just reading for information, to know and understand; you're reading for argument, to follow and assess); and (2) such content is simply more difficult to understand—partly because of its nature and partly because most students (indeed, most people generally) have had so little practice with it.

Keep in mind that reading is writing in reverse: when you write, you come up with a skeleton or plan for your essay, and then you flesh it out—you have an outline of points and then you write the paragraphs with detail, explanation, example, and so forth, to "make" those points; when you read, you're trying to extract that skeleton, that plan—you need to separate the detail, explanation, and example from the points they serve.

The questions accompanying the essays are multi-purpose. Partly, they are designed to highlight the argument of the essay (so use them as guides *as* you read, not *after* you read—even though they're at the end), to develop your ability to read essays like these with critical understanding; you will note that in general there are more questions accompanying the essays at the beginning of the text than at the end (my assumptions are that you will need less guidance as you go on and that you will go through the chapters pretty much in the order in which they're presented). And partly the questions are designed to provoke you to consider alternatives to the positions presented by the authors.

Lastly, at the end of each chapter, you will be presented with a case study, a description of a real situation in Canadian business that illustrates the ethical issue of the chapter. In some cases, you may find action worth imitating—many Canadian companies are trying to do the right thing. In other cases, you may be challenged to figure out what should have been done differently to avoid what happened.

CHAPTER ONE

Whistleblowing

What to Do?—Rivertree's Grocery

You have a summer job as stockperson for your local grocery store, Rivertree's Grocery. One day, as you're unpacking and shelving produce, you notice that many of the crates are marked "U.S.A. Produce" and some are labelled "Product of Mexico." However, the refrigerated shelves on which you're placing the produce have tag labels indicating "Produce of Canada, No. 1." You search in the stockroom for tag labels indicating U.S.A. and Mexico, but you can't find any. When you explain this to your manager, he says, "Don't worry about it."

You think that probably fruits and vegetables from the States are okay—though of course most of it is genetically modified—but still there's the principle of the matter. However, you're aware that some countries, perhaps especially poorer countries like Mexico, don't have the same environmental/agricultural standards as Canada and the US. It's possible, you think, that produce from Mexico has been grown or sprayed with pesticides that are illegal in Canada, possibly even hazardous to one's health. In fact, you recall that a few years ago, grapes from somewhere had to be pulled off the shelves because of some chemical health risk. But, of course, you don't know about this particular produce; it could be fine. And yet, better safe than sorry—people should know.

You consider telling someone—the local paper? They'd probably print some sort of story; they're usually desperate for news. Then again, the manager might be friends with the paper's editor—you're not sure.

There is another grocery store in town, and the town is barely large enough to support both. So unfortunately, it wouldn't take much for Rivertree's Grocery to go out of business.

And in any case, you don't want to get fired: you've worked here for three summers in a row, and you're going into your last year of university; while your parents have agreed

> to cover your food and shelter expenses, the rest is up to you—if you get fired now, you probably won't be able to get another summer job because by this time, mid-July, they're all gone, and then you won't be able to pay for tuition and books come September. Still, apart from the blatant lying, people could get very sick....
> What do you decide to do? Why?

Introduction

Simply defined, whistleblowing refers to *the release of information to the public, by an employee, of his/her employer's wrongdoing*. To many, a whistleblower is a "tattle-tale." But, as is often the case, the ethics that got us through childhood may be inadequate for our adult life. (Indeed, they may have been inadequate for childhood too—what exactly is wrong with being a tattle-tale?) Perhaps a better label, an adult label, is "ethical resister" (suggested by Glazer and Glazer) or simply "person of principle" (suggested by Aldergrove).

Like most ethical decisions, deciding whether to blow the whistle is difficult because there are *conflicting interests* involved. Specifically, one must consider three parties—*the public, the company or organization*, and *the individual*—and somehow measure and compare their interests.

One way of determining whose interests are greater, or whose interests have greater moral priority, is to consider the *consequences*. Very often, consequences are measured in terms of *harm and benefit*. So one important question is "How much harm to the public and to yourself (because if the company goes down, you might go with it) would result if you did *not* blow the whistle?" Another is "How much harm to the company and to yourself would result if you *did* blow the whistle?"

However, you must first define harm and, further, you need to be able to measure it. Perhaps some sort of utilitarian calculus could be used. *How many* people would be harmed? (Is "the public" the community, the country, or the entire planet?) *How severe* would the harm be? (Are we talking about inconvenience or injury? A slight decrease in profits or bankruptcy? A little ostracism or loss of job?) *How long* would it last? *How likely* is it to occur? Sure, saving the entire planet is worth losing your job, but is preventing short-term, somewhat severe, harm to a hundred people worth causing a company to go bankrupt and lay off three times that many?

For such a consequentialist approach, Sissela Bok's comments about the conditions necessary for *successful* whistleblowing may be relevant: if the whistleblowing under consideration is unlikely to succeed, then the harm to the public is unlikely to be avoided, and that changes things.

Bok's comments about considering *alternatives* are also relevant: is whistleblowing the best way to achieve the consequences? (Did you try other things first, such as internal reporting, to minimize the negative consequences?)

Certainly individuals considering whistleblowing have a duty to verify the facts. You may see or hear something that you consider unacceptable and that, if true, could result in harm to others. However, if it's not true, your whistleblowing could put the company in financial jeopardy due to the bad publicity; this, in turn, could have negative consequences for the employees, and perhaps even the community at large. Furthermore, mistaken whistleblowing could make it harder for future whistleblowers, who may be dismissed as misguided alarmists. So you want to have your facts straight. However, verification may not always be easy. Perhaps the degree of certainty that wrongdoing is happening bears on the moral rightness of the whistleblowing.

Consequences are not the only worthy consideration, however. You could determine whether whistleblowing is morally justified solely on the basis of *intent*: if your intentions are good, then whistleblowing is the right thing to do (whether or not it succeeds). In this case, you'd have to define "good." Perhaps "good" corresponds to some list of virtues, and insofar as whistleblowing is telling the truth, for example, it is good; on the other hand, as Bok suggests, motives arising from malice may qualify the whistleblowing as unjustified.

Another area of consideration is that of *rights*, *duties*, and *obligations*. Whistleblowing is seen by many, including Bok but excluding Duska (in the second essay in this chapter), to be a violation of *loyalty* to the company or organization. (Consider that if you were not an employee, informing the public of a company's wrongdoing would, without question, be praiseworthy.) To accept this claim, you must first accept the premise that employees actually have an obligation of loyalty to the company. Upon what basis might this obligation rest? That is, why could an employer demand—or why should an employer expect—that its employees be loyal? And what exactly does "loyalty" mean? Does it include obedience? What are the limits of that loyalty? Does it extend forever or just while you are employed by the company? Does it extend over all company behaviour or just legal behaviour? Whatever the limits, are they absolute or can there be exceptions? What might these exceptions be? What happens when loyalty conflicts with honesty?

Even if you agree that there *is* an obligation of loyalty, you must then determine whether whistleblowing violates that loyalty. This will probably take you back to defining clearly the nature of that loyalty.

Another duty or obligation to consider is that of *confidentiality*. Again, one must determine whether one has a duty to maintain confidentiality, what the limits of that duty are, and whether whistleblowing does in fact violate that duty.

Both loyalty and confidentiality are in the company's interests; what about duties and obligations to yourself and to others? Do you have an obligation to be loyal to your family? Which obligation comes first? Do you have any duties to society at large that might supersede duties to the company? Do you have any duties to future generations?

And what about the rights of others? Does society have a right to freedom of information? Does it have a right to freedom from harm? Perhaps, in light of these rights, one has a duty, an obligation, to blow the whistle. (Duska argues in this direction at the end of his essay.) Consider the comments of Ralph Nader et al.:

> Corporate employees are among the first to know about industrial dumping of mercury or fluoride sludge into waterways, defectively designed automobiles, or undisclosed adverse effects of prescription drugs and pesticides. They are the first to grasp the technical capabilities to prevent existing

product or pollution hazards. But they are very often the last to speak out, much less to refuse to be recruited for acts of corporate or governmental negligence or predation. Staying silent in the face of a professional duty has direct impact on the level of consumer and environmental hazards. (Nader, Petakas, and Blackwell, p. 4)

Indeed, perhaps companies and organizations have a duty to allow, rather than a right to prohibit, whistleblowing. And not "just" a duty to do so, but perhaps also an interest in doing so: Burton and Near found that "a large number of business undergraduates admitted cheating while only a small percentage reported peers' cheating when they observed it" (abstract). They add, "these results should be sobering for managers...." Indeed. Any company committed to high ethical standards—not to mention high-quality products and services and a good public reputation—will *value* its potential whistleblowers: it will have an effective internal program (an ethics office or an ombudsperson, for example) that genuinely supports reports of wrongdoing and truly protects those employees who make such reports—and, of course, corrects the situation quickly and completely. Davis suggests several procedures that could be part of such a program, such as space on evaluation forms specifically for negative things, review meetings specifically for problem identification, and changing the "chain" of command to a "lattice" of command.[1] Of course, prevention would be the best cure: Walters suggests that organizations can reduce the need for whistleblowing in the first place by ensuring that they don't interfere with employees' basic political freedoms and that they are truly socially responsible companies.

> **BOX 1.1 Evan Vokes Blew the Whistle on TransCanada and...**
>
> When Evan Vokes, a machinist, welder, and mechanical engineer working for TransCanada became concerned about the competence of pipeline inspectors and TransCanada's lack of compliance with welding regulations (set by the National Energy Board [NEB]), he sent emails to various project managers. They dismissed his concerns. Vokes then met with the Vice-President of Operations. No change. Then he wrote a letter to the Chief Executive Officer. Still no change. Finally he blew the whistle, making a formal complaint to the NEB.
>
> TransCanada fired him. That was in May 2012.
>
> Then TransCanada said to *CBC News* that "the items raised by the former employee were identified and addressed through routine quality control processes well before any facilities went into service" and "we are confident that any remaining concerns the regulator has about compliance and pipeline safety will be unwarranted."

---

1 See also Kaptein; King; Lee and Fargher; MacGregor and Stuebs; Miceli, Near, and Dworkin; and Moberly for other ways in which companies can increase the likelihood of internal whistleblowing over the more "expensive"—that is, publicized—external whistleblowing.

> Then they confessed that they "did not always follow [the] regulation [that *independent* inspectors be hired] in the past" and that such noncompliance was "industry standard" (Rusnell, Sawa, and Loeiro).
>
> And then in October 2012, they shut down their XL pipeline, saying that "tests showed possible safety issues." Coincidence? Maybe.
>
> *Sources*
> The Associated Press. "TransCanada shuts down Keystone pipeline temporarily." *CBC News*. 18 October 2012. http://www.cbc.ca/news/world/transcanada-shuts-down-keystone-pipeline-temporarily-1.1288847
> Rusnell, Charles, Timothy Sawa, and Joseph Loiero. "Whistleblower forced investigation of TransCanada Pipelines." *CBC News*. 17 October 2012. http://www.cbc.ca/news/canada/whistleblower-forced-investigation-of-transcanada-pipelines-1.1146204

Although corporate whistleblower protection programs have increased in the last decade or so, Monk, Knights, and Page note that even though "there exists an underlying assumption that all those involved in the design of such measures have created them in good faith," research challenges this assumption; they suggest that "some corporate interests deliberately sabotage whistleblower protection law as part of a wider corporate counter-resistance strategy."

Certainly companies will likely do their best to squelch the story as soon as possible, and the whistleblower too may not want publicity that invades privacy and disrupts life, not to mention future livelihood. It's my guess, then, that there are many more people out there than we know about who have stood up and done the right thing, who have made personal sacrifices for principles—not to mention the prevention of harm. Don't underestimate your capacity for small-scale heroism.

But at the same time, don't underestimate the politics either. Note that despite restricting his whistleblowing to internal channels, Roger Boisjoly (one of the engineers aware of and very concerned about the O-rings whose failure resulted in the death of the space shuttle *Challenger*'s crew; see the first reading by Grant, below) was, after his testimony to the government investigation, essentially demoted and reportedly harassed, and he eventually left his job at Morton Thiokol. If, after checking your facts, you *do* decide to blow the whistle, do so after careful planning[1]—you want to make it count!

Kernaghan says that "the number of whistleblowing incidents involving government employees has increased significantly" (35), and he lists several examples: a forester in the Ontario Ministry of Natural Resources reported that it was granting timber-cutting rights where volumes were insufficient, an employee of the Ontario Ministry of Correctional Services reported overcrowding in two Toronto jails, an employee in the Canadian Department of Indian and

---

1 See the material by James and Raven-Hansen for advice.

Northern Affairs reported that it routinely broke financial agreements with Indian bands, and an employee of the Department of Immigration reported that it allowed people with criminal records to stay in Canada illegally.

Even so, why is whistleblowing the exception rather than the rule? Why do so many people, by their silence, allow the bad to continue? MacGregor and Stuebs conclude that "an individual's willingness to remain silent depends upon their awareness that an action is wrong, community ties, moral competence, and professional standards..." (p. 150). I hope that this book improves the first and third factors, but despite my earlier warning, I think people are less politically naïve (and more self-interested?) these days, so I would add a fifth factor to their list: knowledge of the consequences to oneself. "Easy whistleblowing occurs," MacGregor and Stuebs go on to say, "with minimal personal costs, risks, inconveniences, and economic disincentives to the whistleblower (Malm 2000); however, generally there is no easy whistleblowing (Vandekerckhove and Tsahuridu 2010)." Well, there is now—WikiLeaks!

BOX 1.2 WikiLeaks   Making Whistleblowing Easy

In its online "About" page, WikiLeaks describes its purpose as follows:

> With its anonymous drop box, WikiLeaks provides an avenue for every government official, every bureaucrat, and every corporate worker, who becomes privy to damning information that their institution wants to hide but the public needs to know. What conscience cannot contain, and institutional secrecy unjustly conceals, WikiLeaks can broadcast to the world. It is telling that a number of government agencies in different countries (and indeed some entire countries) have tried to ban access to WikiLeaks. This is of course a silly response, akin to the ostrich burying its head in the sand. A far better response would be to behave in more ethical ways.

The site goes on to say that "When information comes in, our journalists analyse the material, verify it and write a news piece about it describing its significance to society. We then publish both the news story and the original material in order to enable readers to analyse the story in the context of the original source material themselves."

For example, on 13 November 2013, WikiLeaks released the draft text for the Intellectual Property Rights chapter of the TPP (Trans-Pacific Partnership)—the "largest-ever economic treaty, encompassing nations representing more than 40 per cent of the world's GDP...[with] wide-ranging effects on medicines, publishers, internet services, civil liberties and biological patents...." (We'll come back to the TPP later.)

> *Sources*
> https://wikileaks.org/About.html
> https://wikileaks.org/tpp/pressrelease.html

> **BOX 1.3   Feel Like Watching a Movie?**
>
> For whistleblowing movies, check out *All the President's Men* (1976), *The China Syndrome* (1979), *Silkwood* (1983), *The Insider* (1999), *Erin Brockovich* (2000), and *The Whistleblower* (2010). All but *The China Syndrome* are based on true stories.

References and Further Reading

Aldergrove, John Romney. *Enemies: The Rationalist View of Human Nature*. Burnaby, BC: Stentorian, 1998.

Bok, Sissela. "Whistleblowing and Professional Responsibility." *New York University Education Quarterly* 11 (Summer 1980): 2–7.

Burton, Brian K., and Janet P. Near. "Estimating the Incidence of Wrongdoing and Whistle-blowing." *Journal of Business Ethics* 14.1 (January 1995): 17–31.

Callahan, Elleta Sangrey, and Terry Morehead Dworkin. "Internal Whistleblowing: Protecting the Interests of the Employee, the Organization, and Society." *American Business Law Journal* 37 (1991): 267–308.

Davis, Michael. "Avoid the Tragedy of Whistleblowing." *Business and Professional Ethics Journal* 8.4 (1989): 3–19.

De George, Richard T. ed. *Business Ethics*. 4th ed. Englewood Cliffs, NJ: Prentice Hall, 1995. 240–62.

Duska, Ronald. "Whistleblowing and Employee Loyalty." In J.R. Desjardins and J.J. McCall (eds.), *Contemporary Issues in Business Ethics*. 2nd ed. Belmont, CA: Wadsworth, 1990. 142–47.

Elliston, Frederick A. "Anonymity and Whistleblowing." *Journal of Business Ethics* 3.1 (1982): 167–77.

Fredin, A. "The Unexpected Cost of Silence." *Strategic Finance* (April 2012): 53–59.

Glazer, Myron. "Ten Whistleblowers and How They Fared." *The Hastings Center Report* 13 (December 1983): 33–41.

Glazer, Myron Peretz, and Penina Migdal Glazer. *The Whistleblowers: Exposing Corruption in Government and Industry*. New York: Basic Books, 1989.

Grant, Colin. "Whistle Blowers: Saints of Secular Culture." *Journal of Business Ethics* 39 (2002): 391–99.

Gundlach, Michael J., Scott C. Douglas, and Mark J. Martinko. "The Decision to Blow the Whistle: A Social Information Processing Framework." *Academy of Management Review* 28.1 (2003): 107–23.

James, Gene G. "Whistle Blowing: Its Moral Justification." In W. Michael Hoffman and Robert E. Frederick (eds.), *Business Ethics: Readings and Cases in Corporate Morality*. 3rd ed. New York: McGraw-Hill, 1995. 290–301.

Kaptein, M. "From Inaction to External Whistleblowing: The Influence of the Ethical Culture of Organizations on Employee Responses to Observed Wrongdoing." *Journal of Business Ethics* 98.3 (2011): 513–30.

Kernaghan, Kenneth. "Whistle-Blowing in Canadian Governments: Ethical, Political and Managerial Considerations." *Optimum* 22.1 (1991–92): 34–43.

King, Granville. "The Implications of an Organization's Structure on Whistleblowing." *Journal of Business Ethics* 20.4 (1999): 315–26.

Klein, Helen A., Nancy M. Levenburg, Marie McKendall, and William Mothersell. "Cheating during the College Years: How Do Business School Students Compare?" *Journal of Business Ethics* 72 (2007): 197–206.

Larmer, Robert A. "Whistleblowing and Employee Loyalty." *Journal of Business Ethics* 11.2 (1992): 125–28.

Lee, Gladys, and Neil Fargher. "Companies' Use of Whistle-Blowing to Detect Fraud: An Examination of Corporate Whistle-Blowing Policies." *Journal of Business Ethics* 114.2 (2013): 283–95.

MacGregor, Jason, and Martin Stuebs. "The Silent Samaritan Syndrome: Why the Whistle Remains Unblown." *Journal of Business Ethics* 120 (2014): 149–64.

Malm, H.M. "Bad Samaritan Laws: Harm, Help, or Hype?" *Law and Philosophy* 19 (2000): 707–50.

Miceli, Marcia P., Janet P. Near, and Terry Morehead Dworkin. "A Word to the Wise: How Managers and Policy-makers Can Encourage Employees to Report Wrongdoing." *Journal of Business Ethics* 86 (2009): 379–96.

Miethe, Terry D. *Whistleblowing at Work, Tough Choices in Exposing Fraud, Waste, and Abuse on the Job*. Boulder, CO: Westview Press, 1999.

Moberly, Richard E. "Sarbanes-Oxley's Structural Model to Encourage Corporate Whistleblowers." *Brigham Young University Law Review* 5 (2006): 1107–80.

Monk, Hilary, David Knights, and Margaret Page. "Whistleblowing Paradoxes: Legislative Protection and Corporate Counter Resistance." In Alison Pullen and Carl Rhodes (eds.), *The Routledge Companion to Ethics, Politics and Organizations*. London: Routledge, 2015. 300–17.

Nader, Ralph, Peter J. Petakas, and Kate Blackwell. *Whistle Blowing: The Report of the Conference on Professional Responsibility*. New York: Grossman, 1972.

Nielsen, Richard P. "Changing Unethical Organizational Behaviour." *The Executive* (May 1989): 123–30.

Perlow, Leslie, and Stephanie Williams. "Is Silence Killing Your Company?" *Harvard Business Review* 81.5 (2003): 52–58.

Peters, Charles, and Taylor Branch. *Blowing the Whistle: Dissent in the Public Interest*. New York: Praeger, 1972.

Raven-Hansen, Peter. "Dos and Don'ts for Whistleblowers: Planning for Trouble." *Technology Review* 83 (May 1980): 34–44.

Vandekerckhove, Wim, and Eva E. Tsahuridu. "Risky Rescues and the Duty to Blow the Whistle." *Journal of Business Ethics* 97.3 (2010): 365–80.

Walters, Kenneth. "Your Employees' Right to Blow the Whistle." *Harvard Business Review* (July/August 1975): 160–62.

Westin, Alan F. *Whistle Blowing! Loyalty and Dissent in the Corporation.* New York: McGraw-Hill, 1981.

Whistle Blowers: Saints of Secular Culture[*]

Colin Grant

[1] On January 28, 1986, the space shuttle *Challenger* exploded 73 seconds after lift-off, killing all 7 astronauts on board. This was especially dramatic because one of them was the civilian teacher, Christa McAuliffe. The Rogers Commission, appointed to investigate the explosion, concluded that "the explosion occurred due to seal failure in one of the solid rocket booster joints" (Boisjoly, Curtis, and Mellican, p. 229).[1] The rocket booster used to launch *Challenger* was made by Morton Thiokol. Engineers at Morton Thiokol were concerned about the O-ring seals. A year before, on January 24, 1985, Senior Scientist at Morton Thiokol, Roger Boisjoly, watched a launch during unseasonably cold weather. When he inspected the solid rocket booster several days later, after it was recovered from the Atlantic Ocean, he saw black marks that indicated hot combustion gasses had escaped past the O-rings. Boisjoly had 25 years' experience as an engineer in the aerospace industry, and was considered the leading expert in the United States on O-rings and rocket joint seals.

[2] A Seal Erosion Task Force was appointed to investigate, but Morton Thiokol engineers expressed frustration over lack of progress on the problem in the summer of 1985. In July of 1985, Boisjoly wrote a memo labelled "Company Private," warning management that the seals could fail, resulting in the loss of human life. The formation of the Seal Erosion Task Force was formally announced in August. Another flight in October provided more evidence and further protests.

[3] Morton Thiokol's contract with NASA specified a temperature range for the rocket boosters between 40 and 90 degrees Fahrenheit. The temperature on January 28, 1986 was 30 degrees, 2 degrees below freezing. The Rogers Commission discovered that four senior Morton Thiokol execu-

---

[*] *Journal of Business Ethics* 39 (2002): 391–99.

tives overruled engineering concerns, and recommended launch. Boisjoly had returned to his office and made a journal entry stating his disagreement with the decision.

[4] On February 25th, Boisjoly testified before the Commission, exposing the disagreement with Morton Thiokol management about the launch. He was later given the title of Seal Coordinator for the redesign effort, but in practice was isolated from NASA and from the redesign effort itself. He was also chastised by an executive for "airing the company's dirty laundry" before the Commission.

[5] On July 21, 1986, Boisjoly requested an extended sick leave from Morton Thiokol. He said: "I have been asked by some if I would testify again if I knew in advance of the potential consequences to me and my career. My answer is always an immediate 'Yes.' I couldn't live with any self-respect if I tailored my actions based upon the personal consequences" (Boisjoly et al., p. 245).[2]

[6] In terms of this motivation, and the consequences endured by Boisjoly, he is representative of whistle blowers as described in the results of extended examinations of sixty-four whistle blowers by Myron Peretz Glazer and Penina Migdal Glazer, *The Whistleblowers, Exposing Corruption in Government and Industry*. His case is also roughly parallel to other cases that have received media attention such as Hugh Salmon in the advertising industry (Lynn, p. 61), and Dr. Nancy Olivieri at the Hospital for Sick Children in Toronto in her challenge to the drug industry (O'Hara). Furthermore, it is in line with cases featured in popular culture in the novels of John Grisham and in films such as *Silkwood*, dramatizing the suspicious highway death of Karen Silkwood, protestor of safety standards in the nuclear industry, and *The Insider*, depicting the tactics used by the tobacco industry to counteract exposure of its efforts to increase the addictiveness of its product. The whistle blower feels compelled to take a stand against practices in his or her own organization. "Whistle blowing may be defined as the attempt by an employee or former employee of an organization to disclose what he or she believes to be wrongdoings in or by the organization" (James, 1995, p. 409). Like the referee in a basketball game, the whistle blower calls a foul. A major difference is that the whistle blower has no authority to do this, and that is where the controversy comes in.

[7] Boisjoly also fits the profile of the typical whistle blower. "Among the research findings that may surprise many readers is that whistleblowers are typically above-average performers who are highly committed to the organization, not disgruntled employees out for revenge" (Graham, p. 683). However, his action is not the clearest example of whistle blowing itself because his whistle blowing was largely internal, and only became external through testimony before the Rogers Commission. The most distinctive and dramatic form of whistle blowing, reflected in most of the examples just cited, involves going outside the government agency or business corporation in a more direct way,[3] even though internal channels may have been tried and found ineffective. Further, although whistle blowing is usually the action of an individual, it is not an isolated act; whatever distortions may be involved in dramatizations of whistle blowing, these depictions, as well as the more sober scholarly examinations, indicate that it raises the most fundamental questions about the standards and expectations that prevail not only in business but in the wider society. These far-reaching implications of whistle blowing are indicative of the inadequacy of the conventional corporate view of whistle blowers as traitors and even of the more sympathetic understanding of them as tragic heroes battling corrupt or abused systems and suggests that they only begin to be

appreciated in their most distinctive form when they are seen as the saints of secular culture.

(1) Tattle-tale, Traitor, Troublemaker

[8] The generally prevailing view of the whistle blower within business, on the part of management and colleagues, is that this person is a traitor to the organization (DeGeorge, p. 225). This sentiment is clearly expressed in the title of a *Fortune* magazine article dealing with laws prohibiting discrimination against whistle blowers, "Rat Protection" (Seligman). A more elaborate version is articulated by former President of General Motors, James M. Roche.

> Some critics are now busily eroding another support of free enterprise—the loyalty of a management team, with its unifying values of cooperative work. Some of the enemies of business now encourage an employee to be disloyal to the enterprise. They want to create suspicion and disharmony, and pry into the proprietary interests of the business. However this is labelled—industrial espionage, whistle blowing, or professional responsibility—it is another tactic for spreading disunity and creating conflict. (Roche, p. 141)

Business corporations anticipate the possibility of disloyalty by requiring employees to sign confidentiality agreements, assenting to the principle that the business of the corporation will remain the business of the corporation. The competitive nature of business makes ingredients and design of products, market prospects and production plans classified information. Employees who are privy to such information must be expected to make confidentiality a paramount consideration among their responsibilities to their employer. Without this understanding, backed by the legal requirements of confidentiality agreements, business as we know it could not function.

[9] Whistle blowers violate their role as loyal agents of the corporation and betray their employers and co-workers. Sissela Bok identifies three central elements of whistle blowing: dissent, breach of loyalty, and accusation (Bok, p. 71), and notes: "Such characteristics of whistle blowing and strategic considerations for achieving an impact are common to the noblest warnings, the most vicious personal attacks, and the delusions of the paranoid" (Bok, p. 73). Whistle blowing is an obvious tactic for those who feel themselves victimized by an employer. It can represent a cover for incompetence on the part of the whistle blower or some kind of vendetta or personal crusade that is imposed on the realities of regular business practice. However, if Bok's reservations are allowed to shape our views of whistle blowing, this could be more reflective of a kind of corporate paranoia than of the reality of whistle blowing in is most typical instances. The dissent, disloyalty and accusation that whistle blowing involves is not usually indulged in frivolously; it is generally evoked by serious concern about what a business is doing, and the harm it may cause or be causing consumers, employees, or the wider community. Consequently, the disruption caused by the practice raises fundamental questions about the operations of the particular business in question, about the procedures for addressing concerns within that business, and about the relationship between business and the wider society.

[10] The charge that whistle blowers are disloyal to their corporation must confront the fact that whistle blowing becomes a reality and a problem not only because of the action of the whistle blower, but also because of circumstances within the corporation. The extent to which corporations will go to silence or retaliate against whistle blowers, and the serious consequences whistle blowers

have suffered in their careers, personally and in their families, indicate that very serious issues of business practice are at stake. This suggests that while the internal business characterization of the whistle blower as a tattle-tale may be justified in some instances, in many cases it is a self-serving attempt of business, officially on the part of boards and management or informally through reactions of fellow employees, to pursue practices detrimental to the wider society.

(2) Tragic Hero Battling the System

[11] While whistle blowing may reflect the actions of disgruntled or incompetent employees, genuine instances are distinguished by certain ethical criteria. In the first place, the issue must be a serious one, where employees, consumers, or the wider public may be harmed by the issue to be exposed. Second, unless there are extenuating circumstances, internal channels of notification must be exhausted before the whistle blower raises the alarm outside the organization. "Once an employee identifies a serious threat to the user of a product or to the general public, he or she should report it to his or her immediate superior and make his or her moral concern known. Unless he or she does so, the act of whistle blowing is not clearly justifiable" (DeGeorge, p. 231). This is a necessary, but by no means a sufficient, basis for justifiable whistle blowing. "If one's immediate superior does nothing effective about the concern or complaint, the employee should exhaust the internal procedures and possibilities within the firm. This usually will involve taking the matter up the managerial ladder, and if necessary—and possible—to the board of directors" (DeGeorge, pp. 232–233). Third, the whistle blower must be convinced of the urgency of the situation, and the lack of alternative to the drastic action of whistle blowing. Finally, the motives of the whistle blower become suspect if he or she profits from their whistle blowing. Whistle blowers may be compensated, or even rewarded. In some ways, this would be a welcomed alternative to the penalties, professional and personal, that many suffer. However, any indication that reward was anticipated, or in any way entered into the decision to blow the whistle, compromises the ethical quality of the act itself.

[12] Circumstances may prevent compliance with the second requirement, that internal channels be exhausted. As Gene G. James notes, some situations may pose too immediate a threat to allow for exhausting internal procedures. "If the wrongdoing is one which threatens people's health or safety, exhausting all channels of protest within the organization could result in unjustified delay in correcting the problem" (James, 1995, p. 413). There are also the related considerations that the immediate superior may be the source of, or heavily implicated in, the problem, that some organizations are more amenable to dealing with such complaints than others, that the internal process can allow for cover up and retaliation against the employee that may be more difficult if the report is made externally. The reservations expressed by James indicate how the issue of whistle blowing readily moves beyond questions of loyalty within the corporation to questions about the nature of the corporation itself. As Richard DeGeorge observes, whistle blowing challenges the amoral view of the corporation promoted by the nee-classical outlook, which would have us see the business corporation operating in its island of economic expertise (DeGeorge, p. 238). The impact of the business corporation on the wider society is much too dramatic for that, especially where that impact may be negative and dangerous.

[13] The whistle blower betrays his or her organization, but the reason for the betrayal may lie with the whistle blower or with the organization. Virtually

by definition, the whistle blower violates the bonds of the *Gemeinschaft* (collegial) connections with co-workers as well as the *Gesellschaft* (organizational) commitments implicit in accepting employment in the corporation in the first place. The perception of a need to blow the whistle may be indicative of the attitudes and practices of company personnel, of the focus of the company or of a former naivety in the employee who now feels this need. The scope and the gap that requires whistle blowing may be due to particular individuals, but it may also be reflective of the structure itself. Isolation of the pursuit of profit in business can encourage subordination of everything, including morality, to this pursuit. Contacts are acquired and maintained by providing what the customer wants, including approving a launch for NASA, despite engineering reservations about the safety of O-rings in freezing temperatures. In these circumstances, the whistle blower then becomes a tragic hero, taking a stand against the system.

[14] If the problem is with the system, the obvious answer is in restructuring. This is Norman Bowie's view. "I believe the only reasonable answer to this question [to how society can be protected from corporate wrongdoing] is to restructure business and social institutions so that these supererogatory moral acts no longer carry such severe personal penalties" (Bowie, p. 148). The effective solution to whistle blowing is to eliminate the need for it. Unfortunately, the effectiveness of the solution is proportionate to the radical revision that would be required. Whistle blowing would not be necessary if the corporation were significantly different from its present form. Whether the business corporation can sustain a revision that would amount to a revolution in economic systems and outlooks is another matter.

[15] Whistle blowing would not be necessary if business corporations provided opportunity for hearing and dealing with ethical concerns internally. What this may involve is suggested by Joseph W. Weiss's outline of steps management could take to internalize the concerns that erupt in whistle blowing. This would include developing internal grievance procedures, encouraging and rewarding use of these procedures, appointing senior executives to be responsible for investigating and reporting wrongdoing, and assessing large fines for illegal actions (Weiss, p. 207). It may not be accidental that these refinements offer procedures for reporting and dealing with moral concerns, but advocate fines for illegal actions. The radical nature of this revision is seriously compromised by this shift because illegality represents a limit imposed by the wider society, as Milton Friedman advocates in his defence of the neo-classical, isolationist view of business, and one with which corporations are expected to comply in any case. This is more indicative of business as usual than of a corporation that will take morality so seriously as to preclude the need for whistle blowing.

[16] A more realistic alternative might be changes in legislation to protect whistle blowers. In the United States, over two-thirds of the states have passed legislation to protect whistle blowers from retaliation and, at the federal level, the Organizational Sentencing Guidelines penalize corporations for not allowing for internal policing, of which whistle blowing would constitute an integral element, and reward corporations that allow for such procedures (Near and Dworkin). Legal protection for whistle blowers is not an obviously unqualified improvement, however. It could invite abuse from malcontents and incompetents, interfere with the rights of employers to run their business in their own terms, and raise questions about what kind of redress would be appropriate for vindicated whistle blowers (Boatright, p. 119). There are answers to these concerns, as Gene James contends (James,

1995, pp. 415–416). Protection would be limited to employees with solid employment records, and such legislation would only prevent retaliation by employers and only protect whistle blowers, and not reward them. Beyond such practical considerations, however, there is the consideration that such promotion and protection of whistle blowing may be contrary to the fundamental nature of whistle blowing itself, a logical contradiction rather than a pragmatic matter of effectiveness.

[17] This more intrinsic problem with attempts to safeguard whistle blowing becomes particularly evident when the focus moves beyond protection for whistle blowers to offering actual rewards. The False Claims Amendment Act of 1986 guarantees whistle blowers fifteen to thirty percent of funds recovered in a successful prosecution of exposed misappropriations, in addition to attorney's fees, back pay, and comprehensive protection from retaliation (Glazer and Glazer, p. 251). The Cavallo Awards, established by financier Michael Cavallo in 1987, provide three ten thousand dollar awards annually to people who show courage in business and government (Glazer and Glazer, p. 246). While these awards may reflect careful selection of candidates after the fact, the prospect of profiting from whistleblowing, encouraged especially by the False Claims Amendment Act, can be seen to be antithetical to the spirit of whistle blowing itself. For far from reward being a credible motivation for whistle blowing, sincere whistle blowers are incapable of being concerned with themselves precisely because they are so preoccupied with what is required of them by the situation they are confronting. Far from being the traitor and tattletale that the whistle blower is generally perceived to be within the organization, the reality may well be that the characterization of tragic hero battling a corrupt or abused system is not strong enough. To appreciate what is at stake in whistle blowing, it may be necessary to move beyond these options to recognize the whistle blower as a primary instance of the saint in a secular culture that has little scope for acknowledging this traditional classification.

(3) True Saint

[18] The phenomenon of whistle blowing poses the issue of the justification of the whistle blower and exposes the precariousness of a corporation that does not provide for ways of dealing with the ethical dimension in its own operations. Ultimately, it represents the question of the significance and form of ethics itself, not only in the corporate context or in terms of standards of society, but in its own right. Although Boisjoly's whistle blowing may not be typical in that he did not make his concerns public directly, but only after the event and through channels provided by the inquiry procedure, he is a typical whistle blower in motivation. His reflection, "I couldn't live with any self-respect if I tailored my actions based upon the personal consequences" (Boisjoly et al., p. 245), reveals the high ethical motivation that tends to characterize many whistle blowers. The profile of the average whistle blower emerging from a 1988 *New York Times* survey shows "a 47-year-old family man who has been a conscientious employee for seven years and who has strong belief in universal moral principles" (Velasquez, p. 455). If this characterization is to be questioned, it may be because it is not strong enough. What serious whistle blowers seem to display is not a universal morality in the modern sense of a Kantian or utilitarian ideal, but a moral sensitivity that is peculiarly individual. "There is such a thing as voluntarily assuming a responsibility and doing so because of commitments to (valid) ideals, to a degree beyond what is required for everyone" (Martin, p. 226). Such action may appear as moral heroism; however, in contemporary secular culture,

it is more apt to appear as foolhardy. It is intelligible in terms of the wider context that used to ground what we have come to think of as morality or ethics, the comprehensive visions of religion. Whether or not self-sacrificial whistle blowers think of their motivation in religious terms, the quality of their action is of these proportions, and, as a result, they represent one of the clearest instances in a secular culture of depths of devotion and dedication that are rare even in explicitly religious cultures.

[19] Consideration of the main directions of modern ethics indicates how the actions of whistle blowers burst such ethical confines. They clearly exceed the minimal level that is required to sustain civil life. The method of maintaining this level is criminal and civil law, and while this minimal level as imposed by the wider society satisfies the classical view of business, it cannot begin to recognize the actions of the whistle blower. The more deliberate modern approaches of Kantian or utilitarian ethics take ethics seriously in its own terms, and in fact establish ethics as a subject in its own right. This represents what everyone who is morally serious would do if their ethical performance matched their aspirations. This is the way that ethics has come to be understood generally and what is usually taken to be at stake in applied fields such as business ethics. Given these possibilities, the whistle blower would have to be seen to occupy this more serious ethical level beyond the minimum level of legality. The problem with this is that this level cannot encompass the radical self-sacrifice that tends to be entailed by significant instances of whistle blowing. In one sense, the problem is the radical nature of whistle blowing itself, but this also rebounds on this universalistic view of ethics, exposing its inability to deal with this level of moral seriousness. The demand for consideration of the common good characteristic of utilitarian approaches will find ways to broaden the burden before the sacrifice of career, family, health, and perhaps life itself are called for. For all its insistence on the encompassing demands of duty, the Kantian deontological approach draws back from the extremes represented by whistle blowing, finding in this not instances of universal moral requirements, but acts of supererogation, praiseworthy for their moral seriousness, but exceeding what can be expected on a rational moral basis. Whistle blowing represents an extreme that defies the reasonable expectation of the most prominent versions of ethics.

[20] The situation is continued and even intensified in prominent recent revisions in ethics. The more social direction of utilitarian ethics has been endorsed recently by feminist care morality. The promotion of the mutuality of give and take in this form of ethics sees itself offering a more realistic and engaging approach to ethics than the individualistic focus of the standard approaches. It also makes the kind of self-sacrificial actions that characterize the whistle blower even more foreign. Such moral heroism reflects a lack of capacity for true mutuality, where people work together, rather than in superhuman isolation. John Rawls qualifies the Kantian duty approach to ethics in the direction of addressing issues of social justice by asking us to imagine ourselves in an original position where we are designing a social system in which we do not know where we ourselves will stand. Since we might occupy the lower rungs on social and economic scales, we would want a system in which those rungs are afforded some measure of social and economic recognition. Here again, the moral heroism of the whistle blower represents an anomaly.

[21] If the most dramatic instances of whistle blowing fall off the ethical landscape, how are we to make sense of these acts other than as simply foolhardy and unintelligible? One possibility is provided by the recognition of the important social

role of saints in what might seem like an unusual source, the pragmatism of William James.

> They are the impregnators of the world [James says of saints], vivifiers and animators of potentialities of goodness which but for them would lie forever dormant. It is not possible to be quite as mean as we naturally are, when they have passed before us. One fire kindles another; and without that overtrust in human worth, they show, the rest of us would be in spiritual stagnancy.... If things are ever to move upward, someone must be ready to take the first step, and assume the risk of it. (James, n.d., p. 358)

Among the most prominent assumers of such risk in our culture are serious whistle blowers. Our need for them may be as profound as our inability to deal with them in business and in the wider society today.

[22]   The distinctiveness, courage and sacrifice of many of the most prominent whistle blowers suggests that what they represent goes beyond ethics in the modern sense of concern with universal moral principles, or social concern with mutuality or the justice of structures, important though these considerations are, to what James alludes to as the spiritual dimension. In this way, whistle blowing may defy clear understanding because it involves not only questions about the nature and practices of business, and how these relate to the wider society, but also such fundamental issues as how ethics and religion relate. If understanding whistle blowing must await clarification of such ancient conundrums, we will not expect crystal clarity on the matter any time soon. Indeed, it is not even clear what kind of evidence could be expected to become available. On the most immediate level, empirical evidence about the significance of religion for whistle blowers is obscure, as the summation of one of the most thorough surveys of the literature makes clear.

> There is some anecdotal evidence that religious views may be related to whistle-blowing. The typical whistle-blower studied by Soeken and Soeken...described himself or herself as 'moderately religious' though it is not clear how this might differ from the self-description of people in general. In another study, some whistle-blowers described their religious faith as contributing to their decision to blow the whistle; however religious belief alone may be insufficient to cause whistle blowing.... (Miceli and Near, p. 115)

One problem is that there have not been enough thorough empirical studies of religious influence on whistle blowers; more significant, however, is the issue of whether this is a subject that lends itself to empirical study. The influence of religion is by its nature comprehensive, and may well be most effective where it is least noticed, even by the person under its influence. Identifying the significance of religion for whistle blowers is bound to involve difficulties similar to those encountered by researchers who have attempted to establish the significance of religion for rescuers of Jews in Nazi Europe (Oliner and Oliner). This result is not entirely negative, however, for it can be taken as further confirmation of the depth and distinctiveness of whistle blowing at its starkest.

Although empirical evidence of the significance [23] of religious influence on whistle blowing is elusive, there is no shortage of anecdotal evidence. In their reports on extensive and sustained examination of sixty-four whistle blowers, *The Whistleblowers: Exposing Corruption in Government and Industry*, Myron Peretz Glazer and Penina Migdal Glazer give extensive consideration to three whistle blowers for whom religion was particularly determinative, a Roman Catholic, a Mormon, and a Jew. What emerges is the way in which the religious sensibility of these individuals allowed them no option but to blow the whistle, and did this by obscuring the general "realism" that allows most people to accept the way things are. "Like the prophets of the Old Testament, religiously committed resisters undertook the task of exposing and condemning widespread corruption, heedless of popular belief that these practices are so deeply embedded in modern society that it is foolhardy to try to change them" (Glazer and Glazer, p. 98). Beyond this alternate vision, the other striking feature that highly religiously motivated whistle blowers had in common is that they acted as individuals. For some this was so much their own issue that it was not seen to involve even their families, in spite of the devastating impact their actions would have on their families. The Catholic subject was adamant about this.

> It's not something you discuss with your wife. That never entered my mind. Your conscience is something you deal with yourself. It is not a committee action. It's whether you believe it is right or wrong. It comes back to a question of faith. I am the one who is going to be held accountable for what I do in my life. My wife is not going to be held accountable for it nor are my children. You've got to decide whether you are going to do something because it is right or wrong. (Glazer and Glazer, pp. 103–104)

[24] While this stance might be seen to betray a simplistic view of ethics, it might be better characterized as a single-mindedness through which the issue is posed with such crystal clarity for the whistle blower that there is no question about what must be done. Such rugged individualism may also be seen to betray a lack of appreciation of the intrinsic significance of the social for ethics, but here again such legitimate concern must not be allowed to obscure the intensity of the personal challenge felt by the whistle blower. This is the direction of religious influence on whistle blowing, a matter of personal inspiration rather than of organizational direction or concern. Indeed, the personal nature of the challenge is matched by a corresponding lack of communal support by religious congregations or fellow believers (Glazer and Glazer, pp. 117, 120). Religiously motivated whistle blowers take their religion as well as their ethics to extremes, or, perhaps more accurately, they are constrained to follow the dictates of their ethics and religion with a consistency that is successfully resisted by most of us.

[25] It is for this reason that the serious whistleblower transcends the level of corporate tattle tale and cannot be contained even by the characterization of tragic hero battling the system. Because they stand out from the rest of us by such conspicuous courage and self-sacrifice, even though it is a sacrifice that is often imposed also on their families, serious whistle blowers can only be appreciated in their full significance when they are viewed as the saints of secular culture. Whatever the direct role of religion in particular cases, what is involved in the most dramatic instances is of religious proportions.

> Only those employees who have a highly developed alternative belief system can withstand the intense pressure to conform to the requirements of management.... The beliefs of religious resisters are unshakable and provide powerful motivation to act out their ideas of individual responsibility. (Glazer and Glazer, p. 97)

Regardless of the explicit awareness of religious motivation on the part of the whistle blower, the self-sacrificial dedication of the extreme cases is only finally intelligible in religious terms. Their moral foolishness is the stuff of saints. They are badly maligned as corporate tattle-tales. They are misunderstood as moral heroes who deserve compensation or even rewards, justified though such compensation may well be, and unjustified as the marginalization and penalties they often suffer are. The most appropriate response to the justified, self-sacrificial whistle blower is the respect and awe elicited by recognition that such saints, who respond to a higher calling, still live among us.

Notes

1. The main source for the Challenger story is: Russell P. Boisjoly, Ellen Foster Curtis and Eugene Mellican, "Roger Boisjoly and the Challenger Disaster: The Ethical Dimensions," *Journal of Business Ethics* 8 (1989), 217–230, reprinted in Deborah C. Poff and Wilfrid J. Waluchow (eds.), *Business Ethics in Canada*, Third Edition (Scarborough, ON: Prentice Hall Allyn Bacon Canada, 1999), p. 229. Another source on the case is: "NASA and the Space Shuttle Booster Rockets," in Marianne M. Jennings, *Case Studies in Business Ethics,* Second Edition (Minneapolis/St. Paul: West Publishing Co., 1996), pp. 69–73.
2. From a speech given at the Massachusetts Institute of Technology, January 7, 1987, in Boisjoly et al.
3. Although whistle blowing occurs in government bureaucracies, sometimes in instances that are as dramatic and sacrificial as anything involved in business, the focus here is on whistle blowing in the business corporation.

References

Boatright, John R. *Ethics and the Conduct of Business.* 3rd ed. Upper Saddle River, NJ: Prentice Hall, 2000.

Boisjoly, Russell P., Ellen Foster Curtis, and Eugene Mellican. 1989. "Roger Boisjoly and the *Challenger* Disaster: The Ethical Dimensions." In Deborah C. Poff and Wilfrid J. Waluchow (eds.), *Business Ethics in Canada*, 3rd ed. Upper Saddle River, NJ: Prentice Hall Allyn Bacon Canada, 1999.

Bok, Sissela. "Whistleblowing and Professional Responsibility." In Peg Tittle (ed.), *Ethical Issues in Business: Enquiries, Cases and Readings,* 1st ed. Peterborough, ON: Broadview Press, 2000.

Bowie, Norman. *Business Ethics.* Englewood Cliffs, NJ: Prentice-Hall, 1982.

DeGeorge, Richard T. *Business Ethics.* 2nd ed. Upper Saddle River, NJ: Macmillan, 1986.

Glazer, Myron Peretz, and Penina Migdal Glazer. *The Whistleblowers: Exposing Corruption in Government and Industry.* New York, Collins Basic Books, 1989.

Graham, J.W. "Blowing the Whistle." *Administrative Science Quarterly* 38 (1993).

James, Gene G. "In Defense of Whistle Blowing." In William H. Shaw and Vincent Barry (eds.), *Moral Issues in Business.* 6th ed. Belmont, CA: Wadsworth, 1995.

James, William. *The Varieties of Religious Experience.* Garden City, NY: Doubleday Dolphin Books, n.d.

Lynn, Matthew. "The Whistleblower's Dilemma." *Management Today* (October 1988), 54–61.

Martin, Mike W. 'WHISTLEBLOWING, Personal Life and Shared Responsibility for Safety in Engineering." In Deborah C. Poff and Wilfrid J. Waluchow (eds.), *Business Ethics in Canada*, 3rd ed. Scarborough, ON, Prentice Hall Allyn Bacon Canada, 1999.

Miceli, Marcia P., and Janet P. Near. *Blowing the Whistle: The Organizational and Legal Implications for Companies and Employees.* New York: Lexington Books, 1992.

Near, Janet P., and Terry Morehead Dworkin. "Responses to Legislative Changes: Corporate Whistleblowing Policies." *Journal of Business Ethics* 17 (1998), 1551–1561.

O'Hara, Jane. "Whistle-Blower." *Maclean's* (16 Nov. 1998), 64–69.

Oliner, Samuel P., and Pearl M. Oliner. *The Altruistic Personality: Rescuers of Jews in Nazi Europe.* New York: Free Press, 1988.

Roche, James M. 1971. "The Competitive System, to Work, to Preserve, and to Protect." In "Vital Speeches of the Day" (May), p. 445, in Norman Bowie, *Business Ethics.* Englewood Cliffs, NJ: Prentice-Hall, 1982.

Seligman, D. "Rat Protection." *Fortune* (18 May 1981), 36.

Velasquez, Manuel G. *Business Ethics: Concepts and Cases.* 4th ed. Upper Saddle River, NJ: Prentice Hall, 1998.

Weiss, Joseph W. *Business Ethics.* 2nd ed. Fort Worth, TX: The Dryden Press, Harcourt Brace, 1998.

Questions

1. (a) According to Grant, and articulated by Roche, what is the prevailing view of whistleblowers?
   (b) In order for exposing a problem or a truth to be considered disloyal, what definition of 'loyal' must be in use?
   (c) Given the increasing prevalence of short-term contracts as well as the increasing absence of pension plans and other employee benefits that accrue over time, is loyalty to a company still a valid expectation?
2. What does Grant think of Bok's reference to "dissent, breach of loyalty, and accusation" (para 9)?
3. What four ethical criteria does Grant identify as distinguishing genuine whistleblowing?
4. What four circumstances does Grant identify that may prevent compliance with the second ethical criterion?
5. Grant says that "[t]he effective solution to whistle blowing is to eliminate the need for it" (para 14). What four steps does Weiss propose in order to do just that?
6. Grant mentions legislation to protect whistleblowers. On what grounds would such legislation be justified? On what grounds would such legislation be unjustified? (If this issue intrigues you, see the Vandekerckhove and Tsahuridu article listed in the References and Further Reading list above, p. 74.)
7. Grant says, "What serious whistle blowers seem to display is not a universal morality in the modern sense of a Kantian or utilitarian ideal, but a moral sensitivity that is peculiarly individual" (para 18). Do you agree? (Read carefully the subsequent paragraph before responding.)
8. What does Grant mean by "minimal level that is required to sustain civil life" (para 19)?
9. Grant says that "the most dramatic instances of whistle blowing fall off the ethical landscape" (para 21). Do you agree? That is, is there no approach to ethical decision making that accounts for whistleblowing?
10. Related to the previous question, does one need religious faith/belief in order to be a whistleblower?

Whistleblowing and Employee Loyalty*

Ronald Duska

Three Mile Island. In early 1983, almost four years after the near meltdown at Unit 2, two officials in the Site Operations Office of General Public Utilities reported a reckless company effort to clean up the contaminated reactor. Under threat of physical retaliation from superiors, the GPU insiders released evidence alleging that the company had rushed the TMI cleanup without testing key maintenance systems. Since then, the Three Mile Island mop-up has been stalled pending a review of GPU's management.[1]

[1] The releasing of evidence of the rushed cleanup at Three Mile Island is an example of whistleblowing. Norman Bowie defines whistleblowing as "the act by an employee of informing the public on the immoral or illegal behavior of an employer or supervisor."[2] Ever since Daniel Ellsberg's release of the Pentagon Papers, the question of whether an employee should blow the whistle on his company or organization has become a hotly contested issue. Was Ellsberg right? Is it right to report the shady or suspect practices of the organization one works for? Is one a stool pigeon or a dedicated citizen? Does a person have an obligation to the public which overrides his obligation to his employer or does he simply betray a loyalty and become a traitor if he reports his company?

[2] There are proponents on both sides of the issue—those who praise whistleblowers as civic heroes and those who condemn them as "finks." Glen and Shearer who wrote about the whistleblowers at Three Mile Island say, "Without the *courageous* breed of assorted company insiders known as whistleblowers—workers who often risk their livelihoods to disclose information about construction and design flaws—the Nuclear Regulatory Commission itself would be nearly as idle as Three Mile Island.... That whistleblowers deserve both gratitude and protection is beyond disagreement."[3]

[3] Still, while Glen and Shearer praise whistleblowers, others vociferously condemn them. For example, in a now-infamous quote, James Roche, the former president of General Motors said:

> Some critics are now busy eroding another support of free enterprise—the loyalty of a management team, with its unifying values and cooperative work. Some of the enemies of business now encourage an employee to be *disloyal* to the enterprise. They want to create suspicion and disharmony, and pry into the proprietary interests of the business. However this is labelled—industrial espionage, whistle blowing, or professional responsibility—it is another tactic for spreading disunity and creating conflict.[4]

---

* Ronald Duska, "Whistleblowing and Employee Loyalty" © 1983 by Ronald Duska. Reprinted with permission of the author.

[4] From Roche's point of view, whistleblowing is not only not "courageous" and deserving of "gratitude and protection" as Glen and Shearer would have it, it is corrosive and not even permissible.

[5] Discussions of whistleblowing generally revolve around four topics: (1) attempts to define whistleblowing more precisely; (2) debates about whether and when whistleblowing is permissible; (3) debates about whether and when one has an obligation to blow the whistle; and (4) appropriate mechanisms for institutionalizing whistleblowing.

[6] In this paper I want to focus on the second problem, because I find it somewhat disconcerting that there is a problem at all. When I first looked into the ethics of whistleblowing, it seemed to me that whistleblowing was a good thing, and yet I found in the literature claim after claim that it was in need of defense, that there was something wrong with it, namely that it was an act of disloyalty.

[7] If whistleblowing was a disloyal act, it deserved disapproval, and ultimately any action of whistleblowing needed justification. This disturbed me. It was as if the act of a good Samaritan was being condemned as an act of interference, as if the prevention of a suicide needed to be justified. My moral position in favor of whistleblowing was being challenged. The tables were turned and the burden of proof had shifted. My position was the one in question. Suddenly instead of the company being the bad guy and the whistleblower the good guy, which is what I thought, the whistleblower was the bad guy. Why? Because he was disloyal. What I discovered was that in most of the literature it was taken as axiomatic that whistleblowing was an act of disloyalty. My moral intuitions told me that axiom was mistaken. Nevertheless, since it is accepted by a large segment of the ethical community it deserves investigation.

[8] In his book *Business Ethics*, Norman Bowie, who presents what I think is one of the finest presentations of the ethics of whistleblowing, claims that "whistleblowing...violate[s] a *prima facie* duty of loyalty to one's employer." According to Bowie, there is a duty of loyalty which prohibits one from reporting his employer or company. Bowie, of course, recognizes that this is only a *prima facie* duty, i.e., one that can be overridden by a higher duty to the public good. Nevertheless, the axiom that whistleblowing is disloyal is Bowie's starting point.

[9] Bowie is not alone. Sissela Bok, another fine ethicist, sees whistleblowing as an instance of disloyalty:

> The whistleblower hopes to stop the game; but since he is neither referee nor coach, and since he blows the whistle on his own team, his act is seen as a *violation of loyalty* [italics mine]. In holding his position, he has assumed certain obligations to his colleagues and clients. He may even have subscribed to a loyalty oath or a promise of confidentiality.... Loyalty to colleagues and to clients comes to be pitted against loyalty to the public interest, to those who may be injured unless the revelation is made.[5]

[10] Bowie and Bok end up defending whistleblowing in certain contexts, so I don't necessarily disagree with their conclusions. However, I fail to see how one has an obligation of loyalty to one's company, so I disagree with their perception of the problem, and their starting point. The difference in perception is important because those who think employees have an obligation of loyalty to a company fail to take into account a relevant moral difference between persons and corporations and between corporations and other kinds of groups where loyalty is appropriate. I want to argue that one does not have an obligation of loyalty to a company, even a *prima facie* one, because companies are not the kind of things which are proper objects

of loyalty. I then want to show that to make them objects of loyalty gives them a moral status they do not deserve and in raising their status, one lowers the status of the individuals who work for the companies.

[11] But why aren't corporations the kind of things which can be objects of loyalty?...

[12] Loyalty is ordinarily construed as a state of being constant and faithful in a relation implying trust or confidence. And according to John Ladd, "The ties that bind the persons together provide the basis of loyalty."[6] But all sorts of ties bind people together to make groups. I am a member of a group of fans if I go to a ball game. I am a member of a group if I merely walk down the street. I am in a sense tied to them, but don't owe them loyalty. I don't owe loyalty to just anyone I encounter. Rather I owe loyalty to persons with whom I have special relationships. I owe it to my children, my spouse, my parents, my friends and certain groups, those groups which are formed for the mutual enrichment of the members. It is important to recognize that in any relationship which demands loyalty, the relationship works both ways and involves mutual enrichment. Loyalty is incompatible with self-interest, because it is something that necessarily requires we go beyond self-interest. My loyalty to my friend, for example, requires I put aside my interests some of the time. It is because of this reciprocal requirement which demands surrendering self-interest that a corporation is not a proper object of loyalty.

[13] A business or corporation does two things in the free enterprise system. It produces a good or service and makes a profit. The making of a profit, however, is the primary function of a business as a business. For if the production of the good or service was not profitable, the business would be out of business. Since non-profitable goods or services are discontinued, the providing of a service or the making of a product is not done for its own sake, but from a business perspective is a means to an end, the making of profit. People bound together in a business are not bound together for mutual fulfillment and support, but to divide labor so the business makes a profit. Since profit is paramount, if you do not produce in a company or if there are cheaper laborers around, a company feels justified in firing you for the sake of better production. Throughout history, companies in a pinch feel no obligation of loyalty. Compare that to a family. While we can jokingly refer to a family as "somewhere they have to take you in no matter what," you cannot refer to a company in that way. "You can't buy loyalty" is true. Loyalty depends on ties that demand self-sacrifice with no expectation of reward, e.g., the ties of loyalty that bind a family together. Business functions on the basis of enlightened self-interest. I am devoted to a company not because it is like a parent to me. It is not, and attempts of some companies to create "one big happy family" ought to be looked on with suspicion. I am not "devoted" to it at all, or should not be. I *work* for it because it pays me. I am not in a family to get paid, but I am in a company to get paid.

[14] Since loyalty is a kind of devotion, one can confuse devotion to one's job (or the ends of one's work) with devotion to a company.

[15] I may have a job I find fulfilling, but that is accidental to my relation to the company. For example, I might go to work for a company as a carpenter and love the job and get satisfaction out of doing good work. But if the company can increase profit by cutting back to an adequate but inferior type of material or procedure, it can make it impossible for me to take pride in my work as a carpenter while making it possible for me to make more money. The company does not exist to subsidize my quality work as a carpenter. As a carpenter, my goal may be good houses, but as an employee my goal is to contribute to making a profit. "That's just business!"

[16] This fact that profit determines the quality of work allowed leads to a phenomenon called the commercialization of work. The primary end of an act of building is to make something, and to build well is to make it well. A carpenter is defined by the end of his work, but if the quality interferes with profit, the business side of the venture supercedes the artisan side. Thus profit forces a craftsman to suspend his devotion to his work and commercializes his venture. The more professions subject themselves to the forces of the marketplace, the more they get commercialized; e.g., research for the sake of a more profitable product rather than for the sake of knowledge jeopardizes the integrity of academic research facilities.

[17] The cold hard truth is that the goal of profit is what gives birth to a company and forms that particular group. Money is what ties the group together. But in such a commercialized venture, with such a goal there is no loyalty, or at least none need be expected. An employer will release an employee and an employee will walk away from an employer when it is profitable for either one to do so. That's business. It is perfectly permissible.

[18] Loyalty to a corporation, then, is not required. But even more it is probably misguided. There is nothing as pathetic as the story of the loyal employee who, having given above and beyond the call of duty, is let go in the restructuring of the company. He feels betrayed because he mistakenly viewed the company as an object of his loyalty. To get rid of such foolish romanticism and to come to grips with this hard but accurate assessment should ultimately benefit everyone.

[19] One need hardly be an enemy of business to be suspicious of a demand of loyalty to something whose primary reason for existence is the making of profit. It is simply the case that I have no duty of loyalty to the business or organization. Rather I have a duty to return responsible work for fair wages. The commercialization of work dissolves the type of relationship that requires loyalty. It sets up merely contractual relationships. One sells one's labor but not one's self to a company or an institution.

[20] To think we owe a company or corporation loyalty requires us to think of that company as a person or as a group with a goal of human enrichment. If we think of it in this way we can be loyal. But this is just the wrong way to think. A company is not a person. A company is an instrument, and an instrument with a specific purpose, the making of profit. To treat an instrument as an end in itself, like a person, may not be as bad as treating an end as an instrument, but it does give the instrument a moral status it does not deserve, and by elevating the instrument we lower the end. All things, instruments and ends, become alike.

[21] To treat a company as a person is analogous to treating a machine as a person or treating a system as a person. The system, company, or instrument gets as much respect and care as the persons for whom they were invented. If we remember that the primary purpose of business is to make profit, it can be seen clearly as merely an instrument. If so, it needs to be used and regulated accordingly, and I owe it no more loyalty than I owe a word processor.

[22] Of course if everyone would view business as a commercial instrument, things might become more difficult for the smooth functioning of the organization, since businesses could not count on the "loyalty" of their employees. Business itself is well served, at least in the short run, if it can keep the notion of a duty to loyalty alive. It does this by comparing itself to a paradigm case of an organization one shows loyalty to, the team.

[23] Remember that Roche refers to the "management team" and Bok sees the name "whistle-blowing" coming from the instance of a referee blowing a whistle in the presence of a foul. What is perceived as bad about whistleblowing in business from this

perspective is that one blows the whistle on one's own team, thereby violating team loyalty. If the company can get its employees to view it as a team they belong to, it is easier to demand loyalty. The rules governing teamwork and team loyalty will apply. One reason the appeal to a team and team loyalty works so well in business is that businesses are in competition with one another. If an executive could get his employees to be loyal, a loyalty without thought to himself or his fellow man, but to the will of the company, the manager would have the ideal kind of corporation from an organizational standpoint. As Paul R. Lawrence, the organizational theorist says, "Ideally, we would want one sentiment to be dominant in all employees from top to bottom, namely a complete loyalty to the organizational purpose."[7] Effective motivation turns business practices into a game and instills teamwork.

[24] But businesses differ from teams in very important respects, which makes the analogy between business and a team dangerous. Loyalty to a team is loyalty within the context of sport, a competition. Teamwork and team loyalty require that in the circumscribed activity of the game I cooperate with my fellow players so that pulling all together, we can win. The object of (most) sports is victory. But the winning in sports is a social convention, divorced from the usual goings on of society. Such a winning is most times a harmless, morally neutral diversion.

[25] But the fact that this victory in sports, within the rules enforced by a referee (whistleblower), is a socially developed convention taking place within a larger social context makes it quite different from competition in business, which, rather than being defined by a context, permeates the whole of society in its influence. Competition leads not only to winners but to losers. One can lose at sport with precious few serious consequences. The consequences of losing at business are much more serious. Further, the losers in sport are there voluntarily, while the losers in business can be those who are not in the game voluntarily (we are all forced to participate) but are still affected by business decisions. People cannot choose to participate in business, since it permeates everyone's life.

[26] The team model fits very well with the model of the free-market system because there competition is said to be the name of the game. Rival companies compete and their object is to win. To call a foul on one's own teammate is to jeopardize one's chances of winning and is viewed as disloyalty.

[27] But isn't it time to stop viewing the corporate machinations as games? These games are not controlled and not over after a specific time. The activities of business affect the lives of everyone, not just the game players. The analogy of the corporation to a team and the consequent appeal to team loyalty, although understandable, is seriously misleading at least in the moral sphere, where competition is not the prevailing virtue.

[28] If my analysis is correct, the issue of the permissibility of whistleblowing is not a real issue, since there is no obligation of loyalty to a company. Whistleblowing is not only permissible but expected when a company is harming society. The issue is not one of disloyalty to the company, but the question of whether the whistleblower has an obligation to society if blowing the whistle will bring him retaliation. I will not argue that issue, but merely suggest the lines I would pursue.

[29] I tend to be a minimalist in ethics, and depend heavily on a distinction between obligations and acts of supererogation. We have, it seems to me, an obligation to avoid harming anyone, but not an obligation to do good. Doing good is above the call of duty. In-between we may under certain conditions have an obligation to prevent harm. If whistleblowing can prevent harm, then it is required under certain conditions.

[30] Simon, Powers and Gunnemann set forth four conditions:[8] need, proximity, capability, and last resort. Applying these, we get the following:

1. There must be a clear harm to society that can be avoided by whistleblowing. We don't blow the whistle over everything.
2. It is the "proximity" to the whistleblower that puts him in the position to report his company in the first place.
3. "Capability" means that he needs to have some chance of success. No one has an obligation to jeopardize himself to perform futile gestures. The whistleblower needs to have access to the press, be believable, etc.
4. "Last resort" means just that. If there are others more capable of reporting and more proximate, and if they will report, then one does not have the responsibility.

[31] Before concluding, there is one aspect of the loyalty issue that ought to be disposed of. My position could be challenged in the case of organizations who are employers in non-profit areas, such as the government, educational institutions, etc. In this case, my commercialization argument is irrelevant. However, I would maintain that any activity which merits the blowing of the whistle in the case of non-profit and service organizations is probably counter to the purpose of the institution in the first place. Thus, if there were loyalty required, in that case, whoever justifiably blew the whistle would be blowing it on a colleague who perverted the end or purpose of the organization. The loyalty to the group would remain intact. Ellsberg's whistleblowing on the government is a way of keeping the government faithful to its obligations. But that is another issue.

Notes

1. Maxwell Glen and Cody Shearer, "Going after the Whistleblowers," *The Philadelphia Inquirer*, Tuesday, Aug. 2, 1983, Op-ed Page, p. 11a.
2. Norman Bowie, *Business Ethics* (Englewood Cliffs, N.J.: Prentice-Hall, 1982), 140. For Bowie, this is just a preliminary definition. His fuller definition reads, "A whistle blower is an employee or officer of any institution, profit or non-profit, private or public, who believes either that he/she has been ordered to perform some act or he/she has obtained knowledge that the institution is engaged in activities which a) are believed to cause unnecessary harm to third parties, b) are in violation of human rights or c) run counter to the defined purpose of the institution and who inform the public of this fact." Bowie then lists six conditions under which the act is justified. 142–143.
3. Glen and Shearer, "Going after the Whistleblowers," 11a.
4. James M. Roche, "The Competitive System, to Work, to Preserve, and to Protect," *Vital Speeches of the Day* (May 1971), 445. This is quoted in Bowie, 141, and also in Kenneth D. Walters, "Your Employee's Right to Blow the Whistle," *Harvard Business Review*, 53, no. 4.
5. Sissela Bok, "Whistleblowing and Professional Responsibilities," *New York University Education Quarterly*, vol. II, 4 (1980), 3.
6. John Ladd, "Loyalty," *The Encyclopedia of Philosophy*, vol. 5, 97.
7. Paul R. Lawrence, *The Changing of Organizational Behavior Patterns: A Case Study of Decentralization* (Boston: Division of Research, Harvard Business School, 1958), 208, as quoted in Kenneth D. Walters, op. cit.
8. John G. Simon, Charles W. Powers, and Jon P. Gunnemann, *The Ethical Investor: Universities and Corporate Responsibility* (New Haven: Yale University Press, 1972).

Questions

1. Duska says that accusing a whistleblower of disloyalty is like accusing a Samaritan (who saves a would-be suicide) of interference (para 7). Do you think this is a good analogy?
2. On what major point do Bok and Duska differ?
3. What is Duska's main reason for claiming that one does not have an obligation of loyalty to a company (para 10)?
4. What reason does he give to support his view that a corporation can't be an object of loyalty (para 12)?
5. As evidence of the inability to be in a mutually-enriching, i.e., reciprocal, relationship, Duska cites the self-interested motive of profit-making that is, he says, the primary function of business (para 13). Do you agree that profit-making is the primary function of business?
6. Larmer (see the References and Further Reading list at the end of the introduction to this chapter) disagrees with Duska, arguing that loyalty *can* be a one-way thing, and he gives as an example the loyalty of a parent to an erring and disloyal teenager. Which do you think is the stronger position, that of Duska or that of Larmer?
7. Duska might concede that loyalty can be one-way, but he would probably still maintain that feeling loyalty toward a company is misguided. Why? (Read carefully paras 20–21.)
8. Why is the appeal to a team and team loyalty in a company's best interests (para 23)?
9. Explain Duska's criticisms of the team analogy (para 24–27).
10. Duska concludes that whistleblowing is permissible. In fact, his conclusion is even stronger than that—how so?
11. Anticipating the objection that his position is not applicable to non-profit organizations (such organizations do not have as their primary function the self-interested pursuit of profit and therefore may be appropriate objects of loyalty), Duska provides a response.
    (a) Explain what it is.
    (b) Could this response also be applied to profit-making organizations? That is, could one argue that the activity meriting whistleblowing is also counter to the purpose of the for-profit business?

Case Study: Dr. Olivieri vs. Apotex

In April 1993, when Dr. Nancy Olivieri was a medical researcher with the University of Toronto and head of a blood-disorder research program at the Hospital for Sick Children, she signed a contract with Apotex Research Inc., a Canadian pharmaceutical company, to conduct a study of the effects of a new drug, deferiprone, which treats a deadly blood disorder, thalassemia.

In September 1995, she and an expert in iron metabolism discovered dangerously high levels of iron in some of the liver biopsies taken from her patients who were on the drug; heart disease and early death could result from such a condition. She contacted Apotex, hoping to put an end to the study.

Apotex, however, maintained that the drug was safe, claiming that other researchers disagreed with her conclusions; they wanted her to continue the study. They also reminded Olivieri of the confidentiality agreement she had signed and threatened to sue her if she made her opinions public.

Olivieri then contacted the hospital's Research Ethics Board: they told her to change the consent forms so that patients would be informed of the risk; they also told her to report her discovery to the Health Protection Branch in Ottawa, which is responsible for granting drug approvals. She did both.

In May 1996, Apotex terminated the trials at the Hospital for Sick Children and removed Olivieri as lead investigator on the international study she was also conducting for them.

The executive of the Hospital for Sick Children did not support Olivieri in her dispute with Apotex. Publicly, they maintained that it was a scientific controversy which was best settled within the scientific community. (In August 1998, the *New England Journal of Medicine* published Olivieri's article, which concluded that deferiprone was ineffective and may be toxic to the liver.) Privately, in e-mail messages sent to many scientists across Canada, the hospital executive stated that "both Apotex and other scientists involved in the [deferiprone] trials disagreed with Olivieri's interpretation of the data." Olivieri and her supporters within the medical and university communities felt betrayed by a prominent public institution they viewed as having "sold out" to commercial interests—and Apotex used the hospital's actions as support for the drug.

The comments of Dr. Allan Detsky, physician-in-chief at Mount Sinai Hospital in Toronto, go to the heart of the ethical issue in the case, at least from one perspective. He stated, "Forget about the confidentiality agreement, forget about the hospital's financial interests [in drug company research funding], forget about the pharmaceutical companies' interest. What was the right thing to do in the case? How could somebody whose motivation is to protect children from harm ever be wrong?"

In early January 1999, reportedly for personnel issues that happened before the Apotex study, Olivieri was demoted by the hospital: though retaining hospital privileges, she was no longer head of the blood research program and could not conduct any clinical trials. However, just a few weeks later, in late January, University of Toronto President Rob Prichard gathered all the parties together and managed to broker a deal that reinstated Olivieri as head of the program and cleared her reputation.

In 2001, the CAUT (Canadian Association of University Teachers) completed a two-year investigation into the matter. "The hospital and the university should have defended vigorously the right of clinical researchers to disclose risks to research subjects and patients," Patricia Baird, one of the CAUT committee members, said. "They had a responsibility to protect the public interest and academic freedom from inappropriate actions by Apotex, but they did not do so."

The CAUT subsequently demanded that the Hospital for Sick Children, the University of Toronto, and Health Canada immediately act on their 31 recommendations, which included the following:

- Contracts involving industrial sponsorship of clinical research should never prevent researchers

from informing patients or the scientific community of any risks.
- All universities and affiliated teaching hospitals should have in place policies and practices that are effective in protecting academic freedom, as well as principles of research and clinical ethics.
- Health Canada should review the current regulation of health research and make appropriate changes to protect the public interest and the rights of patients who volunteer to be subjects of research.
- The university and the hospital should provide redress to Olivieri for the unfair treatment she has received.

The drug was approved in Europe in 1999 and in the US in 2011; it is now used in over 60 countries. In 2009, Olivieri received the AAAS (American Association for the Advancement of Science) Award for Scientific Freedom and Responsibility.

Sources
Baylis, Francoise. "The Olivieri Debacle." *Journal of Medical Ethics* 30 (2004): 44–49.
Boyle, Theresa, and Rita Daly. "Olivieri Pledges to Battle 'Bias.'" *The Toronto Star* 11 Dec. 1998: A1+.
CAUT Bulletin 48.9 (Nov. 2001).
Foss, Krista, and Paul Taylor. "Sick Kids Demotes Controversial MD." *The Globe and Mail* 8 Jan. 1999: A12.
O'Hara, Jane. "Whistleblower." *Maclean's* 16 Nov. 1998: 65–69.
Quinn, Jennifer, and Tanya Talaga. "Blood Research, Hospital Agree to End 2 1/2-year Battle." *The Toronto Star* 27 Jan. 1999: A1+.

Questions
1. We aren't told if there is an existing treatment for thalassemia. Is this information relevant to the moral rightness of Olivieri's decision/action?
2. Do you agree with Detsky—can somebody whose motivation is to protect children from harm ever be wrong?
3. If you were an ethics consultant hired by the Hospital, the University, or Health Canada, what specific policies would you propose to meet the CAUT recommendations?

BOX 1.4 Whistleblowing Legislation in Canada

In Canada, the Public Servants Disclosure Protection Act (PSDPA, 2007) protects government employees who choose to "blow the whistle" by making a report to the Public Service Integrity Commission. In theory. Sylvie Therrien, a whistleblower fired for reporting employment insurance benefits clawback quotas, says, "I know of some other civil servants who have gone all the way through the internal channel, all the way to the commissioner of integrity, who are without a job today...because they complained" (Dib). Employees who suffer retaliation have no recourse after their reports are dismissed by the Commission (and apparently 640 of the 650 claims made in a recent seven-year period were, amazingly, either dismissed or tabled [Olivier]), because the Commissioner is protected from any kind of legal repercussions for omissions or errors by PSDPA provisions. Nor is sidestepping internal retaliation by going public right off the bat possible, as the Federal Court of Appeal in 2013 decided that employees must exhaust internal whistleblowing mechanisms before going public, and that failing to do so constitutes "disloyal and inappropriate conduct" (Avraam and Chow).

Private-sector whistleblowing may qualify for protection under the Criminal Code of Canada, employment law or industry-specific legislation, such as the Employment Standards Act or the Environmental Protection Act. Frequently, however, the misconduct reported may not satisfy the specific terms of those acts. So, for example, reporters of fraudulent appropriation of funds inside a company, although perhaps eligible for civil litigation, would not qualify for whistleblower protection. Furthermore, whistleblowers who do not have employer authorization when reporting externally (and why would they?) forfeit protection. So, for example, whistleblowers like pipeline engineer Evan Vokes are unprotected. He blew the whistle in 2012 on dangerously substandard practices in building the Keystone XL pipeline to the US, but despite his claims having been validated by the National Energy Board, no measures have been taken either to address the retaliation he has suffered or to correct the situation. (And isn't that rather the point of whistleblowing?) Worse yet, our federal government seems to be clamping down with permanent gag orders on security-sector employees and environmental scientists (Bagley).

References

Avraam, G. & Chow, C. "Canada: Whistleblower Protection: The Importance Of Internal Policies." *Mondaq*. 2014. Retrieved from: http://www.mondaq.com/content/company.asp? article_id=318478&company_id=25166

Bagley, K. "Harper Govt Makes Moves to Silence Canada's Leading Environmental Groups." *FAIR Monthly Headlines*. 2014. Retrieved from: http://fairwhistleblower.ca/

Dib, L. "One whistleblower's story: no job, no rent, no recognition, no redress." *O Canada*. 2013. Retrieved from: http://o.canada.com/news/national/whistleblower-law-has-done-little-to-protect-people-who-raise-red-flags

Olivier, F. "Whistleblower law has done little to protect people who raise red flags." *O Canada*. 2013. Retrieved from: http://o.canada.com/news/national/whistleblower-law-has-done-little-to-protect-people-who-raise-red-flags

Prepared by S. Hilary Anne Ivory

CHAPTER TWO

Advertising

What to Do?—In-Your-Face Advertising, Inc.
You have just been offered a job by In-Your-Face Advertising, Inc., a new and exciting firm specializing in pop-into holographic ads: mini-billboard to full-sized holographic advertisements that suddenly pop into existence in front of carefully targeted consumers as they are just walking along. The creative potential of working with a virtually sci-fi technology is very attractive; it would be almost like 3-D gaming. And the salary is great.

You know that you yourself would be irritated by holograms accosting you as you walk down the street, but really, is it that much different than being accosted by the signs that are currently everywhere? At first, people might keep jerking to a stop to avoid walking into them, but wouldn't they eventually get used to them (just as they've gotten used to the pop-up ads on the internet) and keep walking, right through the ads? Of course, if that became the case, wouldn't the ads become ineffective? So would they have to be designed to be more and more realistic or more and more disturbing?

No doubt someone will eventually develop some sort of cloaking device that prevents the holograms from popping into existence—but how much will *that* cost? Certainly it would be more than *you* could afford, at least until your student loans are paid off.

On the one hand, you reason, no one owns public space, so can't you do whatever you want there? You have to expect unwelcome, unwanted stuff to happen when you go out in public. On the other hand, aren't parks and streets and other public spaces *shared* spaces? So what right does I-Y-F have to impose itself on people when they're just out and about? But maybe the ads will pop into existence only in privately-owned spaces like malls; maybe I-Y-F would have to obtain permission to advertise in the mall's "space" just as it would to advertise on the mall's walls.

It's not that the ads themselves are problematic—in fact, yours would be works of art: why wouldn't someone want to be up close and personal with such beauty? It's the coercive

> and persistent nature of their presentation that bothers you. This would be compounded if there *was* a problem with the ads themselves—for example, if they were obnoxiously loud or ugly. True, people *choose* to go out in public—no, that's not right, it's not really a choice: they *have* to go out in public from time to time.... But they don't *have* to go to the malls—they could shop online.
>
> And, if this is the wave of the future, if holographic advertising in inevitable, isn't it better to have people like you designing the ads—so they *won't* be obnoxiously loud or ugly?
>
> What do you decide to do?

Introduction

One might suppose that the main ethical question with regard to advertising is whether it's morally acceptable to *lie* in advertisements. Certainly that's an important question, but perhaps it's too easy. Consider instead whether it's morally acceptable to *deceive*. And what exactly is deception? Is it more or less than *misleading*?

It is reasonably certain that you will never be able to include in an advertisement everything there is to know about your product or service (supposing you wanted to). So you'll have to be selective. And there's part of the issue: what do you leave out—and why?

As for what you put *in*, perhaps the question becomes whether or not it's morally acceptable to *manipulate*. See Sher for a discussion about this; his conclusion is that a manipulative marketing tactic is immoral when "it is intended to motivate by undermining what the marketer believes is his/her audience's normal decision-making process either by deception or by playing on a vulnerability that the marketer believes exists in his/her audience's normal decision-making process" (97).

The question about whether it's morally acceptable for advertisements to manipulate depends on whether advertisements are, in fact, capable of manipulating people.[1] And if they *are* capable of manipulation, perhaps next we must ask why. Can we really hold a company morally responsible if the consumer is too lazy to think clearly and critically about the claims being made and too insecure to resist even the most ludicrous of suggestions ("Wear these jeans and you'll...")? Isn't the consumer the one who's morally at fault?

Another question is whether it's morally acceptable to *try to* manipulate (whether or not one *can*). Whereas the previous question required establishing cause and effect, this one requires establishing intentions.

Either way, we need to define our terms: What exactly is manipulation? Is it different from persuasion? If so, how? Is it different from influence? From coercion? When does influence become control? Or at least controlling enough to be immoral? Does the context matter? The presence of attractive alternatives? How much resistance is it reasonable to expect? In addition to lies and omissions, we need to consider ambiguities, exaggerations, and implications.

---

[1] See Packard for an argument that they are; see Arrington for an argument that they aren't.

Surely it's a matter of degree: manipulating by intentionally withholding information may be worse than manipulating by merely associating two things. Products are often associated with wealth and sexual attractiveness, but perhaps even more insidious is the "greenwashing" that increasingly occurs, in which products that are damaging to the environment (typically vehicles of various kinds) are shown in the context of pretty blue skies and lush green vegetation. Or maybe both kinds of manipulation are equally reprehensible because of their subtlety, whereas manipulation by making explicit but outlandish claims is less reprehensible (because only an idiot would accept your claims).[1]

But perhaps even explicit and outlandish claim making entails subtlety. Advertisers know the power of repetition: it leads to familiarity, which leads to consumer choice (humans choose what's familiar, what's recognizable—science has established that). Even content-free ads—i.e., the mere presentation of the brand name (think of the tab on jeans, the animated television station logo in the corner of the screen, etc.)—can be manipulative.

Does it matter whether the method of persuasion is rational (evidence, reason) or non-rational (emotional, subliminal)? If you argue that advertising fails to respect people's autonomy, then yes, it does matter: rational argument (unaccompanied by intellectual intimidation) would be morally acceptable; only other means of persuasion could be morally unacceptable.[2]

Also, does the medium make a difference? Are we more susceptible to images, especially moving ones (frogs are like that—they can see something only if it moves)? And if so, should television and animated advertising have higher standards?

Now arguments *against* lying, deceiving, misleading, manipulating, and coercing usually involve several concepts we've already covered: respect for persons, which includes respect for their autonomy (recall Kant in Part II; see the article by Crisp); people's rights, such as freedom of choice; fairness; and the social good (recall utilitarianism).

Concerning respect to persons, one can ask whether or not the consumer is being treated as a means to the company's end or as an end in him/herself.

Concerning autonomy issues, it's not just the autonomy of the targeted person that one can consider; the person being used as "bait" is also exploited. Thus, every ad that shows women in child-like or sexual-object roles, and *only* in those roles (and there's the "lie"), restricts the freedom of all women because people, men and women alike, see so often, get used to seeing, expect to see, women in that role and that role only (even though they know it's "just" an ad).[3] Expectations are highly influential: Rosenthal and Jacobson established that, for example, teachers who expect certain students to be very capable ended up giving those students high grades, and vice versa. (The teachers were told ahead of time which students were the "bright" ones and which were the "slow" ones.) Also, people get very angry when their expectations are not met;

---

1 See the magazine *Adbusters* for some heavy and often hilarious critique of manipulative advertisements.
2 See Fulmer and Barry for an examination of the ethics of emotional "management"
3 See Plakoyiannaki et al. on this matter; the answer to their title question, "Does Sexism Exist?," is, unsurprisingly, yes. See also the "Women in Advertisements and Body Image" website at http://womeninads.weebly.com/history.html and the video by University of Saskatchewan students at http://www.upworthy.com/the-next-time-someone-says-sexism-isnt-real-show-them-these-shocking-role-reversal-images.

to use the preceding example, women are often insulted for not meeting people's expectations about how they are supposed to look and act.[1]

But the undermining of autonomy and the consequent restriction of freedom of choice is not the only harm that can occur as a result of deception (let alone advertising in general, given the current state of affairs). Very real physical injury can also occur. Perhaps one of the classic cases of ethically questionable advertising is that of Nestlé's infant formula: it has been argued that its advertising campaign to mothers in developing countries "failed to consider" (intentionally ignored?) the need for clean water (mothers mixed it with polluted water, the only kind available) and the ability to afford enough of the formula (they couldn't, so they diluted the formula)—as a result, babies died. Perhaps "energy drinks" and "protein shakes" pose similar ethical challenges: too many of the former can cause cardiac arrest; too many of the latter can cause kidney problems (Gallagher; Tremblay).

With respect to fairness, expecting the consumer to make a choice based on incomplete or slanted information isn't fair. But nor is expecting a business to thrive if it can't let people know about its products and services. However, "let people know about" isn't the same as "suggest they're inadequate without" your product/service.

As for the social good argument, many claim that advertising doesn't just "make" people *buy*; many argue that it makes them *want*.[2] In this way, it encourages unhappiness and dissatisfaction; in fact, advertisers *count* on people being unhappy (and they therefore try to create such a state): after all, if people were happy with what they had, they wouldn't need (to buy) more. Is advertising, therefore, somewhat to blame for our skyrocketing personal debt? Perhaps not, since at least in Canada, such debt is mainly attributable to the purchase of housing and education. But it might be to blame for our changing climate: the high-consumption Western lifestyle and the industrialization needed to support it are responsible for most of the emissions that have led to climate change. It is so grossly unfair, many argue, that it is the non-Western countries that are being hit the hardest by the changes *and* are being asked to make sacrifices to turn it around, if that is still even possible.

The use of computer-generated (or at least enhanced) images in advertising may also contribute to this unhappiness. Although Spurgin discusses the effect of such perfect images in advertising that portrays "ideal human beauty, bodies, or looks," and concludes that such use is ethically unacceptable, I suggest the effect of colour-enhancement in other ads, perhaps specifically those portraying our natural environment, is equally questionable: eventually, reality seems pale by comparison. (Recently, I went to Yellowknife to see the aurora borealis and

---

1 I can't help but think that the constant presentation of women who appear so very sexually available has had something to do with men's increasing sense of entitlement (to women). Consider Elliot Rodger, who recently killed himself (after killing several other people) because he wasn't getting any sex—the video he made clearly expressed anger at all the girls who wouldn't have sex with him. Consider the increasingly frequent posts by men who are outraged because women decide whether they get sex. Their starting point assumption must be that all women should be sexually available to all men. See "Elliot Rodger and the Price of Toxic Masculinity." Incidentally, Jay Walker-Smith, president of the marketing firm Yankelovich, estimates that we're exposed to as many as 5,000 ads a day.

2 See Galbraith on this point.

was disappointed; I realized that my expectations had been heavily influenced by what I then realized were unrealistically vivid colours in the images I had seen, mostly in advertisements.)

The standard rebuttal to the argument that advertising makes us want what we may otherwise not want is a denial: business merely supplies what the people demand—consider the notion of consumer sovereignty. But one might ask, then, if the people genuinely want to buy X, why does a company need to advertise X? I don't recall ever seeing an advertisement for mittens, yet many people buy them every winter. Well, the response goes, a company needs to advertise X because it needs to inform the consumer of the product's existence. But then the ad should simply say, "X is available at this store." And we all know it says more than that.

Another part of the social good argument is that advertising, perhaps especially manipulative advertising, creates a consumer culture, one in which "going shopping" is a bona fide activity, just like "going bowling." According to Waide, advertising fosters "the ideology of acquisitiveness." Barbara J. Phillips disagrees, however, blaming not advertising but capitalism for our increasing materialism.

Kant's universality principle can also be used to argue against deceptive advertising: if everyone deceived in advertising, it would eventually fail to achieve its goal of persuading to purchase.

A virtue ethicist might measure advertising against honesty, respect, and integrity. Or cleverness and gainfulness.

Now, arguments *for* such advertising also include people's rights, such as to the pursuit of profit and freedom of speech, as well as the social good (it fosters competition, which, supposedly, improves quality). But surely such rights are not absolute. For example, we may have the right to say whatever we want, but still, if we lie or cause harm, it's morally reprehensible—whether we're advertising, proselytizing, campaigning, or "just" talking. (And in fact, maybe deception in the last three instances is more harmful than in the first, because at least with advertising we *expect* the bias of a vested interest.) And why is it the responsibility of the buyer to beware? Why should Person A have to be vigilant against deception instead of Person B having to refrain from deceiving? Shouldn't the right thing be the default mode? (A similar argument is often made about the need for vigilance against assault and, further, the unspoken curfew for avoiding assault.)

As for the social good, in addition to fostering competition, advertisements simply do the public service of informing people about what's available. If this argument is valid, then companies would present an objective "advantages and disadvantages" advertisement of their products. And why not? If a product is good, if it has more (or more important) advantages than disadvantages, won't people choose it? (And if it doesn't have more advantages than disadvantages, why are you making it?) Don't companies who advertise have faith in people's rationality? If not, could it be that in a world bereft of rational argument, a world characterized by mindless and emotional ads, most people haven't had the chance to develop that rationality? Lippke ventures into this area, arguing that "advertising, in concert with other social conditions, deprives individuals of the ability and willingness to critically reflect on their beliefs, desires, aims, and interests" (103).

One might respond, well, if my competition had to do that too, it would be okay, but if I'm the only one to do it, it would be unfair. Okay, so if it is the right thing to do, then should government make such a regulation? (Assuming that business owners won't do the right thing unless they have to—unless everyone else does. Are you going to be that kind of business owner?)

Another social good to consider is the sponsorship aspect of advertising. Without advertising, we'd probably have very few television shows, at least on "traditional" TV. (Does advertising support TV or does TV support the advertisers—on this, see Nelson.) We'd also have fewer arts centres, fewer sports competitions, and so on. But couldn't the expenses just be passed along to the consumer? Unlikely, since already many can't afford a ticket. Well, how do our libraries exist? At the expense of authors who do not get paid, or get paid very little, per loan? Should governments cover the costs?

As mentioned earlier, many deny that ads influence, let alone manipulate—but if they *don't* influence, then why do businesses spend so much money on them? This leads us to another argument, namely that advertising is wasteful. Just think about what advertising's billions of dollars per year could do to the quality of life if they were spent otherwise. And that's not even addressing the resource waste (paper, electricity, etc.). Or just think how much lower the cost of living would be if we didn't have to pay for that advertising when we made our purchases; that cost includes the packaging, which is really just more advertising—the price of packaging can be as much as three times the price of the product. One could argue that advertising increases profit and that profit could be directed toward improvements in product and service quality, or workplace conditions. Possibly. And much advertising could be intended to maintain, not increase, profit.

Another aspect of ethics in advertising focuses on the target, rather than the content, of the ad. Lynn Sharp Paine argues that because young children are not autonomous consumers (they have no sense of self as independent human beings, a prerequisite for self-control and rational choice, nor do they have much of a sense of time), advertising to them is morally wrong. Perhaps, given the relative absence of even *potential* autonomy, *any* advertising to children is especially manipulative, and especially morally wrong. If adults have trouble resisting the slick emotional messages, what hope do children have? Consider this in the context of the fact that in Canada, the average child watches about two hours of television a day and sees more than 20,000 advertisements per year.[1] Should you, therefore, refuse to engage in advertising aimed at children, without waiting for the rest of Canada to follow Quebec and several European countries in banning it? One might counter that it's up to the parents to limit their children's television viewing time, and monitor their internet use, but what about the ads elsewhere? In the kids' school, for example?[2]

"Product placements are especially potent in their effects on children," say Hudson, Hudson, and Peloza, based on the evidence they investigate. Indeed, the blurring of advertisement and entertainment makes the distinction difficult even for adults.[3] And if product placement is

---

1 Robin Marwick writing in 2010 for "aboutkidshealth," a website hosted by the Toronto's Hospital for Sick Children: http://www.aboutkidshealth.ca/en/news/newsandfeatures/pages/target-market-children-as-consumers.aspx.
2 See Landsberg, MacDonald, and "Parents and Educators."
3 See Hackley, Rungpaka, and Preuss for a consideration of product placement from the point of view of utiltarianism, Kantian ethics, and virtue ethics.

perhaps the oldest form of "stealth marketing," the use of blogs is possibly the newest. Although blogs were initially op-ed column repositories, often with exciting and valuable opportunity for discussion, they quickly became thinly veiled advertising. Social media sites are often better described as commercial media sites; consider the evolution of Facebook. Perhaps the most significant ethical issue here is deception; shouldn't you just call it like it is?

Yet another form of "stealth marketing" that is little addressed is the influence of advertisers on editorial content. Rinallo et al. note that "[a]necdotal evidence hints at various cases of advertisers threatening to withdraw or actually withdrawing their advertising budget from media organizations that published undesirable news about the company or its products" (426). It's understandable that a business will not want to spend a lot of money on an ad promoting X only to have it appear beside a well-researched article showing X to be a bad thing. But shouldn't that just be the risk you have to take? After all, *you* choose to *make* X. The problem is advertisers do more than withdraw their ads in that case (which would be a logistical nightmare for both the advertiser and the magazine); they attach strings *in the first place* requiring the magazine to *not publish* ads critical of their product/s. Do you have a moral right to use your power to suppress dissenting views? Though perhaps the problem is with the magazine: on what grounds can it accept such strings attached and *at the same time* convey, explicitly or implicitly, that it presents unbiased journalism?

Not advertising to a certain group could also be morally wrong. For example, Krohn and Milner argue that condom manufacturers failed to adequately promote their product to the male homosexual population, and since AIDS (which is largely preventable via condom use) is life-threatening, such a failure constitutes negligent homicide.

Indeed, it was concern about target group that led Umbro Canada to turn down a profitable cross-promotion marketing campaign for the World Cup of soccer: the partnership would have been with a beer company, but Umbro's target market is primarily youth under the legal drinking age. Because of Umbro's decision, the company won Ethics in Action's 1998 Award for Ethical Decision Making (Ethics in Action).

And how is one's target group identified? Consider what was initially called "data mining"—the use of data discriminator programs to identify people by all sorts of factors (they know how much you make, how much you spend, and when, and where, and on what, how much you owe... they know where you live). Every click of your mouse and every tap of your tablet is recorded by someone—for their use. Is that a legitimate market-research method or an illegitimate invasion of privacy?[1]

Not only "what" and "to whom"—"where" is also an ethical issue. Is there something morally unacceptable about advertising on billboards along a highway? First, people really can't help but see them (closing one's eyes while driving is not really an option), so it's a touch coercive. Second, they can be quite distracting (indeed, many are designed to blink, move, and otherwise divert one's attention away from the road) and, therefore, can increase the chance of accidents. The use of cellphones while driving is now illegal; why are similarly distracting roadside advertisements

---

1 See Pulfer, and we will come back to this in a later chapter.

still legal? One might argue that protestors along the side of the road can also be distracting, but that would be a red herring: it's irrelevant to whether billboards are distracting and therefore immoral, since protestors at the side of the road, especially those who are persistent, and have blinking lights, may *also* be morally unacceptable. Advertising on buses and subways and planes—on my trip to Yellowknife, I was *forced* to watch an ad for BMW before I could watch the safety demonstration; there was no way to skip ahead or even turn down the audio—similarly involve captive audiences, though without the possibility of real physical injury.

Outdoor advertising in general imposes far more than any elsewhere-placed advertising. Consider these comments from the promotional materials of Canada-based MagnetSigns: "Outdoor advertising works. It continually reaches people where they live, work, shop and play.... Outdoor advertising is always on...traditional advertising...is too easily avoided...." Is it a bad thing that people can avoid advertising? Is it acceptable that a company is able to promote itself to us 24/7?

"How much" might also be an issue. Should the extent of advertising—whether on highways, in magazines, on television, or on the internet—be limited? Why, or why not? And are we talking self-regulation by the industry—or government regulation?

"By whom" is another issue. As one person recently remarked, "You can't even take a piss these days without seeing an ad!" (He was referring to ads placed at eye-level on the walls above urinals.) Some argue that it's morally wrong for some businesses to advertise at all; traditionally, "the professions" have been under this prohibition. But why? Why is it okay for a car mechanic to advertise her services but not for a surgeon to do so? Is the assumption that advertising *does* manipulate, and it's particularly immoral to manipulate when serious things (your health, not your car) are at stake? Well, a bad brake job can certainly affect one's health! Or is it that advertising implies varying degrees of quality, of competence, and some professions don't want that thought to even cross our minds (no doctor wants people to wonder whether they were at the bottom of their class). In that case, though, wouldn't the *failure* to advertise be deceptive?

Does it matter *what* you're advertising? Are the moral standards different for baby cribs than for books? Or prescription drugs? Genetic testing?[1] Some have suggested no advertising at all for harmful products, such as tobacco and alcohol. But why? If the product is so bad that we shouldn't advertise it, why is it okay to make it?

De George (288) identifies another ethical aspect of advertising: who is morally responsible for the advertising? The company that paid for it? The agency that created it? The media that aired/printed it? The consumer that responds to it with a purchase? The government that allowed it? Some combination of the above? Are they *all*, in their own way, endorsing or supporting, it? (So as the agency, do you refuse to create it, on moral grounds? As the TV station, do you refuse to air it?)

Advertising is only one marketing tool, and the others are just as subject to concern about truth and autonomy. Product promotion is another area with many ethical questions (or assumptions!)—from the ethics of free samples (are expectations attached?) to the ethics of the packaging (consider the shape of the bottle, the composition of the label). But PR departments are also marketing tools: media releases and even annual reports can be used to attract

---

1 See Beltramini; Berg and Fryer-Edwards.

consumers, customers, clients. They, too, are subject to ethical standards regarding influence and manipulation. Surely a report full of distorted data is as deceptive as the advertisement claiming that X can do the unlikely.

References and Further Reading

Arrington, Robert L. "Advertising and Behavior Control." *Journal of Business Ethics* 1 (1982): 3–12.

Banker, Steve. "The Ethics of Political Marketing Practices, the Rhetorical Perspective." *Journal of Business Ethics* 11.11 (1992): 843–48.

Beltramini, Richard F. "Consumer Believability of Information in Direct-to-Consumer (DTC) Advertising of Prescription Drugs." *Journal of Business Ethics* 63.4 (2006): 333–43.

Berg, Cheryl, and Kelly Fryer-Edwards. "The Ethical Challenges of Direct-to-Consumer Genetic Testing." *Journal of Business Ethics* 77.1 (2008): 17–31.

Crisp, Roger. "Persuasive Advertising, Autonomy, and the Creation of Desire." *Journal of Business Ethics* 6.5 (July 1987): 413–18.

De George, Richard T. *Business Ethics*. 5th ed. Upper Saddle River, NJ: Prentice Hall, 1999.

"Elliot Rodger and the Price of Toxic Masculinity." 26 May 2014. http://www.doctornerdlove.com/2014/05/elliot-rodger-price-toxic-masculinity/

Ethics in Action. http://www.dal.ca/sites/ethicsinaction.html

Fulmer, Ingrid Smithey, and Bruce Barry. "Managed Hearts and Wallets: Ethical Issues in Emotional Influence by and within Organizations." *Business Ethics Quarterly* 19.2 (2009): 155–91.

Galbraith, John Kenneth. *The Affluent Society*. London: Houghton Mifflin, 1958.

Gallagher, Paul. "Energy drinks can trigger sudden cardiac arrest even in healthy young people, study finds." *Independent* 2 April 2015. http://www.independent.co.uk/life-style/health-and-families/health-news/energy-drinks-can-trigger-sudden-heart-attacks-even-in-healthy-young-people-study-finds-10152418.html

Hackley, Chris, Amy Tiwsakul Rungpaka, and Lutz Preuss. "An Ethical Evaluation of Product Placement: A Deceptive Practice?" *Business Ethics: A European Review* 17.2 (2008): 109–20.

Hudson, Simon, David Hudson, and John Peloza. "Meet the Parents: A Parents' Perspective on Product Placement in Children's Films." *Journal of Business Ethics* 80.2 (2008): 289–304.

Hyman, M. "Responsible Ads: A Workable Ideal." *Journal of Business Ethics* 87.2 (2009): 199–210.

Krohn, Franklin B., and Laura M. Milner. "The AIDS Crisis: Unethical Marketing Leads to Negligent Homicide." *Journal of Business Ethics* 8.10 (October 1989): 773–80.

Laczniak, Gene R., and Patrick E. Murphy. *Ethical Marketing Decisions: The Higher Road*. Boston: Allyn & Bacon, 1993.

Landsberg, Michele. "Let's Signal 'No' to TV Network in Schools." *The Toronto Star* 14 Mar. 1999: A2.

Lippke, Richard. *Radical Business Ethics*. Lanham, MD: Rowman and Barry, 1995. (See especially Chapter 5, "Advertising and the Social Conditions of Autonomy.")

MacDonald, Rod. "Students Profit from Classroom TV." *The Toronto Star* 26 Mar. 1999: A20.

Moore, Elizabeth S. "Children and the Changing World of Advertising." *Journal of Business Ethics* 52 (2004): 161–67.

Nelson, Joyce. *The Perfect Machine: TV in the Nuclear Age*. Toronto: Between the Lines, 1987.

Packard, Vance. *The Hidden Persuaders*. New York: Pocket Books, 1958.

Paine, Lynn Sharp. "Children as Consumers: An Ethical Evaluation of Children's Television Advertising." *Business & Professional Ethics Journal* 3.3–4 (1983): 119–25, 135–45.

"Parents and Educators Warned about Proposed YNN Launch." *SchoolNet Weekly*. 15–19 Feb. 1999. http://www.newswire.ca/releases/February1999/11/c5348.html

Phillips, Barbara J. "In Defense of Advertising: A Social Perspective." *Journal of Business Ethics* 16.2 (February 1997) 109–18.

Plakoyiannaki, E., K. Mathioudaki, P. Dimitratos, and Y. Zotos. "Images of Women in Online Advertisements of Global Products: Does Sexism Exist?" *Journal of Business Ethics* 83.1 (2008): 101–12.

Pulfer, Rachel. "Mining Your Business." *This Magazine* 32.5 (1999): 13–15.

Rinallo, Diego, Suman Basuroy, Ruhai Wu, and Hyo Jin Jeon. "The Media and Their Advertisers: Exploring Ethical Dilemmas in Product Coverage Decisions." *Journal of Business Ethics* 115 (2013): 425–41.

Sher, Shlomo. "A Framework for Assessing Immorally Manipulative Marketing Tactics." *Journal of Business Ethics* 102.1 (2011): 97–118.

Sneddon, Andrew. "Advertising and Deep Autonomy." *Journal of Business Ethics* 33.1 (2001): 15–28.

Spurgin, Earl W. "What's Wrong with Computer-Generated Images of Perfection in Advertising?" *Journal of Business Ethics* 45.3 (2003): 257–68.

Tremblay, Sylvie. "The Side Effects of Protein Drinks on the Kidneys." Livestrong.com. 3 Oct. 2015. http://www.livestrong.com/article/323940-the-side-effects-of-protein-drinks-on-the-kidneys/

Waide, John. "The Making of Self and World in Advertising." *Journal of Business Ethics* 6.2 (1987) 73–79.

BOX 2.1   Properties of Responsible Ads

1. Does no harm or unavoidable harm to any stakeholder while benefiting at least one stakeholder
   a. Avoids advertising that could induce harmful behaviors within vulnerable populations
   b. Uses potent appeals (e.g., fear appeals) cautiously
   c. Addresses unintended consequences immediately
2. (Discourages) Encourages behaviors trustworthy evidence supports as (in)consistent with long-run social welfare
3. Maintains consumers' dignity and autonomy

> a. Avoids deception, which may include puffery
> b. Avoids non-consensual persuasion techniques (e.g., subliminal appeals)
> c. Avoids shallow/inane ads
> d. Avoids condescending and paternal ads (e.g., state and recognized authorities know what is best)
> e. Accommodates individual differences in perspectives and preferences
> 4. Respects consumers' egos
>   a. Avoids psychoactive ads with problematic appeals (e.g., appeals that induce shame)
>   b. Placement avoids unintended exposure
>
> Excerpted from Hyman (see References and Further Reading)

The Inconclusive Ethical Case against Manipulative Advertising*

Michael J. Phillips

Introduction

[1] Back in 1982, the *Business and Society Review* sponsored an exchange on advertising (Colloquy, 1982). The occasion was a statement by Robert Heilbroner in the June 11, 1981 *New York Review of Books*:

> If I were asked to name the deadliest subversive force within capitalism—the single greatest source of its waning morality—I would without hesitation name advertising. How else should one identify a force that debases language, drains thought, and undoes dignity? If the barrage of advertising, unchanged in its tone and texture, were devoted to some other purpose—say the exaltation of the public sector—it would be recognized

---

* Michael J. Phillips, "The Inconclusive Ethical Case Against Manipulative Advertising" *Business and Professional Ethics Journal* 13.4 (Winter 1994): 31–64. © 1994 by Michael J. Phillips. Reprinted with permission of the author.

in a moment for the corrosive element that it is. But as the voice of the private sector it escapes this startled notice. (p. 64)

The colloquy's business and advertising participants made several predictable responses to Heilbroner's statement. Advertising, they said, stimulates technological advance by enabling innovative firms to inform consumers about their products. By thus enhancing competition, it also helps prevent market concentration and the stagnation that frequently accompanies it. Because advertising provides the media with financial support, moreover, it helps keep them free from government control. And since people approach advertising more or less rationally, there are limits on its ability to manipulate consumers.

[2] However, William Winpisinger, then president of the International Association of Machinists and Aerospace Workers, saw things differently.

> I am in wholehearted agreement with Professor Heilbroner's view of advertising as a corrosive element in our society. Its major function and purpose has been to feed already bloated corporate beasts. They've discovered that the only way they can keep their revenues up is by paying exorbitant sums to advertising professionals who combine art and psychology to exploit and manipulate the vast range of human fears and needs. (p. 65)

He concluded his remarks with the ritual demand that corporate influence on public policy be neutralized.

[3] This article explores the ethical implications of Winpisinger's perception that advertisers successfully "exploit and manipulate the vast range of human fears and needs." It begins by defining its sense of the term "manipulative advertising." Then the article asserts for purposes of argument that manipulative advertising actually works. Specifically, I make two controversial assumptions about such advertising: (1) that it plays a major role in increasing the general propensity to consume, and (2) that it powerfully influences individual consumer purchase decisions. With the deck thus stacked against manipulative advertising, the article goes on to inquire whether either assumption justifies its condemnation, by considering four ethical criticisms of manipulative advertising. Ethically, I conclude, manipulative advertising is a most problematic practice. If probabilistic assertions are valid in ethics, that is, the odds strongly favor the conclusion that manipulative advertising is wrong. Nevertheless, there still is room for doubt about its badness. Like the apparently easy kill that continually slips out of the hunter's sights, manipulative advertising evades the clean strike that would justify its condemnation for once and all.

What Is Manipulative Advertising?

[4] Some ethical evaluations of advertising (e.g., Crisp, 1987, p. 413) use the label "persuasive advertising" to name the phenomenon discussed in this article. However, because there is such a thing as rational persuasion and because such persuasion seems unobjectionable (Benn, 1967, pp. 265–66), this usage is questionable. Thus, following Tom Beauchamp (1984), I employ the term "manipulative advertising." According to Beauchamp, manipulation occupies a position about midway along a continuum of influences ranging from coercion, at one end, to rational persuasion, at the other (pp. 3–6). He defines it as including "any deliberate attempt by a person P to elicit a response desired by P from another person Q by noncoercively altering the structure of actual choices available to Q or by non-persuasively altering Q's perceptions of those choices" (p. 8). Virtually all of Beauchamp's exam-

ples, however, involve what lawyers call deceptive advertising. Deceptive advertising involves false or misleading assertions or omissions that cause reasonable consumers to form erroneous judgments about the nature of a product.

[5] What, then, is manipulative advertising? As used here, the term relates mainly to the "nonpersuasively altering Q's perceptions" portion of Beauchamp's definition. Building on that language, I define "manipulative advertising" as advertising that tries to favorably alter consumers' perceptions of the advertised product by appeals to factors other than the product's physical attributes and functional performance. There is no sharp line between such advertising and advertising that is nonmanipulative; even purely informative ads are unlikely to feature unattractive people and depressing surroundings. Nor is it clear what proportion of American advertising can fairly be classed as manipulative. Suffice it to say that that proportion almost certainly is significant. As we will see, advertising's critics sometimes seem to think that all of it is manipulative.

[6] Perhaps the most common example of manipulative advertising is a technique John Waide (1987, pp. 73–74) calls "associative advertising."[1] Advertisers using this technique try to favorably influence consumer perceptions of a product by associating it with a nonmarket good (e.g., contentment, sex, vigor, power, status, friendship, or family) that the product ordinarily cannot supply on its own. By purchasing the product, their ads suggest, the consumer somehow will get the nonmarket good. Michael Schudson describes this familiar form of advertising as follows: "The ads say, typically, 'buy me and you will overcome the anxieties I have just reminded you about' or 'buy me and you will enjoy life' or 'buy me and be recognized as a successful person' or 'buy me and everything will be easier for you' or 'come spend a few dollars and share in this society of freedom, choice, novelty, and abundance'" (1986, p. 6). Through such linkages between product and nonmarket good, associative advertising seeks to increase the product's perceived value and thus to induce its purchase. Because these linkages (e.g., the connection between beer and attractive women) generally make little sense, such advertising is far removed from rational persuasion.

The Effects of Manipulative Advertising: What the Critics Think

In the previous section, I tried to describe manipulative advertising in terms of sellers' *efforts*, rather than their actual accomplishments. But does manipulative advertising successfully influence consumers? As might be expected, advertising's critics generally answer this question in the affirmative. Perhaps the best-known example is chapter XI of John Kenneth Galbraith's *The Affluent Society*, where he described his well-known dependence effect. [7]

Galbraith's dependence effect might be described as the way the process of consumer goods production creates and satisfies consumer wants (1958, p. 158). "That wants are, in fact, the fruit of production," he intoned, "will now be denied by few serious scholars" (p. 154). In part, these wants result from emulation, as increased production means increased consumption for some, followed by even more consumption as others follow suit (pp. 154–55). But advertising and salesmanship provide an even more direct link between production and consumer wants. Those practices, Galbraith says: [8]

> [C]annot be reconciled with the notion of independently determined desires, for their central function is to create desires.... This is accomplished by the producer of goods or at his behest. A broad empirical relationship exists between

what is spent on production of consumers' goods and what is spent in synthesizing the desires for that production. A new consumer product must be introduced with a suitable advertising campaign to arouse an interest in it. The path for an expansion of output must be paved by a suitable expansion in the advertising budget. Outlays for the manufacturing of a product are not more important in the strategy of modern business enterprise than outlays for the manufacturing of demand for the product. (pp. 155–56)

All these propositions, Galbraith concluded, "would be regarded as elementary by the most retarded student in the nation's most primitive school of business administration" (p. 156).

[9] To Galbraith, therefore, advertising in general is manipulative. In *The Affluent Society*, it apparently worked mainly to promote aggregate demand, rather than to shift demand from one brand to another. Many of advertising's critics follow Galbraith's lead by stressing how it socializes people to embrace consumerist values (e.g., Held, 1984, pp. 62–63; Lasch, 1978, p. 72; Lippke, 1990, pp. 38–39, 41–48; Waide, 1987, p.75). Some of these accounts flesh out the causal links between advertising and the consumer mentality. To Richard Lippke, for instance, certain background factors—authoritarian management structures, unequal access to quality higher education, the media's insipid program content, and the dependence of political power on economic power—pave the way for advertising's success by depriving people of autonomy (1990, pp. 41–43). With the path thus cleared, advertising's consumerist message triumphs because it is pervasive, is not effectively challenged, and is implanted early in life (pp. 43–44).

[10] From all this, it is a short step to the notion that advertising plays a major role in shaping and sustaining the modern society of material abundance. Implicitly, at least, some accounts of this kind (e.g., Krutch, 1959, ch. II) liken society to a huge machine whose aim is the conversion of natural resources into consumer products. For the machine to work properly, its human components must be motivated to play their role in producing those products. This can be accomplished by (1) implanting in people an intense desire for consumer goods, and (2) requiring that they do productive work to get the money to buy those goods. If this metaphorical picture is at all accurate, advertising obviously plays a major role in sustaining the system. As Joseph Wood Krutch once argued:

> If we could convincingly accuse the advertisers of greed..., we might reasonably ask why they should be allowed to invade our homes, destroy the beauty of the countryside, and deface the sky. But if "prosperity" as currently defined is the only reasonable meaning or measure of the good life, then a strong case can be made...that when I am urged to trade in my car, buy a new washing machine, or try some new gadget, the profit motive of the seller is of less than secondary importance. Primarily, as he will eagerly explain, he is performing a public service by explaining to me my duty to support prosperity by behaving in the only manner in which this prosperity can be maintained. (1959, pp. 28–29)

Galbraith suggested that these social imperatives of production and consumption make the worker/consumer resemble a squirrel who races full-tilt to keep abreast of a wheel propelled by his own efforts (1958, pp. 154, 159).

[11] Although they naturally evaluate the matter differently, business leaders often second Krutch's argument that advertising is essential to prosperity. In another *Business and Society Review* colloquy, this one a 1985 exchange on advertising expenditures by

the fast-food industry, William H. Genge, the chairman of Ketchum Communications' board, wrote:

> I regard the many millions of dollars spent by fast-food companies (and other retailers as well) as healthy and necessary stimulation of the consumption that makes our economy the most dynamic and productive in the world.
>
> Some people talk as though large advertising budgets are wasteful and nonproductive. It just takes one simple question to put that down. The question is: Where does the money go? The answer is: It provides jobs and livelihoods for hundreds of thousands of people—not only in the advertising and communications sector but for all the people employed by fast-food companies and, indeed, all marketing organizations. (1985, pp. 58–59)

"So," Genge concluded, "large advertising expenditures are not a misallocation of economic resources. They are, in fact, an essential allocation and the driving force behind consumption, job creation, and prosperity" (p. 59).

[12] Advertising that is sufficiently manipulative to create a consumer society also might be able to determine consumers' individual purchase decisions. Most often, I suppose, these would be brand choices within a particular product category, although advertising might also steer people toward certain products and away from others. Although advertising's critics often do not mention this particular form of manipulation,[2] some stress it (e.g., Crisp, 1987, *passim*).

Assumptions and Plan of Attack

[13] As we have just seen, many critics of advertising say that it socializes people to a life of consumption. And some regard it as a strong influence on individual brand or product decisions. However, these beliefs are not universally shared. Some students of advertising doubt that ads do much to dictate individual brand choices (e.g., Schudson, 1986, pp. xiv, 85–89). And even if advertising strongly influences consumer decisions, it does not follow that any specific ad invariably compels the purchase of the product it touts. The reason is that a particular product advertisement is only one of many factors—especially competing advertisements—influencing consumers (Hayek, 1961, p. 347). For the same general reason, it is difficult to assess advertising's role in making people lifetime consumers. As Geoffrey Lantos has observed, this question "involves an almost impossible problem of causal inference" due to "the wide variety of institutional influences on our values and lifestyles" (1987, p. 106). "[T]here is," he adds, "no well-developed sociology of consumption" (p. 106).

[14] Despite such difficulties, this article assumes for the sake of argument that manipulative advertising really works. Thus, I assume that such advertising strongly influences individual purchase decisions, and that it plays a major role in producing consumerist attitudes among the populace. In neither case, however, do I wish to specify all the links in the causal chain through which manipulative advertising does its work. In particular, I make no assumptions about the personal traits that render consumers responsive to manipulative advertising. Later in the article, for example, I consider the possibility that manipulative advertising succeeds because consumers want and need it.

[15] Operating under the assumptions just stated, I now consider four possible ethical attacks on manipulative advertising. These are the claims that such advertising: (1) has negative consequences for utility, (2) undermines personal autonomy, (3) violates Kant's categorical imperative, and (4) weakens the personal virtue of its practitioners and its victims. I also consider one qualified defense of manipulative advertising: that even though no moral person would choose it were he writing on a

clean slate, by now its elimination would be worse than its continuance.[3]

[16] For each attack on manipulative advertising, I assume the validity of the relevant moral value or ethical theory, thus precluding defenses of manipulative advertising which attack the value or theory itself. A defender of manipulative advertising, for example, might argue that its inability to satisfy the categorical imperative does not matter because Kant was a fool and his moral philosophy is nonsense; but I do not consider such claims. This agnosticism about the validity of my four values or theories creates difficulties, for it is unlikely that all four could be fully valid simultaneously. To meet this difficulty while preserving as much scope as possible for each value or theory, I treat them as *prima facie* valid; and I assume that their claims must somehow be balanced against one another when conflicts arise.

Utilitarianism

[17] As just stated, this article assumes that advertising can manipulate people in two distinct ways: (1) by socializing them to embrace consumerist values, and (2) by dictating individual purchase decisions. One important utilitarian criticism of manipulative advertising seems mainly to involve the first of these effects. Another implicates the second effect. A third criticism probably involves both.[4] I now discuss each of these utilitarian attacks in turn. Throughout, I explicitly or implicitly compare my assumed world in which manipulative advertising exists and is effective with a world in which all advertising is merely informative.

The Implications of the Dependence Effect

[18] *The Affluent Society* marked Galbraith's arrival as a critic of consumer society and its works. For his critique to be persuasive, he had to counter the argument that America's enormous production of consumer goods is justified because people want, enjoy, and demand them. This required that he undermine at least two widespread beliefs: (1) that consumer desires are genuinely autonomous, and (2) that they produce significant satisfactions. As we saw earlier, he attacked the first assumption by maintaining that consumer wants are created by the productive process through which they are satisfied, with advertising serving as the main generator of those wants. This argument would have enabled Galbraith to contend that advertising is bad because it denies autonomy, but he seemed not to emphasize that point. Instead, he maintained that the satisfaction of advertising-induced desires generates little additional utility. His argument was that if advertising is needed to arouse consumer wants, they cannot be too strong. "The fact that wants can be synthesized by advertising, catalyzed by salesmanship, and shaped by the discreet manipulations of the persuaders shows that they are not very urgent. A man who is hungry need never be told of his need for food" (1958, p. 158).

[19] As a result, Galbraith continued, one cannot assume that the increased production characterizing the modern affluent society generates corresponding increases in utility. Instead, as he summarizes the matter:

[O]ur concern for goods...does not arise in spontaneous consumer need. Rather, the dependence effect means that it grows out of the process of production itself. If production is to increase, the wants must be effectively contrived. In the absence of the contrivance the increase would not occur. This is not true of all goods, but that it is true of a substantial part is sufficient. It means that since the demand for this part would not exist, were it not contrived, its utility or urgency, ex contrivance, is zero. If we regard this production as marginal, we may say that the marginal utility of present aggregate output, ex advertising and salesmanship, is zero. (p. 160)

Because wants must be contrived for production to increase, on Galbraith's assumptions production would be lower were advertising completely informative. Since on those assumptions that contrived production generates little additional utility, however, the loss would not be much felt. Indeed, with resources shifted away from advertising and consumption and toward activities that improve the quality of our lives, overall utility might well grow in manipulative advertising's absence.

[20] Galbraith's basic argument was that because consumer wants are contrived, they are not urgent; and that because they are not urgent, their satisfaction does not generate much utility. One way to attack his argument is to maintain that consumer desires really do arise from within the individual, but my two assumptions foreclose that possibility here. Another is to follow the lead established by Friedrich Hayek's 1961 critique of Galbraith's dependence effect. To Hayek, Galbraith's argument involves a massive *non sequitur*: the attempt to reason from a desire's origin outside the individual to its unimportance (1961, pp. 346–47). If that assertion were valid, he thought, it would follow that "the whole cultural achievement of man is not important" (p. 346).

> Surely an individual's want for literature is not original with himself in the sense that he would experience it if literature were not produced. Does this mean that the production of literature cannot be defended as satisfying a want because it is only the production which provokes the demand? In this, as in the case of all cultural needs, it is unquestionably, in Professor Galbraith's words, "the process of satisfying the wants that creates the wants." (p. 347)

Presumably, the same general point applies to utility-maximization. Just because product desire A originated within Cal Consumer while product desire B came his way through manipulative advertising, it does not follow that satisfying desire A would give him more utility than satisfying desire B. Indeed, as we will see presently, the opposite may be true.

The Frustration of Rational Interbrand Choices

[21] The second major utilitarian objection to manipulative advertising concerns its power to distort consumer choices among brands and products. As R.M. Hare once observed:

> [T]he market economy is only defensible if it really does...lead to the maximum satisfaction of the preferences of the public. And it will not do this if it is distorted by various well-known undesirable practices.... By bringing it about that people decide on their purchases...after being deceived or in other ways manipulated, fraudulent advertisers impair the wisdom of the choices that the public makes and so distort the market in such a way that it does not function to maximize preference-satisfactions. (Hare, 1984, pp. 27–28)

For example, now suppose that Cal Consumer's preferences would find their optimum satisfaction in Product A. Intoxicated by Product B's manipulative advertising, Cal instead buys that product, which satisfies his original preferences less well than Product A. If Cal would have bought Product A in a regime where advertising is purely informative, presumably B's manipulative advertising cost him some utility.

[22] The previous argument, however, might fail if manipulative advertising gives consumers satisfactions that they would not otherwise obtain from their purchases. In that event, the utility lost

when manipulative advertising causes consumers to choose the wrong product for their needs must be weighed against the utility consumers gain from such advertising. Due to the inherent uncertainty of utility calculations, it may be unclear which effect would predominate. Sometimes, though, the gains could outweigh the losses: that is, manipulative advertising could generate more utility than purely informative advertising.

[23] But how can "manipulated" desires and purchases generate more utility than their "rational" counterparts? One answer emerges from the dark masterpiece of the literature on manipulative advertising—Theodore Levitt's 1970 contribution to the *Harvard Business Review*. Levitt's main thesis is that "embellishment and distortion are among advertising's legitimate and socially desirable purposes" (Levitt, 1970, p. 85).[5] His determinedly nonlinear argument for that conclusion may be regarded as proceeding through several steps. The first is his assertion that when seen without illusions, human life is a poor thing. Natural reality, Levitt insists, is "crudely fashioned"; "crude, drab, and generally oppressive"; and "drab, dull, [and] anguished" (pp. 86, 90). For this reason, people try to transcend it whenever they can. "Everybody everywhere wants to modify, transform, embellish, enrich, and reconstruct the world around him—to introduce into an otherwise harsh or bland existence some sort of purposeful and distorting alleviation" (p. 87). People do so mainly though artistic endeavor, but also through advertising. "[W]e use art, architecture, literature, and the rest, and advertising as well, to shield ourselves, in advance of experience, from the stark and plain reality in which we are fated to live" (p. 90). Thus, "[m]any of the so-called distortions of advertising, product design, and packaging may be viewed as a paradigm of the many responses that man makes to the conditions of survival in the environment" (p. 90).

From all this, it follows that consumers demand [24] more than "pure operating functionality" from the products they buy (p. 89). As Charles Revson of Revlon, Inc. once said: "'In the factory we make cosmetics; in the store we sell hope'" (p. 85). Thus "[i]t is not cosmetic chemicals women want, but the seductive charm promised by the alluring symbols with which these chemicals have been surrounded—hence the rich and exotic packages in which they are sold, and the suggestive advertising with which they are promoted" (p. 85). In other words, consumers demand an expanded notion of functionality which includes "'non-mechanical' utilities," and do so to "help...solve a problem of life" (p. 89). Therefore, "the product" they buy includes not only narrowly functional attributes, but also the emotional or affective content produced by its packaging and advertising. "The promises and images which imaginative ads and sculptured packages induce in us are as much the product as the physical materials themselves.... [T]hese ads and packagings describe the product's fullness for us; in our minds, the product becomes a complex abstraction which is...the conception of a perfection which has not yet been experienced" (pp. 89–90).

For all these reasons, advertisements are not [25] *supposed* to be literal representations of the products they tout (p. 90). "[D]eep down inside," moreover, "the consumer understands this perfectly well" (p. 90). Indeed, Levitt maintains, consumers give industry a "fiat...to 'distort' its messages" (p. 89). Thus, while the consumer wants "'truth,'" "he also wants and needs the alleviating imagery and tantalizing promises of the advertiser and designer" (p. 92). As a result, ethical firms with "rational" advertising imperil their survival. "There is hardly a company that would not go down in ruin if it refused to provide fluff, because nobody will buy pure functionality" (p. 92).

[26] To Levitt, therefore, we do not merely buy a physical product, but also a set of positive feelings connected with it by advertising. If his argument is sound, those feelings give us extra utility above and beyond the utility we get from the product's performance of its functions. This extra utility might well outweigh the utility we lose because manipulative advertising has made us buy a product that is suboptimum in purely functional terms and that we would not have bought were advertising only informative.

[27] Is Levitt's argument sound? Although his description may not apply to all people, or even to most, it hardly seems ridiculous. People who object to Levitt's contention that human life is crude, drab, and dull should recall that he is speaking of a human life we infrequently experience—human life absent the embellishments all civilizations try to give it. If his contention is correct, the need to transcend our natural condition is an obvious motive for those embellishments. John Waide, however, insists that our need for embellishment can be satisfied without manipulative advertising—through, for example, ideals, fantasies, heroes, and dreams (Waide, 1987, p. 76). But why assume this? If the need for comforting illusions is strong and pervasive, why should embellishment not extend to the products people buy?

[28] Bigger problems, however, arise from Levitt's assumption that consumers are aware of advertising's illusions.[6] If people know that advertising lies, how can they derive much psychic benefit—i.e., much utility—from its embellishments? Worse yet, products tend not to deliver on manipulative advertising's promises of sex, status, security, and the like. When this is so, how can such advertising deliver much utility to the consumers it controls (cf. Waide, 1987, p. 75)? Indeed, the gap between manipulative advertising's implicit promises and its actual performance may lead to frustrated expectations and significant *dis*utility.

[29] Recall, however, that for Levitt consumers want and need to be manipulated because life without advertising's illusions is too much to bear. If so, it is unlikely that everyone would be *continuously* aware of advertising's illusions and the low chance of their realization. Only intermittently, in other words, would people assume a tough-minded, rational-actor mentality toward advertising. On other occasions, some would effectively suspend disbelief in advertising's embellishments. Although they might retain latent knowledge of those illusions, that knowledge would not be constantly present to their consciousness. And when the illusions rule, they could generate real satisfactions.

[30] Are these assumptions about consumers realistic ones? To me, they are plausible as applied to some people some of the time. If everyone were consistently able to approach manipulative advertising rationally, how often would it succeed? As Waide correctly maintains, moreover, manipulative advertising is easy to spot if people bother to look (1987, p. 74). But as Waide's observation implicitly suggests, people often do not bother. To think otherwise requires one to believe that people are without mood swings and contradictory impulses, and that they consistently prefer undiluted reality to pleasant illusions. Both of these assumptions, I submit, simply are ridiculous. For that reason, there also is nothing ridiculous in assuming that people gain utility by accepting advertising's illusions, while retaining some latent and/or intermittent knowledge of their condition.

Long-Run Harm

[31] Even if manipulative advertising generates utility by associating products with pleasant feelings, and even if this additional utility outweighs the utility lost when consumers buy suboptimum products, manipulative advertising may still produce a negative utility balance in the end. The reason

is the long-run harm that certain "manipulated" purchases may cause. As Alan Goldman asserted while discussing Galbraith's critique of advertising:

> One weak criterion [of advertising] that can be adopted from a want-regarding or utilitarian moral theory relates to whether satisfaction of the desires in question increases overall satisfaction in the long run, whether it contributes to fulfilled or worthwhile lives. Desires are irrational when their satisfaction is incompatible with more fundamental or long-range preferences.... Alcoholism is an example of such irrational desire, the satisfaction of which is harmful overall. Desires for junk food, tobacco and certain kinds of conspicuous consumption are other examples, at least for certain consumers. Processes that create and feed such desires are not utility maximizing, since even the satisfaction of these desires lowers the subject's general level of utility in the long run. (Goldman, 1982, pp. 254–55)[7]

Here, Goldman appears to embrace a kind of virtue ethics ("fulfilled or worthwhile lives"), and seems to feel that a life of virtue and moderation will produce the greatest happiness in the long run. But while this may be true, the "happiness" in question probably cannot be equated with utility—or at least with utility in its Benthamite form. Judged solely in pleasure-pain terms, that is, Goldman's argument is questionable.

[32] From such a standpoint, Goldman's biggest errors are his tendency to overrate the probability and the severity of manipulative advertising's long-run harms, and his complete failure to consider the pleasure generated by it and the products it touts. This is true even assuming (as I have assumed) that manipulative advertising actually can make people drink, smoke, eat junk food, and so forth. On the probability and severity questions, it is initially worth noting that most manipulative advertising tries to make people buy material things, not the harmful items that Goldman's analysis suggests. Even where alcohol, tobacco, and junk food are at issue, how many people actually suffer severe health or other consequences from such items, as compared with those who suffer lesser consequences or none at all? Even if harmful consequences eventually do occur, moreover, they must be balanced against the utility people accumulate during their years of smoking, drinking, and eating unwisely. In my experience, at least, these are pleasurable activities. Furthermore, if Levitt is correct, manipulative advertising could surround those activities with pleasing associations that generate still more utility.

[33] To illustrate some of the previous points, suppose that Joe Camel, a young stockbroker, is induced to smoke, drink, and eat high-fat foods because a series of ads depict these activities as manly and sophisticated. In addition to the pleasure Joe derives from the activities, Joe also gets satisfaction from the advertising-induced perception that he is tougher and cooler than the (to him) growing tribe of health-conscious sissies. After years of dissipation finally take their toll, Joe dies in his sleep of a heart attack at age 55. In this admittedly loaded example, I cannot help but think that manipulative advertising had positive long-term consequences for utility. Nor would this conclusion necessarily change if Joe instead dies an excruciatingly painful death from lung or colon cancer. Even here, Joe's utility account would be positive if the pleasure accumulated during years of unhealthy living outscores the pain associated with the final reckoning. More importantly, Joe might still have faced a painful death even if all advertising were informative and he had lived a life of sanity and moderation. And while it is true that such a life would probably give Joe more time on earth, it is debatable whether those "Golden Years" are a high-utility experience.

Autonomy

[34] All things considered, the utilitarian arguments against manipulative advertising are unimpressive. Indeed, utilitarianism might even support that practice. Galbraith claimed that little utility is generated when we satisfy contrived wants. But the connection between a desire's origin outside the individual and the low utility resulting from its satisfaction is unclear. At first glance, it appears that manipulative advertising robs consumers of utility by inducing them to buy functionally suboptimal products. But while this may be true, the resulting utility losses arguably are counterbalanced by the utility people gain from manipulative advertising. Finally, although manipulative advertising can induce behavior with harmful long-term consequences, those consequences do not always occur and, even when they do occur, do not invariably outweigh the pleasure accumulated during years of unhealthy living.

The Autonomy-Related Objection to Manipulative Advertising

[35] To some people, however, the preceding points may say more about utilitarianism's deficiencies than about manipulative advertising's worth. One standard criticism of utilitarianism emphasizes its indifference to the moral quality of the means by which utility is maximized. Thus, even if manipulative advertising increases consumers' utility, it is bad because it does so by suppressing their ability to make intelligent, self-directed product choices on the basis of their own values and interests. In a word, manipulative advertising now seems objectionable because it denies personal *autonomy*.

[36] Among the many strands within the notion of autonomy, one of the most common equates it with self-government or self-determination (see Christman, 1988, p. 110). According to Steven Lukes, for example, autonomy is "self-direction"; the autonomous person's "thought and action is his own, and [is] not determined by agencies or causes outside his control" (Lukes, 1973, p. 52). At the social level, Lukes adds, an individual is autonomous "to the degree to which he subjects the pressures and norms with which he is confronted to conscious and critical evaluation, and forms intentions and reaches practical decisions as the result of independent and rational reflection" (p. 52).

[37] If manipulative advertising has the effects this article assumes, it apparently denies autonomy to the individuals it successfully controls. On this article's assumptions, people become consumers and make product choices precisely through "agencies and causes outside [their] control," and not through "conscious and critical evaluation" or "independent and rational reflection." To Lippke, moreover, advertising also has an "implicit content" that further suppresses autonomy. Among other things, this implicit content causes people to accept emotionalized, superficial, and oversimplified claims; desire ease and gratification rather than austerity and self-restraint; let advertisers dictate the meaning of the good life; defer to their peers; and think that consumer products are a means for acquiring life's nonmaterial goods (pp. 44–47). People so constituted are unlikely to be independent, self-governing agents who subject all social pressures to an internal critique. Nor is it likely that they would have much resistance to manipulative appeals to buy particular products.

Are Consumers Autonomous on Levitt's Assumptions?

[38] On Levitt's assumptions, however, perhaps consumers do act autonomously when they submit to manipulative advertising. If Levitt is correct: (1) manipulative advertising works much as its critics say that it works; because (2) consumers suspend

disbelief in its claims and embrace its illusions; because (3) they want, need, and demand those illusions to cope with human existence; while (4) nonetheless knowing on some level that those illusions indeed are illusions. In sum, one might say, advertising manipulates consumers because they knowingly and rationally want to be manipulated. That is, they half-consciously sacrifice their autonomy for reasons that make some sense on Levitt's assumptions about human life. In still other words, they more or less autonomously relinquish their autonomy. This might be thought inconsistent with autonomy itself, but on Levitt's bleak assumptions even a "self-directed" person who exercises "independent and rational reflection" (Lukes, 1973, p. 52) might well do the same. Unless autonomy is an inalienable right,[8] it seems difficult to object to such a decision if Levitt's factual argument is sound.

[39] Levitt's argument, however, appears to concern only individual purchase decisions, and not advertising's assumed ability to socialize people to accept consumerism and reject autonomy. But his argument is broad enough to explain this second process. On Levitt's assumptions, people would more or less knowingly embrace consumerism because unfiltered reality is too much to bear, and would reject autonomy in favor of Lippke's "implicit content" because autonomy offers too little payoff at too much cost. If those assumptions are accurate, moreover, people arguably have sound reasons for behaving in these ways.

Arrington's Attempt to Reconcile Manipulation and Autonomy

[40] In the previous section, I argued that Levitt's assumptions at least are plausible. Demonstrating their truth, however, obviously would be a difficult endeavor. For this reason, at least, they are not a decisive objection to the claim that manipulative advertising undermines autonomy. Another way to attack that claim, however, is to adopt a conception of autonomy that is consistent with advertising's manipulations. Robert Arrington attempts just such a reconciliation.

[41] Arrington begins his attempt by asking whether advertising creates desires which are not the consumer's own. His answer is: "Not necessarily, and indeed not often" (p. 7). In reaching this conclusion, Arrington does not deny that advertising frequently manipulates consumers. Instead, he maintains that this manipulation is consistent with autonomous choice. "[T]here is something wrong," Arrington asserts, "in setting up the issue over advertising and behavior control as a question whether our desires are truly ours *or* are created in us by advertisements. Induced and autonomous desires do not separate into two mutually exclusive classes" (p. 7).

[42] How can manipulation and autonomy coexist? As I just suggested, the key to their reconciliation is a particular conception of autonomy. Although Arrington does not explicitly define the term "autonomy,"[9] he does provide a practical test for distinguishing autonomous and non-autonomous desires. He does so by utilizing a distinction between first-order and second-order desires that apparently originated with Harry Frankfurt (1989).

> To obtain a better understanding of autonomous and nonautonomous desires, let us consider some cases of a desire which a person does not *acknowledge* to be his own even though he *feels* it. The kleptomaniac has a desire to steal which in many instances he repudiates.... And if I were suddenly overtaken by a desire to attend an REO concert, I would immediately disown this desire.... These are examples of desires which one might have but with which one would not identify. They are experienced as foreign to one's character or per-

sonality. Often a person will have...a second-order desire...*not* to have another desire. In such cases, the first-order desire [the other desire] is thought of as being nonautonomous, imposed on one. When on the contrary a person has a second-order desire to maintain and fulfill a first-order desire, then the first-order desire is truly his own, autonomous, original to him. So there is in fact a distinction between desires which are the agent's own and those which are not, but this is not the same as the distinction between desires which are innate to the agent and those which are externally induced. (p. 7)

Arrington then asserts that because people generally do not disown or repudiate the products they purchase, those purchase decisions usually are autonomous. "[M]ost of the desires induced by advertising I fully accept, and hence most of these desires are autonomous. The most vivid demonstration of this is that I often return to purchase the same product over and over again, without regret or remorse" (p. 7). In fact, Arrington concludes, even purchase decisions induced by subliminally implanted advertising could be autonomous if the consumer's implanted subconscious desires are consistent with her conscious ones (p. 7).

[43] For Arrington, then, the autonomy of one's desires and one's subsequent actions is determined by after-the-fact, second-order reflection on their congruence with one's nature, and not by their genesis inside the individual. Because it allows for external manipulation, autonomy so conceived may be inconsistent with the notions of self-direction, self-governance, and self-rule described earlier. The problem, however, may rest more with these notions than with Arrington's conception of autonomy. In other words, because so much of our behavior seems to result from external influences, we may need a conception of autonomy, like Arrington's, which reflects that fact. Indeed, such a conception has been the "received model" of autonomy in recent years (Christman, 1991, p. 4). In Gerald Dworkin's statement of this model, "[i]t is only when a person identifies with the influences that motivate him, assimilates them to himself, views himself as the kind of person who wishes to be moved in particular ways, that these influences are to be identified as 'his'" (Dworkin, 1989, p. 60; see also Frankfurt, pp. 69–72). But, Dworkin continues, if "a person resents being motivated in certain ways, is alienated from these influences, would prefer to be the kind of person who is motivated in different ways, then these influences, which may be causally effective, are not viewed by him as 'his'" (Dworkin, 1989, p. 60).

[44] Lippke attempts to dismiss Arrington's argument by claiming that while it may hold for particular choices consumers make (my second assumption about advertising's powers) Arrington has nothing to say about advertising's general tendency to promote a consumer consciousness (my first assumption). "If advertising induces uncritical acceptance of the consumer lifestyle as a whole, then Arrington's vindication of it with respect to the formation of particular desires or the making of particular choices *within* that lifestyle is hardly comforting" (1990, p. 39). But Arrington's conception of autonomy probably is broad enough to include the adoption of a consumer lifestyle as well as specific product decisions. Just as a person can engage in second-order reflection on her product choices, she also could ask herself whether she identifies with her consumer lifestyle.

[45] But if people have been thoroughly socialized to accept consumerism, can second-order reflection on that fact be genuinely autonomous? Even if such people could step back and ask "Is this consumer-person really me?", would not the answer invariably be "Yes"? The same argument probably applies to

individual purchase decisions. If I bought product X because its advertising successfully associated the product with my strong desires for power, status, and sexual conquest, how likely am I to reject it upon second-order reflection?

[46] To deal with such problems, Dworkin has a second criterion for autonomy—one that Arrington's article apparently does not mention. This is the *procedural independence* of the second-order identification process. Procedural independence means that the identification "is not itself influenced in ways which make...[it] in some way alien to the individual"—for example, by being "influenced by others in such a fashion that we do not view it as being his own" (Dworkin, 1989, p. 61). For a person's individual purchases and her acceptance of consumerism to be autonomous, therefore, her second-order reflection on each must be uninfluenced in the sense just described. But can this be the case if advertising is as strong a force as its critics claim? On that assumption, how can our consumer be sure that her second-order reflection is sufficiently free from advertising's influence? To be certain, she may have to make a third-level identification with her second-level judgment. But for the reasons just stated, one also can doubt the genuineness of the third-level identification, which means that a fourth level of reflection is necessary. Because the same doubt can be raised about the fourth level, however, we seem to be forced into an infinite regress (e.g., Christman, 1991, pp. 7–8; Thalberg, 1989, p. 130).

[47] To summarize, Arrington's claim that most advertising-induced purchases are autonomous apparently can be valid only if: (1) his conception of autonomy is sound, and (2) people actually exhibit procedural independence when they identify with their purchase decisions. Both of these assumptions are questionable. It is difficult not to suspect a conception of autonomy so capacious as to include purchases induced by subliminal advertising. On almost any notion of the self, such purchases are not self-determined at the time they occur; the most that can be said for them is that they meet the approval of some later self. Perhaps for this reason, the "received model" of autonomy has not gone unchallenged. For example, one recent competing account of the concept focuses on the conditions under which desires are formed and actions take place, rather than the actor's after-the-fact identification with a desire or an action (e.g., Christman, 1991, pp. 10–18).

[48] As for the second assumption required by Arrington's account, it seems difficult to determine whether a person's subsequent approval of his consumerist orientation or his individual purchases was genuine, or was wholly or partially produced by the advertising that by hypothesis caused each. The question is the procedural independence of the identification process, and determining this may require an infinite series of identifications with one's previous identification.

The Categorical Imperative

[49] One problem with some of the claims discussed thus far is that they present difficult empirical issues. This is plainly true of Levitt's claims. It also is true of Galbraith's assertion that because advertising-induced wants originate outside the individual, they have low urgency and therefore generate little utility when they are satisfied. The same can be said of Hayek's response to Galbraith. Given these problems, maybe manipulative advertising is best addressed by ethical theories whose conclusions do not depend on empirical matters like consumer psychology, or on manipulation's consequences for utility. Kant's categorical imperative is an obvious candidate.

[50] R.M. Hare made two Kantian arguments against manipulative advertising. "Kantians will say...that

to manipulate people is not to treat them as ends—certainly not as autonomous legislating members of a kingdom of ends.... But even apart from that it is something that we prefer not to happen to us and therefore shall not will it as a universal maxim" (Hare, 1984, p. 28; see also Beauchamp, 1984, p. 17). His reference, of course, was to the two major formulations of Kant's categorical imperative. The first, which comes in several versions, underlies Hare's second argument. The version employed here goes as follows: "Act only on that maxim through which you can at the same time will that it should become a universal law" (Kant, 1964, p. 88). According to the second major formulation of the imperative, one must "[a]ct in such a way that you always treat humanity, whether in your own person or in the person of any other, never simply as a means, but always at the same time as an end" (p. 96).

[51] Under either formulation of the imperative, it seems, manipulative advertising stands condemned. Under the first formulation, it seems difficult to identify a maxim that would: (1) clearly justify manipulative advertising, and (2) be universalized by any advertiser. Consider, for example, the following possibility: "In order to induce purchases and make money, business people can use advertising tactics that undermine the rational evaluation and choice of products by associating them with desired states to which they have little or no real relation." Presumably, no one would will the maxim's universalization, because to do so is to waive any moral objection to manipulative advertising aimed at oneself. Manipulative advertising apparently fares even worse under the second statement of the categorical imperative. As James Rachels has noted, under this formulation "we may never *manipulate* people, or *use* people, to achieve our purposes" (Rachels, 1993, p. 129). Instead, we should respect their rational nature by giving them the information that will enable them to make informed, autonomous decisions (Rachels, 1993, pp. 129–30; see also MacIntyre, 1984, p. 44). As the term "manipulative advertising" suggests, businesses that employ it to generate sales obviously try to use people as means to their own ends, and do so precisely by undermining their rationality and their ability to make informed, autonomous decisions.

[52] Even in the Kantian realm, however, empirical concerns intrude. Suppose again that Levitt is right in claiming that people want and need manipulative advertising. Given this assumption, the relevant maxim becomes something like the following: "In order to induce purchases and make money, people can use manipulative advertising tactics that undermine the rational evaluation and choice of products and services, but only when such advertising tactics liberate consumers from their dark, stark, and depressing natural existence." Although I cannot speak for everyone (or for Kant), I might will this maxim's universalization if I found Levitt's conception of the human condition at all plausible. This illustrates a common criticism of the first formulation of the categorical imperative: that one can manipulate the imperative to get the results one wishes by framing the maxim appropriately (cf. MacIntyre, 1966, pp. 197–98).

[53] Even if Levitt's account is perfectly accurate, however, the second major statement of the imperative still creates problems for manipulative advertising. Here, the question seems to boil down to the following: are firms that employ manipulative advertising using a consumer merely as a means to their own ends and therefore violating the imperative if the consumer, in effect, needs and wants to be manipulated? If, as I suggested earlier, the suspension of disbelief required for one to accept manipulative advertising may be more or less reasonable, then advertisers conceivably *are* respecting consumers' rationality by providing them with product-related illusions. Kant, however, thought

that "[r]ational nature exists as an end in itself" (1964, p. 96). For this reason, he probably would not have acceded to any diminution of human rationality, even one arguably justified on rational grounds. This is suggested by his conclusion that committing suicide to avoid a painful situation—an arguably rational termination of rational nature—violates the second major formulation of the imperative (pp. 96–97).

[54] In this article, however, I am assuming that each of my four ethical perspectives is *prima facie* valid, and that their claims should somehow be balanced against each other when conflicts occur. On this assumption, other moral duties may sometimes compete with those established by the categorical imperative, and the conflicting obligations must be reconciled in some fashion. Thus, if Levitt's view of our condition is correct, if we have a *prima facie* duty to maximize utility, and if manipulative advertising in fact makes human life more bearable, *perhaps* that duty might outweigh the duty to respect the rational element of human nature. If so, we have yet another ethical escape hatch through which manipulative advertising might slip.

Virtue Ethics

[55] Earlier I depicted Galbraith as a utilitarian, but other moral aspirations probably were at work within *The Affluent Society*. The book opened with the following quotation from Alfred Marshall: "The economist, like everyone else, must concern himself with the ultimate aims of man." Galbraith's conviction that consumerism does not rank high among those aims pervades much of his writing, and almost certainly informed his critique of advertising. However, the ethical values and theories previously considered in this article do not state and enjoin the desirable substantive conditions of human life. It seems foreign to the notion of autonomy to dictate the choices the autonomous person should make.[10] As Waide (1987, p. 77) accurately notes, for example, Arrington offers "no standard to which we can appeal to judge whether a desire enhances a life." Although utilitarianism obviously has a substantive criterion for actions, utility can be acquired in innumerable ways, some of them ethically questionable. Waide suggests as much when he correctly remarks of Levitt that he "appears to assume that in a satisfying life one has many satisfied desires—*which* desires is not important" (p. 77). As for Kant's categorical imperative, we have already seen that its first major formulation is notoriously manipulable. And while the second major formulation has some content, all it commands is that we treat other people as rational agents when we propose a course of action to them.

[56] Waide's alternative to such approaches is to examine "the virtues and vices at stake" in manipulative advertising (1987, p. 73), and to see "what kinds of lives are sustained" by it (p. 77). Stanley Benn sounds the same note when he suggests that the key question about advertising is whether it promotes "a valuable kind of life," with this determination depending on "some objective assessment of what constitutes excellence in human beings" (1967, p. 273). Because manipulative advertising encourages advertisers to ignore the well-being of their targets and encourages those targets to neglect the cultivation of nonmarket goods, Waide concludes that it makes us less virtuous persons and therefore is morally objectionable (1987, pp. 74–75). Many other critics of advertising make the same general point. The Heilbroner quotation that opened this article is an example. On another occasion Heilbroner called advertising "perhaps the single most value-destroying activity of a business civilization," due to the "subversive influence of the relentless effort to persuade people to change their lifeways, not out of any knowledge of, or deeply held

convictions about the 'good life,' but merely to sell whatever article or service is being pandered" (1976, pp. 113–14). His main specific complaint is that by offering a constant stream of half-truths and deceptions, advertising makes "cynics of us all" (p. 114). Virginia Held makes a related point when she criticizes advertising for undermining intellectual and artistic integrity (1984, pp. 64–66).

[57] To Christopher Lasch, on the other hand, advertising's greatest evil may be its tendency to leave consumers "perpetually unsatisfied, restless, anxious, and bored" (1978, p. 72). In a passage which echoes Levitt, he adds that advertising:

> [U]pholds consumption as the answer to the age-old discontents of loneliness, sickness, weariness, lack of sexual satisfaction.... It plays seductively on the malaise of industrial civilization. Is your job boring and meaningless? Does it leave you with feelings of futility and fatigue? Is your life empty? Consumption promises to fill the aching void; hence the attempt to surround commodities with an aura of romance, with allusions to exotic places and vivid experiences; and with images of female breasts from which all blessings flow. (pp. 72–73)

From Levitt's basically utilitarian perspective, this condition is defensible because the alternative—our everyday natural existence—is even less satisfying, and there is no other criterion by which to judge the worth of social practices. But one suspects that Lasch might reject advertising's consequences as inherently bad even if they did mark an increase in utility. The same probably holds for most of advertising's cultural critics. As a group, Michael Schudson remarks, they see "the emergence of a consumer culture as a devolution of manners, morals and even manhood, from a work-oriented production ethic of the past to the consumption, 'lifestyle'-obsessed, ethic-less pursuits of the present" (1984, pp. 6–7).

[58] Uniting all these varied criticisms of advertising is the notion that it promotes substantive behaviors, experiences, and states of character which are inherently undesirable, and that it is morally objectionable for this reason. Ordinarily, however, those denunciations are not accompanied by any systematic development of the virtues advertising undermines, let alone any effort to justify those virtues. For the philosophers among advertising's critics, the most likely explanation for these omissions is the difficulty of stating and justifying a convincing account of the virtues—especially today. (Heilbroner's putting "the good life" in quotations while attacking advertising on just that presupposition is suggestive here.) In this section's introduction, however, I waived this difficulty when I assumed that each ethical basis for attacking manipulative advertising is *prima facie* valid.

[59] This still leaves open the question whether any existing scheme of virtue ethics would condemn manipulative advertising, but I hope I can dismiss this problem without much discussion. This article assumes that manipulative advertising both creates a consumer culture and strongly influences individual purchase decisions. Its main means for accomplishing the second aim (and perhaps the first) is to associate the product with such non-market goods as sex, status, and power. On those assumptions, manipulative advertising almost certainly undermines such standard virtues as honesty and benevolence in its practitioners, and arguably dilutes its targets' moderation, reasonableness, self-control, self-discipline, and self-reliance (Rachels, 1993, p. 163 (listing these virtues)). Only with difficulty can one imagine Aristotle's proud man succumbing to such advertising or using it to escape reality.

Manipulative Advertising's Last Defense

[60] All things considered, virtue ethics appears to be the best basis for attacking manipulative advertising. In particular, it seems to dispose of a defense that has plagued our other three attacks on such advertising: Levitt's claim that people want and need advertising's illusions and therefore more or less knowingly and willingly embrace it. Like our other bases for attacking manipulative advertising, however, virtue ethics is not assumed to be an absolute. This might mean that the claims of virtue would have to give way if human beings simply could not endure without advertising's illusions or if its psychic satisfactions give people enormous amounts of utility.

[61] In any event, there is yet another possible defense of manipulative advertising. This defense is mainly utilitarian, but it also implicates my other three ethical criteria to some degree. It arises because by hypothesis all my criteria must be weighed against competing moral claims. The defense does not so much challenge the assertion that manipulative advertising is bad, as argue that it is the lesser of two evils.

[62] Throughout this article, I have assumed for the sake of argument that manipulative advertising's critics are correct in their assessment of its effects. As we have seen, these people usually maintain that manipulative advertising plays an important role in socializing people to consume. This means that on the critics' view of things, manipulative advertising is central to the functioning of modern consumer society. But if manipulative advertising is central to the system's operation, how safely can it be condemned? Assuming that the condemnation is effective, manipulative advertising disappears, and all advertising becomes informative, people gradually would be weaned from their consumerist ways. This is likely to create social instability, with a more authoritarian form of government the likely end result. That, in turn, could well mean an environment in which aggregate utility is lower than it is today, human autonomy and rational nature are less respected, and/or the virtues less recognized.

[63] One set of reasons for these conclusions is largely economic. If people become less consumerist as manipulative advertising leaves the scene, aggregate demand and economic output should decline. At first glance, this would seem to be of little consequence because by hypothesis people would value material things less. The problem is that the economic losses probably will be unevenly distributed: for example, some businesses will fail and some will not, and some people will lose their jobs while others stay employed. These inequalities are a potential source of social instability. Both to redress them and to preserve order, government is likely to intervene. This may involve a significant increase in outright governmental coercion.

[64] One obvious objection to the previous scenario is the claim that once people are liberated from manipulative advertising, they will become less egoistic, more cooperative, and more self-sacrificing. As a result, the necessary economic readjustments could be accomplished with very little coercion. But while this conceivably may be true, there is no reason to believe that these traits dominate human nature, and this article has made no such assumption. Earlier, I assumed for purposes of argument that manipulative advertising actually works, but nowhere did I say that people would be predominantly cooperative and caring in its absence. In fact, it is questionable whether manipulative advertising would be effective if these traits are strongly implanted in human nature. To reverse Galbraith's earlier argument, if people are naturally disposed toward his version of the good life, why does manipulative advertising work so well?

Indeed, manipulative advertising's success may be most compatible with the assumption that people are highly malleable because they lack strongly-rooted traits. On this assumption, manipulative advertising's departure creates a void that probably will be filled with *something*, maybe different somethings for different people. Some may settle down to a "sane" lifestyle that respects nature and tolerates diversity while fulfilling our "real needs." Others, however, may develop strong ethnic, racial, or religious loyalties. Some of these loyalties may be antagonistic to others. The likely result is either a degree of social disintegration, or its prevention through a more authoritarian government.

[65] To my knowledge, Waide is the only business ethicist to raise these kinds of problems, and he finds himself without a solution to them. Because "[i]t seems unlikely that [manipulative] advertising will end suddenly," however, Waide is "confident that we will have the time and the imagination to adapt our economy to do without it" (1987, p. 77). Although I suspect that Waide is too optimistic, I have no solution to the dilemma either. Thus, I am left with the unsatisfactory conclusion that while various moral arguments may provide sound bases for attacking manipulative advertising, prudential considerations dictate that none of them be pressed too vigorously. Manipulative advertising's ultimate justification, in other words, may be its status as a necessary evil.

Concluding Remarks

[66] For all the preceding reasons, it seems that there is no completely definitive basis for condemning manipulative advertising. But this obviously is not to say that the practice is morally unproblematic. Of my four suggested attacks on the practice, virtue ethics seems the strongest, with Kantianism a close second, autonomy third, and utilitarianism last. Indeed, utilitarianism may even support manipulative advertising. The main reason is that the practice's three most important defenses—Levitt's argument, the assertion that there is little connection between a want's origin outside the individual and the benefit resulting from its satisfaction, and manipulative advertising's centrality to our economic system—are more or less utilitarian in nature.

[67] Except perhaps for hard-core utilitarians, therefore, manipulative advertising is a morally dubious practice. However, this conclusion may depend heavily on a critical assumption made earlier: that manipulative advertising actually works. Specifically, I assumed that such advertising: (1) socializes people to adopt a consumerist lifestyle, and (2) strongly influences individual purchase decisions. But what happens if, by and large, each assumption is untrue?

[68] On first impressions, at least, it appears that if manipulative advertising is inefficacious, utilitarianism, autonomy, and virtue ethics largely cease to be bases for criticizing it. (On the other hand, manipulative advertising's "last defense" also bites the dust on this assumption. How can manipulative advertising's elimination threaten economic stability if such advertising does not stimulate consumption in the first place?) Manipulative advertising's ineffectiveness, for example, dooms Galbraith's argument that little utility results from the satisfaction of contrived wants, because now the relevant wants are not contrived. If manipulative advertising does not control individual purchase decisions, moreover, it cannot be blamed for the utility consumers lose when they choose the wrong product for their needs. On the other hand, because Levitt's arguments also seem to fail if manipulative advertising is inefficacious, it probably could not *generate* utility either. In addition, the dollars expended on the practice presumably would produce more utility if deployed elsewhere.

[69] If manipulative advertising neither determines people's values nor directs their purchases, it is also hard to see how the practice denies their autonomy. On the same assumption, it likewise seems improbable that manipulative advertising significantly undermines virtues such as moderation, reasonableness, self-control, self-discipline, and self-reliance in its targets. However, because advertisers still would be trying to manipulate consumers, their honesty and benevolence would continue to be compromised by such behavior. This is especially true since by hypothesis they now would be peddling an ineffective marketing technique to the businesses they profess to serve.

[70] However, Kantian objections to manipulative advertising might well remain even if it is inefficacious. On that assumption, admittedly, perhaps one would will the universalization of a maxim permitting such advertising. If manipulative advertising simply fails to work, moreover, maybe it does not treat consumers merely as means to advertiser's ends. But such arguments ignore the strong anti-consequentialism of Kant's ethics, which arguably renders advertising's ineffectiveness irrelevant. More importantly, those arguments ignore Kant's stress on the motives with which people should act. The only thing that is unqualifiedly good, Kant says, is a good will; and the good will is good not because of what it accomplishes, but simply because it wills the good (Kant, 1964, pp. 61–62). Even if manipulative advertising is unsuccessful, advertisers presumably try to make it work. Unless they believe that their efforts would benefit consumers in the end, it is unlikely that they are acting with a good will when they devise and employ their stratagems.

[71] At a first cut, therefore, it seems that if manipulative advertising is ineffective, the only significant ethical objections to it are Kantian. (To these we might add the money wasted on the practice, as well as its effect on the virtue of its practitioners.) For those inclined to ignore Kantian objections, therefore, it seems that manipulative advertising's rightness or wrongness depends less on ethical theory than on empirical questions within the purview of the social sciences. To people who regard ethical theory as hopelessly soft and subjective, and who think that the social sciences are producing genuine knowledge, this might mean that a definite evaluation of manipulative advertising is within reach.

[72] This line of argument, however, ignores the intractability of the factual issues relevant to any ethical evaluation of manipulative advertising. As the preceding discussion suggests, the most important such question is the extent to which manipulative advertising actually affects purchase decisions and socializes people to consume. Even if manipulative advertising actually has those effects, other more or less empirical issues would remain. These include the validity of Levitt's arguments, Galbraith's asserted connection between a desire's origin outside the individual and the low utility resulting from its satisfaction, and manipulative advertising's contribution to gross domestic product. All these questions, I submit, are unlikely to be answered any time soon. Readers who think otherwise are invited to suggest research programs for resolving them. Viewed against that task, ethical theory's interminable debates seem less hopeless. But while this conclusion may give business ethicists some comfort, it further clouds the inconclusive ethical case against manipulative advertising.

Notes

1. In addition to associative advertising, other manipulative techniques mentioned by business ethicists include subliminal suggestion (in which the implanted message is not consciously perceptible at the time of its implantation) and simple repetition (which tries to establish the product in consumers'

minds) (Arrington, 1982, pp. 4–5; Crisp, 1987, p. 413). However, although I say so with my fingers crossed, there is little to suggest that the former is, or has been, much used.
2. In fact, some (e.g., Lippke, 1990, p. 38) reject it.
3. However, I do not consider the "everyone's doing it" defense. On this subject, see Ronald M. Green, "When Is 'Everyone's Doing It' a Moral Justification?" *Business Ethics Quarterly* 1(1): 75–93.
4. Another possible utilitarian argument involves the voluminous scholarly literature on the economic impact of advertising. To oversimplify considerably, one school of thought on this subject regards advertising as primarily manipulative, and sees it as a means by which oligopolists preserve their market position (through, for example, advertising-created brand identification). The result is decreased competition, somewhat lower output, and somewhat higher prices than otherwise would be the case. This means that consumers get somewhat less value per dollar and somewhat less utility. A newer, more laissez-faire, school of thought contends that advertising increases competition by (among other things) providing more information. This probably means that it increases utility by giving consumers a maximum return on their dollars. The many studies on the issues created by this debate apparently are inconclusive. See Mark S. Albion & Paul W. Faris, *The Advertising Controversy: Evidence on the Economic Effects of Advertising* (Boston, MA, Auburn House, 1981); Robert B. Ekelund, Jr. & David S. Saurman, *Advertising and the Market Process: A Modern Economic View* (San Francisco, CA, Pacific Institute for Public Policy, 1988); Julian L. Simon, *Issues in the Economics of Advertising* (Urbana, IL, U. of Illinois P., 1970).
5. However, Levitt did condemn "falsification with larcenous intent" (1970, p. 85)—that is, the *deceptive* advertising described earlier.
6. Some poll data support this assumption. According to Michael Schudson (1986, p. 10), a 1976 survey found that 46% of the public regard all or most television advertising as "seriously misleading," while 83% regard at least "some" television advertising as seriously misleading. Also, those polled in a 1981 *Newsweek* survey rated advertising executives lowest in honesty and ethical standards among several listed professions (including members of Congress).
7. Goldman also raised the possibility that advertising creates desires that will never be satisfied, thus generating even more long-run disutility. In the interest of brevity, I will not consider that argument here.
8. Much recent literature on inalienable rights argues that few, if any, rights are inalienable. See, e.g., J. Nelson, "Are There Inalienable Rights?" *Philosophy* 64: 519–24 (1989); L. Stell, "Dueling and the Right to Life," *Ethics* 90(1): 7–26 (1979); D. Van De Veer, "Are Human Rights Inalienable?" *Philosophical Studies* 37(2): 165–76 (1980).
9. Instead, Arrington said that autonomy is a "complex, multifaceted concept" which must be approached "through the more determinate notions of (a) autonomous desire, (b) rational desire and choice, (c) free choice, and (d) control or manipulation" (Arrington, 1982, p. 6). Here I only consider Arrington's discussion of autonomous desire.
10. However, Benn (1967, p. 274) suggests that within the liberal tradition, the ability to make responsible choices among competing ways of life *is* a human excellence.

References

Arrington, R. 1982. "Advertising and Behavior Control." *Journal of Business Ethics*, 1(1): 3–12.

Beauchamp, T. 1984. "Manipulative Advertising." *Business and Professional Ethics Journal*, 3(3 & 4): 1–22.

Benn, S. 1967. "Freedom and Persuasion." *The Australasian Journal of Philosophy*, 45: 259–75.

Christman, J. 1988. "Constructing the Inner Citadel: Recent Work on the Concept of Autonomy." *Ethics*, 99(1): 109–24.

Christman, J. 1991. "Autonomy and Personal History." *Canadian Journal of Philosophy*, 21(1): 1–24.

Colloquy. 1982. "Advertising and the Corrupting of America." *Business and Society Review*, 1(41): 64–69.

Crisp, R. 1987. "Persuasive Advertising, Autonomy, and the Creation of Desire." *Journal of Business Ethics*, 6: 413–18.

Dworkin, G. 1989. "The Concept of Autonomy," in

Christman, J. (ed.), *The Inner Citadel: Essays on Individual Autonomy* (New York: Oxford U.P.), pp. 54–62.

Frankena, W. 1973. *Ethics* (Englewood Cliffs: Prentice-Hall, 2nd ed.).

Frankfurt, H. 1989. "Freedom of the Will and the Concept of a Person," in J. Christman, (ed.), *The Inner Citadel: Essays on Individual Autonomy* (New York: Oxford U.P.), pp. 63–76.

Galbraith, J.K. 1958. *The Affluent Society* (Boston: Houghton Mifflin).

Genge, W. 1985. "Ads Stimulate the Economy." *Business and Society Review*, 1(55): 58–59.

Goldman, A. 1982. *The Moral Foundations of Professional Ethics* (Totowa: Rowman & Littlefield).

Hare, R.M. 1984. "Commentary." *Business & Professional Ethics Journal*, 3(3 & 4): 23–28.

Hayek, F.A. 1961. "The *Non Sequitur* of the 'Dependence Effect.'" *Southern Economic Journal*, 27: 346–48.

Heilbroner, R. 1976. *Business Civilization in Decline* (New York: W.W. Norton).

Held, V. 1984. "Advertising and Program Content." *Business and Professional Ethics Journal*, 3(3 & 4): 61–76.

Kant, I. 1964. *Groundwork of the Metaphysic of Morals* (New York: Harper Torchbook, H.J. Paton tr.).

Krutch, J.W. 1959. *Human Nature and the Human Condition* (New York: Random House).

Lantos, G. 1987. "Advertising; Looking Glass or Molder of the Masses?" *Journal of Public Policy and Marketing*, 6: 104–28.

Lasch, C. 1978. *The Culture of Narcissism; American Life in An Age of Diminishing Expectations* (New York: W.W. Norton).

Levitt, T. 1970. "The Morality (?) of Advertising." *Harvard Business Review*, (July-August): 84–92.

Lippke, R. 1990. "Advertising and the Social Conditions of Autonomy." *Business and Professional Ethics Journal*, 8(4): 35–58.

Lukes, S. 1973. *Individualism* (Oxford: Basil Blackwell).

MacIntyre, A. 1966. *A Short History of Ethics* (New York: Collier).

MacIntyre, A. 1981. *After Virtue: A Study in Moral Theory* (Notre Dame: U. of Notre Dame P.).

Rachels, J. 1993. *The Elements of Moral Philosophy* (New York: McGraw-Hill, 2nd ed.).

Schudson, M. 1986. *Advertising, The Uneasy Persuasion: Its Dubious Impact on American Society* (New York: Basic Books, 2nd ed.).

Thalberg, I. 1989. "Hierarchical Analyses of Unfree Action," in Christman, J. (ed.), *The Inner Citadel: Essays on Individual Autonomy* (New York: Oxford U.P.), pp. 123–36.

Waide, J. 1987. "The Making of Self and World in Advertising." *Journal of Business Ethics*, 6(2): 73–79.

Questions

1. Give an example, if you can, of a current ad that:
   (a) "debases language"
   (b) "drains thought"
   (c) "undoes dignity"
2. Defenders of advertising claim that:
   (a) it *informs* consumers about their products, which enhances *competition*, which prevents market *concentration* and *stagnation*. Do the ads you described in question one inform consumers about products, and does informing by advertising enhance competition? (Could non-informative ads also enhance competition? Is competition the only way to prevent market concentration and stagnation?)

(b) it provides the media with financial support, which keeps it free from *governmental* control. Is governmental control better or worse than sponsor control?

(c) people approach advertising *rationally* and *therefore* it can't be too manipulative. *Do people approach advertising rationally, and would a rational approach necessarily limit an ad's manipulativeness?*

3. What is Phillips's overall point, his thesis, his conclusion (in one sentence)?
4. Phillips makes two assumptions, accepting as "givens" two claims.
    (a) What are they?
    (b) Do you accept those claims?
5. (a) How does Phillips define "manipulative advertising"?
    (b) Is it a good definition—will it include everything you want to include, and will it exclude everything you want to exclude?
6. (a) What is the first ethical attack against manipulative advertising that Phillips examines (in one sentence)?
    (b) Phillips presents three arguments for this first claim:
    (i) The first argument is that made by Galbraith. Outline the argument (summarize paras 18–19; check your work with para 20), then explain the two objections to it that Phillips presents (pay special attention to the second one, that by Hayek).
    (ii) Referring to Hare, state the second argument. Phillips presents Levitt's argument as an objection—how exactly does Levitt argue that manipulated desires and purchases can provide *more* utility than rational desires and purchases? (Summarize paras 23–24; check your work with para 26.)
    (iii) The third argument seems to be grounded in virtue ethics—explain. Does Phillips think that manipulative advertising will necessarily cause long-term harm, regardless of Goldman's virtues? And does he think any long-term harm will necessarily outweigh the attendant pleasures?
7. (a) What is the second ethical attack against manipulative advertising that Phillips examines (in one sentence)?
    (b) Arrington says that one can be manipulated and at the same time be autonomous—how so? (Look carefully at how he determines whether a desire is autonomous.) Does Phillips accept Arrington's conception of autonomy (para 47)?
    (c) What is Lippke's objection to Arrington? Does Phillips accept Lippke's objection (para 44)?
8. (a) What is the third ethical attack against manipulative advertising that Phillips examines (in one sentence)?
    (b) Both of Kant's imperatives can be used to condemn manipulative advertising. However, if Levitt's view that people want to be manipulated is correct, the support of which imperative is seriously weakened?
9. (a) What is the fourth ethical attack against manipulative advertising that Phillips examines (in one sentence)?

(b) Be sure to highlight the statements against manipulative advertising made by Waide, Heilbroner, and Held (para 56)—all argue from a virtue ethics point of view.

(c) Which virtue does Phillips consider manipulative advertising to most undermine?

10. Phillips argues that a non-consumerist society would be unstable and "a more authoritarian form of government the likely end result" (para 62). Do you agree? (Before you answer, be sure you understand the economic reasons Phillips gives in para 63 and the social reasons he gives in para 64.)

It's All on Sale: Marketing Ethics and the Perpetually Fooled[*]

Andy Wible

Abstract: Discussion of marketing deception has mostly focused on two main areas: first are cases that involve the intentional deception of people who tend to have compromised intelligence, such as children or the elderly, and second are cases that involve intentional falsehoods or the withholding of vital information, such as Madoff's exploits. This article will differ from most in the field by examining marketing practices that are generally truthful, but deceive almost everyone. These practices do not fool just small select groups, but are fooling those usually assumed to be rational. For example, we love "free" merchandise so much that we are willing to irrationally settle for less to get the free product. Behavioral economists and psychologists are proving that, as Dan Ariely puts it, most all of us are "Predictably Irrational." Is it wrong for marketers to take advantage of the mass's foibles as it is wrong to take advantage of children? The article will look at some of the behavioral economists' data, how that data affects the rational and ignorant person standards of marketing, and suggest the reflective rational person standard as a way to morally evaluate marketing techniques given this new data.

Most theorists hold that in marketing persuasion [1] is acceptable, but deception and lying are wrong. Hence, discussion of marketing deception has mostly focused on two main areas: first are cases that involve the intentional deception of people who tend to have compromised intelligence, such as children or the elderly, and second are cases that involve intentional falsehoods or the withholding of vital information, such as Madoff's exploits. This article will differ from most in the field by examin-

[*] *Journal of Business Ethics* 99.1 (2011): 17–21.

ing marketing practices that are generally truthful, but deceive almost everyone. These practices do not fool just small select groups, but are fooling those usually assumed to be rational. Behavioral economists and psychologists are proving that, as Dan Ariely puts it, most all of us are "Predictably Irrational." Is it wrong for marketers to take advantage of the mass's foibles as it is wrong to take advantage of children? The article will look at some of the behavioral economists' data, and how we ought morally to evaluate these marketing techniques.

Art Van: A Common Case

[2] Art Van is a successful statewide furniture chain in Michigan. They have a large advertising budget with loud yelling TV commercials and bright newsprint that announces its new sale every week. One week it is an anniversary sale, the next week it is an inventory reduction sale, the following week it has a "three day only" up to 65% off sale, and this week "it's all on sale." The sales are constant and like many furniture stores, nothing is ever offered at "full price." The customer can always be assured of "saving." The approach seems to have worked on the customer's psyche. They have sales every week, but the masses are still drawn to them. When they say "We have never had a sale like this sale," most of us know the prices are not drastically different than last week. But these buzz words still pique our interest and drive us to buy. Even with all the facts in front of us, we feel good about the "deal" we got on the La-Z-boy recliner.

[3] Art Van's marketing techniques are not unique. They are followed by many if not most large retailers in the country. With such widespread usage, the constant sale technique must be working. But why are more people attracted to stores that have constant "sales" than to a store that has similar prices, but does not run a sale? Also, often the "reasonable person" standard is used to assess the morality of marketing techniques. It seemingly sensibly says that only marketing techniques that would deceive a reasonable person are immoral. Art Van's marketing techniques tend to persuade and perhaps deceive the reasonable masses, so are they immoral?

Predictably Irrational

[4] Dan Ariely is a behavioral economist who has looked into why we are attracted to constant sales and other marketing techniques. The thesis in his book *Predictably Irrational* is that economists have been mistaken in assuming that people are acting rationally within a market system. Economists assume that people in general do quite well making decisions to further their own interests. We do a cost benefit analysis and perform that action which has the most benefits with the fewest costs. We do make mistakes, but "market forces" will cause us to correct our actions. For example, we might buy a SUV because it looks cool, but then be forced to trade it in when we cannot afford to drive it. Behavioral economists like Ariely contend that this is a rosy picture of human nature. Their findings show us that we are often irrational in our decisions, and we are irrational over and over again. We can overcome this irrationality, but the draw will always be there. The illusion of a good deal is similar to visual illusions. The Müller-Lyer illusion is of two lines that seem to be of different lengths due to different types of arrow like lines attached to them, but upon closer measurement are the same. Yet, even when we know the lines are the same length, visually they still look different lengths. Marketing techniques work a similar way and seem to be even more beguiling for they have strong motivational effects even when we know that they are irrational (Ariely 2009).

[5] One of Ariely's examples of irrationality comes from an advertisement in *The Economist*

magazine (*The Economist* claims the ad was accidental). The advertisement was for *The Economist* on-line for $59, the print-only subscription for $125, and the on-line and print subscription for $125. Ariely found that 84% of his smart MIT students wanted joint on-line and print subscriptions and 16% wanted the online only version. No one wisely chose the print-only. He then gave the ad to a similar group of MIT students but took out the print-only subscription that no one chose and which seemed to be irrelevant to their choices. But taking out this option resulted in 68% of the students choosing the on-line only version and 32% choosing the print and on-line option. Ariely calls this the decoy effect where the comparison makes us behave irrationally. The rationally irrelevant addition of the print-only subscription makes us think that we are getting something for nothing, and in many cases an irrational decision is made (Ariely 2009, pp. 4–6).

[6]   Ariely tells of another decoy story that happened at Williams-Sonoma. They had a $275 bread maker that was not selling well. They brought in a marketing expert who recommended that they bring in another bread maker that was larger and fifty percent higher in price. The gimmick worked and the presence of the more expensive bread maker caused the now cheaper looking $275 dollar bread maker to fly off the shelves. The decoy made customers want something that they normally would think was too expensive and they did not need (Ariely 2009, pp. 14–15). Similar examples can be seen all around. I have often wondered why they make five thousand dollar televisions that very few people can afford to buy. One answer is that they help to sell the fifteen hundred dollar sets that with a little stretch many people can afford. The five thousand dollar set makes the fifteen hundred dollar set look like a relative bargain.

[7]   Getting something for free is something that we all like, but behavioral economists show us that free stuff actually makes us irrational. Ariely shows in several examples that we value free things more than we should. His example is of giving people the option of a chocolate truffle at 15 cents or a Hershey's Kiss at 1 cent. 73% chose the truffle. When the truffle price was lowered to 14 cents and the Kiss was free, the whole dynamic changed. Now, 69% of people chose the free kiss over the truffle (Ariely 2009, p. 52). Being free made the product much more valuable. We know that free deals are everywhere in marketing and like the Art Van sales we continue to fall for them. We are told that if we buy three tires, then we get the fourth one free. Amazon.com tells us that if we buy two books then we get free shipping. These free offers sometimes cause us to do irrational things. We might buy a book that we did not want, or buy sale tires even when non-sale tires are a better deal. Thus, free merchandise causes irrational decisions. The irrational attraction to free things might even explain why "buy one get one free" sales are often more successful than 50% off sales.

The Moral Assessment of Marketing in General

Marketers commonly defend their actions by saying that they are simply supplying what the consumer wants and needs. Theodore Levitt claims that advertising is analogous to art. Art fulfills the human desire for beauty, enrichment, imagination, and entertainment (Levitt 1974, pp. 84–92). Entertaining ads during the Super Bowl and Art Van commercials satisfy these uniquely human needs. John Kenneth Galbraith disagrees. He criticizes ads for creating desires rather than satisfying them. People did not want the $275 dollar bread maker until the $400 one was presented. [8]

People are manipulated into developing wants that they would otherwise not have. Galbraith [9] believes that as a result consumers spend their money on private goods like expensive bread makers and then ignore public goods like art, parks, and clean air that without advertising people would desire (1976). Advertising is not like art, it is a substitute for art. For Galbraith it is the bad consequences of marketing, rather than deceptive intentions, that makes it morally suspect. Art Van would have a very different marketing campaign if it was simply supplying what the consumer wants. They get many people thinking: "I don't really need a new sofa, but at 60% off it is very tempting." A second defense of advertising is the claim that we are dealing with adults and adults are rational persons. They can make the choice not to buy the product or perform the action. People are not as irrational as Galbraith suggests and consumers are at fault when they irrationally fall for these marketing techniques. The consumer should have more fortitude. In one sense, this position seems right. People should read books like Ariely's and try to overcome or work within their irrationalities. Ariely even suggests tips to overcome irrationality by using devices, such as smart credit cards that alert one's spouse upon one's giving into a temptation. Nevertheless, focusing on the responsibility of the consumer does not alleviate the entire responsibility of the marketer. Kant rightly teaches us that the marketer should not try to use people. Consumers should not be fools, and marketers should not be foolers. Analogously, I may be unwise to leave my house unlocked, but my doing so does not negate the blameworthiness of the robber.

The Rational and Ignorant Persons Standards

[10] The marketers might reply that they are not trying to fool people. They are simply presenting their product in a persuasive and entertaining way. Some illogical people may be deceived, but that is not the intent and the average "rational person" will not be. Advertisers should not be held to such a high standard. As Manuel Velasquez says, "Advertisers should take into account the interpretive capacities of the audience when they determine the content of an advertisement. Most buyers can be expected to be reasonably intelligent and possess a healthy skepticism concerning the exaggerated claims advertisers make for their products" (2006, p. 286). The rational person approach does seem reasonable. It does not hold either the marketer or the consumer to an unusually high standard. One initial worry about the theory is that marketers would still be allowed to fool the most vulnerable members of society who need to be protected the most. Taking advantage of people such as children and the elderly seems particularly troubling. But there could be extra restrictions put on ads that target those markets. For example, toys and caskets currently have more stringent marketing requirements than cars and running shoes.

[11] Behavioral economists point to a second major problem with the "rational person" standard: its assumption that most people are rational. What we have seen with Ariely is on the contrary most people are irrational. They fall for marketing tricks over and over and over again. We continually fall for free "giveaways" and stores with constant "sales." So, perhaps the rational person theory holds the consumer to an unusually high standard, as most people have very strong irrational tendencies. The free shipping that Amazon gives us is like giving fee drugs to a known drug addict or using Müller-Lyer tricks to make their products look bigger than they are. It is a rare person who can overcome these ingrained tendencies. Much of what we buy does not have such a detrimental effect as hard drugs, but Galbraith seems right that we may be foregoing public goods that we would

value without the constant bombardment of these marketing techniques.

[12] The Supreme Court seemed to recognize this problem in 1937's *FTC vs. Standard Education*. Standard Education's agents gave away a set of encyclopedias for free, and then the buyer only had to pay $69.50 for updated inserts. The "free" approach convinced even doctors and professors to buy the inserts even though the books and inserts were regularly sold for the same price. The courts said that their marketing practices were overly deceptive and the Federal Trade Commission (FTC) could prohibit them. The court declared that intentional deception was wrong and advocated what is frequently called the ignorant consumer standard.

[13] The ignorant consumer standard says that event marketing practices that deceive the naive and ill-informed consumers should be banned. There is a responsibility to protect the trusting as well as the rational and cautious customer. Such an approach might seem appropriate given Ariely's research and the *Standard Education* case which shows most everyone is frequently intellectually naive. Most all of us are now protected from being used. The standard holds that Art Van, *The Economist*, and almost all infomercials which claim "but wait, for free we will include not one but two extra of these amazing devices" are immoral.

[14] Many thought that this standard was too stringent on marketers, and even the FTC eventually found that they could not protect everyone from everything. Thus, the FTC modified their approach by only going after marketers who deceived large numbers of people. The modified standard would still prohibit Standard Education's practices due to the prevalent deception, but what about Ariely's cases? No one is withholding valuable information in *The Economist* or bread maker cases. As the deception is widespread, it should be censured by the FTC, but are they using people?

[15] The main problem of the modified standard is that the masses like these commercials. They watch television often for these advertisements and enjoy the entertainment provided. They know they are being naive, but the thrill of getting something for free or buying on sale is worth it. Consumers want to be entertained and they want to buy; this is why they read or watch the advertisement. They are like a novice swimmer who wants to swim, but gets to the end of the diving board and needs a little push. The marketers are providing this push and Ariely has exposed the psychology behind it. Yet, this does not open the flood gates for any type of marketing technique. Consumers can still be unjustly used as a mere means by being subjected to detrimental deceptions or falsehoods. Thus, we will turn to a sketch of a new approach to marketing protection.

The Reflective Rational Person

[16] The reflective rational person approach says that consumers are not being treated as a mere means if they accept the way they were treated after reflection. The consumer becomes rational after reflection. This approach protects consumers from serious deception, but it preserves the beauty and entertainment of advertisements. The consumer's long-term logical thinking is preserved, even if suspended in the short term. The theory says that if people say things such as, "I know it was irrational to take the free item, but free items are fun and I still like the Hershey kiss" or "I know that the sale at Art Van is a weekly sale, but it felt good shopping there and I like my new couch" then the person is not being used as a mere means. If Art Van's sale prices are actually much higher than the competition's prices or their products are considerably inferior for the price, then they are using the consumer and their action was wrong.

[17]   Another example currently popular in infomercials is to offer a lifetime of free pads for a mop and then in fine print or a hushed voice to say that you must just pay shipping and handling. Unlike the *Standard Education* case, the marketer is not withholding vital information. Also, if the consumer purchases the mop in part due to the free lifetime pads, she will likely only have buyer's remorse if the shipping and handling costs more than pads for a similar mop in a local store. After all, no reasonable person on reflection should think a company could stay in business giving away such things for free for a lifetime.

[18]   The rational reflective person standard does seem to be commonly considered. Most retailers have generous return policies that give buyers 30 days to return the product. These return policies may be what make the consumer and perhaps the FTC more willing to allow deceptive practices. The consumer knows that on reflection she can simply take the product back with little cost. However, many wrongly believe that the rational reflective person standard legally applies to agreements for large purchases, such as houses and cars. Morally, it does seem like there should be a 30-day return policy, but rarely is it the law. Unfortunately, in general, the law is not on the buyer's side, and any return is dependent upon the good will of the seller.

[19]   Although it is an improvement over the alternatives, there are some problems with the reflective rational person standard. First, the most vulnerable consumer is not protected. As mentioned above, this problem can be somewhat alleviated by having special restrictions on marketing practices when such groups are targeted. The FTC does use special precaution when it comes to children and certain products.

[20]   Second, people often do not reflect after a purchase or when they do they are unable to assess if they were treated within fair limits. For example, it was very difficult for consumers in 1937 of Standard Education's encyclopedias to know the standard price for encyclopedias and the inserts. Today, though, the open access to information through easy transportation and the internet should help to alleviate this problem. There is no requirement that people reflect, but, in general, the opportunity is available. Special precaution would need to be given to people, such as the very poor, who do not have ready access to information.

[21]   Third, overtly manipulative marketing practices would be considered permissible if people do not mind them. The marketer is saying "I am going to try to fool you" and the consumer is saying "go ahead, it's fun." It is deception, but perhaps not problematic because people are agreeing to it. The consumer is saying, "Try to fool me, but don't go too far." It is similar to going to a hypnotist to be fooled and entertained, but we expect it to be limited to the performance hall. This consent means that the consumer is not being treated as a means only.

[22]   The consent may be a problem because it seems to be given in retrospect. Consent is normally required before the activity. If the hypnotist tricks us without knowing it, we might feel used even if it was simply for our own entertainment. Marketing techniques might be different because they are so prevalent. We know they are constantly on television, the web, or in print. They are almost everywhere we look. The ubiquitous nature of marketing also means that our knowledge of it in general is quite strong. We should not be and are not usually surprised by marketing techniques that lure us to buy things we normally would not have considered. We are consenting by just being part of an open market society. The reflection part is then less a matter of consent and more one of performance evaluation.

Conclusion

[23] Art Van's ads and similar techniques are part of our everyday life. For many they are entertaining and for most they are alluring. Dan Ariely helps us to understand why it is difficult to avoid being attracted to them. He shows us that most of us are irrational. Sales and free items stupefy the mind. Yet, the exposing of our weakness and marketers' deception does not mean we should prohibit such techniques. Rather we should allow deception within limits. Marketers cannot tell falsehoods and marketers cannot unduly deceive as in the *Standard Education* case. Yet, marketers can deceive as long as consumers in rational reflective mode still look kindly upon the deception. Within these constraints, perhaps consumers can enjoy the entertainment and joy that marketers supply, and not feel manipulated in the end.

References

Ariely, D. (2009). *Predictably irrational: The hidden forces that shape our decisions* (Rev. ed.). New York: HarperCollins.

Galbraith, J.K. (1976). *The affluent society* (3rd ed.). New York: Houghton Mifflin.

Levitt, T. (1974). The morality of advertising. *Harvard Business Review*, 48(July-August), 84–92.

Preston, I.L. (1996). *The great American blow-up: Puffery in advertising and selling* (Rev. ed.). Madison: University of Wisconsin Press, pp. 121–123.

Velasquez, M. (2006). *Business ethics: Cases and concepts* (3rd ed.). Upper Saddle River, NJ: Pearson Prentice Hall, p. 286.

Questions

1. What is the "reasonable person" standard as it is applied to assessing the morality of marketing techniques?
2. If Ariely is correct, what does that say about classical economics?
3. According to Ariely, what is the effect of offering free merchandise?
4. (a) Describe the first defence of marketing that is mentioned by Wible; what refutation does Wible present?
   (b) Describe the second defence of marketing that is mentioned by Wible; what refutation does Wible present?
5. How is Kant relevant to Wible's argument? (What is Wible's argument?)

Pop-Ups, Cookies, and Spam: Toward a Deeper Analysis of the Ethical Significance of Internet Marketing Practices*

Daniel E. Palmer

ABSTRACT. While e-commerce has grown rapidly in recent years, some of the practices associated with certain aspects of marketing on the Internet, such as pop-ups, cookies, and spam, have raised concerns on the part of Internet users. In this paper I examine the nature of these practices and what I take to be the underlying source of this concern. I argue that the ethical issues surrounding these Internet marketing techniques move us beyond the traditional treatment of the ethics of marketing and advertising found in discussions of business ethics previously. Rather, I show that the questions they raise ultimately turn upon questions of technique and the ways in which technologies can transform the fundamental means by which relationships are established and maintained within a social environment. I then argue that the techniques of e-commerce are indeed transforming the means by which businesses relate to consumers, and that this transformation is affecting the applicability of our previous ways of demarcating the imperatives determining the limits of accessibility between consumers *and* businesses. Properly addressing the ethical status of the techniques of e-marketing as such necessarily moves us to consider the changes that Internet commerce are having upon the norms that govern individuals in their relations with others.

Introduction

While the Internet was originally developed for governmental and educational purposes, its commercial potential was quickly realized and as a result Internet commerce has grown at exponential rates in recent years.[1] By 2002, 67 million Americans were buying products on-line, and Internet sales of all kinds have skyrocketed in recent years (Stead and Gilbert, 2001). Perhaps the most significant changes that e-commerce has brought to the business world concern the means technologies available on the Internet give marketers to identify and reach potential consumers. While the mutual benefits e-commerce provides consumers and sellers explains the continued growth of Internet business, some of the techniques used in marketing and advertising on the Internet, such as spamming, pop-ups, and cookies, have been received less than enthusiastically by the general public (Hafner, 2003). Recent efforts at both the federal and state

---

* *Journal of Business Ethics* 58.1–3 (2005): 271–80.

levels to enact legislation regulating spam e-mailing testify to the general sense of concern that many people have in regards to such cyber marketing techniques (Swartz, 2003). However, while a clear sense of dissatisfaction can be garnered within the public discussion surrounding e-commerce related issues, there is less clarity as to the deeper underlying issues involved with concern over these practices. Indeed, by and large, those responding to ethical issues involved in e-commerce have tended to view the issues in a piecemeal fashion without exploring the underlying philosophical issues involved in the transformation of commerce brought about by Internet technologies. In this paper I will argue precisely for the need for such a deeper philosophical analysis if we are properly to come to terms with the ethical ramifications of the technologies of e-commerce and the implications they have for our understanding of the underlying norms that govern business relationships. My aim is threefold. One, I wish to show that the techniques of Internet marketing raise ethical questions that go beyond the standard concerns raised in relation to these topics in discussions of marketing in business ethics previously, and that we cannot thus simply apply our previous analyses of these issues to the distinctive world of e-commerce. Two, to argue that we need to think about the issues raised by e-commerce primarily in terms of questions of technological transformation. Addressing issues of e-commerce primarily in terms of the use of technology, I argue, more fully reveals what is at the heart of the matter with our concern with many of the specific practices involved. And, third, I wish to explore how the transformations that Internet technologies are bringing about in e-commerce have wide implications for many of the basic concepts that have governed moral and legal discussions of relationships between consumers and businesses in the past. Here, I look at some specific ways in which traditional concepts are being affected by this transformation and how we might begin to respond to the ethical implications of these changes in a way that is sensitive to the philosophical challenges involved.

Marketing on the Web: The Techniques of e-Commerce

Until recently, most discussions of normative issues [2] in marketing and advertising ethics have concentrated upon a few narrow topics. For the most part, the ethical issues associated with marketing centered on two main issues: deceptive and/or manipulative advertising and the marketing of harmful or non-beneficial products. An informal survey of several of the major textbooks available on business ethics confirms this view.[2] In regards to the first category, every text surveyed carried articles and case studies dealing with deception in advertising. Topics discussed in this regard typically included such topics as puffery, exaggeration, concealment of information, and psychological manipulation in advertising. Likewise, all of the textbooks dealt with issues involving the marketing of harmful or non-beneficial products, such as tobacco, alcohol, fast food, or nutritional supplements. Of course, the two issues mentioned above are in practice often intertwined as well, since the most questionable advertising in terms of its deceptive nature is often used to market products of the most questionable benefit to the consumer. However, I would argue that there is a deeper conceptual link between these two categories as well: for in each case the underlying ethical concern turns upon issues involving the nature of the product or service being marketed. In the first case, because it is felt that the advertising undermines the rational ability of a consumer to evaluate the nature of that product or service and in the second case because of the very nature of the product or service being marketed itself. As the issue really turns in both of these instances upon the product or the way in which the product is presented to the consumer in the marketing campaign in question, I will term ethical questions of these nature ethical questions of product. And, by and large, traditional discussions of marketing in business ethics have been devoted to such ethical questions of product.[3]

[3] Certainly all of these same questions of product in regards to the ethics of marketing can be applied to many of the marketing practices that one finds on the Internet. Indeed, if, for instance, one actually reads the typical spam she receives on a daily basis, she will find no shortage of paradigm cases for such discussions. Advertisements for putative cures for baldness, impotence, obesity, and other ailments, real or imagined, vie in a dizzying array with offers for credit, business opportunities, sexual material and other goods and services of dubious worth. As such, I certainly do not deny that the traditional ethical issues raised surrounding marketing and advertising retain their importance in the environment of ecommerce. Nonetheless, I want to argue that these matters do not exhaust the general sense of concern that is commonly raised in regards to the marketing practices involved in e-commerce.

[4] Before moving directly to this question, let me briefly review three of the practices of Internet marketing that I have in mind first. My choice of these three should not suggest that I take them to be either exhaustive of, or even necessarily the most important of, the sorts of techniques that are involved in e-commerce. They simply are some of the more common ones with which most Internet users are familiar, and each of them is also illustrative of the deeper issues that I think Internet technologies used in e-commerce raise.

[5] First, there is spam, those ubiquitous messages that fill our inboxes in a seemingly never ending stream. While it turns out that defining spam is more difficult than it might appear at first glance, for the purposes of this discussion it is enough to stipulate that spamming in the context of marketing involves the sending of unsolicited e-mail advertisements, usually repeatedly, to very large lists of e-mail addresses. Often, though arguably not necessarily, spamming campaigns involve an additional feature: the source of the e-mail is difficult to trace and the consumer is not able to remove themselves from the e-mail lists used to generate the spam. Indeed, often the attempt by a consumer to opt out of receiving further e-mail is used by the sender as a way of confirming the legitimacy of the consumer's computer address and results in the person receiving more spam in the future, not less (Hafner, 2003). While estimates vary, at least 2 trillion spam messages are sent to American e-mail addresses on a yearly basis and the amount of spam sent has increased by double digits on a yearly basis over the last few years (Swartz, 2003). For some time now, spam messages have been far more prevalent for most users on their e-mail accounts than legitimate e-mail messages, despite the significant efforts of Internet service providers to block such messages (Hafner, 2003).

[6] While spamming involves sending unsolicited messages to e-mail users, the use of pop-ups can be thought of as a different kind of unsolicited advertising. Pop-ups are separate windows that automatically appear on a user's browser when he or she accesses a web site. The most common use of pop-ups is to advertise some product or service to the person viewing a web site, and often they provide hyper-links for the consumer that will lead them to further windows if pursued. As technology advances, pop-ups have become more sophisticated, with some including video images and/or audio tracks. Other pop-ups will move about a person's browser screen rather than occupy a stationary

position. While most pop-up windows are easy to close, it is somewhat more difficult on others to find the close function. At the worst extreme, there are those nefarious pop-ups that in essence take control of the normal functions on one's browser, so that the attempt to close them or use the back function on one's browser screen instead takes the viewer to new, and usually undesired, windows, so that the user becomes "locked" into viewing a series of new windows from which there is no obvious escape (Newman, 2001). At times, the only way to get out of the loop started by attempting to close these kinds of pop-ups is to shut the computer being used down altogether.

[7] Cookies are small files placed on a user's computer by a third party entity when that person is browsing web sites on the Internet. Such cookies record various information about the user that is later retrieved by the computer that placed them on the user's site. While there are lots of uses for cookies and a number of types of information that they can be used to retrieve, they are commonly used in e-commerce to store database information, customize page settings, or otherwise make a site unique to a specific user. Doing so gives companies, in the words of one Internet business site, "the ability to personalize information (like on My Yahoo or Excite), or to help with on-line sales/services (like on Amazon Books or Microsoft), or simply for the purposes of tracking popular links or demographics (like DoubleClick)" (Tenrox, 2003). Cookies are also sometimes placed by third parties to collect information about a user's preferences or browsing habits. This information, in turn, can be distributed widely and easily on the Internet to other companies who can in turn use it to market other goods and services to these consumers (Stead and Gilbert, 2001).

[8] The basic principle behind the use of cookies involves the ability of businesses (or other entities) to place files or programs on consumers' computers to collect data about those consumers in ways that are often opaque to the user and/or difficult for them to control. This same principle has led to a number of other Internet technologies used by businesses that have caused even more concern on the part of consumers. In this regard, Colin Bennett (2001) even notes that "cookie technology might be the tracking device of the past" (p. 202). Web Bugs, for instance, are very small graphics embedded in Web pages or e-mails designed to monitor and collect information on who is reading the pages or e-mail in question. Again, these bugs allow companies to compile information about consumer behavior online and are often placed on web sites by third parties (Bennett, 2001). In the same regard, many of the techniques involved in such practices as data mining on the Internet involve similar uses of technology to monitor and gather data concerning consumer behavior in ways that consumers are either unaware of or unable to avoid when they engage in Internet use (Tavani, 2000).

[9] Having briefly viewed the nature of some of the marketing practices that have elicited concern from Internet users, we can now see that by and large the ethical issues surrounding these practices cannot be readily viewed in terms of the common ethical topics that discussions of marketing ethics have focused upon in the past. For instance, for many of us who rarely do more than glance at the spam e-mail that we receive, our primary concern is not simply that the appeals contained in such messages are deceptive in nature (though surely many of them are), or that the products or services they advertise are worthless or harmful (though, again, surely a large majority of them are). Similar remarks could be made about the use of pop-ups. In the case of cookies and related information gathering technologies this point can perhaps be made even more clearly, since here we are often unaware

of the very existence of the practice involved and thus of the companies and kinds of marketing connected with them. In each case then, our sense of concern with these practices is not derived primarily from ethical questions of product, but from elsewhere, even if we cannot always articulate the nature of the source of this ethical concern. But many people do at least sense that there might be ethical problems associated with many of these practices, even if they cannot quite put their finger on what the issues really are. Any attempt to deal with the ethical issues raised by e-commerce thus must involve more than a simple application of the questions of product to the context of the Internet. Rather, if we are to fully explicate the ethical issues surrounding e-commerce, we must attempt to unpack the source and significance of this underlying sense of worry about the implications of the kinds of business practices it often involves. In the following sections, I will attempt to do just this, displaying what I believe is the philosophical source of our concern with the practices involved in e-commerce and disclosing more clearly the deeper ethical questions engendered by the technologies of e-commerce.

Questions of Technique and the Transformation of the World of Commerce

[10] So far I have argued that if the practices of e-commerce marketing raise ethical questions for our consideration, then these ethical issues must take us beyond those discussed in the context of marketing in the past. While not denying that e-commerce does involve those issues, what I have termed ethical questions of product, I have also suggested that our real sense of unease with some of the practices involved in e-commerce marketing raise considerations of a different sort. Again, if the problem with spam advertising was merely that the information it contained was deceptive or that the products and services advertised non-beneficial, then the outcry over spam would hardly be as widespread as it is for the simple reason that most of us pay very little attention to the information contained in spam advertisements anyway. Likewise, if the use of pop-ups and cookies in marketing products are morally problematic, it can hardly be because of the nature of the products they advertise or the information about the products they provide, since the techniques involved are neutral as regards to such issues. So, if these practices pose a particular problem, it must be one that moves us beyond questions of product. Our inquiry needs as such to change to reflect the nature of the practices involved in e-commerce themselves.

[11] To properly orient our philosophical focus, we should first consider that if the ethical questions involved in these practices do not primarily turn upon the nature of the products or even the message conveyed about the products, then the obvious response is that they involve the means by which the consumer is accessed in e-commerce. And, this I would maintain, is exactly right. Our real concern with such practices is not with the products involved, or even what is claimed about the products, but with the innovative means by which businesses can relate to potential consumers. Others have made similar claims (see, for instance, Radin, 2001). But why should this pose a problem, and what exactly is the nature of the problem? The answer to these questions is less obvious and has not, to my mind, been fully explored. Here, I will proceed by arguing for two inter-related claims. The first is that we should think of the ethical issues posed by e-commerce primarily in relation to what I will term the questions of technique that they raise. The second is that questions of technique are particularly important to address because they deal with transformations in both the kinds

of relationships that we have with others as well as with the concepts that are used in determining the ethical norms governing these relationships.

[12] The first point is the easier one to see. What I will call questions of technique in business ethics turn on questions involving the means by which a business interacts with its consumers or potential consumers rather than on the nature of the product or service itself or the message put out about that product. They involve questions, for instance, about how a business can access consumers for the purposes of marketing or selling a product in the first place. And, I think it is clear that the underlying sense of unease that is found in many discussions of e-commerce clearly relate to such questions. What has changed radically with the advent and growth of e-commerce is not, at least not primarily, the type of products involved or the types of claims that are made about these products. This is again not to say that problems with these sorts of issues are not present in e-commerce, it is just to say that they are present in e-commerce largely to the same extent that they were present in marketing in the past. Rather, what has rapidly changed is the way in which the Internet allows businesses to interact with consumers. And this, I would argue, is proving to be the real challenge to our understanding of the ethics of Internet marketing. With each of the practices involved in e-commerce discussed here, as with a host of others, what we are finding is that businesses now have fundamentally new ways of interacting with consumers that raise serious and largely new questions for our understanding of business ethics. The most significant ethical questions that can be raised about e-commerce involve questions surrounding the very techniques by which businesses can now interact with consumers and questions as to how these techniques are transforming the nature of the relationship between consumers and marketers. Answering these questions, I will argue, means examining the applicability of many of the concepts we have used in the past to discuss legal and moral issues about the relationship between businesses and the public to the world of e-commerce.

[13] Again, in some sense this is readily obvious. Spamming allows companies to access large numbers of consumers easily and inexpensively. The use of pop-ups allows companies to direct messages to consumers in very unexpected, at least from the consumer's point of view, and selected ways. Likewise, cookies, web bugs, and other data-mining technologies allow companies to gather information on consumers and track consumer behavior in order to market products to consumers in highly targeted manners. In each case, Internet technologies allow businesses to interact with consumers in ways that were not possible in the past. Ethical questions surrounding the use of such innovative technologies to establish connections with consumers are what I am terming ethical questions of technique. The issue I will next turn to is what questions of technique involve and why I believe they are so important.

[14] I would first note that ethical questions of technique are not completely new, nor have they gone completely unnoticed by ethicists (see for instance, Thompson, 1997). The development of a national postal system gave birth to the use of mass marketing and direct mailing. The invention of the telephone eventually led to the use of the unsolicited sales call by marketers. And, television advertising allowed businesses to enter the home of the average consumer in a significant way for the first time. Each of these technologies led to changes in the means by which businesses could interact with consumers, and each resulted in at least some reflection as to the ethics involving the use of these techniques (Radin, 2001). Nonetheless, I would argue that the development of the Internet and the technologies

of e-commerce have made questions of technique more pressing than ever.

[15] My general thesis then is that business relationships, like any sort of relationships, are established on the basis of the means by which the persons involved interact. And, as technology changes the means by which persons interact, there will be ramifications upon the nature of relationships that are possible, as well as upon our understanding of the norms and concepts that govern such relationships. My more specific point is that just such a change is being signaled with the emergence of the technologies of e-commerce, and that such a change is altering the basic nature of the relationship that exists between consumers and businesses. Further, such a change is affecting the way in which we have previously understood the ethical limits and norms governing these relationships in a fundamental manner. In the next section, I will more fully flesh out these claims as well as illuminate the source of this transformation and its normative implications.

Philosophical and Ethical Quandaries: The New World of Business on the Internet

[16] My contention is that the technologies of e-commerce are fundamentally altering the kind of relationships that businesses can and do have with consumers, and with this transformation the applicability of our previous understanding of the norms and concepts governing these relationships. To flesh out this claim, we should note that many persons have quite rightly seen that many of the questions of technique related to e-commerce turn on issues of privacy and property as well (see for instance, Bennett, 2001; Maury and Kleiner, 2002; Radin, 2001; and Stead and Gilbert, 2001). However, what has been less clearly seen is that the issue goes deeper than this. That is, any attempt to simply apply our habitual notions of privacy and property to the context of e-commerce is bound to be unsatisfying since the kinds of relationship from which our understanding of these concepts was derived and to which they are normally applied are themselves being altered. What really needs to be examined is the very nature of the relationships that are made possible by the technologies of the Internet and then, and only then, will the full significance of the issues engendered by e-commerce emerge.

[17] To see this point, we should note that notions such as those of privacy and property are inherently social in nature. These concepts would make little sense and be little needed if we existed as completely isolated individuals, since they essentially concern the limits that we place on the way in which others can access ourselves and the fruits of our endeavors. As social concepts, they are derived in relation to the sorts of social relationships that are present within given social structures. But social structures change, and with them so too do our concepts of such notions as privacy and property. Importantly, changes in technology allow persons to have access to others in ways that were hitherto not possible, and thus change the sorts of relationships that are possible between individuals in a given set of social practices (Winner, 1993). In this paper I am arguing that just such a set of transformations is being brought about by the technologies available on the Internet. Pop-ups, cookies, and spam in this regard are merely illustrative of a deeper set of technological transformations that is fundamentally altering the sorts of relationships that are possible between businesses and consumers. The very fabric of the business world is itself being altered by these technologies in ways that are stressing our previous understanding of the nature and limits of the relationship between consumers and businesses.

[18] There is no doubt that notions of privacy and property have been particularly important to the

Western legal and moral tradition in modern times (May, 1980). These concepts have been shaped by a certain notion of individuality central to the Western understanding of the self (Taylor, 1989). This notion of individuality, in turn, has been defined in reference to the kinds of relationships that our social practices have previously involved. Of course, one of the important set of relationships involved has been those found in commerce. And, this notion of individuality has thus been at the heart of our understanding of the ethical norms governing relationships of commerce. The notion of individual autonomy involved places great emphasis upon an individual's ability to determine the way in which other individuals interact with them (Buss, 2002). Until recently, this notion was largely defined in terms of physical access to a person or to the physical control of the goods that she possessed, and thus so too were the concepts of privacy and property that governed relationships between persons, including those found in the world of business. This is not surprising, since the physical separation between persons and goods were the characteristic way in which the separation of individuals was understood in these relationships.

[19] However, what we are finding is that notions of privacy and property grounded in an understanding of relationships that are defined in terms of physicality are not easily applicable to the context of the Internet and to the technologies of e-commerce. As I have shown, the technologies of e-commerce are unique in that they are redefining the way in which consumers can be accessed by businesses. What is unique about these technologies is that they allow companies to access consumers in ways that do not involve the sorts of physical transactions that have been seen as paradigmatic of definitions of privacy and property in the past. The world of cyberspace, in which businesses interact with consumers, is not a physical world, at least not in the way that shops, offices, and malls are, and the notions of privacy, property and related concepts do not well apply in this world. As Colin Bennett (2001) argues, the Internet is creating a new form of life with its own distinctive kinds of social interactions and practices. The new kinds of relationships that these technologies involve are defined primarily in terms of access to information rather than in terms of physical accessibility. Rather than merely apply our old concepts of privacy and property to these contexts, we need to confront the very conditions of the relationships established in the world of e-commerce themselves.

[20] I would maintain that confronting the larger question of the implication that these technologies have for the kinds of relationships that are possible between businesses and consumers in the world of the Internet needs our attention for at least three reasons. For one, the sorts of technological advances that have occurred with the development of the Internet and related computer technologies have quite simply advanced at a speed that is unprecedented in history. As such we have, as a society, had little time to absorb the significance of these changes for our lives. If the concepts that we use to determine the ethical parameters of business are derived from the type of relationships that are possible within the social sphere, then it is important that we reflect upon the changes that the technologies of e-commerce are bringing to the relationship between businesses and consumers. While such changes have always been occurring, the rate of the transformation is making our attempts to absorb the significance of these changes particularly difficult. The adjustment of the concepts governing the ethics of relationships in the past was easier in part because the progression of the transformation was gradual. However, in the digital age, these transformations are taking place

at a speed that hinders our ability to absorb their impact fully into our conceptual apparatus.

[21] Second, the sorts of techniques that e-commerce involve are largely difficult to avoid and/or invisible to the average consumer, who either is unable to control them while browsing on the Internet or is even unaware of their very existence and the means by which they operate. While the sorts of techniques used by marketers in the past were largely such that the consumer had the ability to determine the extent to which they would be subject to them, the new techniques used on the Internet tend to make the access easier to control from the point of view of businesses and less easier to control from the point of view of consumers. The world of e-commerce in a sense is reversing the direction by which the terms of access between consumers and marketers is dictated. And, much of the unease that is expressed by the general public with Internet interactions reflects this sense of loss on the part of consumers.

[22] Third, these techniques have allowed businesses to largely shift the burden of cost, both in monetary and non-monetary terms, of such access unto the consumer. It is not just that many of the marketing and advertising techniques are much cheaper than traditional means of advertising, though they certainly are. Rather, it is also that they have allowed businesses to transfer a large part of the expenses involved onto other parties. For instance, the costs of spamming, which are not trivial, are largely borne by parties other than those sending them, such as the service providers who must process such e-mail (Spinello, 1999). The environment of the Internet, in effect, allows businesses to engage in marketing practices quite cheaply, but the real costs of this ability are ultimately borne by others. And it is not merely the burden of monetary costs; many of these techniques have also changed who bears the burden of other costs in these relationships. These techniques have also shifted the burden of costs in terms of the time, effort, and knowledge spent in establishing and maintaining relationships with consumers from the businesses involved—onto the consumers. In effect, e-commerce techniques allow companies to very easily have access to consumers and consumer information, while making it relatively difficulty for consumers to prevent such access.

[23] Each of the above points illustrates the importance of the shift in the very nature of the kind of relationship that exists between consumers and businesses in the world of e-commerce. Let me end with some reflections on the philosophical significance of this shift and some suggestions as to where a philosophically sensitive understanding of the ethical implications of the technologies of e-commerce should lead us. As I have argued, an essential element of the Western notion of individuality has concerned an emphasis upon our ability to limit the access that others have to ourselves. Limiting such access has been seen as crucial to our ability to determine our own lives free from undue influence from others. What the world of e-commerce, and the world of the Internet more generally, is transforming is the ways in which others can have access to our lives, by means that no longer rely upon physical interventions and are largely opaque to us. In the past, at least in the context of a capitalist understanding of the market, it was largely assumed that individuals had the ability to control the access that others had to them through assuring them control over their physical self and possessions. Since physical violations of space or control are fairly transparent, the proper limits between individuals were fairly well demarcated and the ethical norms governing relationships were derived from these distinctions.

[24] In the world of e-commerce, it would seem that the sorts of relationships that are possible give busi-

nesses the almost constant ability to have access to consumers in various ways, and to shift the cost of that access back onto the public itself. But the access involved defies the application of traditional concepts governing the limits of access since it does not involve the sorts of physical contacts that were previously seen as paradigmatic of social relationships. What is now needed is to determine what concepts are going to govern the limits of these transformed relationships. I would argue that though the benefits of these new relationships are manifold, they must be balanced by a need to preserve at least part of the central notion of individuality which has been at the heart of our understanding of autonomy. And, this means that we must find new ways of governing the sorts of accesses that businesses have to consumers that preserve at least elements of consumers' ability to determine the limits of this accessibility.

[25] In the past, the norms and limits that were placed on relationships between persons were designed to guarantee this control of access. However, those norms were developed in a social context in which the means of access were primarily physical ones, and our concepts of privacy and property were largely developed in relation to this context. In the world of e-commerce this is what has changed. Access in the world of digital computing is primarily a virtual access, one that involves access to and control over information about ourselves rather than control over the physical boundaries between us.

[26] As such, what is really needed is a way of assuring that individuals retain some degree of control over the accessibility that others have to them. While it is beyond the scope of this paper to go into specific details as to how this might be addressed, I would suggest that at a minimum, this will involve two important elements. One, there needs to be a greater emphasis on transparency regarding the kinds of transactions that are made possible within the relationships between consumers and businesses on the Internet. Since the sorts of connections that exist between consumers and businesses in e-commerce that we have discussed take place, as it were, underneath the surface of the activities that consumers engage in on the Internet, it is often difficult for them to understand that they are being established, how they are being carried out, or how to control them. An emphasis on the need for transparency would stress that it is impossible for someone to control how others are accessing them if they are not aware of the nature and purpose of that access. Ethical e-commerce practices should strive to make any access of customers, whether through e-mails, cookies, etc. as transparent as possible to the consumer, for only then can the consumer truly consent to the kind of interactions that occur between themselves and the businesses involved.

[27] Second, and stemming from the first point, public regulation of the sorts of interactions that are allowed and the conditions of their use will be of paramount importance. Whether through direct government action or through semi-governmental regulatory bodies, a greater degree of independent control needs to be provided to maintain the appropriate uses of Internet technologies in e-commerce. Because the technologies of e-commerce are not readily transparent and because fully understanding their use is often beyond the capability of the average consumer, there is a greater need for third party oversight. While consumers could be expected to easily monitor the access that businesses had to them under models based on physical interaction, they cannot be held to do so in the world of e-commerce. Thus, there is stronger need for public regulation to provide consumers with some assurance about the kind of access that businesses have to them and to make the nature of these

relationships as transparent as possible to consumers who might lack the ability to do so themselves. The goal of such regulation should in part be to put the burden of costs, again monetarily and non-monetarily, of accessibility to consumers back onto businesses. Many businesses have themselves sought stronger legal regulatory control over the way in which consumers can access the products they produce, as in the case of music downloading and related practices. Ironically perhaps, what consumers should demand is the same sort of regulatory control over the accessibility that businesses have to information about themselves and over the use to which it is put.

Conclusion

[28] In this paper I have argued that the various practices that are commonly involved in e-commerce raise deep philosophical issues involving the manner in which technology can transform the nature of business relationships in ways that challenge some of the fundamental concepts that have characterized these relationships in the past. Raising such questions I have argued moves us beyond the typical questions of product that have dominated discussions of the ethics of marketing in the past and into questions of technique that involve the very means by which businesses relate to consumers in the first place. Such questions are both much more important and much more difficult to deal with because they reveal the way in which technology can transform the basic structures of the social sphere itself in such a way as to have deep ramifications for the application of many of the concepts normally appealed to in discussions concerning the ethical and legal norms governing business practices. In specific, I have tried to show that lurking underneath the surface of the general public concern with such now common e-commerce practices such as spamming, pop-ups, and cookies lie a host of philosophical and ethical issues concerning the way in which the technologies of the Internet are fundamentally transforming the nature of the relationship that businesses have with consumers and the public. In turn, I have tried to show that this transformation has deep implications for our understanding of such fundamental notions as privacy and property as well as for our understanding of how the costs, monetarily and otherwise, of doing business are properly allocated.

While I have offered some suggestions as to [29] how we might address some of the ethical implications of these transformations, I have above all attempted to show that it is important that we face up to the challenges brought with these technologies in a more systematic fashion than has been done as of yet. If, as I have argued, technologies bring with them the ability to fundamentally alter the nature of the kind of relationships that exist between businesses and consumers, then it is particularly important that we address the ethical implications of these changes before the transformation is complete.

Notes

1. For a good, brief, survey of the early history and development of the Internet, see Sterling (1993).
2. The textbooks surveyed were Beauchamp and Bowie (2004), Donaldson and Werhane (1999), Hoffman, et al. (2001) and Shaw and Barry (2001).
3. This is not to say that these issues have not been raised by others. Indeed, later in the paper I point out some authors who have addressed what I am here calling questions of technique to some extent. However, these issues have been largely addressed in the context of more general discussions of technology, not from the perspective of viewing them as basic issues in marketing and advertising ethics as I approach them here.

References

Beauchamp, T. and N. Bowie. 2004. *Ethical Theory and Business*, 7th edition. Upper Saddle River, NJ: Prentice Hall.

Bennett, C. 2001. "Cookies, Web Bugs, Webcams, and Cue Cats: Patterns of Surveillance on the World Wide Web." *Ethics and Information Technology* 3(3), 197–210.

Buss, S. 2002. "Personal Autonomy." In E. Zalta (ed.), *The Stanford Encyclopedia of Philosophy*, http://plato.stanford.edu/archives/win2002/entries/personal-autonomy/.

Donaldson, T. and P. Werhane. 1999. *Ethical Issues in Business: A Philosophical Approach*, 6th edition. Upper Saddle River, NJ: Prentice Hall.

Hafner, K. 2003. "A Change of Habits to Elude Spam's Pull." *The New York Times* (October 23).

Hoffman, W., R. Frederick and M. Schwartz. 2001. *Business Ethics: Readings and Cases in Corporate Morality*, 4th edition. Boston: McGraw Hill.

Maury, M.D. and D. Kleiner. 2002. "E-Commerce, Ethical Commerce?" *Journal of Business Ethics* 36(1–2), 21–31.

May, L. 1980. "Privacy and Property." *Philosophy in Context* 10, 40–53.

Newman, D. 2001. "Impersonal Interaction and Ethics on the World-Wide-Web." *Ethics and Information Technology* 3(3), 239–246.

Radin, T. 2001. "The Privacy Paradox: E-Commerce and Personal Information on the Internet." *Business and Professional Ethics Journal* 20(3–4), 145–170.

Shaw, W. and V. Barry. 2001. *Moral Issues in Business*, 8th edition. Belmont, CA: Wadsworth.

Spinello, R.A. 1999. "Ethical Reflections on the Problems of Spam." *Ethics and Information Technology* 1(3), 185–191.

Stead, B. and J. Gilbert. 2001. "Ethical Issues in Electronic Commerce." *Journal of Business Ethics* 34(2), 75–85.

Sterling, B. 1993. "Internet." *The Magazine of Science Fiction and Fantasy* (February).

Swartz, J. 2003. "Senate Passes Anti-Spam Bill, but Many Obstacles Remain." *USA Today* (October 23).

Tavini, H. 1999. "Informational Privacy, Data Mining, and the Internet." *Ethics and Information Technology* 1(2), 137–145.

Taylor, C. 1989. *Sources of the Self: The Making of Modern Identity*. Cambridge, MA: Harvard University Press.

Tenrox Web Site. 2003. "Cookie Q & A." http://www.tenrox.com/en/help/cookies.htm.

Thompson, P. 1997. *Food Biotechnology in an Ethical Perspective*. London: Chapman and Hall.

Winner, L. 1993. "Citizen Virtues in a Technological Order." In E. Winkler and J. Coombs (eds.), *Applied Ethics: A Reader*, pp. 46–68. Cambridge, MA: Blackwell.

Questions

1. What element of spam identified by Palmer makes it especially coercive?
2. Because of cookies, many pop-up ads are now targeted. For example, if collected data indicates that you are interested in purchasing books, pop-up ads specifically for books, rather than chocolate, will start appearing on your screen.
   (a) In what way is this more ethically acceptable?
   (b) In what way is this more ethically disturbing?
3. Regarding Palmer's point about the cost of advertising having been shifted to others, notably to ISPs (who must process the two trillion spam messages sent) and consumers (who must spend time and energy to close pop-ups and delete spam), what's wrong with that?

4. "An essential element of the Western notion of individuality has concerned an emphasis upon our ability to limit the access that others have to ourselves. Limiting such access has been seen as crucial to our ability to determine our own lives free from undue influence from others" (para 23). Do you agree? If so, what changes to current online advertising would you try to implement if you had the chance? If not, which part/s exactly do you disagree with, and why?

....

Case Study: Adbusters

Adbusters Media Foundation is a Vancouver-based organization activist organization that is "concerned about the erosion of our physical and cultural environments by commercial forces" (Adbusters site). Although primarily focused on the media, of note is the fact that its founder and editor-in-chief Kalle Lasn initiated the Occupy Movement.

Adbusters has created a number of "subvertisements" for television broadcast but has repeatedly discovered that television networks refuse to air them.

In 1993, CBC withdrew an Adbusters anti-car ad ("Autosaurus"—you can find it online) after complaints from other sponsors, mostly car companies.

In 1997, NBC, CBS, and ABC refused to air an Adbusters ad in which "an animated pig superimposed on a map of North America smacked its lips while saying 'The average North American consumes five times more than a Mexican, ten times more than a Chinese person, and thirty times more than a person from India.... Give it a rest. November 28 is Buy Nothing Day'" (Hertz).

NBC (owned by GE) said, "We don't want to take any advertising that's inimical to our legitimate business interests" (Hertz).

CBS (owned by Westinghouse) said that Buy Nothing Day was "in opposition to the current economic policy in the United States" (Hertz).

According to Jim Gilliam (who notes that this sort of censorship has been happening for a while; for example, anti-war ads have been refused by all the major networks, and ABC and CBS have aired pro-life ads but refuse to air pro-choice ads), the official policy of the three major American networks is as follows:

ABC: "We have a blanket policy against advocacy ads of any kind."

CBS: "Policy precludes accepting commercials which take an advocacy position on one side of a controversial issue of public importance."

NBC: "It pertained to a controversial issue which we prefer to handle in our news and public affairs programming."

Another source (see "Adbusters Organization" listed below) reports that MTV has refused Adbuster ads because they are "issue-oriented."

By 2003, CanWest Global, Bell Globemedia, and CHUM Ltd. had also refused to air Adbuster ads, one of which exposed the fact that 50 per cent of the calories in a Big Mac come from fat.

Other ads rejected by various television networks have targeted the forestry, pharmaceutical, and high fashion industries.

In September of 2003, Adbusters filed a suit against six major Canadian television broadcasters. (For details, see Dhawan.)

"It's outrageous that the fast food, oil and automobile industries can buy as much TV time as they want in order to promote their agendas, but citizens are not allowed to talk back," says Lasn. "Canadian democracy will not work properly until we the people have the same right to buy airtime as corporations do."

Sources

Adbusters website. https://www.adbusters.org

"Adbusters Organization." Activist Facts. https://www.activistfacts.com/organizations/36-adbusters/

"Can TV stations refuse to carry advertising?" *The Hollywood Reporter* 13 Apr. 2009. http://www.hollywoodreporter.com/blogs/thr-esq/tv-stations-refuse-carry-advertising-63068

Dhawan, Sona. "Courts Hold that Media Corporations Should Prepare for Public Scrutiny." *The Court* 23 Sept. 2009. http://www.thecourt.ca/2009/09/23/courts-hold-that-media-corporations-should-prepare-for-public-scrutiny/

Ewert, James H., Jr. "Adbusters' Ads Busted." *In These Times* 4 Apr. 2008. http://inthesetimes.com/article/3581/adbusters_ads_busted

Gilliam, Jim. "CBS refuses to air Moveon's Super Bowl ad." http://www.jimgilliam.com/2004/01/cbs_refuses_to_air_moveons_super_bowl_ad.php

Hertz, Noeena. *The Silent Takeover: Global Capitalism and the Death of Democracy.* New York: HarperBusiness, 2003.

Morrow, Fiona. "Adbusters wins right to sue broadcasters over TV ads." *The Globe and Mail* 10 April 2009. http://www.theglobeandmail.com/news/national/adbusters-wins-right-to-sue-broadcasters-over-tv-ads/article1150947/

Pickerel, Wendy, Helena Jorgensen, and Lance Bennett. "Culture Jams and Meme Warfare: Kalle Lasn, Adbusters, and Media Activism." 2002. https://depts.washington.edu/gcp/pdf/culture-jamsandmemewarfare.pdf

Questions

1. What definitions of "advocacy," "controversy," and "issue" would you have to have in order to consider an advertisement that promotes eating hamburgers to be *not* advocacy, *not* about a controversial issue, or *not* issue-oriented, but an advertisement promoting *not* eating hamburgers to *be* advocacy, about a controversial issue, or issue-oriented? (Ditto for an ad that advocates driving automobiles versus one that advocates not driving automobiles.)

2. The legal question is, as Adbusters' legal counsel, Mark Underhill, states, "whether private ⁓oadcasters given a license to operate by Parliament have the right to determine who gets ⁓eak on the public airwaves" (cited in Morrow). In the case of the American networks' ⁓l, Lasn cites Article 19 of the United Nations Universal Declaration of Human Rights.

Suppose that private broadcasters didn't have to get a licence from a public body; would it matter whether the program is delivered completely via privately-owned routes (cable, for example, laid completely on/in private land?) or whether the signal at some point travels through air/space (which is public)?
3. What's the moral question? (Especially if there are no public television stations.)

CHAPTER THREE

Product Quality

What to Do?—An Ungodly Insurance Policy

You set the newest version of the house insurance policy aside and wonder whether it's time to look for a new job. You have been selling insurance for five years now, and in that time, as climate change has dramatically increased the frequency of "extreme weather events," your company has just as dramatically expanded the definition of "acts of God"—*exclusions* to coverage.

A tree fell onto your house because of a strong wind? Wind is an act of God. Doesn't matter if the tree was healthy or not; doesn't matter if it was your tree or your neighbour's. Your basement's flooded? Rain is an act of God. The power went out because of a heavy snow storm and you lost a freezer full of food? Snow is an act of God. Sure, you could add a rider, a separate add-on policy, to cover such events. But they're so expensive, you have yet to sell one.

The truth is, the policy is almost a complete waste of money. You've tentatively mentioned this to your supervisor, but of course nothing came of it. The higher-ups are well aware of the limitations of their product.

But so should prospective customers. Of course, the exclusions are indicated in the policy. But it's standard practice not to provide the actual policy; customers just receive the invoice, with their deductibles indicated. They could *ask* for a copy of the policy, but even then, it's written in such convoluted language and in such small print. It would be easy enough to prepare a summary in plain language of what's covered and what's not, and in fact, you've prepared such a summary. But if you showed it to prospective customers, you wouldn't make any sales.

And the problem is that you work on commission. When you were a waitress, you wore tight clothing to get good tips. You thought you could leave that behind once you earned your degree and landed a real job. But working on commission is just like working for tips: The financial incentive—even in the case of performance bonuses, you imagine—is supposed to make people work hard, but it just makes them work bad: it makes them do things they wouldn't otherwise do. Like withhold important information. Don't a lot of real-estate agents do that?

Besides which, you think, there *is* no god, there are *no* gods—so there can't possibly be *acts* of god. Certainly the increasing frequency of extreme weather events isn't some god's fault. You wonder if that's a lawsuit waiting to happen. It would serve the company right.

So what to do? The policy isn't really hurting anyone. Is it? So do you keep telling yourself that if the person doesn't ask the right questions, that's *their* problem? You're not the one who made the policy; you're just the middle guy. Or do you look for another job and once you have it, post the policy, "acts of god" clause highlighted, on WikiLeaks?

What do you decide to do?

Introduction

One might think that it's morally wrong to manufacture or market an unsafe product or service, a product or service that causes harm—and that's that. What else need one say about it? Attention to harm is characteristic of a utilitarian analysis, but one can examine the issue of product safety from other perspectives. A rights-based analysis would consider buyers' rights—for example, the right to be adequately informed and to be protected from harmful products; the right to choice (between degrees of safety, of quality, of price) might also be considered. These would be measured against sellers' rights—for example, the right to decide what to make and sell, as well as how to market it. Obviously, there are conflicts. Which rights take priority? Why?

First, one might do well to ask, "How unsafe?" Surely for many products and services, safety is a matter of degree. How likely is the harm? How severe? How permanent? And what, exactly, counts as harm? Are we talking about just physical injury or should we talk about psychological injury as well? High-school shootings by "disturbed" adolescents have been blamed on violent movies, TV shows, video games, and internet sites. Wright and Funk (see Jacobs) found that men who watch pornography are less likely to support hiring or promoting women (no surprise, given that over 90 per cent of porn shows women happily being degraded) and others (see Layden; Flood) have found that such men are more likely to rape. Are these, therefore, "unsafe" products?

As for "How unsafe is *too* unsafe?," Health Canada's answer might be determined by examining their (on average) 200 product recalls per month.[1] However, we would be assuming that degree of damage is a determining factor for recall. Certainly that wasn't the case when Ford decided *not* to recall their Pinto (see below), which had a propensity to explode in the case of a

---

1 This was for all categories: consumer products, health products, vehicles, and food, the latter including products recalled because of undeclared ingredients such as sesame seeds, milk, and insects. See Health Canada, "Search recalls and safety alerts," http://www.healthycanadians.gc.ca/recall-alert-rappel-avis/index-eng.php.

rear-end collision, because what could be more damaging than loss of life? (I was fortunate in that the window handle of my Pinto fell off, the driver's door jammed shut, and the floor rusted out *before* I was rear-ended.) (I traded the car for a Honda 350, motorcycles being notoriously safer....) Pity they didn't do their utilitarian calculus *before* going to market, because an $11 increase in the price tag (the cost of the fix) wouldn't have affected sales at all.

Second (or rather first, since this question must precede the other), one might ask, "Is it okay to make a product or provide a service that's less than perfectly safe?" Especially if, for some reason, you *can't* make or provide a perfectly safe one? (Is there even such a thing as a "perfectly safe" product or service?)[1]

And if it is okay, is it okay not to advertise the risk associated with the product (because of its less-than-perfectly-safe nature)? Perhaps informing the potential consumer of the risks makes the not completely safe product morally acceptable to make because it puts the moral responsibility for its use on the consumer (respecting their autonomy, their ability to think, and their freedom to choose). Certainly the warnings about content and intended audience that are placed at the beginning of certain movies seem to have this intent, although the paper you have to sign before surgery attesting to the fact that you have been informed of all the risks meets this requirement far better.

But what if the "especially if" clause above doesn't apply—is it okay to manufacture a less-than-perfectly-safe product even when you *can* make a perfectly safe one? Maybe there would be less, or no, profit in the perfectly safe one. But by not making the less-safe (and therefore lower-priced) product, you'd be depriving some consumers of the product altogether. And again, the marketing question must also be asked: is it okay not to advertise the low quality?

Does it *matter* why you're making it? Maybe you *are* making it because it provides more profit. But maybe you *are* making it so people can *afford* it. Maybe you're making it because it has positive features that outweigh the negative features. Does your intent matter? (To determining whether it's morally acceptable for you to do what you do?)

Furthermore, if it is morally permissible for you to make an unsafe product, is it then morally permissible for consumers to sue you for the damage it causes? Consider the lawsuits against tobacco companies and, more recently, against fast-food companies.[2] Consider also the "Cheeseburger Bill" (actually the Personal Responsibility in Food Consumption Act), proposed in the US to prohibit such lawsuits, although it didn't pass into law. No one is forcing consumers to buy the product—to smoke cigarettes, to eat fast food, or to drive a Pinto. Is it enough to inform people of the risk if they do purchase your product? What if it's addictive? (And recent research shows that eating fast food may be addictive—actually physically addictive because of the salt, sugar, fat, and some of the additives.) Does that change things?

And what if your product isn't unsafe per se, but simply not effective. Consider nutritional supplements (multi-vitamins, for example) and holistic remedies (argued by many to be mere placebos). Is the moral issue in these cases just that of misleading advertising?

---

1 From this point, when I write about "products," assume that I mean "products and services."
2 See Mello, Rimm, and Studdert for a good analysis of ethical issues in the context of American law.

What about totally unsafe products, such as land mines? Is it okay to make them? What possible warning could you put on the label that would inform potential users of the risk: "This product is unsafe, anywhere, anytime"? That may inform of the risk, but in doing so, it does nothing to reduce the likelihood of harm (which was the moral point of such warnings)—especially if, at the same time, you make them look like brightly coloured toys which encourage kids to pick them up and thus blow themselves up;[1] since they are *always* harmful, only refusing to make the product would eliminate the potential harm.

And do all weapons fit into that category, from nuclear bombs to hand guns? Can you make a moral argument for their manufacture despite their obvious lack of safety and their risk of harm? (Such an argument would probably be utilitarian—harm outweighed by good. Or principle-based—distinguishing between defensive use and offensive use.)

Not only may carefully considered advertising make a not completely safe product morally acceptable; carefully considered sales may achieve the same thing. For example, one could refuse to sell land mines (and nuclear weapons) to psychopaths. It might be a good idea to include the hand guns here, too.

> ### BOX 3.1 *Caveat Emptor* Comes Back to Haunt You...
>
> Suppose you've just discovered that your company is standing on a toxic dump of sorts. If you do nothing, chemicals will continue to leach out, polluting lakes and streams in the community (such water is used not only for recreational purposes, but also for drinking). However, as far as you can see, doing something means either selling your business property (and you'd have to withhold the truth to get a sale) or excavating and arranging proper disposal (which means you'd go bankrupt).
>
> You feel it's a little unfair—after all, you're not the one who dumped the toxins. But it is your land now. Along with property rights come responsibilities.
>
> Could you say you bought the land under false pretences? Suddenly *caveat emptor* comes back to haunt you. Truth be told, you didn't actually ask about the toxicity of the land; no one actually lied about it—they simply didn't tell you (apparently property assessments don't routinely check for this kind of thing). And, well, you don't tell prospective customers about the downside of what you're selling, either.
>
> No one seems to have dropped dead from the contaminated water (which still sparkles prettily in the sun)—but you know that such harm could be long-term, even next-generational. It may be that drinking the water isn't nearly as bad as, say, eating the fish that live in it (since it is less concentrated), but you don't know.

---

1 See Noorzoy and "Cluster Bombs."

The standard response to these questions (i.e., those involving products that are potentially harmful) has been "let the buyer beware" (*caveat emptor*, i.e., it's the buyer's responsibility to find out, not the seller's responsibility to tell). Perhaps if such information were easily accessible, this would be a reasonable distribution of responsibility. Although maybe not—why should the buyer have to find out? If *you* want the sale, *you* should have to tell—tell me what I need to know. Well, but if *I* want the product, *I* should have to find out! Regardless, such information is often not easily accessible. And perhaps placing the responsibility on the buyer suggests that the default mode is deceit rather than honesty—what's there to "find out" in the first place? If one were honest, why wouldn't one "tell"? (Does honesty rank higher than profit? On what grounds?)

BOX 3.2   How Can We Find Out? Will Researchers Tell Us What's Safe and What's Not?

In 1998, when scientists employed by Health Canada refused to approve rbGH (a bovine growth hormone, given to cows to increase milk production) due to concerns for human health, one (Dr. Margaret Haydon) was taken off the study, her notes were stolen, and she was bribed to keep quiet. Others were "passed over for promotions, given impossible tasks or no assignments at all" (Smith) and yet another was suspended without pay. Three were eventually fired, in 2004. Even so, in 1999 Health Canada did ban the sale of the chemical. (Of possibly ethical relevance, dairy farmer R. Visser said he wouldn't have used it even if it *had* been approved.)

More generally, GMO food (genetically modified or genetically engineered food) is banned in the EU, but not in Canada. Why? (Two separate questions there: Why there? And why not here?)

In other countries where they are allowed, they have to be labelled as such, but not in Canada. Why?

Sources

Bourrie, Mark. "Canada Rejects Bovine Growth Hormone." *Albion Monitor* 25 Jan. 1999. http://www.monitor.net/monitor/9901b/copyright/rbstcanada.html

Smith, Jeffrey. "A Short History of Genetically Engineered Bovine Growth Hormone." Council for Responsible Genetics. http://www.councilforresponsiblegenetics.org/ViewPage.aspx?pageId=125

Suzuki, David. "Understanding GMO." David Suzuki Foundation. http://www.davidsuzuki.org/what-you-can-do/queen-of-green/faqs/food/understanding-gmo/

"Understanding Genetically Modified Foods." Eat Right Ontario. http://www.eatrightontario.ca/en/Articles/Food-technology/Biotechnology/Novel-foods/Understanding-Genetically-Modified-Foods.aspx#.VL_QwKIauUc

Another answer to these questions is the "due care" response: the manufacturer has the responsibility of taking due care, reasonable precautions, to prevent harm. (How reasonable is "reasonable"?) Many service providers, such as electricians, have to be licensed, partly for this reason.

Yet another answer, provided by contract theory, says that the manufacturer is bound only by the terms of the contract—which ideally is explicit and precise, and freely entered into by all parties. (How often is there such a contract?)

And according to those adhering to a policy of strict liability, the manufacturer is "responsible for all harm resulting from a dangerously defective product even when due care has been exercised and all contracts observed" (Boatright 305)—seller beware? This answer is often justified by appealing to affordability: who better can afford to compensate for injuries than the company (i.e., its insurance company, meaning its premium-paying policyholders)? It's also justified by appealing to incentive: it will motivate companies to be extra safe (do you *need* that kind of motivation?). On the other hand, such complete denial of any responsibility on the consumer's or user's part seems unfair, not to mention insulting.[1]

One element of product safety and moral responsibility running through these various views is foreknowledge: did the company know of the risk? And does that make a difference? How much can we expect the company to know about its product? That is, how thoroughly must it test the product? Sometimes side effects don't show up for 30 or 40 years; consider asbestos; even now that we know asbestos is carcinogenic, Canada is the world's second-largest exporter of it, mostly to developing countries. Sometimes the side-effects show up only in the next generation; consider DES (diethylstilbestrol), prescribed to reduce miscarriage but actually increasing the likelihood of cancer in "DES daughters," or consider also thalidomide, prescribed to reduce the nausea of pregnancy but actually causing fetal limb malformation. Does the product sit on the shelf until then? What if it's really important to some people and they're willing to take the risk?

On this matter of obligations to future generations, see the Routley and Routley essay listed at the end of this section; although the development of nuclear power isn't the issue it once was—despite the fact that Ontario nuclear energy accounts for 50 per cent of Ontario's energy, that taxpayers will have to pay some $25 billion to construct and maintain a nuclear waste repository, and that the decision has been made to refurbish several reactors to keep them in operation—the essay is applicable to many of our ongoing resource-depleting and environment-destroying activities. As the authors say, "The risks imposed on the future by proceeding with nuclear development are, then, significant. Perhaps 40,000 generations of future people could be forced to bear significant risks resulting from the provision of the (extravagant) energy use of only a small proportion of the people of 10 generations" (Routley 118). The same may well be true for fossil fuel development: Keep in mind that even though evidence indicates that solar, wind, and tidal power generates seven times more jobs per dollar and is both less expensive to develop and far less destructive, our government subsidizes the oil, natural gas, and coal industries with $34 billion while investing only $6.5 billion in "clean" energy.

---

1 See Velasquez for a discussion of the strengths and weaknesses of these views.

And how will the company know about side effects? That is, is it okay to test the product on living animals? Only on those that can give informed consent? (That is, only human animals?) Only when there are no alternatives? (Colgate has developed an "artificial mouth" which simulates the conditions of the human mouth for testing their oral health products.) Only when the benefits of the product outweigh any pain and suffering caused by the testing? (Do we really need another kind of mascara so badly we have to torture rabbits to get it?) And do these benefits include financial benefits?[1]

In addition to asking, "How safe?," we should also ask, "Safe for what?" Really, is it the company's fault that the consumer stuck his fingers in the snowblower while trying to fix it? Just how many warnings must one put on the label? Indeed, Bucciarelli argues that "idiotproofing" may actually work against safety: "With the user 'out of the loop,' shielded from the details of the device, there is less possibility he or she will act rationally, judiciously, if the unaccounted-for weighs in" (55). Often the answer to this question is something like "whatever the reasonable person might require." But, again, what's "reasonable"? Who decides?

And "safe for whom?" Just people? Or other animals too? Just for the people who use the products or for others who may be affected by that use? (Consider the victims of a drunk driver.) Affected only in the short term or also in the long term? For example, we are *still* experiencing the consequences of CFCs that were released into the atmosphere in the 1970s via the use of common spray cans—namely increased solar radiation getting through the damaged ozone layer.

And finally, given that many products will be in households with children, are you obligated to childproof everything you make or sell? Or is that the parent's moral responsibility?

The phrase "product safety" can be narrowly interpreted to refer only to the finished product or broadly interpreted to refer to the full process of its manufacture—from getting the raw materials to disposing of the waste. The finished product might be harmless, but what if a great deal of harm was done in order to make it? This broad interpretation gives rise to questions that overlap with those in the chapters on the environment (Chapter 10) and on employee rights (most specifically, the right to a safe workplace; Chapter 4). Fossil fuel and nuclear energy production, as mentioned above, is a good example of this aspect of product safety (and an excellent argument for the development of solar and wind energy).

Safety may become an even more difficult issue if you're the distributor, not the manufacturer. Consider grocery stores: pesticides and additives can make a product harmful—how morally responsible is the grocer for ensuring that the produce sold is safe for consumption? Will merely labelling a product "BGH" or "GM" be sufficient to inform potential consumers that the product came from cows injected with the controversial Bovine Growth Hormone or that the product is the result of genetic modification? Perhaps. After all, isn't making the decision for them (deciding not to carry any BGH or GM products) patronizing? Perhaps many people would rather eat an apple that is really red and perfectly round (i.e., grown with pesticides) than one that perhaps has a worm in it.

---

1 See Jamieson and Regan's excellent paper on this issue. If you're having *any* trouble understanding and evaluating argument, especially arguments for or against a particular moral position, read this for its clarity and comprehensiveness.

And a consumer can simply shop at "organic produce only" stores. Well, what if s/he can't—what if there are no such stores in the area? Does that change the only grocer's moral responsibility? Does any of this depend on government regulations? That is, are you morally bound to conform only to safety regulations? Is that a moral minimum or a moral maximum?

If by this stage you're feeling overwhelmed by these questions, then that's good. Doing—determining—the right thing is difficult, and possibly the most important thing you'll ever do. Well, apart from *doing* the right thing.

Canada's "tainted blood scandal" is an example of just how complicated this issue can get. In the 1980s, an estimated 1,200 recipients of Red Cross blood were infected with HIV and 60,000 with Hepatitis C. Part of the problem, according to the *Report of the Commission of Inquiry on the Blood System in Canada* (the Krever Report), was that adequate measures were not taken to track down infected individuals, some of whom unknowingly infected their partners or children. Risks were downplayed and the information eventually provided to the public was vague and confusing. A test for Hepatitis C in blood products, available after 1986, may have saved almost 24,000 people, but Canada did not adopt it for reasons of cost and efficiency. How much financial "compensation" is enough in this case?

Certainly a classic case of product safety involves the Ford Pinto. Some argue that Ford knowingly put an unsafe car on the road, causing pain and suffering, and Ford executives are therefore morally at fault (see Dowie). Ford argued that others caused the accidents that resulted in that pain and suffering (someone had to rear-end a Pinto for it to explode) and so Ford was not at fault—the Pinto was intended for driving, not colliding (see the Ford Motor Company article).

But isn't colliding part of driving, or at least a regular sort of risk involved in driving? If so, then Ford should have foreseen and eliminated (or at least reduced) the risk of harm. But what chance of happening makes an event a reasonable expectation—one in a hundred or one in a million? And does it matter at all how cheap or how expensive the remedy was? (The Pinto could have been fixed for $11 a car.) GM seems to have followed Ford's lead, refusing to recall their Cobalt until February 2015 despite knowledge of a design flaw back in 2004. The fatal flaw (implicated in 13 deaths and 31 crashes) could have been fixed for 57 cents. Dow Corning's silicone breast implants is another classic case in product safety—or lack thereof. Ditto for A.H. Robins's Dalkon shield.[1]

BOX 3.3   How Much Is a Life Worth?

In deciding not to recall the Pinto, Ford estimated how many people would be killed by the defect (180) and then compared how much it would cost to fix it in all cars ($137 million) to how much it would cost to "pay" for those deaths ($49.5 million). That calculation led to the $200,000 figure (it's actually $275,000) touted as what they consider the value of a human life to be. (So if you donate a kidney,

---

1 On Dow Corning, see Boatright; on A.H. Robins, see Buchholz and Rosenthal.

you should be paid $200,000 for it?) (What about if you give blood, without which the other person would die?)

However, the $49.5 million is actually based on paying "death benefits" (as well as medical expenses from sustained injuries and car and/or property damage arising from the incident—which perhaps makes the $200,000 figure correct). So perhaps the problem is one of equivocation: are "death benefits" intended to indicate what a life is *worth* or just what some insurance company is willing to pay as compensation for the loss of that life?

If we *are* going to assign a life with economic value, wouldn't you have to figure out what that life would be worth in *economic* terms? Say a twenty-year-old gets killed when the Pinto is rear-ended. If he had gone on to make an average of $50,000 a year for 40 years, he would have been worth $2 million (ten times Ford's $200,000 figure). Add to this the monetary value of five hours per week of childcare and housekeeping services for his children. Plus the monetary value of a book he might write on the weekends. Plus half of the monetary value of his kids' work (after all, he made them, half of them). Plus a quarter of the monetary value of his grandkids' work. (Yes, minus the value of the resources they use and any destruction they cause....)

Also, if someone were to ask parents how much they would be willing to pay for life-saving surgery for their child, the answer wouldn't be so much an indication of what they would be *willing* to pay as it is of what they could *afford* to pay. In the first case, no doubt they'd say they'd pay an infinitely high amount: their child is worth everything to them, they'd pay anything. But they can't afford to pay, say, $2 million and still be able to support, say, their other child and even themselves. So how does the $2-million figure turn into "what the child's life is worth"? The "price" of something is simply what we are willing to pay, what we *can* pay, *given the constraints of our lives*, when forced to do so.

But let's back up a bit. To determine what a life is worth would require first that you think you *can* put a price tag on everything. *Can you?* Even using a "replacement cost" approach—how could you replace a human being? Even if you could make a clone, could you arrange twenty years of the same experiences?

(And show me one habitat that business-as-usual has destroyed that it has replaced. Or even replaced with a habitat of equal value.) If you can't replace it, you can't put a price on it.

Even if you could, *should* you? Is it morally acceptable to buy and sell people? (Not the temporary use of their bodies via the services they provide, but the people themselves.) Is it morally acceptable to put a price tag on the oxygen we breathe? How can someone charge money for it? It's just *there*. What about the water we

> drink? The ground we walk on? How did the first person to own that ground, that land, come to *own* it? (So he could then *sell* it or rent it....) Who did he buy it from?
>
> Because it if *isn't* morally acceptable to buy and sell people, why would we, how could we, put a price tag on them? Perhaps the problem with "How much is a life worth" isn't the answer—it's the question. (And perhaps companies that make unsafe products should approach the problem of what to do when it hurts someone in a totally different way.)

But then don't forget that J.C. Penney recalled an entire line of radios when it discovered that some—fewer than one per cent—had defective resistors that caused them to catch fire. And Johnson Wax withdrew all its CFC products when the connection was made between CFCs and the ozone layer. More recently, Johnson and Johnson recalled all its Tylenol when seven people in Chicago died as a result of cyanide in tampered-with capsules.

> **BOX 3.4   Maple Leaf and Food Safety**
>
> The day after the Canadian Food Inspection Agency contacted Maple Leaf (in August 2008) about possible contamination of their meat products, the company contacted its distributors and asked them to put their products on hold pending test results. The day after they were notified that their meat did indeed contain *listeria* bacteria, the company recalled the affected products. Three days later, after recalling even more products, they closed their factory to re-evaluate their food safety procedures. Other recalls within the food industry followed. All in all, the meat caused or contributed to 22 deaths.
>
> **Source**
> "Listeriosis Outbreak Timeline" *CBC News* Aug26/08. http://www.cbc.ca/news/
>   listeriosis-outbreak-timeline-1.694467

In addition to safety, obsolescence should also be considered an ethical issue of product quality. On what grounds can you make a product that will not last as long as it could? Obsolescence leads to increased resource use because of the manufacture of replacement products; indeed, *planning* obsolescence (see the Guiltinan reading below) indicates a failure to understand that natural resources are limited. It may also contribute to human abuse, since the manufacture of cheap products is often associated with sweatshop labour conditions.

Making short-lived products also leads to increased resource use because of the "disposal" of the worn-out or broken products—fuel is required to transport the garbage to somewhere else (out of sight, out of mind), depleting energy sources and increasing emissions, which increases temperature, which increases floods and droughts, which decreases food production and human habitat... And where is the 'garbage' transported to? (See the Singh and Lakhan essay in Chapter 10; although their data are outdated now—suffice to say the situation is much worse—the ethical arguments are still sound.) More "landfill" sites (quite a euphemism!) means less land for crops... In addition to countless landfills, there are now five piles of garbage floating around in the Pacific ocean; the biggest one is twice the size of Texas, covering 1.3 million square miles. And Canada produces more garbage per person than any other country on Earth....[1] By contrast, Sweden now recycles 99% of its garbage.

Lastly, let's consider that cutting corners with respect to both safety and longevity/durability is typically done in order to increase profits. So that means that your profit is more important than someone else's injury and death? Your profit is more important than a life-sustaining planet?

References and Further Reading

Anderson, Mitchell. "IMF Pegs Canada's Fossil Fuel Subsidies at $34 Billion." *Tyee* 15 May 2014. http://thetyee.ca/Opinion/2014/05/15/Canadas-34-Billion-Fossil-Fuel-Subsidies/

Blackwell, Richard. "Canada risks being left behind as green energy takes off." *Globe and Mail* 22 Sept. 2014. http://www.bnn.ca/News/2014/9/22/Canada-risks-being-left-behind-as-green-energy-takes-off.aspx

Boatright, John R. *Ethics and the Conduct of Business*. 2nd ed. Upper Saddle River, NJ: Prentice Hall, 1997.

Bucciarelli, Louis. "Is Idiot Proof Safe Enough?" *International Journal of Applied Philosophy* 2 (Fall 1985): 49–57.

Buchholz, Rogene A., and Sandra B. Rosenthal. *Business Ethics: The Pragmatic Path beyond Principles to Process*. NJ: Prentice Hall, 1998. 511–29.

"Canadians produce more garbage than anyone else." *CBC News*. 17 Jan. 2013. http://www.cbc.ca/news/business/canadians-produce-more-garbage-than-anyone-else-1.1394020

"Cluster Bombs, Made in America." *New York Times* 1 June 2008. http://www.nytimes.com/2008/06/01/opinion/01sun1.html?_r=0

Curtis, Gary L. "What Cosmetic Companies Can Learn from Pharmaceutical Testing." *DCI* 157.2 (Aug. 1995): 48–53.

Dowie, Mark. "Pinto Madness." *Mother Jones* 2.8 (Sept./Oct. 1977).

Fern, Richard L. "Human Uniqueness as a Guide to Resolving Conflicts Between Animal and Human Interests." *Ethics and Animals* 2.1 (March 1981): 7–21.

Flood, Michael. "The harms of pornography exposure among children and young people." *Child Abuse Review* 18.6 (2009): 384–400.

---

1 See "Canadians produce more garbage" and "Great Pacific Garbage Patch."

Ford Motor Company. "Closing Argument by Mr. James Neal" (Brief for the Defense, *State of Indiana v. Ford Motor Company*, U.S. District Court, South Bend, Indiana, January 15, 1980). In Lisa H. Newton and Maureen M. Ford (eds.), *Taking Sides: Clashing Views on Controversial Issues in Business Ethics and Society*. 4th ed. Guilford, CT: Dushkin Publishing Group, 1996. 263–71.

Frey, R.G. *Interests and Rights: The Case against Animals.* New York: Oxford University Press, 1980.

"Great Pacific Garbage Patch." YouTube. 31 Aug. 2012. https://www.youtube.com/watch?v=1qT-rOXB6NI

Jacobs, Tom. "Porn Viewing Impacts Attitudes on Women in Workplace." *Pacific Standard: The Science of Society* 16 Sept. 2013. http://www.psmag.com/blogs/news-blog/porn-viewing-impacts-attitudes-women-workplace-66280/

Krever, Horace. *The Final Report of the Commission of Inquiry on the Blood System in Canada.* Ottawa: Public Works and Government Services Canada, 1997.

Layden, Mary Anne. "Pornography and Violence: A New Look at Research." http://www.socialcostsofpornography.com/Layden_Pornography_and_Violence.pdf

May, Steve, and Val Caron. "All forms of energy subsidized in Canada." *Sudbury Star* 13 Aug. 2013. http://www.thesudburystar.com/2013/08/30/all-forms-of-energy-subsidized-in-canada

Mello, Michelle M., Eric B. Rimm, and David M. Studdert. "The McLawsuit: The Fast-Food Industry and Legal Accountability for Obesity." *Health Affairs* 22.6 (2003): 207–16.

Noorzoy, M. Siddieq. "Afghanistan's Children: The Tragic Victims of 30 Years of War." Middle East Institute. 20 Apr. 2012. http://www.mei.edu/content/afghanistans-children-tragic-victims-30-years-war

"Nuclear Power in Canada." World Nuclear Association. Dec. 2014. http://www.world-nuclear.org/info/Country-Profiles/Countries-A-F/Canada--Nuclear-Power/

Routley, Richard, and Val Routley. "Nuclear Power—Some Ethical and Social Dimensions." In Tom Regan and Donald VanDeVeer (eds.), *And Justice for All: New Introductory Essays in Ethics and Public Policy*. Totowa, NJ: Rowman and Allanheld, 1982. 116–38.

Smyth, D.H. *Alternatives to Animal Experimentation.* London: Scholars' Press, 1978.

Turley, Jonathan. "Did GM Pull a Pinto?" 14 Apr. 2014. http://jonathanturley.org/2014/04/14/did-gm-pull-a-pinto/

VanDeVeer, Donald. "Interspecific Justice." *Inquiry* 22 (Summer 1979): 55–79.

Velasquez, Manuel G. *Business Ethics: Concepts and Cases.* 3rd ed. Upper Saddle River, NJ: Prentice Hall, 1992. 277–92.

Creative Destruction and Destructive Creations: Environmental Ethics and Planned Obsolescence[*]

Joseph Guiltinan

[1] When I first started teaching marketing, Vance Packard's (1960) criticisms of planned obsolescence were widely discussed by students and faculty. The prevailing view was that it was unethical to design products that would wear out "prematurely" (i.e., have useful lives that were well below customer expectations), particularly if they were costly to replace. Today, the mounting numbers of functioning durable goods ending up in landfills have led to renewed criticism of product obsolescence. Sources indicate that in North America over 100 million cell phones and 300 million personal computers are discarded each year, and only 20,000 televisions are refurbished each year while 20 million are sold, resulting in tremendous environmental damage from lead, mercury, and toxic glass (cf. Boland, 2001; Slade, 2006). Additionally, when electronics are recycled, 50%–80% are shipped to third world nations where workers use dangerous, primitive processes for extracting recyclable materials, often exposing themselves to toxic gases in the process (Associated Press, 2007). So, while advances in technology and increasingly skillful industrial design have enabled firms to develop innovative products in virtually every durable goods category, the nature of the materials that are often required and the rapid pace of product upgrading have resulted in negative environmental consequences for consumers and society (cf. Calcott and Walls, 2005).

[2] Per Figure 1, two aspects of new product development strategy drive these environmental problems. First, frequent introductions of replacement products increase the opportunities and motivation to replace functioning durables. Mindful of Schumpeter's theory that established firms are often replaced by innovators (through a "creative destruction" process), today's strategists focus on rapid new product development to defend their competitive space. Industrial designers and engineers also drive replacement frequency by incorporating desirable benefits or styles into new products (abetted by marketers who promote the incremental value of these upgrades). Second, the recyclability of new products is influenced by choices of components or materials made by designers and engineers. Thus, environmental problems are exacerbated to the extent that corporate strategies emphasizing continuous improve-

---

[*] *Journal of Business Ethics* 89 (2009): 19–28.

ment and those actually involved in creating and marketing new products are insensitive to the need for sustainable innovation and promote excessive consumerism.[1]

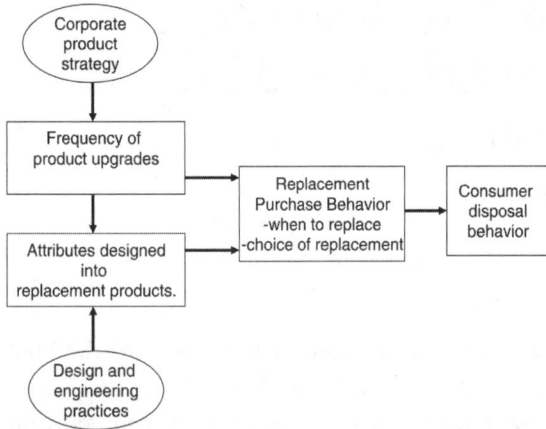

Figure 1. Product obsolescence and the environment: decisions and influences.

[3] In this paper, I specify the set of product development practices that are included under the umbrella of planned obsolescence, and I explain why planned obsolescence is so ubiquitous among durable goods manufacturers. I then examine the ecological responsibilities and responses of technical and managerial product development professionals. I show that design practices (prodded by regulatory initiatives) can be developed for assuring that "creations for consumers" will be less destructive to the environment in the future, but that cultural changes at the product design level are likely to be somewhat constrained by corporate and marketing realities and perceptions. I conclude that the lack of understanding of consumer behavior with respect to replacement and disposal of durable goods is an impediment to marketers and public policy makers seeking this goal, creating an important opportunity for scholars in the field of marketing.

Planned Obsolescence Practices

The objective of planned obsolescence is to stimu- [4] late replacement buying by consumers. The most direct way to speed replacement demand is to shorten the usable life of a product through one or more of the following physical obsolescence mechanisms.

- *Limited functional life design* (or "*death dating*"). In a recent book, Slade (2006) notes that in the 1950s and 1960s death dating was standard practice for many appliances. (At one point portable radios were designed to last for only 3 years.)
- *Design for limited repair.* Disposable single-use cameras were designed to be non-repairable, although a small recycling industry emerged for a time until Fuji and Kodak took these firms to court for copyright violations (Adolphson, 2004; McCollough, 2007). It suggests that the price of repair for consumer electronics encourages disposal, and household income correlates positively with the propensity to dispose of and replace appliances rather than repair them.[2]
- *Design aesthetics that lead to reduced satisfaction.* Cooper (2005) shows how aesthetic characteristics can influence premature disposal. One example is the design of "faultless forms and surfaces" on products like small appliances which leave a pristine and polished appearance which, with everyday use quickly becomes damaged, engendering user dissatisfaction and premature disposal.

Faster replacement can also be achieved through new product replacement strategies designed to foster technological obsolescence. Packard (1960) termed this form of obsolescence "voluntary" because there was no reason that consumers could not continue to be satisfied with their existing products.

- *Design for fashion*. Although comic detective Dick Tracy kept his two-way wrist radio from 1946 until he retired in 1977, today fashion influences many durables replacement decisions. Increasingly designers have applied fashion thinking to watches, mp3 players, cell phones, and even laptop computers. Slade (2006) suggests that the rise of General Motors and its displacement of industry leader Ford was the first victory of fashion positioning over durability positioning among "hard" goods.
- *Design for functional enhancement through adding or upgrading product features*. Technological development frequently allows firms to expand the number of uses or benefits of a product (e.g., adding a camera feature to a cell phone) or to improve the level of performance on existing benefits (as when a laptop maker increases memory and speed or reduces weight). Note that if there are clearly stratified benefit segments in a market, the early generation product may not have a high demand cross-elasticity with the new one because the new level of performance may not be (at least initially) desired or needed by all customers. In such cases older platforms may be retained as long as there is significant demand for them (cf. Saunders and Jobber, 1994) and the obsolescence effect will be minimal. The obsolescence effect is stronger when many consumers perceive the old products to be "unfashionable" (cf. Mason, 1985) or when the incremental features of the new products are universally perceived as beneficial and desirable.

Drivers of Obsolescence and Fast Replacement

[5] Durable goods producers face a specific challenge in maintaining a high rate of sales growth. This "durables problem"—the core driving force behind planned obsolescence in any market structure (from monopoly to intensive competition)—occurs when successful sellers quickly saturate their markets. The more reliable and long-lasting the product, the longer the repeat purchase cycle and the slower the rate of sales growth. If a firm chooses to rent its goods, it would receive a consistent flow of revenue for several years, but once a firm sells its durable goods output it no longer has a vested interest in the value of those goods. Instead its interests lie in the next generation of goods. (To economists this is known as the "time inconsistency" problem.) The existence of a market for used versions of the durable further complicates the problem, because the more durable the product is the greater is the competition between new and used versions and the lower is the price of replacement products (Bulow, 1986). Thus, durability becomes a drag on replacement sales volume and, when a used market exists, on the prices of replacement goods. To mitigate competition from the used market, firms increase the frequency of the revision (upgrade) cycle (Iizuka, 2007). Thus, increasing the rate of replacement through obsolescence will enable firms to: (1) stimulate revenues through faster replacement; (2) reduce competition from any used good markets; (3) by virtue of making used or owned goods less competitive, increase prices for the replacement product.

Competitive Pressure for Technological Obsolescence

[6] While the "durables problem" exists even in monopoly settings, as Sonntag (2000) notes competitive considerations create additional pressures for obsolescence. Pointing out that a consensus has emerged that cost, quality, time-to-market and performance based on distinctive product features are hallmarks of competitive businesses today (see also Hua and Wemmerlov, 2006), Sonntag argues that advances

in manufacturing practice that yield faster product cycles are now a defining force in business strategy. Through the use of flexible, modular, and faster design software and production equipment, concurrent product development processes, and information technology, firms have reduced both the length of the production process and the time required to adapt production to demand and competitive actions. The result is rapid execution of orders and delivery, faster implementation of new product concepts, and reduced capital, inventory, and unit costs. Perversely, such systems demand growth in output because the technologies amplify economies of scale and scope which can only be realized through faster product replacement and increasing consumption of products designed for particular needs. The competitive success of such technologies and processes has led to emulation by other firms. Thus, the incentives for obsolescence in the traditional "durables problem" are compounded in industries in which rapid new product development is embedded in the competitive environment.

[7] Gillette's strategy of regularly replacing its market-leading razors is often cited as an exemplar of the competitive necessity of a self-cannibalizing product replacement strategy. That firm saw the wisdom of this strategy after its experience in 1962 when a small British cutlery and garden tool maker, Wilkinson Sword, created a stainless steel blade that lasted three times as long as Gillette's offering and took away 20% of Gillette's share. Gillette had resisted introducing a stainless steel blade itself due to concern for cannibalization of its existing market leading brands and because of the negative demand impact of the longer lasting feature of the blades (Tellis and Golder, 2001). Thus, the managerial dilemma regarding "willingness to cannibalize" is that if a firm will not cannibalize its own product's sales its competitors will.

Additionally, an idea that has gained currency [8] among marketing managers and strategic planners is that brand loyalty is a route to high profitability because of the higher "lifetime value" of customers who can be retained for multiple repeat purchases. Firms want to facilitate migration of their customers to their own version of the next technological advance rather than risk losing them to competitors because it is generally much less expensive to retain customers than to acquire new ones. Notably, durable goods upgrades may provide avenues to customer retention even in non-durable industries. Witness the cellular phone service competition in which free phone upgrades are offered every 2 years as incentives to consumers to renew cellular service contracts.

Thus, the existence of a highly competitive [9] environment, combined with the fundamental economic motives for obsolescence discussed earlier have created a sort of path-dependence for product development strategies geared toward faster replacement of durables.

The Impact of Consumer Decision-making Processes

The success and consequences of technological [10] obsolescence ultimately depend on consumer behavior in the marketplace. Consumers decide whether and when to replace functioning durables with new versions. In at least some cases, consumers also have choices among replacement products that differ in their durability or in their environmental benefits and liabilities.

In general, little is known about consumers' [11] durable goods replacement decision-making processes. However, technical product obsolescence is clearly a more significant driver of replacement timing than physical obsolescence. Grewal et al. (2004) compared "unforced" replacement decisions driven by technological (including fashion) obsolescence with replacement decisions that were "forced" by poor product performance. They found that durable product replacement intervals were shorter for unforced decisions, explaining the result with the argument that, in the case of voluntary replacement, consumers are more excited about and interested in the decision to replace and thus more motivated to act. (The major exception to the finding that technological obsolescence is more of a driver of replacement purchasing than physical obsolescence is that unexciting, out-of-view durable—the washing machine [Box, 1983].) The Grewal et al. study also identified various attitudinal functions served by durable goods, including social approval, utilitarian, and "value-expressive" functions. It is difficult to speculate on the relative impact of fashion changes versus functional enhancements in replacement buying. However, if "fashion" is defined to include industrial design aesthetics, then it is likely to be a factor in the purchase of luxury utilitarian goods and value-expressive goods as well as goods where replacement is motivated by the desire for social approval.

[12] Interestingly, rates of technological obsolescence influence the value that consumers attach to upgrades. Rapid product improvements can increase the household discount rate (or the "impatience" rate) so that consumers value purchases made in the near term more than the savings from delayed purchase (Winer, 1997). Moreover, even when improvements are not obvious, an empirical study by Boone et al. (2001) indicated that more frequent introductions of upgrades may be interpreted by consumers as cues to higher rates of intergenerational improvement, so a policy of "continuous upgrading" creates a heightened sense among consumers that their existing durable is outmoded. Thus, more rapid introductions appear to motivate faster replacement regardless of the actual level of quality enhancement.

In sum, based on what we do know from the limited studies available, replacement buying behaviors are complex, heterogeneous, and perhaps based more on heuristics and extrinsic cues than on a calculative cost-benefit tradeoff process.

With respect to the process of choosing among [13] alternative replacement durables, there is little evidence that durability is a key consumer buying motive. Economic theory generally assumes that warranties signal higher quality, and that firms that build in quality and signal it through warranties are rewarded with higher prices (cf. Utaka, 2006). But a study in the UK (Cooper, 2004) indicates that consumers who buy premium appliances do not do so because they view high prices as signals of higher durability. Moreover, a recent retail study of TV purchasing concluded that warranty information trailed behind picture quality, brand name, price, and picture size in rated importance (Cervini, 2005). There is also substantial evidence that consumers ignore information on features that reflect product durability (cf. the discussion of the furniture industry consumer in George, 2000). Indeed Cooper's aforementioned study concluded that: consumers are equally divided on whether appliance life spans are adequate; often do not consider durability to be a critical attribute; and see product life span as a quality issue—not an environmental issue (Cooper, 2004).

Similarly, environmental attributes play a modest role at best in durable goods decision-making with green purchasing restricted to a small segment of the population. Right now, any expectation that consumers will suddenly become dramatically pro-environment in their purchasing behavior seems excessively optimistic. A Finnish study by Niva and Timonen (2001) on product purchasing points out why this is the case: (1) consumers lack knowledge about the environmental implications of their purchases—even in product categories where such [14] impacts are widely discussed in the media; (2) consumers believe it is the responsibility of manufacturers to produce environmentally benign products and for distributors to screen for such qualities, and that consumers have little impact on those activities. Of course environment-related attributes will only influence purchase choices when there is some variance among the alternatives offered on the environmental dimension. If competitors do not create or promote such attributes one cannot expect "green" purchasing by consumers.

Ethical Responsibilities and Responses

[15] While innovation and technological progress are good (*ceteris paribus*), the gains from some new products may not always be worth the consumer or societal cost. To the extent consumers and society at large incur the economic and environmental costs associated with disposal of durable goods, the more frequent the replacement and the less recyclable the durable, the greater the problem.

[16] The responsibility for the negative consequences of planned obsolescence is a shared one. First, when technical professionals (engineers and industrial designers) involved in new product development design durables to foster premature physical obsolescence they create corporate (and possible personal) gains at the expense of consumer welfare and the environment. Second, managers responsible for product replacement strategies act in ethically questionable ways if they "psychologically condition" consumers to believe that the utility of a product is diminished simply because a new version becomes available. By extension, offering frequent product "upgrades" while touting minor or illusory benefit improvements might be considered a wasteful and potentially misleading practice (cf. Giaretta, 2005). Third, from the perspective of utilitarian theory, consumers may also act unethically when they add to the public burden with what some might consider frivolous, self-serving replacement behavior as well as when they knowingly use or dispose of products in ways that are environmentally harmful in order to save time or money. Even when new products yield significant increases in consumer benefits, mass replacement of the existing stock can still be a negative if improper disposal is a result. For example, one can anticipate mass replacement of analog television sets as HDTV set ownership diffuses through the market.

[17] What are the options available to firms for addressing the environmental concerns about planned obsolescence? This is a question that must be answered at two levels: (1) the designers and engineers responsible for choosing specific components, materials, architectures, and interfaces, and (2) marketing and business strategists.

Environmental Ethics: Responses from Industrial Design and Engineering

[18] With respect to product development practice, one could argue that significant progress is being made in building a sustainable design culture among industrial designers and engineers involved in new product development. Design trade groups have placed sustainable and ethical design practices high on their educational agendas, and many firms that employ designers and design firms are buying in to such practices (Cooper, 2005). Design is one way of attempting to increase replacement intervals. For example, classic designs (such as the one used for years by Volvo) or local, cultural designs that communicate a community identity are sources of "timeless" designs that make a product's appeal long lasting (cf. Zafarmand et al., 2003). Typologies of strategies for sustainable design are available from several sources (cf. Charter and Tischner, 2001).

[19] Similar kinds of strategies are being developed in engineering. For example, Sonntag (2000) suggests that firms could adapt the current technologies of lean and flexible manufacturing for producing value-added products that will be more intensively used by consumers (such as multi-function products). One option for coping with changing needs driven by culture, fashion, or function is "design for adaptability" (cf. Kasarda et al., 2007)—the development of new products that are amenable to adaptation by replacing subsystems or modules as an alternative to full product replacement.

[20] Many new processes and technologies have also been developed for the cross-functional communication process in firms where sustainable new product development is a priority. These include important tools like "design for environment," "life cycle assessment," and "environmental effect analysis" (cf. Tingstrom and Karlsson, 2006). Pujari (2006) argues that the leading firms in developing eco-innovations are those that have fully integrated such tools into their new product development planning so that they think in a positive sustainability mode rather than a reactive mode of just eliminating environmentally problematic features. For example, King and Burgess (2005), recognizing the strength of the culture of fashion obsolescence, argue for applying platform strategy thinking in which key components and subassemblies can be remanufactured and integrated into new products.

[21] These developments would seem to bode well for the evolution of environmentally friendly product development or, at least, for increased attention on creating products that consumers will keep longer. However, design decisions at the individual product level will have to be consistent with the firm's strategic priorities on positioning and growth objectives. (Per Figure 1, the specific attributes designed into new products will usually, in part, reflect strategic decisions regarding the frequency of product change).

Corporate Responsibility and Marketing/Business Strategy

[22] As noted earlier, relentless product change has become the centerpiece of new product development strategy in many durable goods industries. But to some observers (cf. Giaretta, 2005) relentless product change is a one-sided strategy because it focuses on the needs of the firm at the risk of detriment to the environment and to consumer welfare. She argues that a firm should seek a market positioning that distinguishes it on the basis of true customer satisfaction, environmental friendliness, and reliable long-term usefulness of its products. Adolphson (2004) offers an insight on what is entailed in redefining a firm's agenda to implement such repositioning. Following Werhane's (2002) concept of "moral imagination" he argues that firms need to revise their mental schemas for new product development to include a "biophysical" perspective which places the economic system in the larger context of an ecological system. In this perspective, value cannot always be captured in monetary terms. For example, nature performs work that is valuable without any exchange of money. This occurs when farmers reuse seeds from produce to plant future crops. On the other hand, the single-use camera forces premature disposal and thus wastes energy resources. This constitutes a waste of "natural capital" that would normally be ignored in estimates of the consequences of a given decision.

[23] Such thinking would mean that managers should consider the costs of product disposal to be real costs that someone must bear rather than as "externalities," so that the decision-making "script" (i.e., the protocol by which new product proposals move through the development process from

concept to launch) for each new product development business case includes an ecological dimension. A Swedish example of revising the script is reported by Byggeth et al. (2007). They developed a specific set of "sustainability product assessment modules" for evaluating proposals that could be easily adapted to a variety of established protocols to pro-actively identify opportunities for improved sustainability (such as energy savings, use of recyclable materials, and disposability). A similar initiative being applied in Ireland is reported in Maxwell and van de Horst (2003).

[24] These perspectives are consistent with the "stakeholder" model of corporate responsibility which would acknowledge the possibility that a responsible product replacement strategy may compromise profitability (cf. Godfrey and Hatch, 2006). They are also consistent with the American Marketing Association's statement of Norms and Values. That statement calls on marketing professionals to support specific ethical values including "Responsibility—to accept the consequences of our marketing decisions" and "Citizenship—to fulfill the economic, legal, philanthropic, and societal responsibilities that serve stakeholders in a strategic manner." However, Sonntag (2000) indicates that the World Business Council for Sustainable Development (a CEO-led global association of 200 companies) purposely does not include extending product durability on their list of eco-efficient practices because of the belief that fast repeat purchase is healthy for their bottom lines as well as for the public goal of higher levels of employment. The latter point raises a challenging issue for public policy: when two public goals—employment and the environment in this case—are in potential conflict, how does one resolve this dilemma. It also reflects the reality that individual firms operate in a complex environment that includes investor norms and expectations.

Public Policy Initiatives

To corporate strategists, asking firms for voluntary reductions in the rate at which new product improvements are brought to market would be akin to a request for unilateral competitive disarmament. Moreover, absent a matching response from other firms, the net effect on the total volume of durables sold may not change—just the distribution of market shares. So, it would take industry agreements (anti-trust issues notwithstanding) to reduce such cycles or to assure that all sellers deliver to the market durables which are equally environmentally benign (at the likely cost of reducing some consumer benefits). Because this will lead to the return of the "durables problem" industrywide economic sacrifices are the price of sustainability. Thus, we have a social dilemma. [25]

Such dilemmas also exist at the consumer level. The cost and effort of recycling, trading off lower price or some other desirable benefit to buy a more environmentally friendly product, and denying oneself (or delaying) the benefits of a prospective upgrade are examples of perceived sacrifice that impedes more "green" consumer behavior. [26]

One solution for a social dilemma is public policy action. Many of the strides being made in sustainable design were initially motivated by public policy directives. For example, the EU is stipulating minimum reuse and recovery rates for end-of-life automotive vehicles (cf. Ferrao and Amaral, 2006), and another EU directive on waste electrical and electronic equipment makes manufacturers and importers responsible for the treatment and disposal of products discarded by consumers in those categories. Product "take-back" laws are "on the books" in many parts of Europe and East Asia, and efforts to enact such legislation have occurred in nearly all the 50 States [27] of the United States (Toffel, 2004).[3] These efforts are based on the belief that such laws provide incentives to firms to implement design changes that will reduce the environmental burden created by future new products while shifting the cost from local government.[4]

[28] Because product take-back laws increase the unit cost of new products (when disposal costs are factored in) they are an "upstream solution"—one that is intended to motivate the design and marketing of green products. Current environmental policy wisdom favors "upstream" solutions over "downstream" solutions (those that focus on recycling incentives and taxes) (cf. Thorgerson, 2000). As Calcott and Walls (2000) argue, downstream solutions such as disposal fees only influence upstream behavior when there is a fully functioning recycling market in which recyclers pay each household for each recycled item and the price varies with the value of recyclable components of the product. Because such systems appear infeasible, they argue that the next best approach is a deposit refund system (producers pay a tax and recyclers receive the refund).

[29] Thus, public policy initiatives have the potential to motivate business and marketing strategists to support environmentally friendly designs emerging from new product designers and engineers. But as Malcolm (2005) notes, the effectiveness of upstream solutions ultimately depend on whether "greener" products will be competitive in the mind of the consumer with "less green" alternatives once the costs and benefits of green alternatives are weighed against the cost (tax included) and benefits of less green options. Additionally, the effectiveness of take back laws presumes compliance on the part of the consumer who must still bear the transaction costs of returning durables to manufacturers' recycling drop-off sites.

Conclusion

[30] The World Business Council on Sustainable Development includes the following as a major action point: "Encourage consumers to prefer ecoefficient, more sustainable products and services" (World Business Council for Sustainable Development, 2000). As noted, such products could include goods that pose fewer toxic threats that are more readily recyclable, or that consumers will keep longer. Prospects for achieving this goal are enhanced by the fact that sustainable product development is now a motivating force for many product development engineers and designers. Additionally, this action point is consistent with public policy initiatives focused on "upstream" solutions. However, two impediments exist: (1) the competitive pressure for and consumer expectations of frequent upgrades for durable goods; (2) the lack of consumer concern for environmental consequences when contemplating upgrades of durable goods. Thus, achieving the WBCSD's goal requires not only green design but also effective green marketing by firms and public policy initiatives that offer the right mix of consumer and manufacturer incentives.

[31] Iyer (1999) makes the pessimistic argument that a sustainability paradigm based on encouraging "green" consumer behavior is inadequate. He notes that this "anthropocentric view" presumes that more pressure by green consumers will result in products that do not reduce human quality of life, yet there is little evidence that consumers exercise their market votes in a way that will achieve this outcome. It is not clear that we know why this is the case. However, as Moisander (2007) notes, a consumer's motivation to act partly depends on his/her perception of the degree of behavioral control they have in a given situation. Ecologically responsible purchase/consumption/disposal often requires

practical skills and knowledge that are not readily available to consumers, so for consumers to have behavioral control they need meaningful choices and complete and relevant information about those choices. Managers and public policy makers need to know what constitutes a choice that is "meaningful" to consumers and how information about these choices can best be communicated. Specific questions of interest would include:

- What information content, framing, timing, and sources will be effective in educating and motivating consumers to consider and choose "greener" options or to make more "rational" or cost-effective evaluations of when to purchase upgrades?
- What would the consumer response be to new products that were more resistant to technological obsolescence (e.g., adaptable products per the discussion of sustainable design strategies from above) or to leasing of durables that might be modified or refurbished/remanufactured for next generation production? (Recall that rental of durables reduces the reliance of the manufacturer on repeat purchase demand for future revenue. It also assures that consumers will return the good to the manufacturer or its agent.)
- What incentives (tax credits, rebates, trade-in discounts) or disincentives (deposits, taxes) will influence upgrade purchasing patterns or choices?
- What kind of information about disposal options or costs (personal and societal) of durables will be evaluated and used in the consumer's decision-making process?

[32] Unfortunately, as noted earlier, the marketing literature offers very little insight on the drivers of upgrade behavior or on the decision-making processes involved. Our current theoretical understanding about how consumers perceive, understand, and use environmentally related goods product information has limited managerial utility because of the complexity and variety of the decision situations that might be studied (Leire and Thidell, 2005). Moreover, what we do know about why people are motivated to perform certain green behaviors (e.g., energy saving practices) is not readily translated to other contexts such as durable purchasing behaviors (Cleveland et al., 2005). Thus, marketing scholars would seem to have a great opportunity to contribute to the understanding of how consumers interpret and respond to green marketing overtures and to government incentives for green behavior.

Notes

1. Replacement products also may offer positive environmental benefits if they are more energy efficient, made from more eco-friendly materials, or create fewer undesirable side effects. Van Nes and Cramer (2006) offer an approach to assessing the lifecycle impact (production, distribution, usage, and disposal) of a product on the environment that includes the calculation of both positive and negative benefits.
2. The rationale given for the latter finding is that high income households have a higher opportunity cost of time, and time is required for most repair situations.
3. That the EU is more advanced than the United States on take back laws can be attributed in part to the political strength of Green Parties (notable in Germany which pioneered such laws), in part to the division of regulatory powers between the states and the federal government in the US, and perhaps to a more communitarian political ethos in the EU.
4. Some major firms are offering to take back electronic items. However, by the end of 2007 only Sony had agreed to take back all televisions, breaking from the Electronic Manufacturers Coalition for Responsible Recycling which (along with the Consumer Electronics Association) has opposed take back legislation on economic grounds (Gunther, 2007).

References

Adolphson, D. 2004. "A New Perspective on Ethics, Ecology and Economics." *Journal of Business Ethics* 54, 203–216.

Associated Press. 2007. "Destination of Recycled Electronics May Surprise You," http://www.computer-takeback.com/news_and_resources/destination.cfm. Accessed 11 November 2007.

Boland, M. 2001. "Water and the Environment." *Forbes* 168(6), 60–62.

Boone, D., K. Lemon and R. Staelin. 2001. "The Impact of Firm Introductory Strategies on Consumers' Perceptions of Future Product Introductions and Purchase Decisions." *Journal of Product Innovation Management* 18, 96–109.

Box, J. 1983. "Extending Product Lifetime: Prospects and Opportunities." *European Journal of Marketing* 17, 34–49.

Bulow, J. 1986. "An Economic Theory of Planned Obsolescence." *The Quarterly Journal of Economics* 101, 729–749.

Byggeth, S., G. Broman and K. Robert. 2007. "A Method for Sustainable Product Development Based on a Modular System of Guiding Questions." *Journal of Cleaner Production* 15, 1–11.

Calcott, P. and M. Walls. 2000. "Can Downstream Waste Disposal Policies Encourage Upstream Design for Environment?" *American Economic Review* 90, 233–237.

Calcott, P. and M. Walls. 2005. "Waste, Recycling and Design for Environment: Roles for Markets and Policy Instruments." *Resource and Energy Economics* 27, 287–305.

Cervini, L. 2005. "TV: Shoppers Choose Quality over Size," TWICE June 20, 22.

Charter, M. and U. Tischner. 2001. *Sustainable Solutions: Developing Products and Services for the Future*. Sheffield, UK: Greenleaf.

Cleveland, M., M. Kalamas and M. Laroche. 2005. "Shades of Green: Linking Environmental Locus of Control and Pro-Environmental Behaviors." *Journal of Consumer Marketing* 22, 198–212.

Cooper, R. 2005. "Ethics and Altruism: What Constitutes Socially Responsible Design?" *Design Management Review* 16, 10–18.

Cooper, T. 2004. "Inadequate Life? Evidence of Consumer Attitudes to Product Obsolescence." *Journal of Consumer Policy* 27, 421–449.

Ferrao, P. and J. Amaral. 2006. "Design for Recycling in the Automobile Industry: New Approaches and New Tools." *Journal of Engineering Design* 17, 447–462.

George, R. 2000. "Your Lifetime Guarantee Won't Guarantee Sales." *Upholstery Design & Management* 13, 24–27.

Giaretta, E. 2005. "Ethical Product Innovation: In Praise of Slowness." *The TQM Magazine* 17, 161–181.

Godfrey, P. and N. Hatch. 2006. "Researching Corporate Social Responsibility: An Agenda for the 21st Century." *Journal of Business Ethics* 70, 87–98.

Grewal, R., R. Mehta and F. Kardes. 2004. "The Timing of Repeat Purchase of Consumer Durable Goods: The Role of Functional Bases of Consumer Attitudes." *Journal of Marketing Research* 41, 101–115.

Gunther, M. 2007. "Sony Champions Free Recycling." *Fortune*, August 22.

Hua, S. and U. Wemmerlov. 2006. "Product Change Intensity Product Advantage and Market Performance: An Empirical Investigation into the PC Industry." *Journal of Product Innovation Management* 23, 316–329.

Iizuka, T. 2007. "An Empirical Analysis of Planned Obsolescence." *Journal of Economics & Management Strategy* 16, 191–226.

Iyer, G. 1999. "Business, Consumers and Sustainable Living in an Interconnected World: A Multilateral Ecocentric Approach." *Journal of Business Ethics* 20, 273–288.

Kasarda, M., et al. 2007. "Design for Adaptability—A New Concept for Achieving Sustainable Design." *Robotics & Computer-Integrated Manufacturing* 23, 727–734.

King, A. and S. Burgess. 2005. "The Development of a Remanufacturing Platform Design: A Strategic Response to the Directive on Waste Electrical and Electronic Equipment." *Journal of Engineering Manufacture* 219 (Part B), 623–631.

Leire, C. and A. Thidell. 2005. "Product-Related Environmental Information to Guide Consumer Purchases—Research on Perceptions Understanding and Use among Nordic Consumers." *Journal of Cleaner Production* 13, 1061–1070.

Malcolm, R. 2005. "Integrated Product Policy—A New Regulatory Paradigm for a Consumer Society?" *European Environmental Law Review* 14, 134–144.

Mason, R. 1985. "Ethics and the Supply of Status Goods." *Journal of Business Ethics* 4, 457–464.

Maxwell, D. and R. van de Horst. 2003. "Developing Sustainable Products and Services." *Journal of Cleaner Production* 11, 883–895.

McCollough, J. 2007. "The Effect of Income Growth on the Mix of Purchases Between Disposable Goods and Reusable Goods." *International Journal of Consumer Studies* 31, 213–219.

Mello, Michelle M., Eric B. Rimm and David M. Studdert. "The McLawsuit: The Fast-Food Industry and Legal Accountability for Obesity." *Health Affairs* 22.6 (2003).

Moisander, J. 2007. "Motivational Complexity of Green Consumption." *International Journal of Consumer Studies* 31, 404–409.

Niva, M. and P. Timonen. 2001. "The Role of Consumers in Product-oriented Environmental Policy: Can the Consumer Be the Driving Force for Environmental Improvements?" *International Journal of Consumer Studies* 25, 331–338.

Olson, Walter. "The FDA's Trans Fat Ban: Their Laws, Your Body." Cato Institute, Cato at Liberty, June 16, 2015.

Packard, V. 1960. *The Waste Makers*. New York: David McKay.

Pujari, D. 2006. "Eco-Innovation and New Product Development: Understanding the Influences on Market Performance." *Technovation* 26, 76–85.

Resnik, David. 2010. "Trans Fat Bans and Human Freedom." *The American Journal of Bioethics*, 10(3): 27–32.

Routley, Richard and Val Routley. 1982. "Nuclear Power—Some Ethical and Social Dimensions." *And Justice for All: New Introductory Essays in Ethics and Public Policy*. Ed. Tom Regan and Donald VanDeVeer. Totowa, NJ: Rowman and Allanheld, 1982. 116–138.

Saunders, J. and D. Jobber. 1994. "Product Replacement: Strategies for Simultaneous Product Deletion and Launch." *Journal of Product Innovation Management* 11(5), 433–450.

Slade, G. 2006. *Made to Break: Technology and Obsolescence in America*. Boston: Harvard University Press.

Sonntag, V. 2000. "Sustainability—In Light of Competitiveness." *Ecological Economics* 34, 101–113.

Tellis, G. and P. Golder. 2001. *Will & Vision*. New York: McGraw-Hill.

Thorgerson, J. 2000. "Psychological Determinants of Paying Attention to Eco-Label in Purchase Decisions: Model Development and Multinational Validation." *Journal of Consumer Policy* 23, 285–313.

Tingstrom, J. and R. Karlsson. 2006. "The Relationship between Environmental Analyses and the Dialogue Process in New Product Development," *Journal of Cleaner Production* 14, 1409–1419.

Toffel, M. 2004. "Strategic Management of Product Recovery." *California Management Review* 46, 120–141.

Utaka, A. 2006. "Durable-Goods Warranties and Social Welfare." *The Journal of Law, Economics and Organization* 22, 508–522.

van Nes, N. and J. Cramer. 2006. "Product Lifetime Optimization: A Challenging Strategy Towards More Sustainable Consumption Patterns." *Journal of Cleaner Production* 14, 1307–1318.

Werhane, P. 2002. "Moral Imagination and Systems Thinking." *Journal of Business Ethics* 38, 33–42.

Winer, R. 1997. "Discounting and Its Impact on Durables Buying Decisions." *Marketing Science* 8, 109–118.

World Business Council for Sustainable Development. 2000. *Eco-Efficiency: Creating More Value with Less Impact*. Geneva: World Business Council for Sustainable Development.

Zafarmand, S., K. Suguyama and M. Watanabe. 2003. "Aesthetics and Sustainability: The Aesthetic Attributes Promoting Sustainability." *Journal of Sustainable Product Design* 3, 173–186.

Questions

1. Guiltinan's opening paragraph suggests a great business opportunity. What is it?
2. How often do we *really* need a new version of an existing product (phone, car, etc.)? What does Guiltinan suggest makes us think otherwise?
3. What does Guiltinan identify as the objective of planned obsolescence, and what is the motive for that objective? On what grounds is that a morally defensible motive?
4. Which approach/theory does Guiltinan use in his analysis of the ethics of planned obsolescence? Use a different approach/theory—do you get to the same conclusions?
5. Summarize Guiltinan's analysis of who is responsible for planned obsolescence. Do think the named parties are *equally* responsible? Why/why not?
6. "Value cannot always be captured in monetary terms" (para 22). Do you agree? Why/why not?
7. Guiltinan identifies the concept of "externalities" as part of the problem. On what grounds is that concept morally defensible?
8. What public policy changes would you advocate to solve the problem?

On the Ethics of the Use of Animals in Science[*]

Dale Jamieson and Tom Regan[1]

[1] As you read this, animals are being killed, burned, radiated, blinded, immobilized and shocked. They are being locked and strapped into the Noble-Collip Drum, tossed about at the rate of 40 revolutions per minute and thrust against the iron projections that line the drum. This procedure crushes bones, destroys tissues, smashes teeth and ruptures internal organs. Right now, somewhere, animals are in isolation, deprived of all social contact, while others are in alien environments, manipulated into cannibalizing members of their own species. It is not just a few animals at issue. In the year 1978 alone, about 200 million animals were used for scientific

---

[*] Dale Jamieson and Tom Regan, "On the Ethics of the Use of Animals in Science" from *And Justice for All: New Introductory Essays in Ethics and Public Policy*. Ed. Tom Regan and Donald Van De Veer. NJ: Rowman and Allanheld, 1982. 169–96. Reprinted with permission of the editors and the authors.

purposes, about 64 million of these in the United States. This number includes 400,000 dogs, 200,000 cats and 30,000 apes and monkeys.[2]

[2] ...Before setting forth our own view regarding the ethics of the use of animals in science, two extreme positions will be characterized and debated. By subjecting their supporting arguments to criticism, we hope to show the need for a more reasonable, less extreme position. We shall call the two positions "The Unlimited Use Position" and "The No Use Position." The former holds that it is permissible to use any animal for any scientific purpose, so long as no human being is wronged. The latter holds that no use of any animal for any scientific purpose is morally permissible. We shall first examine the leading arguments for the Unlimited Use Position.

I.

[3] The first argument that we shall consider is the Cartesian Argument. It is named after the seventeenth century philosopher, René Descartes, who held that animals are mindless machines. Here is the argument.

1. If a practice does not cause pain, then it is morally permissible.
2. Unlimited use of animals for scientific purposes would not cause them any pain.
3. Therefore, the use of any animal for any scientific purpose is morally permissible.

So simple an argument is not without far reaching consequences. The tacit assumption of the Cartesian Argument by the scientists of Descartes's day helped pave the way for the rapid growth of animal experimentation in the seventeenth and eighteenth centuries. The following passage, written by an unknown contemporary of Descartes, gives a vivid and unsettling picture of science at that time.

They [i.e., scientists] administered beatings to dogs with perfect indifference; and made fun of those who pitied the creatures as if they felt pain. They said the animals were clocks; that the cries they emitted when struck, were only the noise of a little spring that had been touched, but that the whole body was without feeling. They nailed poor animals up on boards by their four paws to vivisect them and see the circulation of the blood which was a great subject of controversy.[3]

It is well to remember this passage whenever we doubt that ideas can make a difference. Clearly Descartes's idea that animals are mindless machines profoundly influenced the course of science. The influence of an idea, however, is not a reliable measure of its truth, and we need to ask how reasonable the Cartesian Argument is.

[4] A moment's reflection is enough to show that some crucial qualifications must be added if the Cartesian Argument is to have any plausibility at all. Inflicting pain is not the only way to harm an individual. Suppose, for example, that we were to kill humans painlessly while they are asleep. No one would infer that because such killing would be painless it would therefore be quite all right. But even if the necessary qualifications were introduced, the Cartesian Argument would still remain implausible. The evidence for believing that at least some animals feel pain (and it is only those animals with which we shall be concerned) is virtually the same as the evidence for believing that humans feel pain. Both humans and animals behave in ways that are simply, coherently and consistently explained by supposing that they feel pain. From a physiological point of view, there is no reason to suppose that there are features that are unique to humans that are involved in pain sensations. Veterinary medicine, the law and common-sense all presuppose that some animals feel pain. Though some

seem to accept the Cartesian Argument implicitly, it is doubtful that many would try to defend it when it is clearly stated.

[5] ...A fourth argument for Unlimited Use is the Knowledge Argument.

1. If a practice produces knowledge, then it is morally permissible.
2. Unlimited use of animals for scientific purposes would produce knowledge.
3. Therefore, unlimited use of animals for scientific purposes is morally permissible.

Here we should balk at the first premise. Torturing suspects, spying on citizens, vivisecting cousins, all could produce knowledge, but surely that alone would not make these activities morally all right. Some knowledge is simply not worth the price in pain required to get it, whether those who suffer the pain are humans, as in the activities just listed, or animals, as in the case about to be described.

[6] The Draize Test is a procedure employed by many manufacturers to determine whether proposed new products, most notably new cosmetics, would irritate the eyes of humans.[4] The most recent Federal guidelines for the administration of the Draize Test recommend that a single large volume dose of the test substance be placed in the conjunctival sac in one eye of each of six albino rabbits. The test substance is to remain in the eyes of the rabbits for a week, and observations are to be periodically recorded. The guidelines recommend that in most cases anesthetics should not be used. The rabbits are often immobilized in restraining devices in order to prevent them from clawing at their eyes. At the completion of a week, the irritancy of the test substance is graded on the basis of the degree and severity of the damage in the cornea and iris.

[7] The Draize Test is not a very good test by anyone's standards. It is unreliable and crude. In fact, a 1971 survey of twenty-five laboratories employing the Draize Test concluded that the Draize Test is so unreliable that it "...should not be recommended as standard procedures in any new regulation."[5] But even if the Draize Test were a reliable test, the most that we would gain is some knowledge about the properties of some inessential new products. Can anyone really believe that there is a scarcity of cosmetics already on the market? The value of whatever knowledge is provided by the Draize Test is insignificant compared to the cost in animal pain required to obtain it. Indeed, no less a figure than Harold Feinberg, the chairperson of the American Accreditation for the Care of Laboratory Animals Committee, has stated that "the testing of cosmetics is frivolous and should be abolished."[6]

[8] A fifth argument seeks to remedy this deficiency of the Knowledge Argument. Here is the Important Knowledge Argument.

1. If a practice produces important knowledge, then it is morally permissible.
2. Unlimited use of animals for scientific purposes would produce important knowledge.
3. Therefore, unlimited use of animals for scientific purposes is morally permissible.

The Important Knowledge Argument fares no better than the Knowledge Argument. Consider an example. Surely it cannot be denied that it is important to know what substances are carcinogenic in humans. But animal tests for carcinogenicity in humans are often inconclusive. For example, in recent years there has been great controversy over whether one can infer that saccharin or oral contraceptives are carcinogenic in humans on the basis of data collected in animal tests. Some have argued that because of the methods used in such research, such an inference cannot be made.[7] Massive doses are administered to rats and mice in these studies over short periods of time; there is no reason to believe that human cancers develop in response to similar conditions. Moreover, unlike humans, rats and mice tend spontaneously to develop a high incidence of tumors. One prominent medical journal remarked with respect to the oral contraceptive controversy:

> It is difficult to see how experiments on strains of animals so exceedingly liable to develop tumors of these various kinds can throw useful light on the carcinogenicity of a compound for man.[8]

If, however, we were to adopt the policy of unlimited use of *humans*, we could conclusively determine which substances are carcinogenic in humans. Moreover, such a policy would be sanctioned by the Important Knowledge Argument, since unlimited toxicology testing and experimentation on humans would unquestionably produce important knowledge. If the production of important knowledge makes a practice permissible, then unlimited testing and experimenting on humans is permissible. But again, this is a repugnant conclusion. If we are unwilling to accept it, we must give up the Important Knowledge Argument. If, on the other hand, we are willing to accept it, then most and possibly all toxicology tests and experiments carried out on animals in the name of human interests are unnecessary, since better models, namely humans, are available....

II.

[9] The No Use Position holds that no use of any animal for any scientific purpose is ever permissible. Is this position rationally defensible? We think not. We propose to argue for this conclusion in ways analogous to the case made against the Unlimited Use Position. We shall characterize some representative arguments for this position, indicating where and why these arguments go wrong.

[10] Before addressing these arguments, it is worth noting that the reasonableness of the No Use Position does not follow from the inadequacy of the Unlimited Use Position, any more than it follows, say, that no men are bald because it is false that all men are. Those who accept the No Use Position may take some comfort in our critique of the Unlimited Use Position, but they cannot infer from that critique that their own position is on the side of the truth.

[11] We shall discuss four arguments for the No Use Position. Here is the Pain Argument.

1. If an action causes pain to another being, then it is not morally permissible.
2. The use of animals for scientific purposes causes animals pain.
3. Therefore, no use of any animal for any scientific purpose is morally permissible.

We should note first that not all scientific uses made of animals cause them pain. For example, some experimental uses of animals involve operant conditioning techniques, and most of these do not cause pain at all. Other experiments call for minor modifications in animals' diets or environments. Still others require killing anesthetized animals. The Pain Argument does not provide a basis for objecting to any of these uses of animals. Because the Pain Argument cites no morally relevant consideration in addition to pain, it cannot provide a thorough-going defense of the No Use Position.

[12] More importantly, the Pain Argument is defective from the outset. Contrary to what the first premise states, it is sometimes permissible to cause pain to others. Dentists cause pain. Surgeons cause pain. Wrestlers, football players, boxers cause pain. But it does not follow that these individuals do

something that is not permissible. Granted, the presumption is always against someone's causing pain; nevertheless, causing pain is not itself sufficient for judging an act impermissible.

[13] Suppose, however, that, unlike the case of dentists, pain is caused against one's will or without one's informed consent. Does it follow that what we've done is wrong? This is what the Informed Consent Argument alleges. Here is the argument.

1. If an action causes pain to another being without that being's informed consent, then it is not morally permissible.
2. The use of animals for scientific purposes causes animals pain without their informed consent.
3. Therefore, no use of any animal for any scientific purpose is morally permissible.

The second premise is open to the same objections raised against the corresponding premise in the Pain Argument: Not all scientific uses made of animals cause them pain. Thus, one cannot object to every use made of animals on this ground. Besides, animals are not the sort of beings who *can* give or withhold their informed consent. Explanations of what will be done to them in an experiment or test cannot be understood by them, so there is no possibility of "informing" them. Thus, there is no coherent possibility of causing them pain "without their informed consent."

[14] The first premise also falls short of the truth. Suppose that a small child has appendicitis. If not operated on, the condition will worsen and she will die. Scary details omitted, the situation is explained to the child. She will have none of it: "No operation for me," we are told. The operation is performed without the child's consent and causes some amount of pain. Was it wrong to perform the operation? It is preposterous to answer affirmatively. Thus, we have a counterexample to the basic assumption of the Informed Consent Argument, the assumption that it is not permissible to cause others pain without their informed consent.

[15] Still, one might say that there is a difference between hurting others (causing them pain) and harming them (doing something that is detrimental to their welfare). Moreover, it might be suggested that in the example of the child and appendicitis, what we've stumbled upon is the fact that something that hurts might not harm. Accordingly, it might be held that what is always wrong is not causing pain, or causing others pain without their informed consent; rather, what is always wrong is harming others. This suggestion gains additional credence when we observe that even a painless death can be a great harm to a given individual. These considerations suggest another argument. Here is the Harm argument.

1. If an action harms another being, then it is not morally permissible.
2. The use of animals for scientific purposes harms animals.
3. Therefore, no use of any animal for any scientific purpose is morally permissible.

This argument, like the ones before it, has gaping holes in it. First, it is clear that it will not even serve as a basis for opposing all animal experimentation, since not all animal experimentation harms animals. More fundamentally, it is simply not true that it is always wrong to harm another. Suppose that while walking alone at night, you are attacked and that through luck or skill you repel your assailant who falls beneath your defensive blows, breaks his neck, and is confined to bed from that day forth, completely paralyzed from the neck down. We mince words if we deny that what you did harmed your assailant. Yet we do not say that what you did is therefore wrong. After all, you were innocent; you were just minding your own business. Your assailant, on the other hand, hardly qualifies as innocent. He attacked you. It would surely be an unsatisfactory morality that failed to discriminate between what you as an innocent victim may do in self-defense, and what your attacker can do in offense against your person or your property. Thus despite the initial plausibility of the first premise of the Harm Argument, not all cases of harming another are impermissible.

[16] The difficulties with the Harm Argument suggest a fourth argument, the Innocence Argument.

1. If an action causes harm to an innocent individual, then it is not permissible, no matter what the circumstances.
2. Animals are innocent.
3. The use of animals for scientific purposes harms them.
4. Therefore, no use of any animal for any scientific purpose is morally permissible.

This argument, unlike the Harm Argument, can account for the case of the assailant, since by attacking you the assailant ceases to be innocent, and therefore in harming him you have not wronged him. In this respect if in no other, the Innocence Argument marks a genuine improvement over the Harm Argument. Nevertheless, problems remain. Again, since animals are not always harmed when used for scientific purposes, the Innocence Argument does not provide a foundation for the No Use Position. It could also be argued that animals cannot be viewed as innocent. We shall return to this issue in the following section. The more fundamental question, however, is whether the basic assumption of this argument is correct: Is it always wrong to harm an innocent individual, no matter what the circumstances?

[17] Here we reach a point where philosophical opinion is sharply divided. Some philosophers evidently are prepared to answer this question affirmatively.[9] Others, ourselves included, are not. One way to argue against an affirmative answer to this question is to highlight, by means of more or less far-fetched hypothetical examples, what the implications of an affirmative answer would be. The use of such "thought-experiments" is intended to shed light on the gray areas of our thought by asking how alternative positions would view far-fetched hypothetical cases. The hope is that we may then return to the more complex situations of everyday life with a better understanding of how to reach the best judgment in these cases. So let us construct a thought-experiment, and indicate how it can be used to contest the view that it is always wrong to harm an innocent individual, no matter what the circumstances. (A second thought-experiment will be undertaken near the beginning of Part III.)

[18] Imagine this case.[10] Together with four other friends, you have gone caving (spelunking) along the Pacific coast. The incoming tide catches your group by surprise and you are faced with the necessity of making a quick escape through the last remaining accessible opening to the cave or else all will drown. Unfortunately, the first person to attempt the escape gets wedged in the opening. All efforts to dislodge him, including his own frantic attempts, are unsuccessful. It so happens that one member of your party has brought dynamite along, so that the means exist to widen the opening. However to use the explosive to enlarge the escape route is certain to kill your trapped friend. The situation, then, is this: If the explosive is used, then it is certain that one will die and likely that four will escape unharmed. If the explosive is not used, it is certain that all five will die. All the persons involved are innocent. What ought to be done? Morally speak-

ing, is it permissible to use the dynamite despite the fact that doing so is certain to harm an innocent person?

[19] Those who think it is always wrong to harm an innocent individual, no matter what the circumstances, must say that using the dynamite would be wrong. But how can this be? If the death of one innocent individual is a bad thing, then the death of considerably more than one innocent individual must be that much worse. Accordingly, if it is claimed that you would be doing wrong if you performed an act that brought about the death of one innocent individual *because it is wrong to act in ways that harm an innocent individual*, then it must be a more grievous wrong for you to act in ways that will bring equivalent harm to a greater number of innocent individuals. But if this is so, then we have reason to deny that it is always wrong to harm an innocent individual, *no matter what the circumstances*. What our thought experiment suggests is that it is possible that some circumstances might be so potentially bad that morality will permit us to harm an innocent individual. In the thought-experiment it would be permissible to use the dynamite.

[20] Those who incline toward viewing the prohibition against harming the innocent as absolute, admitting of no exceptions whatever, are not likely to be persuaded to give up this view just by the weight of the argument of the previous paragraphs. The debate will—and should—continue. One point worth making, however, is that those who like ourselves do not view this prohibition as absolute can nevertheless regard it as very serious, just as, for example, one can view the obligation to keep one's promises as a very serious moral requirement without viewing it as absolute. Imagine that you have borrowed a chainsaw from a friend, promising to return it whenever he asks for it. Imagine he turns up at your door in a visibly drunken state, accompanied by a bound and gagged companion who has already been severely beaten and is in a state of terror. "I'll have my chainsaw now," he intones. Ought you to return it, under *those* circumstances? The obligation to keep one's promises can be regarded as quite serious without our having to say, yes, by all means, you ought to fetch the chainsaw! There are other considerations that bear on the morality of what you ought to do in addition to the fact that you have made a promise. Similarly, the fact that some action will harm an innocent individual is not the only consideration that is relevant to assessing the morality of that action. In saying this we do not mean to suggest that this consideration is not an important one. It is, and we shall attempt to develop its importance more fully in the following section. All that we mean to say is that it is not the only morally relevant consideration.

[21] There would appear to be cases, then, whether they be far-fetched hypothetical ones or ones that might arise in the real world, in which morality permits us to harm an innocent individual. Thus, even in those cases in which animals used for scientific purposes are harmed, and even assuming that they are innocent, it does not follow that how they are used is morally wrong. Like the other arguments reviewed in this section, the Innocence Argument fails to provide an acceptable basis for the No Use Position. Assuming, as we do, that these arguments provide a fair representation of those available to advocates of this position, we conclude that the No Use Position lacks a rationally compelling foundation, either in fact, or in logic, or in morality....

Notes

1. Readers are referred to Tom Regan's *The Case for Animal Rights* (CA: University of California Press, 1983) for a sustained presentation of his current

views, which differ in important ways from what they will find in the following paper. Dale Jamieson's updated views are presented in *Morality's Progress: Essays on Humans, Other Animals, and the Rest of Nature* (Oxford: Clarendon Press, 2003); see, in particular, essays 9 and 10.
2. For documentation and additional information see J. Diner, *Physical and Mental Suffering of Experimental Animals* (Washington: Animal Welfare Institute, 1979); and R. Ryder, *Victims of Science* (London: Davis-Poynter, 1975).
3. As quoted in L. Rosenfield, *From Animal Machine to Beast Machine* (New York: Octagon Books, 1968) p. 54.
4. In January 1981 Revlon, Inc. the world's largest cosmetics manufacturer, announced that it had awarded Rockefeller University $750,000 to research and develop an alternative to the Draize test. The company also granted $25,000 to establish a trust, the purpose of which is to fund further research into alternatives. Thus other cosmetic companies can join Revlon's pioneering move— (this is the first time a commercial firm has funded the search for alternatives to the use of live animals for testing)—by the simple expedient of contributing to the trust. The political realities being what they are, chances are good that Revlon's efforts will soon be imitated by other firms in the cosmetics industry. Revlon's actions were prompted by an uncommonly well organized campaign, involving more than four hundred separate animal welfare related organizations, conducted over a two year period. Through meetings with representatives of Revlon, through the media, through petitions to the Congress, through letter writing campaigns, and through protest marches and rallies, the Coalition to Stop the Draize Rabbit Blinding Tests, Inc. helped to persuade Revlon to take its revolutionary step. The Coalition's success gives a clear demonstration of what can be done on behalf of animals and what must be done to succeed. When the money required to seek alternatives is on hand, there will be no lack of persons willing to do it.
5. M. Weil and R. Scala, "A Study of Intra- and Inter-Laboratory Variability in the Results of Rabbit Eye and Skin and Irritation Tests," *Toxicology and Applied Pharmacology* 19 (1971), pp. 271–360.
6. Dr. Feinberg made this claim while serving on a panel discussion on animal experimentation, sponsored by the Anti-Cruelty Society of Chicago, in October 1980.
7. Some of these issues are explored in a rather extreme way in S. Epstein, *The Politics of Cancer* (Garden City: Anchor Press/Doubleday, 1979).
8. *British Medical Journal*, October 28, 1972, p. 190. We have taken this example as well as several others from Deborah Mayo's unpublished paper, "Against a Scientific Justification of Animal Experiments."
9. Baruch Brody is apparently one such philosopher. See his *Abortion and the Sanctity of Life: A Philosophical View* (Cambridge: The MIT Press, 1974).
10. The example is given by the contemporary American philosopher, Richard Brandt in his essay "A Moral Principle About Killing," in Marvin Kohl, ed., *Beneficent Euthanasia* (Buffalo: Prometheus Books, 1972). The philosophical propriety of using more or less unusual hypothetical examples in assessing moral principles is critically discussed by the contemporary English philosopher G.E.M. Anscombe in her "Modern Moral Philosophy," *Philosophy*, 33 (1958), reprinted in Judith J. Thomson and Gerald Dworkin, eds., *Ethics* (New York: Harper & Row, 1968).

Suggested Readings

J. Diner, *Physical and Mental Suffering of Experimental Animals* (Washington: The Animal Welfare Institute, 1978).

G. Holton and R. Morrison, eds., *The Limits of Scientific Inquiry* (New York: W.W. Norton and Co., 1978).

T. Regan and P. Singer, eds., *Animal Rights and Human Obligations* (Englewood Cliffs: Prentice-Hall, 1976).

A. Rowan, *Alternatives to Laboratory Animals: Definition and Discussion* (Washington: The Institute for the Study of Animal Problems, 1980).

R. Ryder, *Victims of Science* (London: Davis-Poynter, 1975).

H. Salt, *Animals' Rights in Relation to Social Progress* (Clark's Summit, PA: Society for Animal Rights, 1980).

P. Singer, *Animal Liberation* (New York: Avon Books, 1975).

D. Smyth, *Alternatives to Animal Experiments* (London: The Scholar Press, 1978).

J. Vyvyan, *The Dark Face of Science* (Levittown, NY: Transatlantic Arts, 1972).

Questions

1. (a) Of the products you generally buy, do you know which ones have been tested on animals?
   (b) Of the companies you may seek employment with, do you know which ones use animals to test the safety of their products?
   (c) Do you know how you can find out these things?
2. (a) Of the six arguments supporting *unlimited* use of animals (note that only three are presented in the excerpt),
      (i) which has been rendered unsound because one of its premises is now known to be false?
      (ii) which might certain religionists find convincing?
      (iii) which might appeal to natural law theorists?
   (b) Do Jamieson and Regan make the same objection to both the Knowledge Argument and the Important Knowledge Argument?
3. With regard to the four arguments supporting *no* use of animals...
   (a) Enrich Jamieson and Regan's objection by articulating the conditions necessary for permissible pain-causing (i.e., *when* is causing pain morally acceptable?).
   (b) (i) Jamieson and Regan say that "animals are not the sort of beings who can give or withhold their informed consent" (para 13). Do you agree—for all (nonhuman) animals?
       (ii) Enrich the authors' objection by articulating the conditions necessary for permissible pain-causing that is without consent (i.e., *when* is it morally acceptable to cause pain even though you don't have consent?).
   (c) The authors' example to refute the Harm Argument involves pain and self-defence as a motive/intent. Can you think of an example of morally permissible harm that does not involve pain (but is nevertheless harmful) and uses a different motive/intent?
   (d) Would you use the dynamite?

Trans Fat Bans and Human Freedom

David Resnik

Abstract

A growing body of evidence has linked consumption of trans fatty acids to cardiovascular disease. To promote public health, numerous state and local governments in the United States have banned the use of artificial trans fats in restaurant foods, and additional bans may follow. Although these policies may have a positive impact on human health, they open the door to excessive government control over food, which could restrict dietary choices, interfere with cultural, ethnic, and religious traditions, and exacerbate socioeconomic inequalities. These slippery slope concerns cannot be dismissed as far-fetched, because the social and political pressures are in place to induce additional food regulations. To protect human freedom and other values, policies that significantly restrict food choices, such as bans on types of food, should be adopted only when they are supported by substantial scientific evidence, and when policies that impose fewer restrictions on freedom, such as educational campaigns and product labeling, are likely to be ineffective.

[1] Trans fatty acids (or trans fats) are unsaturated *trans*-isomer fatty acids, which may be monosaturated or polyunsaturated. Small amounts of trans fats occur naturally in meat and dairy products, but the largest source of these lipids in the human diet comes from artificial sources, such as partially hydrogenated vegetable oils used in cooking and food preparation (Institute of Medicine 2002). Trans fats became popular with food manufacturers, bakeries, and restaurants in the 1960s, because they can enhance the taste of some foods and help to preserve texture. Trans fats used in frying also are more durable than other types of oils and have a neutral taste (Severson 2003).

[2] A growing body of evidence has linked consumption of trans fats to cardiovascular disease (Woodside et al. 2008). According to a meta-analysis of four prospective cohort studies, a 2% increase in energy uptake from trans fats is associated with a 23% increased risk of cardiovascular disease. Trans fats are also associated with sudden death from cardiac causes (Mozaffarian et al. 2006). Trans fats are thought to promote cardiovascular disease by increasing levels of low-density lipoprotein (LDL or "bad") cholesterol in the blood and decreasing levels of high-density lipoprotein (HDL or "good") cholesterol (Institute of Medicine 2002; Ascherio 2006). According to some experts, replacing artificial trans fats with healthier oils, such as olive oil or canola oil, could save 30,000 to 100,000 lives per year in the United States (American Medical Association 2008).

---

* *The American Journal of Bioethics* 10.3 (2010): 27–32.

[3] In January 2006, the Food and Drug Administration (FDA) required that nutrition labels on foods include information about trans fat content (Food and Drug Administration 2006). The FDA estimates that trans fat labeling could save up to 500 lives per year in the United States by reducing the incidence of cardiovascular disease (Food and Drug Administration 2006). Consumer groups and public health organizations have argued that product labeling is not a sufficient response to the problem posed by trans fats, and that there should be a ban on all artificial trans fats in food (Ban Trans Fats 2009; Center for Science in the Public Interest 2008; American Medical Association 2008). Several major cities and counties (New York City, Boston, Philadelphia, King County, WA, and Nassau Country, NY), the state of California, and Puerto Rico have heeded this call and passed laws banning the use of artificial trans fats in restaurant food. More bans are likely to follow (Steinhauer 2008; Center for Science in the Public Interest 2008).

[4] While many view trans fat bans as an important policy tool for promoting public health, others are disturbed by the government's encroachment on freedom and autonomy. ABC News's John Stossell writes, "This week, New York became the first big city to ban trans fats. Gee, I'm all for good health, but shouldn't it be a matter of individual choice?" David White (2007) expresses a similar sentiment: "Like smoking, the choice to eat high-calorie foods might not always be prudent. But government prohibition of that choice is a remarkable confiscation of freedom." National newspaper columnist Walter Williams raises slippery slope concerns:

> The nation's food zealots have...started out with a small target—a ban on restaurant use of trans fats. Here's what I predict is their true agenda: If banning a fat that's only two percent of our daily caloric intake is wonderful, why not ban saturated fats, the intake of which is much higher? Then there's the size of restaurant servings. Instead of a law simply requiring restaurants to label the calories in a meal, there will be laws setting a legal limit on portions. (Williams 2007)

[5] Should we embrace trans fat bans as a sound public policy or should we be wary of this strategy for controlling the human diet? Are trans fat bans the best thing since sliced bread or the road to food fascism? In this essay I examine the ethical arguments for and against trans fat bans (i.e., bans on trans fats in foods prepared by restaurants or other commercial food producers). I argue that while trans fat bans may help to improve public health, they represent a worrisome policy trend, because they open the door to further restrictions on food. Though few people will mourn the loss of artificial trans fats from restaurant food, the issue here is much larger than that. At stake is a freedom that most of us exercise every day but often take for granted: the freedom to choose what we eat.

Arguments for Trans Fat Bans

Public Health Promotion

[6] The two main arguments for trans fat bans are consequentialist in form. According to the first argument, trans fat bans are justified in order to promote an important social good, public health. Trans fat bans can promote public health by reducing the consumption of trans fats, which could reduce the incidence and severity of cardiovascular disease. According to one estimate, totally eliminating artificial trans fats from the food supply in the United States would save 50,000 lives per year (Center for Science and the Public Interest 2008). Trans fat bans are cut from the same cloth as other laws that safeguard the food supply, such as quality and safety standards for restaurants and food

manufacturers, regulation of food additives, and product labeling requirements (Fortin 2009). Food safety and quality laws help to prevent food manufacturers from harming the public with unsafe or unhealthy products, and they can assist consumers in making healthy choices. Recent events, such as adulteration of powdered milk in China with the industrial chemical melamine, which killed five children and sickened over 300,000, and contamination of peanut butter with *Salmonella* in the United States, which killed nine people and sickened over 570, illustrate the importance of food safety and quality as a public health matter (Barboza 2008; Martin 2009).

[7] The strength of the public health argument depends on the empirical premise that trans fat bans will promote public health. While this assertion is highly plausible, given what we know about the adverse effects of trans fats on the cardiovascular system, it is not indubitable. Because trans fat bans have been in effect for only a few years, very little is known about how they impact public health. One study has shown that mandatory labeling of products with trans fats reduces consumption of trans fats, but there have been no studies on the effects of trans fat bans (Niederdeppe and Frosch 2009). Trans fat bans could, paradoxically, reduce some unhealthy behaviors but encourage others. Many food manufacturers began using artificial trans fats in commercial products during the 1980s and 1990s to reduce the saturated fat and cholesterol content of food, because the medical consensus at that time was that saturated fats and cholesterol are unhealthy. As it turned out, trans fats are much worse for the human heart than saturated fats; some saturated fats, such as those contained in peanut and canola oils, are good for you; and moderate amounts of cholesterol in the diet are essential to health (Severson 2003). While I am not suggesting that there is no scientific basis for reducing the consumption of artificial trans fats, I do think that much more research is needed on the public health effects of trans fat policies, so that we can avoid repeating the nutrition policy mistakes of the past.

Economic Cost-Savings

The second argument for trans fat bans is an economic one. According to this line of thought, bans on artificial trans fats can save potentially billions of dollars in health care and related costs by reducing prevalence and severity of cardiovascular disease (Ban Trans Fats 2009). In the United States, over 80 million people (36% of the population) have cardiovascular disease (American Heart Association 2009). The direct and indirect costs of cardiovascular disease amount to an estimated $305 billion in the United States in 2009 (Centers for Disease Control and Prevention 2009a). If a nationwide ban on artificial trans fats reduced the costs of cardiovascular disease by only 10%, this would save $30 billion per year. [8]

The strength of the economic argument depends on the empirical premise that a trans fats ban will reduce the costs associated with cardiovascular disease. This assertion, like the empirical premise in the public health argument, is also highly plausible, given what we know about the effects of artificial trans fats on human health, but it is not unassailable. Consider the costs of smoking. For many years, health policy analysts have assumed that smoking places enormous economic burdens on society by increasing costs related to lung cancer, pulmonary disease, cardiovascular disease, and other health problems (World Bank 1999). Smoking costs the United States nearly $200 billion per year in health care expenditures and lost productivity (Centers for Disease Control and Prevention 2009b). A recent study examining the lifetime costs of smoking found that smokers actually cost soci- [9]

ety less than nonsmokers, because smokers die earlier. The investigators examined the costs of three cohorts: an obese cohort, a smoking cohort, and a healthy living cohort. The healthy living cohort cost society the most money, because they lived an average of 7 years longer than the smoking cohort and 4.5 years longer than the obese cohort. During those extra years of life, people in the healthy living cohort had costs associated with various diseases of aging, such as bone fractures, arthritis, stroke, dementia, urinary-tract infections, and loss of hearing and vision (van Baal et al. 2008). Some authors have disputed the policy implications of this study because it does not take into account costs of quality-adjusted life years lost (McPherson 2008). The debate over the costs of smoking suggests that we should be careful about making claims about the potential cost-savings of trans fat bans. While there clearly is a factual basis for claiming that trans fat bans can save society a great deal of money, more research is needed on the effects of these policies, including effects on the food industry.

Arguments against Trans Fat Bans

Restrictions of Freedom

[10] The main ethical argument[1] against trans fat bans is that these laws, whether at the local, state, or federal level, constitute an unjustifiable restriction on the freedom to decide what one eats. One could argue that the ability to decide what one eats, though not as important as freedom of speech or religion, is an important freedom nonetheless. First, food has a significant impact on one's quality of life. People take great pleasure in eating, preparing, and serving food. Food is more than mere nutrition: it is one of life's simple pleasures. Second, food has considerable ethnic, cultural, and religious significance. Different ethnic and cultural groups have their own cuisines and culinary practices. In any medium-sized city in the United States, one can find restaurants that serve Chinese, Japanese, Italian, French, Mexican, Indian, and Thai food. There are also many different foods associated with particular geographic regions in the United States, such as Southern fried chicken, Texas barbeque, Boston baked beans, Philadelphia steak sandwiches, and so on. Food also has religious significance, as different faiths have various rules, customs, and teachings related to food (Montanari 2006). Third, food plays an important role in family traditions and customs. Food takes center stage at family reunions and at gatherings associated with particular holidays, such as Thanksgiving, Christmas, and Independence Day. Families also have special recipes handed down from generation to generation. Thus, the freedom to decide what one eats is an important freedom that should not be restricted unnecessarily.

[11] A proponent of trans fat bans can acknowledge that the ability to decide what one eats is an important freedom but still maintain that trans fat bans are justifiable. First, bans on artificial trans fats do not have a major impact on food consumers, since most people do not care whether they eat products that contain these substances. People do not have a special fondness for artificial trans fats, but rather for the foods that contain them. Removing artificial trans fats from cookies, crackers, hamburgers, and French fries will make little difference to consumers as long as this does not affect how these foods taste, smell, look, or feel. Bans on artificial trans fats mostly affect food producers, not consumers.

[12] Second, even if some consumers have a strong preference for artificial trans fats, laws that ban commerce and trade in these substances can be justified to promote public health. As noted earlier, trans fat bans fit into the safety and quality regulatory framework that operates in the United States and other industrialized nations. Banning

trans fats is no different, in principle, from banning food additives that have been found to be unhealthy, such as cyclamate (Henkle 1999). The reasoning that justifies food safety and quality laws is similar to the reasoning that justifies other public health measures that restrict human freedom, such as mandatory vaccinations, disease surveillance, and isolation and quarantine. Though freedom is an important value, it can be overridden in some circumstances to promote important social goals, such as preventing people from harming themselves or others, and promoting the health of the population as a whole (Kass 2001; Childress et al. 2002; Gostin 2007; Buchanan 2008; Gostin and Gostin 2009).

The Slippery Slope

[13] A critic of trans fat bans could acknowledge that not many people have a particular fondness for artificial trans fats and that food safety and quality laws can be justified to promote public health, but could maintain that there is a larger issue at stake here: the continued erosion of dietary freedom. Trans fat bans are very different from food safety and quality laws because they aim to prevent consumers from making unhealthy choices, instead of preventing producers from causing harm. Requiring food manufacturers to ensure that their products are not contaminated with microorganisms that can cause severe illness or death is very different from preventing manufacturers from selling products that increase the risk of cardiovascular disease if consumed for many years, because most people will not voluntarily choose to eat food that is contaminated or spoiled, while people often choose to eat foods that can cause harm if eaten for many years. Bans on the use of trans fats in restaurant food would lead to additional bans on trans fats, which would open the door to further restrictions on the human diet, since there is no difference, in principle, between banning artificial trans fats and banning other unhealthy foods, such as processed meats and sugared drinks. Today, trans fats; tomorrow, hot dogs.

[14] Support for this empirical slippery slope argument comes from the following facts: (1) we already know about the adverse health effects of many foods and science is likely to discover more; (2) health advocates are likely to continue to push for additional regulations; and (3) health-conscious consumers and politicians are likely to be receptive to additional regulations. For example, consumption of red meat and processed meat increases the risk of colon cancer (Johnson and Lund 2007), and consumption of sugared drinks, especially those high in fructose, increases the risk of obesity, diabetes, and heart disease (Brown et al. 2008). Emboldened by victories against trans fats, health advocates could go after red meats, processed meats, sugared drinks, and other unhealthy foods (Chan 2008).

[15] The social consequences of sliding down the slope toward additional food regulation could outweigh any public health gains that might result. Since restrictions on the human diet can impact quality of life, family traditions, and cultural, ethnic, and religious practices, wide-ranging attempts to control food choices could have adverse consequence on society. Few people would want to live in a world in which government health experts dictate what is on the menu or how it should be prepared.

[16] Additionally, increased regulation of the human diet could lead to social and economic injustices. Policies that make it more difficult to obtain affordable nutrition, such as taxes on food, can exacerbate socioeconomic inequalities (Caraher and Cowburn 2005). For example, hot dogs, bologna, and other processed meat products provide an inexpensive form of protein, but they also are high in saturated animal fat, the consumption of which contributes to cardiovascular disease (Woodside et al. 2008).

If the government taxes or bans these foods on the grounds that they contribute to heart disease, then low-income people might need to seek other, more expensive sources of protein.

[17] A standard response to an empirical slippery slope argument is to assert that the slide toward undesirable outcomes can be avoided by implementing rules, procedures, or definitions designed to stabilize policy and practice (Lewis 1999). A proponent of trans fat bans could claim that society can avoid excessive food regulation by distinguishing between bans on food additives and bans on foods. A food additive is a substance added to food to improve taste, texture, flavor, color, or freshness. Bans on cyclamates, which are food additives that enhance sweetness, have not led to bans on foods that enhance sweetness, such as sugar (Henkle 1999). By limiting the scope of trans fat bans to prohibitions on food additives, such as artificial trans fats, society can promote public health while safeguarding other values.

[18] A proponent of trans fat bans could also point out that there are social and economic forces in place that would counteract a move from trans fat bans to bans on other foods. For example, tobacco companies, automobile manufacturers, and many other corporations have mounted influential (and often successful) campaigns against government regulation. The food industry would be a powerful opponent of any attempt to extend the scope of food regulation beyond trans fats.

[19] While I appreciate the merits of these critiques of the empirical slippery slope argument, I am not convinced that they defuse concerns about excessive food regulation. First, the distinction between foods and food additives is not as clear as one might think. Many substances added to improve the taste, texture, flavor, color, or freshness of food, such as sugar, corn syrup, yeast, citric acid, and vitamins, might also be viewed as foods. It is not at all obvious how one could make a conceptually stable distinction between artificial trans fats and other lipids added to foods. A policy framework that focused on specific kinds of fats defined as "food additives" could collapse under social and political pressure for additional food regulation. Second, although there are powerful forces that would resist attempts to extend the scope of food regulation beyond trans fats, it is not clear to me that these forces would be able to hold the line. Restaurants and food connoisseurs who opposed trans fat bans in New York City, California, and other jurisdictions could not resist effective campaigns by public health organizations and consumer groups.

Toward Rational Food Policies

[20] The empirical slippery slope argument developed in the previous section cannot be easily dismissed as a flight of fancy, since it is firmly rooted in existing political, social, economic, and biological realities. To avoid the undesirable outcomes that could occur from excessive government control over the human diet, food policy decisions should be made with an eye toward not only promoting public health but also preserving human freedom. One of the central dilemmas in public health policy is how to balance health promotion and other important values, such as freedom and justice (Kass 2001; Childress et al. 2002; Gostin 2007).

[21] To develop food policies that appropriately balance public health and freedom, and therefore address slippery slope concerns, it will be useful to establish a set of conditions that must be met to restrict human freedom. These conditions can help to ensure that policy decisions will not be made willy-nilly, but will be appropriately articulated, reviewed, and justified (Kass 2001). The following are some conditions that can be applied to

proposed policies that restrict human freedom to promote public health (Childress et al. 2002):

- Effectiveness: there must be substantial scientific evidence that the policy is likely to be effective at achieving an important public health goal.
- Necessity: there must be substantial scientific evidence that the policy is necessary to achieve the public health goal.
- Proportionality: the potential public health gains of the policy must outweigh the adverse social impacts and other moral considerations.
- Least infringement: the policy must impose the least restrictions on freedom necessary to promote the public health goals.
- Publicity: the policy must be justified to the public, with the reasons for restricting freedom clearly explained.

How might these conditions apply to trans fat bans? The trans fat bans enacted by state and local governments may meet three of these conditions. Trans fat bans probably may be effective, because, as mentioned previously, trans fat bans may help to promote public health, though more research is needed. Trans fat bans may also meet the proportionality condition as well, because the public health gains could outweigh adverse social impacts and other moral considerations. Because few people have special preference for artificial trans fats, trans fat bans probably do not have a significant impact on quality of life, cultural, ethnic, or religious traditions, or family values. Trans fat bans will not exacerbate socioeconomic inequalities by increasing the price of food, though more research is needed to verify this point. Trans fat bans also meet the publicity condition, because they have been discussed and debated at government hearings, public comment meetings, and other public forums (Mello 2009).

The trans fat bans that have been enacted thus [22] far may not meet the other two conditions, however. The bans may not meet the necessity condition, because a combination of other policies, such as education and mandatory labeling, may be equally effective at achieving public health goals. Proponents of trans fat bans have asserted that they are necessary, because the other methods for promoting public health are not effective enough, since consumers may not understand the risks of trans fats or heed warnings or advice (Ban Trans Fats 2009). However, this claim rings hollow, because bans have been imposed before public education and food labeling have been given a chance to work. Trans fats have only been on the public's radar screen since about 2001. Prior to this time, people were more concerned about saturated fats in the diet (Severson 2003). FDA labeling and voluntary labeling by fast food restaurants began in 2006, but the movement to ban trans fats began before then. Admittedly, educational campaigns and product labeling may prove to be ineffective, but then again, they may not. The important point is that we simply do not have enough evidence at this time to declare that educational campaigns and product labeling will fail and that some other policies are necessary.

If it turns out that other methods of decreas- [23] ing the consumption of trans fats are as effective as bans, then trans fat bans also do not meet the least infringement condition as well. To develop this point, it will be useful to classify different trans fat policies with respect to how much they restrict human freedom. Education involves virtually no restriction on freedom, because the objectives of education are to convey information and enhance decision-making, not to manipulate or control individual choices. Mandatory food labeling is more restrictive than education, because labeling controls the decisions made by food producers, even though this helps to promote effective decision making by consumers. Taxation is more restrictive than labeling because it can place financial constraints on decisions made by food producers and consumers. Food safety and quality standards are highly restrictive, because they require food producers to follow specific rules, and impose penalties for noncompliance. Bans on particular food items are the most restrictive methods of promoting public health, because bans prevent people from making some types of dietary choices and they prevent food producers from selling particular types of foods.

[24] Thus, although trans fat bans probably will help to promote public health, a convincing argument can be made that governments have enacted these policies without determining whether other policies, which do not significantly restrict human freedom, are effective at promoting public health. A better way of dealing with the trans fat problem would be give education and product labeling a chance to work, before resorting to the extreme measure of banning trans fats. By enacting food policies that limit the freedom to choose what one eats only as an option of last resort, the government can strike a fair balance between promoting public health and protecting human freedom (Wikler 1978; Mytton 2007).

Conclusion

[25] While it is clear that consumption of artificial trans fats poses a significant risk to human health, it is not clear how societies should respond to this risk. Numerous state and local governments in the United States have banned the use of artificial trans fats in restaurant foods, and other bans may follow. Although these policies may have a positive impact on human health, they open the door to excessive government control over food, which could restrict dietary choices, interfere with cultural, ethnic, and religious traditions, and exacerbate socioeconomic inequalities. These slippery slope concerns cannot be dismissed as far-fetched, because the social and political pressures are in place to induce additional food regulations. To protect human freedom and other values, policies that significantly restrict food choices, such as bans on types of food, should be adopted only when they are supported by substantial scientific evidence and when policies that impose fewer restrictions on freedom, such educational campaigns and product labeling, are likely to be ineffective.

Note

1. Mello (2009) has examined some of the legal issues concerning the trans fat policies adopted by New York City and other cities and states, including preemption by federal laws and insufficient opportunities for public comment. According to Mello, one of the problems with local policymaking on trans fats is that this could create a patchwork of rules that will create compliance problems for businesses and spark legal battles over preemption issues. Though Mello raises some important legal issues, her analysis does not get to the heart of the matter, since she does not voice any ethical objections to trans fat laws. Rather, her article supports the view that trans fat policies should be made at the federal level, not the local or state level.

References

American Heart Association. 2009. Heart disease and stroke statistics, 2009. Available at: http://www.americanheart.org/downloadable/heart/1240250946756LS-1982%20Heart%20and%20Stroke%20Update.042009.pdf (accessed May 31, 2009).

American Medical Association. 2008. AMA supports ban of artificial trans fats in restaurants and bakeries nationwide. Press Release, November 10. Available at: http://www.ama-assn.org/ama/pub/category/20273.html (accessed June 2, 2009).

Ascherio A. 2006. Trans fatty acids and blood lipids. *Atherosclerosis* Suppl. 7(2): 25–27.

Ban Trans Fats. 2009. Available at: http://www.bantransfats.com (accessed June 2, 2009).

Barboza, D. 2008. China begins trial for 9 in tainted milk scandal. *New York Times*, December 30, p. A8.

Bren, L. 2004. Got milk? Make sure it's pasteurized. *FDA Consumer Magazine* September–October. Available at: http://www.fda.govfdac/features/2004/504 milk.html (accessed June 2, 2009).

Brown, C., A. Dulloo, and J. Montani. 2008. Sugary drinks in the pathogenesis of obesity and cardiovascular diseases. *International Journal of Obesity (London)* 32(Suppl. 6): S28–S34.

Buchanan, D. 2008. Autonomy, paternalism, and justice: Ethical priorities in public health. *American Journal of Public Health* 98: 15–21.

Caraher, M., and G. Cowburn. 2005. Taxing food: Implications for public health nutrition. *Public Health and Nutrition* 8: 1242–1249.

Center for Science in the Public Interest. 2008. Trans fat: On the way out! Available at: http://www.cspinet.org/transfat (accessed June 2, 2009).

Centers for Disease Control and Prevention. 2009a. Chronic disease prevention and health promotion. Available at: http://www.cdc.gov/NCCDPHP/publications/AAG/dhdsp text.htm#2 (accessed May 31, 2009).

Centers for Diseases Control and Prevention. 2009b. Economic facts about. U.S. tobacco use and tobacco production. Available at http://www.cdc.gov/tobacco/data statistics/fact sheets/economics/econfacts/index.htm (accessed May 31, 2009).

Chan, S. 2008. A tax on many soft drinks sets off a spirited debate. *New York Times*, December 16, p. A36.

Childress, J., R. Faden, R. Gaare, L. Gostin, J. Kahn, R. Bonnie, N. Kass, A. Mastroianni, J. Moreno, and P. Nieburg. 2002. Public health ethics: Mapping the terrain. *Journal of Law, Medicine & Ethics* 30: 170–178.

Fast Food News. 2006. McDonald's unveils nutrition labeling. February 8. Available at: http://www.foodfacts.info/blog/2006/02/mcdonalds-unveils-nutrition-labeling.html (accessed June 2, 2009).

Food and Drug Administration. 2006. Questions and answers about trans fat nutrition labeling. Available at: http://www.cfsan.fda.gov/~dms/qatrans2.html#s5q5 (accessed June 2, 2009).

Fortin, N. 2009. *Food regulation*. New York: Wiley.

Gostin. L. 2007. General justifications for public health regulation. *Public Health* 121: 829–834.

Gostin, L., and K. Gostin. 2009. A broader liberty: J.S. Mill, paternalism and the public's health. *Public Health* 123: 214–221.

Henkel, J. 1999. Sugar substitutes: Americans opt for sweetness and lite. *FDA Consumer Magazine* November-December. Available at: http://www.fda.gov/FDAC/features/1999/699sugar.html (accessed June 2, 2009).

Institute of Medicine. 2002. Letter report for dietary reference intakes for trans fatty acids. Available at: http://www.iom.edu/Object.File/Master/13/083/TransFattyAcids.pdf (accessed June 2, 2009).

Johnson, I., and E. Lund. 2007. Review article: Nutrition, obesity and colorectal cancer. *Alimentary Pharmacological Therapy* 26(2): 161–181.

Kass, N. 2001. An ethics framework for public health. *American Journal of Public Health* 91: 1776–1782.

Lewis, P. 2007. The empirical slippery slope from voluntary to non-voluntary euthanasia. *Journal of Law, Medicine & Ethics* 35: 197–210.

Martin A. 2009. Peanut plant says audits declared it in top shape. *New York Times*, February 5, p. B10.

McPherson, K. 2008. Does preventing obesity lead to reduced health-care costs? *PLoS Medicine* 5(2): e37.

Mello, M. 2009. New York City's war on fat. *New England Journal of Medicine* 360: 2015–2020.

Montanari, M. 2006. *Food is culture*. New York: Columbia University Press.

Mozaffarian, D., M. Katan, A. Ascherio, M. Stampfer, and W. Willett. 2006. Trans fatty acids and cardiovascular disease. *New England Journal of Medicine* 354: 1601–1613.

Mytton, O., A. Gray, M. Rayner, and H. Rutter. 2007. Could targeted food taxes improve health? *Journal of Epidemiology and Community Health* 61: 689–694.

Niederdeppe, J., and D. Frosch. 2009. News coverage and sales of products with trans fat: Effects before and after changes in federal labeling policy. *American Journal of Preventative Medicine* 36: 395–401.

Severson, K. 2003. *The trans fat solution.* Berkeley, CA: Ten Speed Press.

Steinhauer, J. 2008. California bars restaurant use of trans fats. *New York Times,* July 26, p. A1.

Stossell, J. 2006. Trans fat ban is 'Nanny State' intrusion. *ABC News*, December 6. Available at: http://abcnews.go.com/2020/story?id=2705411&page=1 (accessed June 2, 2009).

van Baal, P., J. Polder, G. de Wit, R. Hoogenveen, T. Feenstra, H. Boshuizen, P. Engelfriet, and W. Brouwer. 2008. Lifetime medical costs of obesity: prevention no cure for increasing health expenditure. *PLoS Medicine* 5(2): e29.

White, D. 2006. Take two servings of paternalism. *The American* December 21. Available at: http://american.com/archive/2006/december/take-two-servings-of-paternalism (accessed June 2, 2009).

Wikler, D. 1978. Persuasion and coercion for health: Ethical issues in government efforts to change lifestyles. *Millbank Memorial Fund Quarterly/Health and Society* 56(3): 303–338.

Williams, W. 2007. Trans fat ban. Townhall.com, January 10. Available at: http://townhall.com/columnists/walterewilliams/2007/01/10/trans_fat_ban (accessed June 2, 2009).

Woodside, J., M. McKinley, and I. Young. 2008. Saturated and trans fatty acids and coronary heart disease. *Current Atherosclerosis Reports* 10(6): 460–466.

World Bank. 1999. Curbing the epidemic: Governments and the economics of tobacco control. Development in Practice Series. Washington, DC: World Bank. Available at: http://www1.worldbank.org/tobacco/reports.htm (accessed June 2, 2009).

Questions

1. (a) What reasons does Resnik give to support a trans fat ban?
   (b) What reasons does Resnik give to reject a trans fat ban?
2. (a) What rights does "business" have?
   (b) If you support the ban, what reasons trump the rights of business? Explain why.
   (c) If you reject the ban, what rights of business trump the given reasons? Explain why.
3. Walter Olson ("The FDA's Trans Fat Ban: Their Laws, Your Body," *Cato at Liberty*, June 16, 2015) calls the ban "frank paternalism." Do you agree? Why/why not?
4. So-called "fast food" is often lumped together with tobacco, alcohol, guns, and casinos.
   (a) In what important ways are any of the listed business products/services similar?
   (b) In what important ways are any of the listed business products/services *dis*similar?

Case Study: Personal Watercraft (PWCs)

The Montreal-based company Bombardier, along with Kawasaki and Yamaha, is a leading manufacturer of personal watercrafts (PWCs—perhaps more commonly known by their brand names, Sea-Doos, Jetskis, and WaveRunners, respectively).

Since the 1990s, when they first became popular, they have been subject to severe criticism for safety issues. First, PWCs didn't have brakes: "The owner's manual for [the] Kawasaki Ultra-150 says 'Leave 348 feet to come to a stop.' That's longer than a football field..." (Rockwell).

Second, also because of the way they were designed, as soon as you cut the throttle, you lost all steering: "When the throttle is off, a speeding jet ski is like a car on ice. It can't stop. It can't turn. The driver has no control" (Rockwell):

> "It wouldn't turn! It wouldn't turn!" cried a PWC driver after she tried unsuccessfully to avoid running into her friend at 30 mph, killing her. Another turned his friend into a quadriplegic. Yet another killed her own five-year-old daughter, who was playing in two feet of water at the beach.

PWCs are designed to travel at speeds in excess of 100 km/h; in the mid-1980s, their engines maxed out at 32hp, but now they max out at 150hp (which is more than that in most cars). Unlike other watercraft, because of their hull and engine design, they can travel at high speeds in shallow water and confined areas, where there are likely to be swimmers, paddlers, and wildlife (which are often displaced, if not killed). Water spray almost guarantees operators' reduced visibility. And, unlike cars and motorcycles, which are required to drive on roads in prescribed lanes, PWCs can go all over the place: they can zig zag, go in circles, turn right, turn left—and there's no way to anticipate where they'll go next because they don't have blinkers. What does one expect to happen with such random, visibility-impaired, high-speed driving?

In fact, PWCs *are* involved in a disproportionately high number of injuries and fatalities. In Canada, from 1991 to 2008, 25 per cent of all recreational boating "trauma deaths" involved PWCs (and it's unlikely that PWCs account for 25 per cent of all registered water vessels—no statistic could be found); 52 per cent of those were the result of a collision (Transport Canada). In the US, from 1996 to 2000, PWCs accounted for only 6.5 per cent of all registered water vessels, but 32 per cent of all boating accidents involved PWCs and 55 per cent of all vessel-on-vessel collisions involved PWCs (Jenkins).

Due to market demand, by 2006, all sit-down PWCs had rudders attached to the jet nozzle, providing some off-throttle steering capacity. In 2009, Bombardier put brakes on some of their Sea-Doos, enabling them to stop in one-half to one-third the distance of the previous models. However, thousands of the older models are, of course, still in use on lakes across Canada.

Not only are PWCs responsible for such immediate harm and injury. One hour of operation releases two gallons of uncombusted fuel into the water. You may as well stand at the end of your dock and pour two gallons of gas into the lake. Jenkins reports that driving a PWC for one hour pollutes the air as much as driving a car for a year. PWC fumes contain carbon monoxide, formaldehyde, and benzene (a carcinogen), known to cause headaches, dizziness, and nausea to anyone within range (for example, swimmers and paddlers).

In addition, the sound of a PWC (and other two-stroke engines, such as those in chainsaws, dirt bikes, and ATVs) registers at around 110dB. For comparison, a garbage truck registers at 100dB. (Keep in mind that the decibel is a logarithmic unit: that 10dB difference means that PWCs are *ten times* as loud as garbage trucks.) The World Health Organization says that 55dB is "highly annoying," continuous exposure to 40–70dB can affect a person's hearing, and hearing protection is recommended even for occasional 85dB noise. Furthermore, the way PWCs are driven means frequently changing pitch and loudness, which is more annoying than a steady pitch and loudness. (Given that sound travels remarkably well across water, this can explain neighbours' screaming and finger gestures as PWCs drive past them.)

Finally, some identify as a design flaw the fact that operators aren't enclosed in any way, so in the case of a collision they're likely to be flung over the handlebars and off the machine.

In 2002, Senator Mira Spivak introduced a bill (Bill S-26, *The Personal Watercraft Act*) that would simply give communities the option of limiting the use of PWCs, much as they can now do with regard to waterskiing. The bill was not passed into law. Subsequent attempts resulted in similar failure. BRP Inc. (in 2003, Bombardier sold its recreational division) aggressively lobbied senators and cabinet ministers to reject the bill. Similarly, Jenkins notes that in the US, "[d]ue to legal threats from PWIA [the Personal Watercraft Industry Association], some localities have been reluctant to prohibit PWC use on waterways." He also points out that the "PWIA and its allies are constantly promoting their agenda and philosophy at meetings of boating-related agencies and organizations."

In response to complaints by PWC operators, Rockwell notes, "[f]ar from being 'singled out unfairly,' personal watercraft are the most protected, privileged vehicles on public waters, operating with tacit permits—a permit to pollute; a permit to make obnoxious noise in violation of laws against disturbing the peace; and a tacit permit to operate outside the traditional 'rules of the road.'"

Captain Brad Cuthbertson, in Hawaii, has been an expert witness in close to 200 PWC product liability lawsuits; in all but three, he reports, an out of court settlement was made. "In each case," Cuthbertson says, "the manufacturer acts like the PWC accident never happened before." Such settlements typically involve a "gag order," and so, Rockwell notes, remain "off the record and out of public scrutiny."

One can hope that PWC drivers change their behaviour, but this is unlikely given that the target market is the same sector of society whose unsafe driving behaviour has led insurance companies to set differentially high premiums just for them. Ads showing strong, muscular men ripping up the water, and telling PWC drivers to "Own the lake!" (Kawasaki) and "Thumb your throttle at the world" (Polaris) don't help.

Sources

Good, Craig. "Personal watercraft: High-speed fun, high-speed defects." 2010. www.plaintiffmagazine.com

Jenkins, David. *Hostile Waters*. American Canoe Association. 2002. http://www.lakeaccess.org/hostile-waters.pdf

Sea-Doo. "Safety Recalls." http://www.sea-doo.ca/owners/safety/safety-recalls.html

Rockwell, Paul. "Why Jetskis Kill: Reckless Endangerment on the Water." http://www.inmotionmagazine.com/opin/jetskis.html

Transport Canada and the Canadian Red Cross Society. "Boating: Immersion and Trauma Deaths in Canada: 18 Years of Research." 2011. http://www.redcross.ca/crc/documents/3-3-4_2011_boating_fnl.pdf

Questions

1. Should Bombardier have marketed their PWC before making the steering and braking modifications? On what grounds do you base your answer?
2. Should they recall all models *without* those modifications? On what grounds do you base your answer?
3. Should they make fuel-emission modifications? On what grounds do you base your answer?
4. Should they make noise-emission modifications? On what grounds do you base your answer?
5. Should the PWIA, or any individual PWC-manufacturer, become involved in debates and other efforts to limit the use of PWCs? To what extent?
6. All things considered, should (and remember, we're talking *morally*) PWC manufacturers insist on a "gag order" when they settle out of court?

CHAPTER FOUR

Employee Rights

What to Do?—IT Tech and/or Hall Monitor?
You're an IT technician. And management wants to implement a "comprehensive, system-wide monitoring" program.

As a result, you're being asked to log employees' keystrokes and their email. You're also being asked to log their browser activity—to keep an actual record of all the sites everyone goes to. Someone else in the department has been asked to spend one day a week looking at the Facebook pages of a number of employees. Yet another person has been asked to track the company's drivers' locations via GPS. What's next, microchipping?

You understand the need to protect the system; if someone's browsing infects the servers, all hell will break loose. But that sort of thing can be stopped with website blocks. And you understand the need to maintain a certain level of productivity. Surfing the net *is* a time-waster. And addictive. But you're not the hall monitor.

And you're certainly not a cop. Yet you're being asked to watch for illegal behaviour as well.

Worse, you're being asked to lie to your co-workers about it. You're not supposed to tell them what you're monitoring. But, you think, wouldn't telling them be *more* effective? If they *knew* they were being watched, wouldn't they be less likely to do things they shouldn't?

If they start to get suspicious—in fact, several people are already quickly clicking and closing sites when you just happen to walk by—your "real" job will be that much more difficult and much less pleasant.

What do you decide to do?

Introduction
If you've read the subsection on rights theories in Part II, you'll know that "*what* rights?" and "on what *basis*?" are two of the first questions that need to be answered if we are to discuss employee rights.

But even before that, you should wonder "why *employee* rights?"—or at least "why not also *employer* rights?" Good question. I suppose that attention tends to focus more on the rights of the employ*ee* because the employ*er* tends to have more power—including the power to ignore others' rights. And traditionally, it seems that employ*ers* have violated employ*ee* rights more often than the other way around. But that's a lame excuse, isn't it, for ignoring a whole half of an issue. Alternatives to this traditional relationship of employee/employer will be addressed in the next chapter.

Another point you should wonder about is why *rights* and not *responsibilities*? Well, one could say that rights entail responsibilities: if I have a right to X, you have a responsibility to provide X or at least to not stand in the way of my acquiring X. Don't skip over that "or" too quickly—which is it? And is it definitely one of the two?

If we were to call this chapter, then, "Employee/Employer Rights and Responsibilities," well, that would pretty much cover the whole text: whistleblowing falls under employee responsibilities; product quality falls under employer responsibilities; profit falls under employer rights *and* responsibilities, as does the chapter on the environment, and the one on advertising, and so on. And certainly this chapter also overlaps with the chapter on international issues to the extent that employee rights are the same *wherever* you set up business.

As to *what* rights employees might have, that may depend on what *basis* you establish. Some argue that the only rights an employee has, or should have, are those stipulated by the employment contract (which would, we hope, stipulate the employer's rights as well, and also both parties' responsibilities).

However, such a contract theory is open to a few criticisms. First, contract theory seems to ignore the reality that many contracts are not entered into freely. Sure, the employee signed it, voluntarily and with full knowledge of its contents, but if there were no other alternatives, no other income-providing jobs, how "free" was that person to *not* sign it? Some argue that for consent to be *truly* voluntary, not only must there *be* alternatives, but there must be *attractive* alternatives—did the person have another just-as-good job offer?

Second, the contract may allow parties to abuse each other: if the contract doesn't include, say, so-called "human rights," then the employer is under no obligation to respect those rights. An employer could, theoretically, be morally in the clear to hit employees, as long as the contract didn't specify that "employers shall not hit employees."

A modified contract theory might say that rights and responsibilities accord to the contract *as long as* no human rights are violated. And, in the absence of a contract, one might simply say that employees are entitled to the basic human rights; in fact, one might ask what's so different about being an employee—how are employee rights any different than ordinary human and civil rights? That is to say, why should we have more, or fewer, or different, rights at work than we do before or after work? (And why should an employer have any more, or less, or different, responsibility than any other person?)

Perhaps they're not any different; perhaps there are just special applications to the business sphere of standard rights. For example, the right to security of person (Article 3 of the United

Nations Declaration of Human Rights includes the right to life, liberty, and security of person) may translate into the right to a safe workplace. The right to marry and to found a family (Article 16) may translate into the right to parental leave and on-site childcare facilities. The right to rest and leisure (Article 24) might translate into the right to breaks and holidays. And so on.

What about the right to freedom of thought and belief, freedom of opinion and expression (Articles 18 and 19)—does that mean you should be able to pray all day long? Or just on your breaks? Does it mean you should have your holy days off? With pay? (Why? Why not?) Maybe the employer can't do anything to stop you from being religious (for example, forbid you to go to church *after* work), but that doesn't mean he or she has to let you be religious *at* work (for example, let you go to church on company time).

Can the company reprimand you for freely expressing your opinion if it's against the company? Why? Why not? Does it matter whether you do so on company time or on your own time? (Can't employees talk and work at the same time? And if they *can* talk, why can't they speak the truth as they understand it?) How far can a company go to project or protect its image? Shouldn't image, appearance, pretence be irrelevant—isn't reality, substance, the point? Why should I censor myself or dress a certain way to maintain a façade? And if it's not a façade, you won't need me to censor myself or dress a certain way; I'll *be* a certain way.

Article 23 of the Declaration is especially relevant to our focus, as it claims that all people have the right to work, to free choice of employment, to just and favourable conditions of work, and to protection against unemployment; the right to equal pay for equal work; and the right to just and favourable remuneration.

I'm not suggesting, however, that the United Nations Declaration is the definitive statement on human rights, let alone employee rights. There are other perspectives. Werhane describes a bill of rights for employees and employers, listing among others, for employees, the right to due process in the workplace, the right to engage in outside activities of their choice, and the right to participate in the decision-making processes entailed in their job.[1]

In addition to asking *what* rights, and on what *basis*, of course, we have to ask what we do when rights collide? My right to freedom of speech steps on your right to freedom from a hostile environment—so now what? If you can rank the principles or virtues involved, perhaps that will provide a solution. So will a utilitarian approach.

So much for rights in general; let's get specific.

The Right to Equal Treatment...

...or the right not to be discriminated against. When considering the issue of discrimination, there are several questions to be asked. First, what *is* discrimination? (Define your terms.) Second, is discrimination *wrong*? Discrimination in general? This particular *kind* of discrimination? This particular *instance* of discrimination? And if so, *why* is it wrong?

---

[1] See Ewing's "An Employees' Bill of Rights" for something similar.

Strictly speaking, the word *discrimination* refers to distinguishing one thing from another, to making a distinction, to noting a difference between things. So we discriminate when we choose ripe fruit over rotten fruit, we discriminate when we say this music has more rhythmic complexity than that music. And we certainly discriminate when we run "discriminator" programs through a database using specific search parameters ("data mining is in essence a kind of automated discrimination," says Pulfer [13]).

However, commonly speaking, the word *discrimination* is a short form for *unjustified discrimination*—distinguishing between two (or more) things on some basis that's not justified. Recall that Aristotle's view of distributive justice says that like cases should be treated alike, so if you have similar merit, you get similar consideration, and irrelevant aspects such as sex and colour are, well, irrelevant. (The trick is in determining what's relevant and what's irrelevant—we'll get to that.) Because of this element of injustice, such discrimination is considered morally wrong.

One can appeal to rights instead of justice (though, of course, the two can be related) to explain the moral wrongness of discrimination. Consider Abella's definition: "practices or attitudes that have, whether by design or impact, the effect of limiting an individual's or a group's right to the opportunities generally available because of attributed rather than actual characteristics" (253). Recall that Rawls argues that we should have an equal right to opportunities, and, presumably, such discrimination makes that impossible (see Narveson, however, for an argument that we don't have the right to non-discrimination).

Note, however, that Abella's definition is different not only in its attention to rights rather than justice but also in its mention of attributed and actual characteristics rather than irrelevant and relevant ones. I believe Abella's point, however, is not that it would not be unjustified discrimination to distinguish according to religion, for example, as long as the subject actually was of the religion at issue, but that it would be discrimination to judge a person dishonest, for example—an attribute—because of her religion rather than because she was actually dishonest.

Thus discrimination is defined in relation to membership in a group: what supposedly happens when people discriminate is that they stereotype or prejudge the individual, attributing certain characteristics according to their view of the group to which that individual belongs. However, perhaps one could be guilty of unjust discrimination without stereotyping: one simply needs to judge according to an irrelevant standard. Nevertheless, insofar as discrimination *does* involve this group scenario, then surely Kantian ethics would argue against it: if we were to universalize the practice of judging an individual according to the characteristics of the group, the very notion of "individual" would come to be meaningless.

Furthermore, discrimination is typically defined as a negative judgement. No doubt, that is what has moved us to identify, and attempt to rectify, this injustice, but I think we should be as vigilant against positive discrimination: is it not as wrong to assume the distinguished-looking man before us is wise and capable? (I know many distinguished-looking men who are complete idiots.)

People often think of unjustified discrimination in the workplace in relation to hiring (and firing) decisions and promotion (and demotion) decisions. However, discrimination can also show up in recruitment methods, benefits plans, and salaries (compare Bell Canada's plan to outsource its construction workers, 100% male, with its plan to outsource its operators, 98% female: the men would keep their union, their seniority, and their wage—the women wouldn't [Rebick, 44]), as well as purchasing and contracts decisions, and even product lines. (Are your "flesh-tone" cosmetics and crayons beige or black? And take a look at your toys with race, ethnicity, age, and ability in mind.)

The questionable criteria, the bases used for distinguishing that usually result in a claim of unjustified discrimination, are often those listed in the Canadian Charter of Rights and Freedoms: age, colour, ethnic or national origin, race, mental or physical disability, religion, sex, and sexual orientation.[1]

Living in a multicultural country, one might think that discrimination according to colour and ethnic or national origin is infrequent. Think again. The twelfth time Kamal El Batal submitted his résumé to Quebec's agricultural co-operative, he changed the name on it to Marc Tremblay—and received a call: the recruiter was impressed with his two degrees and almost twenty years' experience (Patriquin).

One might also think that racial discrimination is rare in Canada. Maybe it is. But maybe it's not as easy to detect as you think. Suppose you choose not to hire the small and soft-spoken Asian shop teacher because you suspect the immature fourteen-year-old students in his classes wouldn't pay attention to him, wouldn't grant him the authority and respect he deserves (yes, some of "them" are qualified and competent in fields other than math and engineering), and serious physical injury would likely result. To the degree that teachers need students to cooperate, he will not, in fact, be a good teacher: when students don't listen to a teacher and don't follow his or her instructions, they won't learn. Would choosing not to hire him count as discrimination?

And though not an example of employee rights, a possible example of so-called "reverse" discrimination on the basis of race or culture is granting to First Nations people the right to hunt and fish when and where non–First Nations people do not have that right. Some justify it on the basis of need: First Nations are allowed because it's their livelihood, but for non-First Nations people, it's just sport. But what about commercial hunting and fishing? Then is it not livelihood for both?[2] The Maritime provinces certainly have an interest in these matters. Of course, we'd have to establish first on whose land and in whose water the hunting and fishing is being done....

As for religious discrimination, why exactly is it morally wrong, for example, to refuse to hire people who believe in a certain religion? Is belief in *any* ideology unjust grounds for discrimination, or just belief in a religious ideology? (Just dominant religious systems or any

---

1 Regarding age discrimination, some jobs have a minimum age requirement, some a maximum, and many enforce mandatory retirement (see Wedeking)—can any of that be fair? See also Ferris and King, who examine the differences between subjective and objective performance evaluations of older workers and conclude that to some extent age discrimination is actually intentional. Henry and Jennings consider age discrimination in lay-off decisions from several ethical perspectives.

2 See *Windspeaker*—e.g., "Hunters and Harvesters" and "Let's Talk about Fish"—for some good pieces on these issues.

supernaturalist cult?) And if you must hire them, must you also accommodate their beliefs in the workplace? How far? And when does "accommodate" become "impose" become "harass"? Is beginning a staff meeting with a prayer considered to be accommodating Christians or harassing non-Christians? Or both? So how do you resolve this conflict?

A common basis for discrimination that's not on the human-rights list is discrimination on the basis of health conditions. Consider AIDS. Is it right to limit people with AIDS to certain jobs? Is it right not to hire them in the first place because of medical costs?[1] Is that justifiably considered a "physical disability"?

And what about discrimination against pregnant employees? When exactly is non-pregnancy a bona fide job requirement? And do fetal protection policies, such as those excluding pregnant women, and even potentially pregnant (i.e., non-sterile) women, from certain jobs, discriminate against women?[2]

Consider, too, genetic discrimination, an issue that is bound to become more prevalent now that the human genome is fully mapped. Brockett and Tankersley thoroughly examine the implications of genetic knowledge for the insurance business (and employers)—individual rights to privacy and employment vs. insurance companies' desire for better informed decisions (fairer decisions? discriminatory decisions?).[3]

Another issue that may become bigger than it currently is, since Canadians are getting fatter,[4] is weight discrimination. In fact, discrimination can occur not only because of weight, but also because of other body-type factors. For example, tall men get promoted over short men. They even get paid more.[5] Certainly airline attendants have a history dealing with this: it has been the case that not only must a certain weight be maintained (though this might be justified on the basis of airplane carrying capacity and aisle size), but female attendants must wear make-up (what does eyeliner have to do with flight attendant skills?). Consider sex-different dress codes in this light.

> **BOX 4.1 Should Your Appearance Matter?**
>
> One might say that appearance should matter only when it's relevant to job performance. What? How *can* one's appearance be relevant to job performance? I don't suddenly forget everything I know about music and teaching when I put on a pair of blue jeans and a sweatshirt, and yet I was fired from a music teaching position in Ontario because of that—because of how I looked. Apparently I didn't

---

1 See Häyry and Häyry.
2 See John F. Quinn, as well as Andiappan, Reavley, and Silver.
3 See Murray as well, who takes a distributive justice approach to the issue; and see also Hubbard and Wald.
4 See http://www.research.utoronto.ca/edge/edgenet/fall2004/48/.
5 On these issues, see Willard; Pummer; Donahue.

look "professional" enough. (Define "professional" and tell me why jeans *aren't* professional, but polyester pants are.)

The same thing happened in a Winnipeg Safeway: a cashier was asked not to wear her nose stud. Apparently the company's Jewellery Policy (yes, they had a Jewellery Policy; they also had several Personal Appearance Policies, one of which prohibited beards) stated that jewellery worn at work must be "conservative in appearance and size" in order to "attract (and maintain) business." (What's the connection between being conservative and getting business?)

And the same thing happened in a Calgary Co-op: an employee was asked not to ear an eyebrow ring. Apparently it suggested "unsanitary standards" and made customers feel "uncomfortable."

Both Safeway and the Calgary Co-op seem to be appealing to community standards to determine what's acceptable and what's not. Is that morally acceptable? (Recall the subsection on relativism in Part II of this text. And consider retailers' refusal to serve black people because it might offend the white customers, and their insistence that women cover themselves top to bottom because the sight of a female forehead or elbow might offend or arouse [I can never figure that out] the male customers....)

The United Food and Commercial Workers' Union claimed that Safeway's jewellery policy was an "unwarranted intrusion into [the employee's] private life." Which part of that, if any, is defensible—"unwarranted"? "intrusion"? "private"?

However, in both cases, the courts sided with the employers, saying more or less that "employers have the right to establish appearance, grooming and dress standards that they think are necessary for the safe and effective conduct of a business." However, as Slattery-Aisling notes, "Last time we looked, we were pretty sure nose rings did not alter the art of bagging groceries." When is personal appearance *really* related to job performance and not just a reflection of the employer's personal preferences?

Okay...you *can* put on a pair of non-denim pants, and you *can* take off the jewellery. And the employers weren't saying you couldn't wear jeans and nosestuds off-hours. But what about when you're not tall enough or not small enough? Are you supposed to get surgery to lengthen your legs or excise your fat—or increase your breast size?

How do people justify, for example, not hiring the fat person? Roehling notes three possibilities: predicted lower performance levels (because they're lazy, less able to get along, and less intelligent); higher costs (higher insurance premiums, greater absenteeism, the cost of special accommodations); and "it's their own fault" (it's only discrimination when the person can't help it).

> Obviously, at least *some* of these justifications are based on incorrect information—just as is the association between eyebrow rings and sanitation. (One has to wonder why *ear*rings didn't similarly indicate "unsanitary standards" and make the customers "uncomfortable"....) But perceptions, mistaken or not, *do* ultimately affect job performance, sales, and so on. So does that mean you *are* justified in asking someone to wear different clothes and different jewellery? *And* in not hiring the fat person—or the black person or the lesbian or the guy with the awful acne....
>
> **Sources**
> Drohan, Paul, and Mario Toneguzzi. "Co-Op Issues Ban on Facial Jewelry." *Calgary Herald* 21 Aug. 1998: B4.
> "Employer Justified in Protecting Its Image." *Focus on Canadian Employment and Equality Rights* 4.31 (July 1997).
> Roehling, Mark V. "Weight Discrimination, in the American Workplace: Ethical Issues and Analysis." *Journal of Business Ethics* 40 (2002): 177–89.
> Slattery-Aisling, Cross-Val. "Minimum Wage Hell." *Spank!* November 1998.
> Teskey, P.S. "Canada Safeway Ltd. and United Food and Commercial Workers' Union, Local 832." *Labour Arbitration Cases* 63 L.A.C.(4th): 256–78.

What about class discrimination: do your well-to-do clients and customers get better service? (Do the others even *get* service?) Is that justified or unjustified discrimination? It may well be justified from an egoistic perspective (well-to-do clients are more valuable to the company), but what about the other moral perspectives?

What makes the many criteria mentioned above questionable is their irrelevance to the decision (to hire, to promote, or whatever). For example, whether you are male or female would seem to be irrelevant to whether you can be an architect, so if only male architects are hired, perhaps some (unjustified) discrimination is going on. That is to say, sex is not a *bona fide occupation qualification (BFOQ)* for the occupation of architect. However, hiring only women to be surrogate mothers would be okay, because the possession of a uterus is most definitely required for the job—it is a BFOQ—and only women have uteruses.

The implication is that only ability or capacity is relevant. However, some have argued that our society is not a meritocracy (despite the belief of the "haves" that they got what they have by merit, and not luck or discrimination—we all like to think we got the job because we were the best candidate, not because we were lucky, or because we look okay, or because we were the last interviewed and the freshest in the interviewer's minds...). Nor should it be a meritocracy, say some.[1] What then should be the criterion for hiring? Need? Desire?

---

1 See Wasserstrom.

Why not simply the preferences of the company's owners? Why shouldn't they be able to hire whomever they want? After all, it's their company. And if they happen just not to want a "mentally challenged" person in their office, why should they hire such a person? Or if they happen to believe, for example, that men are more capable, well, why shouldn't they hire the applicant they believe to be most competent: the man? One might be tempted to suggest to the owners a psychology lesson in emotional bias and/or an epistemology lesson in validity of evidence, but still, why should they not (be able to) do as they see best? People are allowed to be ignorant every day, so why should company owners be any different? Why should they be held to a different, higher standard? Well, first of all, company owners' decisions affect others in a far greater way than most individual personal decisions—maybe *that's* why they should be held to a higher standard. But one can certainly argue that many personal decisions shatter lives in a way no business decision ever will. Second, people are "allowed" to be ignorant every day, yes, but we may still call such people immoral (and we may do so every day)—and *that's* our focus (deciding what's immoral, what's ethically wrong).

To return to the implication behind most claims of unjustified discrimination: *is* ability sufficient? But what if the male attending surgeon doesn't take direction from the female chief surgeon during an operation? What if television viewers don't believe the Jamaican anchor when he reads the news? In these situations, *can* sex or ethnic origin be said to be a bona fide occupational qualification? After all, it seems that being male or "non-ethnic" (whatever that means!) is required for the job—or, at least, for doing the job with any degree of success.

Now, recognizing that discrimination on the basis of irrelevant aspects isn't morally right, we could just stop it. Unfortunately, it's not that easy, for two reasons. The first is that it's so subtle, so unconscious. Even the most vigilant of people find themselves "automatically" making unfair assumptions. Let's consider sex: literally from the moment of birth, we identify, we discriminate, according to sex—"It's a girl!" "It's a boy!" Room decor, toys, and clothes are different according to sex (and not just for babies and kids); even our language is sexist—"he," "she," "Ms.," "Mr." (Why do we even need sex-differentiating pronouns and honorifics? (It's not surprising, then—indeed it may be realistic—to assume that of the two people before you, the woman will be the teacher, the man, the manager. (And the First Nations person in a wheelchair will be neither.)

And it's not just a nurture thing. It could be a very built-in nature thing: men choose other men, whites choose other whites—we choose what's familiar, what's similar, rather than what's different. So as long as white men are doing the choosing....

Even with rigorous interview and performance appraisal techniques, which require that all applicants be asked and scored on the same questions, multiple standards may still interfere with merit as the sole criterion for hiring and promotion. Consider this: women are expected to smile more than men, so even though both a male and a female applicant may actually smile the same number of times during an interview, the woman may be considered less friendly than the man—the friendliness bar was set higher for her. On the other hand, men are expected to be more aggressive than women, so even though both may wait patiently, without interrupting, before speaking, the man may be considered "lacking in initiative" whereas the women is deemed simply "polite."

Lest you think this is just speculation, take a look at Purdy's essay, which includes mention of research findings such as these: male students rated identical course syllabi higher when the instructor was known to be male; male students rated articles higher when the author was thought to be male; when a woman is recognized as having done a good job, her success is attributed to factors other than her ability.

Velasquez reports similar findings of discrimination:

> In 1993, for example, ABC sent a male and female, Chris and Julie, on an "experiment" to apply in person for jobs several companies were advertising. Chris and Julie were both blonde, trim, neatly dressed college graduates in their 20s, with identical resumes indicating management experience.... [W]hen the company recruiter spoke with Julie, the only job he brought up was a job answering phones. A few minutes later, the same recruiter spoke with Chris. He was offered a management job. (370)

Velasquez notes that similar experiments have shown that racial discrimination is happening in much the same way (371).

Besides this subtlety, the other obstacle to just putting an end to discrimination is that it's often systemic; that means that it's not due to any individual's decisions, conscious or otherwise—it's built right into the system. For example, a fire department may swear up and down that it does not discriminate on the basis of sex: if a woman is able to pass the tests, she will be considered alongside the men. Sounds fair enough. Even the tests have been revamped to eliminate any sex bias (for example, push-ups, which give the male body an advantage because of its higher centre of gravity, have been replaced with bicep curls and shoulder rolls as tests of upper body strength), and all the skills and standards are demonstrably required for firefighting. However, the department may store its hoses at a height that makes it much more difficult for a 5'4" person to get them off the wall than for a 5'10" person. So women invariably do worse than men on any test that involves getting the hoses. So they score worse on the physical part of the testing. So they have less of a chance of getting hired. Because they were female. But wouldn't you *want* to have a few small, light people on your firefighting team? Maybe to go up the crumbling staircase and crawl under the bed to rescue the terrified child hiding there?

The same kind of systemic discrimination may apply to a position for which staying late at the office is seen as evidence of the preferred "teamwork," "drive," and "dedication." Anyone responsible for children is unlikely to meet those requirements. And if that is indeed the only demonstration of teamwork, drive, and dedication, being able to work late may be a BFOQ. But my guess is that one could have, and could exhibit, those qualities in other ways—such as taking work home, having shorter lunches, being sensitive to one's colleagues' work, and so on.

Because discrimination has been so hard to root out, many companies institute affirmative action or employment equity programs; in Canada, these are, by law, focused on women,

Aboriginals, visible minorities, and the employable handicapped. First, it's important to note that there are different kinds of affirmative action programs, from tie-breaking (if two candidates are judged to be equally well qualified, you hire the one from the "disadvantaged" group) to quotas (a certain number of positions are for members of those groups only). Each has its problems.

For example, seldom are candidates "equally qualified." And, given that people in the identified groups may have had to work twice as hard and overcome twice as many obstacles to get where they are, getting where they are probably means they're twice as good as the others, so choosing them over the other candidates may well mean you *are* choosing the *better* qualified. Say you've got two runners: Jane starts a few seconds after John (John was told the starting time by his coach, but Jane has no coach, and no one she asked seemed to know); Jane hasn't got her running clothes on (she spent half an hour looking for the women's changeroom—there were signs everywhere directing runners to the men's changerooms, but none pointed to the women's changerooms); and even if she did have her running gear on, she wouldn't be wearing spikes like her competitor (they don't make them in women's size 6); she hasn't warmed up (she spent that time looking for the changeroom); and her lane is strewn with holes and rocks (the holes are there because her lane hasn't been maintained by the field operators; the rocks were thrown there by angry spectators who don't think she should be allowed in the race). (Don't scoff: Kathrine Switzer, the first woman to run the Boston Marathon—one of the officials tried to shove her off the course.) Now if Jane finishes at the same time as John, she's actually the better runner, right? Even if she finishes a little behind, she's better (though you'd have to be able to measure just how much all that stuff affected her time).

Second, one should understand and assess the various justifications for affirmative action programs (see Dimock and Tucker). Achieving a representative workforce is one aim; if 10 per cent of the population is gay, then 10 per cent of your workforce should be gay. But why? Why should every workplace, or every career field, *be* representative of the population at large? To some extent, a representative workforce ensures diversity, and diversity in the workplace is a good thing because more perspectives are available, leading to better solutions (more alternatives will be considered).

And to some extent, such representation ensures role modelling: unless First Nations kids see First Nations lawyers, for example, they might not even consider that career. How many boys thought of being a nurse when they grew up? Diversity helps get rid of the stereotypes; it changes the expectations of both those in the group and those outside the group. It thus increases the freedom of choice for future generations (at the expense of freedom of choice for some of the present generation?) and moves us closer to a meritocracy. Such justifications seem to fit with many of the ethical approaches we've covered: utilitarianism—the consequence is a good society;[1] Kantian ethics—the individual gains respect and autonomy; justice theories—a meritocracy is fair; and rights theories—one's right to one's deserts is upheld (although it depends on which "one" you're talking about).

---

1 Or is it? See Groarke 1996, Ferris and King, and Dimock and Tucker.

Compensation for past injuries (to well-being and prospects) is another aim of employment equity programs (recall Aristotle).[1] One problem with this justification is that you're not compensating the individuals who were actually injured. However, insofar as people identify themselves not as individuals—and more importantly, insofar as others identify them not as individuals—but as members of a group, maybe today's individuals, the ones being compensated, *are* also the ones who have been injured; inheritance (of attitude, of opportunity) should not be lightly dismissed. But how do you measure the extent of injury? And how much compensation is enough?

Also, the ones bearing the burden of compensation may not be the ones guilty of injuring. But again, consider group identity: whether they like/want/accept it or not, white males have benefitted and perhaps continue to benefit from that past discrimination. Similarly, those of us living in North America and Europe have benefitted most from the industrialization that has nearly ruined our planet, so shouldn't we bear most of the burden of fixing the problem? In addition, often these individuals are not asked to give up something they already have; they are merely asked not to take something they have yet to get.

Then again, if it's a case of group injury, it should be a case of group compensation—not individual compensation. Maybe affirmative action programs are unfair on an individual basis, and are thus justifiably called reverse discrimination, but fair on a group basis. This may be especially convincing if one considers the group to be society as a whole.

In addition to the claim that affirmative action programs are wrong because they are simply reverse discrimination, they could be wrong because they cause harm to the target groups themselves, members of which are made to feel that they need special help (the equal start often looks like a head start). However, as Boatright points out, "Success in life is often unearned, but there is little evidence that the beneficiaries of good fortune are psychologically damaged by it" (204)—if white men have not suffered for it, why now should non-whites and women have a problem with it? (Because they *know* they're getting it unearned, perhaps.)

Furthermore, affirmative action programs may perpetuate rather than get rid of the problem of stereotypes (see Heilman's paper for this argument), if only by continually drawing attention to such irrelevant differences. Also, if such programs do lead to hiring and promoting genuinely less qualified or capable people, well, the work just won't be as good (assuming both the more and the less qualified work to their potential), and this could have a negative effect on the society as a whole.

Rooting out discrimination doesn't necessarily stop at affirmative action hiring strategies; to be fair, to do the right thing, one must also provide equal pay for work of equal value. But how do we define "equal value"? Value to whom? To the company? To society? To the worker? And how is that value determined? By effort, skill, productivity, qualifications/training, experience, responsibility, risk, stress? To consider more deeply the factor of responsibility, consider Simon's question: "Is responsibility related to the number of people one supervises, the level

---

[1] See Thomson for a discussion of the compensation argument, and Fullinwider for a critique of Thomson's argument; see also Groarke 1990.

of decision making one holds within a firm, the costs of misjudgment, or what?" (400). And how are these assessed, and by whom? The person who currently holds the position or some middle-manager?

Jennifer Quinn presents an interesting analysis of the role that job evaluations play in determining pay equity: she argues that what usually gets the points on a job evaluation are those skills primarily associated with "men's jobs" (for example, secretaries, usually women, are usually required to do several things at once, with a smile, while being constantly interrupted—that skill is seldom on the list for points); that jobs that are traditionally the same as those women do at home (for free) go unrecognized ("So while men, for example, typically receive points for dirt and grease that they encounter on the job under a factor designated 'working conditions,' nurses, who deal with vomit, blood, and excrement on a daily basis, receive no such points" [396]); that men's jobs such as those in the trades requiring a lot of visible and on-the-job training get credit, but women's jobs such as those in the clerical category requiring the same level of training, but which is often invisible and off-the-job, don't get credit.

Righting our wrongs may not even stop with pay equity; Kavka argues, on the grounds of distributive justice and self-respect, that handicapped people's right to work includes not only a right to non-discrimination in employment and promotion but also a right to compensatory training and education and a right to reasonable investments by society and employers to make jobs accessible.

Right to Respect

Harassment often gets categorized with discrimination, but the one doesn't necessarily involve the other; for example, a bisexual person could harass *everyone* she or he was sexually interested in. It is also important to distinguish between sex*ist* harassment (discriminatory) and sex*ual* harassment (discriminatory or non-discriminatory). And harassment may not be sex-based at all—employees may be harassed for holding certain "unpopular" opinions, for example, or they may be harassed just because they're very annoying.[1]

There are generally two kinds of harassment. "Quid pro quo" ("this for that") cases, in which an employee is promised something (a promotion or a pay increase, for example) in return for sexual interaction (or threatened with loss of job or demotion unless such interaction is provided), are easily understood as morally unacceptable. "Hostile work environment" cases, in which certain employees work in an environment that is intimidating, offensive, or demeaning to them because of comments, gestures, decorations, dress codes, and so on, are a little more difficult—partly because so much behaviour may (or may not) qualify: Rayner, Hoel, and Cooper note that "[i]n the workplace, bullying can include behaviours such as damaging your reputation; humiliating you in public; accusing you of lack of effort; calling you names; insulting, teasing, or intimidating you; preventing your access to opportunities; isolating you

---

1 See, however, Bell, McLaughlin, and Sequeira regarding the relationship between discrimination, harassment, and the "glass ceiling."

physically or socially; imposing undue pressure to produce work; setting impossible deadlines; making consistent unnecessary disruptions; failing to give you credit; assigning meaningless tasks; setting you up for failure; or removing responsibility" (cited in McKay-Panos).[1] Such behaviour may just be an indication of the increasing incivility in society as a whole, but having to face it from neighbours and passing strangers from time to time is one thing; having to deal with it all day while you're trying to work is another.

One big question is "how offensive is offensive?" One way to decide this is according to the "reasonable person" standard. But one of the problems with this is that a reasonable man may react quite differently from a reasonable woman: for example, suppose there is someone walking behind you at night who changes sides of the street every time you do—if you're a woman, you might reasonably fear attack, but if you're a man, you might reasonably just think that some idiot can't make up his mind about which side of the road to walk on.[2]

Another way to decide offence is according to the subjective standard: if the person involved considers the action offensive, it's offensive. Period. But how would you know that your action is going to be offensive, or unwelcome, to that particular person until you do whatever it is? One might suggest that you could just play it safe and wait until after work to ask for that date. But why does asking for a date, which may be harassment if it's done during the workday, suddenly become *not* harassment when it's done after work?

A more fundamental question is "why is it wrong to offend?" Do we have a right not to be offended? Anywhere, anytime? Is it wrong because it causes psychological harm? Does psychological harm count as much as physical harm? Some argue that when the offensive behaviour involves touching, it is wrong because it violates one's privacy, one's physical integrity. (What exactly is that?) It may also be wrong because it violates one's rights to freedom—harassment restricts one's choices in very subtle (and sometimes not so subtle) ways.

But what about offensive behaviour that "just" involves speech? It may be wrong to insult, but some people are offended merely by an opposing point of view. Do we really want to limit speech to what is agreeable to others?

In addition to these rights arguments, one can make a Kantian argument that certain behaviour often identified as harassment does not show respect for persons as persons. Furthermore, a hostile work environment keeps individuals from the offices and positions for which Rawls argues all must have equal opportunity in a just society.[3] One can also make a utilitarian argument: the low morale, not to mention the lower productivity, of harassed employees is certainly not good for the company (or for society as a whole).

Another question is "how interfering is interfering enough?" Is a one-time occurrence considered harassment or must the behaviour be persistent?

---

1 See Namie, as well as Harvey et al., for an identification of factors that elicit bullying behaviour, along with recommendations for addressing it.
2 See Abrams, as well as Paetzold and Shaw, for a discussion of this issue.
3 Again, see Bell, McLaughlin, and Sequeira.

Lastly, one should consider the power relationship. An interaction between a so-called superior and a subordinate may have different value than the same interaction between equals, simply because of the ability, in the first case, of the one party to bring about specific consequences (such as promotion or a pay increase).

Another interesting issue related to the right to respect, and one that Velasquez looks at in his discussion of the political organization of the company, is the ethics of political tactics, the things one does to "get ahead" (467–74). Scott points out that "companies quietly encourage bullies." Their aggressive behaviour tends to keep costs down and profits up; it leads to promotion. And, to the extent that business is male-dominated, and non-aggression is eschewed as feminine, such behaviour will prevail. So it's no surprise that "bully bosses" have become a serious problem—such a problem, in fact, that in Canada the odds are good that workers harassed by their bosses will win lawsuits against them.

The Right to a Job

The right to a job? Is there such a thing? On what basis? De George argues that the right to employment derives from the right to work, which can be derived from the right to life, to development, and to respect. He examines assumptions and conditions involved in this position, one of which is that the supply of labour exceeds the demand (359–65). Weiss argues that we have the right to a job because a job equals social status and self-esteem. (But do we have a *right* to those things?) And once you have a job, is the employer under any obligation to let you keep it? Can he or she take the job away? For any reason or only for some certain specified reason? Why must she have a reason?[1]

As for the reasons for firing or dismissal, the common view is that this may be done only for "just cause." But what's "just"? De George suggests several possibilities: economic recession, inefficiency, immorality on the job, chronic lateness or absenteeism, lack of ability to perform at the level expected, incompatibility with management or with other workers, lack of respect or deference to supervisors, poor attitude toward work, the voicing of dissent, an employer's belief that he or she can find someone who can do the job better, the employer's dislike of the employee for personal reasons (394)—are all of these *just* cause? Where do you draw the line (and why)?[2]

For example, why is lack of deference just cause? Why should I be deferential to another human being, my equal (and quite possibly younger than me, and maybe even less qualified and/or less experienced than me), just because she or he is above me in the organizational hierarchy? And why is voicing dissent just cause? If you want your employees to be thinking, morally responsible adults, how can you also demand deference and acquiescence?

---

1 There are several essays (for example, see those by Ridler and Singer) about plant closings that address the obligation of the employer not to take away your job—they're well worth the read.
2 See Boatright's chapter on unjust dismissal for a good discussion of this very question.

In the case of lay-offs, certainly downsizing brings this ethical issue into the spotlight: Whom do you lay off? How do you lay off? And what about the "survivors"?[1] Di Norcia suggests that downsizing is often reactive and usually not at all the best of the options available to management:

> Not only does it worsen employee morale, it also results in productivity declines, loss of competitiveness and other costs. Nor does cost-cutting itself improve sales or increase market share. Layoffs have costs too: severance payouts, the loss of employees with valuable corporate knowledge, poor morale, and lower productivity. (146)

Alternatives to this "pathological management syndrome" (146) include "cutting overtime, reducing/rearranging the work week; reducing benefits and wages; days off without pay; redeploying and retraining employees" (148). He goes on to say that

> [w]here personnel cuts are necessary they should be distributed equitably across the organization, beginning in the executive suite and moving down, not the other way around. Where employees must be let go, attrition is preferable to layoffs or resignations as a means of workforce reduction. (148)

Lay-offs are often done according to seniority—but should this be the case? Is that morally right? Some associate seniority with loyalty, but are we sure that length of employment at any one company is a measure of the employee's loyalty to that company? Might it be, instead, as is more likely the case today, a measure of the paucity of other employment opportunities for that employee? Or perhaps it is just a measure of the employee's reluctance to take risks, to change directions. Seniority *per se* is merely longevity; it is a measure of quantity, not quality. Quantity *may* affect quality, and longevity *may* increase ability and accomplishment, but then again, it may not. (Many mediocre employees are given raises year after year just because they've been there one more year. Is it any wonder then that so many employees develop a clock-punching mentality, thinking that just being there, just putting in time, is enough? After all, it is: if they put in enough time, they get that wage increase, those extra holidays—and a stronger guarantee that they'll continue to just be there.)

And of course not just *whether* you dismiss or lay-off, but *how* you do so can be an ethical issue: Do you provide notice and a reason? Do you provide the right to appeal, due process? (Why not—are management decisions infallible? But then again, why—just whose company is this?)

The Right to a Fair Wage

The right to a fair wage—what's fair? Recall the justice theories discussed in Part II—do we determine according to need, value, time, effort…?

Shaw (217–18) suggests seven questions that are worth asking to determine what's fair in this case: what is the law, what is the prevailing wage in the industry, what is the community wage

---

1 See Ridler for a few suggestions.

level, what is the nature of the job itself, is the job secure and what are its prospects, what are the employer's financial capabilities, and what are other employees inside the organization earning for comparable work? De George also discusses this right to a just wage (366–70). Sometimes this question is phrased as the right to a *living* wage. But should that mean enough for the one person, the one who's working for you, to live on, or should it mean enough for that person *and* someone else that she or he may want to support? (How many other someone elses? Someone elses they have voluntarily contracted to support? Someone elses they have voluntarily created?)[1]

And does setting a minimum wage (something Gaski argues is immoral), a wage that ensures some minimum standard of living, some minimum justice, imply that you should also set a maximum wage? Why? Why not? Or perhaps, in the interests of justice, you should set a maximum *ratio* of maximum to minimum wage—are the upper-level managers *really* entitled to fifty times what your front-line workers earn? (We'll come back to this.)

BOX 4.2   Do You Have an Obligation to Provide *Any* Pay?

Unpaid internships are becoming increasingly prevalent in Canada, with some 300,000 people currently "working for free for some of the wealthiest and biggest transnational corporations." In theory, internships enable fresh graduates to gain experience and increase the likelihood of employment in their chosen field. In practice, often an intern's duties are low-level scut work, and maybe (just maybe) a reference letter waits at the end. Understandably, many people are wondering whether internships are simple exploitation.

Legally speaking, employers do not have any duty to pay interns (see Kraljevic and Laskoski). But morally speaking?

Consider Kraljevic's comments: "We don't see professional school graduates content to work for free in hospitals, schools, and law firms. Why should there be a stratification of employability based upon the degree that one has earned? Is the work provided by a journalist inherently less valuable than that of a teacher?"

Kraljevic also identifies an important consequence: internships will increase the likelihood that only those able to afford to work without pay in their field eventually get whatever jobs there are. (Because the rest will be working full-time at pizza joints trying to pay off their student loans.)

And yet isn't being an intern just like being a volunteer? If not, why not? And if so, does that mean there is something just as morally reprehensible about using volunteers?

---

1 Vancouver City Savings Credit Union adopted a "living wage policy" whereby 100 per cent of eligible Vancity employees are paid at least $19.14 per hour (salary and benefits), well above B.C.'s minimum wage of $10.25.

> *References*
> Kraljevic, Ana. "Possibly, Maybe, Perhaps: Empty Promises Spell the Death Knell of the Unpaid Internship." *Law Now* 5 Nov. 2014.
> Laskoski, Stephanie. "Unpaid Interns have Little Protection under the Law." *Law Now* 5 Nov. 2014.

The Right to Privacy

This is an issue that is becoming increasingly important, given the development of informational technology: there are many more ways to invade, and perhaps many more reasons for invading, employees' privacy. Both Boatright and De George devote an entire chapter to this issue. To start, let's ask what exactly is privacy? Garrett and Klonoski (47–49) distinguish between psychological privacy (to one's thoughts, feelings, desires, etc.) and physical privacy (to one's physical activities, one's physical appearance, and/or a certain amount of physical space around oneself).

A starting point for a definition of psychological privacy might be that the right to privacy is the right to control access by others to personal knowledge. Next, we'd have to define "personal." A manager or company may be justifiably interested in whatever affects job performance (a narrow view) or whatever affects the company (a broader view), but how far can they go in acting on that interest? Are they, for example, entitled to acquire personal information? Whether to gather, how to gather (overtly or covertly), what to gather (information about sex, age, race, religion, health, performance, income, interests, personality, etc.)—all of these are ethical issues. So too is what to *do* with the information once you have it. Can you give it to other employees, to other companies (database trading), to governments, to landlords, to banks, and so forth?

As for physical privacy, how do we define that? Does it mean you have control over who touches your body or does it also mean you have control over how your body looks? Does it also mean you have a right not to have your "personal space" invaded?

Let's consider first the invasion of privacy that might occur as a result of monitoring job performance. Surely an employer is justified in monitoring job performance. After all, how else can you be sure you have a quality workforce? And certainly first-hand evidence is preferable to rumour. But what, exactly, can you do, ethically speaking? Log the number of calls, the length of calls, or the content of calls? Log keystrokes? Read the employee's e-mail messages? On the latter topic, is it reasonable to demand, or even to expect, that all e-mail messages be bereft of anything personal, any personality? If not, then is it fair to read employees' e-mail? And if so, why exactly would you need to do so? Wouldn't it be far more efficient, and far less invasive, to use any one of a number of sophisticated programs that automatically scans e-mail for very specific content? On the other hand, if employees use the company system for personal communication, why should they expect it to remain private? Should you monitor computer use? (According to a *Forbes* report, 64 per cent of employees visit non-work-related websites every day—that's lost productivity; other reports indicate that up to 30 per cent [males] visit porn sites—that's an increased risk of malware attacks.) Peruse employees' search-engine histories? Surveil by video camera the employee's actions—time away from the desk, trips to the washroom, and so on? (Won't *respecting* privacy, and *trusting*, ensure quality performance? Treat someone like an irresponsible, cheating kid and soon enough they'll act like one.) And should any of this be done without the employee's knowledge?

But job performance isn't the only concern; employers also want to maintain their reputation, their brand, their image. So, at a minimum, they don't want their employees to be breaking any laws—which takes us back to monitoring their behaviour in various ways. (Monitoring and then just firing? Or reporting to the police?) They also want to protect their "trade secrets"—which takes us back perhaps especially to monitoring computer use.

However, invasion of privacy may occur even before you get the job—consider interview questions, reference contacts, and background checks. (In fact, background checks can now be done on an ongoing basis for current employees—see Dell and Kullen.) Prospective employers might also google you. Is that okay?

And it may continue even after you leave the job—can a company tell you not to smoke, even at home? Well, maybe—if they're going to be the ones to pay for your lung cancer treatments. Can they take a look at what you're up to at whatever social media sites you frequent after hours? Do you have a blog?

At this point, perhaps we should (re)examine the whole divide between work life and personal life. Why is there a wall between them? Because what you do at work is not the real you? And why is that? Because the employer wants to maintain some charade about the company's brand or image? Because people jump to conclusions, assuming, for example, that because someone wears sweatpants, she isn't meticulous about the details of her work?

BOX 4.3   Jian Ghomeshi (and a whole bunch of sports guys?)

Jian Ghomeshi, host of CBC Radio's *Q*, was fired in 2014 allegedly because of his assaultive sexual behaviour during off-hours. (Ghomeshi's Facebook post refers to "the risk of [his] private sex life being made public as a result of a campaign of false allegations pursued by a jilted ex girlfriend"; the CBC refers to "information" that "precludes [it] from continuing [its] relationship with Jian" [Tucker].) To determine who did what wrong, would it matter at all....

- whether he's a "star"?
- whether the sexual behaviour in question was consensual?
- whether he voluntarily told management about his off-hours sexual behaviour or whether they asked him about it or found out some other way?

- whether he actually said, "I want to hate fuck you, to wake you up" to a colleague while at work?
- whether that colleague reported the incident (if true) at the time?

And in all these scenarios, *why* would it matter?

Is the problem (have you identified the problem?) caused or exacerbated by the fact that we idealize (or idolize) public figures, we put them on a pedestal, we expect them to be role models in all aspects of life (not just at their job)? Why do we do that? Is it just sloppy thinking, a case of overgeneralization? "X is excellent at playing football, so he must be excellent in his dealings with other people." Or is there something more going on? And does the employer encourage that? Why? So are they complicit?

Sources

"Full text: Jian Ghomeshi's Facebook post on why he believes CBC fired him." *Global News*. 24 Oct. 2014. http://globalnews.ca/news/1637310/full-text-jian-ghomeshis-post-on-why-he-believes-cbc-fired-him/

Gatehouse, Jonathan, Michael Friscolanti, Genna Buck, Rachel Browne, and Martin Patriquin. "Why No One Stopped Him." *Maclean's* 127.45 (17 Nov. 2014): 22–28.

Teitel, Emma. "Sex, lies, and the CBC." *Maclean's* 127.44 (10 Nov. 2014): 124–25.

Tucker, Erica. "Timeline: Jian Ghomeshi charged in Sex Assault Scandal." *Global News*. 3 Dec. 2014. http://globalnews.ca/news/1647091/timeline-sex-assault-allegations-arise-after-cbc-fires-jian-ghomeshi/

So exactly what is *justified* invasion? Only what is relevant to job performance? So if your employees are professional athletes—then is drug testing justified? And—here's an interesting question for you—would those found *not* to be using performance-enhancing steroids be *required to do so*? Might it start with employers encouraging the use of stimulants at "crunch time"? See Caste on this possibility. What if your employees operate heavy machinery? What if they're pilots? Wouldn't breathalyzer tests be justified? Yet the Supreme Court of Canada has ruled that "[a] unilaterally imposed policy of mandatory random testing for employees in a dangerous workplace has been overwhelmingly rejected by arbitrators as an unjustified affront to the dignity and privacy of employees unless there is evidence of enhanced safety risks, such as evidence of a general problem with substance abuse in the workplace…" (Mitchell).

But what if they're bank tellers? Toronto Dominion Bank's drug-testing policy to screen new hires was deemed discriminatory against the disabled, which was taken to include those with a previous or existing dependence on a drug. But is it also unfair to others, if the drug you test for *doesn't* affect job performance? DesJardins and Duska explore the job-relevant criterion, considering both job performance (which affects productivity and profits) and harm to individuals (employees, consumers); they find the first to be inadequate justification for the invasive testing, the second to be adequate, with some conditions or strings attached. (Moore would disagree, arguing that "responsibility for the actions of others does not entitle us to do anything at all to control their behavior" [abstract].)

What about invasions that are relevant to the cost of employee benefits? Is this employee likely to cost us a lot—because of illness? because of pregnancy? because she is a bungee-jumping freak likely to become a paraplegic? But so what—will you not hire that person then? Or will you just demand that she stop bungee jumping—or smoking?[1] Should an employee be able to (be required to?) opt out of medical benefits plans in order to avoid such screening? Would genetic screening be even more invasive than drug testing via blood and urine tests?

Utilitarian arguments in favour of respecting privacy and those in favour of violating privacy weigh the consequences for all involved: maybe it's good for the company and good for the customers to monitor a pilot's off-time alcohol consumption. But maybe covert surveillance of the office floor will just result in distrust, lower morale, and paranoia.

Kantian ethics seem to favour respect for privacy—invasions of privacy not only fail to respect persons, but they also hinder their autonomy. See Lippke about the relationship between privacy and autonomy: "[p]rivacy conveys to individuals the sense that they are capable of acting autonomously, that they are worthy of doing so, and that they are entitled to do so" (83).

Is this issue of privacy (merely) a question of ownership? If so, then how much exactly does the employer own—the office equipment, the workers' time, the workers' ability, the workers' work?

> **BOX 4.4 How Much Does an Employer Have a Right To?**
>
> Employees must often sign confidentiality agreements, which prohibit them from sharing trade secrets. But how can you ask someone to totally forget (and not use) knowledge they've obtained working for you when they leave and work for someone else? Surely in many cases, the line can be blurry between what they "know" and what is a "trade secret." A specific recipe is one thing; additional understanding about the way the world works is another.
>
> Another good question is "On what basis does the product of work belong solely to the employer?" Because it is the result of the employer's resources? Because of the need for fair competition? Is payment for someone's effort and time (i.e., wage/salary) enough (i.e., *fair* enough) when the resulting research or invention brings the company millions?

---

1 In addition to MacDonald and Williams-Jones, see Kupfer; Gunderson, Mayo, and Rhame; Ladd, Pasquerella, and Smith; and Simms—all address testing, hiring (or not), and healthcare costs.

In any case, the employer doesn't own, not in a large business; the stockholders own, don't they? But ownership alone might not justify control; recall the stakeholder theory.

One might also consider whether invasion of privacy is the best—or the only—way to acquire the information needed or desired. Consider your alternatives! Maybe, for example, instead of monitoring internet use, you could just block certain websites.[1]

The Right to a Safe Workplace

A first important question is "Is an employer obligated to provide a healthy and safe workplace?" Yes, because we have a right to survival? Or yes, because an employer who has an unsafe, unhealthy workplace is obviously treating its workers as the means to his/her end and is therefore morally in the wrong (an appeal to Kantian ethics rather than to rights theories)?

A second important question regarding workplace safety is, as with product safety, "How safe is safe enough?" Lowrance presents a valuable insight when he distinguishes between, and then connects, safety and risk: "Safety is not measured. *Risks* are measured. Only when those risks are weighed on the balance of social values can safety be judged: *a thing is safe if its attendant risks are judged to be acceptable*" (224). He goes on to determine acceptability according to a range of factors, including best available practice and detectable adverse effects.

But is it necessarily and completely the employer's decision to make? What if your employees are *willing* to work in a dangerous workplace? (Don't I have the right to be a crash test dummy if that's what I want to be when I grow up?) Especially if it's for more pay? Shouldn't people have the right to choose? (Perhaps a theory of rights can be *too* robust—and can thereby infringe on people's autonomy, their freedom of choice.)

But should a company influence that choice by offering danger pay? (On the other hand, should it expect dangerous jobs to be done at regular pay?) Is that influence or manipulation? Do your employees have alternatives—*attractive* alternatives? (Is that necessary before we call their willingness a free choice?)

Asking whether employees have the right to choose to accept the danger is separate from asking whether they have the right to be *told* about the danger. And then can they refuse any dangerous part without losing their job?

Peskin and McGrath note that "accidents do not happen randomly; they are caused" (66)—by inadequate worker training, lack of understanding of the job, improper tools and equipment, hazardous work environments, poor equipment maintenance, and overly tight scheduling (and hotshot workers who show off or who partied the night before?), suggesting that one's moral responsibility may be not just to passively do no harm but to actively prevent harm. One might add that prevention is important not only with industrial injuries: carpal tunnel syndrome from keyboarding and chronic lower back pain from cashiering are both preventable (why *do*

---

[1] See Arnesen and Weis for a pretty comprehensive (15-point) list of things to be included in any email/internet monitoring policy.

they have to *stand* for eight hours, lifting stuff across the checkout—that's about six inches too high—with the upper body only?).[1]

In the matter of prevention, does foreknowledge matter? A classic case of worker safety is the Johns Manville company, which became aware of the adverse health effects of asbestos exposure in the 1930s but, nevertheless, did nothing to inform its workers. Are they therefore more at fault? With respect to foreknowledge, how much must the employer do to determine any long-term ill effects of the work environment? Is it fair to require over ten years of testing before you even open your business?

Also, with respect to prevention, does the availability of alternatives matter? (Well, one alternative is *always* available—shut down the business.... Yes, that *is* an option.)

Frances Early, focusing on the Canadian nuclear industry, makes an interesting point about discrimination and the right to a safe workplace: traditionally, women of reproductive age, whether pregnant or not, have been kept out of jobs that pose reproductive health hazards; but men, whose sperm may be damaged by the same conditions, have not been so restricted, not so protected. How can that be justified?

The Right to Parental Leave

Before focusing on this particular benefit, we may well ask about benefits in general: Is it the employer's obligation to provide benefits? Why? Why not? What benefits should be provided? Why those and not others? And should benefits be available only to full-time workers or to all workers, on a pro-rated basis?

As for parental leave, why should that be a right—with or without pay? If Person A gets a year off to make a child, why shouldn't Person B get a year off to write a symphony? Is there something special about children? (Let's face it—almost anyone can make a baby, but few people can write a symphony.) Is there something special about children that obligates an employer to provide some benefit to employees? If anything, shouldn't society as a whole bear the burden of maintaining the species? Does it matter whether the child is genetically related to the employee? Legally related?

Shaw supports parental leave, suggesting that we shouldn't have to choose between a meaningful career and meaningful parenthood (though I'd say the latter *is* the former):

> Enhanced opportunities for part-time employment and job sharing, along with generous parental leave arrangements and flexible, affordable, and accessible firm-sponsored child-care facilities, could enable both fathers and mothers to achieve a more personally desirable balance between paid work and family relations. (255)

But again, why is that a *company's* responsibility?

---

[1] See Boatright, who has an entire chapter on occupational health and safety.

> **BOX 4.5   Feel Like Watching a Movie?**
>
> And speaking of hostile work environments, check out the movie *North Country*. It was a real eye-opener, even for me. And stay tuned for the twenty-first-century iteration, featuring the Canadian army (see Noémi Mercier and Alec Castonguay, "Our Military's Disgrace," *Maclean's* 16 May 2014).

References and Further Reading

Abella, Judge Rosalie. *Equality in Employment, A Royal Commission Report*. Government of Canada: Minister of Supply and Services, 1984.

Abrams, Kathryn. "The Reasonable Woman: Sense and Sensibility in Sexual Harassment Law." *Dissent* (Winter 1995): 48–55.

Andiappan, P., M. Reavley, and S. Silver. "Discrimination Against Pregnant Employees: An Analysis of Arbitration and Human Rights Tribunal Decisions in Canada." *Journal of Business Ethics* 9.2 (1990): 143–49.

Arnesen, David W., and William L. Weis. "Developing an Effective Company Policy for Employee Internet and Email Use." *Journal of Organizational Culture, Communications and Conflict* 11.2 (2007): 53–65.

Bell, Myrtle P., Mary E. McLaughlin, and Jennifer M. Sequeira. "Discrimination, Harassment, and the Glass Ceiling: Women Executives as Change Agents." *Journal of Business Ethics* 37 (2002): 65–76.

Boatright, John R. *Ethics and the Conduct of Business*. 2nd ed. Englewood Cliffs, NJ: Prentice Hall, 1997.

Brenkert, George G. "Privacy, Polygraphs and Work." *Business and Professional Ethics Journal* 1.1 (1981): 19–35.

Brockett, Patrick L., and E. Susan Tankersley. "The Genetics Revolution, Economics, Ethics and Insurance." *Journal of Business Ethics* 16.15 (1997): 1661–76.

Caste, Nicholas J. "Drug Testing and Productivity." *Journal of Business Ethics* 11.4 (1992): 301–06.

Connor, Cheryl. "Who Wastes the Most Time at Work?" *Forbes* 7 Sept. 2013. http://www.forbes.com/sites/cherylsnappconner/2013/09/07/who-wastes-the-most-time-at-work/

De George, Richard T. *Business Ethics*. 5th ed. Englewood Cliffs, NJ: Prentice Hall, 1999.

Dell, Kristina, and Lisa Takeuchi Kullen. "Snooping Bosses." *Time*. 3 Sept 2006. http://content.time.com/time/magazine/article/0,9171,1531312,00.html

DesJardins, Joseph, and Ronald Duska. "Drug Testing in Employment." *Business and Professional Ethics Journal* 6 (1987): 3–21.

Dimock, Susan, and Christopher Tucker. "Affirmative Action and Employment Equity in Canada." In Susan Dimock and Christopher Tucker (eds.), *Applied Ethics: Reflective Moral Reasoning*. Scarborough, ON: Nelson, 2004.

Di Norcia, Vincent. "Downsizing, Change and Ownership." In Leo Groarke (ed.), *The Ethics of the New Economy: Restructuring and Beyond*. Waterloo, ON: WLU Press, 1998. 143–54.

Dodds, Susan M., Lucy Frost, Robert Pargetter, and Elizabeth W. Prior. "Sexual Harassment." *Social Theory and Practice* 14.2 (1988): 111–30.

Donohue, Meg. "Why Tall People Make More Money." CNN. 2 Feb. 2007. http://edition.cnn.com/2007/US/Careers/02/02/cb.tall.people/

Early, Frances H. "Reproductive Health Hazards at Work: The Canadian Atomic Industry." In Deborah C. Poff and Wilfrid J. Waluchow (eds.), *Business Ethics in Canada*. 2nd ed. Scarborough: Prentice Hall, 1991. 216–21.

Ewing, David. W. "An Employees' Bill of Rights." In William H. Shaw and Vincent Barry (eds.), *Moral Issues in Business*. 7th ed. Belmont, CA: Wadsworth, 1998. 278–89.

Ewing, David W. *Freedom Inside the Organization*. New York: Dutton, 1977.

Falkenberg, L.E., and L. Boland. "Eliminating the Barriers to Employment Equity in the Canadian Workplace." *Journal of Business Ethics* 16.9 (1997): 963–75.

Ferris, Gerald R., and Thomas R. King. "The Politics of Age Discrimination in Organizations." *Journal of Business Ethics* 11.5–6 (1992): 341–50.

Fullinwider, Robert K. "Preferential Hiring and Compensation." *Social Theory and Practice* 3.3 (1975): 307–20.

Garrett, Thomas M., and Richard J. Klonoski. *Business Ethics*. 2nd ed. Englewood Cliffs, NJ: Prentice Hall, 1986.

Gaski, John F. "Raising the Minimum Wage Is Unethical and Immoral." *Business and Society Review* 109.2 (2004): 209–24.

Groarke, Leo. "Affirmative Action as a Form of Restitution." *Journal of Business Ethics* 9.3 (1990): 207–13.

———. "What's in a Number? Consequentialism and Employment Equity in Hall, Hurka, Sumner and Baker et al." *Dialogue* XXXV (1996): 359–73.

Gunderson, Martin, David Mayo, and Frank Rhame. "AIDS Testing Mandated by Insurers and Employers." In Martin Gunderson, David Mayo, and Frank Rhame (eds.), *AIDS: Testing and Privacy*. Salt Lake City: University of Utah Press, 1989. 165–88.

Harbert, Tam. "When IT Is Asked to Spy." *ComputerWorld* 11 Oct. 2010.

Harvey, Michael, Darren Treadway, Joyce Thompson Heames, and Allison Duke. "Bullying in the 21st Century Global Organization: An Ethical Perspective." *Journal of Business Ethics* 85 (2009): 27–40.

Häyry, Heta, and Matti Häyry. "AIDS Now." *Bioethics* 1.4 (1987): 339–56.

Heilman, Madeline E. "Sex Discrimination and the Affirmative Action Remedy: The Role of Sex Stereotypes." *Journal of Business Ethics* 16.9 (1997): 877–89.

Henry, Eleanor G., and James P. Jennings. "Age Discrimination in Layoffs: Factors of Injustice." *Journal of Business Ethics* 54 (2004): 217–24.

Hubbard, Ruth, and Elijah Wald. *Exploding the Gene Myth*. Boston: Beacon Press, 1993: 133–44.

"Hunters and Harvesters." *Windspeaker* Classroom Edition 1. http://www.ammsa.com/sites/default/files/html-pages/old-site/classroom/CLASS1HUNTERS.html

Hurka, Thomas. *Principles: Short Essays on Ethics*. Toronto: Harcourt Brace, 1994.

Kavka, Gregory S. "Disability and the Right to Work." In Joseph R. DesJardins and John J. McCall (eds.), *Contemporary Issues in Business Ethics*. 3rd ed. Belmont, CA: Wadsworth, 1996. 486–92.

Kupfer, Joseph. "The Ethics of Genetic Screening in the Workplace." *Business Ethics Quarterly* 3.1 (1993): 17–25.

Ladd, Rosalind, Lynn Pasquerella, and Sheri Smith. "Liability-driven Ethics: The Impact on Hiring Practices." *Business Ethics Quarterly* 4.3 (1994): 321–33.

"Let's Talk about Fish" *Windspeaker* Classroom Edition 2. http://www.ammsa.com/sites/default/files/html-pages/old-site/classroom/CLASS2FISH.html

Lippke, Richard. *Radical Business Ethics*. Lanham, MD: Rowman & Littlefield, 1995. (Chapter 4, "Privacy, Work, and Autonomy")

Lowrance, William W. "Of Acceptable Risk." In Michael Boylan (ed.), *Ethical Issues in Business*. Fort Worth, TX: Harcourt Brace College Publishers, 1995. 223–31.

MacDonald, Chris, and Bryn Williams-Jones. "Ethics and Genetics: Susceptibility Testing in the Workplace." *Journal of Business Ethics* 35 (2002): 235–41.

Manning, Rita C. "Liberal and Communitarian Defenses of Workplace Privacy." *Journal of Business Ethics* 16.8 (1997): 817–23.

McKay-Panos, Linda. "Bully Bosses: When Harassment Is Not Discrimination." *LawNow* 4 Nov. 2012. http://www.lawnow.org/bully-bosses-when-harassment-is-not-discrimination/

Mercier, Noémi, and Alec Castonguay. "Our Military's Disgrace." *Maclean's* 16 May 2014.

Mitchell, Teresa. "Bench Press 37-6: Mandatory Workplace Testing." *LawNow* 1 July 2013. http://www.lawnow.org/mandatory-workplace-testing/

Moore, Jennifer. "Drug Testing and Corporate Responsibility: The 'Ought Implies Can' Argument." *Journal of Business Ethics* 8.4 (1989): 279–87.

Murray, Thomas H. "Genetics and the Moral Mission of Health Insurance." *Hastings Center Report* 22.6 (Nov./Dec. 1992): 12–17.

Nagel, Thomas. "A Defense of Affirmative Action." Testimony before the Subcommittee on the Constitution of the Senate Judiciary Committee, 18 June 1981. In Tom L. Beauchamp and Norman E. Bowie (eds.), *Ethical Theory and Business*. 5th ed. Englewood Cliffs, NJ: Prentice Hall, 1997. 370–74.

Namie, Gary. "The Challenge of Workplace Bullying." *Employment Relations Today* 34.2 (2007): 43–51.

Narveson, Jan. "Have We a Right to Non-Discrimination?" In Deborah C. Poff and Wilfrid J. Waluchow (eds.), *Business Ethics in Canada*. 3rd ed. Scarborough, ON: Prentice Hall, 1999. 270–87.

Ottensmeyer, Edward J., and Mark A. Heroux. "Ethics, Public Policy, and Managing Advanced Technologies: The Case of Electronic Surveillance." *Journal of Business Ethics* 10.7 (1991): 519–26.

Paetzold, Ramona L., and Bill Shaw. "A Postmodern Feminist View of 'Reasonableness' in Hostile Environment Sexual Harassment." *Journal of Business Ethics* 13.9 (1994): 681–91.

Patriquin, Martin. "Resumé Being Ignored? Try a Name Change." *Maclean's* 26 Mar. 2007.

Peskin, Myron I., and Francis J. McGrath. "Industrial Safety: Who Is Responsible and Who Benefits?" *Business Horizons* 35.3 (1992): 66–70.

Pojman, Louis P. "The Moral Status of Affirmative Action." *Public Affairs Quarterly* 6.2 (1992): 181–206.

Pulfer, Rachel. "Mining Your Business." *This Magazine* 32.5 (1999): 13–15.

Pummer, Chris. "The Measure of an Employee." *MarketWatch*. 21 Oct. 2003. http://www.marketwatch.com/story/height-bias-found-in-us-hiring-promotion-practices

Purdy, Laura M. "In Defense of Hiring Apparently Less Qualified Women." *Journal of Social Philosophy* 15 (1984): 26–33.

Quinn, Jennifer M. "Visibility and Value: The Role of Job Evaluation in Assuring Equal Pay for Women." *Law & Policy in International Business* 25 (1994): 1403–44. Rpt. in Tom L. Beauchamp and Norman E. Bowie (eds.), *Ethical Theory and Business*. 5th ed. Englewood Cliffs, NJ: Prentice Hall, 1997. 393–98.

Quinn, John F. "Business Ethics, Fetal Protection Policies, and Discrimination against Women in the Workplace." *Business & Professional Ethics Journal* 7.3–4 (1988): 3–27.

Rayner, C., H. Hoel, and C. Cooper. *Workplace Bullying: What We Know, Who Is to Blame and What We Can Do*. London: Taylor and Francis, 2002.

Rebick, Judy. "Collect Call to Ma Bell." *This Magazine* 32.5 (1999): 44.

Ridler, Jim. "Ethical Downsizing: How to Walk the Talk." *Engineering Dimension* (July/Aug. 1997): 40–41.

Roehling, Mark V. "Weight Discrimination, in the American Workplace: Ethical Issues and Analysis." *Journal of Business Ethics* 40 (2002): 177–89.

Schwoerer, Catherine E., Douglas R. May, and Benson Rosen. "Organizational Characteristics and HRM Policies on Rights: Exploring the Patterns of Connections." *Journal of Business Ethics* 14.7 (1995): 531–49.

Scott, Sarah. "You *#%&!" *Maclean's* 3 Sept. 2007.

Shaw, Bill. "Affirmative Action: An Ethical Evaluation." *Journal of Business Ethics* 7.10 (1988): 763–70.

Shaw, William H. *Business Ethics*. 2nd ed. Belmont, CA: Wadsworth, 1996.

Simms, Michele. "Defining Privacy in Employee Health Screening Cases: Ethical Ramifications Concerning the Employee/Employer Relationship." *Journal of Business Ethics* 13.5 (1994): 315–25.

Simon, Robert L. "Comparable Pay for Comparable Work?" In Tom L. Beauchamp and Norman E. Bowie (eds.), *Ethical Theory and Business*. 5th ed. Englewood Cliffs, NJ: Prentice Hall, 1997. 398–409.

Singer, Joseph William. "The Reliance Interest in Property." *Stanford Law Review* 40/611 (1988): 614–733.

Southerst, John. "What Price Fairness?" *Canadian Business* 64.12 (1991): 67–72.

Stewart, Wayne H., Donna E. Ledgerwood, and Ruth C. May. "Educating Business Schools about Safety & Health Is No Accident." *Journal of Business Ethics* 15.8 (1996): 919–26.

Thomson, Judith Jarvis. "Preferential Hiring." *Philosophy and Public Affairs* 2 (1973): 364–84.

Velasquez, Manuel G. *Business Ethics: Concepts and Cases*. 4th ed. Englewood Cliffs, NJ: Prentice Hall, 1998.

Wasserstrom, Richard. "A Defense of Programs of Preferential Treatment." *National Forum (The Phi Beta Kappa Journal)* LVIII.1 (1978): 15–18.

Wedeking, Gary A. "Is Mandatory Retirement Unfair Age Discrimination?" *Canadian Journal of Philosophy* 20.3 (1990): 321–34.

Weiss, Joseph W. *Business Ethics: A Managerial, Stakeholder Approach*. Belmont, CA: Wadsworth, 1994. 188–96.

Wells, Deborah L., and Beverly J. Kracher. "Justice, Sexual Harassment, and the Reasonable Victim Standard." *Journal of Business Ethics* 12.6 (1993): 423–31.

Werhane, Patricia H. *Persons, Rights and Corporations*. Englewood Cliffs, NJ: Prentice Hall, 1985. 168–70.

Willard, L. Duane. "Aesthetic Discrimination against Persons." *Dialogue* XVI.4 (1977): 676–92.

Affirmative Action and Employment Equity in Canada[*]

Susan Dimock and Christopher Tucker[1]

I. Introduction

[1] Canada is a country committed to the principle of legal equality amongst its citizenry. This principle is enshrined, among other places, in the fundamental law of the land: the Canadian Constitution. In particular, the *Canadian Charter of Rights and Freedoms* (1982) lays down in s.15 (1) that "Every individual is equal before and under the law and has the right to the equal protection and equal benefit of the law without discrimination and, in particular, without discrimination based on race, national or ethnic origin, colour, religion, sex, age or mental or physical disability." Notwithstanding this commitment to equality, the subsection of the *Charter* immediately following this allows for the implementation of affirmative action programs. Thus s.15 (2) states that "Subsection (1) does not preclude any law, program or activity that has as its object the amelioration of conditions of disadvantaged individuals or groups including those that are disadvantaged because of race, national or ethnic origin, colour, religion, sex, age or mental or physical disability."

The affirmative action programs which s.15(2) [2] permits may take a number of forms. They may be adopted by educational institutions, employers, financial institutions, landlords, insurance companies and many other institutions that are in a position to award benefits within society; depending upon the benefit in question, the specific details of the affirmative action plan will vary, of course.

---

[*] Susan Dimock and Christopher Tucker, "Affirmative Action and Employment Equity in Canada" © 1999 by Susan Dimock and Christopher Tucker. Printed with permission of the authors.

Moreover, even within a single sector there is considerable variation as to the steps that an institution might take by way of adopting affirmative action policies. Take, for example, affirmative action programs within the area of employment. It may be decided that the best way to ameliorate the disadvantages of those discriminated against in the past is to adopt a tie-breaking mechanism: if two candidates are otherwise equally qualified for a job, but one is from a disadvantaged group, then the company will hire that person. Or the company may decide that, because of past discrimination, persons from disadvantaged groups cannot compete on a fair footing with those from more privileged groups, and so it may adopt a policy of ranking applicants which gives minority candidates extra credit, as it were, just for being members of the minority group. Alternatively, a company might decide that more aggressive measures are needed to attract persons from previously disadvantaged groups into their workforce. Thus it might adopt a policy whereby certain positions are set aside for members of minority groups, or it might adopt a quota system which sets hiring targets for specific groups. Though many people think that the exact nature of the program adopted matters to its justification (typically people tend to think that tie-breaking measures are easier to justify than quota systems, for example), we shall not be concerned with the differences between these approaches in what follows. For we believe that all affirmative action programs stand or fall together.

[3] Our concern in this paper is with the justification of affirmative action programs. That they stand in need of justification can be seen from a number of different perspectives. First, the allowance (and in some cases requirement) that educational institutions, employers and others adopt affirmative action programs seems problematic in a society committed to equality. For such programs clearly privilege some over others; they treat people unequally. Secondly, it would seem that affirmative action policies must be inefficient in a certain way. For such programs allow that a candidate may or must be admitted to the institution or hired even though he or she is not the most qualified for the position, because he or she belongs to an historically disadvantaged group. Finally, for every person who is benefited by an affirmative action plan, there is another person who is disadvantaged by it. Those who would have received the benefit on the basis of merit in the absence of affirmative action seem to have some legitimate grievance: they have been adversely discriminated against. Those who view affirmative action programs in this light tend to refer to them as policies of "reverse discrimination." Whatever we call it, though, it is clear that affirmative action stands in need of justification for these reasons.

We shall concentrate on affirmative action as it [4] applies only to employment in what follows. Our concern will be to examine the arguments that are offered in favour of affirmative action policies in hiring, particularly those which have played an important role in setting Canadian policy and law on matters of affirmative action and employment equity. We shall conclude that the reasons typically offered in defence of affirmative action are inadequate.

The basic argument will proceed as follows. [5] Those who wish to defend the use of affirmative action programs typically do so on one of two importantly different grounds. The first general approach to justifying affirmative action programs is to argue that they are required by justice. The second approach is to argue that they produce good consequences for society. We shall argue that the arguments from justice are problematic, and that only consequentialist reasons seem capable of providing a defensible justification of affirmative action. But whether a particular policy like affirmative action actually produces good consequences is an empirical matter. So while we can agree with those consequentially-minded philosophers and legal theorists that *if* affirmative action programs produced significant goods for society then they could be justified, we shall question whether they actually do produce such goods. And we shall find that most of the goods which it is suggested are made available by affirmative action programs not only are not produced by such programs, but are actually retarded by them. Thus the second approach to defending affirmative action policies is also unsuccessful.

II. Justice-Based Defenses of Affirmative Action

[6] Those who wish to argue that affirmative action programs are justified because they are required by justice have two routes available to them, and both have had numerous followers. They each correspond to the kind of justice that affirmative action is supposed to serve: compensatory justice or distributive justice.

II.1 Compensatory Justice

[7] The first argument from justice has it that affirmative action is required as a matter of *compensatory* justice. The idea is this: members of the groups that are now to be favoured by affirmative action have in the past been adversely discriminated against. As a result of that discrimination, they now occupy a significantly disadvantaged position relative to those who were not discriminated against in the past. Because the past discrimination was unjustified, based on attributed rather than actual characteristics, it was unfair. Therefore, the resulting advantages for some and disadvantages for others were equally unfair; some benefited unjustly at the expense of others. As a matter of justice, then, we must right this wrong.

Now this argument has been subject to considerable attack. Most important, we think, is that it is incompatible with the actual way in which affirmative action programs must work. For affirmative action programs identify those who are to be favoured by group membership. Thus, for example, the Canadian Employment Equity Act which was passed in 1986 identified four designated groups whose members were to be advantaged via affirmative action programs: women, aboriginal peoples, persons with disabilities, and persons who are, because of their race or colour, in a visible minority in Canada. If we adopted the compensatory justice model for defending such legislation, we should have to say that every member of these groups has been disadvantaged relative to others who are not members of these groups, such that those who were not disadvantaged gained benefits unfairly at the expense of those who were disadvantaged. And this is precisely the position that the courts have in fact taken in Canada. Group membership alone is taken as sufficient evidence that a person has been discriminated against or is entitled to affirmative action assistance. Under s.15(2) of the Charter, "The court would be spared assessing the situation of every individual covered by an ameliorative program to determine whether he or she were entitled to be included in the class of *disadvantaged* persons. Every member of the disadvantaged group would be assumed to have been disadvantaged and thereby entitled to the benefit of the program...."[2] [8]

But of course the presumption that every member of a disadvantaged group has thereby been disadvantaged is highly implausible! We cannot assume that just because an individual belongs to an historically disadvantaged group, that that individual has been disadvantaged and so deserves compensation. It may be true, for example, that [9] women as a group have been discriminated against to their detriment in employment, but that surely does not alone entitle someone like Princess Diana or Jackie Kennedy-Onassis to compensatory benefits. For they simply have not suffered from adverse discrimination and so have no claim to compensation. The point of all this is a general one, though: because we cannot identify individual victims of past discrimination on the basis of group membership alone, affirmative action programs which make entitlements to compensatory benefits available just on that basis cannot be justified. They will extend benefits to those who do not deserve them. Furthermore, they are unlikely to benefit those who are most entitled to compensation on this model because, even with affirmative action programs that grant them extra points or that reserve positions for members of their group, those individuals who have been most severely disadvantaged by past discrimination will not be able to compete for valuable employment positions; they will lack the skills needed to compete even for an affirmative action position.

[10] A similar problem arises if we concentrate, not on the beneficiaries of affirmative action, but on those who lose out as a result of such programs. According to the compensatory justice approach, we may disadvantage those who belong to groups that have benefited from past discriminatory practices (white, abled, non-aboriginal males, in particular). The reason given for this is that they have gained unfair benefits at the expense of others, and so must now provide compensation for their ill-gotten gains. But the group problem re-emerges here: not every white, abled, non-aboriginal man has participated in discriminatory practices or benefited from them. Just as we cannot identify the victims of discrimination by group membership alone, nor can we identify the beneficiaries of discrimination in that way.

[11] Consideration of those who are to be relatively disadvantaged by affirmative action programs on compensatory grounds raises a further concern. The discrimination at issue is an historical event, which has produced significant disadvantages for those in the designated groups. But the people who have participated in that discrimination are long since dead; they are certainly not the same people who are now told that they must suffer loses in order to compensate those who have been historically disadvantaged. But is this not a case of "the sins of the father being visited upon his sons"? In other words, is this not a clear case of holding the descendants of those who have committed past wrongs responsible for those wrongs, even though they in no way participated in them or had control over them? And do not societies committed to justice abhor such practices?

[12] Whatever the deficiencies of the compensatory justice argument for affirmative action may be and whether its advocates can meet the challenges raised here need not concern us any longer, however, for this argument has not been particularly important in Canada (unlike the United States). It certainly has not been a significant influence in the development of our legislative programs, at least, and since we are concerned with assessing the reasons that have actually been given in support of our affirmative action policies and laws, we can safely move along.

II.2 Distributive Justice

[13] A second argument founded on justice is offered by those in favour of affirmative action as well. In this approach affirmative action is defended as a matter of distributive justice. Those in the designated groups have been unjustly deprived of opportunities and benefits in the past, which make them unable to compete now on the same terms with others who have not been similarly disadvantaged. The

result is distributively unjust, because some have a vastly greater share of the goods which society makes available than others do, through no fault of their own. This injustice in the distribution of society's benefits has to be rectified, and affirmative action is one way to do that.

[14] It is frequently taken as evidence of past discrimination, on this view, that different groups are under-represented in various positions in society relative to their percentage of the population at large. Thus, for example, the fact that only 7% of upper management positions in the private sector are held by women, despite the fact that women make up just over 50% of the total population, is taken as evidence of discrimination against women in employment and career advancement. Not surprisingly, then, the goal of affirmative action which defenders of this view usually adopt is that of having in all sectors of employment a level of representation for each group which is equal to their proportion of the general population.

[15] As with the previous argument from justice, however, this approach faces some very serious challenges. Problems of identifying individuals solely by group membership arise again here, for example, though in a different form. For individuals are not typically identifiable as members of a single group. Is a disabled woman who occupies a managerial position to count as increasing the representation of one group or two?

[16] More importantly, this argument rests upon two very dubious assumptions. The first is that, in the absence of past discrimination, there would in fact be participation in all sectors of the economy equal to representation in the population. This is very unlikely. Given that some differences are genetic, some are a contingent feature of such circumstances as geography, and others are cultural without being based on discrimination, it is unlikely that people will be drawn to or excel at different occupations proportionately with their share of the general population.

[17] The second problem is that this approach assumes that the just distribution of economic positions in society will be equal across groups. This is a controversial moral judgement; those who wish to defend it must shown that a distribution of the economic rewards of society which maintains an equality between a group's percentage of the population and their participation in all sectors of society is better than (more just than) alternative principles of distributive justice. Such alternatives include principles which hold that economic rewards should be distributed according to merit, need, virtue, contribution, etc. Though we cannot enter into the debate concerning the proper conception of distributive justice here, we need not; for again, such arguments have not played a central role in the development of Canadian public policy and law.

[18] Though these arguments from justice have occupied much of the attention of philosophers and other theorists in thinking about affirmative action, they are at best highly contentious and they have failed to generate any consensus concerning the permissibility of such programs. Indeed, for every defender of affirmative action on the grounds that it is required by justice (compensatory or distributive), one can find opponents who insist that it is a subversion of justice. It subverts justice, moreover, in exactly the same way that discrimination of the type to be resisted does, because it makes benefits available to people on such arbitrary grounds as skin colour or gender, rather than on relevant grounds such as merit.

[19] Those who think that affirmative action is in fact discriminatory against those who have been privileged in the past may nonetheless think that it is justified, as a necessary means to eliminating the gross inequality that characterises our society

and as a way of providing those who have previously disadvantaged with a fair opportunity of bettering their fortunes. To take this kind of line, however, is to adopt a very different approach to the justification of affirmative action, one which looks not to its justice but to its good social consequences.

III. Consequentialist Justifications of Affirmative Action

[20] Those who argue that affirmative action is justified because it will lead to significant social benefits are offering a consequentialist position. Consequentialism is the view that an action, policy, law or what have you is justified when it produces good consequences. The best action is that which, of the alternatives available, produces the best consequences. The most common consequentialist position is typically some form of utilitarianism, which holds that the consequences that matter are those affecting the welfare, happiness, well-being or utility of all those affected by the action, policy or law in question. Utilitarianism then says that the right thing to do, or the morally justified thing to do, is whatever, among the alternatives, will maximise the welfare, happiness, well-being or utility of all those affected by the choice. This has been the route adopted by most Canadian philosophers who have sought to defend affirmative action, as well as by our legislators in setting public policy and developing laws designed to achieve employment equity and eliminate discrimination in the work-place.

[21] Now those who wish to defend affirmative action on the grounds that it will produce good social consequences (and that nothing less invasive of freedom will do so) must explain what good consequences are to be expected from such policies. A number of good consequences have been proposed in this regard.

III.1 To Better Serve the Needs of Minority Cultures

[22] It is frequently claimed in support of affirmative action that the needs of minority cultures are unique in important ways, and that the best way of ensuring that those needs are met in a way that is sensitive to their differences is to have representatives from the minority cultures themselves providing the services. This is typically taken to require affirmative action programs specifically designed to increase the spaces available to members of the minority cultures in advanced educational and training programs, rather than affirmative action designed to achieve employment equity in all sectors of the economy.

[23] This argument may be able to provide a limited defence of affirmative action programs, particularly in relation to fields such as medicine in which cultural differences are often very significant and dictate a different approach to the physician/patient/family relationship, death, medical procedures, consent and patient autonomy, etc. A similar case may be made with respect to the legal profession. In such cases it may be plausible to conclude that medical and legal services provided by members of one's own community would be better than those provided by others from outside of one's cultural group.

[24] This argument faces some serious challenges, however. First, it is simply not possible to ensure that members of the various ethnic, racial, linguistic and cultural groups that constitute Canada's diverse population be served by professionals drawn from their own communities exclusively or even primarily. The resources that would be required to implement such a system are simply not available. Most communities can only support a small number of specialised professionals, whether they be medical, legal or financial specialists, for example. Furthermore, if one were to attempt to

increase the participation of various minority cultures' members in the different professions as a means of providing better service to those groups, one would not only have to adopt affirmative action policies to ensure that training was available to these individuals, but one would then also have to ensure that they practised their professions in centres whose population is made up of a sufficient number of the minority group's members. This would be a significant invasion into the freedom of those who are to be the beneficiaries of such programs, and it is certainly not a policy that has received political support or expression in Canada. Finally, such an argument seems to run a serious risk of isolating minority communities, of maintaining their distinctiveness and homogeneity at the price of cutting them off from other communities and their members. This model seems ill-suited to achieve the Canadian vision of a multi-cultural society, in which distinct and diverse peoples come together, not into a melting pot which eliminates their differences, but into a mosaic where each piece of the pattern is unique but related to all the rest in a way that renders the result unified and beautiful. The Canadian vision of multi-culturalism depends upon interaction between peoples, which will give rise to knowledge and tolerance of differences. Any policy which presupposes that individuals in minority cultures can only receive adequate service from members of their own group flies in the face of our national ideal.

[25] Thus while increasing the participation of various minority groups within such professions as medicine and law would, perhaps, improve the quality of service available to members of those groups, this approach provides only a very limited defence of affirmative action programs at best. For the good that such a policy would make available can be provided to only a few groups, likely in large urban centres, and even there members of minority groups would still have to receive a considerable amount of service from non-member specialists. Furthermore, this good cannot be achieved by affirmative action programs alone but must be conjoined with restrictive requirements designed to ensure that those who receive the professional training use their skills in the service of their minority group; this is a serious cost which may offset any good that such a policy might make possible. Finally, this approach runs the risk of isolating and marginalizing the groups it is designed to assist. For these reasons, this consideration is not sufficient to justify the wide-spread use of affirmative action programs in society at large.

[26] This case does, however, raise an issue that permeates our discussion of the various consequentialist defences that are offered in favour of affirmative action programs: those who wish to employ consequentialist arguments must consider *all* of the consequences a policy is likely to achieve. For it is not enough to establish that a policy would have some good consequences, if those are vastly outweighed by bad consequences that would also attend it. Furthermore, this case, like those to follow, should serve as a warning. In particular, philosophers are notorious for speculating about the likely consequences of various proposals, without much empirical investigation. Thus while a good consequence of affirmative action might on first glance seem plausible in the abstract, the details often belie the suggested benefit. When discussing empirical matters, it is best to get out of our armchairs and consult the experts in the field, as we shall see.

III.2 To Promote Diversity

[27] Affirmative action policies are often advocated on the grounds that they will promote diversity in employment situations. Philosophers and other academics are often among those who advance

diversity as a reason for adopting affirmative action programs. It is likely that this is a case in which a specific good for a very unique profession has been inappropriately applied to others where it fits less well. For there may indeed be good reason to think that universities and other centres of research and learning benefit from a diversity of views, cultural influences, histories, etc. It is not surprising, therefore, that professional philosophers and other academics should promote diversity as a value in its own right; within their professions diversity is a significant good. But it would be problematic to conclude from this that affirmative action as a general program in society is justified, for it is not at all clear that diversity is a value in its own right. Rather, it seems vastly more likely that diversity is promoted as a good because people believe that it will be instrumental in achieving other goods: tolerance, understanding, an undermining of the racist/sexist/ablist attitudes that produce the invidious discrimination in the first place, different groups will then have role models available upon which their members can draw, etc. These goods, which diversity in the population of various employment sectors is supposed to generate, all depend on diversity itself leading to some fundamental changes in attitudes, both by those who are to be the beneficiaries of affirmative action and those who are thereby forced not to discriminate against those whom they otherwise would discriminate against. Since the effect on attitudes has occupied a central place in Canadian justifications of affirmative action, both in the political and academic arena, we shall examine this claim closely in what follows.

III.3 Attitudinal Changes and the Reduction of Prejudice

[28] Those who adopt a consequentialist approach to affirmative action typically relate the good consequences that they anticipate from affirmative action programs ultimately to a change of attitudes among the members of society. This is not surprising, of course, since the discrimination that affirmative action policies is supposed to ameliorate ultimately stems from prejudicial attitudes based on arbitrary characteristics of persons such as race, ethnicity, gender, physical disabilities, etc. If these attitudes are fundamentally responsible for discriminatory practices, then policies aimed at eliminating these attitudes seem the best approach to eliminating discrimination. It would seem, furthermore, that changing attitudes is really behind the more specific consequentialist arguments that are advanced in favour of affirmative action: that it will promote diversity, lead to better service for minority groups, provide role models for members of groups which have been previously disadvantaged because of prejudice and the like are all held out as good because they will lead to greater tolerance and understanding between groups. Those who have been prejudiced against in the past will come to be seen as competent and contributing members of their professions, both by those who previously undervalued them and by themselves. Through participation, previously disadvantaged groups will gain not only the esteem they deserve from others, but self-respect as well. As prejudicial attitudes are eroded, people from previously disadvantaged groups will be increasingly able to simply compete on a fair basis with others, for they will no longer have to overcome the arbitrary biases against them that racism, sexism, etc. put in their way in the past. The end result of this process, consequentialists hope, is a society in which people are judged and rewarded purely on the basis of merit. When such a state is reached, affirmative action programs will no longer be needed; affirmative action is at best a temporary means to overcoming the prejudice that denies some people the opportunities they deserve, and once those prejudicial attitudes have

been overcome affirmative action commitments can simply wither away.

[29] Now these are some very sweeping generalisations about what all or most consequentialists think on the matter of affirmative action. They are borne out, however, by an examination both of the writings of our most prominent philosophers and of our legislators and policy makers. Take, for example, the work of L.W. Sumner. Sumner argues that affirmative action, or positive discrimination as he calls it, cannot be defended on grounds of corrective or compensatory justice. He does think that it can be defended on consequentialist grounds, however, and he rests his argument on using affirmative action as a means of overcoming certain prejudicial attitudes. Concentrating just on the use of affirmative action policies that favour women in employment, Sumner argues that affirmative action programs are needed principally to combat the effects of sexism, and ultimately to eliminate sexist attitudes themselves. He identifies two forms of sexism: primary (direct or overt) sexism and, more importantly, what he calls "secondary sexism," which consists in a host of attitudes by which the abilities or commitment of female candidates for employment or promotion are undervalued because of prejudicial attitudes about women. Secondary sexist attitudes include such things as the belief that women will be less committed to their jobs because of family responsibilities, that a female candidate will not be able to fit into a male dominated work environment, etc. Now Sumner thinks that secondary sexism is "one of the main mechanisms whereby employment practices continue to discriminate against women"[3] and that affirmative action programs must discriminate in favour of women in order to neutralise the immediate effects of such sexist attitudes and thereby ultimately eliminate those attitudes: "The centrepiece of the consequentialist argument is the claim that introducing a measure of discrimination against men will be the most effective means of eliminating discrimination against women, and thus of minimising discrimination in the long run."[4]

Likewise, Thomas Hurka believes not only [30] that sexist attitudes lead to discrimination against women in employment, but that changing those attitudes is one of the principal benefits of affirmative action. Indeed, he thinks that affirmative action will produce positive changes not only in men's attitudes toward women but also in women's attitudes towards themselves:

> If the belief that women are inferior persists in Canada, either consciously or sub-consciously, it's partly because women aren't sufficiently prominent in Canadian life. Moving them quickly into important jobs can help dispel that belief and the many harms it does.
>
> Equally important are the changes in women's attitudes. What you aspire to in life depends on what you think you can do, which depends on what people like you have done before. Women in prominent jobs can be role models, encouraging young women to work for similar success. If the young women achieve success this will benefit both them and society, which now wastes much of their potential.[5]

In this quotation we find Hurka appealing to two of the consequentialist reasons discussed above—increasing the representation of a given group in a particular field and the role model argument—though his reason for doing so is not that these benefits alone are sufficient to justify affirmative action, but that they will lead to the change in attitudes that will ultimately eliminate discrimination based on the prejudicial belief that women are inferior to men.

Let us turn now to an examination of the legal [31] literature supporting affirmative action, and particularly employment equity. The Supreme Court of Canada, for example, has made it clear in a number of rulings that the purpose of s.15 of the Charter, as well as the various Provincial Human Rights Codes, is to prevent the deleterious effects of discrimination. In so doing, they have adopted a consequentialist position at two levels. First, whether a particular law, labour practice, insurance provision or what have you is discriminatory depends upon its effects, not the intent of those who have adopted it. No intent to discriminate or other foul motive is necessary in order to establish that discrimination has occurred. Secondly, they have attributed to anti-discrimination and equity legislation a consequentialist justification or purpose: to remove the negative effects of prejudice.[6]

[32] The Supreme Court's position is not unique in this respect. Indeed, as we shall see, the approach taken by the members of our legal community has been thoroughly consequentialist, with the goal of changing prejudicial attitudes as a means of reducing discrimination occupying a prominent position in their deliberations about the justification of affirmative action policies. This concentration on creating a climate in which attitudes of fellow-feeling, respect, inclusivity and mutual understanding replace those of prejudice, ascriptions of inferiority upon whole groups and exclusion of those who are different than oneself, as a means of effecting greater equality within society, is reflected in virtually all of the Provincial and Territorial Human Rights Codes. Thus we read in the Preamble to the Human Rights Code of Ontario, for example, that "WHEREAS it is public policy in Ontario to recognise the dignity and worth of every person and to provide for equal rights and opportunities without discrimination that is contrary to law, and having as its aim the creation of a climate of understanding and mutual respect for the dignity and worth of each person so that each person feels a part of the community and able to contribute fully to the development and well-being of the community and the Province...."[7] The Canadian commitment to affirmative action and employment equity must be understood against the backdrop of this more sweeping commitment to equality and the goal of creating a society free of invidious prejudice.

[33] In 1986 the federal Government of Canada passed the Employment Equity Act. In that Act four groups of persons were identified as victims of prejudicial discrimination in employment and designated as groups for whom employment equity was immediately needed: women, aboriginal peoples, persons with disabilities, and persons who are, because of their race or colour, in a visible minority in Canada. It is clear from writings related to this Act that its framers intended it to have the effect of increasing the participation of members of the designated groups in employment situations from which they had traditionally been excluded on grounds that they belonged to one of the designated groups: "Employment Equity is a result-oriented program which seeks evidence that employment situations for the designated groups are improving, indicated by their greater numerical representation in the workforce, improvement in their employment status, occupations, and salary levels in jobs for which they are available and qualified."[8]

[34] Now the government of Canada clearly recognises that the factors contributing to the relative employment disadvantage of persons in the designated groups are diverse. Many which they identified in discussing the Employment Equity Act might be categorised as structural, involving the way employment activity is structured: thus lack of day-care facilities for women, lack of ramps and elevators for disabled persons, the organisation of the work-day into standard eight-hour shifts and the like present barriers to certain groups. These can be easily remedied, however, and the Supreme

Court of Canada has made it clear that the equality guaranteed to all Canadians under the law requires that employers take reasonable steps to accommodate workers with special needs.[9] Much more important for our purposes are the attitudinal causes which the government identified as leading to the under-representation of the designated groups in the workforce, particularly at the managerial or professional levels. For these attitudes are not only a barrier in and of themselves, but they retard the willingness or ability of employers to see the value of making the needed structural changes. Among those attitudes, identified in the Government of Canada Background Paper to the proposed Employment Equity Act, are the following: "Foremost is the attitude of many non-disabled persons: there is a widespread misunderstanding and underrating of the abilities of disabled persons." And in relation to aboriginal peoples, "Native people face attitudinal and cultural barriers to their equitable participation in the economy. Racial intolerance and misunderstanding" are chief amongst them. Likewise, "Research attests to the existence both of prejudicial attitudes to non-whites and systemic discrimination based on racial factors."[10] It is clear from these and similar claims that the authors of the Background Paper believe that prejudicial attitudes play a crucial role in the perpetuation of discrimination against the designated groups, and insofar as they adopted employment equity (affirmative action) as their response to such discrimination, they believe that affirmative action policies can (help to) eliminate those pernicious attitudes.

[35] The perceived relation between prejudicial attitudes and discrimination in employment was perhaps nowhere more clearly articulated than in the report of the Royal Commission on Equality in Employment, headed by Judge Rosalie Abella. In their report the members of the Royal Commission made it clear that they understood both discrimination and equity to essentially involve certain attitudes. Thus "the goal of equality is more than an evolutionary intolerance to adverse discrimination. It is to ensure, too, that the vestiges of these arbitrarily restrictive assumptions do not continue to play a role in our society."[11] And as to their understanding of discrimination, they characterised it this way: "Discrimination in this context means practices or attitudes that have, whether by design or impact, the effect of limiting an individual's or a group's right to the opportunities generally available because of attributed rather than actual characteristics."[12]

[36] Group membership and prejudicial attitudes based on group membership are central in the approach adopted by the Royal Commission on Equality in Employment:

> Remedial measures of a systemic and systematic kind are the object of employment equity and affirmative action. They are meant to improve the situation for individuals who, by virtue of belonging to and being identified with a particular group, find themselves unfairly and adversely affected by certain systems or practices. System remedies are a response to patterns of discrimination that have two basic antecedents:
> a) a disparate negative impact that flows from the structure of systems designed for a homogeneous constituency; and
> b) a disparately negative impact that flows from practices based on stereotypical characteristics ascribed to an individual because of the characteristics ascribed to the group of which he or she is a member.[13]

[37] Judge Abella does not believe that voluntary programs can effect a significant reduction in employment discrimination; mandatory programs are necessary. "Given the seriousness and appar-

ent intractability of employment discrimination, it is unrealistic and somewhat ingenuous to rely on there being sufficient public goodwill to fuel a voluntary program."[14] Apparently coercion will effect an end of discrimination even in the absence of a change of attitude (increase of goodwill), contrary to everything else that we have seen!

IV. The Real Consequences of Affirmative Action

[38] In the introductory paragraph of the last section, we suggested that if it is believed that prejudiced attitudes are responsible for discriminatory practices then any policy designed to eliminate these attitudes seems to be the best way to eliminate discrimination. We then went on to make clear that affirmative action policies, at least in Canada, have been traditionally defended on the grounds that the increased representation of target groups in the workforce would eliminate these prejudiced attitudes, as well as arrest (or at least retard) the discriminatory hiring practices which result from them. The appropriateness of these policies, then, must be evaluated by how effectively they serve their ends. In other words, these affirmative action policies may only be deemed appropriate responses to discriminatory acts and prejudiced attitudes if they serve to eliminate these acts and attitudes; insofar as the former largely stem from the latter, moreover, the efficiency with which affirmative action eliminates those prejudiced attitudes will determine whether it can be justified on consequentialist grounds.

[39] As we have argued above, that the elimination of prejudiced attitudes is of paramount import to the Canadian philosophical and legal communities is clear: Sumner focuses primarily on the importance of changing sexist attitudes, while Hurka believes that the overcoming of prejudiced attitudes is one of the principal benefits of affirmative action. The Ontario Human Rights Code states explicitly that creating a prejudice free environment in which its citizens can live is one of its principal aims. Canada's Employment Equity Act, likewise, must be understood as an attempt to overcome prejudicial attitudes.

[40] So, then, affirmative action policies may be viewed as appropriate responses to discriminatory hiring practices only insofar as they can be thought to aid the overcoming of prejudiced beliefs. Unfortunately, as we shall see, there is no good reason to believe that these policies serve this end. The psychological literature on the subject indicates that affirmative action policies would actually frustrate efforts geared towards the elimination of prejudiced attitudes held by persons against others because of their membership in historically disadvantaged groups, building resentment in prejudiced individuals, and further entrenching their previous discriminatory behaviours. This literature also fails to indicate that the 'role model' approach to overcoming negative attitudes that disadvantaged persons hold regarding their own social group is served by affirmative action.

IV.1 The Alteration of Others' Attitudes

[41] It is easy to understand why someone would suppose that a workforce which well represents minorities at large would be one in which prejudiced attitudes dwindle off and die. A bigot, prejudiced against each and every type of person who is different than himself, when at work would first be forced to get to know people of type X, Y, and Z, and, through continued interaction with these persons, would then come to respect them, or at least tolerate them. After watching presentation after presentation by persons of groups X, Y, and Z, the bigot would have to reason to the conclusion that he was wrong after all, and that these groups

are not lazy and stupid (to take common prejudiced beliefs). After sharing a change room with them, the bigot would be forced to conclude that they did not smell. And after a very long time, it may even be the case that the bigot is forced to reason to the conclusion that all the members of these groups are not out to get him, and do not even hate him *en masse*. This is a fairly persuasive presentation, and no reasonable person would ignore its power. Unfortunately, there is data available to justify supposing that the bigot is not appropriately described as being 'reasonable'.

[42] Persons with no prejudice imagine themselves in the situation just described, and come to the conclusion that they would end up as unprejudiced persons. They then hastily conclude that anyone in that situation, whether previously prejudiced or not, would likewise come to judge people from minority groups fairly upon getting to know them better. But the results of imposing affirmative action programs upon non-prejudiced people is not particularly telling, since all it amounts to is this: those who are not already prejudiced will not become so if they are forced through affirmative action to interact in the workplace with members of previously disadvantaged groups. But this is not the group that affirmative action must reform in order to eliminate discrimination. What reaction can we expect to our scenario from those who are prejudiced?

[43] People with prejudice need not find the evidence undermining their prejudiced beliefs compelling, and it is far from clear that the imagined scenario would have the desired effects. Persons with prejudiced attitudes have incentive to reason to entirely different conclusions than non-prejudiced persons when confronted with a workplace enhanced by affirmative action policies. In fact, there is ample evidence to suggest that workplaces affected by affirmative action policies would have negative, rather than positive or even negligible, consequences on the bigot's opinions. There is evidence that suggests that affirmative action policies, and indeed "politically correct" (PC) environments more generally, lead to the entrenching of a bigot's disposition, and lead to more radical, but perhaps less obvious, discriminatory behaviours.

[44] For the last several decades, it has been recognised by several psychologists that transgressing a personal standard or conviction creates mental costs for the transgressor. If you maintained throughout your life that John Denver's songs were all a bit cheesy, and then actually heard a song which you said you quite liked, and were then informed that it was by John Denver, you would experience some mental discomfort (and some razzing). It is also recognised quite generally (indeed, it is sometimes treated as a tautology) that one avoids discomfort when one can. To tie this together to the point at hand: if a racist was forced to admit that race X was not so bad after all, then he would experience some psychological costs. Further, if a racist was going to experience some psychological harm, then he would have reason to avoid it if it were possible.

[45] It turns out that in the case in question—the discomfort associated with coming to the conclusion that being a racist is wrong—it is possible to avoid the harm. Ziva Kunda has presented us with a compelling argument which suggests that a person's choice of rules of inference to reason with depends upon the conclusion desired.[15] While there are limits to how wild the reasoning may be, if there is a seemingly plausible argument which may be constructed that allows for the conclusion desired to continue to be endorsed, then it will continue to be endorsed. Bigots, then, are able to construct an argument which allows them to maintain that their racist attitude is warranted, and thus avoid the psychological discomfort which would result from coming to the conclusion that their racist attitudes are incorrect, and must be changed. We

certainly recognise these types of rationalisations: "I have to work with an X, but *he's not like the others, he...*", or "You're O.K., for a skirt", or the somewhat more disturbing, "I wonder who she's getting assistance from, and why?" It is worth noting that the stronger one's racism is, the more discomfort may be expected to obtain after realising that one's personal opinions regarding race X are incorrect. Deeply racist persons would have stronger motivation to avoid coming to the conclusion that their attitudes are inappropriate.

[46] Interestingly enough, it was likely the recognition of the desire to minimise the discomfort associated with an action that contravened one's ideology which led people to the conclusion that affirmative action policies were a good idea to begin with. It was previously thought that by forcing one to say that something was the case, one would then modify one's previous position with regard to the opinion in question. To turn back to our previous example, upon being told that the song was played by John Denver, one may then modify one's previous position and say "Well, at least *that* wasn't cheesy, like his earlier material" or something similar which allows you to maintain some form of consistency. In the case of affirmative action, then, once forced to the conclusion that the co-workers from group X aren't lazy/stupid/smelly, etc., the bigot would then be motivated to conclude that X's, overall, aren't that bad, really. Unfortunately, this is not how cognitive dissonance is believed to actually work. The discomfort associated with expressing something that is inconsistent with one's personal values only arises when one freely chooses to engage in the expression.[16] Forced expressions of non-prejudiced sentiments do not result in a bigot being motivated to become less bigoted.

[47] Being forced to publicly endorse non-racist/sexist sentiments, and to recognise that one is apt to react in a way that society at large prohibits, leads to stress of quite another type, as well. Bigots who recognise that they are living in a PC environment are likely to alter their public behaviours to appear to conform to PC standards, and feel threatened and fearful. E. Ashby Plant and Patricia Devine have recently run several tests which measure the degrees to which people have adopted anti-racist attitudes due to personal endorsement of non-prejudiced beliefs, compared with others who have adopted anti-racist behaviours due to external pressure.[17] Their findings indicate that people who 'cave in' and conform to anti-racist behaviours in response to external pressure do not thereby internalise anti-racist sentiments. Racists can retain their racist sentiments, and feel threatened and fearful, in proportion to how deep the racism runs—the more racist, the more threatened they feel.

Plant and Devine write: [48]

> We are much less sanguine about the likelihood that threat-related feelings, in the absence of guilt, will lead to prejudice reduction... simply avoiding situations in which non-prejudiced social pressure is experienced and/or situations involving contact with outgroup members would be effective strategies to remove the anticipated threat.... [18]

When possible, then, it is likely that these racist individuals would engage in anti-social behaviour, or band together in closed communities. It is not always possible to avoid members of a given group, or a PC society, especially when in the workforce, and especially in a workforce in which affirmative action policies are implemented. What then of the results of the tension created by a racist's fear?

> It seems plausible that such resentment could ultimately culminate in these people lashing out against the...norms...or even outgroup members...under anonymous conditions.... [19]

Incidents of a group of masked individuals gathering and beating members of minority cultures/lifestyles are certainly not rare enough to make this chilling speculation as implausible as one may desire.

[49] To summarise, then: If one consults the psychological literature of the day, affirmative action policies cannot be thought to result in a change of attitude of the racist/sexist/ablist. All that they can reasonably be thought to result in is increased hostility towards already disadvantaged groups. This is not a result to be applauded, nor even tolerated. And insofar as the purpose of affirmative action policies is to change the dispositions of the racists/sexists/ablest at large, these policies must be thought to utterly fail.

IV.2 Changing Attitudes about Oneself

[50] Even if affirmative action cannot change the attitudes of racists/sexists/ablists, does it not still have value insofar as it provides role models for members of disadvantaged groups and raises their self-esteem? Certainly changing the attitudes of members of previously disadvantaged groups about themselves has been seen as integral to the purpose of affirmative action in Canada. Hurka, for example, explicitly mentions the inspiring of individuals to achieve as one of the goals of such programs. So, while failing to justify affirmative action policies on the grounds that they would lead to the eradication of racist attitudes, advocates may still find grounds to justify affirmative action because of the positive effects a role model could have to the members of the relevant group.

[51] Members of disadvantaged groups, having been raised in a culture that inculcates the belief that they cannot achieve success in a given field, do not attempt to do so, even if they have the desire. To this extent we can agree with Hurka. In order to overcome this belief, and realize their dreams, it is thought that a role model would allow disadvantaged persons to come to the conclusion that they, too, could achieve such success. A successful group member in the field of figure-skating could, for example, provide the necessary example for a member of a disadvantaged group to say to himself, "That person is an X, and he is a good figure skater. Therefore people who are from group X can succeed. I am an X, and therefore, despite what I previously thought, I can probably succeed at what I wish to do."

[52] Unfortunately, it turns out that this is a simplistic expectation. It is generally accepted in the literature that *relevant* others are necessary to inspire. An aspiring academic is not inspired by a successful football player of the same group, for example; to be relevant, the role model must have achieved success in the same particular field as the person to be inspired desires success in. By hypothesis of affirmative action supporters, it is also necessary that the role model be relevant in another respect, namely, be of the same group membership. This is also supported by the literature on the subject of how relevance is determined.

[53] The existence of even relevant role models may nonetheless fail to inspire others or boost their self-esteem. Penelope Lockwood and Ziva Kunda have presented strong evidence that suggests that when another person is perceived as relevant, that person will only inspire if his or her success is seen as achievable by the person engaging in the comparison.[20] An aspiring football-player from group X, seeing a quite successful football-player of the same group membership, will not be inspired if the star player's success is due to the fact that he weighs 325 pounds, and the football-player-to-be weighs only 165 pounds, and has little chance at gaining the weight necessary to achieve the success of the role model in question. In fact, if the role model's success is seen as unattainable, the person whom one hopes would be inspired is likely to be discouraged, insofar as the comparison is seen to be relevant. Whatever the profession, the message is the same: only per-

ceivably attainable success will inspire, while perceivably unattainable success will deflate.

[54] This has disastrous consequences for the advocate of affirmative action. Each role model must be successful in order for him or her to inspire anyone at all. This success will be seen as attainable by some, unattainable by others, according to how highly they value their own potential. For those who do not think that they can achieve the same level of success, this example will deflate, leaving them worse off than before. For affirmative action to have as a goal the raising of certain people's self-esteem, it must be thought that these people have low self-esteem. If they have low self-esteem, it is then more likely that they will perceive the role model's success as unattainable, which would then deflate their feelings of self-worth. We are not claiming that all members of group X will find the success of any relevant role model unattainable; we are merely claiming that it is likely that *most* of the members of this group X, interested in achieving success at activity Y, will find that success unachievable because of their low self-esteem. If this is the case, overall affirmative action policies would be causing more harm than good on their supporters' own terms.

[55] It may be argued that people's self-esteem is not *so* low, and that overall they feel that they can achieve the success showcased by the relevant role model. But that being the case, the need for affirmative action policies to raise the self-esteem of the members of these groups is puzzling, to say the least.

[56] Lastly, to consider the middle ground, it could be suggested that the group's self-esteem is low enough to warrant an attempt to have it raised, yet high enough to make it the case that a typical role model will, overall, have a positive effect on the group in question. In this case, we would have to weigh the relative success of affirmative action in achieving both of its stated objectives—changing the opinions of bigots, sexists, and ablists on the one hand, and inspiring members of the disadvantaged groups to reach for their dreams on the other. We would then have to suggest that it fails to achieve the first objective, indeed it achieves quite the opposite effect, and would only marginally achieve the second. When looked at in this light, then, it seems to us that the conclusion to draw is that affirmative action programs are not justified on their stated grounds, and ought to be rescinded.

V. Conclusion

[57] We have argued that none of the common defenses of affirmative action programs are successful. Employment equity policies are not required by justice, and they fail to significantly reduce the prejudice that produces invidious discrimination against the members of identifiable groups within society. Given that such policies have the significant costs outlined in the introduction of this paper, their failure to provide significant counter-balancing benefits requires that we declare them unjustified. This is not to say, of course, that racism/sexism/ablism must be countenanced nor that those who are committed to eradicating prejudice and the discrimination it inspires should relax their efforts. But to those who suggest that, while not perfect, affirmative action is the only solution we have, we suggest turning instead to focus their efforts on education, paying particular attention to the young, in order to ensure that racist/sexist/ablist attitudes fail to obtain in our society.

Notes

1. I wish to thank SSHRC for its support of my research—Christopher Tucker.
2. Report of the Commission on Equality in Employment, *Employment and Immigration Canada* 1984 (Supply and Services, Canada); reprinted in Wesley Cragg, ed., *Contemporary Moral Issues* 3rd edition

(Toronto: McGraw-Hill Ryerson Ltd, 1992). Hereafter cited as Abella, for its chief author, Judge Rosalie Abella; page numbers refer to Cragg, p. 191.
3. L.W. Sumner, "Positive Sexism", *Contemporary Moral Issues* 3rd edition, ed. Wesley Cragg (Toronto: McGraw-Hill Ryerson Ltd., 1992), p. 221; originally published in *Social Philosophy and Policy* 15:1. He takes the term "secondary sexism" from Mary Anne Warren, "Secondary Sexism and Quota Hiring", *Philosophy and Public Affairs* 6:3 (1977).
4. *Ibid.*, p. 223.
5. Thomas Hurka, "Affirmative Action: How Far Should We Go?", *Contemporary Moral Issues* 3rd ed. Cragg *op. cit.*, p. 209; originally published in *The Globe and Mail*.
6. *Cf.* Law Society of B.C. et al *v* Andrews et al, Supreme Court of Canada (1989) 1 S.C.R. 143; Ontario Human Rights Commission et al and Simpson-Sears Ltd., Supreme Court of Canada (1985) 2 S.C.R. 536; Brooks *v* Canada Safeway Ltd., Supreme Court of Canada (1989) 1 S.C.R. 1219.
7. Preamble to the Human Rights Code of Ontario 1990, Chapter H.19.
8. Government of Canada Paper, "Outline of the Employment Equity Act", reproduced in *Ethical Issues: Perspectives for Canadians*, ed. Eldon Soifer (Toronto: Broadview Press, 1992), p. 418.
9. *Cf.* Ontario Human Rights Commission et al and Simpson-Sears Ltd., Supreme Court of Canada (1985) 2 S.C.R. 536.
10. Government of Canada Background Paper, "Employment Equity and Economic Growth", reproduced in *Ethical Issues*, ed. Soifer *op. cit.*, p. 420.
11. Abella *op cit.* p. 185.
12. *Ibid.*
13. *Ibid.*, p. 189.
14. *Ibid.*, p. 192.
15. Ziva Kunda, "The Case for Motivated Reasoning", *Psychological Bulletin*, 1990, Vol. 108, No. 3, p. 480–498.
16. *Ibid.*, p. 484.
17. E. Ashby Plant and Patricia G. Devine, "Internal and External Motivation to Respond without Prejudice, In Press: *Journal of Personality and Social Psychology*.
18. *Ibid.*, p. 44.
19. *Ibid.*, p. 45.
20. Penelope Lockwood and Ziva Kunda, "Superstars and Me: Predicting the Impact of Role Models on the Self," *Journal of Personality and Social Psychology*, 73:1, p. 91–103.

Questions

1. With respect to justification, do Dimock and Tucker believe it matters what *kind* of affirmative action program is being judged?
2. What three reasons do Dimock and Tucker give in support of their claim that affirmative action programs need justification (para 3)?
3. In para 4, Dimock and Tucker state, "We shall conclude that the reasons typically offered in defence of affirmative action are inadequate." Does it necessarily follow that affirmative action programs are indefensible or unjustified?
4. Dimock and Tucker first examine justice-based arguments for affirmative action.
   (a) With respect to the compensatory justice argument, they identify and reject its key assumption—what is it (para 9)?
   (b) However, even if they accepted that assumption, affirmative action programs, they argue, would fail to provide compensatory justice to those disadvantaged in the past—why?
   (c) With respect to distributive justice, under-representation of some groups in various posi-

tions relative to their percentage of the population-at-large is taken to be due to discrimination; Dimock and Tucker offer three alternative explanations—what are they (para 16)?

(d) Explain Dimock and Tucker's second objection (to distributive justice arguments for affirmative action programs).

5. Dimock and Tucker next examine consequence-based arguments for affirmative action.

(a) What is the first good consequence said to result from affirmative action programs? For such a consequence to result, Dimock and Tucker argue, freedoms must be violated—explain.

(b) Dimock and Tucker claim the argument for diversity depends on what other argument?

(c) Dimock and Tucker proceed to show that "increased representation of target groups in the workforce" (diversity) does *not* "eliminate...prejudiced attitudes"—why not? (Be sure to include the main points of paras 44 and 46.)

(d) Do you agree with Dimock and Tucker's analysis of the role-model argument as failing to result in attitude change (consider the effect of the presence or absence of role models in your own life) and/or as failing to justify affirmative programs?

6. What, if *not* adopt affirmative action programs, can business do to eradicate discrimination?

Ethics and Genetics: Susceptibility Testing in the Workplace[*1]

Chris MacDonald and Bryn Williams-Jones[2]

Introduction

[1] The rapid advances made in genetic research and technology over the last few decades have led to a host of important advances in the detection (and hopefully soon the treatment) of genetic conditions and diseases. These developments have also raised ethical concerns about how resulting technologies will be implemented, and about how their implementation will impact different communities. One particular set of concerns surrounds the use of genetic testing in the workplace. Though not yet common, workplace genetic testing is bound to become a real option for employers as genetic technologies improve.[3]

* *Journal of Business Ethics* 35: 235-41, 2002. © 2002 Kluwer Academic Publishers.

[2]   Genetic testing comes in two forms: screening and monitoring. Genetic *monitoring* (which tends to be supported by labour advocates) detects genetic abnormalities potentially caused by exposure to workplace toxins: an alert to hazards in the workplace, similar in principle to radiation detection badges. By contrast, genetic *screening* (the focus of this paper), is used to detect hereditary disease or susceptibility to workplace toxins. This could be used for pre-employment testing, employee placement, and risk avoidance—all useful tools for employers (Department of Labor et al., 1998).

What Can Be Screened for and Why?

[3] Genetic screening can be used to detect which individuals have a genetic makeup associated with particular hereditary diseases, such as sickle cell anaemia, cystic fibrosis, and Huntington disease. Screening can also detect genes that confer increased susceptibility to workplace toxins or environmental factors, e.g., N-acetyltransferase phenotype (increased risk of bladder cancer in those exposed to carcinogenic arylamines (Vineis and Schulte, 1995)), or Glu-69 (heightened susceptibility to beryllium, which can cause pulmonary disease (American Nuclear Society Environmental Sciences Division, 1998)).[4]

[4]   Employers might benefit from genetic screening through reduction in costs associated with occupational disease, e.g., lost productivity, excess absenteeism, worker's compensation payments, health insurance premiums, and legal liability (Andre and Velasquez, 1991). While some tests are still relatively expensive, they will become more affordable as technologies develop (e.g., DNA chips, cf. Wickelgren, 1998), and through cost savings from maintaining a healthy workforce. A further argument in favour of genetic screening is that in order to maintain a healthy and productive workforce and safeguard corporate interests, companies have to be selective about who they hire or retain as employees. It can be argued that companies are not unfairly discriminatory in selecting against employees at risk for hereditary disease or genetic susceptibility. Workplace discrimination is generally not thought to be unfair if the issue is a "bona fide" requirement of the job. And it may simply not be economically feasible for the employer to eliminate all substances that put a few hypersensitive employees at risk. It may be more sensible, from an economic point of view, not to hire susceptible workers or to transfer susceptible workers to different positions. Finally, if challenged that using genetic screening in the workplace is unfairly discriminatory, employers can reply that prospective (and current) employees do not have a right to work at a specific company, and that those who object to screening can seek employment elsewhere. Of course, this reply is plausible only while workplace genetic testing remains rare—if it becomes common practice, some people may become unemployable because of genetic susceptibility.

It can also be argued that workplace genetic [5] screening will benefit both workers and employers by helping to maintain a healthy workforce. Employers have a general ethical obligation to minimize the likelihood of workplace illness and injury. One way to approach this obligation is to improve the workplace—that is, to tailor the workplace to needs of the worker. But, since workplace illness and injury typically involve interaction between some characteristic of the workplace and some characteristic of the worker, another way to approach this obligation is to tailor the worker to the workplace. If the latter approach is taken, it will generally mean not modifying particular workers, but changing which workers have which jobs. That is, it will mean avoiding placing workers into work environments that, because of particular characteristics of those workers, are particularly dangerous to them. This was the rationale for DuPont's voluntary sickle cell anaemia screening program in the 1970s, and for the widespread restrictions in the chemical industry that preclude women from working in environments that expose them to chemicals known to cause birth defects (cf. Draper, 1991).

[6] Screening may also benefit workers directly by providing information that will allow them to avoid placement in potentially harmful environments, thereby sparing workers and their families the physical, emotional, and financial burdens of disabling disease or premature death. The suggestion is that, once informed of their increased risk, workers can evaluate their situation and take voluntary preventative measures to avoid exposure.

Opposition to Workplace Screening

[7] The above arguments in favour of genetic screening will be unsatisfactory to many. Screening, it may be argued, is unjustly discriminatory, is a threat to privacy, offers only a questionable degree of accuracy, and does not ensure a safe working environment. On these grounds, some will argue that genetic screening should be restricted.[5]

[8] Justice requires people be treated equally unless there are *relevant reasons* for different treatment. Differences in skill, knowledge or experience would be relevant criteria for hiring or placement. However, traits that are not within the control of the individual, such as gender, ethnicity, or disability, are commonly held (e.g., in the Canadian *Charter of Rights and Freedoms*, and the U.S. *Americans with Disabilities Act*) to be unjust grounds for discrimination. Thus it has been argued that one's genetic makeup, like disability, should not be reason for discrimination (cf. Annas, Glantz et al., 1995; Task Force on Genetic Information and Insurance, 1993; Murray et al., 2001). Further, given that predispositions to genetic diseases may be associated with specific ethnic backgrounds (e.g., sickle cell anaemia in people of African descent or TaySacks disease in Ashkenazi Jews) there is concern that screening could stigmatize and negatively impact historically disadvantaged groups (cf. Task Force on Genetic Information and Insurance, 1993).

[9] The usefulness and scientific validity of workplace genetic screening have also been challenged (Draper, 1991; Department of Labor et al., 1998). Screening is not diagnostic, but predicts only *risk* or *susceptibility*. The information provided by means of genetic testing will not determine whether a person will *in fact* develop a condition, only that they are more *likely* to do so than others.[6] Moreover, there are problems with the sensitivity and specificity of the screening methods—a test may be accurate but still miss people who are at risk (a "false negative"), or on the other hand, label some people as at increased risk who are not actually susceptible (a "false positive"), thereby increasing anxiety and possibly resulting in the unwarranted termination of a position. To be "at risk" implies a *probability* of developing a condition that *might* affect performance—even with a positive result on a test, a person might never develop the condition. Nor does being at risk directly affect current ability to perform, except to the extent that this information creates fear and anxiety, which could affect a person's performance. Confidence in genetic screening may also be unreasonable given the complexity of the human genome and the complexity of its interaction with the environment (Lewontin, 2000). Most of the conditions that would likely be of interest for workplace testing are multifactorial, i.e., there are numerous factors involved in the development of disease, only some of which are genetic. And even when there is an association between a specific gene and development of disease, there may be

other (unknown) genetic factors necessary before the target gene gets "turned on" and causes cancer, for example. Thus a person who tests positive for "the gene" in question may still never develop the disease (Baird, 2001).

[10]   There is also concern that genetic screening will lead to employees not being treated as individuals, but as "risk groups" who are in some way to blame for their conditions, thereby distracting from the responsibility borne by the company for workplace safety—employers should be improving safety and removing hazards, not shifting responsibility to employees (Kegley, 1998).[7]

[11]   Given that the gap between diagnosis and treatment is still great for most genetic disorders, screening will likely be of dubious direct medical benefit to employees. Even if an employee is found to be at risk, the best that can be offered is transfer to a different position and increased monitoring. But genetic information can be a significant psychological and social burden, especially if one is told one has "a defective gene" or is "at risk." Such news might affect a person's conception of health and identity,[8] lead to stigmatization, or even make a person unemployable or uninsurable. (Such risks might be mitigated through genetic counselling, but counselling is unlikely to eliminate such risks altogether.) For these reasons, it is widely argued that genetic information should be treated as personal and private,[9] and that access by third parties should require convincing justification (Secretary's Advisory Committee on Genetic Testing, 1999). Forcing an employee to undergo genetic screening also forces the employee to deal with the resulting information, and studies on the psychological impact of genetic testing have shown that it may sometimes be better "not to know" (Benjamin et al., 1994; Codori, 1997; Cox and McKellin, 1999).

Is There Room for Compromise?

Those in favour of genetic screening are probably justified in citing employee benefit, corporate responsibility, and economics as reasons for using genetic testing to select against certain employees while protecting those already employed who may be susceptible. Opponents to screening also provide persuasive arguments for the need for concern about justice and discrimination, scientific validity, and privacy. There are further concerns, particularly in the U.S., regarding risks to employees' insurability (for both health care and life insurance) (Murray et al., 2001). While we find the arguments against screening at this time are in general more persuasive (given the rather low accuracy of testing, the low utility of risk information, and the clear potential for injustice and discrimination), screening may be a viable option—both technically and ethically—in certain specifiable situations either now or in the future. Obviously the accuracy of testing methods must be improved, but more importantly, testing must be administered in a just and respectful manner. [12]

Given that workplace genetic testing is a technology both full of promise and fraught with ethical peril, we suggest a pragmatic approach that allows for the possibility of workplace genetic testing, but that attempts to minimize its negative effects. Each of the positive and negative factors alluded to above warrants serious ethical investigation. Such work has begun, but is far from adequate to provide satisfying answers. In the meantime, we propose a set of criteria, the satisfaction of which would make it *prima facie* permissible for employers to offer genetic testing to workers. *Requiring* workers to submit to genetic testing is significantly more problematic morally. Forced testing would constitute an invasion of privacy, and expose the worker—on a non-voluntary basis—to a range of poorly under- [13]

stood risks. Thus it may not be possible to identify circumstances in which such a requirement would be ethically permissible. We do not attempt that task here. As a result, we restrict our discussion to the search for conditions under which it would be permissible for employers to offer employees the *opportunity* to be tested.[10] We contend that it is *ethically permissible* to offer genetic testing to employees if the following six conditions are met:

1. A genetic test (for a specific condition) must be available which is highly specific and sensitive and offers an acceptably low incidence of both false positives and false negatives; such a test must test for a gene that is sufficiently penetrant for the test result to have some important health implication;
2. Testing should be carried out by an independent lab, and results of genetic tests should be given to workers directly, either by a geneticist or a genetic counsellor; test results should be held confidential, and revealed to the employer only at the employee's request;
3. Pre- and post-test genetic counselling must be available from a qualified health professional, and paid for by the employer, regardless of the outcome of the test;
4. The gene being tested for must not be prominently associated with an identifiable and historically disadvantaged group;
5. Where relevant, the employer must guarantee continued access to group insurance;
6. The employer must ensure that if the employee chooses to reveal that she has tested positive, suitable policies are in place to ensure a reasonable degree[11] of job security.

[14] We feel that if the above criteria were met, it would be ethically permissible to offer (but not to *require*) workplace genetic testing. Meeting these criteria would allow employers to offer genetic testing, and further to have reasonable answers in the face of most of the objections noted above. The only concern *not* directly addressed by meeting these six criteria is the worry that, in focusing on tailoring the workforce to the workplace environment (by using genetic testing to weed out those workers who are particularly susceptible to workplace hazards) employers may neglect improvements to the workplace that would benefit *all* employees. It would of course be possible to further stipulate that, in order for it to be permissible to offer genetic testing, employers must also ensure that other appropriate measures are taken to clean up the workplace so that the interests of "normal" workers as well as "at risk" workers are served. We feel, however, that the obligation to provide a safe workplace for all employees is a general issue that can be separated from the issue of genetic testing.

[15] If the six criteria above are met, then any genetic test that is offered holds the promise of being good for all involved. The employer reduces costs associated with employee illness; at-risk employees gain the information needed to remove themselves from work environments that pose special risks for them; and employees found *not* to be at increased risk gain the comfort of that knowledge. These advantages (in the absence of the disadvantages avoided through meeting our six criteria) justify offering testing. They do not justify failure to maintain a reasonably safe environment for all employees: employees found not to be at risk gain only psychological comfort from testing, and untested employees gain nothing at all from testing. The availability of testing does little if anything to change employers' health-and-safety related obligations to these employees.

[16] Next, let us ask, is it ever ethically *mandatory* for employers to offer genetic testing? We believe that it is, and suggest that it be considered

mandatory for an employer to offer genetic testing to employees if conditions 1 through 6 above are satisfied, and if, in addition, the following conditions are met:

1. Knowing their status with regard to the genetic characteristic in question can reasonably be expected to influence at least some employees' decision to remain in their current position;
2. The cost of the test is "reasonable" (e.g., is similar to the costs of other insured medical services, or other normal workplace benefits).

[17]   We think that the possibility of an obligation to offer testing to employees—and the financial burden that would imply—goes hand in hand with the possibility of *offering* genetic testing to employees, and the risks such testing would imply for them.[12] In considering whether they favour a world in which employees *may* be tested, employers should also consider whether they also favour a world in which they may be *obligated* to offer testing.

[18]   The future is likely to see a rapid expansion in the number of genetic conditions or susceptibilities that can be tested for, and testing will become cheaper, more accurate, and more widely available (Silverman, 1995; Secretary's Advisory Committee on Genetic Testing, 1999; Williams-Jones, 1999). This could provide for better monitoring and screening of employees to increase safety, but only if both the motivation and the process are fair and non-discriminatory. Given the often restrictive nature of many governmental responses to developments in genetic research and technology (e.g., the response to fetal cell research, cloning, etc.), screening tests will almost certainly be restricted unless they are proven scientifically valid and used in a just and equitable manner. Genetic technologies are becoming increasingly important in our lives—something that is not soon likely to change. Careful thought needs to go into the conditions under which such technologies should be welcomed into our lives.

Notes

1. Authorship of this paper is shared equally. The authors wish to thank Charles Weijer, Susan M. Cox, Jason Scott Robert, and Paul Miller for helpful comments on various drafts. Many of the ideas here have also benefited from ongoing critique and discussion with the Genetics and Ethics Research Group at the UBC Centre for Applied Ethics.
2. Bryn Williams-Jones's research is supported in part by The Canadian Health Services Research Foundation (CHSRF), the Social Sciences and Humanities Research Council (SSHRC), and the Faculty of Graduate Studies and Centre for Applied Ethics at UBC.
3. For a review of some of the forms of genetic testing currently becoming commercially available (and the social, ethical and policy implications of these developments), see (Williams-Jones, 1999; Burgess, 1999).
4. We refer here primarily to laboratory tests indicating the presence of a particular gene. Similar information can sometimes be acquired simply by means of taking a family history, when the inheritance characteristics of a particular gene are known. For example, since the gene for Huntington disease is dominant, an individual whose family history includes a parent with the disease would have, based on family history alone, a 50% chance of inheriting the gene (and thus of manifesting the disease), while their children would in turn be at 25% risk. Some of the worries about genetic testing thus should also apply to the gathering of family histories.
5. The scenario in which workplace genetic testing is carried out in an oppressive manner is exemplified in the 1997 science fiction movie, "Gattaca." But not all examples come from science fiction. In 1970, a test was developed to screen for carriers of sickle cell trait, a recessive genetic condition that causes a severe form of anemia, and affects 1 in 500 African Americans. The U.S. Air Force used this

test to refuse African-Americans with this trait from becoming pilots. The Air Force was afraid that reduced oxygen levels in cockpits would trigger the disease. However, this recessive condition only occurs in individuals who have both copies of the faulty gene (and will thus have a history of disease) as opposed to carriers who have one copy, but are unaffected (those the test was picking up). This test was used as justification to discriminate against a group of people, who would never actually develop the condition. The Air Force ended its sickle cell screening program in 1981 (Draper, 1991). More recently, The Burlington Northern & Santa Fe Railroad Co. was sued (for violating the Americans with Disabilities Act) by the U.S. Equal Employment Opportunity Commission, on behalf of the employee union, for obtaining blood samples and conducting genetic testing on employees claiming work-related carpal tunnel syndrome (Ceniceros, 2001).

6. There are rare exceptions, such as the test for Huntington disease. Individuals who test positive for the expanded number of tri-nucleotide repeats associated with HD have (nearly) a 100% chance of developing this degenerative neurological disorder at some point in their lives. (Such a gene is called "highly penetrant" by geneticists.) It would be too easy to be misled, by examples like Huntington disease, into thinking that genetic tests usually provide certainty.

7. As Trudo Lemmens has noted (1997, p. 60), the focus on genetic susceptibility ignores the fact that workers who do not have the gene associated with *increased* susceptibility to some hazard can nonetheless still be affected by that hazard. Focusing on genetic screening obscures the needs of "normal" workers.

8. We might reasonably wonder, of course, whether the impact of genetic testing is different in this regard from the impact of, for example, intelligence testing.

9. Note that the possibility of misinterpretation of genetic information may be a greater threat than simple lack of control over personal information.

10. Some will wonder why we need justification even to *offer* testing; that is, they will wonder why employees' consent to being tested is not sufficient. The answer lies primarily in the possibility that a) the offer may in some sense be coercive; and b) employees may not in all cases understand the ramifications of consenting to be tested. As a parallel, note that consent is not always considered sufficient to justify subjecting patients to medical research. See (Weijer et al., 1997).

11. Just what would constitute a "reasonable" degree of job security is an important question; an employer's justification in offering genetic testing would depend, in part, upon justifying suitably the degree of job security that was ensured.

12. In a similar vein, Lemmens (1997, p. 70) argues that when reliable genetic monitoring is available, providing such monitoring should be considered obligatory.

References

American Nuclear Society Environmental Sciences Division. 1998. *Proceedings of the Topical Meeting on Risk-Based Performance Assessment and Decision Making.* Pasco, WA: Richland.

Andre, Claire and Manuel Velasquez. 1991. "Read My Genes: Genetic Screening in the Workplace." *Issues in Ethics* 4(2), <http://scuish.scu.edu/Ethics/publications/iie/v4n2/genes.shtrnl>.

Annas, George J., Leonard H. Glantz and Patricia A. Roche. 2000. *The Genetic Privacy Act and Commentary.* Human Genome Project Information 1995 [cited 25 July 2000].

Baird, Patricia A. 2001. "Will Genetics Be Used Wisely?" *ISUMA: Canadian Journal of Policy Research* 2(1), 94–101.

Benjamin, C., Adam S., S. Wiggins et al. 1994. "Proceed with Care: Direct Predictive Testing for Huntington Disease." *American Journal of Medical Genetics* 55, 606–617.

Burgess, Michael M. 1999. "Marketing and Fear Mongering: Is It Time for Commercialized Genetic Testing?" In T.A. Caulfield and B. Williams-Jones (eds.), *The Commercialization of Genetics Research: Ethical, Legal, and Policy Issues.* New York: Kluwer Academic/Plenum Publishers.

Ceniceros, Roberto. 2001. "Genetic Screening Faces Lawsuits." *Business Insurance* 35(8), 1, 42.

Codori, A.-M. 1997. "Psychological Opportunities and Hazards in Predictive Genetic Testing for Cancer Risk." *Colorectal Neoplasia, Part II: Diagnosis & Treatment* 26(1), 19–39.

Cox, Susan M. and William McKellin. 1999. "'There's This Thing in Our Family': Predictive Testing and the Construction of Risk for Huntington Disease." *Sociology of Health & Illness* 21(5), 622–646.

Department of Labor, Department of Health and Human Services, Equal Opportunity Commission, and Department of Justice. 1998. 'Genetic Information and the Workplace.' Department of Labor, U.S. Government, Washington, DC.

Draper, Elaine. 1991. *Risky Business: Genetic Testing and Exclusionary Practices in the Workplace.* Cambridge: Cambridge University Press.

Kegley, Jacquelyn Ann K. 1998. "Genetic Information and Genetic Essentialism: Will We Betray Science, the Individual, and the Community." In J.A K. Kegley (ed.), *Genetic Knowledge: Human Values & Responsibility.* Lexington, KY: International Conference on the Unity of the Sciences.

Lemmens, Trudo. 1997. "'What About Your Genes?' Ethical, Legal and Policy Dimensions of Genetics in the Workplace." *Politics and the Life Sciences* 16(1), 57–75.

Lewontin, Richard C. 2000. *The Triple Helix: Gene, Organism, and Environment.* Cambridge, MA: Harvard University Press.

Murray, William D., James C. Wimbush, and Dan R. Dalton. 2001. "Genetic Screening in the Workplace: Legislative and Ethical Implications." *Journal of Business Ethics* 29(4), 365–378.

Secretary's Advisory Committee on Genetic Testing (SACGT). 1999. "A Public Consultation on Oversight of Genetic Tests." *Federal Register* 64 (67273), http://www4.od.nih.gov/oba/sacgt12-99.htm.

Silverman, Paul H. 1995. "Commerce and Genetic Diagnostics." *Hastings Center Report* 25(3), S15–S18.

Task Force on Genetic Information and Insurance. 1993. "Genetic Information and Health Insurance: Report of the Task Force on Genetic Information and Health Insurance." Washington, DC: National Institutes of Health.

Vineis, Paolo and Paul A. Schulte. 1995. "Scientific and Ethical Aspects of Genetic Screening of Workers for Cancer Risk: The Case of N-Acetyltransferase Phenotype." *Journal of Clinical Epidemiology* 48(2), 189–197.

Weijer, Charles, Bernard Dickens and Eric Meslin. 1997. "Bioethics for Clinicians 10: Research Ethics." *CMAJ* 156(8), 1153–1157.

Wickelgren, I. 1998. "Gene Readers." *Popular Science* (Nov.), 56–61.

Williams-Jones, Bryn. 1999. "Re-Framing the Discussion: Commercial Genetic Testing in Canada." *Health Law Journal* 7, 49–68.

Questions

1. The authors distinguish between genetic monitoring and genetic screening: is there, in your opinion, an *ethical* difference between the two?
2. (a) What two arguments do the authors present in favour of genetic screening that address employer benefit?
   (b) The authors anticipate an objection and provide a reply, but their reply is dependent on what being the case?
   (c) What two arguments do the authors present in favour of genetic screening that address employee benefit?
   (d) Why do the authors mention DuPont?

3. Why do the authors talk at some length about probability?
4. Of the three arguments suggested by the authors against genetic screening, which do you consider the strongest? Why?
5. What is your evaluation of the authors' "compromise" argument? (Consider both the distinction between requiring and offering, as well as the six conditions. Also, of course, consider the authors' reasons for that distinction and the conditions.)
6. The authors conclude, further, that not only *may* employers offer genetic testing, but that in some cases, they *must* do so. Under what two conditions? Would you add any conditions?

Case Study: The Westray Mine Disaster

The report of the public inquiry into the coal-mine disaster at the Westray mine in Nova Scotia called the mine "an accident waiting to happen." On May 9, 1992, the accident happened. On that day, a methane gas explosion in a 300-foot-deep seam of the mine killed 26 miners.

While the proximate cause of the explosion was a spark coming from a mining machine, the public inquiry found that the mine had an inadequate ventilation system, inadequate treatment of coal dust, and inadequately trained workers. A proper ventilation system would have diluted the potentially flammable methane gas, eliminating the risk of an explosion; stone dusting (which makes coal dust non-explosive) should have been done on a regular basis; and properly trained workers would have been more familiar with the equipment and safe work methods.

The testimony of witnesses at the public inquiry reveals the virtual absence of a "safety mentality" at the mine. In the months leading up to the explosion, Westray management, according to the inquiry, had "ignored or encouraged a series of hazardous or illegal practices"—despite a history of rock falls, cave-ins, and even roof collapses. Managers hired by Westray were unqualified (a senior engineer had no experience in underground coal mines and a surveyor failed to obtain provincial certification), and miners could not follow safety methods because of the pressure to keep production levels high.

Many of the workers were certainly aware of the dangers. For example, one of the mine mechanics noticed one of the mine supervisors recalibrating a monitor so that excessive levels of methane would not cause an automatic shut-off. But when he said he would report the tampering, he was threatened with losing his job. Others reported high methane gas and coal dust levels to visiting mine inspectors on more than one occasion.

The public inquiry was particularly harsh in criticizing government regulators for their role in the tragedy. The Nova Scotia Department of Natural Resources was responsible for ensuring, before permits were granted, that mining plans were not only efficient, but safe. However, "the department did not insist that the company submit sufficient information to support its application. Furthermore, it did not insist that the company submit any changes to approved plans. Consequently, for a critical period, the department was not aware that Westray was working an unapproved section of the mine." The Department of Labour, the report points out, also "failed to carry out its mandated responsibilities to the workers at Westray and to the people of Nova Scotia": there were repeated violations of regulations governing mine operations, and the report insists that "the Department of Labour's mine inspectorate should have detected these violations and ensured compliance."

An expert in mine ventilation, Andrew Liney, testified that it would have been relatively easy to eliminate the dangerous gases in the mine, which would also have increased worker productivity. There were so many violations of Department of Labour regulations that he doubted the competence and commitment of the provincial mine inspectors. Overall, Liney viewed the situation at Westray to be "an absolutely unbelievable disgrace." Two of the Westray managers were charged with criminal negligence causing death and manslaughter, but the charges were stayed.

Sources

Di Norcia, Vincent. *Hard Like Water: Ethics in Business*. Toronto: Oxford University Press, 1998. 79–81.

Richard, Peter. *Report of the Westray Mine Public Inquiry*. Province of Nova Scotia, 1997. www.gov.ns.ca/legi/inquiry/westray/

Questions

1. If you had to apportion blame for the Westray disaster, how much would you say should go to the Westray management, how much to the provincial regulators (Natural Resources and Labour), and how much to the workers who were aware of the hazards? Would you also include shareholders and consumers who demand the high returns and low prices that can come only from high production levels?
2. By accepting and keeping a job as a miner (indeed some Westray miners quit in the months preceding the disaster), isn't one also accepting the risk that goes along with that occupational choice?
3. If, as Liney claimed, the improvements in safety would have also improved productivity, why do you think Westray management failed to make those improvements?
4. What if improvements in safety did not also improve productivity—how obligated (morally speaking) would management be to nevertheless make those improvements?

CHAPTER FIVE

Management, Corporate Governance, and CSR

What to Do?—Union's in the Air

You've heard that some of your employees are trying to start a union. You figure this is bad news because every time a place becomes unionized, profits decline. Actually, you don't really know if that's true, but it stands to reason, doesn't it? Because they always ask for more pay and more benefits. In any case, if they thought management was doing a good job, they wouldn't be wanting a union, right? So the whole thing is making you look bad.

You could transfer the "troublemakers." After all, you know who's behind it. Or at least you have your suspicions. It would be easy to do. You wouldn't even have to demote them. They'd have to uproot their lives though.... Well, not your problem.

You could even fire them. A good manager can always find a reason. Though that seems extreme.

Or…you could promote them. The troublemakers. Yes, that would be "buying them off," but so what? The greater good and all that.

Maybe you could just give them whatever it is they want. A bit more pay? A few more benefits? You remember that at the first ever unionized McDonalds, in Squamish, BC, back in 1998, the employees wanted a union simply because management was treating them like shit. When management heard about it, they started having meetings to hear complaints, they introduced free meals, they fixed faulty electrical outlets, they even bought a new stereo for the staff room—Maybe you could do that. Buy a new stereo for the staff room.

What do you decide to do?

Introduction

The traditional corporate structure—hierarchy—seems to leave little room for respect for the person. The very words *subordinate* and *insubordination* suggest this (*insubordination* basically means criticizing one's superiors—one's *organizational* superiors—and is usually considered just cause for dismissal). So too do the starting and quitting time buzzers that sound like a school bell; the regimented morning and afternoon 15-minute coffee breaks, reminiscent of recess; performance reviews treated like report cards; disciplinary hearings that feel like being called in to the principal's office; dress codes like school uniforms. Isn't this organizational structure founded on a very insulting view of people, people who *are* adults (and often have been for quite some time)? See the essay by Maguire in this chapter for a more academic discussion of this issue.

Consider also the standard corporate view of responsibility: the subordinate actually *does* X, but the superordinate (I will not say "superior") is *responsible for* X. If there's a problem, she's the one who'll be held accountable. This conception of responsibility infantilizes the subordinate. A sign of maturity is that one takes responsibility for one's actions. Only with children and the mentally incompetent is someone else held responsible. Denying the subordinate that responsibility, then, is insisting on juvenile or incompetent status. (It also puts a great deal of strain on the superordinate: it's very stressful to be responsible for someone else's behaviour. Ask any parent. One has the responsibility, but not the power, not the control. No wonder superordinates develop ulcers. And no wonder they can develop into control freaks: if one is responsible for something, one is surely going to try to have some control over that something. Which of course will be resented by any truly mature and autonomous "subordinate"....)

Perhaps virtue ethics can play a valuable role here in deciding what's right: respect, trust, honesty, integrity, dignity, self-development, well-being, security, pride, choice, freedom...are these fostered in such an environment?

Not only does the traditional corporate structure leave little room for respect and the like; it also leaves little room for participation. Do employees have a right to democratic participation in the company's decision making? McCall argues that there is an ethical basis for such participation. Shaw supports this view, pointing out that worker dissatisfaction results from a company's "preoccupation with quantity, not quality; the rigidity of rules and regulations;...the lack of opportunities to be one's own boss..." (255, referring to a 1970s study by the US Secretary of Health, Education, and Welfare). But should employees have input into company policies and procedures? Owners would argue that since employees didn't help to start or fund the company, they have no right; employees could argue that lack of worker input turns companies into dictatorships. Maybe that's why employees want a union....

Of course no company is a dictatorship. It can't be. Isn't that what boards are for? To protect against dictatorships? Nordberg identifies four theories of corporate governance: agency theory (in which the board is accountable to shareholders, and assumes ethical egoism on the part of executives and utilitarianism on the part of outside directors); shareholder value (in which the board is accountable to shareholders, and assumes utilitarianism); stakeholder theory (the board is accountable to customers, suppliers, employees, competitors, shareholders, and society at large, and assumes a duty-based ethic); and stewardship theory (board members are accountable to themselves, their conscience, and assumes a duty-based ethic). Analysis of these theories of corporate governance go beyond the scope of this text; I mention them only to show that whatever model your business is based on *isn't the only option*. Turnbull, for example, recommends the inclusion of stakeholders in the governance architecture of firms. In Germany, half the seats on supervisory boards *must* go to representatives of the workforce (Nordberg 39).

Speaking of boards, Fogarty et al. (in their analysis of the rise and fall of Nortel) recommend "an independent board of directors composed of non-executive directors, that is nominated and elected by shareholders" (171). Nortel did have that, but according to Fogarty et al., the problem was that it was too large: "[as] board size increases, boards become less effective at monitoring management because of free-riding problems amongst directors and increased decision-making time" (171). They go on to say that "[a] further reason for board dysfunction can be attributed to the multiple obligations that nonexecutive board members had" (172). Except for one, each of the Nortel board members had on average 5.8 directorships, and four board members were CEOs of other companies. How can such people possibly have time to fulfill their responsibilities? They don't.

Similarly, the Canadian Coalition for Good Governance includes among its best practices that boards have a majority of independent directors, that board members hold significant stock, and that compensation is aligned with performance (Gagne et al.). I'd question the second recommendation, which seems to assume egoism (that people will be more apt to make good decisions when they personally have a lot to lose), and the third recommendation as well, which may introduce the problem with commissions—when compensation is linked directly to performance, one is tempted to cut corners and do "whatever it takes" to get the commission (or bonus or whatever).

"One of the most important changes in capitalism since World War II," Fogarty et al. note, "has been the diversification of ownership interests." So when we consider governance, we must look not only at boards but also at shareholders. If you own part of a company, are you not partly responsible for it? *Morally* responsible? For what it does and does not do? Ownership has its privileges, but it also has its responsibilities. (We'll come back to this when we discuss limited liability.) And yet investors often don't even know what companies they're part owner of, what companies they're supporting—let alone what those companies are doing. How many people take a good look at the list of companies in their pension and mutual funds? Let alone take a good look at what those companies are doing? Perhaps one is morally obligated to get into "shareholder activism." (See Alinsky, perhaps the first to organize "ordinary" citizens to influence corporations through shareholding.)

Your own business may in fact not only *have* shareholders; it may *be* a shareholder—won't you have investments? Given that, consider Forsey's comments:

> The claim than an "ethical" mutual fund can bring principles and corporate profits cozily together
> is at bottom a moral fraud. Even if the screening process could be made to work more or less as

intended, any significant corporate profit still has to come from someone else's labour or from the finite and precious resources of the Earth itself. Nothing comes from nothing, so if you're getting a windfall, someone else is getting shafted. (2)

(Or are your dividends just your payment for letting someone else use your money? People pay you for the use of your time and effort, and your property, so why not also for the use of your money? But then why aren't dividends a fixed amount—like wages or rental fees?)

> **BOX 5.1   What Companies Do *You* Want to Be Part-owner Of?**
>
> Some people use a *negative screen*. That is, they *exclude* all companies that do X, Y, and Z—ethically bad actions such as dumping untreated waste products, engaging in unfair hiring and firing practices, and contributing to the arms trade. However, for this method to be completely successful, your list of no-nos will have to be complete. And that might be difficult. (Did you screen out "obscenely high salaries for its CEOs"?)
>
> Some use a *positive screen*: they *include* all companies that do A, B, and C—ethically good actions such as developing environmentally friendly technologies, providing a safe workplace, and operating a daycare for employees' kids.
>
> Of course, you could use a combination of negative and positive screens. And, of course, it can be tricky. Referring to ethical screening processes and drawing attention to their potential difficulties, Leonard J. Brooks asks, "Why is it unethical for a company to provide food or telephones or pencils to the military? On the other hand, why are banks considered ethical investments, even though they lend to the companies that supply the food, phones and pencils?" (1).
>
> Whichever way you go, you'll soon find out that, like people, companies are not usually all good or all bad. What do you do with a solar heating company that never hires First Nations people? Do you put it in your ethical investment fund or not? And that gets us to the *really* big question: *How do you solve moral conflicts?*
>
> Consequentialist theories, you may recall, provide one way. You can rank your options according to the severity or extent (or whatever) of the consequences. So, for example, supporting solar technology may actually contribute to saving the planet—which, you may decide, is more important than offering jobs to a few specific people. So you support the company.
>
> What about principle- or value-based theories? How do you decide which principle or value takes priority? One way is according to logical primacy. For example, if we don't save the planet, *no one*'s going to get jobs—because no one's going to exist. Saving the planet must logically precede equal employment opportunities. So you support the company.

> However, logical primacy may not always work: life is logically prior to pleasure, but many would say that a life without (at least a certain amount of) pleasure isn't worth living, so they'd put pleasure before life.
>
> One could, instead, rank according to some other criterion. Perhaps rational values are worth more than emotional ones—so justice outranks compassion, for example. See Irvine, as well as Hayden, for more on this matter.
>
> But don't forget, in any case, to be creative and consider alternatives: you could, along with your investment cheque, send a letter to that solar company endorsing their environmentally responsible attitude but encouraging them to reconsider their employment equity policy.
>
> And remember not to be discouraged by the inability to make *pure and perfect* moral decisions—making *better than* decisions is an achievement in itself.

In his discussion of the moral responsibilities of shareholders, Warren shows, using asbestos as a case study, that the orthodox model of corporate governance (employees are accountable to the company, which is in turn accountable to the shareholders, who are in turn accountable to neither company nor employees—and who, exactly, is accountable to the society in which the company operates and on which it has a multitude of effects? we'll come back to this too) is one in which so-called unencumbered shareholders are actually irresponsible shareholders. It is no surprise that he concludes thus:

> It is contended then that our corporate governance structures are in need of reform, and that the obligations of shareholders need to be reappraised. Where there are burdens to be borne, they should be laid on every shareholder, but the responsibility to improve corporate governance processes should weigh more heavily upon the relatively broad shoulders of the institutional investors [pension funds, insurance companies, mutual funds, and the like]. The responsible shareholder needs to be encumbered by the bonds of society and have a sense of commitment to the common good. Shareholding should be an embedded role where the virtues of the investors, either individual or collective, should have a part to play in their deliberations. Responsible shareholders and corporate governance reforms can help restore company legitimacy as institutions that serve the common good in society. (24)

One of the dominant buzzwords at the moment is *transparency*. Full disclosure about one's business is presumed to reduce ethical misconduct. Does it? And is transparency always good? *Complete* transparency? About *everything*? To *everyone*? That bar is quite a bit higher than the one we set for individuals. On what grounds do we insist on a higher standard for business? Because their withholding of information causes, potentially, *far greater harm*? And yet, consider Turnbull's comment that "it may not be in the interest of employees to report negative community impacts of the business, especially if they could be held responsible and/or it could diminish their ability to further their careers" (244). But then what about the community members who wouldn't then know about those negative impacts.... Is utilitarian calculus an appropriate tool to use here?

Transparency and accountability (another buzzword) not only affect the relationship between management and the company's employees; they also affect the relationship between management and its board (and, ultimately, society as a whole). As Fogarty et al. note, "a large literature has developed examining the monitoring function of the board of directors, audit committees, compensation structures, contracts, financial analysts and institutional investors, and regulatory activity" (166). Certainly Enron is the poster child for transparency and accountability, at the very least to shareholders. Lying about profits? Concealing debts? ("Among other things, Enron was logging the entire revenues from decade-long contracts as single-year sales" [Thompson].) No, maybe World.com takes first prize. Shareholders lost $180 billion, compared to, in Enron's case, $75 billion[1] (http://www.accounting-degree.org/scandals/).

But transparency and accountability may not be the only issues in corporate governance to consider when you're looking at ethical behaviour. Morck, noting our possibly hardwired tendency for obedience, says, "Misplaced loyalty lies at the heart of virtually every recent scandal in corporate governance" (180).[2] Given that, independent boards should lead to better corporate governance, but apparently this is not necessarily so: "The directors of Enron, WorldCom, Hollinger, Parmalat, and all the other companies currently embroiled in scandal attended regular meetings to favourably assess the performance of their CEOs. Despite increasing attention being drawn to their legal and ethical responsibilities, directors seem paralyzed in the presence of powerful CEOs. To social psychologists, this paralysis is not surprising" (184). Morck goes on to analyze the problem and concludes (this is an oversimplification) that "[i]ndividuals can err either by acting for themselves when they should act as agents of others, or by acting as agents when they should be thinking for themselves" (194). His recommendation? "Corporate governance reforms that envision independent directors (dissenting peers), non-executive chairs (alternative authority figures), and fully independent audit committees (absent authority figures)... [to enable] real debate to expose poor strategies before they become fatal" (196).

> **BOX 5.2 Transparency   Just Do It!**
>
> Nike outsources its manufacturing of shoes, clothing, and sports equipment. It's not by any means the only company to do so (for example, Walmart, Sears, the Gap, and Apple also outsource), but it has become one of the more famous for doing so. Since outsourcing is motivated by low expenses, it's often accompanied by poor working conditions—"sweatshops."

---

1 See "The 10 Worst Corporate Accounting Scandals of All Time," http://www.accounting-degree.org/scandals/.
2 Read about the famous Milgram study if you haven't already done so; there's an excellent summary in Morck's paper.

How did Nike respond to accusations of low wages and other employee abuses? They established a code of conduct, and a team to enforce it.

But accusations (and, presumably abuses) continued.

They increased the minimum age for their workers, they increased their monitoring (auditing 600 of their factories), and they created the Fair Labor Association (fairlabor.org), "a non-profit group that combines companies, and human rights and labor representatives to establish independent monitoring and a code of conduct, including a minimum age and a 60-hour work week, and pushes other brands to join."

Accusations (and presumably abuses) lessened, but nevertheless they continued.

So they published a 108-page report "revealing conditions and pay in its factories and acknowledging widespread issues, particularly in its south Asian factories." And they continue to make public their audits (http://about.nike.com/pages/manufacturing).

That's how, says Nisen, Nike solved their problem: "by becoming a leader instead of denying every allegation, Nike has mostly managed to put the most difficult chapter in its history behind it and other companies who outsource could stand to learn a few things from Nike's turnaround."

And yet abuse still continues: "Workers at the Sukabumi plant, about 60 miles from Jakarta, say supervisors frequently throw shoes at them, slap them in the face, kick them and call them dogs and pigs" (Daily Mail Reporter).

(But is that a Nike problem or an Indonesian problem [maybe most Indonesian bosses/men treat workers/women that way] or just a human nature problem [power, even supervisory power, corrupts]. Or all three?)

References

Daily Mail Reporter. "Nike workers 'kicked, slapped, and verbally aubsed' at factories making Converse." *Daily Mail* 11 July 2013. http://www.dailymail.co.uk/news/article-2014325/Nike-workers-kicked-slapped-verbally-abused-factories-making-Converse-line-Indonesia.html

Nisen, Max. "How Nike Solved Its Sweatshop Problem." *Business Insider* 9 May 2013. http://www.businessinsider.com/how-nike-solved-its-sweatshop-problem-2013-5

Unions

Insofar as the purpose of a union is to ensure some level of participation and to define and protect employees' rights through the collective agreement, management/union issues overlap with employee rights issues. However, many issues are unique to the management/union relationship.

Let's start with whether or not there should even *be* unions. As Shaw explains, the formation of unions is

> based on the indisputable premise that employers have tremendous power over individual workers. They can hire and fire, relocate and reassign, set work hours and wages, create rules and work conditions. Acting individually, a worker rarely is an employer's equal in negotiating any of these items. The position of most workers acting independently is further weakened by their lack of capital, occupational limitations, and personal and family needs. (222)

To the extent that this initial inequality exists—and to the extent that such an inequality is morally unacceptable (on what grounds?)—the existence of unions seems legitimate.

De George argues that the right to form unions derives from the right to pursue one's own ends and the right to associate with others to achieve common ends.[1] However, is *collective* action necessarily morally good? Could it be coercive? Does it appeal to "majority rule"? Democracy is all very well if the majority is right, but even then, what about "the tyranny of the majority"? Does collective action appeal to "might (and intimidation) is right"? Or does it just recognize, as Shaw suggests, that "united we stand, divided we fall"—especially if the employer tries to divide and conquer? As a collective, a union may well restrict rather than enhance individual rights: one is no longer free to negotiate one's terms of employment (not that most workers ever really were).

If a unionized company is more expensive to run than a non-unionized company (because of wages and benefits), how can a unionized company compete? So perhaps unions are not in the best interests of the company (at least in the short term). And if being unionized eventually leads to poor sales, layoffs, and even closure, well, such consequences suggest that unions may not be in the best interests of the employees either (at least in the long term?).

But while wages and benefits may cost, do *all* union "demands" cost? Not necessarily. Maybe workers want to go from one shift arrangement (rotating days and nights, for example) to another (steady days or nights, for example), or from rigid hours to flextime, or from regular sick days only to sick kid days in lieu of regular sick days—these changes need not cost the company.

What about recruiting members? How and when and where a union does so may be ethical questions. And should management intervene (interfere)? When does a "goodwill visit" become "union-busting"? For example, what moral justification can you as a manager give for asking for the names of those employees who attend a union information meeting, off-hours and off-site? And what moral justification can you as an employee give for using the company list of employee names and phone numbers for the invitations to such a meeting? Are both unjustified invasions of privacy? Is the latter just cause for dismissal? Do you as the employer keep a union out of the

---

1 De George, like Shaw, is one of the few business ethics text authors to address union matters—both are worth checking out.

workplace this way (and by refusing to hire people who have previously worked at unionized workplaces) or do you do so by paying a fair wage and providing good working conditions?[1]

Another question is whether the union should be a closed or open shop. That is, should membership be compulsory? If not, which means it's an open shop, then management can hire non-unionized workers at lower wages, so it won't be hiring unionized workers (which defeats the union's purposes); and if management hires non-unionized workers at the same wages, then non-unionized workers benefit from the union's efforts without paying the dues (which isn't fair). Both of these points support a closed shop. However, freedom of choice and freedom of association both support an open shop. And yet, as Gibson observes, "There is no way the 'independents' can avoid benefiting from the presence of the union, and no way they can, acting as independents, avoid weakening the union" (104). Is that true? Would independents always benefit from a union? What if the presence of a union makes management grudging in all interactions with all its employees? A middle way may be that dues deduction is mandatory, but actual membership is not; this addresses the second point in favour of a closed shop, but not the first. And again, consider Gibson: "We don't allow individuals to avoid paying their share of the police or national defense or air pollution control budget on the grounds that they prefer to go it alone. Why should this case be different?" (104). But why compare a union with the state? Why not compare it to a business and ask that it operate in that manner, showing the workers what it can do and in that way persuading them to "buy in"?[2]

Collective bargaining is another area of ethical concern. In particular, there are several negotiation tactics (used not just in collective-agreement bargaining but in any negotiation context, such as contract bidding) that have come under ethical scrutiny. One such tactic is bluffing. Some may think that the ethics of bluffing should be considered. During negotiation (and not just collective agreement bargaining, but any negotiation—contract bids, for example), some may think that bluffing is morally acceptable, if only because it's the convention, the "understanding," to overstate one's wants, and to conflate wants and needs, in order to achieve one's ends (see Carr). Carson suggests that deception in negotiation is morally acceptable self-defence against the harmful actions of the other side. Strudler also argues that it's acceptable, but on the grounds that it's a "mutually beneficial solution to a problem confronted by negotiators who, for morally benign reasons, cannot trust each other" (806). Others disagree: negotiation is supposed to be in good faith—how can it be when one side deceives? It's hard enough to reach an agreement when two parties have different objectives; to lie about those objectives makes it harder, not easier. Certainly Kantian ethics would say tell the truth; recall the categorical imperative (if everyone lied, the very notions of 'truth' and 'lie' would logically fall apart into meaninglessness). But a utilitarian analysis might yield another prescription.

---

1 See the article by Patricia D'Souza, which focuses on unions and Canada's grocery stores, especially Sobeys.
2 See Gibson (98–105) for a fuller discussion of these issues.

BOX 5.3 Questionable Negotiation Tactics

1. *Lies*—Statements made in contradiction to the negotiator's knowledge or belief about something material to the negotiation. Subject matter for lies can include limits, alternatives, the negotiator's intent, authority to bargain, other commitments, acceptability of the opponent's offers, time pressures, and available resources.
2. *Puffery*—Exaggerating the value of something in the negotiation. Among the items that can be puffed up are the value of one's payoffs to the opponent, the negotiator's own alternatives, the costs of what one is giving up or is prepared to yield, importance of issues, and attributes of the products or services.
3. *Deception*—An act or statement intended to mislead the opponent about the negotiator's own intent or future actions relevant to the negotiations. Acts and statements may include promises or threats, excessive initial demands, careless misstatements of facts, or asking for concessions not wanted.
4. *Weakening the opponent*—Actions or statements designed to improve the negotiator's own relative strength by directly undermining that of the opponent. The negotiator here may cut off or eliminate some of the opponent's alternatives, blame the opponent for his own actions, use personally abrasive statements to or about the opponent, or undermine the opponent's alliances.
5. *Strengthening one's own position*—Actions or statements designed to improve the negotiator's own position without directly weakening that of the opponent. This tactic includes building one's own resources, including expertise, finances, position, and alliances. It also includes presentations of persuasive rationales to the opponent or third parties (e.g., the public, the media) or getting mandates for one's position.
6. *Nondisclosure*—Keeping to oneself knowledge that would benefit the opponent. Includes partial disclosure of facts, failure to disclose a hidden fact, failure to correct the opponents' misperceptions or ignorance, and concealment of the negotiator's own position or circumstances.
7. *Information exploitation*—Using information provided by the opponent to weaken him, either in the direct exchange or by sharing it with others. Information provided by the opponent can be used to exploit his weaknesses, close off his alternatives, generate demands against him, or weaken his alliances.
8. *Change of mind*—Engaging in behaviours contrary to previous statements or positions. Includes accepting offers one had claimed one would not accept, changing demands, withdrawing promised offers, and making threats one promised would not be made. Also includes the failure to behave as predicted.

9. *Distraction*—Acts or statements that lure the opponent into ignoring information or alternatives that might benefit him. These acts or statements can be as simple as providing excessive information to the opponent, asking many questions, evading questions, or burying the issue. Or they can be more complex, such as feigning weakness in one area so that the opponent concentrates on it and ignores another.
10. *Maximization*—The negotiator's single-minded pursuit of payoffs at the cost of the opponent's payoffs. Includes demanding the opponent make concessions that result in the negotiator's gain and the opponent's equal or greater loss. Also entails converting a win-win situation into win-lose.

Source
H. Joseph Reitz, James A. Wall, Jr., and Mary Sue Love, "Ethics in Negotiation: Oil and Water or Good Lubrication?" *Business Horizons* 41.3 (May/June 1998): 5–15.

Let's back up a step to recognize that bluffing, deception, presumes in the first place an adversarial relationship—and that's another issue: is the adversarial model of management/union right? Is it honest? Is it in everyone's best interests? Consider this excerpt from a piece I wrote after attending a leadership workshop held by a major union:

"Negotiations is a game." One seminar leader said it. And another illustrated it. The ice breaker in her seminar was a game called "Diverse Points." Basically the game went like this: the Leisure Area was for single players to form pairs in preparation for negotiation; the Negotiations Area was for negotiation—people met in pairs and tried to reach agreement on how to divide 100 points between them in any of four proportions, 90/10, 80/20, 70/30, 60/40 (a division of 50/50 was not permitted); the object of the game was to accumulate as many points as possible and the player with the highest total score wins.

Well. First of all, trying to get as many points as possible is not negotiating, it's competing.

Second, why isn't a split of 50/50 permitted? In the absence of significance (the points have no meaning) and therefore rationale, a split of 50/50 is, to my mind, most fair. Why structure a game that excludes fairness as a possibility? Could it be that achieving fair agreement is not the point?

Third—the Leisure Area. I suppose it simulates the golf course, the tennis court, the cocktail lounge—you butter up your associate, pretending to be friends, doing the leisure thing together, and then you saunter over to the Negotiations Area. Talk about mixing business with pleasure. "How to Use Your Friends" couldn't be written more clearly over the entrance. Instead, why not just show up at the Negotiations Area when you want to negotiate?

I played the game, with great reluctance and after considerable thought, trying to average 50 points per negotiation. It was the best I could do in terms of fairness (I believe a split of 90/10 could also be fair—it depends on context, which was absent). To my pleasant surprise, many of the people I interacted with were quite happy with this approach, and we easily and peacefully decided who would get 40 and who would get 60, based on each of our totals so far; sometimes we agreed on 70/30, or even 80/20, if one was quite a bit over an average of 50 and the other quite a bit under.

However, at least one person lied to me about her point average. This was not surprising, given the preceding instruction. She may have been the winner, I'm not sure; to be honest, I didn't care much who won. But, of course, the winner was applauded for her high point total.

The last thing I remember about this "leadership workshop" was this statement: "Collective bargaining has nothing to do with logic or reason." Apparently it has nothing to do with ethics either.[1] (Tittle)

To strike or not—this one is always a big question. Does the right to bargain necessarily entail the right to strike?[2] Should it depend on what you do—for example, on whether you're providing essential or non-essential services? (How are we defining "essential"?) Does a strike involving essential services give the union an unfair advantage (unfair, that is, if the company is at all sensitive to the pain and death that may be caused by a lack of medical, firefighting, or police personnel)? But if essential-service providers don't have the right to strike, is the company at an unfair advantage? Are there no satisfactory alternatives in between?[3]

But even if you're providing *non*-essential services, do you have the right to inconvenience or to use others (clients, customers) for your ends? According to Gonsalves,[4] strikes are justified when they are with just cause, with proper authorization, and as a last resort. (And what is "just cause"?) Furthermore, Gibson points out that although a strike might seem in the short term to inconvenience the recipients of the service, that may not be the case in the long term: "Welfare workers demanding lighter case loads, teachers insisting on smaller classes, air traffic controllers complaining about obsolete equipment, understaffing, and compulsory overtime are all instances of government workers attempting to secure adequate conditions in which to do their jobs. The rights of the recipients of these services are not protected by prohibiting the providers from using what may be the only effective means of securing such conditions—quite the contrary" (105). De George argues that if one has the right to refuse employment and the right to refuse or accept employment only on certain conditions, then one does have the right to strike (379). But *does* one have those rights? And just because we may have a right to do something, that doesn't mean it's morally good to do that something: maybe overall good trumps rights—consider a utilitarian analysis of the consequences if you go on strike; maybe

---

1 Consider also Bowie, who rejects the adversarial model because it "undermines trust and ignores the cooperative features of business" (abstract); he argues that the values of dignity and fairness should characterize labour/management negotiation. (See also Koehn's commentary on Bowie's paper.) Also, check out Post, who proposes, in lieu of the adversarial collective bargaining process, a five-stage collaborative collective bargaining process (commitment, explanation, validation, prioritization, and negotiation), which insists on honesty and teamwork.
2 See Yates on this matter.
3 See the relevant chapter in Gibson's book for an excellent analysis; Burton also addresses public sector strikes but the ethical standard he uses is jurisdictional law; also see Gotbaum, for something rather provocative.
4 See Fagothey and Gonsalves, also in Shaw.

intent trumps rights—consider whether one is going on strike just for vengeance at the current management. (See Liesch's paper for an analysis of teachers' strikes.)

Assuming strikes are justifiable, are sympathetic strikes *also* justifiable? Shaw defines a sympathetic strike as one in which "workers who have no particular grievance of their own and who may or may not have the same employer decide to strike in support of others" (224). One might argue in favour of such strikes on the basis of obligations of loyalty; however, in the case of different employers, the consequences would be suffered by innocent people, the owners. (And, as with any strike, the clients and customers are also innocent victims—though some may be perfectly happy to be so.)

Now, what about "scabs"—workers who cross a picket line to accept work, who are hired by the employer to fill the positions left vacant by the striking workers. What's wrong with someone who's unemployed taking over a union member's job while that person is on strike? They're unemployed! Don't they have the right to look out for themselves—as the union members are doing? And why shouldn't a company hire such workers? If the company can safely operate with workers who may (*or may not*) be untrained, well, why not? Keeping them on *after* the strike, however, and firing the strikers is another matter. Management backlash actions—dismissals, pay cuts, benefits reductions—how are these justified? (Well, how were the poor conditions which prompted the strike, perhaps even the union formation in the first place, justified?)

Let's take a look at this tendency, this unquestioned mandate, of unions to look out for themselves at the expense of others. Fully employed union members often get first chance at extra work (for example, at many universities, spring and summer courses are offered first to full-time faculty members)—shouldn't extra work go to the un/underemployed (for example, the [typically] non-unionized part-time faculty)? Is it right for a union to limit the numbers of people working in a certain occupation so supply doesn't exceed demand, thus ensuring the value of each individual in the occupation? Doesn't that infringe on people's freedom of choice? In short, if corporations have social responsibilities, responsibilities for those outside the corporation, don't unions have the same social responsibilities? (See Dawkins for arguments that unions *do* have social responsibilities.)

One final issue to consider is that unions may be becoming less and less part of Canadian business, something that is due, indirectly, to globalization: sometimes (often?) companies facing undesirable union "demands" or "threatened" with union formation simply shut down. That happened in 2012 with the Electro-Motive (owned by Caterpillar) plant in London, Ontario: "Contract talks collapsed...after [the] locomotive maker issued a final offer that would cut the wages of union members in half [from \$35/hr to \$16.50/hr], eliminate pensions and gut other benefits" and a month later they shut down the plant. They could pay people \$12–18/hr if they relocated to Muncie, Indiana. It also happened with Walmart in Jonquière, Quebec: employees voted in 2004 to unionize (a first for Walmart), but then attempts to reach a collective agreement failed; when the matter was sent to arbitration, Walmart announced that it would be closing the store. (The Supreme Court of Canada ruled, a decade later, that Walmart owed the workers compensation.)

Is that sort of response morally defensible? Those using a utilitarian approach must consider that any time you close down a business, whether temporarily or permanently, the consequences spread out in all directions: the suppliers of the now-closed business suffer, the now-unemployed workers suffer, the businesses previously supported by those workers suffer. This effect was perhaps most evident with the NHL lockout in 2013: "For every Sidney Crosby or Daniel Alfredsson making millions on the ice, there is an entire ecosystem of managers, announcers, hotdog vendors, and Zamboni drivers who only have jobs because hockey is being played" (MacDonald 2013). Those using a rights approach would have to weigh the rights of the employees against those of the employer, and, given the comments about consequences, those of people who are neither. And those using an intuitionist approach would just have to figure out what feels right, I guess.

Co-ops

If we consider unions to be a response to corporate dictatorships (especially when they're not benevolent dictatorships), then perhaps co-ops are best considered as corporate democracies. They may also be the least adversarial.[1] Indeed, the Canada Business Network says "Co-operatives are owned by an association of people or businesses that pool their resources to meet a common need. *A co-operative offers democratic control—each member gets one vote*" ("Co-operatives"; emphasis mine). Democracy may accord with a justice-based ethic, but does it accord with a utilitarian ethic? I suppose it depends on the decisions made by the group.

Given that every member has a vote, whether they're skilled in management or not, one must wonder whether co-ops can be successful business ventures:

> During its 13 years as a worker-owned cooperative, Tower Colliery could be considered an economic success. Internally, the organization and management were emancipatory and empowering to the workers, and this allowed them, collectively, to reassert some degree of control over their economic and social space. Consequently, over the same period, where coal prices were stable and the global market contracting, Tower increased its sales and output, diversified its activities, created additional jobs, invested with a view to the long-term, and distributed part of its increased surplus to support local community initiatives. Furthermore, the continued existence of Tower ensured that capital was effectively anchored in the local community. In addition, Tower's activities contributed to the economic security and well-being of the local community. (Smith et al., 297)

> Consolidated sales for Tennessee Farmers Cooperative (TFC) and its subsidiaries reached an all-time high of $584 million in 2007, an increase of $63 million from 2006. In a year full of

---

[1] And let's face it, the standard business model *is* adversarial: sports metaphors abound; competition seems mandatory. In fact, at a 2005 retreat for Bell executives, participants were encouraged, even expected, to engage in martial arts—to kick, punch, and choke each other. It must also be said that the two female VPs who refused to participate were later fired, despite having "surpassed the performance of their male predecessors, posting better results and earning shares and praise, respectively, from Bell Canada's top boss, Michael Sabia" (MacCharles).

challenges—including a late-spring freeze, summer drought, short hay supplies and higher input costs—the sales record was welcome news for Tennessee farmers. (Campbell, 39)

There are many success stories in Canada as well: Battle River Railway New Generation Co-operative in Alberta, in which farmers took ownership of a railway system; TREC Renewable Energy Co-operative in Ontario, which includes WindShare (the first large-scale wind energy co-op in Canada) and SolarShare (Canada's largest solar co-op); numerous credit unions across the country; and so on. In fact, Cameron notes "The world's 300 largest co-operatives, nine of which are Canadian, have an aggregate turnover of $US 1.1 trillion, the size of the 10th largest economy in the world." He goes on to say "Co-op brand names include Nordica cottage cheese, Sunkist, Welchs, Green Bay Packers, Sealtest, Ocean Spray and Blue Diamond."

In addition to the difference in structure (though co-ops typically still have a board and "management," as well as bylaws, policies, and so on), Davisson has identified a difference in communication:

> The second major difference [between managing a co-op and managing an investor-owned company] is the method of communication used. The publicly traded corporation is very formal in this regard, by requirement. The cooperative is much more informal and hands-on, directly one-on-one with the customer. Communication is much more open regarding operations and the direction of the company because cooperatives do not need to be as concerned that what they say may affect their stock price. Cooperative CEOs must be prepared to spend a lot of time with their customer-owners. (Davisson 39)

Does this increase the likelihood that co-ops will be more "moral" companies? If so, how so?

Of course, another major difference is that although the co-op may (but likely does not) seek to *maximize* profits, profits are distributed among the members according to their work activity. Is this more or less fair than distribution among shareholders according to number of shares held? And is it "just reward" or does it introduce the problem with commissions mentioned above?

BOX 5.4 The Co-operative Advantage

Co-operatives and credit unions are community-based organizations that care not only about the bottom lines of their businesses, but also about the needs of their members and the quality of life in their communities. They bring many obvious benefits to their members such as sharing costs or financial dividends. But the process of being an active member brings its own rewards, allowing member-owners to solidify social and economic links in the community. Perhaps most importantly, membership provides a common ground and support to reduce isolation, and build confidence and skills.

Co-operative organizations differ from other businesses in three key ways:

- A Different Purpose: Co-ops and credit unions meet the common needs of their members, whereas most investor-owned businesses exist to maximize profit for shareholders.
- A Different Control Structure: Co-ops and credit unions use a system of one-member/one-vote, not one-vote-per-share. This helps them to serve common interests and to ensure that people, not capital, control the organization.
- A Different Allocation of Profit: Co-ops and credit unions share profits among their member-owners on the basis of how much they use the organization, not on how many shares they hold.

There are a multitude of benefits that come from successful co-operatives and the ones that will apply to your situation will be as unique as your co-op is itself.

Philosophical benefits
- People trump money in terms of priorities
- Modest savings for all instead of the excessive accumulation of profits by a few
- Opportunities to strengthen community bonds by helping one another
- You can define your own needs instead of letting a conglomerate do it for you
- Product and service development by the people for the people
- Control of your own future
- Greater community autonomy
- More honest and ethical business practices
- Freedom from homogenized mass-market-driven goods and services

Community benefits
- Better access to quality products and services
- Fair market prices
- Strong customer/client loyalty
- Greater employment opportunities
- Ability to change things that don't work
- Economic and social growth in the community
- Access to new markets

Source
http://www.coopzone.coop/about-co-operatives/the-co-operative-advantage/

Corporate Social Responsibility (CSR)

Another buzzword—or buzzacronym—at the moment is CSR: Corporate Social Responsibility. Although often spoken in the same breath as "transparency" and "accountability" and even "corporate governance," it actually goes much further and includes the corporation's role in, or influence on, the community. At the same time, it doesn't go far enough. First, why limit the discussion to corporations? Why not include other businesses? Second, why limit the discussion to *social* responsibilities? As we've seen, responsibilities to employees and shareholders are significant too. Third, as I've mentioned elsewhere in this text, rights and responsibilities are flip sides of the same coin. Or *should be* considered as such. So if we're discussing the responsibilities of corporations (and other businesses), we should also discuss their rights. For example, should the right to *commercial* speech be any different from the right to "regular" speech?

That said, there is a very serious (if somewhat limited) question posed by the notion of CSR: do corporations and other businesses have any social responsibility? Or can they just merrily go on their way pursuing profit? Note the somewhat different, and larger, question: what should the role of the corporation be in society?

Note, however, that the two—being socially responsible and pursuing profit—are not necessarily mutually exclusive. Milton Friedman is, of course, known as the grandfather of the notion that the role of business is to pursue profit, everything else be damned. Colin Grant understands Friedman to be saying that business should "concentrate obsessively on profitability, and that ethics should be marginalized" (907). McAleer has a similar interpretation and shows that all six of Friedman's arguments are unsound.[1] However, although Friedman *did* call social responsibility a "fundamentally subversive doctrine" (1962, 133), he also said that corporate executives have responsibilities to stockholders "to conduct the business in accordance with their desires, which generally will be to make as much money as possible while conforming to the basic rules of society, both those embodied in law and those embodied in *ethical custom*" (1970, p.33; my emphasis). Furthermore, as Scherer, Palazzo, and Baumann point out, "Profit-orientation *is justified by* its expected contribution to societal growth and stability and the increase in public welfare that it generates from which all members of a society benefit" (511).

And if your answer to the question about the role of business isn't "to pursue profit" but "to provide needed and wanted products and services," then it's even more likely that you can claim social responsibility at the same time.

But back to the question: does, or *should*, business have any social responsibility? We might say that we all have a responsibility to make the world a better place, or at least to refrain from making it a worse place—so why should a business be any different? Why should it have any less—or any *more*—such responsibility than individuals?

For example, many people seem to think that a business should provide health care and a pension to its employees. But if those are basic needs, why shouldn't they be the government's

---

[1] See also Mulligan's concise critique of Friedman.

responsibility? (We do assume that the state should cover everyone's basic needs.) And indeed, in Canada, the government does provide basic health care and a pension. (But not food—why not?) So why does business also provide those benefits? Are they extras? To entice employees? To compensate employees? Isn't the pay being offered sufficient? Wouldn't it be better, more respectful of people's autonomy, to just pay employees the "extra," so they can decide for themselves whether to set up a personal pension/health-care supplement? (They may want instead to go back to school.) Isn't it a bit patronizing for the business to just decide to do that for them? (Is it patronizing for the state to do so?) Or is it that the government programs are inadequate? Well, why should business have to pick up the slack?

> **BOX 5.5 Corporate Responsibility in Practice**
>
> 1. The separation of the corporation from the rest of life must be eliminated. Corporations are merely an economic instrument composed of and attending to a series of stakeholders and groups and to the individuals that compose them. Corporations have no independent identity, no reason for being except to serve their stakeholders. Corporate leaders must stop seeing the corporation as a separate entity and begin to recognize interdependencies that exist at a number of levels. These leaders must align personal and corporate values. The desire of corporate executives that their grandchildren enjoy full and good lives must be reflected in the policies and practices undertaken by the corporation.
> 2. Effective long-term planning must replace the current focus on short-term profit, and the long-term approach must be implemented and supported by corporate systems. Reward systems must be reworked to direct attention to long-term success and away from only short-term gain.
> 3. Life-cycle (full) cost accounting practices must be adopted. The full impact of a product must be accounted for in design and costing, for the entire life of the product. This involves accurately valuing all resources, including raw materials, labour, energy, air, water, land, and the impact of emissions. The impact of ultimate disposal will also have to be valued and included.
> 4. Corporate associations must be further developed and must be challenged to promote collective, voluntary, responsible action. Corporations must take the lead in educating their consumers about potential environmental impact and designing their products to limit negative effects.
> 5. An expanded concept of stakeholders and their legitimate involvement in decision making should be accepted. Ideas from all sources should be considered and integrated into corporate decision making.

> 6. Corporations must voluntarily apply equivalent standards regardless of where they are operating. Duty cannot be confined within national borders when the impacts of actions refuse to be so restricted.
> 7. Corporations must operate in an efficient manner, using minimum resources to ensure both short-term profit and long-term supply of raw material.
>
> **Source**
> Wayne Stewart and Peter Dickey, "Corporate Responsibility." Previously published in *Ethics and Climate Change: The Greenhouse Effect*, Ed. Harold Coward and Thomas Hurka. Waterloo: Wilfrid Laurier University Press, 1993. 99–113. © 1993 by Wilfrid Laurier Press. Reprinted with permission of the publisher and the authors.

Why is it so hard for corporations to see that they *are* socially responsible, whether they like it or not? One might suggest that a business has more social responsibility simply because it has more power. (The top 200 corporations in the world have almost twice as much economic clout as four-fifths of humanity [Fraser].) (Even our standard of living is measured by economic performance indicators, by trade in goods and services—by business; that's a lot of power.) So does that mean that individuals with greater power (greater political power, greater economic power) have more responsibility? It's certainly a notion worth considering.

And the argument for why business should have *less* responsibility than individuals? "Only people have responsibilities," Friedman says (1970). "A corporation is an artificial person and in this sense may have artificial responsibilities, but 'business' as a whole cannot be said to have responsibilities, even in this vague sense" (Friedman 1970). (And yet it has rights. How does that work?) So...a business shouldn't have social responsibility because it's not a person. *Should* it be? Should a corporation be considered a person? It's an important question.[1] But it's a relevant question only if we accord legal responsibility only to persons. And only if we're talking only about *legal* responsibility.[2]

As for *moral* responsibility, perhaps one must first ask whether the corporation is a *moral* person.[3] Perhaps it's sufficient to recognize that a business consists of persons with intent and autonomy and agency; there are persons who are members of the corporation who are making decisions—indeed the company doesn't exist *without* such persons. Doesn't *that* make moral responsibility incontestable? Do we need to determine whether we consider the collective a person? (Furthermore, if its status as a non-person exempts it from social responsibility, wouldn't it exempt it from *all* responsibility? Even toward its employees? And shareholders?)

---

1 See French; Ladd; and Goodpaster and Matthews for some answers.
2 See Chris MacDonald's blog post on this issue.
3 See French on this matter.

And yet, "[t]he point to *incorporation* is to create a legal entity *independent of* the people who create it" (Bishop 194; my emphasis). So maybe that's the problem. Maybe *incorporation* is ethically unacceptable.

For as Bishop points out, "Businesses do not have to be corporations; there are individuals and families who conduct businesses in their own names, and there are partnerships, co-ops, associations, and other sorts of businesses" (194). So why incorporate? "One of the distinctive features of corporations is their legally recognised autonomy; corporations do business in their own names, not in the name of investors or employees" (Bishop 194). So if the company directors or owners (or both) were held *personally* responsible for their behaviour, like sole proprietors, would they act more responsibly? Perhaps. If only out of self-interest.

Bishop goes on to say, "The autonomy rights of corporations include, for example, the right to sign contracts and the right to sue" (194). But, again, if the corporation has rights… "[T]he autonomy of corporations also means that they are legally responsible for their 'actions'; corporations can be sued and can be held liable" (Bishop 194).

But businesses often have *limited* liability. Maybe *that's* the problem. Limited liability ensures that shareholders, the owners of the company, aren't personally liable, responsible, for debts, damages, and so on. So when you limit your liability, you're just limiting your responsibility. On what moral grounds can you do that? For example, consider the recent BP oil spill. The Oil Pollution Act caps the amount BP owes in damages for the spill at $75 million (Wang). Current laws (well, one is 160 years old) limit how much victims' families can sue for. As a result, either taxpayers or injured parties have to pay for damage and injury they didn't cause. How is that right? If business entrepreneurs have a right to all the profits, surely they have a responsibility for all the losses. If not, why not?

After all, in sole proprietorships, the owners are responsible for all the losses, all the damages. I can appreciate that individual investors should be limited in their liability to the amount they've invested, but the total liability should add up to 100% so that all losses are covered—by someone! Then again, maybe I don't appreciate limiting liability: if I as an individual "invest" only twenty bucks in an archery set from Canadian Tire, and then accidentally or negligently shoot someone, fatally, in the heart, should I be able to limit my liability to twenty bucks? Am I not responsible for ending someone's life? So why do we allow limited liability? One justification is that it encourages entrepreneurial activity. So that's more important than responsibility for one's actions? Another related justification is that it encourages investment: "People might not want to invest their money in companies if they have to take an active role to make sure the company is behaving morally, legally, and responsibly" (James W. Gray). But that's just encouraging *ir*responsibility.

Let's accept that the people who own or run the company have moral responsibility for their decisions and their actions—does that responsibility extend beyond the company's doors to the broader society? (After all, we're considering corporate *social* responsibility.) Again, I suggest that an affirmative answer is incontestable, if only on utilitarian grounds: what the company does or does not do has consequences beyond its doors; what the company does or does not do affects people *other than* employees and shareholders, so *certainly* the company is responsible to those people. This is the essence of Freeman's stakeholder theory.

Even from the perspective of ethical egoism, surely you have at least *some* responsibility to society if you're looking at all at the long term, because without society, you'll have neither employees nor customers/clients. (This perspective justifies social responsibility, and indeed any ethically correct behaviour, on the grounds that it's good for business—doing the right thing is profitable. But understand that that's not really an ethical argument: the end is not goodness, but profit; goodness is seen as a means to that end.)

Furthermore, the company doesn't exist without society. It is *part of* society. It obtains its employees from society. It obtains its ideas from society, indirectly, as a result of the knowledge base upon which society is built. Cragg makes this intriguing argument for CSR:

> [T]he modern corporation is a legal artifact. It exists because communities create the legal framework necessary for its existence. Individual corporations can therefore be said to owe their existence to a partnership (what might be called a social contract) between shareholders and governments, a partnership that is itself built on the shared though often implicit understanding that corporations have an unconditional (categorical) obligation both to obey the law and to treat their stakeholders ethically while generating wealth for their shareholders. (abstract)

Bishop also implicates the social contract (which has a long history in political philosophy—people become citizens by entering into a sort of contract with others to respect each other's rights and to assume certain responsibilities) when he investigates "if the existence of for-profit corporations is consistent with the fundamental principles of a just society" (192). He concludes that yes, for-profit corporations ought to exist, and "society and the law ought to recognise their definitional rights to autonomy, to pursue private interests, and to engage in economic activities" (192). But at the same time, he says, "[c]orporations have a responsibility to respect the freedom and human rights of all people, and not to interfere with government programs that ensure people have the education and training they need to find and keep corporate employment and that provide a safety-net that prevents destitution" (abstract).

Although not an ethical question *per se*, it might be useful to ask why it's so hard for business to *be* socially responsible? Among common answers are the profit motive, conflicting responsibilities to shareholders, market conditions, and the regulatory environment. Perhaps another part of the problem is that corporations are *collectives*. And when there is more than one person involved, responsibility becomes diffused. Another feature of collectives is groupthink or, even less flattering, the herd mentality.

Returning to the ethical question, from a practical point of the view, the question of whether business *should* have social responsibility may be moot. As Scherer, Palazzo, and Baumann point out, "many TNCs have already assumed state-like roles when and where state agencies fail or are unwilling to contribute to the public good" (508):

In a globalized world..., *global governance*—referring to rule-making and rule-implementation on a global scale—is no longer a task managed by the state alone. Today, transnational corporations (TNCs), as well as civil society groups, increasingly participate in the formulation and implementation of rules in policy areas that were once the sole responsibility of the state or international governmental organizations. The activities of TNCs and civil society groups include, e.g., involvement in peace-keeping, protecting human rights, or implementing social and environmental standards. This development indicates a shift in global business regulations from state-centric forms toward new multilateral, non-territorial modes of regulation, with the participation of private and non-governmental actors. (506; references deleted)

Michalos describes a very good example: Canada's Business Council on National Issues was founded on the idea that "corporations and their leaders have a responsibility not merely to their traditional constituents but to society as a whole" (225)—to "help build a strong economy, progressive social policies, and healthy political institutions" (226). However, Michalos points out that "some Canadian companies and families have more than one voice at the Council's table. For example, the Bronfman family interests may be expressed through the C.E.O. of Brascan Ltd., John Labatt Ltd., Noranda Inc., Noranda Forest Inc., MacMillan Bloedel Ltd., Norcen Energy Resources Group, or Joseph E. Seagram and Sons." He adds that "the most glaring absentee is a representative from the Canadian Federation of Independent Business" and concludes that "it would be more accurate for the Council to describe itself as the 'voice of big business'" (226). As for doing what it says it's to do, for society as a whole, Michalos points out that the Council has never suggested that there is anything wrong with a tax system that allows big companies to frequently pay no income tax or with a system that makes lobbying expenses in the private interests of businesses tax-deductible while those expenses in the public interests of antipoverty groups are not tax-deductible.

Big business is running society, Scherer, Palazzo, Baumann essentially say, because "within a context of globalization, nation states and their agencies are severely constrained in their ability to monitor and protect the rights of their citizens and to provide sufficient public goods" (508); consequently, "the state is incapable of recognizing and anticipating all possible conflicts and coordination issues that can arise from an increasingly interconnected and highly complex environment" (511). (But business *is*?)

Note that businesses have assumed these state-like roles even though, as Friedman notes, they are "neither democratically controlled nor trained to identify or solve social problems" (509–10). In other words, not only do they lack the expertise, but they also lack legitimacy: no one elected business people to run society.[1] This lack of expertise would be a good argument *against* corporate social responsibility: business isn't any more equipped to solve social problems than the ordinary citizen, and such endeavours should be left to those who know something

---

1 On this note, check out the TV sci-fi series *Continuum*. Its premise is that corporations have totally replaced governments and the world is ruled by the "Corporate Congress."

about them, presumably social experts and policy makers. (And yet we all assume a certain minimum of social responsibility when we accept the social contract and agree to live in society....)

As for the lack of legitimacy, apparently it doesn't matter. So if there is to be a blurring of government and business—and let's face it, there is, with governments acting like businesses, arranging trade agreements, and businesses acting like governments, as just pointed out—then business had *better* adopt some social responsibility.

> **BOX 5.6 Feel Like Watching a Movie?**
>
> Check out *Norma Rae*. And, if you're in the mood for a documentary, *Wal-Mart: The High Cost of Low Price*.

References and Further Reading

Adler, Robert S., and William J. Bigoness. "Contemporary Ethical Issues in Labor-Management Relations." *Journal of Business Ethics* 11.5–6 (May 1992): 351–60.

Alinsky, Saul. *Rules for Radicals*. New York: Random House, 1971.

Bataille-Chedotel, Frederique, and France Huntzinger. "Faces of Governance of Production Cooperatives: An Exploratory Study of Ten French Cooperatives." *Annals of Public and Cooperative Economics* 75.1 (2004): 89–111.

Bishop, John Douglas. "For-Profit Corporations in a Just Society: A Social Contract Argument Concerning the Rights and Responsibilities of Corporations." *Business Ethics Quarterly* 18.2 (2008): 191–212.

Boatright, John R. *Ethics and the Conduct of Business*. 2nd ed. Englewood Cliffs, NJ: Prentice Hall, 1997.

Bowie, Norman E. "Should Collective Bargaining and Labor Relations Be Less Adversarial?" *Journal of Business Ethics* 4 (1985): 283–91.

Brooks, Leonard J. "Ethical Investing: Helpful or Heresy." *The Corporate Ethics Monitor* 9.5 (1997): 1.

Burton, John F., Jr. "Public Sector Strikes: Legal, Ethical, and Practical Considerations." *Ethics, Free Enterprise, and Public Policy: Original Essays on Moral Issues in Business*. Ed. Richard T. De George and Joseph A. Pichler. New York: Oxford University Press, 1978. 127–54.

Cameron, Peter. "What Is a Co-op?" Ontario Co-operative Association. http://www.ontario.coop/all_about_cooperatives/what_is_a_coop

Campbell, Dan. "Newsline: Tennessee Farmers' Co-op Sets New Sales Record." *Rural Cooperatives* March/April 2008: 39–40.

Canadian Coalition for Good Governance. www.ccgg.ca

The Canadian Press. "Electro-Motive Locks Out 420 CAW Union Members at London, Ontario Plant." *Huffington Post* 2 Jan. 2012. http://www.huffingtonpost.ca/2012/01/02/electro-motive-locks-out-union-members_n_1179218.html

Carr, Albert Z. "Is Business Bluffing Ethical?" *Harvard Business Review* 46.1 (1968): 143–53.

Carson, Thomas. "Second Thoughts about Bluffing." *Business Ethics Quarterly* 3.4 (1993): 317–41.

Cohen-Rosenthal, Edward. "Should Unions Participate in Quality of Working Life Activities?" *Quality of Working Life: The Canadian Scene* 3.4 (January 1980).

"Co-operatives." *Canada Business Network*. http://www.canadabusiness.ca/eng/page/4725/

Cragg, Wesley. "Business Ethics and Stakeholder Theory." *Business Ethics Quarterly* 12.2 (2002): 113–42.

D'Souza, Patricia. "Food Fights." *This Magazine* 32.5 (March/April 1999): 30–35.

Davisson, Bill. "Management Tip: How managing a co-op differs from running an investor-owned firm." *Rural Cooperatives* March/April 2011: 29, 39.

Dawkins, Cedric. "Beyond Wages and Working Conditions: A Conceptualization of Labor Union Social Responsibility." *Journal of Business Ethics* 95 (2010): 129–43.

De George, Richard T. *Business Ethics*. 5th ed. Englewood Cliffs, NJ: Prentice Hall, 1999. 375–85.

Donaldson, T. *Corporations and Morality*. Englewood Cliffs, NJ: Prentice Hall, 1982.

Fagothey, Austin, and Milton A. Gonsalves. *Right and Reason: Ethics in Theory and Practice*. St. Louis: Mosby, 1981. 428–29.

Fogarty, Timothy, Michel L. Magnan, Garen Markarian, and Serge Bohdjalian. "Inside Agency: The Rise and Fall of Nortel." *Journal of Business Ethics* 84 (2009): 165–87.

Forsey, Helen. Letter. *This Magazine* 32.3 (November/December 1998): 2.

Fraser, Chris. "Taking Stock." *Conscience Canada* 76 (November 1994): 4.

French, Peter A. "Corporate Moral Agency." *Business Ethics: Readings and Cases in Corporate Morality*. Ed. W. Michael Hoffman and Jennifer Mills Moore. New York: McGraw Hill, 1984. 163–71.

———. "The Corporation as a Moral Person." *American Philosophical Quarterly* 16.3 (1979): 207–15.

Friedman, M. *Capitalism and Freedom*. Chicago: University of Chicago Press, 1962.

———. "The Social Responsibility of Business Is to Increase Its Profits." *New York Times Magazine* 13 Sep. 1970. Rpt. in *Business Ethics in Canada*. Ed. Deborah C. Poff and Wilfrid J. Waluchow. 3rd ed. Scarborough, ON: Prentice Hall Allyn and Bacon Canada, 1999. 43–47.

Gagne, Claire, Zena Olijnyk, John Gray, and Denis Seguin. "MBAs on the March." *Canadian Business* 77.21 (2004): 133–39.

Gibson, Mary. *Workers' Rights*. Totowa, NJ: Rowman & Allanheld, 1983.

Goodpaster, Kenneth E., and John B. Matthews, Sr. "Can a Corporation Have a Conscience?" *Business Ethics: Readings and Cases in Corporate Morality*. Ed. W. Michael Hoffman and Jennifer Mills Moore. New York: McGraw Hill, 1984. 150–62.

Gotbaum, Victor. "Public Service Strikes: Where Prevention Is Worse than the Cure." *Ethics, Free Enterprise, and Public Policy: Original Essays on Moral Issues in Business*. Ed. Richard T. De George and Joseph A. Pichler. New York: Oxford University Press, 1978. 155–69.

Grant, C. "Friedman Fallacies." *Journal of Business Ethics* 10 (1991): 907–14.

Gray, James W. "Ethical Implications of Corporations. *Ethical Realism* 3 May 2011. https://ethicalrealism.wordpress.com/2011/05/03/ethical-implications-of-corporations/

Gray, John. "Is Labour's Mac Attack a Losing Battle?" *The Globe and Mail* 9 Sep. 1998: A1+.

Hayden, Anders. "Capitalist Crunch." *This Magazine* 32.1 (July/August 1998): 23–26.

Irvine, William B. "The Ethics of Investing." *Journal of Business Ethics* 6.3 (1987): 233–42.

Jeurissen, Ronald. "Institutional Conditions of Corporate Citizenship." *Journal of Business Ethics* 53 (2004): 87–96.

Koehn, Donald R. "Commentary upon 'Should Collective Bargaining and Labor Relations Be Less Adversarial?'" *Journal of Business Ethics* 4 (1985): 293–95.

Ladd, John. "Morality and the Ideal of Rationality in Formal Organizations." *Ethical Issues in Business: A Philosophical Approach.* Ed. Thomas Donaldson and Patricia H. Werhane. 2nd ed. Englewood Cliffs, NJ: Prentice Hall, 1983. 125–36.

Liesch, James R. "Strikes and Sanctions: A Moral Inquiry." *Educational Theory* (1968): 253–61.

Lu, Vanessa. "McMemories Resurface." *Toronto Star* 28 Aug. 1998: A4.

———. "Stand Up, Speak Out, Unionists Say." *Toronto Star* 28 Aug. 1998: A4.

MacCharles, Tonda. "Ex-Bell execs allege sexism." *The Star* 14 Jan. 2008. http://www.thestar.com/news/canada/2008/01/14/exbell_execs_allege_sexism.html

MacDonald, Chris. "NHL Lockout and the Ethics of Labour Disputes." *The Business Ethics Blog* 7 Jan. 2013. http://businessethicsblog.com/2013/01/07/nhl-lockout-and-the-ethics-of-labour-disputes/

———. "Why Corporations Must Be Legal Persons." *The Business Ethics Blog* 27 Sept. 2009. http://businessethicsblog.com/2009/09/27/why-corporations-must-be-legal-persons/

McAleer, S. "Friedman's Stockholder Theory of Corporate Moral Responsibility." *Teaching Business Ethics* 7 (2003): 437–51.

McCall, John J. "An Ethical Basis for Employee Participation." *Contemporary Issues in Business Ethics.* Ed. Joseph R. Desjardins and John J. McCall. 3rd ed. Belmont, CA: Wadsworth, 1996. 199–206.

Mendleson, Rachel. "Electro-Motive Lockout: Caterpillar to Close London, Ont. Plant, Company Says." *Huffington Post* 3 Feb. 2012. http://www.huffingtonpost.ca/2012/02/03/electro-motive-lockout-ca_n_1252510.html

Michalos, Alex. "Issues for Business Ethics in the Nineties and Beyond." *Journal of Business Ethics* 16.3 (1997): 219–30.

Morck, Randall. "Behavioral Finance in Corporate Governance: Economics and Ethics of the Devil's Advocate." *Journal of Management & Governance* 12 (2008): 179–200.

Mulligan, Thomas. "A Critique of Milton Friedman's Essay 'The Social Responsibility of Business Is to Increase Its Profits.'" *Journal of Business Ethics* 5 (1986): 265–69.

Nordberg, Donald. "The Ethics of Corporate Governance." *Journal of General Management* 33.4 (2008): 35–52.

Pava, Moses L. "Why Corporations Should *Not* Abandon Corporate Responsibility." *Journal of Business Ethics* 83 (2008): 805–12.

Phillips, Robert, R., Edward Freeman, and Andrew C. Wicks. "What Stakeholder Theory Is Not." *Business Ethics Quarterly* 13.4 (2003): 479–502.

Post, Frederick R. "Collaborative Collective Bargaining: Toward an Ethically Defensible Approach to Labor Negotiations." *Journal of Business Ethics* 9.6 (1990): 495–508.

Public Policy Forum. *At the Vanguard of Canadian Innovation: A Compilation of Co-operative Case Studies.* October 2014. ppforum.ca

"Quebec unionized Wal-Mart workers win Supreme Court victory." *CBC News* 27 June 2014. http://www.cbc.ca/news/canada/montreal/quebec-unionized-wal-mart-workers-win-supreme-court-victory-1.2689646

Reitz, H. Joseph, James A. Wall, Jr., and Mary Sue Love, "Ethics in Negotiation: Oil and Water or Good Lubrication?" *Business Horizons* 41.3 (May/June 1998): 5–15.

Rosenberg, Hilary. *A Traitor to His Class: Robert A.G. Monk and the Battle to Change Corporate America.* New York: John Wiley & Sons, 1999.

Scherer, Andreas Georg, Guido Palazzo, and Dorothee Baumann. "Global Rules and Private Actors: Toward a New Role of the Transnational Corporation in Global Governance." *Business Ethics Quarterly* 16.4 (2006): 505–32.

Shaw, William H. *Business Ethics.* 2nd ed. Belmont, CA: Wadsworth, 1996. 219–26.

Smith, Russell, Len Arthur, Molly Scott Cato, and Tom Keenoy. "A Narrative of Power: Tower Colliery as an Example of Worker Control through Cooperative Work Organization." *Working USA: The Journal of Labor and Society* 14 (2011): 285–303.

Strudler, Alan. "On the Ethics of Deception in Negotiation." *Business Ethics Quarterly* 5.4 (1995): 805–22.

Thompson, Clive. "Cooking the books: in the wake of Enron, WorldCom, and ImClone, the corporate annual report may be one of our finest contemporary works of fiction." *This Magazine* (Sep/Oct 2002).

Tittle, Peg. "Leadership?" http://www.pegtittle.com/leadership.html

Turnbull, Shann. "Defining and achieving good governance." In Aras, G., and Ingley, C. (Eds.) *Corporate Behavior and Sustainability: Doing Well by Being Good,* Farnham, UK: Ashgate Gower Publishers, 2016: 234–51.

Wang, Marian. "A Year After Gulf Tragedy, Offshore Oil Companies Still Shielded by Liability Limits." *ProPublica* 19 Apr. 2011. http://www.propublica.org/blog/item/a-year-after-gulf-tragedy-offshore-oil-companies-still-shielded-by-liability

Warren, Richard C. "The Responsible Shareholder: A Case Study." *Business Ethics: A European Review* 11.1 (2002): 14–24.

Yates, Charlotte A.B. "In Defense of the Right to Strike." *University of New Brunswick Law Journal* 59 (2009): 128–37.

The Discourse of Control*

Stephen Maguire

[1] Organizational control is deeply embedded in the discourse of management. Most management texts agree that control, the process of setting performance standards, monitoring performance, and taking corrective action to achieve organizational goals, is one of the four major management functions (Daft & Fitzgerald, 1992; Donnelly et al., 1995; Gatewood et al., 1995; Schermerhorn et al., 1995). These texts describe a variety of control systems such as strategic planning, financial forecasting, budgeting, operations management systems, performance evaluations, and management information systems. There are also much broader forms of organizational control, and three have emerged as the most relevant to large contemporary organizations: bureaucratic, clan, and concertive (Barker, 1993; Ouchi, 1980). These three forms of organizational control describe ways to control employees through technical and social control (Graham, 1993). Each form of control describes different ways in which employees are told what to do, how to do it, and how long to take. They also describe ways to manipulate employee attitudes to their work so that organizational goals may be more effectively and efficiently accomplished.

[2] Bureaucratic control structures work activities through a hierarchical division of positions assigning to each specific tasks, responsibilities, and a level of authority. Bureaucratic control is usually recommended in circumstances where tasks are routine and the external environment is relatively stable (Perrow, 1995). Clan control regulates employee behavior through a system of shared goals, values, and traditions and is usually recommended when non-routine tasks are situated in unstable environments (Ouchi, 1980). Recently a new form of control called "concertive control" has been described in the literature (Barker, 1993). Concertive control is achieved by the pressure of peers in self-managed teams and has been successfully adopted for routine and non-routine tasks and in stable and unstable environments (Barker, 1993; Stayer, 1990).

[3] It is too early to tell whether concertive control will become another recommended form of control, but it is clear that bureaucratic and clan control already are. Couched in the scientific discourse of organizational behavior and organizational theory, the recommendations to match appropriate forms of control to specific environments appear to be the logical consequence of a synthesis of organizational strategy and environmental dynamics. The problem here, however, is not which form of control is appropriate to specific

---

* Please note that this is a slightly revised version of the paper that appeared in *Journal of Business Ethics* 19.3 (March 1999): 109–14. © 1999 by Kluwer Academic Publishers. Reprinted with permission of the publisher and the author.

situations. The problem is whether we should be talking about controlling people at all. The problem is essentially a moral one which has been given a scientific hearing.

[4] Organizational control was first legitimated by Max Weber's theory of bureaucracy (1947) and Frederick Taylor's theory of scientific management (1916). Taylor in particular formalized the shift in the knowledge of production from worker to manager (Braverman, 1974). Taylor's concern with management control and with doing more with less workers continues to influence the contemporary discourse of control. Recent management trends including management by objectives, total quality control, delayering, restructuring, re-engineering, downsizing, just in time workers, outsourcing staff functions, and the new employment contract have all been interpreted as ways of increasing organizational control over workers. Team talk, in which business is compared to sport, is also a means of legitimating unquestioned loyalty, fragmentation of labor, the sacrifice of self-interest to organizational interests, and acquiescence to hierarchical authority (Jackall, 1988). Sometimes control talk is legitimated by humanistic discourse which we find in discussions of management's manipulation of cultural rituals, symbols, and stories (Ray, 1986) or in the use of such terms as mentoring, teamwork, and empowerment (Simons, 1995). So successful has our immersion been in the paradigm of control that we are now beginning to talk about controlling for ethical behavior (Johnson, 1996; Lindsay, 1996; Treviño, 1995; Weaver, et. al., 1999). In this paper I will argue that the use of such morally problematic discourse is indicative of a much deeper problem, a failure to understand the fundamental conditions which sustain moral practices.

[5] I will also argue that the discourse of control objectifies workers, denies their moral agency, and violates the principle of moral equality. Control talk also undermines our notion of reciprocity which is a fundamental condition of moral communities and organizations. Finally, I will suggest an alternative discourse, a discourse of accountability which appropriately highlights the reciprocity necessary to build ethical organizations.

Is "Control" an Apt Description?

[6] Before I can begin, however, I first need to consider an argument which suggests that organizational control of employees is pervasive and hence unavoidable. If employees are always subject to subtle and pervasive means of organizational control, then doing away with the discourse of control as a description of organizational life amounts to undermining the integrity of science and submitting to the worst elements of political correctness. I do not propose, however, to dispense with the discourse of control in general. Instead I suggest that we (1) separate its descriptive and normative components, (2) more carefully examine the range of its descriptive scope, and (3) do away with the normative component of the discourse of control.

[7] The normative discourse of control is legitimated if we believe that every conceivable work environment is subject to organizational control. If organizational control is impossible to avoid, then there is some justification for discussing appropriate ways to control employee behavior. Pessimism about achieving freedom from organizational control is supported by two findings. First, employee behavior is controlled through the internalization of organizational culture which is impossible to avoid (Treviño, 1995). If organizational culture is inescapable, then so too is organizational control. Second, self-managed work teams, the exemplars of employee autonomy in the workplace, have been found to be stronger than traditional forms of organizational control (Barker, 1993; Graham, 1993).

If, therefore, the best autonomy supportive conditions in the workplace ultimately result in stronger organizational control, then it seems that whatever employees do in the workplace is a result of organizational control.

[8] Let us first examine the issue of controlling employee behavior through organizational culture. And let us concede that organizational culture is internalized by employees. It does not follow, however, that if we concede that organizational culture is internalized, organizational culture is pervasive in controlling employee behavior. If we accept that internalization of knowledge, beliefs, and values is tantamount to being controlled, we would no longer be able to specify conditions in which we are free from control. We always act from an internal source. All of our actions must be accompanied by a desire to act (Bond, 1983). What we desire to do will be based on a synthesis of our knowledge, beliefs, values, and situational contingencies. Some of those situational contingencies, such as close supervisory control, may be coercive. Many other situations, such as new responsibilities or promotions, may be construed as opportunities. Hence we need to distinguish those conditions under which desires are coerced from those in which they are not.

[9] Similarly it would be a mistake to argue from the fact that all human experience is situated within an historical context of knowledge, values, and interests, that all human social behavior is controlled by historical and cultural forces. It is impossible to conceive of persons independent of cultural and historical conditions. Nonetheless the struggle for freedom and self-determination takes place within such a context of social constraints. Just because we are never entirely free of such constraints does not mean that autonomy is illusory. If autonomy is "the capacity of persons to make rationally reflective choices about their ends and activities" (Lippke, 1997, p. 331), then freedom is the exercise of our rationally reflective choices made within the context of a given cultural and historical situation.

[10] How does this discussion bear on organizational culture? Precisely because some organizational cultural values which are readily internalized are consistent with our rationally reflective choices. Organizational cultural values which support living a meaningful life are more likely to be willingly adopted and sustained in workplace practices. These are instances of self-determined behavior. Values which are inconsistent with living a meaningful life are likely to be resisted or experienced as controlling. Supportive organizational cultures, on the other hand, will value openness, dialogue, and collaboration, values which promote self-determination and self-fulfilment. Whether a culture is supportive of self-determination or is instead controlling will be determined by the relationship between organizational cultural values and the living of a meaningful life.

[11] Nor does it follow from specific studies which highlight organizational attempts to control the values of self-managed teams (Graham, 1993) or from studies which emphasize the pressure of peers in controlling behavior (Barker, 1993) that self-managed teams are inevitably controlling. What these studies implicitly provide are fascinating accounts of the ways in which ostensibly autonomy enhancing conditions are undermined. Other research also supports the view that autonomy supportive conditions may be jeopardized if a threshold of such conditions is breached. Research into the contextual factors which facilitate internalization of regulations supports the view that a threshold of supportive conditions must exist to facilitate integration of external regulations in a self-determining style (Deci, et al., 1994). Once this threshold is undermined, individuals experience external regulation as controlling rather than

supporting (Deci, et al., 1994). The studies which have concluded that self-managed teams are inevitably controlling have failed to differentiate between autonomy supportive conditions and controlling conditions. With this difference in mind, we will be in a better position to explain how autonomy supportive conditions are undermined.

Controlling Conditions versus Autonomy-enhancing Conditions

[12] On the basis of established research by Deci and colleagues, we can distinguish between controlling conditions and those which enhance autonomy. Controlling conditions are experienced as compulsion, of having to do what one has to do. They are characterized by an absence of choice, a lack of opportunity to provide meaningful input, and an obligation to perform work which is not valued for its own sake or for the ends it provides (Deci & Ryan, 1987; Deci, Connell, & Ryan, 1989; Deci et al., 1994). In general, routine work which is highly specialized, standardized, and formalized is experienced as controlling. Close supervision whether by persons or technology, is also controlling. So too is corrective action issued as commands, or as one ought to do "x", or one should do "x" (Deci & Ryan, 1987). Even positive feedback can be experienced as controlling according to the context of evaluation; if you are told that you have done well *as expected*, the experience is one of control (Deci, Connell, & Ryan, 1989). To summarize, if one does work which one does not value, and does what one is told to do under close supervision or because of rewards, threats, and externally imposed deadlines, and is peremptorily corrected for making mistakes, the experience is one of external control.

[13] Autonomy enhancing conditions contrast with controlling conditions. If individuals are able to exercise choice among meaningful options in the absence of pressure, if they are able to initiate action and take responsibility for their actions, if they have opportunities to provide meaningful input, if their perspective is acknowledged, if rationales are provided with requests, if the work they are able to perform is inherently meaningful or helps to achieve meaningful ends, and if individuals are allowed to develop their competencies through the exercise of their judgment and skill, then organizations which sustain such conditions have a supportive rather than a controlling culture (Deci & Ryan, 1987; Deci, Connell, & Ryan, 1989; Deci et al., 1994).

[14] We should reasonably expect self-managed teams, decentralized organizations, and learning organizations to foster such autonomy supportive conditions. Nevertheless even within such organizational structures, conditions may develop which undermine the threshold of autonomy supportive conditions. I claim that in general such organizational structures are more likely to be supportive of employee autonomy in the workplace. Bureaucratic rule bound organizational cultures, autocratic cultures, and high risk cultures are much more likely to foster controlling conditions. Responsive cultures, cultures which value their employees, are much more likely to support conditions which enhance the autonomy of their employees (Di Norcia, 1998). In summary, control is an apt description of how some organizational cultures do attempt to determine employee behavior. The range of its descriptive application, however, ought to be limited only to those cultures which can be observed as exhibiting controlling conditions.

How Ethical Is Control Talk?

[15] It ought to be clear that, at least in some organizations, control will not be an apt description of the ways in which employees are encouraged to go about their work. Nevertheless, if control talk

remains an appropriate way to describe how many organizations structure employee behavior, we still need to determine whether the normative discourse of control is also appropriate. Suppose we concede, for the sake of argument, that controlling organizations are more efficient and effective for routine tasks and stable environments. Is this not a powerful utilitarian justification of control? Does not the good which society enjoys as a result of tightly controlled organizations justify arguably immoral methods? I will argue that the assumptions underlying the discourse of control are sufficiently disturbing to give us cause to consider this question more deeply than we presently do. In particular, we need to consider whether control talk presupposes a denial of individual autonomy, moral agency, and the possibility of moral community.

[16] One of the underlying assumptions of control is that those who command are more knowledgeable and capable, and those who serve need direction. Hence management does the thinking and employees do what they are told to do. Compliance with externally imposed standards, however, undermines an individual's autonomous self concept. To be autonomous, one must be able to conceive of oneself as being able to act autonomously (Kupfer, 1987; Lippke, 1997). To act autonomously, one must be able to deliberate about one's actions by examining the relationship of those actions to values which contribute to the living of a meaningful life. In the workplace, this suggests that workers ought to be given reasons to act and the power to criticize, modify, reject or accept those reasons. They ought to be given the opportunity to engage in dialogue about the way things are done, or could be done. They ought to be able to "buy in" to organizational goals. Control talk, on the other hand, presupposes that individuals will not rationally accept organizational goals and as a consequence obviates opportunities for employees to develop and exercise autonomy and to voluntarily commit to organizational goals. Instead, control talk perpetuates the view that people are objects to be manipulated in accordance with organizational goals.

[17] Insofar as one's self-esteem is dependent on the successful exercise of one's abilities and insofar as control minimizes the need for employees to exercise their rational abilities, their self-esteem will at best be modest, at worst constantly undermined. The perception of worthlessness is directly related to one's being valued only as a means to an end. Control talk, particularly that which emphasizes ethical compliance, ignores a human need to experience self-worth. Programs which are meant to control for ethical compliance stress obedience. Self-worth is dependent upon the exercise of virtue, particularly moral virtue. Self-worth grows from valuing one's judgments about doing what is right and good. One values these judgments because one has become engaged with others in determining and acting on shared moral beliefs. Compliance denies opportunities to exercise judgment and discursively engage in the determination of what is right. In doing so, compliance programs eliminate the conditions upon which self worth and moral agency depend.

[18] The same conditions which preempt moral agency also preempt the formation of a moral community. One encourages autonomy by providing choice, by providing a rationale for requests, by acknowledging the perspective of the other, and by engaging in collaborative reflection. These are also conditions which support dialogue with others. Dialogue is further supported by the values of trust, openness, and a willingness to learn, conditions which are also necessary for the development of a moral community. Kant (1959) also recognized that the conditions which support autonomy are necessarily linked to the supporting conditions of moral community. Autonomous agents are able to

recognize the role which reciprocity plays in developing a community of autonomous moral agents. Agents who recognize and value the development of rationality will be motivated to foster its development in others. Through such reciprocal action friendship, fraternity, and solidarity may blossom.

[19] If we are interested in building ethical organizations, then we need to give up the normative discourse of control, particularly the more recent discourse which is committed to "controlling" for ethical behavior. The relationship between discourse and reality is now so much more apparent to us all. There is no need to review why racist language is offensive or why feminists advocate non-sexist language. There is no need to explore the deeper philosophical underpinnings of language and world expressed in the Greek concept of *logos* (Gadamer, 1976). It is clear that language expresses and creates our reality. If we continue to use the discourse of control, the reality we will create will be organizations bereft of the fundamental conditions for the exercise of autonomy, self-worth, and moral community. We will continue to objectify workers and legitimate an instrumental view of employees as another resource to exploit.

Accountability as an Alternative Discourse

[20] Where does this leave us? How ought we to describe the way in which organizations coordinate individuals to pursue organizational ends? How do we ensure that workers responsibly pursue those ends? How do we reframe managers' control orientations and practices (Winter et al., 1997)? If we concede the importance of reciprocity in fostering moral community, then why not adopt a discourse of accountability? To be accountable means to be responsible for one's actions and to be willing to engage in dialogue to explain and defend them. It means a willingness to be questioned, to ask for, or to provide clarification. It involves a willingness to share in the construction of explanations. Dialogical rationality presupposed by accountability in turn presupposes a collaborative and reciprocal spirit of inquiry. It both presupposes and strives to achieve mutual understanding (Gadamer, 1989).

[21] Accountability cuts both ways. Status and authority do not provide immunity from accountability to subordinates. To hold others accountable is to be subject to reciprocal action, to be accountable for asking the right questions, and for contributing in a spirit of inquiry to a collaborative partnership in resolving issues at hand. Accountability presupposes autonomous agents willing to discursively settle their differences and agree on common worthwhile goals. The practice of being accountable and demanding accountability helps to build and sustain moral organizations.

[22] Accountability encourages self-responsibility, self-monitoring, and self-management. It encourages the kind of autonomous reflection necessary for recognizing moral issues and voicing moral doubt, disagreement, or protest (Bird, 1996). By voicing one's concern, one invites a dialogical analysis and resolution of moral problems. If building and sustaining moral organizations is our goal, then dialogue which grows from accountability is the kind of talk we need. And the first thing we ought to be accountable for is the way we talk about the people with whom we work.

References

Barker, J.R. 1993. "Tightening the Iron Cage: Concertive Control in Self-managing Teams." *Administrative Science Quarterly* 38, 408–437.

Bird, F.B. 1996. *The Muted Conscience: Moral Silence and the Practice of Ethics in Business*. Westport, CT: Quorum Books.

Bond, E.J. 1983. *Reason and Value.* Cambridge: Cambridge University Press.

Braverman, H. 1974. *Labor and Monopoly Capital: The Degradation of Work in the Twentieth Century.* New York: Monthly Review Press.

Daft, R.L., and P.A. Fitzgerald. 1992. *Management.* Toronto: Dryden.

Deci, E.L., J.P. Connell, and R.M. Ryan. 1989. "Self-determination in a Work Organization." *Journal of Applied Psychology* 74, 580–590.

Deci, E.L., and R.M. Ryan. 1987. "The Support of Autonomy and the Control of Behavior." *Journal of Personality and Social Psychology* 53, 1024–1037.

Deci, E.L., H. Eghrari, B.C. Patrick, and D.R. Leone. 1994. "Facilitating Internalization: The Self-Determination Theory Perspective." *Journal of Personality* 62, 119–142.

Di Norcia, V. 1998. *Hard Like Water: Ethics in Business.* Toronto: Oxford.

Donnelly, J.H., Jr., J.L. Gibson, and J.M. Ivancevich. 1995. *Fundamentals of Management.* Chicago: Irwin.

Gadamer, H.G. 1976. "Man and Language." In *Philosophical Hermeneutics.* Berkeley: University of California Press, 59–68.

Gadamer, H.G. 1989. *Truth and Method.* New York: Crossroad.

Gatewood, R.D., R.R. Taylor, and O.C. Ferrell. 1995. *Management: Comprehension, Analysis, and Application.* Chicago: Irwin.

Graham, L. 1993. "Inside a Japanese Transplant: A Critical Perspective." *Work and Occupations* 20, 147–173.

Jackall, R. 1988. *Moral Mazes: The World of Corporate Managers.* Oxford: Oxford University Press.

Johnson, P., C. Cassell, and K. Smith. 1996. "The Management Control of Ethics: The Case of Corporate Codes." *Business Ethics and Business Behaviour.* London: International Thomson Business Press, 163–181.

Kant, I. 1959. *Foundations of the Metaphysics of Morals.* Trans. Lewis White Beck. Indianapolis: Bobbs-Merrill.

Kupfer, J. 1987. "Privacy, autonomy, and self-concept." *American Philosophical Quarterly* 24, 81–89.

Lindsay, R.M., L.M. Lindsay, and V.B. Irvine. 1996. "Instilling Ethical Behavior in Organizations: A Survey of Canadian Companies." *Journal of Business Ethics* 15, 393–407.

Lippke, R.L. 1995. "The Importance of Being Autonomous." *Radical Business Ethics.* Lanham, MD: Rowman and Littlefield, 27–48.

Lippke, R.L. 1997. "Work, Privacy, and Autonomy." *Moral Issues in Business* 7th ed., eds. W.H. Shaw and V. Barry. Belmont, CA: Wadsworth.

Ouchi, W.G. 1980. "Markets, Bureaucracies, and Clans." *Administrative Science Quarterly* 25, 129–141.

Perrow, C. 1995. "Why Bureaucracy?" *Foundations of Organizational Communication: A Reader.* White Plains, NY: Longman, 28–50.

Ray, C.A. 1986. "Corporate Culture: The Last Frontier of Control." *Journal of Management Studies* 23, 287–297.

Schermerhorn, J.R., Jr., R.J. Cattaneo, and A. Templer. 1995. *Management.* Toronto: John Wiley & Sons.

Simons, R. 1995. "Control in an Age of Empowerment." *Harvard Business Review* March-April, 80–88.

Stayer, R. 1990. "How I Learned to Let My Workers Lead." *Harvard Business Review* Nov-Dec, 66–83.

Taylor, F.W. 1995. "The Principles of Scientific Management." *Foundations of Organizational Communication: A Reader.* White Plains, NY: Longman, 65–75.

Treviño, L.K., and K.A. Nelson. 1995. *Managing Business Ethics: Straight Talk about How to Do It Right.* New York: John Wiley and Sons.

Weaver, G.R., L.K. Treviño, and P.L. Cochran. 1999. "Corporate Ethics Programs as Control Systems: Influences of Executive Commitment and Environmental Factors." *The Academy of Management Journal* Feb., 41–57.

Weber, M. 1947. *The Theory of Social and Economic Organizations,* ed. and trans. A.M. Henderson and T. Parsons. New York: Free Press.

Winter, R.P., J.C. Sarros, and G.A. Tanewski. 1997. "Reframing Managers' Control Orientations and Practices: A Proposed Organizational Learning Framework." *The International Journal of Organizational Analysis* Vol. 5, No. 1, 9–24.

Questions

1. (a) Do you think it is necessary for managers to be in control? Of what? Why?
   (b) Do you think such control can be morally acceptable?
   (c) Does the contractual nature of employment bear on this at all?
2. (a) What is "the discourse of control"? Give some examples, if you can, from your own employment experience (as employee or employer).
   (b) "It is clear that language expresses and creates our reality" (para 19)—do you agree?
3. Maguire claims that "control talk" does four things.
   (a) What are they (para 5)?
   (b) How does it do these things (paras 16–18)?
4. Kantian ethics and virtue ethics seem to provide the strongest basis for Maguire's argument.
   (a) Would a rights-based approach strengthen or weaken his argument?
   (b) What about a justice-based approach?
5. Maguire disagrees with the opinion that it is impossible to avoid organizational control, presenting and refuting two arguments in support of that opinion. What are the arguments and how does he respond to each (paras 7–11)?
6. (a) Explain and assess Maguire's alternative to the discourse of control.
   (b) Could his alternative enable managers to meet the three functions of setting performance standards, monitoring performance, and taking corrective action to achieve organizational goals (see para 1)? How?

In Defense of the Right to Strike[*]

Charlotte A.B. Yates

[1] In October 2007, the Canadian Autoworkers (CAW) signed an historic deal with the automotive parts firm, Magna International, that gave up the right to strike in exchange for the opportunity for Magna employees to vote to join the CAW unimpeded by their employer. This voluntary concession of one of labour's fundamental rights sparked a furor of debate over the importance of the right to strike in contemporary industrial relations. Was this deal a sell-out of labour rights or a harbinger of innovation and change to labour-management relations in Canada?

---

[*] *University of New Brunswick Law Journal*, Volume 59 (2009): 128–37.

[2] The CAW's concession of the right to strike came at the very moment that the Autoworkers had joined with other unions in Nova Scotia to form a coalition of health care unions to defend the right to strike from provincial governments' attempts to remove health care workers' right to strike. Since then, the Ontario provincial government has ordered striking Toronto transit workers back to work while the newly elected federal Conservative government introduced an economic statement that included provisions to suspend federal government employees' right to strike.

[3] These instances illustrate the renewed debate over the place of the right to strike in current economic affairs. Ironically, these encroachments on the right to strike come at the very time when levels of strike activity in Canada are at an all time low. These low rates of strike activity underline questions about the real importance of the right to strike for unions and their capacity for effectiveness. Do low strike rates suggest that the 'age of strikes' has come to an end? Have we reached a time when unions can and should give up the right to strike as a weapon more suited to the 'old' economy, or 'old' unions who are themselves better suited for the industrial than the post-industrial age? Or should unions continue to defend the right to strike and if so why? This research note explores some answers to these questions that underline the critical importance of defending the right to strike.

Strike Statistics

[4] To begin the discussion we need to examine patterns of strike activity and unionization in Canada. Whether measured in terms of total number of strikes or person days lost due to strikes, Canada's strike rate has declined precipitously over the last twenty-five years (See Table 1), with the low point reached in 2003. Between 2003 and 2005 there was a noticeable increase in the number of strikes and person days lost as a result of strikes, although these numbers remained low in historic comparison. According to Ernest Akyeampong of Statistics Canada, strikes in the period from 2003–2005 were concentrated in Quebec and Ontario and, most interestingly for the purpose of this article, were concentrated in manufacturing, education, and health and social services.[1] Although strikes in the information and cultural industries only accounted for 2 percent of total strikes, this industry accounted for approximately 25 percent of total workdays lost to strikes in Canada in 2005 due to the effect of the strike at the Canadian Broadcasting Corporation. Such an impact on lost time is explained by the fact that this strike was prolonged, a characteristic of many strikes in Canada. Briskin shows that strike duration has increased significantly in Canada since the 1960s, with average strike duration growing from 22.3 workdays in 1960–64 to 41.1 workdays in 2000–2004.[2]

Year	Total Number of Strikes	Person Days Not Worked	Number of Employees
1980	1,028	9,130	9,621
1985	829	3,126	9,901
1990	579	5,079	11,250
1995	328	1,583	11,212
2000	379	1,657	12,391
2003	266	1,736	13,271
2005	293	4,107	13,658

Table 1. Strikes and person-days not worked, Canada 1980–2005. Source: Ernest Akyeampong, "Increased Work Stoppages," *Perspectives on Labour and Income*, August 2006. Statistics Canada.

[5] It is not surprising that unions and their core activities of collective bargaining and collective action, including strikes, have come under attack.

Increased economic competition, the neo-liberal celebration of individualism at the expense of collective action, and a deluge of commentary that compares unions to dinosaurs which have served their purpose has eroded the legitimacy of unions and opened them up for criticism and attack. For the last twenty-five years, employers have stepped up their opposition to unionization[3] and demanded concessions from unions, threatening plant closure or de-investment if their demands are not met. For their part, governments have systematically curtailed unions' collective bargaining rights and right to strike. In addition to sweeping re-writes of many provincial labour codes that have made it harder for unions to organize workers or gain effective redress from employers that break the law, governments have relied increasingly on back-to-work legislation, with a noticeable upswing in its usage since 2000.[4] In a recent article, Joseph Rose noted that governments have moved away from assigning arbitrators to settle disputes ended by back-to-work legislation, and instead have begun unilaterally imposing terms of agreement. The penalties for defying such legislation are harsh. Governments have withdrawn the right to strike from some groups, such as nurses in Alberta, or used the designation of 'essential' services to all but withdraw the right to strike for other public sector workers.

[6] Not surprisingly, under this kind of pressure union density in Canada has been slowly though steadily declining, with especially steep declines in the private sector. In 1997, union density in Canada stood at 31 percent compared to 29 percent in 2008, and in the private sector dropped from 22 percent to 16 percent in the same period.[5] Unions have had increasing difficulty in recruiting new members over the past ten years.[6] Under these conditions, it is not surprising that strike rates are in decline and that unions such as the CAW look to cutting deals with employers that exchange increased membership and union density in their core industry, the automotive industry, for the right to strike. Do these recent trends and events justify giving up the right to strike as part of adjusting to the 'new' economy? In the remainder of this article, I will advance three reasons why the right to strike continues to be critically important to unions and why it must be defended by unions as well as governments.

'You Can't Give Up What You Didn't Have': Industrial Citizenship and the Right to Strike

In defence of its decision to give up the right to strike [7] for Magna employees who voted to join the CAW, the CAW argued that workers were not giving up anything, as they could not give up something that they had never had. This logic makes sense if we see workers and labour power as commodities that can only be possessed if traded, bought or sold. But the right to strike is more than a commodity; it is a crucial part of a bundle of rights and responsibilities associated with industrial citizenship and membership in a union.

Unionization, with its intended goal of granting workers some influence over the terms and conditions of their employment, only becomes meaningful when associated with certain activities, responsibilities, and rights. Thus unionization without the ability to engage in free collective bargaining limits the effectiveness of union membership but also strikes to the heart of the debate over whether union membership and collective bargaining are essential components of freedom of association. Arguments made by organized labour to the Supreme Court of Canada in the early 1980s insisted that protecting the right to belong to a union as part of freedom of association was hollow if the actions of that collective organization [8] were not also protected. Although organized labour initially lost this argument in the famous labour trilogy decisions of the Supreme Court in the late 1980s, the Supreme Court revisited these issues in 2007 and issued a decision in the case of the *Health Services and Support-Facilities Subsector Bargaining Association v. British Columbia* that reversed the decision in the Trilogy. The 2007 decision endorsed a more expansive definition of freedom of association that included protecting the right of unions to engage in collective bargaining.[7]

[9] Rights, whether human, political, civil, or social, are associated with belonging to a particular community that brings with it entitlements as well as obligations and responsibilities. Although more contentious than basic human, civil or political rights, the rights of industrial citizenship are associated with belonging to unions, communities of workers who come together to exercise influence over the terms and conditions of their employment, most often through negotiations with an employer. The bundle of entitlements associated with belonging to unions includes a series of collective as well as individual rights such as the right to engage in collective bargaining with employers and the right to withdraw labour to put pressure on an employer in the event that negotiations fail. This right to withdraw labour can be seen as attempting to balance capital's right to close down places of employment and withdraw or reduce investment. In addition to the various responsibilities associated with belonging to a union, unions in Canada experience several limitations on their rights, many of which are codified in laws such as, for example, laws ordering unions not to take workplace action during the life of a collective agreement, ordering the provision of essential services by public sector workers in the event of a labour-management dispute, or requiring a vote to ratify or reject a collective agreement. Thus, through Canadian labour law originally framed in the 1940s, a form of industrial citizenship was extended to workers which limited the rights associated with commerce and property ownership.

[10] Without these rights intact, unions are unable to fulfill their responsibilities, which include effectively negotiating the terms and conditions of their members' employment. By taking away or giving up the right to strike, unions deprive workers of one of the fundamental rights of industrial citizenship, which in turn erodes the very foundation of freedom of association in the workplace. Further, once unions begin to give away some of their rights in exchange for representation of workers they are in danger of creating two classes of citizens within their own organizations. Just as political citizenship requires that all citizens having certain rights, such as the right to vote, so too does industrial citizenship require that all union members have the same rights. However, by giving up the right to strike, unions also undermine the basis for their defence of free collective bargaining, as both these rights rest upon an acceptance by the state that workers have the right to form and act as independent unions as part of their rights to industrial citizenship. By giving some of these rights away, unions are in danger of unwittingly undermining their capacity to defend their other rights, opening the door for further erosion of workers' freedom of association and the basis for industrial citizenship. The importance of negotiating the terms of employment, which includes backing up negotiations with the threat of a strike, has become increasingly evident as more and more working people who are not represented by unions fail to make a living wage, working and living in poverty.

[11] What gets lost in debates over whether the right to strike should be retained or constrained is how prudently unions exercise their rights-including the right to strike. Although it is true that the most recent downward trend in strike activity has

only partly to do with union choice, and a lot to do with economic uncertainty and the pressures of globalization experienced by workers, the history of collective bargaining and industrial citizenship in Canada points to a remarkably limited use of strikes to settle contract disputes. The large majority of contracts in Canada are settled through collective bargaining without industrial action. Furthermore, when strike levels have been especially high, this has often reflected the impact of political strikes (such as Ontario's Days of Action, protests against national wage and price controls, or the Newfoundland public sector strikes, protests against restructuring). Given their political motivation, these kinds of strikes are unlikely to be discontinued because of changes to regulations about the use of strikes during regular collective bargaining. Therefore, legislative or voluntary concession of the right to strike is unlikely to have the desired effect, if that effect is to reduce workplace disruption through industrial action.

Right to Strike in Unions' Strategic Repertoire

[12] Beyond the debates around legal rights and responsibilities, the right to strike needs to be situated in the context of union effectiveness and strategic capacity. Unions are organizations whose purpose is to shape the terms and conditions of employment for members as well as others in the labour market. For more than one hundred years unions have used a certain set of strategies to pursue these goals, including collective bargaining, strikes or other industrial workplace action such as work to rule, and political activism. Upholding the right to strike—even when it is used as infrequently, as it is in the current era—is critical to union effectiveness as striking is an essential part of unions' strategic repertoire.

Unions have very few means by which they can [13] push their demands onto reluctant employers. If negotiations for a new collective agreement break down there are a limited range of options open for unions to advance their positions. This limited range of options stems from the particular nature of power resources available to unions with which they might exercise influence. Information pickets are legal and may inform the general public about the nature of an industrial dispute, but such information dissemination has a limited effect except in areas of the economy most vulnerable to public pressure. Even there, as we saw in the two-week elementary school teachers' strike in Ontario in the 1990s, strike action accompanying information sharing is often critically important to pressing home the importance of issues such as funding of elementary schools and class size.

Various forms of arbitration have and are used [14] in Canada as a substitute for strikes. Certainly arbitration was the CAW and Magna Corporation's agreed means for resolving their disputes once they agreed to give up the right to strike. Yet a growing mass of evidence points to the negative consequences of arbitration.[8] Robert Hebdon and Maurice Mazerolle's analysis of arbitration in the public sector examined the impact of arbitration on bargaining behaviours and concluded that compulsory arbitration had both a "chilling" and a "narcotic" effect on the bargaining process, resulting in much higher rates of bargaining impasse than occurred in those sectors in which the right to strike was maintained.[9] Arbitration reduced the likelihood that the two parties would agree to compromises or make trade-offs due to the perception that arbitrators made decisions by splitting the difference between the last bargaining positions of both parties. This understanding of arbitration discouraged compromise as the party that agreed to a compromise was perceived to be more likely to lose in the arbitration process. This experience under arbitration had a 'narcotic' effect as parties to the negotiations became dependent on arbitration and, according to Hebdon and Mazerolle, lost their ability to negotiate. The long-term effect of this dynamic was to discourage the creation of positive collective bargaining relationships.

[15] A third option, in the absence of the right to strike, is to allow employers unilateral capacity to determine the terms and conditions of work. Although this 'option' may seem absurd, evidence from the United States and growing actions by governments in Canada, including the tendency to use back-to-work legislation and unilaterally impose contract conditions, suggests that this is the intent of governments and employers as they increasingly restrict the place and capacity of unions to recruit new members, bargain and strike. It is therefore worth considering the effect of allowing employers free rein in determining the terms and conditions of employment. Non-union employers pay lower wages than unionized employers, with the effect that overall wage rates are significantly reduced in countries with low rates of unionization. Moreover, the spread of wages between the richest and poorest is greater in countries where unionization rates are low. Provincially regulated minimum wages in Canada are set significantly below what is required for a "living wage," which means that poverty rates would be likely to increase under non-union labour market conditions. Finally, there is a significant body of literature that underscores the negative impact of declining unionization on the state of social policy and level of government social provisions such as pensions, health care, and public education.[10] Low rates of unionization are also strongly correlated with low levels of public social investment and infrastructure. A decline in social benefits such as health care, unemployment insurance and pensions has commensurate negative effects on a person's income, their health and their capacity to cope with and possibly recover from a 'disaster' in their lives, such as a long-term lay-off or an injury at work.

[16] So what is wrong with unions having the right to strike? When do they use it and under what conditions? Unions use the threat of a strike more often than they actually go on strike in pushing their bargaining agenda. Approximately 97 percent of collective agreements are settled without industrial action of any kind. If anything the past ten years in Canada have shown that unions use strikes as a last resort. Strikes are high risk for unions as there is no guarantee that workers on strike will recoup what they lose by unpaid days on the picket line or that jobs will remain as factories close and employers relocate.

[17] But statistics alone do not tell the full tale of why the right to strike continues to be an important tool, if one that is now rarely used. Increased competition, the rise of global markets in which governments play only a small regulatory role and the "cult of the individual" have laid the conditions for tilting the balance of power in employers' favour. Employers have responded to these threats and opportunities with downward pressure on wages and working conditions, a consequence of which is seen in deteriorating real wages in many parts of the private sector, most notably in manufacturing where unions at one time had been able to drive up wages. Workers in the meat packing industry, for example, have seen wages halved and working conditions become increasingly dangerous; they now face hostile employers who repeatedly violate human rights and employment regulations. In the face of these conditions, workers have seen no option other than to go on strike, as when the meatpacking plant in Brooks, Alberta, took to the picket lines. In the public sector, teachers, nurses

and other public sector workers have decided that the only way in which they can protect standards of public service and mobilize public support is through strikes, though these are often illegal. In a large number of instances the public has been supportive of their demands, linked as they are to the provision of social, education, and health services that Canadians define as essential. Without the right to strike, the capacity of workers to defend their rights and protect their dignity is eroded, undermining basic tenets of industrial democracy and internationally recognized worker rights.

New Economy, New Workers: The Right to Strike in the New Economy

[18] Many commentators have argued that as unions lose their relevance in the new post-industrial economy, the rights to strike and bargain collectively are no longer as necessary as they were in the past. Those who put forth these arguments see unions as having declining relevance to new workforces or new types of work; unions were needed in the old heavy industries such as automotive manufacture and steelmaking, but not in information, service, and cultural industries. Evidence used to support this line of argument tends to include the low rates of union density in many of these "post-industrial" sectors, the decline in employment and therefore union membership in older industrial sectors, and cultural arguments that proclaim that new workers have no interest in collective organizations or solutions but are more attuned to individual and flexible options.

[19] Ironically, there is a growing amount of evidence that it is exactly in 'new' or growing post-industrial service industries as well growing parts of the workforce—namely new Canadians, racialized groups and women—that strikes are being used to uphold workers' rights, and where some of the most creative new forms of industrial action are being developed. On the question of strikes in emerging sectors where employment of racialized groups is often high, education, along with health and social services, posted the second highest proportion of strikes nationally between 2003 and 2005, after manufacturing. This sector is one that has expanded considerably but has also undergone significant restructuring through outsourcing, privatization and work intensification. Teachers have become increasingly militant across the country, using the strike to defend class size and investment in public education. In the case of the British Columbia elementary teachers' union, a two-week strike in October 2005 was led by a woman and Indo-Canadian, Jenny Sims, who was able to mobilize widespread support [...] for teachers to protest the government's declaration of teachers as an essential service whose right to strike and demands for a wage freeze could therefore be taken away.

[20] Ancillary and support workers in the education sector, many of whom are racialized minorities or new immigrants, have also turned to the strike to defend their claims for better wages and working conditions. The cleaning staff strike at Seneca College in March 2008 was made more poignant by the fact that these workers were not fighting the College, but a large American multinational, Aramark, that had subcontracted cleaning services. This strike was to achieve a first contract. Many cleaners were new immigrants who were stuck in these jobs despite having university or college educations and managerial or professional job experience. Workers were paid $9.90 per hour, far below a living wage. Insult was added to injury when the company offered workers a mere 1.25 percent pay increase, or an additional $0.10 an hour. The company also refused to pay for benefits that it had promised employees when hired. This strike

[20 cont.] was part of a wider North American campaign by the union to protest Aramark's poor wages and labour standards.

[21] Meanwhile, hotels have been the site of several creative industrial disputes, characterized by the mobilization of public support and an air of festivity in struggle.[11] These and countless other strikes in small manufacturing and service based organizations, such as taxi companies, point to the changing face of strikers as more women and racialized workers lead union struggles for better wages and workplace rights.

[22] The strikes of technicians, journalists, and administrators at the Canadian Broadcasting Corporation, as well as those of Hollywood writers, illustrate the use of 'old' industrial tactics by cultural and creative workers who are most often associated with the new, rather than the old economy. These strikes included high-profile celebrities, who, in the CBC dispute, played leadership roles and were clearly visible on the picket lines. Many hosts of programs began doing guerrilla programming as a new form of protest, framing the dispute as one of the protection of national culture. In these strikes, old tactics were often framed and strategized in new ways, at the core of which, nonetheless, lay the right to strike.

[23] Another group that has become increasingly prominent in labour activity, notably during strikes, is women. Women have been the fastest growing segment of the workforce in the post-war market around the world. Although women have historically been involved in strikes, they have taken on a new leadership role in strikes and industrial disputes. Whether we examine the illegal strikes of nurses, teachers and other public servants who use the strike weapon to defend social services and resist government cutbacks, or we look at strikes amongst University staff in Ontario many of whom have joined forces—and memberships—with older industrial unions such as the United Steelworkers of America or the Canadian Autoworkers, women continue to use and need to strike to press their bargaining demands.

[24] All this evidence points to the endurance of the right to strike as a critical right for workers, especially for new groups of workers and new types of work. Just as industrial unions used the strike to make breakthroughs in bargaining and the extension of the workplace rights, so too are new generations of workers in emerging sectors of the economy.

Conclusion

[25] Low strike rates are a reflection of the enormous constraints under which unions and workers operate in the contemporary economy, as well as the caution exercised by unions when entertaining the possibility of a strike. Patterns of strikes suggest that there have been shifts in the sectors and workers involved in strikes. Emerging sectors of the economy, including health, education, and culture, have seen increases in the incidence of strikes coincident with the rise in participation in industrial action by women, new immigrants and racialized minorities. There has also been a rise in the length and political use of industrial disputes and strikes. Thus strikes have survived the transition to a new economy, whether defined as a post-industrial, knowledge or service economy, and are being transformed.

[26] However, at the root of the defence of the right to strike lies its importance as one of a bundle of rights associated with industrial citizenship. Just as voting is one of our political rights, so too must the right to strike be seen as an essential component of industrial citizenship. With encroachment on the right to strike comes the erosion of the capacity of independent unions to engage in meaningful collective bargaining and play a role in

shaping the terms and conditions of employment. Without unions, income inequality rises and the wages and working conditions of the most vulnerable in society deteriorate. Engaging in debate about the right to strike brings us squarely into a debate about the kind of society in which we want to live.

Notes

1. Ernest B. Akyeampong, "Increased Work Stoppages," *Perspectives on Labour and Income* (August 2006) Statistics Canada at 7–8.
2. Linda Briskin, "From Person-days Lost to Labour Militancy: A New Look at the Canadian Work Stoppage Data" (2007) 62(1) *Ind Relat Quebec* 31–65 at 51.
3. Karen Bentham, "Employer Resistance to Union Certification: A Study of Eight Canadian Jurisdictions" 57(1) *Ind Relat Quebec* 31–65 at 51; Charlotte Yates & Felice F. Martinello "Union and Employer Tactics in Ontario Organizing Campaigns" David Levin & Bruce Kaufman, eds., *Advances in Industrial and Labor Relations*, vol. 13 (New York: Elsevier, 2004) at 157–190.
4. Joseph B. Rose, "Regulating and Resolving Public Sector Disputes in Canada" (2008) 50(4) *Journal of Industrial Relations* at 556.
5. Ernest B. Akyeampong, "A Statistical Portrait of the Trade Union Movement" *Perspectives on Labour and Income* (Winter 1997) Statistics Canada; "Unionization" *Perspectives on Labour and Income* (August 2008) Statistics Canada.
6. Charlotte Yates, "Missed Opportunities and Forgotten Futures: Why Union Renewal in Canada has Stalled" in ed., Craig Phelan, *Trade Union Revitalisation: Trends and Prospects in 34 Countries* (Oxford: Peter Lang Publishing, 2007) at 57–74.
7. Judy Fudge, "The Supreme Court of Canada and the Right to Bargain Collectively: The Implications of the Health Services and Support Case in Canada and Beyond" (2008) 37(1) *Indus. L. J.* at 25–48.
8. The one exception to this is first contract arbitration which is seen by most analysts to be a positive way of establishing collective bargaining in a newly unionized workplace.
9. Robert Hebdon & Maurice Mazerolle, "Regulating Conflict in Public Sector Labour Relations: The Ontario Experience (1984–1993)" (2003) 58(4) *Ind Relat Quebec* at 671.
10. Lane Kenworthy & Jonas Pontusson, "Rising Inequality and the Politics of Redistribution in Affluent Countries" (2005) 3(3) *Perspectives on Politics* at 449–471.
11. Steven Tufts, "Renewal from Different Directions: The Case of UNITE-HERE, Local 175" in Pradeep Kumar & Chris Schenk, eds., *Paths to Union Renewal* (Peterborough: Broadview Press, 2005) 201–208

Questions

1. Throughout most of the article, the author simply assumes the right to strike. However, there is reference to an argument for that right: "Arguments made by organized labour to th e Supreme Court of Canada in the early 1980s insisted that protecting the right to belong to a union as part of freedom of association was hollow if the actions of that collective organization were not also protected" (para 8).
  (a) Elaborate on that reference; that is, on what is the right to strike based? (Read carefully the two paragraphs that follow; they contain several reasons for the right to strike.)
  (b) Do you think it's a strong argument? Why/why not? (Consider the merits of each reason.)
2. Yates says that the rights of industrial citizenship are "more contentious than basic human, civil or political rights" (para 9). Why might that be?

3. Yates says that membership "brings with it entitlements as well as obligations and responsibilities" (para 9). She mentions two rights associated with belonging to a union; what responsibilities might there be?
4. Yates presents the right to strike as one of three options, the other two being arbitration and the employer's "unilateral capacity to determine the terms and conditions of work" (para 15).
(a) Which option does Yates endorse? For what reasons?
(b) Which option do you think is most ethically acceptable? For what reasons?
5. What is the relevance of the section titled "New Economy, New Workers"?
6. "Engaging in debate about the right to strike brings us squarely into a debate about the kind of society in which we want to live" (last para). What do you think Yates means by this statement?

Why Corporations Should Not Abandon Social Responsibility*

Moses L. Pava

[1] Robert Reich, Secretary of Labor in the Clinton Administration, and currently Professor of Public Policy at Berkeley, is an old-fashioned liberal. He is deeply concerned about broad societal issues like equity, justice, human rights, global warming, environmental degradation, and increasing corporate power. Unlike many liberals, however, Reich, in his recent book *Supercapitalism: The Transformation of Business, Democracy, and Everyday Life* (2007), rejects outright the call for increased corporate social responsibility. He believes that social responsibility advocates are wasting resources and efforts on a doomed project.

[2] This article suggests that while Reich raises several interesting concerns in his counter-intuitive book, especially about the rise in corporate political power, ultimately his argument is unconvincing. Worse yet, a careful reading suggests that Reich does not contemplate fully what it is he is asking business and society to give up in his call to jettison corporate social responsibility. Reich's own idiosyncratic understanding of corporate social responsibility is a thin and highly constrained substitute for the broader and deeper conceptions held by most of its advocates. For those who continue to push for more and better corporate social responsibility, there is a demand to respond to Reich's argument. Such a response must articulate fully

---

* *Journal of Business Ethics* 83 (2008): 805–12.

and convincingly the rich and fertile understanding of corporate social responsibility that has become an essential foundation for business ethics and for modern capitalism.

Robert Reich's "Supercapitalism"

[3] In an era of "supercapitalism," as Reich dubs the current age, investors demand and get maximum stock market returns while consumers demand and get the lowest possible prices. Markets, enhanced by several technological advances, are more efficient now than ever before. Stock prices are near historical highs and the diversity of consumer products is staggering. As Reich states, "In supercapitalism, the corporation as a whole must, for competitive reasons, resist doing anything that hurts—and will place a very low priority on anything that doesn't help—the bottom line" (2007, p. 169). Nevertheless, Reich bemoans, that as *citizens*, our ability to participate in the democratic process is at an all-time low.

[4] The solution to this seeming paradox, according to Reich's book, is to cease immediately blurring the boundaries between business and government and to define sharply the parameters of each of these unique domains. Business managers should focus (as they must in any event if they want to survive in efficient markets according to Reich) on satisfying customer demands and maximizing corporate profits for shareholders. On the other hand, it is the unique role of government to set the rules of business and to enforce them vigorously and fairly. It is Reich's contention that to re-energize civic participation and to restore informed and reasonable public dialogue, we must jettison the advocacy of corporate social responsibility and corporate citizenship altogether. After all, he states, it is only as individual citizens that we even possess ethical and social responsibilities.

[5] If this argument sounds eerily familiar, it should. It is an almost verbatim reiteration of Milton Friedman's 1970 claim that the sole responsibility of business is to increase profits for shareholders. What is new and interesting in Reich's book is that more than 35 years later, it is now an unrepentant liberal making this argument and not a conservative, libertarian economist.

[6] Why is Reich so belatedly embracing Friedman's single-minded view of business? Reich is not making these arguments to advertise and promote an ideological change of heart. Rather, he is doing so because, from a practical point of view, he no longer believes (as he once did, by the way) that corporate social responsibility works. Tersely put, from a politically liberal perspective, the social responsibility movement has failed the test of pragmatism. It has, in Reich's view, on net, caused more harm than good.

[7] It is Reich's contention that it is virtually impossible for corporations to engage in real socially responsible actions. While businesses increasingly use this and similar terms to describe themselves, they do so only to make themselves appear to the public as if they are socially responsible. In fact, according to Reich, business is necessarily an amoral enterprise with a single goal. Businesses exploit the shared language of corporate social responsibility only to serve shareholders' interests. Here, in a typical passage, is how Reich puts his case:

> It is easy to understand why big business has embraced corporate social responsibility with such verve. It makes for good press and reassures the public. A declaration of corporate commitment to social virtue may also forestall government legislation or regulation in an area of public concern where one or more companies have behaved badly, such as transporting oil care-

lessly and causing a major spill or flagrantly failing to respect human rights abroad. The soothing promise of responsibility can deflect public attention from the need for stricter laws and regulations or convince the public that there's no real problem to begin with. Corporations that have signed codes of conduct promising good behavior appear to have taken important steps toward social responsibility, but the pressures operating on them to lure and keep consumers and investors haven't eased one bit. In supercapitalism, they *cannot* be socially responsible, at least not to any significant extent. (2007, p. 170, emphasis in original)

[8] Over time, the language and practices of corporate social responsibility have become a mere tool in the hands of managers and public relations experts used to manipulate the beliefs and expectations of citizens. Corporate social responsibility rhetoric is a kind of sedative doled out by business to calm a jittery but almost completely inattentive public. It is a device designed to deflect away attention, real criticism, and dialogue among uninformed, naïve, and detached citizens.

[9] Obviously, there is *some* truth to Reich's exaggerated thesis, and no doubt one can cite much anecdotal evidence (as Reich does in his book) to show how some companies do misuse the language of corporate social responsibility in an attempt to fool and mislead investors and other stakeholders—think tobacco companies here as one obvious example. His chapter on the increasing political power of corporations (Chapter 4: Democracy Overwhelmed) is insightful, provocative, and well worth reading. In addition, the book, as a whole, serves as an important warning to the advocates of corporate social responsibility not to ignore the appropriate role of government in society.[1]

[10] Nevertheless, the sum total of his evidence is insufficient to prove his most important and provocative point that corporations should now abandon social responsibility altogether. This is an especially extreme thesis to promote and it should be pointed out that even if it could be demonstrated that corporations only use the language of social responsibility as a public relations tool (which, in any event, I don't think it is possible to do), it does not necessarily follow that disallowing such language (whatever that might really mean) would improve civil discourse and political dialogue in society in any real or measurable way. It is not even clear that a culture without corporate social responsibility would reduce corporate power and lobbying efforts. Might it not just as easily increase such power?

[11] While corporations may, in part, be contributing to a deterioration in the overall quality of political dialogue, surely some of the blame must be placed upon governments and political leaders, too. Nothing in Reich's book, including his list of new proposals (for example, doing away with corporate income taxes), convinces a reader that governments, even without undue corporate influence, would do any better than they now do at solving social problems like global warming, economic degradation, and human rights abuses. In fact, many believe that without the active cooperation, stakeholder engagements, hard-won information advantages, and undeniable expertise of corporations, many social problems will continue to get worse and not better in the foreseeable future.

The Empirical Evidence

[12] For Reich, the issue of corporate social responsibility is now seemingly as black and white as it was for Milton Friedman back in 1970 (oddly—and unexplained in the book—is how Friedman came to these same stark conclusions even before the rise of Reich's era of supercapitalism). In his own

words, "Competition is so intense that most corporations *cannot* accomplish social ends without imposing a cost on their consumers or investors—who would then seek and find better deals elsewhere. Even if individual consumers or investors believed in the virtuousness of a particular sacrifice, absent laws requiring all companies and therefore all other consumers and investors to forbear as well, the individual's actions would have no effect" (p. 173).

[13] In order to support this and similar claims throughout the book, Reich sends the reader to David Vogel's book, *The Market for Virtue* (2006). He describes this book in an endnote, as first "among the *best* recent books I have found" (p. 245, emphasis added) on corporate social responsibility. Surely then, one might surmise, Reich's Berkeley colleague David Vogel must agree with his radical conclusion. However, surprisingly to the reader of *Supercapitalism* here's how Vogel summarizes his extensive and rigorous analysis of the available empirical evidence. Contrary to Reich, he believes corporate social responsibility has produced many positive and quite *significant* changes in corporate behavior including:

- A reduction in the employment of child labor and improvements in health and safety conditions in many of the factories and workshops that supply clothing, athletic equipment, toys, and rugs to Western manufacturing and retail firms;
- An increase in the prices some agricultural producers in developing countries receive for their products;
- A reduction in the quantity of wood products produced from tropical, old-growth, and endangered forests;
- A decrease in greenhouse gas emissions or in their rate of growth;
- The withdrawal of many companies from Burma;
- The amelioration of some of the negative environmental and social impacts of natural resource development in developing countries.

To be sure, Vogel notes that in some cases social welfare would be enhanced even more if voluntary standards were written into law, but he emphasizes that this "should not be allowed to obscure the significance of the improvements that *have* taken place" (p. 163, emphasis in original).

Vogel is extremely sensitive to the issue of corporate political power as is Reich, but his reading of the empirical evidence and his overarching conclusion is very different. According to Vogel, "The definition of corporate social responsibility needs to be redefined to include the responsibilities of business to strengthen civil society and the capacity of governments to require that all firms act more responsibly" (p. 172). While Reich reads the literature and calls for the outright abandonment of corporate social responsibility, Vogel interprets this same literature and calls for an *expansion* and *deepening* of it. [14]

Toward a Broader Understanding of Corporate Social Responsibility

Reich reaches his conclusion, in part, because he envisions corporate social responsibility in the sparsest possible terms. In Reich's view: [15]

> Corporate initiatives that improve the quality of products without increasing their price, or increase efficiency and productivity so that prices can be lowered, or otherwise generate higher profits and higher returns for investors, are not socially virtuous. They're just good management practices. (p. 173)

[16] This holds regardless of how much or how little such actions benefit society. Hence, for example, Reich believes that it is misleading to describe Starbuck's decision to provide health coverage to part-time employees, as a socially responsible action. Rather, if such a decision leads to more profits, it's simply good business. If it leads to less profits, it's bad business and shareholders would be "justifiably upset" (p. 172). This definition, however, is needlessly restrictive and certainly does not explain why other companies in the same industry do not provide their employees with health benefits. It makes much more practical sense to judge the degree of social responsibility in terms of social outcomes *only*. For advocates of corporate social responsibility, an activity or action is socially responsible just to the extent that it benefits society *regardless* of its effects on the business itself.

[17] The best run businesses search actively and imaginatively to find and invent solutions that produce more profits *and* better social outcomes simultaneously (see Porter and Kramer, 2006; Savitz and Weber 2006, for especially good, contemporary descriptions of the link between competitive advantage and corporate social responsibilities). There is simply no reason to regress and resurrect Milton Friedman's either/or stance, as Reich is now doing.

[18] Companies that did follow such outdated advice would quickly learn that even if *they* don't care about social responsibility many powerful and strategically sophisticated stakeholders do. It is far better (both from a company's own point of view and from a social point of view) to engage stakeholders in honest, transparent, and forthright debate about social values and the limitations of what any one business can accomplish than to simply claim from a philosophically dubious high ground that businesses possess no responsibilities and leave it at that.[2]

Enhancing Ethical Dialogues

[19] One of the most important advances in corporate social responsibility in recent years has been a formal recognition on the part of businesses that performance cannot be measured with a single yardstick. Corporate performance, especially for global corporations, is now almost universally understood as multi-dimensional. It includes economic, environmental, and social aspects. This is why more companies are reporting triple bottom line reports than ever before. In 2005, almost 70% of the top 250 corporations in the world published a stand-alone triple bottom line report. This is an astonishing increase from an earlier 2002 survey that found only 15% of companies reported a stand-alone sustainability report (KPMG, 2005).

[20] The evolution of triple bottom line reports underscores a remarkable change in society's understanding of corporate accountability. There has been an almost continual broadening of the scope of corporate accountability over the past 40 years. Annual reports now include a statement of cash flows, enhanced verbal descriptions, more forward-looking information, and a much higher degree of transparency than ever before. Among the most important advances in our understanding of corporate accountability has been an almost revolutionary change in conceiving of accountability as a dialogue among stakeholders rather than as a monologue on the part of a solitary business (Pava, 2007).

[21] As a matter of course now, businesses are expected to not only set a strategy and to move towards it, but businesses are expected to actively participate in "ethical dialogues" with stakeholders concerning the appropriate boundaries of business behavior. In a dynamic and highly interdependent world, accountability can no longer be thought

of as centralized, fixed and pre-determined, but accountability is decentralized, fluid, contested, and constantly changing. It requires a give and take on the part of business and its stakeholders. Most importantly, it requires open channels of communication—with information flowing in two directions, from businesses to external stakeholders and back again.

[22] Robert Reich's suggestion to jettison corporate social responsibility altogether would be a step backward rather than a move forward. It would mark a return to an older and outmoded understanding of corporate accountability. Corporations must necessarily participate in these continuous ethical dialogues and to do so competently demands a vision of corporate social responsibility on everyone's part that goes beyond a single responsibility to shareholders. Thinking that we can return to a time when corporations fully met accountability requirements by publishing a completely standardized financial report to shareholders once a year is anachronistic, at best.

The Search for Meaning in Business

[23] For sure, advocates of corporate social responsibility are concerned with the fair allocation of goods and services in society. Business is like a machine (or a black-box) that produces consumer goods for customers and profits for shareholders. From a social responsibility perspective such outputs must be allocated fairly among all stakeholders. This machine-like conception of social responsibility, however, misses a deeper dimension of business and organizational life.

[24] For many advocates of corporate social responsibility, business can also be thought of as a location where one pursues friendships, solidarity, spirituality, purpose, and human meaning. To return to Friedman's conception, as Reich would have us do, would be like moving from a three dimensional world back to a two dimensional one.

[25] If business is only about the pursuit of corporate profits there is no vocabulary inside businesses, other than the profit and loss statement, to convey meaning, values, and purposes. In such a world there are no words to communicate with one another about higher level needs. A question like whether or not a corporate mission is compatible with one's most closely cherished values would make no sense whatsoever (i.e., unless one's highest value was the unbridled pursuit of money). The whole notion of social entrepreneurship would become completely incoherent. Issues like advertising unhealthy food to children, promoting the use of tobacco products, doing business with countries that violate human rights, paying wages below subsistence levels, and increasing pollution within legal limits, would become unintelligible (there would simply be no meaningful way to frame these issues) from the point of view of businesses managers, employees, and board members.

[26] In fact, Reich would have us return to a situation where consideration of any of these issues, for their own sake (and not for the sake of maximizing corporate profits) would be illegal. Imagine corporate managers faced with a dilemma like the one Johnson & Johnson faced when it had to decide whether or not to remove Tylenol from stores after several customers had already died from tainted Tylenol. In the world that Robert Reich would like us to return to all such decisions would have to be grounded only in profitability considerations. Executives might be concerned about the lives of customers and their own responsibility in such a situation *on a personal level*, but would be prohibited from including this line of thought in their professional decision making process. According to Reich the bottom-line is the *only* line.

Living an Integrated Life

[27] "The awkward truth is that most of us are of two minds: As consumers and investors we want the great deals. As citizens we don't like many of the social consequences that flow from them" (Reich, p. 89). This is an important insight and one that deserves careful attention and thought. Reich suggests that this kind of schizophrenia implies that we must abandon the notion of corporate social responsibility altogether. This article argues that his is a radically extreme response to a real problem; i.e., how to find the best balance between business and ethics.

[28] Corporate social responsibility, appropriately understood, demands a change in consciousness. Business educators must emphasize the reality of ethical and social goals and constraints. Graduates must choose careers that enhance our world and lead to sustainable solutions rather than just profitable ones. Investors must pick the stocks of those companies that are good corporate citizens. Managers must choose what products to manufacture and sell not just by thinking about the bottom line, but also by thinking about what kind of business and business environment it is that they want to create. Consumers must begin to factor in social as well as personal concerns. One cannot simply disassociate oneself from his or her actions by stating "I took such and such an action in the context of business so it doesn't really 'count'." The above suggestions may seem obvious to most readers, but the point is that without a well-defined notion of corporate social responsibility as a foundation, they make little or no sense.

[29] Is it really feasible to believe that human beings can turn their ethical radar on and off depending on whether they are making a business decision or a political one? It seems to me, Reich's advice to accept the chasm between business and ethics as a given once and forever, and to pursue ethics only in one's part-time role as a citizen (in opposition to one's other part time roles in business as managers, employees, investors, and consumers), is a giving up before one has really started. It is no doubt difficult to live a life of integrity and balance in today's complex world, but to many it still seems to be a worthwhile aspiration.

Corporate Social Responsibility and an Active Government

[30] There is no question that many (perhaps even most) of today's social problems require government intervention and action. After all, how many of us would like to ingest pharmaceuticals approved by an industry-run agency rather than the Food and Drug Administration? as Andrew Savitz correctly asks (2007). However, social responsibility advocates believe that businesses can work with government agencies and other stakeholders to promote a better world and are not destined or fated always to work against them.

[31] Perhaps the best example of this is the above discussed triple bottom line reports. Certainly, an important question to ask here is should these newly emerging reports become mandatory by government. After all, how can we trust companies to report truthfully and fully in every instance? Some European countries have already answered this question and now require sustainability reports. In the United States, however, this is still an open question. The point that I would like to make is that however this decision is ultimately made, sustainability reports would never have happened in the first place without the cooperation and experimentation on the part of global business corporations. In an interconnected world such as ours, this is how it must be.

[32] Triple bottom line reports are not an isolated example. Just about all of today's social problems

require the joint efforts of business and government. Issues related to environmental pollution, global warming, renewable energy, and the equitable availability of health care, require stakeholders to come together in good faith and work out good enough, practical solutions.

[33]   Progressive thinkers who are now beginning to join Reich in his one-sided denunciation of business believe that social responsibility advocates are being naïve in thinking that business can play a positive role in society. The well-known economist and op-ed writer for the *New York Times*, Paul Krugman, for example, writes that drug and insurance companies should have no voice in helping to formulate a health care strategy in a new administration. "Anyone who thinks that the next president can achieve real change without bitter confrontation is living in a fantasy world" (Krugman, 2007).

[34]   Advocates for social responsibility respond that any proposed solution that is generated from civic dialogues that purposely shut out business would be highly improbable to succeed and, perhaps even more importantly, would lack political legitimacy altogether. Krugman hearkens back to a time when Franklin Delano Roosevelt was able to unilaterally impose his will on a recalcitrant business community. Today's fast-changing, wired, and interconnected world is so different from the world of the 1930s, however, that one wonders who is truly being naïve here.

[35]   There is no good reason to view business and government as mortal enemies. If Reich and Krugman are talking about bringing in new voices into the political process, voices that have gone unheard in the past, I agree with them wholeheartedly. If they are advocating limiting corporate lobbying (even dramatically) and making the process much more transparent, again, there is strong agreement. However, these progressives, and others, are going further still, and advocating the complete removal of business's seat at the table. This kind of either/or thinking is regressive and counter productive.

Educational Implications

[36]   Robert Reich notes seemingly disapprovingly of the large and growing number of business schools that now offer courses on corporate social responsibility. Would he really have those of us responsible for business education eliminate these courses and replace them with yet one more finance or marketing course? Further, would he advocate that these finance and marketing courses eliminate all references to social responsibility? In addition, if his suggestions were actually implemented, might this not become a self-fulfilling prophecy where indeed it would become impossible for business to take on a social perspective? It seems absolutely implausible to me that he would really pursue his own vision to this extent. However, if not, he should then tone down his anti-business rhetoric and begin to work with scholars like David Vogel and many others who are trying to clarify and expand the concept of corporate responsibility and not eliminate it altogether.

Conclusion

[37]   There are a very large number of people whose view of human nature is so gloomy that no amount of well-meaning endeavour to reform or even transform contemporary capitalism warrants any credibility whatsoever. According to this worldview, we've got the economic system that we've got because it's the one that most powerfully reflects our true human nature: greedy, aggressive, self-interested, short-termist, irresponsible and cruel. It is the job of politicians and social institutions to 'manage' those characteristics and to mitigate their most destructive

impacts.... We have all met those who subscribe to such a worldview. (Porritt, 2007 p. 320)

Jonathan Porritt, author of the above quote and leading thinker and activist on sustainable development in the UK (he served as Chairman of the UK's Sustainable Development Commission) is perhaps as suspicious of corporations as is Reich, Krugman, and other progressives. However, he maintains a kind of faith in the intelligence, resiliency, and adaptability of "human nature" in the face of dramatically changing circumstances. He points out that it is only "in the last 30 years or so that we have woken up to today's sustainability crisis" (p. 320) and, it is now possible, for the first time, to map a possible transition scenario.

[38] However, will we succeed? Porritt is hopeful, yet extremely cautious in his predictions. If we are to succeed, he notes, it will require us to exploit "our extraordinary capacity for the deepest feelings of empathy and compassion for other people and for the living world" (p. 324). Perhaps these are soft and unreliable sentiments with no role to play in our public lives as Reich and others would have it. Porritt, however, maintains that progress is dependent upon the motivating effects of just such feelings. Will business be part of a solution?

> If our knowledge has been growing for the last 30 years, it is only during the last 10 years or so that some of the world's most powerful multinationals have begun to internalize that knowledge about the state of the world and to change their ways. The changes to date are modest, slow, inadequate and inconsistent. There are still very few companies that have really got to grips with sustainable development; for most the business model remains largely unchanged. But it is happening, and it's not all for show and public relations glory, as so many campaigners would still have you believe. For whatever reason, this is an upward curve moving in the right direction—and, even more astonishingly, doing so at a time when the utterly aberrant pressures of short-term profit maximization to boost shareholder value have been at their most intense and most destructive. (p. 322)

[39] A book like Robert Reich's can play a positive role in sharpening our understanding of corporate social responsibilities and its realistic potentials. It can serve as a useful reminder about the limits of what business can really do. However, such a book, if taken literally, can do much harm.

[40] If one were to take Reich at his word, we should give up altogether on the possibilities of business playing an important role in building a better future. It would make it nearly impossible to teach business ethics to a new generation of would-be business leaders. It would prevent us from distinguishing between the "very few" companies that are legitimately engaging in change projects with real bite and other companies who are merely trying to manipulate a naïve public for private profit. The bottom line is that if one were to accept Reich's thin view of corporate social responsibility and deeply pessimistic vision, civic dialogue would not be enlarged and enlivened as he promises, but it would be cut short, delegitimized, and weakened.

[41] The notion of corporate social responsibility is itself an extremely, valuable, and hard-won social asset. It is a vehicle for promoting transparency, more nuanced accountability, integrity, better communication, high ideals, mutually beneficial exchange, and sensible development. In providing a language and vocabulary to critique business from both inside and outside its boundaries, it has become a necessary condition for business ethics and modern capitalism to flourish. It is especially important in a world of increasing global economics. Nevertheless, it is an extremely fragile asset.

Books, like Reich's *Supercapitalism*, that dismiss corporate social responsibility in such a facile way, are dangerous and risky in ways that perhaps even the authors themselves are unaware.

Notes

1. Unfortunately, there is almost no discussion of global governance mechanisms to help resolve the problems associated with global corporations. This is a strange oversight, especially for a book concerned exclusively with government solutions to social problems.
2. For one of the most understandable yet philosophically grounded discussions on this topic see Goodpaster (2007).

References

Friedman, M. 1970. "The Social Responsibility of Business Is to Increase Profits." *New York Times*, September 13.

Goodpaster, K. 2007. *Conscience and Corporate Culture* (Blackwell Publishing).

KPMG. 2005. *KPMG International Survey of Corporate Social Responsibility Reporting* (KPMG Global Sustainability Services).

Krugman, P. 2007. "Big Table Fantasies." *New York Times*, December 17.

Pava, M.L. 2007. "A Response to 'Getting to the Bottom of Triple Bottom Line.'" *Business Ethics Quarterly* 17(1).

Porritt, J. 2007. *Capitalism as if the World Matters* (Earthscan, London, Revised Edition).

Porter, M.E. and M.R. Kramer. 2006. "Strategy and Society." *Harvard Business Review* 84, 78–92.

Reich, R. 2007. *Supercapitalism: The Transformation of Business, Democracy, and Everyday Life* (Alfred A. Knopf, New York).

Savitz, A.W. 2007. "Robert Reich: Right on 'Supercapitalism,' Not so Right on CSR." *The Triple Bottom Line Blog*, retrieved on December 7, 2007 at http://www.getsustainable.net.

Savitz, A.W. and K. Weber. 2006. *The Triple Bottom Line* (Jossey-Bass, San Francisco).

Vogel, D. 2006. *The Market for Virtue: The Potential and Limits of Corporate Social Responsibility* (Brookings Institution Press, Washington DC).

Questions

1. According to Pava, why does Reich think corporations can*not* be socially responsible?
2. According to Pava, what is Vogel's opinion of corporate social responsibility?
3. In what way does triple bottom line reporting indicate an ethical advance?
4. Pava redefines business. Explain.
5. (a) Do you agree with the description of human nature that Porritt reports?
   (b) Does it describe *your* nature?

Case Study: The Mountain Equipment Co-op

The Mountain Equipment Co-op—a brief history (for the most part excerpted from their website):

1971—The Co-op is formally incorporated with six members and $65 operating capital.
[The Co-op was run by volunteers for the first three years; lifetime memberships/shares cost $5; and people who wanted products—basically, mountain climbing gear—had to pay for them in advance and trust the Co-op to deliver.]

1972—Their first catalogue is a single page, typed and taped to a door in the UBC Student Union Building. Membership grows to 250.

1974—MEC catalogues are sent through the mail to 700 members. [They don't advertise, and they foster equipment swaps, another "anti-sales" move. This inspired Gordon Harris of Harris Consulting Inc. to call them an "anti-retailer" (The Canadian Encyclopedia).]

1976—The Board votes to return patronage dividends to members in proportion to their purchases.

1981—Membership has grown to 57,000.

1987—MEC established the Environment Fund and makes a donation to the Federation of Mountain Clubs of BC to help purchase the property containing the Smoke Bluffs, a well-used climbing area threatened by development. Members receive a share redemption of $350,000.

1988—They create an in-house product development department. The first major product produced is the Névé Gore-Tex Parka. The group initially thought a product run of 1600 would suffice, but by the end of the year they'd produced 10,000.

1990—Membership reaches 250,000, 1% of the population of Canada.

1991—The Co-op reaches $36.5 million in annual sales.

1997—By now, they're online and have several stores across Canada.

2001—Members receive a share redemption of $1.2 million.

2007—MEC joins 1% For The Planet, a group of businesses who donate 1% of gross sales to environmental causes.

2009—Membership reaches 3 million, 10% of the population of Canada.

2011—The Co-op has been in business for 40 years.

It has $261 million in annual sales, and 3.3 million members. [This makes it "the fourth largest democratic entity in Canada, after the governments of Canada, Ontario and Québec" (Strashok).] Members receive a share redemption of $2.4 million.

In 2013, "rather than waiting for the implementation of carbon taxes, Mountain Equipment Co-op (MEC)... [starts] integrating the cost of emissions into all its operations, from staff travel to product shipping" (Public Policy Forum, 15).

It still costs only $5 to become a member, but the 2000+ employees are paid. MEC's 21 stores and website now carry gear and clothing for outdoor activities beyond mountain climbing, including cycling, running, watersports, and camping.

Sources

"Mountain Equipment Co-op." *The Canadian Encyclopedia*. http://www.thecanadianencyclopedia.ca/en/article/mountain-equipment-co-op-profile/

Mountain Equipment Co-op. www.mec.ca

Public Policy Forum. *At the Vanguard of Canadian Innovation: A Compilation of Co-operative Case Studies*. October 2014. ppforum.ca

Strashok, Chris. "Mountain Equipment Co-op: A Co-operative Business Model." Community Research Connections. 13 May 2011. http://crcresearch.org/community-research-connections/crc-case-studies/mountain-equipment-co-op-co-operative-business-model

Questions

1. Visit the Product Development, Governance, or Sustainability page on MEC's website, and then choose one of the ethical perspectives covered in Part II and explain how MEC "did it right."
2. How would their success have been different if they had not been a co-op?

CHAPTER SIX

International Business

> ### What to Do?—The Processing Fee
> Part of the process of setting up shop in a certain foreign country involves obtaining a certain permit. You discover that your application for the permit has not been forwarded to the appropriate person; nor will it, apparently, until you pay the clerk a "processing fee" equal to 40 per cent of the permit fee. There is no mention of this processing fee in the guidelines for permit acquisition—it seems to be blatant bribery, and you are reluctant to start doing that kind of thing. One, it's illegal. Two, bribery compromises the level playing field. (Assuming there is a level playing field.) Three, what if you pay and you're application *still* doesn't get forwarded.
>
> And yet, it also seems expected—there is no shame or secrecy about the request. You know the clerk's wages are minimal, and you suspect that such clerks may actually depend on such additional payments, much like waiters in Canada depend on tips. However, tips are paid after the fact, and even non-tipping customers get served.
>
> You reconsider the financial wisdom of your plans: if these sorts of expenses are common, your financial projections will be significantly off. You even reconsider the ethical wisdom of your plans: do you really want to do business this way?
>
> But then you wonder, call it bribery or not, why is it so wrong?
>
> What do you decide to do?

Introduction

It is almost impossible to avoid international issues—business, indeed life itself (at least for those in the "western" world), has become globalized. The huge multinational corporations (MNCs) may be the key players, but even small and medium-sized enterprises (SMEs), thanks to the internet, are often global in some way. Many ethical questions arise when one does business with or in nations other than one's own, and they present themselves at every stage of the business cycle.

To begin, consider your financing, your stockholders. Should you let your company be partially, or mostly, foreign-owned? To be fair, responsibilities entail rights: do you want non-Canadians to have any rights of influence or control? To those who, like Einstein, think "nationalism is an infantile disease," this may be a non-issue: humanity transcends political boundaries, so what's the problem?

Well, the problem, some may respond, is that value systems often have an unnerving respect for political boundaries: do you want someone who believes that some people are "untouchable," for example, to have any influence over your company? (Of course, values vary *within* political boundaries as well, and this is an equally important ethical question for domestic ownership: do you want a Canadian racist, for example, to have any influence over your company?)

Next, let's consider your acquisition of materials. The ethics of "cross-border shopping" are the same, whether you're an individual buying clothes or a business buying supplies. And again, for some, the "Buy Canadian!" campaign was merely a show of patriotism (or a convenient display of self-interest). But, given our existing economic system, it could be more than that: when you buy here, you keep the jobs here, so there's less unemployment, so there's less stress on the social systems, so taxes go down—or at least don't go up. Now, of course, every one of those "so" statements is arguable, but the general gist is that there are economic consequences for many people, besides yourself (presumably you shop non-Canadian because it's cheaper—at least in the short term), and these are consequences that you may want to consider when deciding what to do.

However, the flip side of "Buy Canadian" is "Buy Nicaraguan" (or whatever)—reverse boycotting. Consider the Bridgehead line of products; consider the Body Shop's purchasing policies. You may want to support a certain nation for certain reasons—and so certain cross-border shopping may be the right thing to do.

Next, let's consider production. Should you outsource? Should you set up a branch of your company in another country? The nationalist and economic/quality of life issues raised in the preceding paragraphs are writ larger here. It's not a matter of indirectly keeping the jobs here, but a matter of *directly* doing so. And yet what if the Mexican needs the job more than the Canadian? Is nationalism a sort of collective egoism that puts self-interest first, just defining "self" a little more broadly? (See Henderson.)

Lastly, consider the by-products of your production: your trash. Is it morally acceptable to ship your garbage outside the country? Well, if they get your products, why shouldn't they get your by-products? Especially if you pay them a good price (what exactly *is* a "good" price?) and they willingly enter into the arrangement. (Does everyone affected by the contract willingly enter into it?) This issue is incredibly significant due to the environmental consequences of ordinary trash, let alone toxic trash, and for that reason will be considered in Chapter 10. But see Sende for a preview.

Now, if you *do* establish in other countries, there are further ethical questions to answer. One is this: "Do you conduct yourself and your business according to *their* ethical standards or according to your own (assuming they're different)?" (And assuming you know what their ethical standards are; many countries lack clear laws regarding human rights and environmental protection, which is relevant for those who take the legal moralism view that ethics are embodied in law). For example, *is* child labour as horrible as we in the "western" world think it is, or is it a productive (and, therefore [?], a morally acceptable) use of human resources? After all, we insist that our children do their chores to earn their allowance; how is it any different to insist that they do something at a factory to earn income for the family? The moral relativist would say conduct yourself and your business according to the other country's ethical standards ("When in Rome, do as the Romans do"); the moral absolutist would say conduct yourself according to your own standards (assuming your own standards *are* your own not just because they're your country's standards, but because you believe they represent some universal good). The utilitarian would consider the consequences—and the big issue here is that the consequences may be quite different in one's own country than in the other country *for the same action* (so you really have to know the customs, the local cultures—at the very least to avoid giving unintentional offence, and at best to adequately judge the consequences of your action).[1]

But note that I said "assuming they're different"—there may be many values and principles that both countries have in common that can be maintained. Consider, for example, the rights listed in the United Nations Declaration of Human Rights. Consider also the Caux Round Table Principles for Business (perhaps the first international ethics code created in collaboration by business leaders in Europe, Japan, and the US). And these common values may—or may not—be sufficient.[2]

However, deciding on absolute/universal values and principles is only a first step. Translating them into action may present problems, which can be magnified in international business. For example, maybe both countries value respect for people, but in the one this is shown by paying for X and in the other it is shown by *not* paying for X. For a very practical approach to ethics in international business, see Treviño and Nelson.

Hugh Lehman has written an excellent analysis of the importance of context with respect to wages, examining the possible interpretations of setting wages in developing nations according to the "equal pay" principle: does that mean we should pay workers the same number of dollars per hour as they're paid in our own country for that job (which might make a factory worker a member of the rich elite and draw all the skilled workers away from local companies that can't compete with those wages, harming those local companies); or does it mean we should pay enough so that their standard of living in their country is the same as that of workers at comparable jobs in our country (which would certainly make them very well off—factory workers here can generally afford a house, car, phone, and TV); or does it mean we should pay enough so that their standard of living relative to other people in their country is the same as the standard of living of their comparable workers relative to other people in our

---

1 In addition to Kohls and Buller, see Wines and Napier.
2 See De George, Donaldson, and Weiss for discussions of international codes of ethics. And lest you assume that when the standards *are* different, your own are *higher*, read Singer's article.

country (which might mean they starve—lower class here is okay, but lower class there...). So sweatshops may not be all that bad, at least with respect to wages? (So-called sweatshops are also characterized by unsafe working conditions and other employee rights abuses, which are discussed in an earlier chapter.)

The same sort of analysis would be needed for other employment rights issues. Discrimination can be particularly thorny: What if the other country believes that it's immoral for women to work? Or that it's okay for children to do so, even chained to the machines?[1]

The decision to become a transnational (or multinational, as the case may be) is not a simple one. On the positive side, transnational companies can benefit their host countries by providing jobs (though note Klein's comment that factory jobs in Shenzhen and Dhaka "are by this point so degraded that some employers install nets along the perimeters of roofs to catch employees when they jump" [2014, 82]), capital, technology, and training, and by boosting the local economy directly and indirectly (e.g., through local purchases). Arguing in favour of transnationals (and providing replies to anticipated objections), Krugman says

> A country like Indonesia is still so poor that progress can be measured in terms of how much the average person gets to eat; since 1970, per capita intake has risen from less than 2,100 to more than 2,800 calories a day.... These improvements have not taken place because well-meaning people in the West have done anything to help—foreign aid, never large, has lately shrunk to virtually nothing. Nor is it the result of the benign policies of national governments, which are as callous and corrupt as ever. It is the indirect and unintended result of the actions of soulless multinationals and rapacious local entrepreneurs, whose only concern was to take advantage of the profit opportunities offered by cheap labor.

However, transnational companies can also be detrimental by widening class divisions, encouraging urbanization, providing unnecessary and harmful consumer goods, changing the way—and quality—of life, supporting morally corrupt governments,[2] pre-empting the development of local business, causing local unemployment through the use of capital-intensive technology, and causing environmental destruction.[3] Along with the power to do all of the above comes the responsibility not to do whichever are morally wrong.

Next, let's look at marketing. One issue to consider is *how* you advertise in other countries. Recall the case of Nestlé's infant formula discussed in Chapter 2—it provides a number of lessons about marketing in developing countries and highlights a number of questions one should ask: Will your potential consumer understand the ad? Will it be unduly manipulative, given the context in which it will appear? (*We* may not be suckered in by a character in a lab coat, but

---

1 See Di Norcia (185), referring to the Asian carpet industry; see also Luetge.
2 Consider what the Canadian oil company Talisman did, or did not do, in the Sudan; see Bakx. See also Gardner's insightful analysis of Nexen's involvement in Equatorial Guinea.
3 Both Cavanagh and De George provide good discussions of these benefits and detriments.

people in countries where medical personnel are rare and revered may be.) Or would you be patronizing and stereotyping to market your product in a special way just for them?

Another issue is *whether* you market your product in another country. Should one sell nuclear-reactor parts to a country that could and might use them in nuclear weapons? Is there something wrong with pushing high-priced status-symbol non-necessities (jeans and running shoes come to mind) to a country that can barely feed itself? (Coca-Cola now reaches areas where there is no clean drinking water.) On the other hand, don't all people, even those living at subsistence level, deserve some modest diversions, some little shred of luxury to make their humdrum lives a bit more bearable?

Not only might you ask whether you're morally obligated *not* to market your product in another country; you might also want to ask whether you're morally obligated *to* market your product to another country. If you're sitting on cheap water-purification tablets, aren't you morally compelled to market them to countries without clean water?

This brings us to sales—and pricing. The issue shares some features with that of wages. Should you charge the same price in the Third World market as you do in the First World market? Many consider dumping (selling a product in a foreign market at a lower price than in the home market, a price that doesn't cover export costs) to be morally wrong because it damages competition and hurts workers in the other country. In fact, it can be illegal if it reduces competition. But since when is competition more important than people? What if the product is much needed and would be unaffordable to many at "competitive prices"? Wouldn't the *right* thing be to sell it at that low price, to dump it?

Of course, that's a consequentialist analysis. An intent analysis may render a different judgement: if your reason for dumping were to enter and capture a market—get in with low prices, get people wanting your product, and then increase the price—perhaps dumping is *not* the right thing to do.

Should you charge a price at all? Perhaps the right thing to do would be to give your product away. Consider the case of the pharmaceutical company Merck and the cure for river blindness: those who needed it simply could not afford it—so they did indeed give it away. And why not? If income from Third World sales isn't necessary to the survival of your company and your product *is* necessary to the survival of Third World people.... But what about your obligations to your shareholders? Well, which is more important, curing blindness or higher returns?

Let's back up a bit and expand the intent analysis: why are you interacting with other countries in the first place? To escape home tax laws? Labour laws? Environmental laws? Safety laws? Well, without the tax advantages, the cheaper labour, and the lenient standards, you may say, I'd have no reason to go to other countries. Hmm. You can't think of any reasons other than those of self-advantage? Well, what's wrong with self-advantage as long as you do no harm to others? But aren't you doing harm by avoiding those taxes, by doing more environmental damage than you would in your own country?

BOX 6.1 Gildan: "The Ultimate Fruit of Globalization"

"As a young company, Gildan benefited from being in Canada, receiving government subsidies, and, when it hit a rough patch during the '90s, even borrowing from Quebec's labour-sponsored fund, the Fonds de solidarité FTQ, which invested $3.5 million in Gildan shares starting in 1996 and lent the company up to $30 million in debentures....

"The Chamandys [the founders of Gildan] soon realized staying in business meant following their competitors overseas....

"Finding cheaper labour was not, however, the only method Gildan used to cut costs—it also chopped its tax bill. In 1999, the company opened a subsidiary in Barbados to manage marketing and sales. Barbados has a treaty with Canada that permits multinationals to repatriate profits they earn abroad without being taxed here. The result: Gildan no longer pays much corporate income tax in Canada....

"Indeed, between fiscal 2009 and fiscal 2013, despite earning $1 billion (U.S.) in net profits, the company has paid only $10.5 million (U.S.) in income taxes (or about 1%). If one includes recoveries Gildan received stemming from acquisitions and restructurings, it paid no corporate income tax at all from 2009 to 2013. 'To us, it's totally immoral,' says Robert Bouvier, president of Teamsters Canada, which once represented Gildan workers. 'Immoral in the sense that you start your company in Canada...you benefit from the health system...you benefit from the banks that loan you money. You benefit from everything. And after you've established all of this, then you move out.'"

Source
Livesey, Bruce. "Gildan workers in Haiti, Honduras complain of harassment, pay too meagre to live on." *Globe and Mail* 27 Nov. 2014.

One might consider that merely doing trade with, selling anything to, another country is a gesture of support. This is the notion underlying Klein's suggestion that the Export Development Corporation, a Crown corporation that finances export and investment deals, "take measures to ensure the projects it supports in no way contribute to the denial of human rights, labour rights or to environmental damage" (1999, A21). Be careful, however, of the false dichotomy: in addition to "do" or "not do," there may be a third option, "do with strings attached." The Sullivan Principles, adopted by multinationals operating in South Africa, are such strings.[1]

Let's next consider product safety and product quality. Is it morally permissible to sell products that wouldn't pass *our* safety standards in a country with*out* such standards? Perhaps it depends on the harm—severity, likelihood, duration, etc. And on the alternatives—is it a drug

---

[1] See the Werhane article.

that would nevertheless in most cases improve their life? (Or is it a croquet set whose mallet heads come off too easily?)

Lastly, focusing on business with so-called "developing" countries (recognizing that international business is often with other developed countries), perhaps we have to ask, "Why *is* the Third World still developing and still so poor?" (Though perhaps we need to reconsider our terms—in many ways, such countries may be far more developed than so-called developed countries: can we really say that at 2 kg/person/day, the world's most prolific garbage producer—yes, remember, that's Canada—is developed?)

The First World has had the resources to remedy illness, malnutrition, and so on worldwide for quite a while. According to The United Nations *Human Development Report 1998*, it would take a mere US$40 billion ($58 billion today) to provide basic education, health, nutrition, safe water, and sanitation for everyone in the world. There is more spent on ice cream in Europe ($11 billion) than on water and sanitation for all ($6 billion). The following more recent numbers are somewhat different, but they make the same point: "To end extreme poverty worldwide in 20 years, Sachs [in his 2006 book, *The End of Poverty: Economic Possibilities for Our Time*] calculated that the total cost per year would be about $175 billion. This represents less than one percent of the combined income of the richest countries in the world" (Harack). What's our problem? What is it about our system that makes it so impossible to distribute these benefits to all who need and want them? Do we lack the ability? Or the will? Why can't we figure this out?[1]

Many developing countries are so crippled by foreign debt that they can't keep up with the interest, let alone chip away at the principal. According to Michalos,

> The Ecumenical Coalition for Economic Justice pointed out that "Total less developed country debt has doubled from approximately US$819 billion in 1982 to US$1,712 billion in 1993 despite their having repaid over US$14 trillion in debt service. The reasons for such massive payments include the compounding effect of high real interest rates and the need to take on new debt just to service old loans." (220)

A more recent source indicates that "indebted countries are repaying $100 million each day (most of which is compounded interest)" (Makwana). Can we honestly say that this state of affairs is just? Canada's debt forgiveness suggests it's not; to date, Canada has forgiven the debts of 15 countries, over $1 billion in total (Canada, Department of Finance).

But how did they get into such debt—by living beyond their means? Have they squandered their money on frivolous items? Or are they just not trying, not working hard enough? Or have their corrupt governments taken it all for themselves—and their war games? Do their elected governments sell their resources to buy mercenaries to fight the mercenaries hired by those trying to get those resources? (See the Grant article.) Or did we, do we, steal their stuff—and call it colonialism and free trade?

---

[1] Read some of Stiglitz's work for some answers.

Speaking of which, our consideration of international issues wouldn't be complete without a consideration of free trade agreements (FTAs). According to Barry and Wisor, among the "commendable features" of free trade agreements are the following: voluntary participation, the creation of reliable conditions of mutual market access, non-discriminatory treatment, impartial adjudication of disputes, and the improvement of human welfare by reducing inefficiencies in the exchange of goods and services. Among the "concerns" are the "outright bullying, coercion, deception and manipulation" that occurs during negotiation, the closing of an agreement with "partners that do not have the time, resources or expertise to fully understand the implications," and the high economic costs that come with refusing (Barry and Wisor).

Free Trade Agreement—the words *sound* so warm and fuzzy.... But of course the "free" refers to being free from regulation by governments. Which means that business trumps government. More specifically, and horrifically, the Trans-Pacific Partnership (TPP), the currently-under-consideration FTA, will allow businesses to sue governments for loss of potential profits; for example, "if a country passes an environmental law, corporations can figure out how it will affect their profits and sue the country for these imagined profits" ("Stop the TPP"). That is to say,

> The TPP would... *elevate individual foreign firms to equal status with sovereign nations*, empowering them to privately enforce new rights and privileges, provided by the pact, by dragging governments to foreign tribunals *to challenge public interest policies* that they claim frustrate their expectations. The tribunals would be authorized to order taxpayer compensation to the foreign corporations for the "expected future profits" they surmise would be inhibited by the challenged policies. (Public Citizen; my emphasis)

And "trade"? *Whose* trade? Although arranged by governments, not businesses, the agreements determine what businesses can and cannot do; they advantage and disadvantage business. (Directly. *In*directly they advantage and disadvantage everyone else.) Which is, no doubt, why business lobbies hard to determine the terms of such agreements. (*Big* business. SMEs can't afford that kind of influence.) In fact, there are 600 (big) business advisors writing the TPP, as well as many unelected trade representatives. Taliano elaborates on what this means:

> The significance of this distorted representation necessarily means that those who are represented are empowered, while those who are absent, are disempowered. Corporate monopolies such as Monsanto and Walmart are well-represented at the table. The track record of such corporations, over the last thirty years or so, shows that they are devoted to a de-humanizing economic theory known as neoliberalism, which erodes the middle class, creates huge income disparities in the population, and strangles both democracy and the economy, by handcuffing economic, social, and political self-determination. Significantly, polls show that the majority of Canadians do not support the consequences of these economic policies.

And *what* trade? Of TPP's 29 draft chapters, only five deal with traditional trade issues. The other chapters amount to "corporate protectionism," many say. For example, one affects Canada's food safety—in that our regulations could be considered "illegal trade barriers" (Hightower and Frazer). Other chapters affect drug prices and our use of the internet.

And 'agreement'? As the Public Citizen website described it at the time of the TPP's drafting, "We only know about the TPP's threats thanks to leaks—the public is not allowed to see the draft TPP text. Even members of Congress, after being denied the text for years, are now only provided limited access" (Public Citizen). Canadians were pretty much left in the dark as well.

On that note, an alternative to business-as-usual for those engaging with other countries is to become part of the "fair trade" movement. In Canada, Fairtrade Canada sets the standards that define what products qualify as fair trade. According to their website, "producers have to meet a variety of criteria that focus on a range of areas including labour standards, sustainable farming, governance, and democratic participation" in order to qualify for Fairtrade certification. "Companies that buy products from Fairtrade-certified producer organizations must also adhere to strict standards, regularly report, and submit to on-site audits. These standards focus on the terms of trade—specifically they spell out the minimum prices that can be paid to producers, the expectation for longer-term contracts, and the requirement to provide up to 60% of the value of a contract in advance should the producers request" (Fairtrade Canada). But is fair trade really fair?[1]

Another alternative to business-as-usual is to become part of the microcredit movement:

> The idea grew out of a shock experienced by [Muhammad] Yunus as a young professor of economics in the mid-1970s in Bangladesh when he saw people suffering and dying outside his campus, not because of a disease, bombs or war, but simply because they had nothing to eat. After investigation, he realized that they were suffering terribly for lack of very tiny amounts of money. But if they borrowed money from money lenders or loan sharks, it came with unbelievable conditions imposed on them. Yunus made a list of people who were suffering from this problem, amounting to 42 names and needing all together only $27. He simply gave the money to the 42 people and was surprised by the excitement and the happiness created by those tiny sums of money in each of those 42 people. This made him want to repeat the experience and with larger numbers of people. Yunus looked for some institutional arrangement so that people in need could find low-cost money whenever they needed it, and thus the first Grameen bank was launched. (Enderle)

I'm reminded here of Peter Singer's claim that in order to lead a morally decent life, people in the well-off countries should give a mere 1 per cent of their income to those in not-so-well-off countries. My guess is that if people *knew* their money would go to those less-well-off rather than the bureaucracy of some NGO.... (So there's a business opportunity for you: establish a Canadian International Microcredit Bank. Wouldn't most people bank at least *some* of their

---

[1] See McMurtry; see also Reed et al., who consider fair trade specifically in the Canadian context. And does the current system leave room for "fairwashing" (akin to "greenwashing")? Again, see McMurtry.

money there if they knew it would be used for such game-changing microloans instead of investments that simply maintain the wealth-distribution status quo? I know I would.)[1]

According to the Grameen website, the Grameen Bank now has 2,565 branches, and in 81,379 villages has 8.349 million borrowers (97 per cent of whom are women—"Studies have shown that the overall output of development is greater when loans are given to women instead of men, as women are more likely to use their earnings to improve their living situations and to educate their children"; despite this, in many cases, microloans go disproportionately to men—see the United Nations report listed below). And 65 per cent of those 8.349 million people no longer live in poverty. Of further note, "Since its inception, Grameen Bank made profits every year, except for the years 1983, 1991 and 1992."

And Grameen isn't the only one: according to Forbes, there are more than 12,000 microfinance institutions (as you might guess, microfinance includes more than microcredit).

One of the interesting things about the microcredit model, in addition to the "small amounts make big differences" element (consider $50 for a sewing machine...), is that loans are made without collateral (poor people don't *have* collateral). What happens instead is that borrowers are organized in groups, which guarantee the loans: if the borrower doesn't repay the loan, the rest of the group must do so. Typically, very *very* few loans are *not* repaid (under 1 per cent).

And yet Bateman claims that microloans *aren't* working. In response, one can point out that macroloans don't always bring about their intended outcome either. Does that affect the morality of the loans? What exactly makes microloans morally good? Perhaps even morally better (than business-as-usual)?

BOX 6.2   Feel Like Watching a Movie?

Check out *El Contrato*.

References and Further Reading

Amba-Rao, Sita C. "Multinational Corporate Social Responsibility, Ethics, Interactions and Third World Governments: An Agenda for the 1990s." *Journal of Business Ethics* 12.7 (1993): 553–72.

Bakx, Kyle. "Oil, politics and human rights: A look back at Talisman." *CBC News*. 22 Feb. 2015. http://www.cbc.ca/news/business/oil-politics-and-human-rights-a-look-back-at-talisman-1.2964715

Barry, Christian, and Lydia Tomitova. "Fairness in Sovereign Debt." *Social Research* 73.2 (2006): 649–94.

---

1 Of course, microloans can be made domestically as well; see Hudson and Wehrell for an analysis of the Royal Bank/Calmeadow partnership in Nova Scotia.

Barry, Christian, and Scott Wisor. "The Ethics of International Trade." Draft of "International Trade," in Darrel Moellendorf and Heather Widdows (eds.), *The Routledge Handbook of Global Ethics*. New York: Routledge, 2014. 216–29.

Bateman, Milford. "The Developing World's Tragic Engagement with Microcredit." *E-International Relations* 20 Oct. 2014. http://www.e-ir.info/2014/10/20/the-developing-worlds-tragic-engagement-with-microcredit/

Canada. Department of Finance. "Canada's Contributions to Bilateral and Multilateral Debt Relief Initiatives." 20 Sept. 2012. https://www.fin.gc.ca/access/dri-iad-eng.asp

Cavanagh, Gerald F. *American Business Values with International Perspectives*. 4th ed. Englewood Cliffs, NJ: Prentice Hall, 1998.

Chakrabortty, Adidtya. "It's time to cancel unpayable old debts." *Guardian* 9 Jan. 2012. http://www.theguardian.com/commentisfree/2012/jan/09/time-cancel-unpayable-old-debts

Chossudovsky, Michel. *The Globalisation of Poverty: Impacts of IMF and World Bank Reforms*. London: Zed Books, 1997.

De George, Richard T. *Business Ethics*. 5th ed. Englewood Cliffs, NJ: Prentice Hall, 1999. (Chapters 19, 20, and 21 deal with "Moral Issues in International Business.")

———. *Competing with Integrity in International Business*. New York: Oxford, 1993. 19–21.

———. "International Business Ethics: Russia and Eastern Europe." *Social Responsibility: Business, Journalism, Law, and Medicine* 19 (1993): 5–23.

Di Norcia, Vincent. *Hard Like Water: Ethics in Business*. Toronto: Oxford University Press, 1998.

Donaldson, Thomas. *The Ethics in International Business*. New York: Oxford University Press, 1989.

"11 Facts about Global Poverty." *Do Something*. https://www.dosomething.org/facts/11-facts-about-global-poverty

Enderle, Georges. "Global Competition and Corporate Responsibilities of Small and Medium-sized Enterprises." *Business Ethics: A European Review* 13.1 (2004): 51–63.

Fairtrade Canada. http://fairtrade.ca

Forbes. "The World's Top Microfinance Institutions." http://www.forbes.com/2007/12/20/top-microfinance-philanthropy-biz-cz_ms_1220intro.html

Frederick, William C. "The Moral Authority of Transnational Corporate Codes." *Journal of Business Ethics* 10.3 (1991): 165–77.

Gardner, Dan. "Nexen and the Dictator." www.dangardner.ca. 5 Nov. 2005. http://www.dangardner.ca/articles/item/312-nexen-and-the-dictator

Grameen Bank. http://www.grameen.com

Grant, Dale. "Canadians Cry 'Havoc,' and Let Slip the Dogs of War." *Toronto Star* 9 Mar. 1999: A19.

Harack, Ben. "How much would it cost to end extreme poverty in the world?" *Vision of Earth*. 26 Aug. 2011. http://www.visionofearth.org/economics/ending-poverty/how-much-would-it-cost-to-end-extreme-poverty-in-the-world/

Henderson, Michael J. "Ethical Outsourcing in UK Financial Services: Employee Rights." *Busi-

ness Ethics 6.2 (1997): 110–24.

Herman, Barry. "Doing the Right Thing: Dealing with Developing Country Sovereign Debt." *North Carolina Journal of International Law & Commercial Regulation* 32.4 (2007): 773–818.

Hightower, Jim, and Philip Frazer. "The Trans-Pacific Partnership is not about free trade. It's a corporate coup d'état—against us!" *Hightower Lowdown*. Aug. 2013. http://www.hightowerlowdown.org/node/3402#.VSg8j6IhG0g

Hudson, Richard, and Roger Wehrell. "Socially Responsible Investors and the Microentrepreneur: A Canadian Case." *Journal of Business Ethics* 60 (2005): 281–92.

Klein, Naomi. "Dusting the Cobwebs off Canada's Conscience." *Toronto Star* 4 Feb. 1999: A21.

———. *This Changes Everything*. New York: Simon & Schuster, 2014.

Kohls, John, and Paul Buller. "Resolving Cross-Cultural Ethical Conflict: Exploring Alternative Strategies." *Journal of Business Ethics* 13.1 (1994): 31–38.

Krugman, Paul. "In Praise of Cheap Labor." *Slate* 21 Mar. 1997. http://www.slate.com/articles/business/the_dismal_science/1997/03/in_praise_of_cheap_labor.html

Lehman, Hugh. "Equal Pay for Equal Work in the Third World." *Journal of Business Ethics* 4 (1985): 487–91. Reprinted in Deborah C. Poff and Wilfrid J. Waluchow (eds.), *Business Ethics in Canada*, 2nd ed. Scarborough, ON: Prentice Hall Allyn and Bacon, 1991. 444–49.

Luetge, Christoph. "Economic Ethics, Business Ethics and the Idea of Mutual Advantages." *Business Ethics: A European Review* 14.2 (2005): 108–18.

Makwana, Rajesh. "Cancelling Third World Debt." *Share the World's Resources*. 20 Feb. 2006. http://www.sharing.org/information-centre/reports/cancelling-third-world-debt

Marleau, Diane. "Canada's Role in Alleviating Poverty in the Third World." *Toronto Star* 19 Mar. 1999: A17.

Mayer, Don, and Anita Cava. "Ethics and the Gender Equality Dilemma for U.S. Multinationals." *Journal of Business Ethics* 12.9 (1993): 701–08.

McMurtry, J.J. "Ethical Value-Added: Fair Trade and the Case of Café Femenino." *Journal of Business Ethics* 86 (2009): 27–49.

Michalos, Alex. "Issues for Business Ethics in the Nineties and Beyond." *Journal of Business Ethics* 16.3 (1997): 219–30.

Pogge, Thomas W. "The Bounds of Nationalism." *Rethinking Nationalism* (*Canadian Journal of Philosophy* Supplementary Volume 22). Ed. Jocelyne Couture, Kai Nielsen, and Michel Seymour. Calgary: University of Calgary Press, 1998. 463–504.

Public Citizen. "Trans-Pacific Partnership (TPP): Job Loss, Lower Wages and Higher Drug Prices." *Public Citizen*. n.d. http://www.citizen.org/TPP

Reed, Darryl, Bob Thomson, Ian Husssey, and Jean-Frédéric Le May. "Developing a Normatively Grounded Research Agenda for Fair Trade: Examining the Case of Canada." *Journal of Business Ethics* 92 (2010): 151–79.

Sachs, Jeffrey. *The End of Poverty: Economic Possibilities for Our Time*. New York: Penguin Books, 2006.

Sende, Marthe. "Toxic Terrorism: A Crisis in Global Waste Trading." *Anamesa* (Spring 2010): 30–67.

Singer, Andrew W. "Ethics: Are Standards Lower Overseas?" *Across the Board* (Sept. 1991): 31–34.

Skelly, Joe. "The Caux Round Table Principles for Business: The Rise of International Ethics." *Business Ethics* (March/April 1995): 2–5.

Smith, Stephen L.S., Christopher B. Barrett, Daniel Rush Finn, and Roland Hoksbergen. "Christian Ethics and the Forgiveness of Third World Debt: A Symposium." *Faith & Economics* 35 (2000): 8–19.

Stiglitz, Joseph E. "Ethics, Economic Advice, and Economic Policy." Document included in the Digital Library of the Inter-American Initiative on Social Capital, Ethics and Development. www.iadb.org/etica/ingles/index-i.htm

———. "Ethics, Market and Government Failure, and Globalization." https://www0.gsb.columbia.edu/faculty/jstiglitz/download/papers/2003_Ethics_Market_and_Government_Failure_and_Globalization.pdf

"Stop the Trans-Pacific Partnership: Bad for Jobs, the Environment, Labor and Consumers." *It's Our Economy*. http://itsoureconomy.us/occupy-the-tpp-stop-the-global-corporate-coup/

Taka, Iwao. "Business Ethics: A Japanese View." *Business Ethics Quarterly* 4.1 (1994): 53–78.

Taliano, Mark. "TPP negotiations: What is our government hiding behind closed doors?" *Rabble.ca*. 3 Sept. 2013. http://rabble.ca/news/2013/09/tpp-negotiations-what-our-government-hiding-behind-closed-doors

Treviño, Linda K., and Katherine A. Nelson. *Managing Business Ethics: Straight Talk about How to do It Right*. 2nd ed. New York: John Wiley and Sons, 1999.

United Nations, Department of Economic and Social Affairs. *2009 World Survey on the Role of Women in Development: Women's Control over Economic Resources and Access to Financial Resources, including Microfinance*.

United Nations Development Programme. *Human Development Report 1998*. New York: Oxford University Press, 1998.

Van Gerwen, Jef, and Vandevelde, Toon. "Ethical Aspects of Debt Reduction for the Poorest Countries." *Ethical Perspectives* 8.1 (2001): 3–17.

Weiss, Joseph W. *Business Ethics: A Managerial, Stakeholder Approach*. Belmont, CA: Wadsworth, 1994. 242–44.

Werhane, Patricia H. "Globalization and Its Challenges for Business Ethics in the 21st Century." Center for Business Ethics at Bentley University. 2012.

———. "The Moral Responsibility of Multinational Corporations to Be Socially Responsible." *Emerging Global Business Ethics*. Ed. W. Michael Hoffman et al. Westport, CT: Quorum Books, 1994. 136–42.

Wines, William A., and Nancy K. Napier. "Toward an Understanding of Cross-Cultural Ethics: A Tentative Model." *Journal of Business Ethics* 11.11 (1992): 831–41.

Ethics and Multinational Corporations vis-à-vis Developing Nations

James R. Simpson

ABSTRACT. The ethical dilemma of large-scale multinational corporations is presented. The list of complaints and issues is summarized. A case is made for the concept of multinationals being inherently beneficial in today's world of high technology and dependence on international trade. The difficulty is extreme power wielded by some groups. It is concluded that a philosophical ideal is for control on size and power as well as international rules to prevent abuses of power. The concern is that today the worthiness of being relatively small is slowly but surely being eroded.

[1] "For the World Managers the underdeveloped world is the supreme management problem.... A Global Shopping Center in which 40 to 50 percent of the potential customers are living at the edge of starvation without electricity, plumbing, drinkable water, medical care, schools, or jobs is not a marketable vision." (Richard J. Barnett and Ronald E. Muller, *Global Reach*)

Advances in world economic and political structure should be positively related to globalization of the private productive system but, for the most part, the required institutional changes in national government have not taken place, with consequent and predictable political and societal tensions. The lag between technological advance and institutional change was envisioned by Marx in his analysis of the historical progression of capitalism to communism and is, ironically, probably doing more to foster interest in socialism among the educated than any discontent which might be fomented among the so-called proletariat. The situation is of such magnitude that economic liberalists will have to depend on a major redefinition of legislation and philosophy of production and distribution, especially those relating to large corporations with a multinational dimension, to prevent Marx's prophecy of the inevitable movement to communism from being fulfilled.

Parallel to the new internationalism of business [2] has been the coining of new jargon. The rise of the 'global corporation', as Barnett and Muller euphemistically call it (they dislike the term 'multinational' corporation for that implies international ownership while globals are almost always owned by one company from one country), has led to the creation of what they term a 'global shopping center' to serve the 'world customer'. The global corporations are operated by 'globalists' and, as might be expected, they 'think globally'. Apart from the chal-

---

* *Journal of Business Ethics* 1982 (1): 227–37.

lenge of making profits through integrating global marketing with superior management techniques, is the creation of what Daniel Boorstin calls the 'consumption community', which is a bond transcending race, geography, and tradition based on drinking, eating, smoking, wearing and driving identical things.[1] The World Managers who are orchestrating the 'Great Crusade' are convinced that they have a 'historic mandate' to participate in the creation of a 'postpolitical world order'.

[3] Many Globalists in the top decision-making ranks believe that politicians have created chaos in the world with their patriotic wars, antiquated borders, and national pride, and that it falls to the international businessmen to save the world. They further argue that social progress stems from the little decisions on production and marketing rather than those of politicians. To them, the great steps forward in a country's progress come about through internationalizing production so that widely dispersed productive facilities can be integrated by such innovations as containerized shipping and automated record keeping into what is, conceptually, a global factory without geographical ties. Although most global corporations, in terms of management and ownership, are either American, British, Dutch, German, French, Swiss, Italian, Canadian, Swedish, or Japanese, they are gradually becoming companies without a country. Carl Gerstacher, chairman of Dow Chemical Company, reportedly even dreams of buying land owned by no nation for his headquarters. A unique feature is that unlike corporate philosophies of just a decade ago, overseas factories and markets are no longer viewed simply as adjuncts to home operations. Rather, the world is visualized as one economic unit with the nation state as an obstacle to planetary development. The irony is that even though many 'futurists' are discussing and planning for a world without borders, the twentieth century is characterized by a wave of nationalism.[2]

[4] It is generally agreed that the driving force behind the global concept is a revolution in managerial organization which has made it possible to centralize industrial planning on a global scale.[3] A key to success is delegation of authority with supreme efforts being made to build the global factory into one big happy participating family. As top managers increasingly receive stocks, options, bonuses, overrides, and special opportunities as a part of their income, the distinction between them and owners begins to disappear, and they acquire the same personal interest in maximizing corporate growth and profits as the largest shareholders. Loyalty is a watchword and, while the globals base their appeal for allegiance on building a faith in their being a principal means of bringing world peace and progress, "its most powerful appeal for loyalty is to the general public, and its message is simple and insistent: Consumption is the key to happiness and the global corporation has the products that make life worth living".[4] The Globalists as well as the Club of Rome[5] are in agreement that there will be a shortage of many products sought by an international community at the global shopping center due to rising populations and depletion of natural resources, and are naturally concerned about a lack of inputs.

[5] Recognizing the dangers from potential resource scarcity as well as other conflicts about globals, at least three groups have arisen in direct opposition to the multinational's efforts to fill the shelves and construct new stores. The first of the global managers' mortal enemies are advocates of a 'zero growth economy'. Second are members of the 'anticonsumption movement' who are especially concerned with finding solutions to the problems of global poverty. The third is a group which resists global centralization on a variety of economic, political, moral, scientific, or aesthetic grounds. This third group can be further subdivided into several subgroups, one of

[6] which consists of those whose economic interests are affected, such as organized labor in developed countries which views the cheap manpower of LDC's [Less Developed Country] as a real threat. An example of this opposition is the United States' textile industry.

[6] The second sub-group of 'enemies' are those motivated as much by political feelings as economic interest. Of special significance are officials and bureaucrats of LDC's who are bent on promoting even greater feelings of nationalism. Paramount in a third subgroup are concerned reformers, idealistic young people, and followers of other economic systems (such as communism) who view the large corporation as another tool of capitalism designed to further exploit the world's masses. There is also a countercorporate movement emerging within universities, and the global managers are reported to be sufficiently upset that they are bringing pressure on universities by reducing grants and through reminders that the funds of most universities are usually tied up in stocks. As an offensive tactic, there is a proposal by the globals to create a University of the World, whose

> curriculum would be geared to the needs of the 'real world'—i.e., the emerging Global Shopping Center. Criticism of the underlying values and assumptions of the establishment would be muted. Doubt, searching for alternative visions, and other inefficient intellectual activities would be discouraged.[6]

[7] The discussion about globals is confined to a new corporate structure comprising a few hundred businesses which deal internationally. They represent the culmination of a process which has led to a concentration that is dangerous in the sense that the globals do not compete according to the traditional liberal economic philosophy.[7] It is this lack of competition and the undesirable effects from their size which form the crux of the global corporation problem vis-à-vis society. Although we must recognize that growth is the driving force behind oligopolistic competition, the late Joseph Schumpeter, a giant among economists, feared that large corporations would rob capitalism of its vitality by dichotomizing the structure into owners who do not manage and managers who do not own. John Kenneth Galbraith, well known for his book, *The Affluent Society*, feels that large corporations become laws into themselves thus preventing Adam Smith's 'invisible hand' from acting as an effective market regulator. The global manager takes a different view though, for to him bigness is next to godliness. It is a law of nature, or to be more exact, of life, since a lack of growth would mean losing confidence from the stock market and other money lenders. Bigness is also important in social hierarchy. The manager (or any employee for that matter) of IBM is more esteemed than one from a little company of 100 employees making parts for the big computer manufacturers. In the same vein, the ambassador from a large industrialized country is held in higher esteem and is more 'important', than one from a small, recently formed African nation. This leads us to one of our tasks which is to determine how a small person's or nation's dignity can be raised in the face of the global corporation problem and how development can be given needed stimulus. First we must examine the globals in more detail.

A Closer Look at Globals

[8] Global corporations have been around for a long time. Witness the East India Company of the 1800's and the banana companies which came into their own after the turn of this century. The real proliferation in globals came about after the Korean War, though, as better methods of communication became available, transportation was improved, the

cost of labor rose rapidly in the developed countries, and there was a general growth in the size and scale of business. Along with improved managerial techniques came a discovery of tax loopholes in the developed countries and encouragement by leaders in various developing nations to build plants in their countries. As the globals ventured forth, they were well received; the news spread that the LDC's offered many advantages for setting up business not found in developed countries.[8] Furthermore, as international economic development has taken place, the sheer size of markets in many LDC's has made them attractive. Finally, if a global locates within a common market, it realizes many economic and political advantages which are not available if it is situated in a developed country which does not belong to a common market.

[9] The principal longer term problem facing the world managers is how to legitimize their actions. They base their claim to a world role on superior management skills, their corporation's efficiency, and a belief that they can bring about world peace through international trade. The globalists support proposals for breaking down world borders and believe that governments are behaving irrationally because they are tied to territories with such uneconomic goals as pride, prestige, and power. The 'transnational corporations' claim great achievements in their contributions toward an unprecedented standard of living in their own countries and argue that they can assist in replicating this economic progress in other countries if given a chance. The global managers argue that a person's self esteem is, in large part, determined by what is purchased. It can be interjected that the sales of transnational corporations come about largely through advertising, which can have both positive and negative effects. On the positive side, most advertised products, such as transistor radios or bicycles, are processed products which have a higher economic multiplier than many of the so-called basic necessities such as milk, bread, rice and fish. In effect, for every dollar's worth of sales there is more economic activity generated in the economy due to more processing. More people are given jobs and incomes improve. On the other side of the coin, advertising leads to the consumption of goods which have a questionable tradeoff with the basic necessities, such as a father purchasing a brand name shampoo while his children are malnourished. Advertising also leads to a dependence on satisfying the desire for goods.

Irrational consumption habits in LDC's should [10] not necessarily be blamed on the advent of T.V., radio, and billboards, no matter how important the globals have been in promoting their use. Since the dawn of civilization, men have squandered their money on wine, women, and song. Thus, if it is deemed desirable that consumption habits be 'improved' in some manner, the problem should be recognized as one of mounting an educational program to accomplish this. Objective reasoning indicates that it is illogical to expect large corporations to take over the function of improving consumption habits *except* to the extent that they are in the business of processing and marketing the type of food deemed 'acceptably nutritious'. This brings us to the topic of globals being change agents or adopting a social role.

While no attempt is being made here to determine [11] the extent to which multinational corporations are engines of development or retard the growth of LDC's, a few comments are in order. First, exhaustive studies are required to determine their input, and certainly it will be difficult to generalize as each country is different. The key point is that global corporations, like any other business, operate to make a profit. They assist in developing a social conscience only to the extent they deem it advisable or the top management happens to have more of an altruistic outlook. It should hastily be pointed out that *if the company were owned by the state, it would have no more altruism than a private corporation.* In fact, there would probably be less spirit of benevolence since state corporation managers in a socialist system receive their rewards from fulfilling production quotas, not in improving the common weal. Anyone who has attempted to solicit donations or assistance will testify that it is harder to get them from government than from private business. The point is that private corporations can be instruments of development, but only within the context of their production and sales capabilities and it is irrational to expect any other attitude.

[12]   The arguments and counterarguments about global corporations being major suppliers of capital, their providing technology when it would be otherwise unavailable, and their helping solve balance-of-payments problems are quite complex. Statistics can be manipulated to prove almost any point and, certainly, abuses by globals have been many and varied. Furthermore, the past serves only as a reference point. What is becoming clear is that globals are enjoying a greater control over technology, finance capital, and marketing. The difficulty, as with any oligopoly or monopoly, is that they frequently have an inordinate amount of power which can be, and frequently is, used to the detriment of other businesses.[9] One factor is that global corporations are not major suppliers of foreign capital to poor countries and often compete with local corporations for scarce financing. A bank would rather loan to Sears, Roebuck and Company than to a new national department store chain because it is less risky.

[13]   Knowledge is the critical component of power.

> The same power that enables corporations in Latin America to conceal their ownership, plans, and intracorporate dealings and hence frustrate government control over them operates also in the United States. It is one key structural reason why, in our view, the world's richest society is looking more and more like an underdeveloped country.[10]

The power shifts which have occurred as a result of global transformations in the private productive system have not been reflected in governmental modifications either in the LDC's or in the first world countries. The relative loss of power by governments is translated as a detriment to small businesses because there is little countervailing power to resist corporate take-over mainly because of structural weakness in major public institutions which theoretically are expected to balance off the power of global corporations. This situation is exactly what global corporations desire, for they want to stimulate government-big business relationships in which the future is planned to meet tomorrow's challenge. The world managers see government's future role as development of a good business climate which will create the needed infrastructure for a global economy. This is why global corporations require a different kind of nation state, one that provides them with stability, since anticipation and projection of the future are vital for efficient planning. It is also why they will do business with fascists, communists, or dictators if there is a profit. They don't like dealing with a state, but state planning does provide an element of stability.

[14]   If the government of a global corporation's home country were to be in league with its multinational corporations to a greater extent than at present, the result would be frightening. Think, for example, of the pressure now brought to bear on weaker countries which dare to stand in the path of U.S. based global corporations. The major role which the globals have played in setting foreign policy both of their own 'home' country as well as the 'host'

country in which they operate is well known. The names of ITT in Chile, Litton Industries in Greece, United Fruit in Costa Rica, and Gulf in Bolivia are cases in point. What appears on the horizon, though, is a clash between governments and global corporations, as neither one is desirous of giving up the planning function that each have accepted as their own domain. To protect their interests, governments have gained a secure foothold on the futurism bandwagon in predicting, planning, and prevention. Numerous government committees in all countries dedicated to these functions have sprung up in the past few years.[11] A bill introduced in the United States Congress by Senators Humphrey and Javets entitled the Balanced Growth and Economic Planning Act of 1975 is the first attempt at centralized national planning in the United States since the 1930's. The clear trend in the United States is a growing demand for tighter coordination between national policy and corporate policy, and while this seems admirable on the surface, there are drawbacks.

[15] Some further considerations of the United States experience are instructive in considering policy about globals as there is evidence that increased planning directed at *coordinating* policies with big business is not the ethical solution for regulating globals. In the United States, big government is not able to control an ever bigger business because

> politicians who achieve high office and the public administrators they appoint have little desire to control the expansion and exercise of corporate power. The dominant ideology in midcentury America is the celebration of growth and bigness. No government dedicated to steady, spectacular economic growth as the prime tool for maintaining social peace can afford to take a tough line with corporations.[12]

The same holds true in most other developed countries. Oddly enough, big business has achieved its power through a conception that the best people to manage, advise, and assist the government are those from big business. The result has been a big business–big government interlock. (An interlock, in business terms, is a corporation electing an executive or director of another corporation to be on its board of directors.) In the United States, there has not appeared to be an overt fundamental conflict in corporate and public interests so that the federal government has regulated the economy by people 'on loan' from corporations and banks. The result is that government is able to exercise little countervailing power against big corporations. In Japan, there is outright collaboration between government and business, management, and labor.

[16] Considering that the power to dominate seems to be a principal element of concern about multinationals, a major question is: How big is too big? A few statistics provide some illuminating facts. The largest ten 'world corps' are, by sales, bigger than some 80 nations as measured by GNP, and the largest 40 firms are bigger than some 64 nations. Whereas the world's GNP increases at about five percent annually, the world's multinational community grows at some ten percent annually. With assets of more than $200 billion along with human and financial resources that come with that financial power, the multi's have access to data that is unavailable to the majority of nations.[13] The problem of size is not new and has faced U.S. government and academics since the late 1800's when the Sherman Antitrust Act was passed. In the 1960's, conglomerates received a lot of bad press, and orders from justice departments to break up their power were commonplace. Although attention in the 1980's continues to be focused on the size and power of corporations, there are no hard and fast guidelines in what is one of the most cloudy areas

of jurisprudence. The sad and disagreeable thing is that many governments are losing their regulatory power because they do not have a clear policy on what they should be regulating.

> What once were laws in such areas as tax, banking, securities, and controls are now looked upon in the sophisticated corporate world as little more than shoals to be avoided by careful steering. The U.S. government is a little like the orchestra conductor who discovers midway through the symphony that the principal players have left.[14]

[17] The list of complaints, some with reason, others without justification, is long. In an effort to summarize the issues, the following list has been prepared:

- Just being big is 'bad'.
- Bigness reduces bargaining power of governments and competitors.
- Global corporations (G.C.'s) enter into cartels which hurt smaller businesses.
- G.C.'s only deal in high profit items and leave low profit items for nationals.
- G.C.'s promote luxury items rather than necessities.
- G.C.'s earn excess profits.
- G.C.'s do not reinvest in the country.
- G.C.'s exploit LDC's natural resources.
- They unfairly compete with local companies for scarce development capital.
- G.C.'s transfer prices deviate considerably from market prices to avoid taxes.
- G.C.'s reap double benefits by selling to themselves.
- They have little "social consciousness."
- They are not development agents.
- G.C.'s exploit indigenous labor.
- They introduce machinery rather than using labor intensive techniques.
- Global corporations reduce jobs in the developed countries.
- Globals fail to introduce new technology, and when they do it is a type which LDC's least need, or it is antiquated.
- They over-use advertising.
- They desire to make the world homogenous, i.e., reduce cultural differences and this is 'bad'.
- The developed countries benefit rather than the LDC's.
- Large corporations plan centrally and act globally, but nation states do not.
- Globals are able to escape national regulation.
- They have an inordinate amount of power in their own and host countries, and interfere in policy making.
- Global interdependence has transformed the world political economy in such a way that former stabilizing effects are now destabilizing effects.

Prior to discussing the allegations, some more [18] evidence—from the viewpoint of ethics—will assist in evaluating the case. We must recall that moral judgments, and this is the crux of this article for we are making a determination if globals are 'good' or 'bad', should be made with full knowledge of the relevant facts to be objective. The situation must be viewed impartially, but with sympathy. Furthermore, another formal requirement for a moral judgment is universality, i.e., that the judgement would hold in a relevantly similar situation. But let's get into the problem.

Ethics and the Global Corporation

Problems of moral philosophy are divided into [19] three parts: value, the good, and duty. The pros and cons of the multi's from a moral point of view can be discussed within this organizational framework.

The problem of value, it will be recalled, revolves around goodness and badness, opinions, attitudes, customs, law, interest, obligation, virtue, control over people; i.e., values or properties which people hold dear. With respect to globals, the heart of the problem revolves around their size. Recognizing that economic organization on a 'sufficiently' large scale is necessary to reach even minimum productive efficiency, the difficulty, from both a practical and ethical viewpoint, is that conflicts of interest arise which threaten order and progress toward many of the values held in highest esteem such as human dignity and the belief by economic liberalists that the 'little guy' should be able to develop a business by working hard enough and possessing the necessary business acumen.

[20] In all fairness to globals, they do use their size and scale to enhance economic freedom by promoting upward mobility and greater choice making. In this sense, they contribute to modernity of the LDC's. On the opposite tack, and probably the most damaging of all arguments, is that power situations arise which cause conflicts of interest and subsequent social problems. By having unequal power, globals can also restrict the range of choice to consumers by driving out competition and consequently reducing freedom of the less powerful. On the personal level, they can act in a negative manner through advertising to coerce us into accepting partial freedoms.

[21] Let's move on to the problem of 'the good' and its special case, happiness. Can globals be shown to be intrinsically good, i.e., worthwhile on their own account? If one listens to the global managers, one will come away believing that globals are the salvation of humankind on a par with happiness. More sober analysis in the academic field known as industrial organization leaves one less optimistic. In fact, it is generally concluded that as concentration of power and sales grows, the social function of the market as a price regulator and resource allocator is diminished. Concentration also leads to violations of good market conduct such as tax evasion, overuse of advertising, escaping certain regulations, and inordinate amounts of interference in policy making, thus fulfilling many of the allegations set forth in the last section. Following up further on the problem of 'the good', we recall that intrinsic (ultimate goods) are ones which are valuable in and of themselves, while non-intrinsic or instrumental goods are those which are valuable by virtue of their being related to intrinsic goods. As such, globals, just like any other corporation or type of business, are non-intrinsic in nature and, furthermore, are instrumental in nature, i.e., those valuable as a means to achieve an intrinsic good. The upshot of the matter is that being a global corporation, or any type of business organization for that matter, is simply a means to an end. It is a tool to assist us achieve happiness or some other higher good rather than being a higher good. Thus, in judging whether globals are 'good' or 'bad', the problem is determining how well they contribute to intrinsic goods or the highest good (whatever that may be). In effect they are judged on their conduct and performance—the same thing that economists hold in their theory of industrial organization.

[22] To what extent are globals' actions appropriate to their position and to what degree do their actions reflect conduct resulting from a sense of morality and justice, i.e., duty? Adopting a normative position to define what 'ought' to be the ideal action, it is clear that globals cannot be lumped together. Just as any business organization, some do carry out their 'social duty' in a commendable fashion while others abuse power vested in them. Witness the flurry in 1976 from discoveries of bribes paid by globals and other large corporations to government officials all over the world. On the more positive side we observe that they *generally* do fulfill their duty of

improving the condition of humankind by providing some articles for life sustenance, enhancement, and luxury. However, they also place emphasis on esteem through materialism, thus probably reducing some inner-self rewards.

[23] In all likelihood, globals do help attain the 'good life' by providing an ever greater amount of goods and services but, to the extent that advertising 'forces' people to accept their products after which there is a feeling of repentance, they detract from quality of life. They provide new jobs and services to us through higher standards of living. They 'pull' development by stimulating wants and desires which in turn generates greater economic activity, but negates principles of austerity. They help attain happiness through economic means, but foster homogenation of cultural values. They do help humankind become masters of their own destiny by helping raise standards of living, but are a potential hazard to economic freedom to the extent that they are interlocked with government. They increase freedom of choice by providing more goods and services, but reduce freedom for the individual entrepreneur or small businessman to self-actualize. In brief, they have desirable traits but difficulties with respect to conduct. How then, should they be finally judged from a moral point of view?

An Assessment

[24] The fundamental objectives of economic policy—full employment, relatively stable prices, equitable income distribution, and quality of life—are compatible with the profit motive providing it is controlled. 'Think, maybe we can avoid work' is a sign frequently observed in both public and private offices. Governments in LDC's could well heed this advice with respect to multinational corporations. By writing the rules clearly, delineating their goals, and using psychology, LDC's can use globals to gain desired development. One place to start is with the world managers themselves.

[25] The Global Manager receives satisfaction from the use of imagination, which translates into the generation of corporate profits. Probably, there are few managers who are concerned with reaching some *absolute* profit level, as a profit figure is just a number. There is nothing magic about 40 percent versus 15 percent, for it is *relative* profits which are important to them. The manager is concerned about what others are doing, so the game is played by pitting one corporation's balance sheet against another's. We can hypothesize that global corporations work at the international level because there is a higher percentage of profits abroad than within their home country, as well as a chance to increase sales and consequently total profits. Probably there are also other economic and non-economic goals. The challenge to the manager is seeing how much profit he can make *within the rules of the game*.[15] Naturally, they will complain and attempt to change the rules, as this is an integral part of good management—it is a rationale for lobbying. If rules are made which set restrictions on all global corporations, none are disadvantaged in terms of the others. If the rules are set even at fairly disadvantageous levels, it is likely that the global managers will not complain too loudly *providing* they are maintained for everyone, i.e., that stability accompanies them. A spinoff would be greater innovation. Overall, the key to using globals is fomenting regulations that take advantage of the firm's propensity for profits; the sin is leaving loopholes in the law or 'rules of the game'.

[26] As Professor Gordon has pointed out, it is difficult to measure the extent of the multinational's influence on the culture, economics, and political structure of the third world and, consequently, it is difficult to set goals or controls. The magnitude of the global's power is impressive, though. Con-

sider, for example, that United Brands has higher net sales than the GNP of Panama or Costa Rica, Del Monte is higher in sales than Honduras is in GNP, and Quaker Oats is higher than Paraguay. This can lead to a playing, by multi's, of one nation against another. Gordon says

> One must wonder why Third world governments have been so directly subject to the control of multinational enterprises. Using Latin America as an example, the governments tend to be feudalistic, highly structured, and centralized, and thus easier to penetrate than a broadly based government.[16]

[27] Recognizing that globals need to be controlled, the United Nations General Assembly recently published a history-making document called the 'Charter of the Economic Rights and Duties of States'. In the second chapter 'transnational corporations', (TNC's) are considered in some detail with the major point being that sovereign states have the right to deal with and regulate TNC's. Recognizing that many states don't have the sophistication to deal with TNC's, the Economic and Social Council (ECOSOC), a United Nations agency, established a Commission on Transnational Corporations as well as an Information and Research Center, both of which are aimed at a comprehensive and continuous monitoring of the TNC's.[17] A similar project is being carried out in the U.S. Congress.[18] Among the first action programs have been special workshops to assist in training government officials in negotiating techniques, taxation laws, and bargaining.[19] This positive action follows up on the 1973 Algiers conference out of which it was decided to establish a center for studying the 500 leading global corporations.

[28] By 1975, the United Nations launched a 48 member intergovernmental body called The Commission on Transnational Corporations which is charged with drafting a code of conduct for transnational corporations. Their subgroups deal with accounting practices, corruption, data retrievals, original research, impact of multi's and conduct workshops.[20]

[29] In summary, when we realistically and rationally study the problem, we cannot help but believe there is nothing 'wrong' or 'bad' about corporations doing business on an international level.[21] The difficulty lies in their wielding an exorbitant amount of power. The approach to take, then, from both moral and practical stands seems to be obtaining general world agreement on regulating globals, as our concern about them falls back to their size.[22] There seems to be nothing wrong with a multinational corporation that is relatively small and controlled.[23] However, the worthiness of being little is slowly but surely being eroded as a part of the liberal economic ethic as the corporation and the state merge into one being.[24]

[30] What should be done? Specific legislation should be enacted in both host and client countries, as well as at the international level, to effectively control the size and activities of globals while concomitantly encouraging them to be innovative.[25] It implies recognition that the problem is much like pollution control; all nations must participate to optimize benefits and prevent any one organization or nation from being unduly disadvantaged. We are living in an international era and, realistically, it is not feasible to propose doing away with international corporations.

[31] The challenge, in which philosophers can play an important role, is drafting the guidelines for dealing with globals from an ethical point of view, recognizing that the end purpose of production and consumption is furthering the happiness of the entire world's population.[26] The problem is defining economic organization in such a way that

our physical and mental wellbeing are promoted to the greatest possible extent. It is recognizing that there is a difference between growth and equity and between growth and development.

Notes

1. As cited by Richard J. Barnett and Ronald E. Muller, *Global Reach* (Simon and Schuster, New York, 1974), p. 33.
2. See Lester R. Brown, *World Without Borders* (Random House, New York, 1972), especially Chapter II on the multinational corporation.
3. Abdul A. Said and Luiz R. Simmons (eds.), *The New Sovereigns: Multinational Corporations as World Powers* (Englewood Cliffs, New Jersey, Prentice-Hall, Inc., 1972).
4. Barnett and Muller, *Global Reach*, p. 89.
5. Donella H. Meadows et al., *The Limits to Growth* (The New American Library, Inc., Signet Books, New York, 1972).
6. Barnett and Muller, *Global Reach*, p. 118.
7. For more detail, see Robert Staiffer, *Nation-Building in a Global Economy: The Role of the Multinational Corporation* (Sage Publications, Inc., Beverly Hills, California, 1974).
8. A summary of the difficulties faced by multinationals is given by Joseph P. Cummings in 'Is the Fear Justified?' and Dion de Beer in 'What Multinationals Should Know'. Both are in the summer, 1977 *World* published by PMM & Co., pp. 8–10 and 11–17 respectively. A major conclusion is that comprehensive planning and reporting in a context of mutual trust and respect are needed for multinationals to fulfill their true role.
9. For example, when the global corporations invade a country, "available statistics indicate that the usual outcome is that the family business is sold off". Barnett and Muller, *Global Reach*, p. 139.
10. *Ibid.*, pp. 252–253.
11. Constance Holden, 'Futurism: Gaining a Toehold in Public Policy', *Science* 189 (1975), 120–124.
12. Barnett and Muller, *Global Reach*, p. 248. For more information on this theme, see Richard Barnett, *The Lean Years* (Simon and Schuster, New York, 1980).
13. See *Action UNDP*, United Nations, New York, May/June, 1977, p. 2.
14. Barnett and Muller, *Global Reach*, p. 261.
15. A number of books and articles have been written on business practice ethics. See for example, Frank Knight's *The Ethics of Competition* (George Allen and Unwin, London, 1951) or Marquis W. Childs and Douglas Cater, *Ethics in a Business Society* (Mentor Books, New York, 1963).
16. Gordon, Michael W., 'The Impact of the Multinational Corporations and the Third World', ed. by K.R. Simmonds, *Legal Problems of Multinationals* (British Institute of International and Comparative Law, London, 1977), pp. 21–42.
17. For a complimentary report see *The Impact of Multinational Corporations on Development and on International Relations*, U.N. Publication Sales No. E.74.11.A.5 (United Nations, New York, 1974). Another good reference is Raymond Vernon, *Storm Over the Multinationals* (Harvard Univ. Press, Cambridge, Mass., 1977).
18. See for example 'A Congressional-Parliamentary Draft Code of Principles on Multinational Enterprises and Governments', office of Congressman Sam M. Gibbons, U.S. House of Representatives, 1976. Activities and publications on multinationals are put out by the International Management and Development Institute, 2600 Virginia Ave. N.W., No. 905, Washington, D.C. 20037 in their bimonthly release *International Corporate Citizenship*.
19. For a summary of the U.N. document and the workshop see *Action UNDP*, United Nations, New York, May/June, 1977. Other periodicals on multi's are *Multinational Monitor*, Corporate Accountability Research Group, P.O. Box 19312, Washington, D.C. 20036, and *The New Internationalist*, 113 Atlantic Ave., Brooklyn, N.Y. 11201.
20. For a summary of the Commission's activities see 'Getting the Measure of the Transnationals', *Development Forum*, Volume V, No. 4, May, 1977, p. 2.
21. Ray Goldberg concludes "the evidence shows" there are many examples of the new breed of socially useful, as well as functionally practical, multinational corporations. *Am. J. Agr. Econ.* 63 (1981), 374.
22. The problem can be conceptualized in the framework similar to pollution control, i.e., no single

LDC will be hurt if all nations adopt the same regulations on globals, just as no one individual company will be disadvantaged with respect to the rest if all are subjected to the same controls. The difficulty arises when one company has an advantage, such as a large multi obtains favorable interest rates while a small company has to pay higher rates.

23. One way to bring about reduction in size is trustbusting'. This same principle could hold on an international level. For a good discussion on the United States situation in food, see Russell C. Parker, 'Antitrust Issues in the Food Industries', *Am. J. Agr. Econ.* 58 (1976), 854–860. For methodology, see Bruce W. Marion and Thomas L. Spoerleder, 'An Evaluation of the Economic Basis for Antitrust Policy in the Food Industry', *Am. J. Agr. Econ.* 58 (1976), 867–873.

24. The Honorable Ted Weiss of New York, for example, has argued that "the corporate state is not individualistic, it is collectivist to the extreme. It is not humanitarian, it is animalistic." See his speech 'Development of the Corporate State' given to the House of Representatives Wednesday, April 30, 1980, *Congressional Record* (126), p. 68.

25. The following suggestions are given to stimulate thought on worldwide control of globals. Certainly I do not possess the credentials for setting up complete guidelines on this complex issue, but at least the following list brings some ideas together and demonstrates that economics cannot be separated from ethics. Many of these proposals are being incorporated in draft legislation in the United States and the EEC.

    (1) Demand competitive bids when appropriate, rather than depending on a brand name.
    (2) Set worldwide minimum wages through international corporations.
    (3) Fight for stronger bargaining on investment, such as time limits and pricing control.
    (4) Look toward worldwide bargaining in which the LDC's form committees to study proposals of global corporations so that one G.C. cannot play one country against another.
    (5) Use the United Nations and congress of various countries to develop a good set of standards, ethics and procedures for relations between multinationals and nation-states.
    (6) Consider strikes as a last resort as this diminishes confidence from potential investors, especially smaller ones.
    (7) Place greater emphasis on auditing global corporations.
    (8) Organize and coordinate international trade plans with other LDC's.
    (9) Place greater emphasis on common market policies.
    (10) Set up rules and improve coordination between the internal revenue service of foreign countries and tax offices in local countries.
    (11) A novel approach—If you can't lick 'em, join 'em. The LDC's could create their own global corporations just as the Union of Banana Exporters is doing in Central America. See *Action UNDP* (United Nations, New York), May-June, 1977, p. 1, for information on COMUNBANA.
    (12) Promote 'Nadarism'.
    (13) Encourage relatively small businesses in the developed countries to invest in LDC's, especially by showing how invested capital can be repatriated.
    (14) Find ways to keep more finance capital in the country. Do not allow large foreign companies to borrow finance capital on local money markets, but help small foreign companies in obtaining loans.
    (15) Increase coordination between LDC's and developed countries on the problem of globals rather than fomenting diametric opposition.

26. For more detail, see Martin A. Alugbuo, 'American Multinational Corporations: What Role Could They Play in Fostering Good Business Ethics in the Lesser Developed Countries?' Staff Paper Series No. 160–77, Unemployment and Underemployment Institute, Southern University and A&M College, Baton Rouge, Louisiana, 1977. Caterpillar Tractor Co. has published *A Code of Worldwide Business Conduct*, Peoria, Ill., 1977. The Interreligious Task Force on U.S. Food Policy presented their view in 'Multinational Corporations and Global Development', *Hunger* (24), July, 1980.

Questions

1. This essay is over thirty years old.
   (a) Has anything changed with respect to Simpson's description of the status quo (paras 1–6)?
   (b) Does it appear that the fears of Schumpeter and Galbraith (para 7) were justified?
2. Do you think the best, most-likely-to-be-successful, road to world peace is economic (the global shopping centre, international trade) or political (nation states of tradition and geography)? Or some third option?
3. Do you agree with Simpson's comments in para 11 about global corporations?
4. Many of the current free trade agreements were made since Simpson wrote this paper. What relevance do such agreements have on his comments of para 14?
5. (a) Despite Simpson's note that "globals cannot be lumped together" (para 22) and that "it will be difficult to generalize as each country is different" (para 11), perform a utilitarian analysis of multinational corporations, listing and weighting their benefits and drawbacks. (Don't restrict yourself to para 17—Simpson speaks of good and bad consequences of MNCs throughout.)
   (b) Is your end evaluation compatible with your (i) intuition? Is it compatible with your view of (ii) rights? (iii) justice? (iv) virtuous behaviour?
6. What is Simpson's answer to the question "how big is too big?"
7. What would you include in the legislative guidelines for globals that Simpson suggests as a solution?

Ethical Value-Added: Fair Trade and the Case of Café Femenino[*]

J.J. McMurtry

ABSTRACT: This article engages various critiques of Fair Trade, from its participation in commodification to providing a cover for "Fair-washing" corporations, and argues that Fair Trade has the potential to answer the challenges contained within them if and when it initiates an ongoing process of developing the "ethical value-added" content of the label. This argument is made in a number of ways. First, by distinguishing between economic and human development impacts and ethics, this

[*] *Journal of Business Ethics* 2009 (86): 27–49.

article argues that these impacts are necessary but not sufficient conditions for ethical trade. Second, it engages the question of the possibility of ethical practice in economics generally; developing the idea that when economics is concerned with securing the material basis of a broad range of life capacities it becomes ethical. Third, Fair Trade practice itself is examined from this standpoint, and is conceived of as both comprising a promising ethical value-added practice as well as posing a problem in its current formulation that the framework of ethical value-added can help understand and resolve. Finally, an examination of these theoretical ideas in practice is undertaken through a case study of Café Femenino, a Fair Trade coffee produced in Peru. In conclusion it is argued that for Fair Trade to build upon its economic and human impacts, and therefore remain a meaningful ethical and economic alternative to corporate capitalism and globalization, it must distinguish itself clearly in ethics from those market relations it wishes, explicitly or implicitly, to challenge.

Introduction

[1] Since its formal inception with Max Havelaar in Holland in 1988, the Fair Trade label has made considerable inroads into public and market consciousness based on the perceived strength of its economic and human development impacts.[1] These impacts have largely been framed in terms of the creation of "fair" economic benefits to producers in the economic South through access to markets and distribution networks for their goods in the economic North. Economic gains, including a social premium built into price, are then invested by producers in a variety of community economic development projects, such as schools, wells, roads and transportation. There is a little doubt that the claims made by and for the Fair Trade label in terms of relative market success and community economic development are to a significant degree justifiable given the range of these impacts.[2] These are made all the more remarkable when one considers the fact that the Fair Trade "brand" has existed for less than twenty years and had no access to standard start-up capital to initiate or sustain its development. Indeed, an optimistic observer would be forgiven for assuming that these economic and human development impacts will continue to expand as new Fair Trade products are added (such as quinoa and cotton), and that market penetration in the non-European economic North will follow a similar pattern of growth.

What is largely missing in both popular and academic discussions of Fair Trade impacts of this kind is a critical examination of the qualitative claims and results of this form of trade, which in fact are its defining feature. There are a number of questions to be asked along these lines. How directly are economic impacts and ethics related? Are these economic and human development impacts enough to justify the label of "fair," or should the bar be set higher for such claims? If so, on what grounds? Are there desirable impacts that are not contained in dominant conceptualizations of economic and human development? What contribution, if any, has Fair Trade made to ethical ideas and practices in economics? Finally, are the often-exploitative economic and social relations characterized by corporate globalization meaningfully altered when trade is conducted through Fair Trade channels, or do the same critiques of this internationalized economic process apply (e.g., Goldsmith and Mander, 1996; Klein, 2000)? In other words, in an assumed climate of strong market-utilitarian ethics and "no-alternative" market solutions, can Fair Trade production and distribution be argued to constitute not just "better" practical human and economic development impacts, but also to form an ethical [2] economic practice which alters, challenges, or, in its proponents' strongest claims, exist in opposition to, the dominant economic order?[3]

[3] This article will engage these questions, and argue that Fair Trade has the potential to answer the challenges contained within them *if and when it initiates an ongoing process of developing the "ethical value-added" content of the label*. I have developed this concept to highlight a process towards development of more inclusive economic and social practices within existing economic and social forms, a process that Fair Trade might be considered the most developed articulation.[4] Like the concept of economic value-added, where the focus is on understanding how the economic value of production is captured at each stage of its production, ethical value-added focuses on how the ethical value of a good or practice is developed *throughout each stage of the production process*. The argument here is that to establish and maintain ethical status there should be an on-going process of improving the ethical (including human development and economic) impacts of a particular economic activity. The process of ethical value-added improvements to trade have in fact been the distinguishing feature of Fair Trade, as well as other "conscious commodities," so far. Thus, conversely, when this process is halted, or even reversed, the Fair Trade label is morally undermined and loses its ethical status even if some positive impacts remain.[5] This question of reversal has become more urgent recently as the idea of an "ethical" or "fair" label has come under threat from the mass-market push towards weaker standards and corporate self-monitored labels rather than broad adherence to Fair Trade principles. This push is only possible because the absence of a clear ethical framework in Fair Trade has left open the space for purely for-profit market organizations to claim inclusion in the ethical "brand" market.

[4] In order to understand the concept of ethical value-added as it relates to Fair Trade, this article will proceed with the following sections of analysis. First, economic and human development impacts and ethics are unwound from each other, with these impacts considered finally *as necessary but not sufficient conditions* for ethical value-added. Second, the question of the possibility of ethical practice in economics is engaged, developing the idea that when economics is concerned with securing the material basis of a broad range of life capacities it becomes ethical. Third, Fair Trade itself is examined from this standpoint, and is conceived of as both a promising example of ethical value-added as well as posing a problem in practice that the framework of ethical value-added can help understand and resolve. Finally, an examination of these theoretical ideas in practice is undertaken through a case study of Café Femenino, a Fair Trade women-run coffee-producing organization in Peru.

Distinguishing Ethics from Impacts

[5] There are four basic issues that highlight the need to distinguish between economic and human development impacts and ethics in economics. The first of these is the recognition that raw numbers of either people involved in, or of developmental capacities created by, Fair Trade goods do not alone justify this trade's ethical claims. Simply put, economic activity is not *necessarily* ethical activity, even if it is a basic condition of realized ethics. Conceived of in the framework of dominant economic practice, if participation in markets, infrastructure development, and waged labour were themselves a priori ethical, then any increase in economic activity, for example the movement of child activity from play to sweatshops, could be seen as "fair" or "just" economics or trade.[6] While such a claim is patently absurd, this has not stopped *its premise of the a*

priori ethical nature of the capitalist market from propping up many arguments within the literature, including an extreme version wherein Fair Trade is itself criticized in some cases as unethical because it eliminates competitive advantage and the "natural" functioning of the market[7] (Maseland and de Vaal, 2002). This assumption in the literature is reinforced by its prevalence in the broader mass media and the work of "ethical" market advocates, such as Jeffery Sachs. Rather than accepting this assumption, the broader question of ethics must be asked of Fair Trade *alongside the question of economic impacts*. For example, one might question the *assumed* ethical premise that greater market participation of actors in the economic South through commodity trade is an economic good given that it maintains, and even encourages, replacement of sustainable and diversified agricultural production with wildly fluctuating and often environmentally destructive mono-crops. However, this kind of questioning has not generally occurred in the literature since the market, and its measurable economic impacts, are largely assumed to underwrite Fair Trade's ethical claims.[8]

[6] The problem of ethics in Fair Trade is however, not limited to the assumption of the a priori moral nature of capitalist market economics. There is also an ethical "glow" that Fair Trade is assumed to give to the trade channels, prices, and business structures of the Northern distributors of these commodities. That is, a business in the North is often assumed to be "more" ethical simply by participating in Fair Trade, despite the fact that their historical role has been minimal at best in initiating the production of these goods that in turn generally comprise only a tiny percentage of their business.[9] Such "Fair-washing" is achieved on the grounds that participating corporations have created positive economic impacts in the South, while in fact these distributors maintain questionable ethical practices in their global organizations and their majority methods of sourcing have generally created the *lived impacts* which form the basic argument *for* Fair Trade (e.g., Starbucks).[10] ... [T]he distinction between trade that is "fair" and trade which is merely "Fair-washing" is therefore crucial for the ethics of the Fair Trade movement and label. However, this distinction can only be made on the basis of a broad-based conception of ethics that extends *beyond* economic impacts to a framework increasingly inclusive of the range of issues confronting producers in the economic South *as well as* the conditions of distribution and consumption in the economic North.

[7] In addition, the ethical nature of Fair Trade may be questioned from the perspective of consumption. Fair Trade is assumed to lend an ethical validity to the process of consumption of luxury items (coffee, chocolate, tea, bananas, etc.) because this consumption increases economic and human development impacts in the economic South (see endnote 8). However, there are clearly a number of issues here. First, there is the conception of consumption itself as a good. That is, Fair Trade avoids the issue of the amount of consumption that is ethical; an issue which any claim to ethical economic production must address. Specifically, the *consumption* of particular Fair Trade goods is not considered for the negative impacts that their production has on the people and ecosystems that produce them. The demand and consumption of goods in the economic North should at least be questioned ethically from the perspective of their negative social and environmental impacts as well as their positive ones. Second, Fair Trade promotes the belief that it is the citizens of the economic North who, as consumers, are (and in some versions should be) responsible for creating, through market activity, developmental infrastructure in the economic South. (e.g., Waridel, 2002, Ch. 6).[11] This assumption

overlooks the possibility of the state taking on the role of a re-distributor of wealth and guarantor of "fair" trade, both nationally and internationally through legal agreements, while at the same time giving consumption based on personal choice in the market an ethical pass. Again, the focus on economic and human development impacts that has dominated Fair Trade discourse does not generally address any of these substantial questions on which its ethical claims at least partially depend.[12]

[8] There is at least one further problem. Since the economic and human development impacts of Fair Trade are broadly recognized as justifying its ethical claims, almost all commentators and actors assume these ethics to be central to the label's success in marketing terms. Ethics is, in important ways, Fair Trade's identity or "brand". Given the above problems with conceptualizing impacts as ethics, there is a circular argument at the heart of most Fair Trade literature—by increasing market economic activity and thereby impacts for producers, Fair Trade is ethical, and it is this ethical nature that increases its market activity. One can see this circular reasoning in play through the variety of ethical "goods" that are attributed to Fair Trade production and consumption without detailed critical justification of these claims. For example, Geoff Moore claims that "empowerment has become a fundamental element of fair trade not only in its own right, but also as a means to enabling producers to deal directly with mainstream buyers," yet "empowerment in its own right" is not explained or defined by Moore, rather, this quote is followed by a series of figures outlining economic impacts (Moore, 2004, p. 80).[13] The problem of this circular reasoning is substantive since even those who are critical of claims for the alternative nature of Fair Trade agree that the success of these commodities is based upon the *belief* that they create "fairness" and even economic justice in international economic relations through trade (e.g., Blowfield, 1999; Ferrie and Hira, 2006; Low and Davenport, 2005).[14] This assumption is bolstered by the fact that those who discuss the nascent ethical challenge to market relations contained within Fair Trade (e.g., Crowell, 2006; Goodman, 2004; Jaffee et al., 2004) do not engage in a sustained examination of the content of the ethics of the label.[15] This circular reasoning around Fair Trade ethics and market activity therefore must be questioned alongside the particular problems of market ethics, corporate "Fairwashing", lionized consumption and the *perception* of ethics in Fair Trade on the part of consumers and commentators. This can be done by getting behind these particular issues by (re)turning to the question of how ethics is conceived of in contemporary economic activity.

Can Economics Be Ethical?

The problems outlined above can be conceptualized as, on the one hand, that there is a belief that Fair Trade is deeply provocative in its implicit ethical critique of the dominant economic paradigm, a belief that seems to be increasingly appealing to consumers and commentators. Yet on the other hand, this challenge to the existing economic paradigm maintains a policy solution of commodity-centred trade and consumption patterns that assumes *at its base* the capitalist market. Consequently, while most Fair Trade literature is constructed along the lines of a debate between those supportive (e.g., Jaffee et al., 2004; Raynolds, 2000; Taylor, 2005; Waridel, 2002) and critical (e.g., Bryant and Goodman, 2004; Johnston, 2002; Maseland and De Vaal, 2002) of Fair Trade's role in developing the practice of global economic justice through the impacts mentioned above, the underlying *economic* framework upon which these rest is assumed by all "sides" rather than developed. [9]

Clearly, as outlined above, Fair Trade practice and theory needs to be judged not solely on its economic and human development impacts, but also on its ability to substantiate its moral claim to provide "fairness" through market, or other, means. For if there is no substantive ethical economic content provided in defence of Fair Trade, then its economic and development impacts can be seen as marketing phenomenon substantially indistinguishable from a myriad of possible "socially conscious" products like an "organic Twinkie" (Joan Dye Gussow's term) which claim to provide some ethical good but in fact continue the conditions of production which created the need for that good.

[10] In order to engage in an examination of the ethics of Fair Trade then, the deeply problematic and fundamentally assumed frameworks of contemporary economic activity must be analysed *as ethical objects themselves* as opposed to "norm free" institutional arrangements (e.g., Friedman, 1993; Habermas 1984, 1987). This poses a problem for the researcher (let alone the practitioner), given the dichotomous and underdeveloped nature of dominant understandings of market ethics from Marx through Hayek to Friedman. When market relations are questioned ethically, the debate has tended to be polarized between those who believe the market is always-already ethical (i.e., as with Market Utilitarianism, Libertarianism), those who believe the market is a value-free economic tool (e.g., Habermas, Communitarianism), and those who believe the market is a necessarily unethical system to be overcome, usually through social revolution (e.g., Anarchism and Communism). What is crucial to all three positions however is *the belief that economics in the contemporary context is only and always capitalist and therefore all economic activity is substantively the same*. Furthermore, the material economic *form of production* (i.e., ever increasing resource extraction, industrial production, and consumption) *developed by capitalism is assumed in present and future production as economic and good*, even when the process is seen to be in need of ethical direction by the state or through revolution. As a result of this one-sided *productivist* understanding of economics, the *practical* versions of these philosophies tend in their policy solutions towards this *a priori* position—from the religiously neo-liberal "no alternative" policies of various parties of the "right" or "centre", to the varieties of European Democratic Socialism which accept capitalist market operations while arguing that their effects can and should be modified marginally by "third way" social programmes, to the "twenty-first century socialism" of Hugo Chavez which is attempting a state and personality-directed "Bolivarian Revolution" of production and ownership in the name of the citizens of Venezuela based on an economy almost wholly reliant on its production of raw material for the oil-addicted capitalist economies.[16] There is, in short, a deficit of conceptions of ethical economics that are not reliant on the form, practice, or theory of the capitalist market.

Fair Trade is no exception to this problem in [11] either practice or theory. Much like the positions outlined above, it overlooks or underplays the role of existent non-market economic relations as an ethical space from which moral economic alternatives can be built and life-needs of the people met—the ideal focus of all economic[17] activity. It thereby continues the dominant view that commodified relations are the only relationships of economic and historical value (McMurtry, 2001). In other words, the possibility of consciously articulating the ethical framework of existent "moral economies" (Thompson, 1991a) as building blocks of understanding and thereby developing economic and political regimes built on human life-needs is overlooked (McMurtry, 2002). Traditional ethical economic theory and alternative economic practices such as Fair Trade *tend* therefore to assume the capitalist market economy as a historically developing, ethically neutral process of increasingly rationalized exchange rather than as a system that carries within it various questionable normative assumptions.[18] Thus even though Fair Trade actors and analysts can be (and are) critical of the inequalities of the capitalist system in its distribution of economic benefit, they do not usually develop an analysis of *the functions of the system itself* as a fundamentally flawed form of economic organization. When they do, they rely on the existing paradigms outlined above and the assumption of the nature of economic activity. However, if this is so, on what basis can a critical examination of economic ethics and Fair Trade be launched?

[12]   This article argues against the above trend and for a conception of the productive framework of any society as being in fact irreducibly ethical. Analysis of these ethics, specifically economic ethics, has to occur from a life-centred value framework focused on meeting vital needs and developing capacities as opposed to producing profit which is the life-blind logic of dominant economics (McMurtry, 2002). By using this position heuristically, one can examine economic processes (in this case Fair Trade) from a more revealing perspective. For example, those Fair Trade commodities (coffee, coco, handicrafts, tea, bananas, etc.), so far developed are almost exclusively built upon the colonially imposed economic relations of a raw material and "curio" (e.g., handicraft) producing South and an economic value adding and consuming North. While one cannot change these relations overnight, neither can one simply give them a moral "pass" when examining relationships of economic fairness and trade. Yet, the literature is remarkably mute on the immoral nature of these historical relationships that are extended by Fair Trade, despite the fact that it is the *consequences* of these unequal relationships that comprises the *raison d'être* for developing the first Fair Trade products. For Fair Trade to be considered to be "fair" or "just," then, there must be an articulation of, and action towards creating, other, more sustainable systems of trade and economic production for the fulfilment of vital needs and human capacities. In other words, *there must be an ethical value-added component in its nature, from inception to strategic planning, which is increasingly responsive to issues of economic and social exclusion.*

Taking this point further one might examine [13] the problem, as identified by a number of authors (Fridell, 2007; Johnston, 2002; Low and Davenport, 2005) and mentioned above, that within Fair Trade the Northern consumer's "ethical" duty seems to begin and end in the consumption of the products of the South. However when consumption is examined and engaged from a life-value perspective,[19] the ethics and assumptions of international trade and capitalism are brought more clearly into focus.[20] For example, with community need in mind one might critique the economic viability of raw material production without value-added components (e.g., plantation tea harvesting) as a recipe for long-term economic failure, human misery and pollution. The decision to produce commodity cash crops to be sold at below sustainable prices is not a free choice made by producers, but one which relies on unequal social, political and economic conditions that must be challenged. While Fair Trade recognizes that current market conditions create, sustain, and exacerbate these inequalities, they do not generally articulate a process by which a transition from existing conditions to a more ethical system of trade and consumption could be realized. Without recognition of the systemic, as opposed to the specific, inequalities of the market a sustained ethical economic claim cannot be identified. Production and consumption of goods produced in Fair Trade therefore cannot in itself support the ethical claims of the label. There must be a more developed conception of ethics in order to sustain these claims that challenge the assumed patterns of economic activity. Lest one believe that the argument here is for the development of unsustainable ethical regime based on abstract principles as opposed to economic realities, the developmental nature of the concept of ethical value-added should serve as a corrective. That is, what is argued for here is that organization both take on proven "best practices" (like those developed by Fairtrade Labelling Organizations International [FLO] and the International Federation for Alternative Trade [IFAT]) as well as *engrain the process of innovation and development of further best practices* in their organization structure and their partners in trade and production.

[14] Having outlined the problem of ethics for Fair Trade and the method with which the label will be heuristically examined (ethical value-added and life value), this article will now develop these issues. First the history and practice of Fair Trade ethics will be examined using these frameworks, and second an examination of a distinct Fair Trade initiative in Peru (which is currently being "exported" to other coffee producing regions)—Café Femenino—will be undertaken. In conclusion it will be argued that the new organizational structure represented by Café Femenino, while by no means ethically "pure," points the way forward to an "ethical value-added" concept of Fair Trade through its conscious recognition and targeting of the economic and social issues of marginalized women in both the economic North and South.

Fair Trade: Promise and Problem

[15] In order to develop an understanding of how the practice of ethics in Fair Trade emerged (both as promise and problem), an examination of the historical lineage of the label must be undertaken.

Generally, the ethics of Fair Trade have been built upon the foundations of previous social and "ethical consumerism" movements (e.g., Jaffee et al., 2004, p. 172). These movements emerged as various social actors that questioned the conditions of production and the quality of consumable goods that increasingly flooded the markets of the economic North in the early twentieth century. This developing economic consciousness was the direct antecedent to the more familiar varieties of social, political and environmental activism that surged throughout the 1960s, 1970s and 1980s. Vegetarianism, anti-war activism, environmentalism, civil rights and feminism are just a few of the more famous of these movements, but just as important to the development of Fair Trade are the less recognized social justice development initiatives loosely organized under the umbrella term Alternative Trading Organizations (ATOs) (Dickson and Littrell, 1997).[21] What is important to identify is that these movements all attempt to make linkages between the movement in its activist form and the broader public as "consumer" using ethics as the motivational lever.[22] In important ways, Fair Trade is indebted to the techniques of these movements in that it attempts to solve social justice issues through economic means.

[16] Outside of ATOs, the food movement in its "organic" form is the most relevant of these precedents for Fair Trade because of its focus on the creation of consumer-based change through the development of an ethical product label.[23] Frontiers were opened up for "conscious commodities" or "ethical consumerism" by the mainstreaming of "organic" foods, providing the market space within which Fair Trade could grow. In fact, a significant component of Fair Trade produce, notably coffee, chocolate and tea, have incorporated the organic label on its products, demonstrating the symbiosis between the movements.[24] However, while

important in influencing the form and practice of labelling, Fair Trade's ethical claims are not based on this association with organics (which is merely a voluntarily added market and ethical value for some products), but rather on their development out of ATOs. These organizations, such as OXFAM, helped to establish the idea of "fair" trade by leveraging their social justice reputation to support the development of "alternative trade" products that returned to producers a significantly better price for their product. The aim was to make explicit the link between deplorable conditions for producers in the economic South and the low prices paid by consumers in the economic North, while at the same time providing an alternative "fair" product. It was this idea of "trade not aid" developed by these ATOs that inspired the idea of a Fair Trade label to encapsulate this issue and, in 1988, Max Havelaar was launched followed by a number of other labelling initiatives. These labels quickly began to work together and their relationship was formalized by the foundation of FLO International in 1997 and the 2002 launch of the Fair Trade certification logo with which many consumers have become familiar.[25] The ethical purpose of the label was clear; to create awareness of development issues and a real choice for consumers at the same time as money flowed back to producers to facilitate self-directed social and economic change.

[17] However, as markets expanded for Fair Trade goods so too did the problem of continuing to highlight the ethics of the label while engaging with organizations built upon dominant economic practice. The problem is that the Fair Trade labels emerged in part to *encourage production and consumption of goods* to create impacts in the economic South. What *has come* to distinguish Fair Trade goods is therefore not the quality or uniqueness of the particular product itself (coffee or clothing, e.g.), or a marketing campaign in the traditional sense, but rather the *idea* that consumption of these goods contributes to ethical development. In other words, the label, not the unique content of the particular product itself, pushes demand.[26] However, the label on its own does not clearly reveal production process for consumers, nor does it in itself educate, two key ethical claims of Fair Trade. Thus, while the Fair Trade label provides convenience by removing the need for time-consuming ethical research and activism (which is provided "free" by non-profit organizations as a social good or borne by the producer through licensing fees), the consequence is that the general consumer can be unaware of the issues that drive the label. This is especially true if the consumer is purchasing their product at some remove from the Fair Trade movement, such as at a Big Box store. Since this education is one of the primary ethical value added features of Fair Trade, the label confronts a paradox—its success appears to reduce its ethical impact when consumption stands in for ethics.

[18] The question arises, if the label cannot on its own educate consumers, what has been the complementary conduit for its ethics to be realized? Historically, ethics have been achieved not only through the label but also through the site of distribution, from the health food store to the alternative-trading outlet, the church basement to the solidarity group. These contexts enable ethical learning through direct interpersonal interaction between consumer and distributor, as well as within these organizations if they are organized democratically (worker cooperatives). However, for ethical goods to reach consumers *within a capitalist market system on a mass scale* there has to be distribution through mass-market sites and supply channels. As a result, while outlets of distribution, such as health food stores, independent coffee roasters, or cooperative buying clubs, were originally a central part of Fair Trade goods' educative function (as

well as to some degree guarantors of ethical value), this role has been, perhaps unconsciously, undermined in exchange for increased impacts through sales. These sites solidified the ethical idea of Fair Trade not only because they are information-laden contexts, but also because *consumers had to actively choose to participate* (such as mail ordering Bridgehead coffee or seeking out distribution sites) in the process of obtaining the product itself. Without this requirement of a modicum of activity by the consumer, the ethical component of the label in terms of education in the economic North is diminished and even reversed while the economic and human development impacts in the economic South, in the short term, increased.

[19] Much of contemporary Fair Trade literature overlooks this crucial ethical value-added feature of distribution in a blanket critique of the commodification process perceived to be at the core of Fair Trade's success (i.e., Bryant and Goodman, 2004; Fridell, 2007). For example, Bryant and Goodman (2004) in their influential article define Fair Trade as "a 'solidarity-seeking' *commodity* culture in order to emphasize the distinctive focus on social justice through fair labour and exchange practices" (Bryant and Goodman, 2004, p. 344, emphasis added). For Bryant and Goodman what distinguishes fair trade is that it is a "consumption-centred political strategy" which commodifies resistance "insofar as protest over perceived environmental degradation or social injustice is expressed through the strategic manipulation of consumption practices and exchange relations" (Bryant and Goodman, 2004, p. 345). They continue by pointing out that while Fair Trade de-fetishizes the commodity by exposing the production to consumer chain, it also re-fetishizes through commodification of the "ethical" relationship. "And yet, ironically, through the very act of revealing the production–commodity–consumer relationship in its 'full glory,' the effect is to commodify, in turn, the ethical relationship deemed to be at the heart of fair trade—that is, small-scale farmers, producer cooperatives and 'sustainably' managed second nature" (Bryant and Goodman, 2004, p. 359). While there is much truth to the argument here, this framing of Fair Trade as consisting of commodified ethical relationships and transparency throughout the "production–commodity–consumer" trajectory of a "good," is only true if the distribution component of the label is short circuited by mass-market consumption and distribution through undemocratic, profit seeking corporations with no commitment to social and economic issues. As discussed above, Bryant and Goodman ignore the possibility of alternative structures of exchange for economics as ubiquitously conforming to the practices of market capitalism. However, by so doing they inadvertently raise the important point that to be ethical Fair Trade must actively engage products *in all phases of their economic life from production through distribution to consumption*. This is not an abstract demand placed on Fair Trade; it is the process out of which the label emerged historically and one that remains active in numerous distribution sites such as worker cooperative roasters and alternative trade outlets. The lack of awareness of the importance of distribution reveals the fact that Fair Trade practitioners and theorists have never been overly *concerned with ethical distribution or consumption in the economic North*. While Fair Trade's ethical strength may in fact rely upon maintaining and developing this component of trade, the focus on the label as its unifying feature has led to a situation in which the goal of consumer education has been usurped by the goals of consumer convenience and increasing sales.

[20] This change in focus has parallels in the economic South as the label has expanded its range of products. Varying rules for "fair" production has

lead to confusion over the basic parameters of Fair Trade practice itself. A brief case study is instructive here. Tea has traditionally been produced on plantations, whereas coffee grows best in mountainous, forested areas and has traditionally been produced by small independent producers. As a result, the development of the rules of production and distribution required to garner Fair Trade certification are notably distinct. FLO labelling requires that Fair Trade coffee must be produced by cooperatives or associations of small producers, whereas Fair Trade tea can be produced either by cooperatives or by "hired labour" (which dominates). FLO insists in the latter case that there must be "freedom of labour," which usually means organization through unions (FLO Standards, 2005a, b). In a hired labour situation, rather than the social premium going to a worker-owned economic institution it is given to a union body to be used solely for community benefit, not capital investment. The "fair trade premium goes directly back to the tea pickers themselves. For plantations, a committee called a Joint Body, elected by the workers, decides how these funds will be used to meet the community's needs. Both co-operatives and plantations have used the Fair Trade premiums to hire school teachers, build maternal health clinics, and bring electricity to their villages, among other projects" (Transfair Canada, n.d.). Furthermore, there are basic labour standards which must be met by the employer: no child under 15 employed, the workers can form unions, and salaries must be equal to or higher than the regional average or minimum wage (Transfair Canada, n.d.). On the surface it would seem as if despite the difference in practice the Fair Trade label is as consistent as possible in ensuring that similar ethical goals (i.e., worker control, social premium used for development, and increased community capacity) are achieved by Fair Trade, given the distinct historical conditions that exist for each product.

However, the problems resulting from these different standards are multifaceted. First there is no mechanism within Fair Trade to alter the conditions of production in either case towards increasingly ethical practices. Historical inequalities in terms of land-ownership and international trade (raw material versus value-added production) are therefore *solidified* in Fair Trade practice, with no incentive to change these economic realities. Second, there is a substantial distinction between a social premium that is directed towards developing an independent worker-controlled *economic* entity, as well as social development, and one that only focuses on social development.[27] Again, there is no mechanism to conceive of aiding in the development of democratic and autonomous producer controlled organizations in Fair Trade tea rather than accepting existing historical forms of production. Third, while the rules are clearly laid out for the producers by FLO, the label does not make this distinction in production conditions clear for the consumer in the economic North or explain why they are necessary, let alone enable them to meaningfully engage in the argument for why these forms of production are "more ethical" than other forms of production. In short, the ethical implications of these different types of production are significant for the producer, the consumer, and for the conception of ethics in economic activity.[28] These problems are a result of the fact that *there is no shared ethical framework upon which to develop an understanding of what constitutes fair, or unfair, conditions of production, nor is there a broader conception of ethical value-added to bridge current economic reality and a more ethical economic reality.* [21]

The problem within the Fair Trade labelling regime is further exacerbated by the activities of mass-market Northern distributors. Not only is there no ethical consistency as the product moves from "ethical" production to distribution, but also [22] the larger distributors of Fair Trade have developed parallel labels and "ethical" practices which serve to confuse the consumer and the issue of ethical trade further. While Starbucks is often, rightly, a target for this kind of critique given their market power and lead role in contentious labelling activities (i.e., their role in trying to secure trademark rights to Ethiopian heirloom coffee names) the issue does not end here with one corporation or trademark case (e.g., Foek, 2007; Fridell, 2007). Within Fair Trade there is no means of addressing the question of trans-national corporations themselves as arguably unethical legal institutions in a society marked by unequal distribution of economic power and goods, since the movement has come to significantly rely on these organizations as sites of distribution (Bakan, 2004; Glasbeek, 2002).

[23] The question then emerges why it is the producers in the economic South who have to conform to an externally imposed regime of monitoring while the often-questionable economic practices of distributors in the economic North are not subject to any parallel process. While this double standard is occasionally recognized in the literature, a concrete solution to it has not been substantively engaged. For example, Crane and Davies have recognized that "although the adoption of fair trade principles means that [distribution] companies [in the economic North] are bound by a strict code of practice governing decisions about their supply agreements, all aspects of decision making are not subject to strict external scrutiny and control" (Crane and Davies, 2003, p. 80). Thus, as these authors' case study of Day Chocolate demonstrates, Northern distributors can practice unethical behaviour in their own activities, such as making "considerable use of unpaid volunteer workers for routine tasks, many of whom seemed to be under the (false) impression that they were helping out a charity," all the while claiming to facilitate ethical consumption and production (Crane and Davies, 2003, p. 84). The consequences of this structural imbalance between Fair Trade in the economic North and economic South are serious given that it further obscures the educative role and ethical nature of Fair Trade for the consumer and producer. This imbalance could serve as an opportunity to conceptualize possibilities for the development of ethical value-added interventions. For example, some in the literature have argued for an extension of Fair Trade to Northern production (Jaffee et al., 2004, p. 171): "we suggest that a more expansive application of the term fair trade to encompass agro-food initiatives within both North and South as well as *between* North and South has considerable analytic and practical utility. Fair trade, we argue, is not necessarily *fair* trade." While domestic Fair Trade in the North and South is an exciting idea, the means by which it would be distinguished from existing trade has as yet not been extensively articulated either practically or ethically.[29]

[24] This problem of clarity around Fair Trade practice combined with *a priori* acceptance of market practice has led to confusion about the distinction between Fair Trade and "regular" trade, within the literature and amongst Fair Trade advocates. One can think of the common "Freudian Slip" which substitutes free trade for fair trade in casual conversation that occurs with alarming regularity as an example.[30] This is not just a problem of occasional speech inversion, or even always a conceptual mistake on the part of the speaker, as the Fair Trade literature often makes the connection between the two explicit (Dobson, 1993; MacMaolain, 2002; Maseland and de Vaal, 2002; Parrish et al., 2005). For example, Dobson argues that there is an increasing convergence between free and fair trade based on an increasing global trade awareness: "The economics of free trade is becoming entwined with the ethics

of fair trade as the tradition of GATT—as a tool for rich nations—is exposed" (Dobson, 1993, p. 574).[31] The question of *how* the ethical economics of Fair Trade (i.e., premium and stable pricing, low interest capital investment, long-term contracts, and sustainable production practices in many cases) can coexist unproblematically with the market economics of "free trade" (i.e., profit maximization through constant cost reduction especially in labour, risk of capital flight, just-in-time production, and avoidance of labour and environmental standards) is unclear. Without a clear conception of the ethical purpose of Fair Trade, such confusion is almost inevitable.

[25] This problem has become entrenched in the literature over time. For example, LeClair (2002, pp. 949, 950) defines Fair Trade (or alternative trade) as "the marketing of products at greater than free market prices" even though it is "not entirely clear what constitutes a 'fair' price for the export of developing countries." Again the definitional framework is misleading, based solely on market parameters as opposed to ethical conceptions or, in this case, even human development goals. The price point differential highlighted by LeClair, while a common perception based on a belief in the efficiency of the free market, is both demonstrably not true (what is a free market price? Some specialty non-Fair Trade coffee for example is marketed at a higher price through the "free market") and, more importantly, obscures the social aspects of the model which translates premiums into non-market goods such as education and health care as opposed to shareholder profit. The social aspect of Fair Trade is thereby eliminated from view by the notion that the only activities that producer groups participate in are export market-focused. Thus LeClair (2002, p. 950) can argue that Fair Trade is "conducted largely by producer groups that provide a variety of services to their members, such as marketing, product development, financing, and distribution services." Market ethical discourse again obscures the very thing that makes Fair Trade distinct. In short, because there is no *consistent definitional framework for Fair Trade as an ethical practice* there is no means by which its forms on the ground and across commodities can be evaluated.

What should be clear is that the focus of ethics [26] in Fair Trade cannot rely solely on the impacts of its specific practice, but requires a developed understanding of the process of creating fairness in trade. Part of this depends on the extent to which the ability to define the conditions of production is controlled by producers in the economic South. That is, the conditions of Fair Trade practice should at least be partially the result of the self-directed and democratically decided developmental trajectory of the producers themselves, as opposed to the marketing of already existing conditions of poverty as comprising ethical trade.[32] This recognition returns us more urgently to the question of understanding the positive ethical framework of this label. An admirable attempt at such a framework is made by Waridel (2002), who argues that, despite fluctuation in practice, there are minimum conditions of production for Fair Trade:

> a fair-trade product must be bought from democratically organized small-scale producers at a price that will provide them with a decent standard of living. The purchasing must be as direct as possible in order to prevent speculation and to cut out unnecessary intermediaries. Southern partners must have access to credit from their Northern counterparts and both parties must be encouraged to develop long-term relationships. Production techniques must be environmentally friendly and the producer organizations must be democratically managed. (Waridel, 2002, p. 94)

[27] However, within this ambitious, impact-centred view of Fair Trade as economic South focused production there is a great deal of ambiguity since the terms employed (e.g., "decent standard of living" or "environmentally friendly") are contested in meaning and practice. For example, Tim Hortons, a large coffee chain in Canada, argues that it achieves all of Waridel's desired impacts (although "working directly with the growers" is substituted for "democratic management") through its coffee sustainability programme (Tim Hortons, n.d.; Schroeder, 2005). These claims are not unique, as Sue Mecklenburg, Starbucks Vice-President of Business Practices, states, "Starbucks doesn't purchase 100 percent of its coffee as fair-trade certified, but 100 percent of the coffee we buy is under conditions that are fair to farmers" (Rogers, 2004). Clearly the conditions need to be clarified if this type of "Fair-washing" is to be challenged.

[28] Waridel's framework also does not directly confront the problem that the economic impacts corporations have, if this is the only measure of ethics, will always outstrip smaller distributors. As Paul Rice, CEO of TransFair USA, explains, "If a corporate giant roasts a million pounds of fair-trade coffee in one year, they are still doing far more than some of the smaller 100-percent roasters will in their entire history" (Rogers, 2004). There is no inclusion of the distribution of Fair Trade goods in Waridel's framework. Finally, in this conception, the economic North has no ethical duty but to provide credit and distribution. In short, this economic impact focused view of Fair Trade is epitomized by a focus on economic indicators and development as the essence of Fair Trade. Yet as outlined above, to continue to survive Fair Trade must develop an explicit ethical response to the discourse of assumed market framework to expose the "Fair-washing" claims of multinationals that create the conditions for Fair Trade in the first place. If not, the concept falls into the capitalist market framework of prioritizing market share and expansion instead of ethical value.

[29] How then might one build upon what Waridel outlines above—those clear, ethical, as opposed to market, goals that should serve as guiding principles for the Fair Trade movement?[33] While Southern producers have had and should continue to have the central voice in constructing these principles, they cannot be solely responsible for setting up international standards for fair economic production. The market and political power of producers in the economic South is not sufficient to make these changes, nor can they be held responsible for creating the conditions within which they struggle. Northern citizens must be involved in moving the debate and practice further than it is currently. The options presented in the literature so far however have been two-fold, ignoring this possibility of involving the economic North in the Fair Trade process. The choices have been constructed as either state-controlled labelling of Fair Trade to ensure ethical consistency, or a reconceptualization of the labelling initiatives providing either more flexible or rigid standards on producers. The state-focused position, such as that of MacMaolain, makes the argument that Fair Trade labelling is, lacking a statedeveloped standard, only self-imposed and therefore subject to abuse. "Only legislative intervention, creating a standard voluntary, legally supported and accountable social label, can realistically achieve that aim [i.e., to improve the working conditions of those presently exploited]" (MacMaolain, 2002, pp. 295–296). Since "there is currently no legal definition of what constitutes fairtrade," this argument continues, the state is the only agent to fill that gap (MacMaolain, 2002, p. 310). While it may be the ultimate goal of Fair Trade to enshrine principles of Fair Trade through the state, the example of organics give one pause

when considering this option. That is, like independent control of the Fair Trade label, corporate demand has created constant pressure on the content of organic labelling whenever it has been legislated, with the lowest common denominator often serving as the default position. The argument here is that the option available to Fair Trade which has the chance to carve new ground and avoid this corporate pressure is to *raise the ethical value-added of its products and enshrine the process of an ever more inclusive label into the "brand" itself.* This of course must happen on the ground first for it ever to be considered as policy. It is to this possibility that we now turn, using the example of Café Femenino.

The Case of Café Femenino

[30] Coffee has been grown and harvested in the Andean foothills of Agua Azul in Northern Peru for centuries. This is an area of Peru that, like so many other coffee producing regions around the world, has a long history of economic destitution and social inequality. For example, the average per-capita income in this region is about USD $1,300.00, but this is much lower for coffee producers (Hoagland, 2005), and it is estimated that the women of Agua Azul are at anywhere from a 40% to 70% risk of sexual assault even though they are married often between the ages of 12 and 16 (Café Femenino Foundation, n.d.; Planet Bean Coffee, n.d.). However, out of these difficult social relations (made all the more imposing by the isolation of communities by the rugged terrain) has emerged an innovation in Fair Trade that demonstrates the potential of the conception of ethical value-added.

[31] Café Femenino is the brand name given to Fair Trade coffee produced in these foothills by cooperatively organized women on land that they own. The women have been able in its short existence to turn the social capital raised from sales of their unique "brand" into a number of community development initiatives, such as new transportation routes, a project for women's healthcare, women's self-esteem projects, community literacy, and a variety of community committees (e.g., a Milk Committee to ensure distribution of fresh milk to community members) (Moore, 2004).[34] The focus of these projects is not just on improvements to the economic infrastructure of the community, but to its social fabric as well. For example, this model of production and social development has inspired the youth of the community to stay in their communities and participate in their own well being not just through work but also through participation in social development projects such as the self-esteem meetings. As Isobel La Torre,[35] an organizer who helped found Café Femenino, explains, "The majority of the women who participate are under 35 years of age. In other words, there is an important incorporation of young and medium-mature women" (Moore, 2004).

While these achievements are impressive, they [32] are not in themselves unique in Fair Trade practice. What is unique is that Café Femenino provides an extra two cents a pound *on top of the Fair Trade premium* that goes directly to female producers, who decide on its use in the community (Café Femenino Foundation, n.d.).[36] This has given women in the communities an independent economic role far greater than they have historically held, and one that is distinct from other male producers of Fair Trade coffee in the region. All of this means that, compared to "normal" coffee producers, the women of Café Femenino make 17 cents more per pound of coffee produced, which is a difference of about 30% (Hoagland, 2005), and have received extra development money, tens of thousands of dollars, from the Café Femenino Foundation on top of this (Café Femenino Foundation, n.d.). The impact of this difference can be demonstrated in what the members of Café Femenino have chosen to use these extra funds for. Their focus has been on improving conditions in the household, such as more efficient cooking spaces and home/market gardens, which in turn benefits the community (Moore, 2004).

[33] However, the improvements for women are not limited just to the coffee producing communities. Café Femenino has constructed itself to have impacts on the communities in which it is distributed in the economic North. That is, unique to Café Femenino in Fair Trade practice, an additional 2 cents a pound is collected by the roasters/distributors in the economic North to go towards a women's shelter in the community where the coffee is sold. Café Femenino mandates further, female participation in distribution in the economic North through requiring that a woman must sign the contract for the Northern partner (Hoagland, 2005). By adding these levels of income, by focusing on a socially and economically marginalized group in both producing and consuming regions on top of the usual benefits accrued to producers under Fair Trade, Café Femenino has engaged in a process of ethical value-added, adding to the minimum requirements of Fair Trade from production to consumption. It has, perhaps most importantly amongst these additions, made steps towards including the economic North in the ethical process of Fair Trade.

[34] These claims of uniqueness can be slightly tempered by the fact that Café Femenino is not alone in the world of Fair Trade as an organization that focuses on the social and economic well-being of women in producing nations. For example, in Nepal the Fair Trade Group provides its marketing services for handicrafts to a majority of women; PREDA Fair Trade[37] in the Philippines helps women and children by selling their handicrafts and dried fruit, and National Association of Women Organizations in Uganda (NAWOU) focuses on handicraft production whose artisans are almost entirely women (LeClair, 2002, p. 951). However, despite the surface similarity of a shared focus on women, all of these other organizations focus on *traditional* women's work such as food and handicraft preparation, whereas Café Femenino focuses on challenging male-dominated land ownership, which is culturally rooted, and on creating a central role for women in the business development of the world's second most valuable commodity, coffee.[38] As La Torre explains, "In the production, the women have always been involved. The part in which they have not had a part is in the sale of the product" (Moore, 2004). Importantly, the developments of female landownership and control of production from planting through sales emerged from the women themselves. This came about through the relative crisis in the price and markets for organic coffee in the 1990s and early 2000s (Moore, 2004). La Torre recalls the process of conceiving Café Femenino in the following way: "In 2003, during the reunion [of women—a yearly event], we discussed this proposal to separate the coffee, of course we didn't have the brand but we had the idea and we had a system to guarantee the consumer that the coffee is grown by the women." When La Torre brought this concept to Vancouver-based Organic Produce Trading Company (OPTCO) on behalf of the women producers, the idea came to realization. La Torre however attributes the idea of a specific brand to market this separated coffee to consumers in the economic North to OPTCO which: "saw the possibility of the brand and an additional premium that would serve as an incentive for the women" (Moore, 2004). In sum, while other women-focused Fair Trade organizations exist, one can consider Café Femenino unique within Fair Trade for its entry of women into economic areas over which historically they had no control, entry that is a result of self-development of existing ethical trade forms and based on critical

self-assessment of both social conditions and the current economic climate.

[35] Critical, therefore, for the development of Café Femenino is the fact that the women did not create the infrastructure of trade from the ground up; they built from already existing organizations and thereby added value to the community's capacities. This type of development is not unique in form in Fair Trade, but in practice there are important developments in that these organizations continue to add ethical as well as economic value as a matter of purpose and survival. Three tiers of cooperative organization—CECANOR, CICAP and PROASSA—had already organized the organic coffee market in order to address the crises in production that gave rise to Café Femenino, with some success. Each cooperative developed to serve a specific function in the production of coffee in the region, and to address particular crises or opportunities as they emerged—specifically the emergence of organic coffee, its collapse, and revival through Fair Trade. Importantly all three are seen by the community not to be in competition with each other but to be working in harmony towards the overall social good of the communities involved. La Torre describes the functional relationship between the three cooperatives and between the cooperatives and the community in this way:

> We have come together with one single objective in order to improve the livelihoods of small producers according to each of our specialties. CICAP focuses on building capacity for the small producers through technical assistance and training. PROASSA promotes the product and is more oriented toward business management for the producers and their farms, as well as promoter. CECANOR works on keeping the producers together in the same organization to enable them to access services that they would otherwise not have: technical assistance, training, marketing and credit. (Moore, 2004)

[36] In 1994 the organic coffee market bottomed out and CICAP, the original cooperative, ran into financial trouble. PROASSA formed out of this crisis, creating a separate cooperative of coffee producers to better manage local production, thereby liberating CICAP to focus on broader issues. This allowed the cooperatives to survive until CECANOR was conceived of and formed in 1999 to unite the three separate coops at this time operating under PROASSA, in order to gain Fair Trade Certification (Moore, 2006). The willingness of the cooperatives to take the lead to enable community is part of the unique conditions out of which Café Femenino's development of ethical value-added emerges.

[37] This, one might argue, is the *raison d'être* of the cooperative organization of Fair Trade coffee production, to improve the living conditions of those living in a marginalized community. However, the process of inclusion of the most marginalized into these organizations is important. As La Torre explains: "There are six associations, 2500 producers and 50 local committees that are all a part of CECANOR. We have two organizations that are fundamentally indigenous, living in areas of extreme poverty and with generally low production—2–3 or 4–6 quintals. Their resources are very limited and they make up about 50% of our associates" (Moore, 2004). The cooperatives' membership is therefore mainly composed of the *most disadvantaged* in the area and its infrastructure is geared to bringing the benefits of Fair Trade to these families and communities. It is this focus on the most disadvantaged as a priority that, while not unique in Café Femenino and the associated cooperatives, demonstrates a commitment to going beyond the minimal conditions set out in the Fair Trade standards.

The cooperatives do not just focus on production and distribution however; they also provide small bridge or micro loans during the "off" season for members, and operate classes and training in coffee production and in social well being. The goal, as expressed by La Torre, is to address "not just economic issues, but also social…we are interested in health for everyone" (Moore, 2004).

[38] This community capacity building is further facilitated through democratic decision making at all levels of the cooperative structure from grassroots local gatherings to regional meetings. Again La Torre provides a clear synopsis of the organizational structure:

> The decisions are always made at the grassroots level. CECANOR has a general assembly of delegates, once or twice a year where they make central decisions affecting the entire organization, women and men. But specifically with regard to Café Femenino, with the orientation toward the general agreements of the assembly, there are regional and zonal meetings of the women to make these decisions. They talk about how to improve the quality of the coffee or about generating funds for improving the infrastructure. (Moore, 2004)

[39] This focus on improving the lives of the most marginalized, overall community social health, and democratic decision making may not be unique to Café Femenino in the world of Fair Trade, but the seamless integration of the specific issue of women's oppression within these existing structures models the possibility of ethical value-added embedded in label development.

[40] This background brings into focus the area where ethical value-added is demonstrated most uniquely in this case. Women's land ownership is a singular feature of Café Femenino, made centrally important by the fact that it is the primary condition for membership: "The requirement to participate in the organization is that the woman has control of the farm, that she has control of a piece of land. One has to have a farm in her name, in her possession, this is the condition" (Moore, 2004). The import of this condition is made clear by the fact that it would be difficult for women in an agricultural producer cooperative in the economic North to meet this condition, let alone the foothills of the Andes. How this unique situation was secured is again a combination of existing social conditions, active female self-determination, and the possibilities generated by ethical trade. As La Torre explains, land was always considered to be shared by couples in these communities, but was in actuality and convention usually held in the husband's name until death. Through inheritance women could gain official title to the land, but usually not while the husband or father was alive (Moore, 2004). The result was that in practice women had little economic independence. However, with the crisis in organic production, the women of this community decided to transform the conventional understanding of ownership to more broadly applied legal reality, using the premium of Café Femenino as incentive to encourage women to meet the membership requirement, beginning with women who already had title to land. As La Torre explains,

> The wife has always had a piece of land that was hers. Now there is a tendency amongst the parents considering the conditions of the marketplace to put a piece of land in the name of the daughter, or the son, or in the name of both. They are small pieces of land, a quarter hectare, or half a hectare. But it is very important because of the commitment of the person, to feel like the owner of a piece of land and the income they can generate. (Moore, 2004)

[41]   An example of this pattern can be found in one of Café Femenino's members, Maria Sabina Hernandez Queva. Mrs. Queva and her husband Enrique have worked together for over 35 years. They own and work a small coffee farm high in Agua Azul and a few years ago they decided to split up their property to take advantage of the emergence of Café Femenino. Now they have his and her parcels of land that they farm separately, and Mrs. Queva has emerged from her domestic duties to be an active member of the cooperative and sometimes spokesperson for Café Femenino (Moore, 2004). More importantly, Sabina has been able to recognize herself not only as a member of a family unit, but also as a breadwinner for the family and an associate in the cooperative structure (Moore, 2004). Both continue to be members of the larger cooperative structures, and therefore work together in some meaningful senses, but Sabina has been given a voice in both the domestic and public sphere where she did not have it before. Her personal capacities and those of the community are simultaneously enhanced. As La Torre explains, "the problem of the women is not just a cultural problem, it's an economic problem. We are trying to give both aspects the same importance" (Moore, 2004).

[42]   This change in economic status and independence for the women has lead to not just Sabina but the women of the area as a whole taking a much larger role in the economy through the cooperative organizations. As La Torre explains,

> Before the emergence of Café Femenino, we did have 15% female associates in the organization...but we weren't having the impact that we were looking for.... Now we have 30% female members, the incorporation of women in the organization is somewhat massive. They feel capable of doing things with security. But there's a change that is very important for us, the change that is happening in the mentality of the male members. Now they accept the involvement of the women in the organization, they accept that they go to meetings, and they are also helping out in activities that they never used to do in order that the women might attend meetings. You can see men staying at home with the children, cooking something while their wife is in a meeting. As well, when we have large gatherings in the communities, they prepare food for everyone in the meeting, something that you could never see before. It's a very important change that for us is fundamental. (Moore, 2004)

[43]   In other words, the entire community has been transformed by women's active enfranchisement within the cooperative and their critical mass in its active membership women. The community experiences the benefits of ethical value-added. This does not mean that the women's issues are isolated from the men's, but that the community's resources are directed from the perspective of female experience and from their work that has previously been undervalued by social and economic development in the area. As La Torre explains, "We don't want to separate them [men and women], given our perspective that we are interested in the family's development, in the community's development and the development of the country, which is work for both men and women, together, the same rights, the same opportunities. This is fundamental" (Moore, 2004). However, the conception that money earned is the man's to spend as he wills has been replaced by the understanding that money earned from coffee production is to be applied for the betterment of the family and the community as a whole in both economic and social terms. Mrs. Queva attests to this new reality when she explains that rather than the Fair Trade premium being spent on alcohol by the men at the bar, women have turned their pre-

mium towards improvements in "our living conditions" (in Moore, 2004).[39] The ethical value-added of improving women's lives—in fact the prioritization of this goal within Café Femenino—has led to the possibility of development of better economic impacts.

[44] All of these changes in production have led to a sense of community both within the membership of Café Femenino and the larger community itself. This in turn has created a sense of awareness amongst members that these changes in their community exist in a larger economic context that must be observed, understood, and resisted if necessary, through community social and economic strength. For them, the entry of larger market organizations into Fair Trade is seen as a potential threat, not a boon. This is to a large degree the result of the fact that the community has seen how development projects can fail because of external market conditions, as it did for organics in the 1990s. The community has foreseen similar trials coming for Fair Trade, and considers this an inspiration to develop ethical value-added components to their product as a means of distinguishing themselves. As La Torre explains:

> When the big exporters can offer a price equal or better than what the [cooperative] organization can offer, it will create a great discontentment amongst the producers and weaken the organizations. This is dangerous and we have to prepare ourselves. I believe that the only way is through strengthening our organizations.... the large businesses have entered into organics, they are entering into fair trade, more as a result of their market orientation and the direction the market is taking.... They are not there because they are interested in the development of the producers, they are not interested in the sustainability of the environment. (in Moore, 2006)

[45] This "strengthening" of the cooperatives is done through the development of ethical values within their economic organizations as a matter of survival as well as a matter of development. As La Torre understands it: "One has to see honesty, transparency and loyalty. We have to consider how we can sustain those values in order to move forward. Because in the end, if one can't give more to the producers, then the producer has to see that the organization is managed in a way that is transparent and honest" (Moore, 2004). The ethical value-added of Café Femenino is therefore seen not only just as a marketing tool, or an economic necessity, but also as a means of protecting individual dignity, community, and a way of life.

[46] Similarly the larger cooperative structures shared by the producers are seen by the members as more than mere economic tools because they serve as social sustainability organizations. La Torre describes this view in the following way: "I believe that it's [the cooperative] both [Economic and Social]. It's an economic instrument... [but] PROASSA is not a business based in the idea of being a business, it's more like a tool for changing things. Fundamentally, it's a social project, an instrument to help us be sustainable" (in Moore, 2004). Further, the economic activity that these cooperative organizations participate in is not an end in itself, but a means by which a community can meet vital needs collectively. "The sales are the motive by which people meet, but in the end it's about the change. It is what generates the active participation of the women such that the women have the same opportunities as the men. It's not enough to give compassion; it's necessary to give the same opportunities for us to be able to develop ourselves" (Moore, 2004). In this context there is a sense that capitalist economic relations are a potential threat to the viability of the community (as experienced in the collapse of organic coffee sales),

and to women in particular, unless these can be brought under community control and made sustainable. The Fair Trade impacts for Café Femenino are therefore not a matter of economic calculation, but of a continuous process of *social and economic* development—a process of adding of economic and social value through the lens of ethics. In so far as the non-market ethical concerns are forefronted, and the development of Fair Trade seen as an ongoing process of adding values to production throughout the commodity chain, Café Femenino forms a unique contribution to Fair Trade practice. It is not that some features are reminiscent of other instantiations of Fair Trade organization that is of note, but how these features are expanded and added to in recognition of the fact that development of ethical distinction from "Fair-washing" alternatives is the key to social and economic survival.

Conclusion

[47] Fair Trade is in a process of redefinition given its rapid success in creating economic and human development impacts for producers in the economic South and its market penetration in the economic North. However, this success has been in important ways illusory, as it has encouraged the entry of large corporations into the "ethical" market before the label had clearly developed its own value identity. The possibility however to develop an ethical value-added conception to Fair Trade has not been lost; in fact the process has already begun with Café Femenino's emergence and success. What is needed is for this conception to be developed in practice in a variety of different venues, especially within the international labelling regimes, such as FLO and IFAT.

[48] The concept of ethical value-added is not a closed formula, but rather a conception that requires an ongoing process dependent on the existing conditions that determine possibilities for development and the capabilities of actors to realize them coupled with the idea that economic practice must conform to a higher ethical standard than profit. This conception of improving life conditions based on developing and/or challenging existing economic and social realities can be conceived of as having a number of general areas of direction for Fair Trade practice, some of which have been partially enacted in existing labelling regimes (FLO's generic standards for small producer organizations, and IFAT's ten principles mentioned in note 33). However, what is crucial in ethical value-added is that these principles be engaged both for Northern and Southern producers, from production to consumption. This requires a number of principles be adhered to as a starting point for ethical value-added. These principles develop out of the practice of Fair Trade, but also engage with its experienced shortcomings, and move them towards an understanding of the lifeneeds of the people involved. They are as follows. First, Fair Trade needs to institutionalize in practice the principle of structurally addressing social exclusions in the particular contexts within which it operates—from the marginalization of women to the cultural genocide of First Peoples. Second, there needs to be a prioritization within Fair Trade of developing the capacities of the most economically marginalized in the production process. Projects need to be inclusive of those denied the access to economic and social well-being. Third, in recognition of its marked shortcomings up until this point in this area, there should be a conscious movement for radical inclusion of the economic North in the ethical processes of Fair Trade through the agents of distribution and the education of the consumer. Fourth, the environmental practices of all organizations involved in the Fair Trade process must continue to evolve

towards and develop best practices such as organic production techniques. Fifth, there must be development of processes of democracy and worker control within all aspects of the Fair Trade commodity chain from production to distribution and, importantly, between these normally cloistered economic entities. With these five principles as guides, the development of ethical value-added as a central component of the Fair Trade label can be instituted and developed, and the distinction between "fair" and "Fair-washed" trade clearly established.

[49] Lest one believe that such demands are utopian in their conception, or unrealistic economically, it should be remembered that the process of ethical value adding is in fact the basis of Fair Trade itself. The label cannot suffer, to borrow a phrase from Tessa Jowell, a "poverty of aspiration which comprises all our attempts to lift people out of physical poverty". Before the label, there were no established practices for Fair Trade, and before the ATOs there were precious few avenues for ethical consumption, or economic means to develop ethical production. Each development charted new conceptual and practical territory in a quest to create "ethical" economic activity. The claim here is merely to continue this process, rather than freezing it at a particular point in time around the somewhat arbitrary levels that have been achieved by Fair Trade to date.

[50] As the example of Café Femenino demonstrates, developing a concept of ethical value-added is becoming increasingly necessary as crises for Fair Trade producers emerge around increasing costs and competition with larger market players. These crises are not only squeezing smaller producers but also confusing the consumer and weakening the appeal of the Fair Trade label. Ethical value-added is therefore a way of strengthening the label through a process of re-establishing the distinction between "Fair-washed" trade and Fair Trade. One can look beyond Café Femenino for inspiration on this front, as there are further examples of ethical value added occurring in nascent form within the Fair Trade movement—for example, Equita, a Montreal-based Fair Trade distributor has been working with Le Transit to employ their physically and mentally disadvantaged members in the packaging and roasting of their Fair Trade coffee (TransFair Canada: 2006, p. 4). In 2006, Equita switched their packaging to fully biodegradable bags (after 60 days), which require 30–50% less fossil fuels to produce (TransFair Canada: 2006, p. 4). Such innovations in the economic North must be combined with practices in the economic South in order to educate anew consumers and activists about the already existent possibilities for development of a more ethical economy. For if the Fair Trade label is to live up to its promise of "ethical trade" and is to survive the aggressive entry of multinational corporations into the Fair Trade market it must make itself relatively immune to "ethical raiding." It must develop this immunity because [of] the perceived "economies of scale" in impacts that multinationals offer through higher volume sales in mass market distribution outlets in exchange for the "halo effect" of the label of Fair Trade which in fact undermine the label's perceived and actual ethical legitimacy. In short, for Fair Trade to build upon its economic and human impacts and therefore remain a meaningful ethical and economic alternative to corporate capitalism and globalization, it must distinguish itself clearly in ethics from those market relations it wishes, explicitly or implicitly, to challenge.

Acknowledgements

The author would like to thank SSHRC for funding which has enabled part of this research. Stephan Dobson, Jennifer Moore, Darryl Reed, Lisa Schincariol and the anonymous reviewers also deserve acknowledgement and thanks for their support and comments throughout the construction of this piece.

Notes

1. It is important to recognize that the Fair Trade label is not a straightforward singularity. For example, handicrafts are largely certified by the International Fair Trade Association (IFAT) and agricultural commodities by Fair Trade Labelling Organization (FLO). While many features are shared, even this basic distinction is not straightforward, as there are complex relationships within and between products (such as cotton and the manufacture of handicrafts) as well as varying standards for product certification.
2. For example, the largest of the labelling initiatives, the Fair Trade Labelling Organization (FLO), claims that by December 2006 Fair Trade covered 569 producer organizations in 57 countries in the economic South with over 1,400,000 producers directly involved in the production process and many more reaping the benefits of the community projects (Fairtrade Labelling Organization, 2005c, p. 3). In the economic North, Fair Trade labels (while not dominant) have developed significant profiles in particular commodity markets. A recent FLO document highlights the fact that, in Switzerland, 47% of bananas, 28% of flowers and 9% of sugar sold annually are Fair Trade certified, and in England, 5% of tea, 20% of coffee and 5.5% of bananas are sold annually using a Fair Trade label (Transfair Canada, 2006, p. 3). The growth of these markets year over year is also impressive, with Fair Trade sugar and wine sales volume increasing 84% and 83% respectively from 2004 to 2005, and even more established products such as coffee and tea have increased 40% and 33% in sales volume (Fairtrade Labelling Organization, 2005c, p. 3).
3. The concept of ethics used in this article is the general philosophical definition of the study of goodness and right action. The question of ethics in Fair Trade centres around the study of goodness and right action in economic activity, specifically trade.
4. Two other well-known forms of ethical value-added economic practice are organic food and no-sweat apparel.
5. Caoimhin MacMaolain's piece "Ethical Food Labelling: The Role of European Union Freetrade in Facilitating International Fairtrade" (2002) discusses some of these issues from a European perspective.
6. The argument for understanding movement into a capitalist economy as "ethical" has been analysed in depth both historically and in a contemporary context by numerous authors (e.g., McMurtry, 2002; Thompson, 1991a, b; Wood, 1996). The forcible removal of common economic infrastructure to private control and the resulting compulsion into wage labour for the majority has in fact been the unethical modus operandi of capitalism from the enclosures through British colonial hut taxes to Maquiladora production. The consequences for those affected have been devastating.
7. This assumption of the market form by the Fair Trade movement as a whole is revealingly stated by Maseland and de Vaal: "the fair trade movement does not resist the market mechanism nor inequality in principle, but objects to inequality in outcomes as a result of unjustified unequal starting positions" (2002, p. 255).
8. Randall provides another clear expression of this tendency when she argues that the goal of her research is "to explore the business strategies of fair trade craft organizations that market and sell products in Western markets and evaluate whether they are adequately taking advantage of opportunities in the market.... An implied part of the argument presented here is that fair trade groups must expand business in order to impact a higher number of third world producers" (Randall, 2005, p. 56). Even the pieces usually cited as opposing this trend such as Jaffee et al., Goodman and Goodman, and Raynolds, essentially affirm it. For example, Jaffee et al., while referencing Raynolds and Goodman and Goodman positively, highlight the need for "social and political challenges to the conventional global agro-food system and the overarching set of corporatist and capitalist relationships in which that system is embedded" (2004, p. 171). Yet, while these authors believe in the importance of such a chal-

lenge, Fair Trade is not seen as being adequate to the task, but rather an essentially market response to market problem: "There is a deep sense of the unfairness of markets as currently constituted, but no direct calls to link fair trade to a transition to a non-market society...Fair trade, then, represents not a challenge to the existence of the market itself, but rather to how markets are constructed and administered, how they deliver and apportion economic benefit to participants" (2004, p. 192).

9. This of course does not apply to the 100% Fair Trade organization in the North, such as worker-owned cooperative roasteries or solidarity-based alternative trade organizations.
10. The impacts of coffee production on communities and ecosystems are well documented. For a brief synopsis one can look at Waridel (2002, pp. 34–36).
11. There are dissenting voices in the literature to this discourse of "consumer activism". Fridel for example argues that Fair Trade in its current commodity form cannot overcome the pervasive commodity fetish relationships and therefore are not truly alternative (Fridel, 2007).
12. Fridell's book *Fair Trade Coffee: The Prospects and Pitfalls of Market Driven Social Justice* (2007) reviews some of the pieces that counter this trend. The combination of the concerns raised here however have not been systematized in any one piece.
13. Moore employs ethical literature in this article in the same manner, citing Nozick and Rawls amongst others, although he does not develop their relevance to Fair Trade substantively. Moore seems to recognize this problem, concluding that: "there is clearly work to be done in developing and articulating theoretical perspectives within which Fair Trade makes sense" (2004, p. 77).
14. Ferrie and Hira state that on "the ground level, fair trade implies that ethical principles are intimately and necessarily tied in with the process of production" (2006, p. 108).
15. Goodman, for example, who engages the question of ethics as substantively as anyone in the literature, conceives of Fair Trade's ethical strength as its discourse which exposes consumers to the process of production of their consumable goods. It is this "relational ethic" and "ethic of care" which forms the basis of Fair Trade's moral claim. "Fair trade seeks to expand the everyday experiences of care and responsibility to include the 'needs of distant strangers'...through the everyday-ness of eating, drinking, and situated commodity production. In the narratives of fair trade, an ethics of care is materialized across the spaces of globalization in a moral economy of both a politics of recognition and redistribution" (Goodman, 2004, p. 906, citing Corbridge). However, nowhere in his discussion of ethics does Goodman engage the question of the capitalist market itself as an ethical system; rather for him it is the sine qua non of economic activity and the limit of discursive possibility.
16. Significantly, Venezuela is increasingly encouraging capacity development and ownership by the people through cooperatives initiated, maintained, and owned by the communities in which they operate. This is an important move away from the aforementioned polarity, and should be closely watched and studied.
17. "Economy" here is defined in its non-ideological form as the efficient (non-waste) production, distribution and consumption of goods otherwise in short supply.
18. Marxism and Anarchism are exceptions to this trend in that they base the revolutionary overthrow of capitalism on an implicit moral critique of its social, political and economic forms. However, even here the value basis of this critique is not developed.
19. McMurtry defines "life-value" as a parametric that stresses "satisfaction of vital needs...to enable universally compossible enjoyment and expression of human life capabilities (of thought, experience and action)" (McMurtry, 2002, p. 124).
20. Is one more ethical if they consume more Fair Trade coffee? On what grounds would it be ethical to consume less given the Fair Trade ethical framework?
21. The roots of these movements themselves are in the abolitionist, working class unionism and socialist/communist movements of the early and late 19th century as well as the anti-colonial struggles, for example in China and India, which gathered steam at the turn of the twentieth century—the last being a connection that is normally overlooked. For

example, Gandhi's non-violent, non-cooperation with British rule had a significant economic component (i.e., salt production or cotton spinning), which could be seen to be a powerful form of ethical consumerism (Schell, 2003, pp. 134–135).

22. Almost all of the political and social movements outlined above have a consumer element to them, from boycott campaigns to solidarity trade, ethical production to environmental consumption. While not the dominant feature in all movements (e.g., Civil Rights), ethical consumption is a central identifiable feature of them all (e.g., lunch-counter or bus boycotts). Similarly, while other, older, social issues such as racism (Civil Rights) and patriarchy (Feminism) had a more central role in inspiring these movements, the radically new conditions of production and consumption created post-World War II shaped (and limited) the structure and goals of these movements to a large degree.

23. A good history of the development of the organic label can be found in Samuel Fromartz's recent book Organic, Inc. (2006).

24. While outside of the scope of this work, a comparison between the ethical value-added of organic and natural food in comparison to Fair Trade is needed.

25. Much of this history is common knowledge. If curious, one can consult the FLO website at http://www.fairtrade.net/about_us.html?&L= or IFAT's history at http://www.ifat.org/index.php?option=com_content&task=view&id=10&Itemid=12&limit=1&limitstart=1 for these and more details.

26. While organic goods can claim to be unique in both production and content (e.g., no pesticides) a Fair Trade good as Fair Trade only claims a different method of production.

27. Unions, while economic in focus, are not economic entities in the same sense that a cooperative is. The latter is an organizational means of production; the former is an organizational means of protest and expression with no direct control over the production process.

28. One can think of numerous other potential problems with the different standards. For example, union independence in the economic South is notoriously uneven, and while the Fair Trade label tries to ensure a degree of worker voice in Fair Trade (FLO Standards), it is almost impossible to ensure. The security of work is also itself difficult to ensure under these conditions. Cooperative structures however, as long as they are not state controlled, ensure independent worker voice, ownership and control.

29. In Canada, there is such an initiative currently being articulated by farmers called Fair Deal. Their website is www.farmerdirect.ca. In the United States, Equal Exchange has tried to initiate a Domestic Fair Trade label and have come up with ten principles for it (Cooperative Grocer, November–December 2006).

30. I personally experience others making this slip regularly.

31. It is important to note that nations, not international corporations, are identified here as creating the problems addressed by Fair Trade.

32. The ethical content of Fair Trade is too often based upon pre-existing conditions rather than social developments initiated by the label itself. For example: "For many small coffee farmers, their production practices are organic by default, since they have been too poor to afford chemicals" (Bryant and Goodman, 2004, p. 355, quoting Rice).

33. One could also examine the recently (2001) established ten IFAT Fair Trade principles (1. Creating Opportunities for Economically Disadvantaged Producers; 2. Transparency and Accountability; 3. Trading Practices; 4. Payment of a Fair Price; 5. Child Labour and Forced Labour; 6. Non-Discrimination, Gender Equity and Freedom of Association; 7. Working Conditions; 8. Capacity Building; 9. Promotion of Fair Trade; 10. Environment) for a basis to develop ethical value-added. Conformity with these principles is achieved through a three prong monitoring process (self, peer, and IFAT 5–10% per year, monitoring). However while the idea of principles to ensure ethics in trade is an important move forward, the impetus to push these principles from minimum to a process of increasing conformity has not yet been developed—that is what moves an organization from non-discrimination to active inclusion? Even this minimum has

had some success however in limiting distributor membership in IFAT to worker cooperatives and ATOs (although this does not stop other distributors from selling IFAT goods). Further, the larger labelling organization, FLO international, has not yet developed even these principles, choosing instead to have "social," "economic" and "environmental" development as their guiding principles. Finally, in none of these versions of principles are the type of goods produced, systems of distribution employed, or, for FLO and Waridel, conformity to these principles by Northern distributors, engaged.
34. Jennifer Moore, an independent Canadian journalist based in Ecuador, has done a significant amount of on-the-ground research for this article, including asking specific questions of principle actors on behalf of the author. The information cited (i.e., Moore, 2006) comes from transcripts of interviews conducted and translated by Ms. Moore during 2006. The author is very grateful that Ms. Moore provided full access to her material.
35. Isobel La Torre's role in the movement and development of Café Femenino cannot be underestimated as she is a constant in the region's development going back to her student days when she was first involved in the union movement and then organic agriculture as well as the foundation of the cooperatives discussed below.
36. The extra 2 cents for women producers and to women's shelters in the North are "paid" for by the distributor, OPTCO, and roasters/retailers. While these costs might be passed on to the consumer ultimately, there is no price differential usually for Café Femenino and similar quality coffee at the point of purchase. On top of this premium, there is also a Café Femenino Foundation organized by the northern distributor of Café Femenino coffee, Organic Products Trading Company (OPTCO) to solicit funds for community economic development in the coffee producing regions (Café Femenino Foundation).
37. PREDA is currently in a public debate with FLO around the licensing of their products as Fair Trade. Some of the details of this debate can be found on their website at http://www.preda.net/index.htm.
38. The UN Chronicle of Higher Education in 2007 puts coffee trade at an $80 billion industry; the only commodity with higher trade is oil. See http://www.un.org/Pubs/chronicle/2007/webArticles/111407_coffee_trade.html.
39. While this expenditure would clearly be a violation of the conditions of the Fair Trade premium, it would be acceptable for the farmer's take from the sale of coffee to the cooperative. The cultural and economic shift marked by the emergence of Café Femenino is clearly marked by this example.

References

Bacon, C. 2005. "Confronting the Coffee Crisis: Can Fair Trade, Organic, and Specialty Coffees Reduce Small-Scale Farmer Vulnerability in Northern Nicaragua?" *World Development* 33(3), 497–511.

Bakan, J. 2004. *The Corporation*. Toronto: Penguin.

Bird, K. and D.R. Hughes. 1997. "Ethical Consumerism: The Case of 'Fairly-Traded' Coffee." *A European Review* 6(3), 159–167.

Blowfield, M. 1999. "Ethical Trade: A Review of Developments and Issues." *Third World Quarterly* 20(4), 753–770.

———. 2004. "Implementation Deficits of Ethical Trade Systems." *Journal of Corporate Citizenship* 13, 77–90.

Bryant, R.L. and M.K. Goodman. 2004. "Consuming Narratives: The Political Ecology of 'Alternative' Consumption." *Transactions of the Institute of British Geographers* 29, 344–366.

Café Femenino Foundation. Available from http://www.cafefemeninofoundation.org/index.html.

Crane, A. and I.A. Davies. 2003. "Ethical Decision Making in Fair Trade Companies." *Journal of Business Ethics* 45, 79–92.

Crowell, E. 2006. "Bringing Fair Trade Home." *Cooperative Grocer* 127.

Dickson, M.A. and M.A. Littrell. 1997. "Alternative Trading Organizations: Shifting Paradigm in a Culture of Social Responsibility." *Human Organization* 56(3), 344–352.

Dobson, J. 1993. "TNC's and the Corruption of GATT: Free Trade Versus Fair Trade." *Journal of Business Ethics* 12, 573–578.

Fairtrade Labelling Organization. 2005a. "International Standards." Available from: http://www.fairtrade.net/fileadmin/user_upload/content/Generic_Fairtrade_ .

———. 2005b. "International Standards." Available from: http://www.fairtrade.net/file admin/user_upload/content/Generic_Fairtrade_Standard_Hired_Labour_Dec_2005_EN_01.pdf.

———. 2005c. Available online at: http://www.fairtrade.net/figures.html.

Ferrie, J. and A. Hira. 2006. "Fair Trade: Three Key Challenges for Reaching the Mainstream." *Journal of Business Ethics* 63, 107–118.

Foek, A. 2007. "Trademarking Coffee: Starbucks Cuts Ethiopia Deal." CorpWatch. 8 May. Available online at: http://www.corpwatch.org/article.php?id=14474&pr intsafe=1.

Fridell, G. 2004. "The University and the Moral Imperative of Fair Trade Coffee." *Journal of Academic Ethics* 2, 141–159.

———. 2007. *Fair Trade Coffee: The Prospects and Pitfalls of Market-Driven Social Justice.* Toronto: University of Toronto Press.

———. 2007. "Fair Trade Coffee and Commodity Fetishism: The Limits of Market Driven Social Justice." *Historical Materialism* 15(4), 79–104.

Friedman, M. 1993. "The Social Responsibility of Business Is to Increase Its Profits." In T. White (ed.) *Business Ethics: A Philosophical Reader.* Toronto: Macmillan. pp. 162–167.

Fromartz, S. 2006. *Organic, Inc.* Orlando: Harcourt.

Glasbeek, H. 2002. *Wealth by Stealth: Corporate Crime, Corporate Law, and the Perversion of Democracy.* Toronto: Between the Lines.

Golding, K. and K. Peattie. 2005. "In Search of a Golden Blend: Perspectives on the Marketing of Fair Trade Coffee." *Sustainable Development* 13, 154–165.

Goldsmith, E. and J. Mander (eds.). 1996. *The Case Against the Global Economy.* San Francisco: Sierra Club.

Goodman, M.K. 2004. "Reading Fair Trade: Political Ecological Imaginary and the Moral Economy of Fair Trade Foods." *Political Geography* 23, 891–915.

Habermas, J. 1984. *The Theory of Communicative Action: Volume 1.* Trans. T. McCarthy. Boston: Beacon.

———. 1987. *The Theory of Communicative Action: Volume 2.* Trans. T. McCarthy. Boston: Beacon.

Hamilton, C. 200. "The Case for Fair Trade." *Journal of Australian Political Economy* 48, 60–72.

Hoagland, S. 2005. "Female Coffee Growers Find New Freedoms in Peru." WeNews, February. Available online at: www.womensnews.org.

Hudson, I. and M. Hudson. 2003. "Removing the Veil? Commodity Fetishism, Fair Trade, and the Environment." *Organization and Environment* 16(4), 413–430.

Jaffee, D., J.R. Kloppenburg and M.B. Monroy. 2004. "Bringing the 'Moral Charge' Home: Fair Trade Within the North and Within the South." *Rural Sociology* 69(2), 169–196.

Johnston, J. 2002. "Consuming Global Justice: Fair Trade Shopping and Alternative Development." In J. Goodman (ed.), *Protest and Globalization: Prospects for Transnational Solidarity.* Annandale: Pluto. pp. 38–56.

Jowell, T. 2004. "Government and the Value of Culture." Department of Culture, Media, and Sport. May. Available online at: http://www.culture.gov.uk/NR/rdonlyres/DE2ECA49-7F3D-46BF-9D11-A3AD80B F54D6/0/valueofculture.pdf.

Klein, N. 2000. *No Logo.* Toronto: Vintage Canada.

LeClair, M.S. 2002. "Fighting the Tide: Alternative Trade Organizations in the Era of Global Free Trade." *World Development* 30(6), 949–958.

Letson, P. 2002. "The Road Up: Free-Market Reforms Fuel Growth of Ethiopia's Co-ops." *Rural Cooperatives* March–April, 15–20.

Loureiro, M.L. and J. Lotade. 2005. "Do Fair Trade and Eco-Labels in Coffee Wake Up the Consumer Conscience?" *Ecological Economics* 53, 129–138.

Low, W. and W. Davenport. 2005. "Postcards from the Edge: Maintaining the 'Alternative' Character of Fair Trade." *Sustainable Development* 13, 143–153.

MacMaolain, C. 2002. "Ethical Food Labelling: The Role of European Union Freetrade in Facilitating

International Fairtrade." *Common Market Law Review* 39, 295–314.

Maseland, R. and A. De Vaal. 2002. "How Fair Is Fair Trade?" *De Economist* 150(3), 251–272.

McMurtry, J.J. 2001. "Commodity Cul-de-Sac." *Socialist Studies Bulletin* 65, 5–21.

———. 2002. *Value Wars: The Global Market Versus the Life Economy.* London: Pluto.

Mellor, M. and G. Moore. 2005. "Business for a Social Purpose: Traidcraft and Shared Interest." *Development* 48(1), 84–91.

Moore, G. 2004. "The Fair Trade Movement: Parameters, Issues and Future Research." *Journal of Business Ethics* 53(1–2), 73–86.

Moore, J. 2006. Unpublished Interviews. Trans. J. Moore.

Nelson, J. 2005. "From Vancouver to Peru, Women Lead a Coffee Revolution"; "Helping Each Other, 5,000 Miles Apart"; "Farmers are Paid More for Fair Trade Coffee"; and "Humility, Intellect and Taking Charge." Four-part series on Café Femenino in *The Columbian*, 6, 7, and 8 November. Available online at: www.columbian.com.

Parrish, B.D., V.A. Luzadis and W.R. Bentley. 2005. "What Tanzania's Coffee Farmers Can Teach the World: A Performance-Based Look at the Fair Trade-Free Trade Debate", *Sustainable Development* 13, 177–189.

Pearce, H. 1994. "Ethical Dilemmas." *New Statesman and Society* 7(285), 30–31.

Planet Bean Coffee. n.d. "Introducing Café Femenino." Flyer. Guelph, Ontario.

Randall, D.C. 2005. "An Exploration of Opportunities for the Growth of the Fair Trade Market: Three Cases of Craft Organizations." *Journal of Business Ethics* 56, 55–67.

Raynolds, L.T. 2000. "Re-embedding Global Agriculture: The International Organic and Fair Trade Movements." *Agriculture and Human Values* 17, 297–309.

Raynolds, L.T., D. Murray and P.L. Taylor. 2004. "Fair Trade Coffee: Building Producer Capacity via Global Networks." *Journal of International Development* 16, 1109–1121.

Rogers, T. 2004. "Small Coffee Brewers Try to Redefine Fair Trade." *The Christian Science Monitor*, 13 April. Available online at: http://www.csmonitor.com/2004.

Sachs, J.D. 2005. *The End of Poverty: Economic Possibilities for Our Time.* Toronto: Penguin.

Schell, J. 2003. *The Unconquerable World: Power, Nonviolence and the Will of the People.* New York: Henry Holt.

Schroeder, D.B. 2005. Letter to OXFAM at Guelph, 28 December.

Smith, S. and S. Barrientos. 2005. "Fair Trade and Ethical Trade: Are there Moves Towards Convergence?" *Sustainable Development* 13, 190–198.

Stolle, D., M. Hooghe and M. Micheletti. 2005. "Politics in the Supermarket: Political Consumerism as a Form of Political Participation." *International Political Science Review* 26(3), 245–269.

Talbot, J.M. 2004. *Grounds for Agreement: The Political Economy of the Coffee Commodity Chain.* Toronto: Rowman and Littlefield.

Taylor, M.P. 2003. "Building Better Co-op Law." National Cooperative Business Association. Available online at: http://www.ncba.coop/clusa_news_ss_ghana.cfm.

Taylor, P.L. 2005. "In the Market but Not of It: Fair Trade Coffee and Forest Stewardship Council Certification as Market-Based Social Changes." *World Development* 33(1), 129–147.

Thompson, E.P. 1991a. "The Moral Economy of the English Crowd in the Eighteenth Century." In *Customs in Common.* New York: New Press. pp. 185–200.

———. 1991b. *The Making of the English Working Class.* Toronto: Penguin.

Tim Hortons. n.d. "Coffee Sustainability." Available from http://www.timhortons.com/en/about/faq.html#Fair_Trade.

TransFair Canada. 2006. Fair Trade Echoes: *The Transfair Canada Newsletter*, 1, 1–5.

———. n.d. *Discover Fair Trade Certified Tea.* Brochure.

Waridel, L. 2002. *Coffee with Pleasure: Just Java and World Trade.* Montreal: Black Rose.

Wood, E.M. 1996. *Democracy Against Capitalism.* Cambridge: Cambridge University Press.

Questions

1. What does McMurtry mean by "ethical value-added"?
2. (a) What does McMurtry think of the relationship between ethics and economics?
   (b) When would McMurtry consider a business to be engaged in "Fair-washing" rather than "Fair Trade"?
   (c) What does McMurtry think of the conception that consumption itself is a good?
   (d) Explain the problem of circular reasoning McMurtry identifies (para 8).
3. Explain McMurtry's answer to the question "Can economics be ethical?"
4. What three problems for Fair Trade does McMurtry identify?
5. What double standard does McMurtry identify?
6. What issues does McMurtry raise regarding Waridel's framework?
7. What element of the case of Café Femenino do you consider most important?

Case Study: Scotiabank's Microfinance Services: A Good Thing?

Scotiabank is the only major Canadian chartered bank active in microfinance. "Small-scale entrepreneurs and micro-business owners comprise a large element of productive society in Latin America and the Caribbean, accounting for over 75% of all businesses," they note on their website. "However, due to their small size and informality, they frequently fall outside traditional banking activity" (scotiabank.com).

And although their focus is on "improving financial access in under-served and under-banked communities," they do recognize that "the health of micro-businesses is critical to economic and social development" (scotiabank.com). As of 2013, Scotiabank made loans totalling $446 million to 150,200 people; in Peru and Chile, the size of the loan averaged $3,000, in the Dominican Republic, $2,500, and in Jamaica, $800. They intend to expand into Mexico, Colombia, and Uruguay.

So far, so good. But Pulfer notes that their interest rates are 21% (which is, actually, relatively low for microfinance). "The reason is cost: it's expensive and labour-intensive to deliver tiny loans to large numbers of people without collateral" (Pulfer).

Although Yunus has criticized this "commercial model" of microfinance, Carlos Danel and Carlos Labarthe, CEOs of Mexico's Compartamos Banco (the largest microfinance bank in Latin America, with $80 million in profits and a 40% return on equity), say that their microloans will help more poor people than will "donor money." But, as Alex Counts, president of the Washington-based Grameen Foundation, points out, Compartamos's poor clients generate the profits they are excluded from (Malkin). At Pro Mujer, a nonprofit microfinance group in Latin America, profits are reinvested in clients.

References

Malkin, Elizabeth. "Microfinance's Success Sets Off a Debate in Mexico." *The New York Times* 5 Apr. 2008.

Pulfer, Rachel. "Microfinance Loans: Big Business." *Canadian Business* 16 June 2008 http://www.canadianbusiness.com/business-strategy/microfinance-loans-big-business/

Scotiabank website. www.scotiabank.com

Questions

1. (a) The comment by Danel and Labarthe indicates that they're using which ethical measuring stick?

   (b) And which ethical measuring stick is Counts using?

2. So.... If you do establish the first Canadian international microfinance bank...?

CHAPTER SEVEN

Profit and Capitalism

What to Do?—No Limits, Ltd.

You are an upper-level manager of a very successful company, No Limits, Ltd. Call it a mid-life crisis, call it an awakening, but the thought occurred to you that *maximizing* profit may not be the be-all and end-all of life, let alone of business—more importantly, it may even be immoral to get everything you can all the time. You're considering suggesting a profit ceiling to the Board of Directors.

Maybe relaxing the bottom line will enable you to pay a fairer price to your suppliers or afford the costlier but more environmentally responsible materials; maybe it will enable you to lower prices; maybe it will enable you to increase wages and benefits; maybe it will enable you to afford peripheral programs that have been on the proverbial back-burner forever.

However, you begin to consider the possible downside of a profit ceiling. Current and potential future investors are likely to sell or not buy your company's shares—why would someone settle for a 6-per-cent rate of return when they can get 7 or 8 per cent elsewhere? What broker would recommend the stocks of a company that has put a voluntary limit on its profits?

Then you get to thinking about your own interests. As a senior executive of the company, you receive bonuses if profits are higher. Those bonuses help to fund some extras which improve your family's quality of life; for example, part of the bonus money goes toward your children's university education. And you recognize that those bonuses have, in fact, been earned with a lot of after-hours work, creative thinking, and commitment to your employer. Finally, you know that profits are never guaranteed: high (even obscenely high) profits are simply a reflection of successful risk-taking *this year*—you know it can all turn around next year.

Then you think to yourself, instead of limiting profits, maybe the company should use the profits that they make to enhance its stability and reputation and hence increase the level of job security for all its employees. Perhaps the company could give part of its after-tax profit to certain charities. Perhaps some of the profits could go to worthy environmental projects or community recreation programs. Perhaps the company could institute a profit-sharing program with its workers; this would improve productivity as well as the quality of future job applicants. But are these profits justifiably the company's to spend—or are they dirty money? Maybe you should suggest the profit ceiling after all.

What do you decide to do?

Introduction

Many students participating in discussions about ethical issues in business seem to take the pursuit of profit as a given. But it's not, at least not from an ethical point of view. And, remember, that's the point of view we're taking in this book; that's what this book is all about. From a *business* perspective (whatever that is—I'd argue that there isn't just one unified "business" point of view—consider Nordberg's four models), perhaps the pursuit of profit is a given. Then again, perhaps it's not. There *are* not-for-profit *businesses*. And there are co-ops. But from an *ethical* perspective, it must be justified—and it must be justified on *ethical* grounds. (See, for example, Arnold's position in Jacobsen's essay in this chapter.)

Further, most business students seem to assume that profit is *good*. Certainly many assume that the pursuit of profit should be their reason for being in business. (Let me remind them again that not-for-profits and co-ops are businesses too.) Many go further still and believe that the *maximization* of profit is good, and should be their reason for being in business. Some even assert that the pursuit of profit is not just a good, but a *right*. And, of course, I'm going to try to get you to question those assumptions and, in the process, to justify profit—on ethical grounds.

"It [is] perhaps…ironic," Fischer notes, "that the method for the objective calculation of business profits [double-entry accounting]—so central to our system of modern capitalism and debates of business ethics—was first broadly communicated by not only a Catholic clergyman [sic], but by a follower of St. Francis of Assisi, who is so often linked with the ideal of 'poverty'" (300). Fischer goes on to say, however, that the clergy member in question, Luca Pacioli, believed that profits should be honest and reasonable. (For another analysis from a religious perspective, see Abbas et al.)

You may, of course, decide that you don't care about ethical justifications, that you don't care about whether what you're doing is right or wrong. Okay, then you *can* consider profit (or power, or whatever) to be your unquestioned need-not-be-justified priority. But then you should have closed this book and withdrawn from this course long ago—because this is about business *ethics*, about the *moral reasons for our decisions and our actions*. (Take another look at Part I if you need to.) And please reconsider: don't be one of those people who think or say, "I can't go around all day thinking about how my actions affect other people." Imagine if you could. Imagine if you *did*. Imagine how business would change if it were guided by consequences (*all* or even *most* consequences, not just the consequence of profit), if it were guided by simple cause and effect. Go ahead. Imagine. Change the world. (If you take away just one thing from this textbook, take away that.)

Or you may want to do the right thing but argue that the pursuit of profit can sometimes override morality (assuming that the pursuit of profit can't be ethically justified, can't be morally good). This is the question Goldman examines, and he concludes in the negative:

> [T]he manager is not to violate moral rights in the interest of his corporation... [h]e must make decisions within a moral framework defined by principles and rights *applicable with the same force* in *non*professional contexts. Adherence to such principles does not require any special expertise at judging cumulative economic effects; *often it requires only the removal of institutional blinders.* (284–85; my emphasis)

BOX 7.1   A Lesson from Medicine on Profit Maximization?

Business ethics—both stockholder and stakeholder theories—makes the same mistake as the one made by the traditional ethics of medicine. The traditional ethics of medicine was a teleological ethics predicated on the assumption that the goal of medicine was to prolong life and promote better health. But, as bioethicists have made plain, these are not the only or even the overriding goals of most patients. Most of us have goals and values that limit our desire for medical treatments. Similarly, the view of the stockholder in business ethics is that the stockholder has only one interest—profit. If stockholders have no other values or interests that would limit their desire for additional profit, their sole interest is in profit maximization. But investors are real people with interests and values that balance and limit their desire for profit. It would be an extremely odd individual who cared for nothing except more profit. And institutional investors are supposed to serve the interests of individual investors. Stockholders hold many stakes in the firms in which they invest. The conclusion that most stockholders have interests that would limit the pursuit of maximum profit has significant implications both for business ethics and for the management of for-profit corporations. Something like 'informed consent for investors' is needed. Corporate managers, to the extent that they are to be agents of their stockholders, must not simply pursue profit maximization. They must ascertain the interests and values of their investors that limit the single-minded pursuit of profit. (Hardwig, abstract)

Source
Hardwig, John. "The Stockholder—A Lesson for Business Ethics from Bioethics?" *Journal of Business Ethics* 91.3 (2010): 329–41.

So.... An ethical justification for profit. Let's start by defining our terms. Accounting profit is different from economic profit, and the layperson's definition/understanding is different still. But simply put, profit is the difference between income (revenues) and expenses (costs). Actually, that's the definition for loss, too—if the difference is positive, it's called profit; if the difference is negative, it's called loss.

The complicated part is what's included in "expenses." If everything is included—everything required to maintain the business, such as fair payment for everyone's labour, including that of the owner, fair return to investors, reserve funds for upgrading, etc.—then there's no need, no reason, for profit. The very existence of a profit (or loss) indicates a miscalculation—either you charged more than you should have for your product or you paid less than you should have for your supplies and/or labour (or vice versa). And if your profit is thus the result of some unfairness (the "should" being a *moral* "should"), then the ethical remedy seems clear: just charge/pay what you should have—decrease your price and/or increase your wages, returns, etc. (or vice versa). Otherwise, your profit means you got back more than you put out, and as such, it should be considered undeserved and unfair. Correct? And if you don't deserve your profits, you don't have any right to keep them. Correct? (What's wrong with breaking even? Isn't that a win-win situation? Whereas profit—if your profit exists because of someone else's loss—is a win/lose situation.)

Note, however, that this analysis assumes that there is, or can be, a fixed fair price for things. But this is not so in a free-market system—in such a system, there is no "fair," only "whatever the market will bear." (We'll come back to markets later.)

Note, also, that the implication is that the miscalculation entails an injustice—and this isn't necessarily so. Maybe the surplus (or deficit) wasn't the result of exploitative pricing or waging, but of unexpected sales or supplies (there could be a number of reasons for "legitimate" profit, but we don't need to go into them). One can't know the future; one can only predict it. So if sales were unforeseeably higher or lower than anticipated, where's the injustice in that miscalculation?

And if everything is *not* included in expenses, why not? On what moral basis do you *not* include all your costs? Are "externalities" morally defensible at all? Klein writes, "[E]missions from the transportation of goods across borders—all those container ships, whose traffic has increased by nearly 400 percent over the last twenty years [and set to double or even triple by 2050]—are not formally attributed to any nation-state and therefore no one country is responsible for reducing their polluting impact" (Klein 79). Talk about externalizing. Some argue that shareholder value is rigged in this way, that is, by discounting externalities and by postponing expenditures to the future—by playing fast and loose, dishonestly, with real costs, creating value where none exists.

Yet another justification for profit appeals to the motivating role of "extra" and "excessive": without profit (or, more accurately, without the expectation of profit), there would be little incentive to do what entrepreneurs do. First, it is arguable that people *are* motivated by economic self-interest. Even if they are, it's arguable that they are happiest and healthiest when so motivated. Furthermore, if they are, consider my comments in Chapter 5 about the danger of commissions tempting people to cut corners and do whatever it takes to get the sale: if that's what happens at that scale, with decisions that affect only a few people, imagine the consequences when that kind of thinking happens at the larger scale, with decisions that affect whole companies, and more. These concerns prompt, I think, the reluctance to privatize education, health care, and prisons. For example, Aspinwall notes that "[p]rivate prison companies are active in pursuing a broader definition of what constitutes 'criminal,' thereby increasing imprisonment rates" (8). But are non-privatized companies any less focused on or driven by profit? (Are they supposed to be?)

Second, most of us who are motivated by economic self-interest are motivated by payment (our basic wage/salary), not by profit (the extra, the excessive payment)—why should the entrepreneur, or the shareholder, be any different? And, in any case, the fact that the entrepreneur and/or shareholder *is* different—*does* require extra and excessive—doesn't make it right. But nor does it make it wrong. Saying that profit motivates simply isn't ethically relevant. (Fear and curiosity motivate, too, but whether either is morally good is independent of those observations. In order to prove that X is good because X motivates, one would need to establish that "motivating" in itself is good—and I suspect that would strongly depend on what one is motivated to do!)

Still others, attempting to justify profit, especially high profit, point to the equally excessive incomes of some actors and athletes. This, however, is a red herring—their incomes may be equally undeserved, so pointing them out adds nothing to the case for deserved profit (though it may add something to the case for societal consistency).

So the very *existence* of profit may, or may not, be morally unacceptable. What about the *distribution* of that profit? Should the profit be used for upgrading and expansion? Should it go to the shareholders? To the employees? Should the owner pocket it? Let's consider the moral acceptability of each of these in turn.

Upgrading and expansion may well be good. Be careful, though, of the circular argument: profit is good because it enables expansion, and expansion is good because it increases profit. Growth should be the means, not the end. And be careful not to *assume* that growth is good. Sometimes growth, certainly *unlimited* growth, is bad—think cancer. Consider that life may be better when we limit our growth. After all, isn't there a point at which you have enough? Don't we all learn, when we're about two years old, to "say when"? ("No," one of my students once quipped, "we didn't learn that lesson. That's why we're in Business.") Cute quip aside, expansion without restrictions is now recognized as one of "our" major mistakes. E.F. Schumacher was among the first to note the problem (in *Small Is Beautiful*), but even most economists now see that we should have been aiming all along for sustainable growth. Or no growth. See, for example, books by Jackson and Daly.

If, however, after upgrading, better products and services can be provided (better, not just more—unless we truly don't have enough), why not provide them? And if, with expansion, more jobs (good jobs, needed jobs) can be created, why not create them? But then why not build this into your price as an operating or development cost? (This particular justification for profit is closely related to the notion of social responsibility, which we'll come back to.)

Okay, what about your shareholders? Is it true that if someone invests in your company, giving you money to use, you have an obligation to give them the best return on their money? The *best*? Why not set a *fair* rate of return and make *that* your obligation? Have you *asked* your shareholders if they're willing to accept a lesser return in order to lower prices or increase wages or whatever? Perhaps there are more people than you think who would rather be (morally) right than be rich. And why not include that return as an expense, rather like the interest on a loan?

And what about stakeholders—all those who are affected by your company (consumers, suppliers, the local community, perhaps even the global community)? Why do you have a responsibility only to, or even first to, your shareholders? Recall that distributive justice according to contribution is not the only option.[1] Recall, further, that shareholder value isn't the only model of corporate governance.

Should the profits go to the employees? This is what co-ops do. But even profit-motivated companies could do this: see the Tembec case study at the end of this chapter.

Next, let's consider the owner/entrepreneur—doesn't she deserve to profit from, to benefit from, her endeavours? Perhaps it is this argument that causes the most moral outrage—on both sides. Certainly most people would agree that one deserves payment for one's work. But as long as the entrepreneur takes her payment from the profit rather than, or in addition to, taking it from the expenses (as a fixed wage), there are two ethical problems: the payment is potentially extra (if indeed she is also getting/taking a wage), and that needs to be justified; and/or the payment is potentially excessive (in the case of high profits), and that needs to be justified too.

One justification appeals to the hard work, the late hours often extending over years, that the owner has put in. Well, most people work hard for many years—are they not as entitled to an eventual payback that exceeds their normal wage? Certainly profit-sharing plans seem to endorse such entitlement. As for the late hours, which is often used as justification for profit-dependent bonuses going to a select few at the top as well as the owner, yes, perhaps they put in twice as many hours, but they'd have to work 100 times as hard during each of those hours to justify some of those bonuses—I don't think that's even possible. (Maybe they've never experienced how hard it is to be on the assembly line or to be a nurse or a receptionist/secretary—there are different kinds of "hard" when it comes to work.) Some companies, perhaps thinking along these lines, put a proportional limit on incomes—those at the top can't make more than, for example, four times as much as those at the bottom.[2]

---

1 See Freeman; Weiss; and Donaldson and Preston for discussions of this.
2 Which is, by the way, considerably different from the status quo: "the average top-100 CEO [in Canada] earns as much in *four hours* as the average Canadian makes in an *entire year*" (MacDonald). MacDonald goes on to say, pointedly, that "even those of us who believe fervently in the value of free markets can see that it's *not a good thing* that a CEO can afford to build a $50-million home while others living in the same country can't afford a roof over their head at all." Indeed. "It is unjust by almost any measure, socially divisive, and potentially socially disruptive." It is little wonder that the Occupy Movement took off like it did. See Kaplan and Walsh on this issue; see also Bogle, who addresses Kaplan's three arguments and indicates that from 1980 to 2004, the average worker's salary went from $14,900 to $35,000, an increase of 136%, while during the same time period the average CEO's income rose from $625,000 to $9,840,000, an increase of 1147%.

Another justification for owner-takes-profit appeals to the risk taken by the owner. Again, I think many would agree that one deserves payment for work-related risk-taking. But why isn't the payment for risk a fixed amount? Miners, police officers, firefighters, and many other workers risk their health, often even their lives, and supposedly their wages reflect that *as a fixed amount*. And this is typically a much lower amount than most entrepreneurs' profit. Why should a person get more for risking money (and often not even their own money, and certainly seldom money they need—i.e., for food, clothing, and shelter) than for risking health or life? No dangerous occupation pays several million dollars per year.

Another good point, raised by Grant, is that "bankruptcy laws...allow entrepreneurs to absolve themselves of certain losses they have incurred, pushing them onto creditors and former employees" (112). The $20 billion "stranded debt" of Ontario Hydro that Ontario residents have been paying off comes to mind, as does the famous bank bail-out: "during the financial crisis [2008–09], when it was suddenly plausible that homes [might] fall significantly in value and lenders might take large hits on their uninsured mortgages, CMHC allowed Canadian banks to transfer the risk on over $90 billion of previously uninsured mortgages from their balance sheets on to Canadian taxpayers" (Rabidoux), to the tune of $3,400 per person (according to CBC News)—and yet the banks reported $27 billion in profits in 2008–10. You want to bear the profits of your risk-taking, but not the losses? "You can't have your cake and eat it too" comes to mind. At the very least, there's a consistency issue here.

As a side note, this leads to a related question: When loans are "unpayable"—whether they're mortgages (think of the so-called "subprime lending fiasco" in the US) or car loans or student loans—what should happen? People take a risk when they borrow money, and they experience, at least temporarily, benefits from the loan. So if the risk doesn't work out the way they'd hoped and they can't pay back the loan, haven't they temporarily, at least partly, stolen those benefits? Why should someone else bear the responsibility of paying back their loans? Consider personal bankruptcy laws in this light. And whose responsibility is it in the first place? If a lender doesn't think the person *can* pay back the loan, is it their moral responsibility to refuse? Isn't that patronizing? (Of course, if the lender takes the loss in the event of non-repayment....) On the other hand, if the person can't repay the loan because of unfair interest rates and calculation methods...then what? And of course, we're not talking only about people here. Often whole countries are in the same situation. Many are obligated (morally?) to keep paying and paying and paying...long past having paid off the principal.

So the heart of the ethical issue seems to be not only the existence of profit (does it imply a legitimate miscalculation or an injustice?) but also the distribution of profit (if its existence is just, who should get it?). Consider, as a summarizing example, the billions of dollars in profit made by the very banks who have laid off thousands of workers. Were some of those billions made *because* the jobs were eliminated? (Is that why such a profit existed?) Shouldn't some of those billions be used to reinstate those jobs?

An examination of the morality of profit is, however, just the tip of an iceberg: what should precede it, perhaps, is an examination of the morality of capitalism. Isn't it capitalism that *enables* the pursuit of maximum profit? Does capitalism, further, make the pursuit of maximum profit *necessary*?[1]

Let's define capitalism as the economic system in which trade and industry, the provision of goods and services, is controlled by private owners competing for profit in a free market. (Is that an accurate definition?) In theory, it sounds fine. So why has it taken us to a dying planet? What went wrong? Do we need to ditch capitalism or just regulate it a bit more? Or do we need to *de*regulate it a bit more? Klein suggests that the problem is the lack of regulation: she speaks of "[t]he failure of deregulated capitalism to deliver on its promises…" (154) and says, "The idea that capitalism and only capitalism can save the world from a crisis created by capitalism is no longer an abstract theory; it's a hypothesis that has been tested and retested in the real world.… We've tried it.… The soaring emissions speak for themselves" (252). Others suggest that the problem is the presence of regulation: if markets were really free, it would all work out. (By some invisible hand…?) But those "soaring emissions"—that's clearly a harm, so capitalism has clearly done wrong—or is wrong.

We've already looked at profit, so let's look at the other elements of capitalism as defined: private ownership, competition, and the free market. I can't think of any ethic that would argue against private ownership *per se*. (Can you?) The controversial issues are how you came to own all the stuff you own (which has to be related to how much you can own) and what you do with the stuff once you own it. If one owns one's body and its labour (surely a solid starting point), then one should be able to own the product of one's labour. But certainly to *some* extent, what one's body is capable of is highly variable: is it fair that those less fortunate in this regard end up with less stuff?

And *no one's* labour produced air, water, or earth, or any other natural product. So how much of what a person makes *out of* those natural resources belongs to that person? And given, then, that some things *can't* be owned (according to the theory of the product of one's labour) and some things *can* be owned, is the most just system some hybrid of private and public ownership? What kind of hybrid? Is the political state necessarily implicated? More specifically, what should be the role of government—what are its rights and responsibilities? (The Sethi et al. anthology has a few good essays on this matter.) According to Collins, citing Neale Donald Walsch, "the next stage of political economy should be a synthesis between capitalism and socialism, a system which guarantees: (1) the meeting of basic needs/dignities…and (2) the opportunity to advance socially and financially. Socialism ensures freedom to live a sustainable life and capitalism ensures freedom of upward mobility" (333). Democratic Social Capitalism is the name Collins gives to this synthesis, which allows a free market but has both upper and lower income limits.

It's interesting that so many people balk at anything socialist. I thought that response was a relic of the Cold War, but Klein suggests another reason: "Real capitalists don't plan…they unleash the power of the profit motive and let the market, in its infinite wisdom, create the best possible society for all" (125). But that can't be right. Don't real capitalists have solid and extensive business plans? Business *plans*? Isn't centralized planning a cornerstone of a successful

---

1 De George and Shaw are good starting points, but many others are now (finally) writing and thinking about the ethics of economics.

business? So why not accept it as a cornerstone of a successful society? Or is the problem that businesspeople want their *own* plans to be unfettered by *other people's* plans. Okay, so what's the ethical response to this?

As for competition, apart from the obvious issue of fairness—nature and nurture, not to mention inheritance, financial and cultural, always give some people a head start—are we really convinced it gets us to a better world than co-operation does? Wells and Graffland state, "It is often supposed that if competitive markets are good, more competition must always be better" (abstract). Not so, says even Adam Smith (according to Wells and Graffland).

Somewhat related to this, since the valuing of competition arises, I think at least to some extent, from the valuing of hard work, are Handy's comments:

> The European example, with its five- to seven-week annual holidays, legally mandated parental leaves for fathers and mothers together, growing use of sabbaticals for senior executives, and working weeks of fewer than 40 hours, helps promote the idea that long work is not necessarily good work, and that the organization serves its own interests when it protects the overzealous from themselves. Many French companies were surprised that productivity increased when their last government required them to restrict the working week to 35 hours on average (a requirement being repealed by the current government). Europe's approach is one manifestation of the concept of the organization as community. The growing practice of customizing workers' contracts and development plans is another. (Handy, 53)

So perhaps it's not capitalism *per se*, but how we *do* capitalism: it doesn't have to be all-consuming (and I choose that word carefully, with at least two meanings).

And as for the market, Harries argues that "the market...acts as an essential signal from consumers to firms telling them how much to produce, when to produce it, and what sort of quality to make" (in Gray). Gray argues, further, that "a market system enhances the individual's scope for and frequency of acts of choice" (Gray). This endorsement of autonomy surely suggests that the market is a morally good thing.

But as for the *free* market, most people by now realize that there simply is no such thing. Not only governmental regulations but also trade treaties attach strings to the market—lots of strings, complicated spiderwebs of strings.... Consider, for example, the TPP (Trans-Pacific Partnership), to which Canada is about to become party: it's "an agreement written by and for transnational corporations including creating a trade tribunal court system that allows corporations to sue governments for potential lost profits, e.g., if a country passes an environmental law, corporations can figure out how it will affect their profits and sue the country for these imagined profits" ("Stop the Trans-Pacific Partnership"). This surely illustrates the difference between a legal right and a moral right. On what grounds does a company's "right" to profit trump others' right to happiness, health, and life itself? Am I being extreme to phrase it that way? (You decide, but wait until you read the last chapter.)

In fact, many would argue that our current system is, therefore, *not* capitalist:

It seems to be generally assumed that relying on markets for economic transactions is a necessary condition for an economy to be identified as capitalist.... However, if [this is a necessary requirement], are the economic systems we currently have, for example, in Europe and America, genuinely capitalist?

All affluent countries in the world—those in Europe, as well as the US, Canada, Japan, Singapore, South Korea, Australia, and others—have, for quite some time now, depended partly on transactions and other payments that occur largely outside markets. These include unemployment benefits, public pensions, other features of social security, and the provision of education, health care, and a variety of other services distributed through nonmarket arrangements. (Sen, 2009)

There is also the question of whether a completely free market would, in fact, be good. The WTO "provides a forum for negotiating agreements aimed at reducing obstacles to international trade and ensuring a level playing field for all, thus contributing to economic growth and development" (www.wto.org). But Silfab, a company in Toronto that was about to produce solar modules with impressive efficiency, never really got off the ground because although the local-content provisions of Ontario's green energy plan would have ensured a stable market for Silfab's products, the WTO determined that the provisions were illegal (Klein, 65–69). Better to be fair than environmentally responsible? (And as Stiglitz puts it, "Should [we] let a group of foolish lawyers, who put together something before they understood these issues, interfere with saving the planet?" [Klein, 72].)

This sort of thing is standard for trade agreements. Like the TPP, the FIPPA (the China-Canada Foreign Investment Protection and Promotion Agreement), with an arbitration institution that doesn't answer to any court in China or Canada, enables companies to sue a country (i.e., its taxpayers) if it gives preferential treatment to its own. Companies like Silfab might object, but maybe it *is* fair. After all, why should any company get preferential treatment by its government? Just because of its location? The chance location of its owner's birth? Or maybe the right question is this: "Why shouldn't Canada, and other industrialized countries, give preferential treatment to China?" Especially if carbon treaties are going to cripple China and other countries not yet as fully industrialized—haven't we had an unfair advantage, having been able to grow when there *weren't* such carbon limitations? Then again, echoing Stiglitz, maybe Klein asks the right question about these treaties: "How would the vastly increased distances that basic goods would now travel—by carbon-spewing container ships and jumbo jets, as well as diesel trucks—impact the carbon emissions that the climate negotiations were aiming to reduce?" (76).

I'm not sure which elements are responsible for this, but capitalism seems to enable a very few to "make" and keep a great deal. According to the *Human Development Report 1998*, the world's 225 richest people (that's about .000004% of the world's population) at that time had, combined, just about as much wealth as the bottom half of the world's people had, combined.[1]

---

[1] The 2015 Report phrases it thus: "[A]round 80 percent of the world's people have only 6 percent of the world's wealth" (5); "the world's richest 1 percent had an average wealth of $2.7 million per adult in 2014" (11).

And things only got worse. In 2014, the 85 richest people had as much as the bottom 3.5 billion people. Yes, 3.5 *billion*. "To put it another way, if the 48 poorest nations pooled their resources, they'd still own less than the three richest guys in the world" (2011 Year in Review).

Consider Michalos's observation about the consequence of such a system, if one assumes that wealth equals power:

> [A]fter people around the world have made Steven Spielberg rich by their individually modest but collectively huge purchases of his products, they might well have second thoughts about putting all that power into the possession of one person. After all, ignoring luck, the virtue that allowed Spielberg to accumulate his vast fortune may be far out of proportion to his virtue in spending it. For all I know, Spielberg is a saint and every dime he spends is well-spent, and there certainly are many others with more money and perhaps less virtue of any kind than he has. But my point is that an economic and political system that would allow such people to spend all their money, say, buying and levelling large chunks of the remaining forest of cash-starved Third World countries or promoting North American football around the world is a dangerous system. It seems to me that the world would be a better place for more people if no one were allowed to have such power. Since twenty of the twenty-two countries in the OECD [Organization for Economic Cooperation and Development] have some sort of wealth taxation, modest as it is in every country, other people apparently have shared some of my intuitions about these things. (222–23)[1]

Another criticism of capitalism is its apparent addiction to unlimited growth: "[O]f all the technical weaknesses in capitalism..., probably the most immediately dangerous is its absolute inability to process the finiteness of resources and the mathematical impossibility of maintaining rapid growth in physical output" (financier Jeremy Grantham, in Allen). The word "weakness" here is a bit understated; consider instead: "Capitalism, by ignoring the finite nature of resources and by neglecting the long-term well-being of the planet and its potentially crucial biodiversity, *threatens our existence*" (Jeremy Grantham, in Klein 233; my emphasis). Not only are we getting it wrong; moreover, "[w]e know that we are trapped within an economic system that has it backward: it behaves as if there is no end to what is actually finite (clean water, fossil fuels, and the atmospheric space to absorb their emissions) while insisting that there are strict and immovable limits to what is actually quite flexible: the financial resources that human institutions manufacture, and that, if imagined differently, could build the kind of caring society we need" (Klein 347).[2]

Whatever else we say about capitalism, surely we have to say it hasn't taken us where we want. Do we want soil too poor to grow food in? Do we want lakes we can't swim in, let alone drink out of? Do we want to have to wear sunscreen whenever we go outside? And oxygen masks? But no, wait, is that the fault of capitalism or only of certain capitalists? Because didn't capitalism

---

1 Canada and the US are the two countries without wealth taxation.
2 See Jackson and many, many others who argue that prosperity is possible without growth; it's being called sustainable economics.

also give us indoor plumbing and ibuprofen and phones? Or could we have got that stuff with some other economic system?

> **BOX 7.2 Is There a Problem with Economic Growth?**
>
> "In virtually every nation, the government aims at economic growth with high levels of employment and low inflation. But the growth element of this set of objectives is incoherent for at least three reasons:
>
> "Growth is not a measure of benefits, but a measure of overall economic activity. That we have more of it means only that we have more of it—not that we are better off. Much economic growth creates negative side effects like pollution, but current measures don't take this into account. Indeed, the money we spend to protect ourselves from pollution creates more growth!
>
> "Incomes can rise while wealth falls. If we cut trees, income can rise during the cutting but the ability to sustain it falls after the trees are gone.
>
> "Growth contains no measure of distribution, so poverty and inequality can and do rise at the same time that overall economic activity increases."
>
> *Source*
> Brown, Peter G. "Why We Need an Economics of Stewardship." *University Affairs* Nov. 2000: 37.

Maybe. But Grantham goes on to say, "There is no single theory that is used in economics that considers the finite nature of resources" (in Hickman). So the problem isn't capitalism, but economics? This is certainly the view of E.F. Schumacher: "The judgment of economics...is an extremely fragmentary judgment; out of the large number of aspects which in real life have to be seen and judged together before a decision can be taken, economics supplies only one—whether a thing yields a money profit to those who undertake it or not" (35). (See Jacobsen's essay in this chapter for a similar point.) Schumacher goes on to say, "[The modern economist] is used to measuring the 'standard of living' by the amount of annual consumption, assuming all the time that a man who consumes more is 'better off' than a man who consumes less. A Buddhist economist would consider this approach excessively irrational: since consumption is merely a means to human well-being, the aim should be to obtain the maximum of well-being with the minimum of consumption" (47–48).

Waring also questions what we value and how we measure what we value, and she comes up with some very disturbing answers. For example, as long as income passes through the system, it's considered a contribution to growth, which is considered a good thing. So the Exxon Valdez oil spill, because it generated clean-up jobs, was a good thing. (So would be the car accident that maims three people, because it makes work for insurance companies and auto shops and physiotherapy clinics....) And "Ben," who spends his days in a bunker practicing to push the button that will annihilate the planet is more valuable, is contributing more to society, than "Cathy," who spends her days in the home, nurturing children into maturity. As Waring says, "this is not a sane state of affairs" (20).

> **BOX 7.3 Feel Like Watching a Movie?**
>
> Check out *The Corporation: The Pathological Pursuit of Profit and Power.*

References and Further Reading

Abbas, J. Ali, Abdulrahman Al-Aali, and Abdullah Al-Owaihan. "Islamic Perspectives on Profit Maximization." *Journal of Business Ethics* 117 (2013): 467–76.

Allen, Frederick E. "Jeremy Grantham Says Capitalism May Destroy Us All." *Forbes* 1 Mar. 2012. Forbes.com

Arrow, Kenneth J. "Social Responsibility and Economic Efficiency." *Public Policy* 21 (Summer 1973).

Aspinwall, Emily. "Prisons Hit the Stock Market." *Kinesis* (Mar. 2001): 8.

Bogle, John C. "Reflections on CEO Compensation." *Academy of Management Perspectives* May 2008: 21–25.

Brown, Grant A. "Are Profits Deserved?" *Journal of Business Ethics* 11.2 (1992): 105–14.

Brown, Peter G. *Ethics, Economics and International Relations: Transparent Sovereignty in the Commonwealth of Life.* Edinburgh: Edinburgh University Press, 2000.

———. *Right Relationship: Building a Whole Earth Economy.* San Francisco: Berrett-Koehler Publishers, 2009.

CBC News. "Banks got $114B from governments during recession." 30 Apr. 2012. http://www.cbc.ca/news/business/banks-got-114b-from-governments-during-recession-1.1145997

Chomsky, Noam. *Free Market Fantasies: Capitalism in the Real World.* AK Press. Audio CD.

Collins, Denis. "Virtuous Individuals, Organizations and Political Economy: A New Age Theological Alternative to Capitalism." *Journal of Business Ethics* 26 (2000): 319–40.

Daly, Herman E. *Beyond Growth: The Economics of Sustainable Development.* Boston: Beacon Press, 1997.

De George, Richard T. *Business Ethics.* 5th ed. Englewood Cliffs, NJ: Prentice Hall, 1999. (See chapters 6 and 7.)

Donaldson, Thomas, and Lee E. Preston. "The Stakeholder Theory of the Corporation." In S. Prakash Sethi, Paul Steidlmeier, and Cecilia M. Falbe (eds.), *Scaling the Corporate Wall: Readings in Business and Society*. 2nd ed. Englewood Cliffs, NJ: Prentice Hall, 1997. 233–52.

Eight Arguments about the Morality of the Marketplace. In Praise of the Free Economy (Centre for Independent Studies), 2000.

Estes, Ralph. *Tyranny of the Bottom Line: Why Corporations Make Good People Do Bad Things*. San Francisco: Berrett-Koehler Publishers, 1996.

Fischer, Michael F. "Luca Pacioli on Business Profits." *Journal of Business Ethics* 25 (2000): 299–312.

Freeman, R. Edward. "The Politics of Stakeholder Theory." *Business Ethics Quarterly* 4.4 (1994): 409–12.

French, Peter A. "Corporate Moral Agency." In W. Michael Hoffman and Jennifer Mills Moore (eds.), *Business Ethics: Readings and Cases in Corporate Morality*. New York: McGraw Hill, 1984. 163–71.

Goldman, Alan H. "Business Ethics: Profits, Utilities, and Moral Rights." *Philosophy & Public Affairs* 9.3 (1980): 260–86.

Grant, Colin. "Friedman Fallacies." *Journal of Business Ethics* 10.12 (1991): 907–14.

Gray, J. "The Moral Foundations of Market Institutions." IEA Health and Welfare Unit, Choice in Welfare Series No. 10, London. 1992.

Handy, Charles. "What's a Business For?" *Harvard Business Review* 80.12 (2002): 49–55.

Hardwig, John. "The Stockholder—A Lesson for Business Ethics from Bioethics?" *Journal of Business Ethics* 91.3 (2010): 329–41.

Harries, R. "Is There a Gospel for the Rich?" London: Mowbray, 1992.

Hickman, Leo. "Jeremy Grantham on how to feed the world and why he invests in oil." *Guardian* 16 Apr. 2013. http://www.theguardian.com/environment/blog/2013/apr/16/jeremy-grantham-food-oil-capitalism

Jackson, Tim. *Prosperity without Growth: Economics for a Finite Planet*. New York: Routledge, 2011.

Kaplan, Steven N. "Are U.S. CEOs Overpaid?" *Academy of Management Perspectives* (May 2008): 5–20.

Klein, Naomi. *This Changes Everything*. New York: Simon & Schuster, 2014.

MacDonald, Chris. "CEO Salaries and Justice." *The Business Ethics Blog*. 7 Jan. 2014. http://businessethicsblog.com/2014/01/07/ceo-salaries-and-justice/

Michalos, Alex. "Issues for Business Ethics in the Nineties and Beyond." *Journal of Business Ethics* 16.3 (1997): 219–30.

Morales, Alex. "Kyoto Veterans Say Global Warming Goal Slipping Away." *Bloomberg*. 4 Nov. 2013. http://www.bloomberg.com/news/articles/2013-11-04/kyoto-veterans-say-global-warming-goal-slipping-away

Mulligan, Thomas. "A Critique of Milton Friedman's Essay 'The Social Responsibility of Business Is to Increase Its Profits.'" *Journal of Business Ethics* 5.4 (1986): 265–69.

Nordberg, Donald. "The Ethics of Corporate Governance." *Journal of General Management* 33.4 (2008): 35–52.

Phillips, Charles F., Jr. "What Is Wrong with Profit Maximization?" In W.T. Greenwood (ed.), *Issues in Business and Society*. 3rd ed. Boston: Houghton Mifflin, 1977. 77–88.

Rabidoux, Ben. "The REAL Canadian Bank Bailout." *Maclean's* 24 May 2012. http://www.macleans.ca/economy/business/the-real-canadian-bank-bailout/

Schumacher, E.F. *Small Is Beautiful: Economics as if People Mattered*. London: Sphere Books, 1974.

Sen, Amartya. "Capitalism: Beyond the Crisis." 2009. http://www.nybooks.com/articles/archives/2009/mar/26/capitalism-beyond-the-crisis/

———. *Development as Freedom*. Rockland, MA: Anchor, 2000.

———. *On Ethics and Economics*. Oxford: Basil Blackwell, 1987.

Sethi, S. Prakash, Paul Steidlmeier, and Cecilia M. Falbe. *Scaling the Corporate Wall: Readings in Business and Society*. 2nd ed. Englewood Cliffs, NJ: Prentice Hall, 1997.

Shaw, William H. *Business Ethics*. 2nd ed. Belmont, CA: Wadsworth, 1996. (See chapters 3, 4, and 5.)

"Stop the Trans-Pacific Partnership: Bad for Jobs, the Environment, Labor and Consumers." *It's Our Economy*. http://itsoureconomy.us/occupy-the-tpp-stop-the-global-corporate-coup/

Turner, Graham. "Is Global Collapse Imminent?" Research Paper No. 4, Lauren, Rickards, (ed.), MSSI Research Papers. Melbourne, Australia: Melbourne Sustainable Society Institute, The University of Melbourne. Aug. 2014. www.sustainable.unimelb.edu.au

2011 Year in Review. http://2011.yearinreview.yahoo.com/2011/us_top_news/#10occupy_wall_street

United Nations Development Programme. *Human Development Report 2015*. http://hdr.undp.org/en/2015-report

———. *Human Development Report 1998*. New York: Oxford University Press, 1998.

Walsch, N.D. *Conversations with God: An Uncommon Dialogue*, Book 2. Charlottesville, VA: Hampton Roads Publishing Company, 1997.

Walsh, James P. "CEO Compensation and the Responsibilities of the Business Scholar to Society." *Academy of Management Perspectives* (May 2008): 26–33.

Waring, Marilyn. *If Women Counted: A New Feminist Economics*. San Francisco: Harper and Row, 1988.

Weiss, Joseph W. *Business Ethics: A Managerial, Stakeholder Approach*. Belmont, CA: Wadsworth, 1994.

Wells, Thomas, and Johan Graffland. "Adam Smith's Bourgeois Virtues in Competition." *Business Ethics Quarterly* 22.2 (2012): 319–50.

Economic Efficiency and the Quality of Life*

Rockney Jacobsen

ABSTRACT. A classical moral defense of profit seeking as the social responsibility of business in a competitive market is examined. That defense rests on claims about the directness of relationships between (a) profit seeking activity and standards of living and (b) standards of living and the quality of life. Responses to the classical argument tend to raise doubts about the directness of the first relationship. This essay challenges the directness of the second relationship, argues that the classical argument is invalid, and claims that an alternative description of the social responsibility of business is entailed by the classical premises.

I.

[1] Profits, we are told by the classical and neoclassical strains in economic thought, are the best measure of a firm's contribution to the welfare of others. If our contributions to the social good are relevant to what we merit or deserve, then profits clearly seem to be deserved. The classical story is sometimes told in a more dramatic form: the mechanisms of the free market work to yield a high quality of life for a community when, and only when, the participants in the market are driven by a motive of profit maximization. If the participants suffer a motivational lapse and direct their market activities to ends other than profits, the machine falters, and the community lapses into hard times; thus, if the participants in the free market bear a responsibility for the well-being of bystanders, then that responsibility can only be met by engaging in the pursuit of profits.

These kinds of stories about the relationships [2] between economic activity and ethics, ending with claims about the moral status of profit seeking, have been widely challenged outside the classical[1] traditions in economic thought. The dispute tends to focus on the truth or falsity of claims about the capability of a free market, fueled by the energies of profit seekers, to deliver the promised goods efficiently to the community. It thus becomes a series of skirmishes over how direct the relationship is, at various points, between increasing profits and increasing contributions to the social well-being. If the relationship turns out to be direct, the classical liberal or contemporary libertarian is thought to win the day; if the relationship is discovered to be indirect or, better yet, inverse, then the case is thought to be lost.

---

* Rockney Jacobsen, "Economic Efficiency and the Quality of Life." *Journal of Business Ethics* 10.3 (March 1991): 201–09. © 1991 by Kluwer Academic Publishers. Reprinted with permission of the publisher and the author.

[3] I will not enter into the fray along this front, for two reasons. First, the claims about the delivery capabilities of a free market of competing profit seekers is often acknowledged to be an empirical claim which, according to its proponents, has not yet been subjected to an adequate or fair test in the market place.[2] Thus, if the consequences of profit seeking in any particular case can be shown to be morally odious, the defender of profit seeking is more likely to call for revisions in the economic system than concede that the odious consequences derive from a motive to acquire profits. Secondly, I suspect that the moral upshot of disputes about the status of profit seeking depend less on the soundness of classical economics than is generally assumed. My strategy in what follows will be to grant as much as possible to the claims of classical economics, but question the moral consequences which are thought to follow. Since his writings are the most articulate contemporary expression of the classical cause, I will use the libertarian views of Milton Friedman[3] as my chief stalking horse. Although most of my attention will be directed towards an argument which operates only as "deep background" to Friedman's own presentation of his case, we will see in the final section how the ruin of this classical argument takes the wind out of the contemporary libertarian addenda.

II.

[4] I noted in opening that the classical argument can take more or less dramatic forms, resulting in a stronger or weaker conclusion; in its weaker form, the argument concludes that profit seeking is always morally justifiable (morally permissible); in its stronger form, the argument concludes that profit seeking is morally obligatory. Both conclusions agree in suggesting that there is certainly nothing wrong with pursuing profits—that it is not morally forbidden. I will state and examine an argument for both the weaker and stronger conclusions; the argument will be found lacking, but in noting how it fails, we shall see an alternative statement of the social responsibilities of business emerge.

[5] The central classical argument for these conclusions, which I will refer to as the economic efficiency argument, is of distinguished pedigree, making an early appearance in the writings of Adam Smith. In a deservedly famous passage, Smith, writing of merchants who intend only their own interest and gain, says that in a free competitive market such a merchant is

> led by an invisible hand to promote an end which was no part of his intention. Nor is it always the worse for society that it was no part of it. By pursuing his own interest, he frequently promotes that of the society more effectually than when he really intends to promote it. I have never known much good done by those who affected to trade for the public good.[4]

This passage, which Friedman quotes[5] with obvious approval, does not actually state an argument, but the spirit of one shines clearly through. The justification of the pursuit of private interest and gain in the market place is derived from the fact that such a pursuit promotes the public interest or good; furthermore, designs on the part of merchants to promote the public good directly will be less efficient in doing so than is the pursuit of gain and may even damage the public interest. If pursuing individual profits effectively promotes the public welfare, then it is morally justified; if pursuing individual profits is the *only* effective means of promoting social ends, then it is morally obligatory, and if pursuing desirable social ends directly is destructive of those ends, it is morally forbidden.

[6]   The first premiss employed in such reasoning may be stated as follows:

> (1) A free competitive market, in which the participants act always so as to maximize their individual profits, is the most (or, the *only*) efficient mechanism for the production and distribution of safe, high quality, affordable goods and services for consumers.

This claim about the delivery capabilities of a free market is offered both in defense of a certain design for the market place—it must be free and competitive—and in defense of a profit motivation on the part of its participants. My strategy will be to suppose that both parts of the claim are true, and see what follows. I will, therefore, suppose that a free competitive market is the most (or, the only) efficient mechanism for the delivery of the goods, and, the efficiency of the mechanism depends upon the self-interested pursuit of profits on the part of persons doing business in the market place. The additional premisses needed to support the desired conclusion are less contentious and less frequently criticized. I suggest the following premisses as a plausible route to the weaker and stronger conclusions of the classical argument:

> (2) The production and distribution of safe, high quality, affordable goods and services for consumption increases the standard of living throughout the community by alleviating scarcity and its attendant moral evils—hunger, disease, crime, etc.
> (3) Alleviation of, and security against, scarcity and its attendant evils is an essential part of promoting and maintaining a high quality of life for persons, human well-being, human flourishing, the good life, etc., and these are morally good things.

[7] Before completing the argument, we should pause here to deflect a misunderstanding which might otherwise affect the outcome of the argument. The joint claim of the first three premisses might easily be obscured by talk about "the quality of life," "human well-being," etc. The claim being made is not that the maximal contribution which *persons in business* can make to our quality of life is made by the self-interested pursuit of their own profits. Rather, the somewhat weaker claim is being made that the maximal contribution such persons can make to our quality of life *in their capacity as persons in business* is made by their self-interested pursuit of profits. Milton Friedman does not deny[6] that I can make, and even *should* make other contributions to the quality of your life in other capacities—e.g., as your friend, as your spouse, as your priest, etc. But, in doing business with you, I can make the fullest contribution to your welfare which it is possible for me to make *in that capacity or role*, by pursuing my own profits in a free and competitive market. Contributions which I might make by serving you well in other capacities may be far greater than any I can make by doing business with you. But in making such contributions to your well-being I can only be viewed as meeting the responsibilities which accrue to me in the roles of friend, spouse, or priest; I am not thereby meeting the responsibilities of business. The question we should have before us is not "what can I do to contribute to the quality of your life?" but, rather, "what can I do, *qua* businessman, to meet the responsibilities which I have in that capacity?"

[8] With this qualification in mind, the argument can be completed as follows:

> (4) Participants in a free competitive market can (or, can only) promote and secure a high quality of life throughout a community by acting always so as to increase their profits.

(5) Those who can contribute to the promotion of moral goods, or the alleviation of moral evils, are morally justified in doing so (or, have a moral responsibility to do so).
(6) Participants in a free competitive market are morally justified in (or, have a moral responsibility for) acting always so as to increase their profits.

We are in a position to see that, even granting the truth of the premises of this argument, there are difficulties in supposing that it supports any moral advice or moral prescriptions which can be used to guide participants in the market place as they do business. In the following sections, I will point to three weaknesses in argument, in order of increasing degree of seriousness, and *en route* arrive at an alternative statement of the responsibilities of business. Only in the concluding section will I address directly Friedman's libertarian addenda to the argument. We shall see that when the economic efficiency argument is answered, and its import better understood, then those addenda lose their force.

III.

[9] It should first be noticed that to concede the argument in its entirety is not yet to concede that persons in business are justified in, or obligated to, pursue profits. The moral justification which the economic efficiency argument provides for either permitting or requiring the pursuit of profits does not depend upon the implausible assumption that there is something intrinsically good about making profits; rather, the pursuit of profits is argued to have intrinsically desirable consequences for the quality of life in our communities. The entire weight of the argument is borne by those consequences. Thus, if there should arise any need for a trade-off between promoting the ends of profit seekers and promoting social ends, then only those trade-offs which favor the promotion of socially desirable ends will receive the moral backing of the efficiency argument. But our present economy is agreed by all sides to be one in which such trade-offs *are* required.[7] Trade restrictions, corporate taxes, and a whole net of government constraints on business make ours a market in which there is not a direct relationship between increasing profits and increasing the quality of our lives. Consequently, even if the argument is sound, the conclusion which it yields is not that participants in any actual market are morally justified in pursuing, let alone morally obliged to pursue their individual profits at every point in their market activities. It may well be true that this only points to flaws in our economic systems as they stand, and the defender of the argument will, perhaps, justly respond that the point only requires us to urge deregulation of the present market. Nonetheless, the conclusion we are forced to by the economic realities is that the efficiency argument cannot be used to support saying that persons in business ought always to act in such a way as to increase their profits. Furthermore, the nature of the support which the argument does try to throw behind profit seeking reveals that at all points where our less than free and competitive market requires a trade-off between the public good and profits, morality will demand that we sacrifice profits for the public good. If an increase in the quality of our lives can work to ground the morality of profit seeking in a free economy, then surely it will work to ground the charge that profit seeking is immoral at any point that it decreases the quality of life.

IV.

It might be thought that the case made in the previous section only establishes that, in our fallible world, the moral advice to people in business to [10] pursue their profits is defeasible on special occasions and, so, allows occasional exceptions. We should therefore see what happens in a less imperfect world. Let us suppose that not only are the premisses of the argument true, but that we also have an ideal libertarian market, of perfect freedom and perfect competition. In this happy world, a firm's profits are thought to be a perfect measure of the contributions which the firm makes to our standard of living. Consumers will be assured that those contributions, in the form of goods and services, which business is capable of making to our well-being are being made to the fullest, and business can be assured of the greatest profits commensurate with that contribution. In such a world, the entrepreneur who lived according to the maxim "act always so as to increase your profits" would at the same time always act so as to increase the standard of living throughout the community. Nonetheless, I shall argue that even in such a world, there are limits on the extent to which the pursuit of profits receives moral justification *via* the economic efficiency argument.

[11] Recall that the moral justification which the pursuit of profits receives from the economic efficiency argument derives solely from the contribution which that pursuit makes to the *quality of our lives*; it does not derive from the intrinsic value of the activity of seeking profits, but, nor does it derive from the contribution which pursuing profits makes to the *standard of living* in the community. It is only in so far as seeking profits promotes the quality of life that we defend profit seeking; but, even in an ideal economy, how far is that? The third premiss of the argument states, quite plausibly, that the "delivery of the goods" is an essential part of promoting human well-being. The larger, more complex, and more interdependent human communities become, the more likely it is to be true that that part of a life of desirable quality will be provided by market mechanisms. Our standard of living, as it is measured by production and consumption, may be granted to be an essential component in our quality of life without thereby granting very much of moral interest. Perhaps there are rare individuals (though this is doubtful) who measure the quality of their lives by their standard of living alone, where that standard is viewed in terms of the goods and services made available for them to use as they will. But in general, however much we differ in what we take a high quality of life to contain, our view of it is much more capacious than our view of our standard of living. Most of us view it as containing certain ingredients which it is no part of the capabilities of a market, however perfect, to deliver—such "intangibles" as love, friendship, virtues, enjoyable activities, and so on.

[12] So long as there is a difference between what makes up a high standard of living and what makes up a high quality of life, there will be limits to the extent to which the economic efficiency argument can justify the pursuit of profits. The reason is this: the moral value which we place on any increase in our standard of living derives from the contribution which that increase makes to our quality of life; but so long as our standard of living is only one of the components of our quality of life, then the moral value of an increasing standard of living will obey a principle of "diminishing moral utility." Equivalent consecutive increases in the standard of living will not yield equivalent consecutive increases in the quality of life; as our standard of living increases up to a certain point, the contribution which such increases make to the quality of our lives will diminish towards zero. Let us see why.

[13] Suppose, contrary to what has been suggested, that increases of equivalent size in a person's standard of living always resulted in increases of equivalent size in that person's quality of life. Now consider the case of a person who lacks love,

friendships, the promise of salvation, or whatever in your view goes into a high quality of life beyond a high standard of living. Suppose that this person has the same high standard of living as others in the community, but that they, unlike him, also have the intangibles to which he has been denied access. We would surely think that those who have an abundance of these "intangible goods" are better off than the one who lacks them. But, now, suppose that the man who lacks the intangibles acquires the means to increase his wealth, and so, his standard of living, without limit. By hypothesis, as he does so, he will at some point acquire a higher, more desirable quality of life than the others, despite the fact that, unlike them, he will never be blessed with the intangibles. Thus, it would appear, love, friendship, and the like, are no essential part of the quality of life we enjoy. Any quality of life which can be achieved by having those things can also be reached, and even surpassed, merely by acquiring a high enough standard of living. But this consequence runs entirely against the grain of our view of a desirable quality of life as containing such intangibles, however much we may differ as to what they are. The consequence is avoided by denying that increases in our standard of living are always accompanied by commensurate increases in our quality of life, and conceding that there are limits on the extent to which greater access to goods and services can make for a better life. No doubt an increase in our standard of living which lifts us from hunger and disease to satiation and health will be assigned a high moral value; but the move from economic sufficiency to affluence need not be thought to have as great a value to us, and the further move from affluence to opulence will have even less value. At some point, further affluence will always become superfluous in the pursuit of a better life.

[14] We can see now why the fact of diminishing moral utility limits the range of the efficiency argument in justifying the pursuit of profits. In a community in which a level of affluence is reached which is sufficient for doing its part in contributing to a desirable quality of life, further increases in our standard of living cease to make any additional contribution, and, so, further profit seeking cannot be given moral justification by citing consequences for the quality of our lives. The very best that the economic efficiency argument can do to defend the pursuit of profit, even in an ideal economy, is justify the pursuit of profit up to the point where the community has reached some level of economic sufficiency or affluence; beyond that point, profit seeking lacks the backing of the argument. Furthermore, before that point is reached, but as it is more and more closely approached, the strength of the support which the efficiency argument gives to profit seeking diminishes.

[15] I have not made the claim that our society has already reached the point of zero moral returns from profit seeking; but it seems arguable that we are approaching it, and the claim is always worth seriously entertaining. The market place, fueled as it is by the profit motive, stands to benefit from obscuring our sense of how close we might be, and when we may have had enough of what it can provide.

V.

[16] I have argued thus far that even if the economic efficiency argument is sound, it does not yield moral advice or prescriptions for persons who do business in our present economies; also, it has been argued that the considerations raised in the efficiency argument do not support unlimited pursuit even in an ideally free and competitive market. Both arguments against the classical cause have assumed that the argument for the cause contains only true premises; the first counterargument assumes the soundness of the efficiency argument and the

second counterargument challenges only the range of application of the conclusion. In this section, the soundness of the argument will be challenged.

[17] It may be replied to the considerations raised in the preceding sections that they show only that profit seeking is not *always* morally justified or obligatory. Nonetheless, in so far as our present markets approximate a free and competitive ideal, and in so far as our standard of living has not (or, has not *clearly*) reached a point of zero moral returns on profit seeking, some (or even much) profit seeking is still justified by the efficiency argument. Furthermore, nothing I have said addressed directly the stronger form of the argument which leads to the conclusion that profit seeking is morally obligatory. If maintaining and securing our standard of living depends upon profit seeking, and if directing the attention of persons in business to desirable social ends and, thereby, away from profit seeking would undermine the efficiency of the market to such an extent that we would run the serious risk of lapsing into scarcity and its attendant evils, then participants in the world of business are morally obliged to pursue their individual profits.

[18] But it is, we shall now see, a mistake to suppose that these considerations, even if all true, would support thinking that business has a social responsibility to pursue profits. Seeing why they fail will lead us to an alternative statement of the responsibilities of business.

[19] Let us assume, once again, that the first premiss of the efficiency argument is true, and that when and only when market participants (in an ideally free and competitive market) pursue their individual profits, can we be assured of security against the evils of scarcity. We noted earlier that the economic efficiency argument gives whatever justification it does to market activities only by reference to the contributions which such activity makes to the quality of our lives. That fact would not be changed simply because the economy was so arranged that we had a perfectly direct relationship between increasing profits and increasing (or maintaining) the quality of our lives. But it is only supposing that a perfectly direct relationship between these two factors does make a difference to the *source* of our rights and obligations which could lead us to suppose that there is a moral responsibility on the part of business to increase its profits. An analogy should make clear why this is so.

[20] Consider a boiler tender who is responsible for keeping the pressure in a boiler within a specified range; he proceeds by opening and closing valves and adjusting the temperature while watching a pressure gauge. As long as the gauge is functioning properly and is properly calibrated, all he need attend to is the position of the needle on the gauge. If he should come to describe his own responsibility as being that of keeping the needle within a certain range, his description of his responsibilities is perfectly harmless, but it is a harmless *mis*-description of his responsibilities. That it is a misdescription, and not merely an alternative reformulation of his duty, is shown by the fact that if the gauge were faulty, he would be clearly duty bound to try as best he could to keep the pressure within its proper range, despite the fact that, then, the needle would no longer stay within the range which ought to, but does not, indicate that pressure. In such a situation, to let the pressure go where it will, in order to ensure that the needle stays where it ought, would be the height of negligence. To take his "harmless" misstatement of his responsibilities seriously would be an invitation to catastrophe.

[21] In a world of perfect pressure gauges, our boiler tender would not be forced to choose between describing his duty as a duty to keep the needle in a certain position or describing it as a duty to keep the pressure in a certain range; in practice, they will come down to the same thing. Likewise,

if we grant that the first premiss of the economic efficiency argument is true, and if we supposed that we lived and worked in a perfectly free and competitive market where profits were a perfect gauge of a firm's contributions to our quality of life, then it would be a harmless *mis*statement of the responsibilities of business to say that their sole social responsibility was to increase their profits. Nonetheless, what the efficiency argument supports as a proper description of the social responsibilities of business is not increasing profit, but, rather, producing and distributing safe, high quality, affordable goods and services for consumers. In the case of the boiler tender, it was only because maintaining the pressure and positioning the needle on the gauge came down to the same thing (given an ideal gauge) and because *maintaining the pressure was his real responsibility*, that we were at all tempted to accept the misstatement of his responsibility as keeping the needle in position. Likewise, it is only because delivering the goods and making profits are thought to come down to the same thing (in an ideal market), and because the delivery of the goods is the social responsibility of business, that we are at all tempted to accept the misstatement of the responsibility of business as increasing profits.

[22] If we think that delivery of the goods, to whatever extent is sufficient for maintaining a desirable quality of life, is a desirable social end, then what this argument shows is that business does, after all, have a moral responsibility to promote desirable social ends. According to my conclusion, it is *no part* of the social responsibility of business to increase its profits though, assuming the truth of the first premiss of the economic efficiency argument, and taking into account the considerations raised in previous sections, pursuing profits may sometimes be morally permissible. In the following and concluding section I will raise and address two objections to my conclusion.

VI.

[23] The doctrine that firms have a social responsibility, combined with the claim that they have no responsibility to make profits, is argued (by the contemporary libertarian descendants of Adam Smith) to have dangerous consequences.[8] The libertarian addenda to the classical efficiency argument proceed by indicating the dangerous social and political consequences of the doctrine of social responsibility. Since I have argued for a version of that doctrine and rejected in total the strong libertarian conclusion that business has a social responsibility to increase its profits, it will be necessary to speak directly to the so-called "dangerous" consequences.

[24] It might first be objected that by following a moral prescription to meet their social obligations, and not attending to profits, corporate executives will be distracted from that course of action on which the efficient operation of the market depends. Businesses attending to their social responsibilities, and not to their profits, are like the boiler tender who attends to the pressure in the tank, and not to the needle on the pressure gauge. Even if their responsibility is to promote certain social ends, they cannot accurately gauge how well they are doing that except by attending to their profits. Even if profits are not a perfect measure, in our less than perfectly free and competitive market, of a firm's contributions to our quality of life, they are nonetheless the best measure we have. The problem here is epistemic, not moral. Just as the boiler tender has no way to gauge the pressure other than by watching the pressure gauge, so the person in business has no way to gauge contributions to our quality of life, except by attending to profits. To allow boiler tenders and firms to exercise their own best judgement without recourse to such aids as gauges and profits is to invite catastrophe. But this objection is misguided.

[25] The heart of the defense of the free competitive market, and the pursuit of profits, was the assumption that business best promotes the public good by seeking profits precisely because it will discover that the best way to make profits is to provide safer, cheaper, lower cost goods and services for consumers. Thus, the self-regulatory nature of the market which is meant to lead (albeit unintentionally) to desirable social ends requires that persons in business will be able to judge what counts as a safer, higher quality, or lower priced commodity. But that is all that I have argued they have a social responsibility to do. If they can do those things well enough for the purposes of the defenders of the first premiss of the economic efficiency argument, then they can do it well enough for the purposes of meeting their social responsibilities *qua* business.

[26] A second objection which might be leveled against my conclusions derives from the contractual agreements which are made by individuals in doing business. Thus, a corporate executive, for example, is described by Milton Friedman as

> an employee of the owners of the business. He has a direct responsibility to his employers. That responsibility is to conduct the business in accordance with their desires, which generally will be to make as much money as possible....[9]

Now this point, by itself, does nothing at all to support the claim, which Friedman is defending, that corporate executives have a social responsibility to increase profits. As is well-known, no one has a responsibility to keep any contracts or agreements if it should turn out that what has been promised, agreed, or contracted to, is itself immoral. But, even if we add the additional premiss that making profits is not immoral, such responsibilities as Friedman mentions would not count as moral or social responsibilities. Even though society has a strong interest in seeing that just agreements and contracts are kept, and so we have a general obligation to keep our agreements, it does not follow that the contents of our agreements have a similar status. Thus, although I may owe a general duty to society to keep my promises, and though I have promised to lend you my car for the weekend, it does not follow that I owe a duty to society to lend you my car for the weekend. Though it turns out, that, on this occasion, the only way I can meet my obligation to society to keep my promise is by lending you my car, my doing *that* (lending the car to you) is not a duty owed to society. My doing that is no part of what society has an interest in, though my keeping my promises is.

[27] Friedman's worry, thus far, simply mistakes the notion of a social responsibility. But he goes further:

> What does it mean to say that the corporate executive has a "social responsibility" in his capacity as a businessman? If this statement is not pure rhetoric, it must mean that he is to act in some way that is not in the interest of his employers.[10]

and:

> The executive is exercising a distinct "social responsibility," rather than serving as an agent of the stockholders or the customers or the employees, only if he spends the money in a different way than they would have spent it.[11]

Friedman is here creating a false dilemma. He represents as incompatible alternatives the options of meeting social responsibilities and abiding by agreements with employers and stockholders. But if the social responsibility which a person has *in his capacity as a businessman* is simply the production and distribution of safe, quality, affordable goods and services, then, according to the doctrines of the free market, by meeting *those* responsibilities, he will be keeping his agreements to make profits for his employers. They are not incompatible alternatives; rather, the one is supposed to be the most efficient means to the other. If that turns out not to be true, then the moral defense of the free market collapses.

[28] Finally, an objection to the view that business has a social responsibility to promote desirable social ends, and no responsibility to increase profits, comes from those who, like Friedman, are concerned to protect the liberties of persons in a free society. The promotion of social ends is the business of those we elect to represent our interests. By inviting corporate executives to promote social ends, we are in effect inviting private citizens to exercise their sometimes considerable influence to shape policy according to their personal visions of what makes for a better quality of life. When there is no consensus as to what makes for a better quality of life, we do not want powerful corporate executives, whom we cannot remove by the ballot, forming public policy according to their private visions.

[29] This argument against the doctrine that businesses have a social responsibility mistakenly supposes that the social responsibilities of businessmen go beyond doing what they can to ensure the production and distribution of safe, high quality, affordable goods and services. But nothing in the efficiency argument supports that supposition. What it supports saying is only that business has a moral responsibility for the delivery of the goods. Of course, not all the responsibilities which persons in business have accrue to them in their capacity as businessmen. Meeting the responsibilities *of that role* does not involve activities which could threaten the liberties of free persons or which could undermine the roles of elected representatives. On the other hand, by doing what they can to meet those responsibilities which they take themselves to have *outside* of their roles in business, businessmen may well undertake to do things which have dangerous consequences. But so may we all. Any individual with sufficient power or wealth is capable of doing things which either promote or destroy the quality of life of others, and we should no doubt maintain close controls on the extent to which any person is capable of so influencing others. Friedman's fear that businesses, when aiming to promote some vision of a better life for the community, will undermine our liberty to pursue our own and varied visions, is not a fear of the consequences which might ensue if businesses meet *their* social responsibilities. The responsibilities which come with doing business—i.e., effectively delivering the goods—are too narrow to pose that threat. The responsibilities which individuals may take themselves to have as citizens, as members of a political party, as members of a church group, and so on, *do* pose the threat which Friedman sees, but even there the threat is contained by limiting the powers of individuals to impose their views on others, not by *denying* that there are such responsibilities.

[30] The error which I have just been attributing to Friedman dates back to Plato. In his argument with Thrasymachus in the first book of the *Republic*, Socrates argues that the doctor who charges a fee is acting in two different capacities. In charging a fee, he is acting *qua* businessman. So, on the account which emerges, it becomes the function of the person (who happens also to be a doctor) to make money *in so far as he is doing business*. But my suggestion has been that this dichotomy—the doctor/businessman dichotomy—is a false dichotomy. Even though it is not the doctor's function to make money but, as Plato rightly says, to promote the health of his patients, it may still be true that the function of the businessman is to promote health, if the businessman *is* a doctor, and his line of business is practicing medicine. In a world in which medical services are acquired in the market place,

to practice medicine is to do one's business, and so one's function *in that line of business*, is to promote health. Likewise, if one is engaged in the business of manufacturing automobiles, one's social "function" is to produce a safe, quality product at a reasonable price.

[31] We thus find that granting the assumption that a free competitive market is the most (or, the only) effective mechanism for promoting a better quality of life does not have the consequence that persons in business have a responsibility to increase their profits; it does not have the consequence that it is always (or, even in general) morally permissible to seek profits; nor does that initial assumption conflict with the doctrine that business has a social responsibility to promote certain desirable social ends. Whether or not that initial assumption should be granted is yet another problem.

Notes

1. I will be using the expression "classical" more broadly than usual, referring to systems of thought which share certain assumptions about the self-regulatory nature of the market. It thus encompasses the theories of [Adam] Smith and [David] Ricardo, the neoclassical or "marginalist" theories of [Alfred] Marshall and his followers, as well as contemporary libertarian figures like [Friedrich] Hayek and [Milton] Friedman.
2. See, for example, Narveson, Jan: 'Justice and The Business Society', in *Ethical Theory and Business*, 2nd ed., Tom L. Beauchamp and Norman E. Bowie (eds.), Prentice-Hall, Inc., Englewood Cliffs, New Jersey. Especially pp. 620–21.
3. 'The Social Responsibility of Business Is to Increase Its Profits', *New York Times Magazine* (Sept. 13, 1970); reprinted in 1983, *Ethical Issues in Business*, 2nd. ed., Donaldson and Werhane, (eds.), Prentice-Hall, Inc., New Jersey. Page numbers cited below are from this reprint. Also see Friedman, M.: 1962, *Capitalism and Freedom*, The University of Chicago Press, especially Chapter VIII.
4. *The Wealth of Nations*, Bk. IV, Chapter ii.
5. Friedman, *op. cit.*, p. 133.
6. On the contrary, he insists on it. Discussion of his conclusion often proceeds by ignoring this important qualification. His *New York Times Magazine* essay emphasizes the need for the qualification in several explicit passages, though his earlier defense of what I am calling "the stronger conclusion" does not make the qualification explicit (see *Capitalism and Freedom*, *op. cit.* pp. 133–36).
7. All sides agree that the pursuit of profits in the present market has morally undesirable consequences in particular cases; what they disagree about is the diagnosis and the cure. Libertarians trace the cause to inadequate freedom or competition, and so call for revisions in the present system to increase these; their opponents trace the cause to excessive zeal in the pursuit of profit, and so call for closer regulation of market activity. But all agree that things are not as they should be in the market place.
8. See Levitt, Theodore: 1958, 'The Dangers of Social Responsibility', *Harvard Business Review* (Sept.–Oct.).
9. *op. cit.*, 'The Social Responsibility of Business Is To Increase Its Profits', p. 239.
10. *Ibid.*, p. 240.
11. *Ibid.*, p. 240.

Questions

1. What are the six premises of the economic efficiency argument, according to Jacobsen?
2. What is Jacobsen's point in Section III?
3. (a) What relationship between standard of living and quality of life does Jacobsen establish in Section IV?

(b) Rewrite the third premise, by adding no more than four words, to incorporate his point.
4. Explain Jacobsen's point about what the social responsibility of business is, with reference to the boiler tender analogy.
5. Consider the notion that profit can be maximized by producing and distributing unsafe, low-quality goods and services.
 (a) Which premise would this, if true, undermine?
 (b) What then would be the implication for the conclusion that "profits... are the best measure of a firm's contribution to the welfare of others" (para 1) and are therefore deserved?
6. The starting point for Jacobsen's paper is based on a consequentialist approach—profit is morally acceptable because of the consequences of its contribution to the social good. What defence of profit-seeking might the following suggest?
 (a) an intuitionist
 (b) a Kantian
 (c) a natural law proponent
 (d) a religionist

Capitalism and Its Regulation: A Dialogue on Business and Ethics[*]

Martin Parker and Gordon Pearson

Preface

"What nonsense has possessed you two all this time Socrates? What do you mean by all your polite bowing and scraping? If you have a genuine desire to know what justice is, don't confine yourself to asking questions, and making a show by refuting any answer that is given. You know that it is much easier to ask questions than to answer them. But answer yourself, and say how you define justice; and don't dare to tell me that it is the obligatory, or the expedient, or the profitable, or the advantageous, but make your answer precise and accurate, for I will not have any rubbish of that kind from you."

(Plato, *The Republic*)

---

[*] *Journal of Business Ethics* (2005) 60: 91–101.

[1] Thrasymachus wants clarity. He wants to know what justice is, and thinks that if Socrates begins to answer questions, rather than endlessly asking them, it will be a more productive strategy for finding the essence of justice. Following the conventions established in a previous paper in this journal (Pearson and Parker, 2001), we here use the Socratic form of dialogue in order to explore issues that we disagree about, and try to discover some answers. But for the reader to find this format engaging, you might like to know something about the two characters who are staging their disagreement here. We have both taught courses on Business Ethics since 1996, and published various books and articles on the topic (for example, Parker, 1998; Pearson, 1995). Despite this shared academic interest, and friendship, our very different biographies lead us to understand the area in rather different ways. Gordon spent more than 30 years in various companies before becoming an academic with a particular interest in strategy. He is convinced that theory and idealism should be tempered by a practical understanding of how businesses can be profitable and sustainable. Martin, on the other hand, has spent most of his working life as an academic and believes that imagining alternatives to market managerialism is vital. He teaches and writes about organisation and culture, and has recently published a book entitled *Against Management* (2002). So, the two participants below might be characterised as a 'business pragmatist' (Gordon) and an 'academic idealist' (Martin).

The Dialogue

[2] *Martin*: We have agreed that the topic of our discussion this time should be capitalism. Putting it glibly, I am against it, and you are for it. But that is too simple, and I assume that the purpose of this dialogue is to clarify exactly what I am against and what you are for. And perhaps after establishing what you are for, a question that has always puzzled me, we might seek some common ground. I do think there is a real danger that, given the legitimacy crisis that market managerialism is currently facing, we could easily end up dramatising our differences too much. So let me begin with some simple provocations and then, in the spirit of dialogue that Socrates encouraged, see if we can be a little more precise about our objections. Not, I should add, that I expect to convince you to change your mind, since you are far too clever to be convinced by mere argument.

[3] Some grand beginnings then, and let's see where we go from there. I do not believe that globalising capitalism is the only or the one best way for human beings to organise themselves. Rather, the current situation benefits the selfish interests of a few (the privileged elites of the developed world), and damages the interests of everybody else on the planet. Basically this is because (following Marx's theory of surplus value), when a capitalist makes a profit, they are essentially stealing value which is produced by labour (Marx, 1979). But you don't need to understand Marxist theory in order to see that the economic structure of capitalism has some very damaging social consequences. Basically, it discourages the local production of useful things and encourages the growth of gigantic corporations that exploit local labour for profits elsewhere. It is a system that maximises inequalities and encourages an extreme competitive individualism that results in alienated labour for many, and is damaging to any meaningful senses of community and co-operation. Do you really want to defend such a system?

Gordon: I really will answer your question, [4] but first I want to ask another one. It might seem rather old fashioned but, instead of haranguing me about selfish interests, stealing value, not to mention "the legitimacy crisis that market managerialism (whatever that is) is currently facing" and so on, why don't we start by saying what we mean by capitalism? Trying to agree on a definition might well prove beyond us because any definition is likely to be loaded with the sort of emotional stuff with which you have gushed forth. But we might divide the term into 'capital' and 'ism' and have a cool, detached look at each.

[5] Capital itself, and its accrual, has an economic logic that was explained by Adam Smith using his pin factory example (Smith, 1986: 109–10). It is probably unavoidable. Can you get terribly worked up about the fact that twenty individuals dividing their "labour" so that they each specialize on a particular bit of the pin making process can produce a 100 times as many pins in the same time as 20 individuals each making their own pins from start to finish? And can you get even more outraged by the fact that with some tools and equipment those same twenty individuals can produce a further hundredfold increase in pin production?

[6] Or is it the 'ism' where the problem lies?

[7] *Martin*: Well, you are talking about the division of labour, which is a common feature of capitalist societies but not a defining one (Durkheim, 1991). Lots of societies and organisations throughout history have allocated different tasks to different people. However, what happens in a capitalist society is that the surplus value produced by this divided labour is taken by the capitalist as a matter of right. So, the increase in the productive power of labour is not owned by labour, but by someone else. This means that capitalist societies have a whole class of people who simply live off other people's work and have an interest in intensifying this work as much as possible. Furthermore, the work that they do is hence "alienated," done for others and not for themselves (Wray-Bliss and Parker, 1998). For me, these are the defining features of capitalism, and also the key thing that makes it an unfair system. Does that clear things up a bit?

Gordon: A bit, but not completely. I was talking [8] about the division of labour to which I arbitrarily attributed a hundredfold increase in productivity. More importantly I also mentioned the provision of tools and equipment (that is to say, capital) to which I attributed another hundredfold increase in productivity over and above that achieved by specialisation. The division of labour will certainly improve productivity in a situation where production is purely craft based. But that is a rather limited improvement in a limited situation (though one that was common enough in the pre-industrial golden age that you appear to yearn for). The use of capital in the form of plant and equipment has a far greater impact on productivity in situations that are more commonly found nowadays.

Whatever economic or political system you [9] aspire to, you must surely acknowledge the importance of capital. Without it the Russians would never have been able to launch a sputnik, or Ford bring the cost of an automobile within the reach of the masses. Even this journal needs capital for its production and distribution. So what exactly is your problem with capital?

Martin: There are some interesting assumptions [10] in your analysis about the need for all this growth, but let's leave that aside for a moment. I agree with you that appropriate buildings and machinery will often (though not always) be required for a particular form of work organisation to take place. But choosing to call this 'capital' already suggests that these buildings and machinery are going to be owned by someone else. If we call them 'resources,' then the question of ownership is left open. Some forms of work organisation might be reliant on borrowing money to buy or borrow resources, but we don't have to assume that this will be a general requirement. Neither do we have to assume that the "rents" paid for money or resources should allow a particular class of individuals to simply sit back and enjoy their luck. Many co-operatives are based on the idea that you can't own shares in the organisation unless you are a worker for the organisation, which is to say that all members share a collective fate. The division of labour, and the need for resources, are general problems for all organising—co-operative, capitalist or whatever. What is distinctive about capitalism is that it allows (and celebrates) gigantic profits being made by people who do no productive work, and appear to care little about the lives of those that do.

[11] *Gordon*: There is something here about the incommensurability of our world views which in the end may frustrate our attempt at dialogue. But I think it would be worthwhile trying to make you understand something about the way that business works. The word capital clearly means different things to different people. But let us try and separate it from the emotional stuff you invest in it. In 1817, David Ricardo identified three factors of production: land, labour and capital, the last being exactly what I was suggesting: plant and equipment for the purposes of production. Accountants include land as part of capital. Balance sheets today record fixed capital as typically including land, buildings, plant, equipment, vehicles and so on. Your distinction between resources and capital on the grounds that capital implies a particular sort of ownership seems to me quite spurious.

[12] The point about these items, as I tried to show previously, is that though they are not part of the daily transactions of a business they are essential to its viability, even to an 18th century pin factory. Whatever you call them they have to be paid for. They can be paid for by borrowing, or by selling risk bearing shares in the business, or by setting aside some of the daily surplus created by the business (which you call stolen value). Most business organisations find it necessary, or desirable, to tap all three sources of finance. That is how the funds are raised to pay for the capital that is necessary to keep the business going. So what is your alternative? You seem to want to go back to some utopian golden age where we live in self-sufficient little co-operative communities living in peace and harmony. But who will make the pins, and who is going to brew the beer?

[13] Just to pick up on your final slightly self-indulgent sentence, what is distinctive about capitalism is not that it just allows excessive profits to be made, but that it allows both profits and losses. As a system, it is essentially permissive. But this permissive framework is not without some natural limitations. Excessive profits encourage competitors to enter who compete profitability away; large scale losses in the end lead to bankruptcy. Or, would you prefer not to have profits and losses?

[14] *Martin*: Odd you should pick the example of beer, since I have seen you drinking 'real ale' made by small regionally based owner-managed breweries on more than a few occasions. Perhaps excessive consumption has clouded your judgement with respect to the selection of examples?

[15] Let us be clear what we are debating here. I accept that many (though not all) organisations will need to borrow money in order to use resources that allow them to do whatever it is that they do. I also accept that some will be successful at doing this, and make profits, whilst others will make losses. I am not against competition in itself, or markets in themselves, or the development of new products and services. However, I do not believe that the current celebration of aggressive "market" discipline, hypercompetition, and corporate giganticism as the solution to all organisational and global problems is a wise one. Rather, it is an arrangement that benefits the wealthy, and delegitimises alternative arrange-

ments. You seem to refuse to acknowledge this, and instead assume that there is no alternative. Let's take a particular example. The growing dominance of the big supermarket chains over British retailing has been well documented (Lawrence, 2004; Monbiot, 2000 for example). In the name of consumer choice, most people now have very little choice. As a result, huge profits are being made by a few organisations, whilst a wide variety of local businesses disappear altogether. Farmers, garage owners, butchers and bakers end up being re-employed on minimum wages pushing trolleys around windy car parks. Do you think this is a desirable state of affairs? Do you think that it is an *inevitable* state of affairs?

[16] *Gordon*: Martin, you make so many outrageous assertions I hardly know where to begin. Your reeducation needs to begin at an even more basic level. You say that not all organisations need to borrow, as if to suggest that the use of capital is in some way voluntary. It isn't. All organisations need to acquire some capital, either by borrowing or in exchange for a share of the business, in order to get started. The nearest to an exception I can think of is, perhaps, the professional practice: lawyers, accountants or management consultants. There is no escape from the requirement that business organisations need to be financed in order to exist. Could you tell me what exceptions you had in mind?

[17] The brewing example merely proves that not all sectors of the economy are dominated by global players, despite your rhetoric. So there is no inevitability about what you call giganticism, because it all depends on what consumers want. Supermarkets might be a safer bet for your argument. But even though they are powerful, it can be argued that the consumers are still their masters (McRae, 2003). It is by responding to us, to you and me, that they have become successful and so improved our quality of life. It is surely that thought that has driven William Morrison ever since he first set up shop in Keighley in the aftermath of the last war. By excessive hard work and attention to his customers' needs, Morrison's has now become the 4th largest supermarket chain in UK. At what point in its progress would you have demanded that they be stopped?

You say you are not against competition, but [18] the natural outcome of competition is that some will succeed and some will fail. By and large it is those that offer a better deal to the customer who succeed. Thus some grow and some go bust. The unhappy results you refer to spring directly from competition, not from the necessity of employing capital. (Yet you have claimed not to be against competition.)

Finally, it is outrageous of you to suggest that [19] there is a current celebration of aggressive market discipline and corporate giganticism. What is your evidence for this? There's plenty to the contrary (see for example, Klein, 2000; Malachowski, 2003; Monbiot, 2004). There is no such celebration; the truth is that you are on a bandwagon of popular suspicion and disquiet. Nor do I distance myself very much from the disquiet.

Martin: My arguments may seem outrageous, [20] but that doesn't make them wrong. What I have been trying to question is a particular form of common sense that suggests that there are "natural" relationships between capital, competition and customers. But, in suggesting that these are inevitable, and that they result in the highest levels of aggregate benefit for all concerned, it then becomes difficult to question them without seeming outrageous. So, if I suggest that the alternative to large supermarket chains is small local businesses, is this outrageous? If I suggest that many of these local businesses will not need to borrow huge amounts of money from commercial banks in order to make their owners a living, is this outrageous?

[21] One of the flaws in your reasoning, if I may be so bold to suggest that it is reasoning at all, is to assume that because something exists it must be what consumers want. Leaving aside the fact that "wants" are manipulated by the billions spent on marketing, are you sure that people want the same retail chains on every high street? Or that they want to drive coffee farmers into poverty because of the monopolistic buying power of a few firms? Or that they want to drive retail wages down because of the demand for dividends coming from city investors? The consequences of capitalism are not always clear to someone who has no choice but to shop in a Morrison's, but they are real enough for those on the sharp end. Rather than accepting that these 'unhappy results' are inevitable, it would be quite possible to begin with some conception of what a particular community wanted. Local mutual banks, for example, could lend money to local businesses because having a particular kind of business in a particular area was widely seen to be beneficial. The ethic was not profit taking, but service to the members of a community. Indeed, this was pretty much the pattern for the early co-operative movement, building societies and forms of medical insurance.

[22] Excellent beer can be brewed and sold in the same place, reducing transport costs, enhancing local diversity against McDonaldisation (Ritzer, 2000), and providing both jobs and pleasure along the way. Why insist that this is the exception, rather than putting forward policies that promote it as a general rule?

[23] *Gordon*: Would you therefore insist that beer has to be made locally? Would you impose a mileage tax on beer that travelled more than x miles? You need to be precise. Woolly good intentions are no good. I recall the "buy British" campaign in the 1960s with union flags everywhere. It was disastrous! Anything featuring the union flag became identified with a product that couldn't compete on its own merit. Before the campaign was dropped the Union Jack was coming to be synonymous with poor quality.

[24] Your arguments are unrealistic. In being "against capitalism" you are forcing yourself to go back to some semi-rural dream world where happy artisans sit in the tavern drinking the local ale and everyone makes their own pins. It won't work. The application of capital is a great force for good and evil. We can have the good but I agree that we don't necessarily have to have all the undesirable outcomes, on which we are probably broadly in agreement. They may be, as I said previously, the natural outcome of competition, but they are not inevitable. However they won't be modified or eradicated by wishful thinking.

[25] I was trying to encourage you to a more hard-nosed analysis by asking you the questions. Like what are the businesses you had in mind that didn't need capital? Not surprisingly you refused an answer. At what point in an entrepreneur's progress would you prevent them from further success? Again you were silent. And I might add: how, in practice, would you go about preventing their further progress? And probably the most interesting question is why are you not "against competition"? Your argument seems to be compromised by that assertion, which really needs to be examined. What is it about competition of which you are in favour?

[26] It may be that you could incorporate what you claim to like about competition within a model which utilises capital for the creation of a surplus, while not destroying local enterprise, and which can pay for our education, health and social services. Or maybe you couldn't. Perhaps you would actually prefer warts and all capitalism to continue so that you have something to be against?

[27] *Martin*: It is nice to have something to be against, you for example, but again that isn't enough to dis-

miss my arguments. Indeed, we seem to be coming closer together on our diagnosis here in some crucial respects. I do agree that there are many examples of discontent being expressed against the current phase of globalised corporate capitalism. However, I do not believe that these various resistances are actually having any substantial effect on corporate and state policies. So it does seem to me that the market managerialist view of the world is dominant, and is being endlessly proselytised in the World Trade Organisation, a thousand Business Schools and endless airport book shops. That, I think, is a problem. Discontent is not being heard in the places where it matters most.

[28] With respect to alternatives to capitalism. Surely the issue here is one of the regulation of unrestrained competition. The dominant view is that all barriers to trade should be knocked down in order that the 'market' can deliver on its heroic promise of making sure that the supply and demand curves meet in the optimum places. The problem is that the 'market' is not in any sense a level playing field, and is actually dominated by large corporations and the institutions that speak on their behalf. This is causing wealth to be further concentrated with certain classes of people and certain parts of the globe. Adam Smith was quite clear that competition, in his local sense, was harmed by "corporations." In its earlier meaning, the corporation was an association of independent people practising the same trade, and Smith felt that such associations tended to harm the public interest. "People of the same trade seldom meet together, even for merriment and diversion, but the conversation ends in a conspiracy against the public, or in some contrivance to raise prices" (Smith, 1986: 232). I agree with him, and would simply add that the role of the state could be to restrict such conspiracies against the public. This might mean setting a defined limit on the acceptable ratio of profit to turnover, or a maximum size on corporations, or even a geographical limit to their trading range. If we are happy to let the state regulate in other areas, why should we exempt profit making organisations from more meaningful forms of intervention that might benefit communities across the globe?

Gordon: "Discontent is not being heard in the [29] places where it matters most"! I can just feel the revolutionary class-consciousness dripping from every syllable. (A nice pose, for a Business School Professor.) But despite your rhetoric, you seem not to be against capitalism after all, just some of the excesses that are permitted in its name. All you want to do is tweak it at the edges. That's rather disappointing. Is this the onset of middle aged complacency, the collapse of moral fibre as a result of taking so many more of capitalism's pennies, or a recognition that there is no viable alternative, so let's try and make it work?

Your suggestion of regulation as an "alternative" [30] requires capitalism to be, by definition, unbridled and unregulated. I think perhaps the debate is over. Although you claim to be against capitalism, you seem to agree it is unavoidable and only needs limitation. Rather than indulge any unbecoming triumphalism, I suggest we move the dialogue on to consider what nature of limitation might work. Yours wouldn't. Consider what a corporation would do that was up against its maximum permitted profit margin, size (however defined) or geographic area. Do you imagine it would donate its "slack" to the deserving poor?

Has your Marxist conviction really collapsed so [31] far that you now profess support for Adam Smith in his objection to any frictions which reduce competition? As well as serving the public interest (solely) by keeping prices down, competition also leads to some succeeding and some failing, some growing and some dying and so to small numbers of large corporations. It doesn't lead to the localised, non-capitalist, craft based idyll that you seemed settled on such a short time ago.

[32] Would it be fruitful to consider some limitations on capitalism that might work?

[33] *Martin*: Far be it for you to indulge in triumphalism, but I fear the debate is far from over. I also fear I may have given you the impression that I was some species of agricultural Marxist, and hence that my alleged lapse into the language of state regulation was some sort of problem. My arguments against corporate capitalism are not intended to imply a hostility to competition per se. It depends, as far as I can see, on who benefits from particular forms of competition, and will hence really be a utilitarian judgement based on the greatest good of the greatest number (Warnock, 1962). My judgement, as I have hopefully made clear, is that benefits are spread most unevenly, both within and between nations, and that corporate dominance is one of the causes of this inequality.

[34] Now it seems to me that one of the things that we ask states to do is to regulate and redistribute. This can be done minimally, as it is in most pro-capitalist states at present, or with some genuine bite. So, using the example of maximum permitted profit margins, this would be an attempt to ensure that organisations made profits that did not go beyond an agreed return on investment. Or, to take another example, that executive pay was limited to a defined multiple of the lowest paid employee. Neither of these measures would in themselves end unfairness and alienation, but they would do much to raise the standard of living of the poor. Now I don't think that you are against regulation of this sort in principal, but because you think that it wouldn't work. Which is to say that your defence of capitalism isn't one based on a political philosophy of the rights to freedom from state interference (Nozick, 1974), but on more pragmatic considerations. So, why do you believe that aggressive state regulation wouldn't work?

[35] *Gordon*: We are agreed then that capitalism works. At least it works better than any of the alternatives that have been tried so far. The question you seem to be posing now is how to make it work (more) equitably.

[36] You are right that I am not motivated by commitment to any political philosophy such that might claim rights to freedom from state interference. Such philosophies bring with them all sorts of baggage of the sort you demonstrated earlier in this dialogue. I would far rather argue things from basic principles, making sure one is clear in one's understanding of each principle involved. We don't need to stand on the shoulders of giants to achieve a workable solution to this little problem.

[37] I'm not sure about aggressive state regulation—I don't think I know what you mean by aggressive or state. What is needed is a legal framework, preferably with international standing, within which enterprises are free to do their own thing, even to maximise profits, whatever that means, if that is what drives them. Your two proposals wouldn't work because they would frustrate and ultimately kill the vitality of free enterprise. I invite you to think through how businesses would respond to your proposals.

[38] *Martin*: There are two related issues here. You are attempting to force me to be either "for" or "against" capitalism. Fair enough, I am against capitalism and you are for it. But that doesn't really help if we don't agree on the meaning of the word in the first place. Your attempt to insist that any economic system that involves competition is capitalist seems to mean that only the most extreme forms of state communism would stand outside your definition. However, surely you would acknowledge that there are many choices and alternatives between complete *laissez-faire* and complete centralisation?

In practice, you believe that some measure of legal regulation is necessary and I believe that local competition of certain forms is desirable. That does not mean we agree on many other issues, merely that we both stand in the grey area between two absolutisms.

[39] So, I think we are really debating what forms of regulation might be appropriate. My regulatory framework would be aimed at protecting ordinary people against powerful businesses, and I have indicated some of the measures that I would like us to discuss. You have claimed that they 'would frustrate and ultimately kill the vitality of free enterprise'. Fine words indeed, and just as rhetorical as anything I have deployed so far. But how far will you take this? I assume you would agree that businesses should be taxed on the profits that they make? Would you agree that they have to meet health and safety at work legislation? Would you agree that businesses should be fined if they pollute the environment? Is there a line that you can draw between legislation that damages 'vitality' and legislation that doesn't?

[40] *Gordon*: I think so. It's definitely a distinction worth making because capitalism works so well. World poverty, using the World Bank's measure of income of $2 a day or less, dropped from 56% of the world's population in 1980 to 23% in 2000 (Bhalla, 2003) a period characterised by the global breaking down of trading barriers. Tinkering with permitted levels of profit or income differentials between the highest and lowest paid wouldn't work. They remind me of the Labour party's attempts to peg prices and incomes in the early 70s when inflation was getting out of hand. They set up the Prices and Incomes Board to control it. The result was that the maximum permitted increases in prices and incomes automatically became the minima and inflation had a new built in accelerator. Government attempts to interfere are invariably counterproductive. Businesses quickly discover ways around such regulation and the overall effect is to make it harder to satisfy customers, and generate the wealth that brings people out of poverty.

[41] Rather than interfere in the internal workings of organisations, we should make sure there is an effective system of self-regulation. Within the capitalist system there are many checks and balances. The most powerful of these is unfettered competition which rewards those that deliver customer value and punishes those that don't. There are many others. For example, shareholders recently threw out a proposed executive share bonus scheme because they thought it was excessive, but that sort of thing is done all too infrequently. In principle, independent directors have power over strategic decisions on a very wide front, but they rarely exercise it because in the main they are not truly independent. Businesses have found ways to avoid many of these checks and balances and those who should exercise them don't, either because they are speculators rather than owners, or because they are otherwise compromised. The checks and balances need reinvigorating.

[42] Here are a few suggestions that might inhibit the greedy and just plain criminal:

1. Employees of any target company should have a vote equivalent to 25% of the voting equity on any merger or takeover proposition.
2. Shareholder voting rights should only accrue 3 months after share purchase.
3. No individual can be an executive director of more than one quoted company, or two non-quoted companies.
4. Independent non-executive directors must be appointed by shareholders.
5. Independent directors must be genuinely independent with no professional, consultancy or supply relationships with the company.

6. No individual can be a non-executive director of more than two quoted companies or four non quoted companies.
7. No individual can be a director of any quoted company that already has a director who holds a directorship of any other quoted company of which he or she is a director.
8. Shares acquired through an executive stock option scheme should not be saleable until a minimum of 5 years after the option is exercised.
9. Shareholders with more than 2.5% of a company's shares must vote on all shareholder voting issues.
10. A company's auditors must not have any relationship with the company other than auditing.
11. A company's auditors can only serve for a maximum of 5 years.
12. If any shareholder fails to register a vote on executive pay 3 years running then those shares lose their voting rights.

These proposals aim to break some of the "conspiracies against the public" that Adam Smith identified. However, they don't compromise competitive capitalism, unlike yours. Now can you see the difference?

[43]   *Martin*: A splendidly interventionist set of rules that nicely demonstrates my point. You are clearly not against regulation if it helps to establish a new version of shareholders' "rights and responsibilities." Indeed, you seem to be quite a creative regulator when the mood takes you. In general, your ideas seem to rest on the assumption that the movement of capital needs to be slowed down and given some friction so that it does not flee too quickly. Essentially this is an attempt to ensure that rapid profit taking is not easily possible, and that shareholders are involved in governance issues. This is a responsible and laudable approach to develop. But what I do not understand is what sort of difference there is between my proposal to limit the pay differentials between the highest and lowest, and yours which limit profit-taking from share incentive schemes? What is the philosophical distinction between an intervention that insists (for example) on the breaking up of large organisations into smaller ones, and one that limits inter-locking directorships? Isn't this merely a question of degree?

We are both, I contend, regulationists. You are [44] not a free market libertarian, and I am neither a state communist, nor a pre-industrial utopian. However, we do differ in terms of our preferences. You claim that your regulation is intended to prevent "greed and criminality." This is certainly useful—though how you distinguish between (what you must regard as) proper self-interest and greed is beyond me. Criminality is easier to define since it assumes the existence of legal sanctions, though laws are often broken because of greedy self-interest (Punch, 1996). The point is that you wish to use the state, and the legal system, to prevent certain things, and to encourage others. I agree wholeheartedly, and am merely pushing your approach a little further. I would prefer a world characterised by smaller and more local organisations with a variety of ownership arrangements, and limitations on pay differentials and profitability. Another way to put that is to say that I would regulate in favour of a particular vision of a future world (see Monbiot, 2004 for a developed example of this). In favour of co-operatives, mutuals, small businesses, local supply networks, carbon neutral organisations and so on. Is this a world that you would dislike, or a world that you believe is utopian?

Gordon: You can't see the difference between [45] my regulation and yours because of the different paradigms we inhabit. Your interventions would

[46] all serve to inhibit and frustrate competition; mine seek to revitalise it. Competition works. It has built in checks and balances, but we must nonetheless work to protect the public against conspiracies and that's what my regulation seeks to do.

[46] For example, FTSE100 company directorships are more or less a closed shop. The market for such directorships has effectively been cornered (Whitley, 1992). The 1999 Cadbury report sought to establish rules of good governance, for example requiring independent non-executive directors to set the pay of executive directors. But most non-executive directors actually have multiple directorships and a personal interest in claiming that £2 m–£3 m is barely sufficient compensation for a FTSE100 CEO. My rules 3–7 are intended to break this particular cartel. Rules 9 and 12 are intended to revitalise shareholders' responsibilities, while rule 8 reinforces the ownership role of manager shareholders rather than allowing shares to become merely a source of added income. Rules 10 and 11 are intended to reinforce the independence of audit firms while rules 1 and 2 are intended to limit the opportunity of dawn raid type abuses.

[47] These sorts of regulations protect the capitalist system from anti-competitive behaviour. They are not driven by personal preferences or a particular vision of a brave new world. Neither do they require me to distinguish between 'proper self-interest' and 'greed.' They are simply based on what works. A few years ago the big brewers had more or less cleaned up or closed down the small independents. But the consumer demanded, and the system enabled, the spawning of lots of new small breweries. You said earlier the supermarkets were now limiting consumer choice, but the consumer is demanding, and the system enabling, all sorts of new initiatives: organic produce, fair-trade products, farmers' markets, web based selling and so on. The consumer actually has more choice than ever before.

[48] That wouldn't happen with your regulations limiting profits, pay differentials, size and geographic spread, even if you could specify a realistic form that such regulation would take. They would kill innovation and change and the result would be a sterile, hollow parody of your utopia.

[49] *Martin*: Different paradigms indeed. I claim that we are both regulationists, but you claim that your regulations enable markets to do their work, whilst mine do not. For me the difference is only one of degree, not of substance, and I see nothing in any of your assertions to persuade me otherwise. But, if we set this definitional issue aside for a moment, we are still left with a more fundamental problem. You seem to believe, as an article of faith, that "competition works." Much of your bluster is based on the idea that the pure market is somehow inherently superior to planning and control. Hence your attempt to characterise my arguments as being centralising and paternalist, as preventing freedom and shackling Smith's hidden hand. Yet you happily acknowledge that your pure market needs to be regulated into being. You seem to accept that if capitalists are left to their own devices they will behave in self-interested ways that (to put it mildly) do not serve the common good. Regulation is therefore a fact of life in all but the most brutal circumstances, but still you insist on praising the virtues of this abstract entity called the market. Well what is this thing? Where can I see it? It's a bit like claiming that football would be a better game if it wasn't for the rules and the referee.

[50] I, on the other hand, do not concern myself overmuch with such metaphysical baggage. It seems obvious that markets, states, organisations (and football) can only exist because a certain set of rules (formal and informal) calls them into being. Social justice involves working out, by trial and error, what sort of rules best guarantee the greatest happiness of

the greatest number. (Utilitarian arguments usually being useful for large scale matters of social and economic policy.) So if we look at the present age, what do we see? It seems clear enough that just as those in the west and the north grow more obese and polluting, so do those in the south and the east continue to starve. It also seems obvious that big business benefits from highly indebted countries, from wars and post-war reconstruction, and hence that the foreign policies of the obese nations are often driven by what happens in (or to) the corporate towers. It seems obvious that business gurus, students, academics and managers benefit so greatly from feeding at the trough that they rarely lift their snouts far enough to see what working life is like in the call centre, the burger bar or the export processing zone. And then you say that all this must not be legislated away, because the great god market might disapprove. (Though this god has never been seen in a pure form, and only manifests themselves properly if there are regulations to prevent them from disappearing.) But then, as I said at the start, you are far too clever to be convinced by mere argument.

[51] *Gordon*: It is disappointing to see you give up on sweet reason and resort simply to polemic. Are you really suggesting that planning and control are inherently superior to market processes? The idea of control is fascinating—is it what Rousseau referred to as chains, or more like Mao's barrel of a gun? How can you ignore the fact that half the world tried planning and control and found it didn't work? That's not an idea but a demonstrable fact.

[52] But let's ignore all that and have a look at those lurid shirts you have a fancy for. Where does the cloth come from? And the colours or dyes, the buttons and the thread, the machines that cut the fabric and machines that stitch the bits together? And who dreamed up the outrageous pictures that feature on your sort of shirt and how did they get printed on the fabric? And what brought all these things together to produce such a seductive result? Your shirt is a product of the market—which, incidentally you can't see because, as Smith pointed out, it's invisible! On the other hand with all the tools of planning and control at your disposal I doubt you could organise the daily bread for Stoke-on-Trent. Central planning and control has been replaced everywhere for the simple reason that the market works while planning and control don't. I've just finished supervising a PhD looking at the various Chinese experiments in capitalism and it is clear they succeeded more or less to the extent to which the communist party passed control to enterprise management (Xiao, 2004).

[53] I agree that some self-interested capitalists would abuse the system if they could and exploit the weak and so, I agree, the market has to be regulated. But regulation should seek to prevent abuse, not undermine or replace the market itself. Your conspiracy explanation of capitalism holds no water. A system that does not work will not have the resources to clean up its act. Nor could unsuccessful economies afford to dispense social justice to the third world.

[54] *Martin*: And so, despite all my attempts to be reasonable with you, we seem to always end up in the same place. I was rather hoping that the use of Socratic dialogue would allow us to examine our prejudices, and perhaps find common ground. Instead I think we have merely rehearsed our differences. I wonder whether we were trying too hard to "win" our arguments, rather than constructing shared positions. But that also seems to tell us something about debates in this form. Socrates rarely used his conversations with others in order to learn something himself, though he liked to claim that he was doing just that. Instead he used whatever rhetorical moves he could muster in order to shame or trick his opponent into renouncing their common sense or imprecise thinking. The problem is

that when you have two people doing that, they are often too busy being clever to learn from each other.

[55]　Gibson Burrell has claimed that "dialogue is a weapon of the powerful" (2001: 19). Perhaps one implication of that phrase is that dialogues can be meaningless rituals in which two aged contrarians debate with each other from opposite sides of a dusty parliament. The other implication of Burrell's aphorism might be that the powerless don't have weapons, or that they have different weapons. It is, after all, unlikely that someone who makes trainers for Nike in an export processing zone will read journals about business ethics. Even if they did, I wonder how much they would learn from our display of differences, or how helpful they would find it for their struggles? It seems to me that business ethics must begin to engage much more directly with the politics of business, to the point where business ethics and the politics of business become indistinguishable. Of course this would also mean that the dismal science of economics, with all its hidden normative claims about efficiency and the morality of possessive individualism, would become subjected to ethical and political critique too (Jones et al., 2005). You will be sceptical about my grand ambitions I'm sure, since you seem so seduced by common sense economics, but nonetheless I have enjoyed our exchange. Your version of regulated capitalism is a small step towards a social order which values equity and justice, so I am happy enough to begin with that. But not to end with it.

[56]　*Gordon*: It is disappointing that you feel we have not found common ground. Surely we both agree that a regulated version of the market economy is what is likely to provide the greatest happiness for the greatest number, or at least the potential for it. We may not agree as to the nature, form and degree of regulation—but you can't have everything.

[57]　At the outset of this dialogue, I was surprised at the extent to which you were driven by feelings and emotion. You claimed to be outraged at the inequalities of income and wealth between the fat cat capitalists "who do no productive work" and those exploited in call centres and burger bars and between what you referred to as the obese and polluting nations with their trotters in the trough and the starving millions. And I was amazed at your quaint utopian notion of a world of small craft based organisations, needing only limited capital, restricted to, faithfully serving and in harmony with, their local community. I personally wouldn't want to live in such a world, but more importantly, if such a world is not possible what is the point in yearning for it?

Such emotion may be laudable, even heroic. [58] Without it we wouldn't have revolution. But revolutions don't seem to produce lasting solutions to the sort of problems we both recognise with the established capitalist market system. Lasting solutions seem to me to be more a technical matter. We need to understand the system and how and why it works and how it relates to human beings. And then we need to make considered adjustments through regulation to limit the inequity in distributing the benefits from the wealth the system creates. But we need to be careful in regulating not to do too much damage to the system itself, because there is no other system that seems to work. Capitalism may produce its discontents but heroic utopianism has generally failed to put bread on the table. Capitalism works, and that is quite enough for me. People can't eat idealism, and hungry people cannot engage in dialogue. We have tried to learn something from each other, but have not come to any precise and accurate answers. Perhaps that should not surprise us. As Socrates responded to Thrasymachus—

"We are in earnest, my friend, believe me; but the task, I fancy, is beyond our powers; and, therefore, you clever people should rather pity than scold us."

References

Bhalla, S. 2003. *Imagine there's no country.* Institute for International Economics, quoted in *Radical Thoughts on our 160th birthday: A survey of capitalism and democracy.* The Economist, 28th June, 2003.

Burrell, G. 1996. "Ephemera: Critical Dialogues on Organisation." ephemera [http://www.ephemera web.org] 1/1: 11–29.

Cadbury, A. 1999. *Cadbury Report: Compliance with Best Practice.* London: Gee Publishing.

Durkheim, E. 1991. *The Division of Labour in Society.* Basingstoke: Macmillan.

Jones, C., M. Parker and R. ten Bos. 2005. *For Business Ethics.* London: Routledge.

Klein, N. 2000. *No Logo: Taking Aim at the Brand Bullies.* London: Flamingo.

Lawrence, F. 2004. *Not on the Label.* London: Penguin.

Malachowski, A. 2003. "Corporate crises: A philosophical challenge." *Philosophy Now* 39, Jan.

Marx, K.: 1979, *Capital Volume 1.* Harmondsworth: Penguin.

McRae, H. 2003. "Like them or not, supermarkets have improved our quality of life." *The Independent* 15 Jan. 2003.

Monbiot, G. 2000. *Captive State: The Corporate Takeover of Britain.* London: Macmillan.

Monbiot, G. 2004. *The Age of Consent.* London: HarperCollins.

Nozick, R. 1974. *Anarchy, State and Utopia.* Oxford: Blackwell.

Parker, M. (ed.). 1998. *Ethics and Organisation.* London: Sage.

Parker, M. 2002. *Against Management.* Oxford: Polity.

Pearson, G. 1995. *Integrity in Organisations: An Alternative Business Ethic.* Maidenhead: McGraw-Hill.

Pearson, G. and M. Parker. 2001. "The Relevance of Ancient Greeks to Modern Business? A Dialogue on Business and Ethics." *Journal of Business Ethics* 31, 341–353.

Punch, M. 1996. *Dirty Business.* London: Sage.

Ricardo, D. 1817. "On the principles of political economy and taxation." In P. Sraffa (ed.), (1951), *The Works and Correspondence of David Ricardo.* Cambridge: Cambridge University Press.

Ritzer, G. 2000. *The McDonaldization of Society.* Thousand Oaks, CA: Pine Forge.

Smith, A. 1986/1776. *The Wealth of Nations.* London: Penguin.

Warnock, Mary (ed.). 1962. *Utilitarianism.* London: Collins.

Whitley, R. 1992. "Societies, firms and markets: the social structuring of business systems." In R. Whitley (ed.), *European Business Systems: Firms and Markets in Their National Contexts.* London: Sage.

Wray-Bliss, E. and M. Parker. 1998. "Marxism, capitalism and ethics." In M. Parker (ed.), *Ethics and Organisations.* London: Sage. pp. 30–52.

Xiao, Y. 2004. Management Issues in the Transformation of State Owned Enterprises. Unpublished PhD thesis, Keele University, Staffordshire.

Questions

1. (a) If you had to choose, would you rather have a job making the head of a pin eight hours a day or making whole pins eight hours a day?
   (b) Why is that question a red herring, according to Martin, with respect to the matter at hand?
2. What elements of capitalism, as Gordon defines it, does Martin accept?
3. (a) What is Gordon's response to the three elements of capitalism that Martin criticizes?
   (b) And what is Martin's response to Gordon's response?
   (c) And what is Gordon's response to Martin's response (to his response)?

4. (a) What is Martin's argument regarding regulation of "unrestrained competition" (para 28)? (b) And what is Gordon's response?
5. Gordon goes on to reject two specific ways in which the state can "regulate and redistribute" (para 34)—on what basis?
6. Martin has suggested state regulation. What does Gordon suggest? With whom do you agree? Why?
7. "Competition works" (para 45). That's Gordon's premiss.
   (a) In support of what conclusion?
   (b) Is his premise true?
   (c) Is he appealing to ethical grounds?
8. Martin's response suggests a very good question: is freedom maximized when there are no controls/rules? What about justice? What about quality of life?
9. Gordon's response alludes to the failure of communism. Did communism fail? (Define your terms.) If your answer is yes—because it had controls/rules or because of *which* controls/rules it had (or both)?
10. Do you agree that "a regulated version of the market economy is what is likely to provide the greatest happiness for the greatest number, or at least the potential for it" (para 56)? If so, what regulations would *you* argue for?

Case Study: Tembec: Losses to Profits to??

In 1972, the multinational corporation Canadian International Paper Company decided to close a pulp and paper mill in Temiscaming, Quebec. "Within three months, 500 people were out of work, and the town itself was on the verge of collapse" ("Tembec Inc. History"). (See what happens in a monoculture? Life needs diversity.)

Believing the mill to be financially viable, several ex-employees organized to buy it. Despite resistance from CIP, they eventually succeeded, in part due to demonstrations and the support of both the Quebec government and the Canadian Paperworkers Union.

Tembec became incorporated in July 1972. And things changed. First, since it was employee-owned (a number of employees reinvested their severance pay to buy the company, but they'd also obtained other funding), employees shared in the profits. True, their salaries decreased, and, in bad times, so did their income; but in good times, their income increased. This arrangement means everyone has a vested interest in the company—in quality, performance, and so on.

Second, management implemented a participatory model: all employees could become members of the several committees that were established; each committee had equal representation from management and the union.

Third, transparency and accountability became the norm: all financial information was made available to employees on a regular basis. "As a result of this management model...labor agreements that might take several months to hammer out at other companies were finalized in a matter of days at Tembec" ("Tembec Inc. History").

In 1979, the company became public, but employees retained 50% ownership.

Although the company has policies about social responsibility (for example, the company spends at least 1% of its pre-tax profits to promote health, education, culture, and recreation in the community) and environmental responsibility (for example, the company plants more trees than it cuts and five of their operations cogenerate electricity), its stated aim is to be profitable. The company earned a profit of $9.3 million in its first year and for the next twenty-five years, except for 1983, was consistently profitable. In its 1998 annual report, it pledged to restrict capital investments to projects that meet minimum return (profit) guidelines, to cut costs by a minimum of $25 million, and to improve management accountability and effectiveness. It has used some of its profits to modernize, building some state-of-the-art facilities. It has expanded into new product lines (particle board, flooring, furniture-quality wood) and markets its products around the world, to Japan, Taiwan, Indonesia, Iraq, Italy, France, Germany, Cuba, England, and eastern Europe. It has established or purchased production facilities in Timmins, Mattawa, Ville Marie, Huntsville, and other Canadian locations. It has even become an international company, with a facility in France and sales offices in Switzerland and China.

Eventually, there would be more sawmills than available lumber in North America; eventually, energy prices would rise; eventually lower-priced competition from Brazil, China, and Russia would emerge. But "Tembec had proven over the course of three decades that its employee-empowered business approach was flexible enough to meet any challenge" (Tembec Inc. History). That was said in 2004.

In September 2014, Tembec's gross profits were $159 million (down considerably from $669 in 2005), but still, it was a profitable company. In November, 2014, Tembec workers went on strike.

What do you think happened?

References

Hamilton-McCharles, Jennifer. "Tembec on Strike." *The Nugget* 26 Nov. 2014. http://www.nugget.ca/2014/11/26/tembec-on-strike

Tembec website. www.tembec.com

"Tembec Inc. History." Funding Universe. 2004. http://www.fundinguniverse.com/company-histories/tembec-inc-history/

Questions

1. (a) Does Tembec show that profit-making is compatible with profit-sharing (with employees)?
(b) If a profit-sharing company can be just as profitable, and is ethically better (*is* it?), why don't all private, for-profit companies have a profit-sharing plan for their employees? Can you think of some reasons why employees might not be interested in such a plan?
2. Does profit-sharing make "obscenely high" profits more morally acceptable?
3. So...what do you think happened?

CHAPTER EIGHT

The Medical Business

What to Do?—The Fetal Tissue Transplant Business

As government continues to privatize services such as health care, opening it up to marketing and profitability, the medical technology business may provide attractive opportunities. Indeed, one of these opportunities has caught your attention: fetal tissue transplants.

Like the now-common organ and bone marrow transplants, fetal tissue transplants may prove to be life-saving. It's been said that fetal tissue (from aborted fetuses or from lab cultures) can be used to treat brain and spinal cord injuries, some forms of epilepsy, as well as Parkinson's and Alzheimer's diseases.

It is true that the completion of the Human Genome Project may render these conditions obsolete, but that is unlikely to happen for a while. And certainly as the baby boomers age, which is happening now, the demand for a cure at least for Alzheimer's will surely increase.

However you have some concerns about the supply. You can't imagine a company actually coercing anybody, but you're not sure it's right for someone to even voluntarily sell their fetus. And yet surely that's better than just throwing it away. (It?) Regardless, are fetal rights violated? Do fetuses even *have* rights?

In any case, it's not really your decision. Or at least, that's not the decision you're trying to make at the moment. You're wondering whether, if you become part of the fetal tissue transplant business, you'd be endorsing whatever it takes to keep you in business. Such as abortions. Mightn't the price your company pays actually *encourage* women to get pregnant and then abort?

What do you decide to do?

Introduction

Business reaches into all areas of life, and each kind of business is a little different; these differences may give rise to unique ethical issues—not all products and services (or employees or clients/customers) should be considered in the same light.

Consider the education business. Many people think there's something morally wrong with students having to go into debt to pay tuition; the implication is that there should be a change in pricing, perhaps through a change in salaries or subsidies. But we go into debt for houses and cars—why not for education? If you really want it now and can't afford it, you borrow the money and thus go into debt; otherwise, you save for many years, and then you buy it all on your own. Some would respond that education is different: it's not a possession—it's a need; access to education is a fundamental right that should be available to all. Well, food is a need too; so, similarly, access to food should be a fundamental right—but we have to pay for it.

Consider the sports business. Perhaps there, the biggest ethical challenge is to justify the incredible amounts of money spent—not only on athletes' salaries, but on the activity itself. My guess is that building and operating a sports stadium costs more than building and operating a school. (Certainly your high school football team may well have cost more than all the other teams put together.)

Consider the military business. (And watch the 2005 documentary *Why We Fight*.) That's another business that is plagued with justifying exorbitant expenses. The ethics of rigid hierarchy and obedience is another issue to be considered (and one that has recently been highlighted by media coverage of military hazing rituals). And of course there's the primary service provided by the military and, increasingly, private security forces—killing.[1] How right is that? Does it matter whether you actually *do* the killing or "merely" provide the means (the people, the weapons—mechanical, biological, chemical, etc.) for killing? That is, does it matter *ethically*?[2]

Choosing the medical business as the special focus for this chapter wasn't completely arbitrary: both the current trend toward privatization and the development of medical technologies seem to present new challenges to the business—and you will be the ones facing them. Are you ready for cancer-killing nanobots? You should be, because almost 30% of all deaths in Canada are caused by cancer. What about 3-D printing? 3-D *bio*-printing. It's like Star Trek's replicator. Here and now.

So what issues might you face? Given our inability to curb our population, our ability to lengthen our lives, and the predicted influx of immigrants (environmental refugees due to

---

[1] The Canadian firm GardaWorld claims to be the largest privately owned security company in the world. See http://www.garda-world.com/about.

[2] See Byrne for an interesting analysis of the US arms industry on the basis of what he identifies as CSR (corporate social responsibility) requirements regarding the environment, social equity, profitability, and use of political power. He finds that the industry fails to meet any of those CSR requirements. Further, "[c]ountering a claim that these failings should not be held against arms manufacturers because their products are crucial to national defense, [he contends] that many of these companies function not as dutiful agents of a nation-state but as politically powerful entities in their own right" (abstract). He concludes that "they should be held responsible for the foreseeable consequences that flow from use of their products. This responsibility should include civil liability and, in cases involving war crimes and violations of human rights, responsibility under international human rights standards" (abstract). I suspect that an analysis of the Canadian arms industry would yield the same findings and conclusion.

climate changes), there will probably be serious resource-allocation problems; whether the resource is hospital beds, pharmaceuticals, or organs, you may have to "choose" your customers—you may have to choose who lives and who dies. Is a utilitarian approach appropriate here? Or a justice-based approach?

Resource allocation becomes particularly critical during epidemics, which are likely to increase due to climate change (and not just because of the predicted influx of environmental refugees—disease vectors will also change because of global warming). Where do you put your human and medical resources? Not from an efficiency point of view, but from an *ethical* point of view? What ethical principles should guide the handling of epidemics/pandemics? (Consider advertising, remedy production, distribution, disposal, employee rights, consumer rights—the full cycle.) Are you ready for another SARS or H1N1 or Ebola? Are you ready for bioterrorism? Biological warfare? (Will that be your business?)

Client confidentiality may be increasingly important (and perhaps increasingly problematic, given some of the issues mentioned in Chapter 9). Do you or do you not give certain information to your patients' sexual partners? To blood donor clinics? To insurance companies? Whose rights take precedence?

Should you, and how should you, advertise your services and products? Will you hold yourself to "higher" ethical standards in this regard (with regard to full disclosure)? Why? Why not? Should you, as a pharmaceutical firm, give free samples to physicians? All-expenses-paid trips to conferences? Doesn't that sort of "advertising" behaviour put undue pressure on physicians to prescribe your products? That is, doesn't that create a conflict of interest? According to a policy statement released by the Canadian Medical Association, "Although many physicians deny that these relations compromise the independence of their judgment as to what is best for their patients, research suggests otherwise" (Kondro).

And what about those services and products? Will you provide abortion, physician-assisted suicide, euthanasia? Religionists would argue against, appealing to the sanctity of life. Blood transfusions are also considered morally unacceptable by some.

What about in vitro fertilization? Surrogacy? Sex selection? Natural law theorists might draw their line here.

What about stem cell research, fetal tissue transplants, cloning? Are *those* morally acceptable business endeavours?[1]

What about genetic research? Genetic screening? Do you want to be the business hired by employers who make genetic screening mandatory? And use the results for hiring and firing decisions? What about genetic modification? And who owns the genetic material you'll be working with—you, the business who hired you, or the person who provided the material?

What about 'smart drugs' that can enhance concentration and memory. Ritalin during exam week? How about Provigil during the work day? Every day, because your boss insists. As

---

[1] See Herder and Brian for an analysis of the attempt by Canadian company Aggregate Therapeutics to commercialize stem cell research.

mentioned in Chapter 4, on what ethical grounds can you, as a boss, insist? On what ethical grounds should you, as an employee, do it anyway? And on what ethical grounds can you, or maybe *should* you, as a pharmaceutical company, *develop* smart drugs?[1]

Another big issue, especially for business, is whether you should patent your "products." What is your motive for patenting—merely to recover expenses for discovery? (Patents provide the right to exclude all others from using, making, selling, or importing your invention for 20 years.) Is that just an egoistic approach or could it be utilitarian? Di Norcia notes that "manipulating patents is the most popular means of suppressing a technology" (120) and says that the oil companies have suppressed solar energy technology. Would you do that? Suppress an alternative remedy or cure so that yours is the one everyone buys?

Perhaps a prior question is "*Can* you patent your products?" That is, are they really yours for the owning? Forbes raises an interesting issue when he proposes a First Nations Intellectual Property Act that would "provide that royalties must be paid for the use of Native American inventions and products including kayaks, toboggans, tipis, rubber, design motifs, plants, *medicinals*, tribal names and personal names" (my emphasis). Citing the attempt by chemical and biomedical corporations to establish ownership of herbs, herbal extracts, food plants, and plant fibres, as well as the past appropriation (theft?) by Europeans of North American foods and medicines (such as corn, potatoes, cacao, peanuts, quinine, and golden seal), he speculates that "the payment of royalties on Native American inventions might well be enough to completely replace the federal contributions to tribes in the U.S. and Canada."

A very current issue is whether human genes can be patented. Inventions, rather than discoveries, typically qualify for patents, so on the one hand, whether or not to allow patents for human genes is a definitional problem. And human genes are not inventions (right?), which is why the US Supreme Court ruling in 2013 makes sense: human genes can't be patented, but synthetic versions of them can be. In Canada, at the moment, genes *can* be patented, but in November 2014 the Children's Hospital of Eastern Ontario filed a lawsuit regarding the long QT gene, essentially becoming Canada's first test case protesting human gene patents. They argue that "restricting access to genetic information by researchers and clinicians undermines patient care and is morally and legally untenable" (Picard).[2]

As for the ethical issues, can bodies, even parts of bodies, *be* owned? Post argues against the commercialization of body parts: only the poor will need to sell their organs and fetuses and only the rich will be able to buy them—this will exacerbate class inequities and it may also result in low-quality parts. Matthews argues in favour of it, refuting both of Post's concerns: a poor person could use the money from the sale of a kidney to start a business and perhaps escape poverty; free market mechanisms increase rather than decrease product quality. Furthermore, an organ market would save lives.[3]

---

1 See Kirby for an entry-level discussion on this issue.
2 See Lipkus for a brief introduction to the legal issues.
3 See also Chadwick, who provides a Kantian argument against such a market. Then see Tadd's response to Chadwick; he argues that there's no difference between selling one's body parts and selling one's labour. See also Andrews.

Another consequence to consider is whether patents promote or inhibit research. There are arguments on both sides: without patents, the initial research may not have been undertaken, but with patents, further research may not be undertaken.

Given the special nature of biomedical technology, not only might researchers *not* have the right to patent, but they also might have a moral *obligation to share*. Gold and Caulfield note that "[i]n some countries, patents are not granted if the sale of the invention would contravene fundamental ethical standards. In Europe, for example, processes to clone human beings, modify human germ lines, use human embryos for commercial purposes, or alter the genetic identity of animals so as to cause pain without a substantial medical benefit to people, are thought to be in breach of these standards" (2268).[1]

A question related to patents is whether you should try to prohibit generic versions of your drugs. This is what Amgen and Genentech are trying to do, claiming that generic versions of their biologics (which, unlike regular drugs, are produced inside genetically modified living cells) could be harmful to consumers (Pollack). If that's the whole truth and nothing but the truth, okay. But of course one wonders if the companies are, as in the case of patents, trying to protect/recover their investment. But what's wrong with that? Isn't it fair? But what if in doing so, they're preventing competition, which, some argue, harms society? Where is the evidence for that?) Is there another way, a win-win way, in which we can arrange things?

Although research ethics may seem to go beyond business ethics, pharmaceutical companies engage in research directly or indirectly (according to Neergaard, in the US, they provide about 70 per cent of the financing for studies of medications), so it's actually extremely relevant. Consider the somewhat recent case in which Dr. Aubrey Blumsohn discovered that results of a study were submitted to a scientific meeting under his name, even though he had neither written nor reviewed the report (Neergaard). And then there are the many claims that critical data are withheld to make a product appear less risky than it actually is. Is the problem merely a conflict of interest? Is the solution *independent* research? Paid for by...? From a virtue ethics perspective, the issue is quite simple: be honest. But from a utilitarian perspective, perhaps a risky drug is better than no drug at all—but shouldn't that be up to the person taking the drug? And *are* there no other drugs? (How do we account for Celebrex, which works just as well as acetaminophen, but has far greater risks of cardiovascular and stomach problems?)

Is it right to test your products on animals who are unable to refuse consent? Does it matter whether your product is life-saving or just life-enhancing? Does it matter whether it benefits only humans or the animals used for testing as well? Does it matter what effect, what degree of harm, your testing has on the animal—discomfort, pain, death?

Must you test all of your products to certain safety? By that point, some prospective customers could be dead. Should people have the right to buy drugs or procedures that are not completely tested—especially if that's their last chance and they're going to die otherwise? What risk is

---

1 See Industry Canada's webpage "Intellectual Property Policy: Patenting and Human Beings" for an overview of the ethical issues.

acceptable? (And, as just mentioned, whose decision is that?) Standard product safety issues should be considered as well. (Remember, or research, the Red Cross "tainted blood" affair.)

Speaking of product safety, workplace safety issues are also an important issue, perhaps more so in the medical business because they often involve life and death, or at least serious quality-of-life consequences. Consider the potential for contagion. And consider it in both directions: would it be unjust discrimination to refuse to hire an HIV-positive surgeon?

Management/union issues may be especially problematic in the medical business—should physicians and nurses be able to go on strike? Does management have an extra responsibility to make sure that doesn't happen? Why/not?

Here's another question: should doctors be able to refuse demands for futile treatment? (Or any other treatment they have reasons to refuse?) Are *other* businesses obligated to provide whatever the customer wants? Should the patient be considered a customer? To what extent *is* the medical business like other businesses?[1]

Lastly, recalling the patent issue, let's reconsider profit in the medical business. According to Zimmerer and Preston (see Donaldson and Werhane, 186), Plasma International Company bought blood in underdeveloped countries and then sold it with a price mark-up in the US. When it was in great demand because of a disaster, they marked it up even more and made quite a profit. Is that morally right? Not just exploiting underdeveloped countries, not just capitalizing on others' misfortune, but capitalizing on life and death? Reversing your perspective for a moment, do you want to consult a doctor whose bottom line is his/her profit margin?[2]

And speaking of profit, consider what Poitras and Meredith call "economic medicalization": transforming non-medical problems into medical problems in order to profit from them. ("Erectile dysfunction"—and hence Viagra, Cialis, and Levitra—is the obvious example.) Again, is that a morally acceptable thing to do? If so, on what grounds? If not, on what grounds?

> **BOX 8.1   Feel Like Watching a Movie?**
>
> Check out *Sicko*. And if you're not in the mood for a documentary, try *Gattaca*, *Elysium*, *Eternal Sunshine of the Spotless Mind*, and *The Fifth Element*.

References and Further Reading

Agich, George J. "Medicine as Business and Profession." *Theoretical Medicine* 11 (1990): 311–24.
Andrews, Lori. "My Body, My Property." *The Hastings Center Report* 16.5 (1986): 28–38.
Byrne, Edmund F. "Assessing Arms Makers' Corporate Social Responsibility." *Journal of Business Ethics* 74 (2007): 201–17.

---

1 See Agich and Wicks.
2 See Relman and Wicks for opposing views about whether medicine is better or worse off as a free market enterprise.

Chadwick, Ruth F. "The Market for Bodily Parts: Kant and Duties to Oneself." *Journal of Applied Philosophy* 6.2 (1989): 129–39.

Di Norcia, Vincent. *Hard Like Water: Ethics in Business.* Toronto: Oxford University Press, 1998.

Donaldson, Thomas, and Patricia H. Werhane. *Ethical Issues in Business: A Philosophical Approach.* 5th ed. Englewood Cliffs, NJ: Prentice Hall, 1996.

Forbes, Jack D. *Columbus and Other Cannibals: The Wetiko Disease of Exploitation, Imperialism and Terrorism.* New York: Semiotexte-Autonomedia, 1992.

———. "Intellectual Property Rights of Indigenous Peoples." *Windspeaker* Classroom Edition 3. http://www.ammsa.com

Gold, E. Richard, and Timothy A. Caulfield. "The moral tollbooth: a method that makes use of the patent system to address ethical concerns in biotechnology." *The Lancet* 350 (29 June 2002) 2268–70.

Herder, Matthew, and Jennifer Dyck Brian. "Canada's Stem Cell Corporation: Aggregate Concerns and the Question of Public Trust." *Journal of Business Ethics* 77 (2008): 73–84.

Hurley, Jeremiah. "Ethics, economics, and public financing of health care." *Journal of Medical Ethics* 27 (2001): 234–39.

Kirby, Jason. "Going to Work on Smart Drugs." *Maclean's* 13 Oct. 2008. http://www.macleans.ca/safety/health/going-to-work-on-smart-drugs/

Kondro. Wayne. "Threats to medical professionalism tackled in Canada." *Lancet* 360.9329 (27 July 2002) 316.

Lipkus, Nathaniel. "Gene Patents in Canada: A Myriad of Possibilities." *JustBioTech*. 3 July 2013. http://www.justbiotech.ca/gene-patents-in-canada-a-myriad-of-possibilities/

Matthews, Merrill, Jr. "Have a Heart, But Pay For It." *Insight* (9 Jan. 1995). Reprinted in Stephen Satris (ed.), *Taking Sides: Clashing Views on Controversial Moral Issues.* 5th ed. Guilford, CT: Dushkin Publishing Group, 1996. 114–17.

Neergaard, Lauren. "Disputes over industry-funded medical research a growing problem." *U-T San Diego* 22 Feb. 2006. http://legacy.utsandiego.com/news/health/20060222-1426-researchconflicts.html

Picard, André. "'Bad patents' on human genes hinder health care, hospital says." *Globe and Mail* 3 Nov. 2014. http://www.theglobeandmail.com/life/health-and-fitness/health/bad-patents-on-human-genes-hinder-health-care-hospital-urges-court/article21423222/

Poitras, Geoffrey, and Lindsay Meredith. "Ethical Transparency and Economic Medicalization." *Journal of Business Ethics* 86 (2009): 313–25.

Pollack, Andrew. "Biotech Firms, Billions at Risk, Lobby States to Limit Generics." *New York Times* 28 Jan. 2013: A1.

Post, Stephen G. "Organ Volunteers Serve Body Politic." *Insight* (9 Jan. 1995). Reprinted in Stephen Satris (ed.), *Taking Sides: Clashing Views on Controversial Moral Issues.* 5th ed. Guilford, CT: Dushkin Publishing Group, 1996. 118–21.

Relman, Arnold S. "What Market Values Are Doing to Medicine." *The Atlantic Monthly* 269.3 (1992): 90–104.

Resnik, David. "The Morality of Human Gene Patents." *Kennedy Institute of Ethics Journal* 7.1 (1997): 43–61.

Tadd, G.V. "The Market for Bodily Parts: A Response to Ruth Chadwick." *Journal of Applied Philosophy* 8.1 (1991): 95–102.

Ubelacker, Sheryl. "CHEO launches lawsuit against owners of gene patent." The Canadian Press/*CTV News*. 3 Nov. 2014. http://ottawa.ctvnews.ca/cheo-launches-lawsuit-against-owners-of-gene-patent-1.2084430

Wicks, Andrew C. "Albert Schweitzer or Ivan Boesky? Why We Should Reject the Dichotomy between Medicine and Business." *Journal of Business Ethics* 14.5 (1995): 339–51.

Ethics, Economics, and Public Financing of Health Care[*]

Jeremiah Hurley

Abstract

There is a wide variety of ethical arguments for public financing of health care that share a common structure built on a series of four logically related propositions regarding: (1) the ultimate purpose of a human life or human society; (2) the role of health and its distribution in society in advancing this ultimate purpose; (3) the role of access to or utilisation of health care in maintaining or improving the desired level and distribution of health among members of society, and (4) the role of public financing in ensuring the ethically justified access to and utilisation of health care by members of society. This paper argues that economics has much to contribute to the development of the ethical foundations for publicly financed health care. It focuses in particular on recent economic work to clarify the concepts of access and need and their role in analyses of the just distribution of health care resources, and on the importance of economic analysis of health care and health care insurance markets in demonstrating why public financing is necessary to achieve broad access to and utilisation of health care services.

---

[*] *Journal of Medical Ethics* 27 (2001): 234–39.]

Introduction

[1] Is there an ethical rationale for publicly financed health insurance? It would seem there is a variety of (sophisticated, complex, and sometimes mutually incompatible) arguments rooted in different ethical frameworks. However, because public financing is a particular institutional arrangement that is valued not intrinsically but only to the extent that it contributes to achieving a higher end, a wide variety of such arguments share a common structure.[1] Although these arguments differ considerably in detail, they share a structure built on four logically related propositions regarding: (1) the ultimate purpose of a human life or human society; (2) the role of health and its distribution in society in advancing this ultimate purpose; (3) the role of access to or utilisation of health care in maintaining or improving the desired level and distribution of health among members of society, and (4) the role of public financing in ensuring the ethically justified access to and utilisation of health care by members of society. Because the dominant concern of modern economic analysis is the consequences of alternative institutional arrangements of economic activity, economic reasoning has much to contribute to the development of such ethical arguments. Indeed, economic analysis is a necessary ingredient since the rationale for public financing rests at least in part on demonstrating that the ethically required access to and utilisation of health care cannot be achieved through a system of solely private financing. Equity arguments alone are not sufficient: if markets function well a system of public subsidies for the purchase of private insurance could deal with equity concerns. Rather, full public financing for health care requires demonstrating that, even in the presence of appropriate subsidies, private financing through insurance markets fails to promote the requisite access to or utilisation of health care. Economic reasoning is crucial to any ethical argument that proceeds in this fashion.

[2] The paper is organised around the four propositions listed above, focusing on propositions (3) and (4) where economics offers the greatest potential contributions. To help make matters more concrete, I illustrate key points with reference to ethical analysis of public financing within three specific ethical frameworks: (1) classical utilitarianism; (2) extra-welfarism, particularly as developed in the health sector;[2,3] and (3) Rawlsian-style contractarianism.[4,5] I choose these because they are commonly used in health sector analysis, they represent broad approaches to social ethics for which there are numerous particular refinements, they differ in their focus for valuation and in the decision rules used to rank institutional arrangements, and they derive from very different philosophical and ethical traditions. Space constraints mean that I can give each only the most cursory treatment; their use is meant purely to illustrate points, not to develop the fundamental argument.

The Structure of Ethical Arguments regarding Public Financing of Health Care

The Purpose of Life, Ultimate Ends and a Just Society

[3] The purpose of life has of course been a central question in moral and political philosophy for thousands of years and a question to which philosophers have provided a wide range of answers. All theories of justice and the "good" society are based (implicitly or explicitly) on such an ultimate end, and within any such theory the characteristics of a just society are those that foster the posited ultimate end. For Bentham, Mill and classical

utilitarians the ultimate human end was happiness and the good society maximised happiness among its members. Extra-welfarists, in contrast, eschew utility in favour of more objective outcomes such as functionings and capabilities and the good society allocates resources to foster these among its members.[6–8] For Rawls the ultimate end was "the satisfaction of [a person's] rational desire" in the form of a rational plan of life,[9] and in a good society deviations from equality of basic primary goods can be justified only to the extent that they improve the lot of the least advantaged member of society.[4]

Health

[4] Health is ethically good to the extent that it contributes to the realisation of the ultimate end sought—happiness, capabilities and functionings, fulfilment of a rational life plan, etc. Among the various "goods" that contribute to the ultimate end, health is often accorded special ethical significance because it is necessary to achieving most intermediate and ultimate ends; ill health and injury are unpredictable and largely beyond the control of an individual (most of those who fall ill have done nothing knowingly to deserve or cause the ill health); and ill health represents a time of considerable vulnerability and dependency on others, giving society's response to those who suffer illness and injury particular ethical salience.

[5]   But simply arguing that health is ethically important is not enough. A crucial question is: what does an ethical analysis demand about the just level and distribution of health in society? Maximising the level of health in society is unlikely to be ethically justified given that health is only one contributor to an ultimate end and that health cannot be directly redistributed among members of society (though of course it can be indirectly redistributed via the allocation of health-influencing resources). Welfarist reasoning cannot identify the just distribution of health a priori because the just distribution depends on the structure and distribution of preferences in society with respect to health and other things. The just level and distribution of health is the one that maximises average utility among members of society. If one assumes diminishing marginal utility, then utilitarianism would have a bias toward more equal distributions of health (up to the point where the additions to utility from this are offset by reductions in utility from transferring additional resources from other activities to health). From an extra-welfarist health perspective, Culyer and Wagstaff argue that the only ethically defensible distribution of health is an equal distribution, subject to some side constraints such as the imperative not to deliberately reduce one person's health status to equalise health levels.[10, 11] Rawls did not include health or health care in his set of primary goods, but more recently he has explored how health might be integrated into his framework.[12] Rawls's difference principle would permit a deviation from an equal distribution of health if it improved the health and wellbeing of the least advantaged member of society; it is silent on the characteristics of the distribution above this minimum level. (See Williams and Cookson[13] for an analysis within an economic framework of the demands of a wide variety of equity criteria with respect to the distribution of health among members of society.)

Access to and Utilisation of Health Care

[6] Health care, which is generally defined to include those goods, services and activities the primary purpose of which is the maintenance or improvement of health,[14] is one of a complex array of factors that determine health.[15] Health care as such is not intrinsically ethically valuable; it is ethically valuable because it contributes to health. From this it follows directly that the ethically justified distribu-

tion of access to and utilisation of needed health care is the one which generates the desired level and distribution of health.

[7] This conclusion rests on two controversial, often confusing concepts—access and need—central to many discussions of ethics and health care. Economic reasoning has contributed in recent years to clarifying access, need and competing definitions of these concepts (see, for example Culyer and Wagstaff, Mooney, Le Grand, Pereira, and Wagstaff and Van Doorslaer[10, 16–20]) even if it may not have generated greater consensus. Economics identifies access with the concept of feasible choice sets.[10, 18, 22] A person's feasible choice set includes all those things it is possible for them to obtain or accomplish given their resources and constraints beyond their control. Therefore, access is greater in situation B compared to situation A if the feasible choice set under B is larger than (and fully encompasses) the feasible choice set in A. Two individuals have equal access if they have identical feasible choice sets. Empirically measuring access remains a tremendous challenge, but this analytic approach provides considerable insight into the implications for resource allocation of calls for differing types of access.

[8] It is not access to or utilisation of health care services *as such* that is ethically justified, but access to or utilisation of *needed* health care services. The notion of need is highly contested,[21, 23–28] but economists generally favour instrumentalist conceptions of need: a need exists when there is a good, activity or service that is effective (and some would add cost-effective[23]) in attaining an ethically legitimate end for a person. The question of effectiveness is in large part technical; the question of what constitutes an ethically legitimate end is in large part social, political and moral. Unlike most areas of economics, for which goods are assumed to contribute directly to welfare, the technical production relationship between health care and health allows for a more precise use of the concept of need than is possible even in other areas where needs talk is prevalent (for example, housing, food, education). This production relationship means that a health care need is very specific—one needs a specific health care service that has been shown to be effective for the particular health problem, for which there are often few substitutes. Unlike most goods, health care itself is often a "bad" that causes considerable short term pain and suffering, but which is consumed only because of its expected health benefits. This provides a sounder basis for third party judgments of need, especially need in relation to socially defined objectives.

[9] The fact that the primary purpose for consuming health care is to improve health and that there is a basis for third-party judgments of need (as opposed to mere wants) generates good-specific distributional concerns about health care. Welfarist frameworks model this through utility interdependences that generate good-specific caring externalities associated with health status and the consumption of needed health care.[29, 30] That is, person A's utility depends in part on person B's health status and, by implication, her consumption of needed health care; where access itself is the focus of concern, person A's utility depends in part on person B's access to health care (though person B may choose not to consume even needed care).

[10] Welfarists seldom investigate the underlying source of such utility interdependence (for example, the view that health care is a right, notions of solidarity with other members of society, etc), but regardless of that, such externalities imply that within welfarist frameworks broad access to and utilisation of needed health care may be ethically justified. As ever, the preferred distribution depends on the precise nature of preferences and utility interdependences, but a priori such externalities give rise to distributional concerns not

associated with most goods and services. Culyer and Wagstaff's health-oriented extra-welfarism calls for access to and utilisation of health care services that generate an equal distribution of health. This will call for broad access to health care services for all members of society, though they specifically note that the ethically justified distribution is unlikely to coincide with allocation according to need and equal access to health care.[10] A Rawlsian demand for a minimal level of health for all in society would also demand a minimal level of access to or utilisation of needed health care services by all in society.

[11] What is noteworthy is that each of these frameworks calls, to some extent, for utilisation of health care to be associated with need and health status, not simply ability to pay, and that this fact demands broad (but not necessarily equal) access to needed health care services by all members of society.

The Role of Public Financing

[12] The last link in the chain of reasoning is the demonstration that public financing of health care is either necessary to generate the ethically justified distribution of access and utilisation or that it does this better than other financing arrangements. This requires examining the properties of alternative private market and public financing arrangements. In the discussion I distinguish four configurations of financing with increasing reliance on public financing: (1) fully private financing through private insurance purchases and direct payments by patients to providers; (2) public subsidies to support the purchase of insurance in private markets, and/or public insurance for certain population sub-groups (for example, as in the US); (3) single-source, universal, first-dollar (free of charge) publicly financed insurance, with a parallel private insurance sector offering coverage for the same services insured by the public sector (for example, as is the case in the UK); and (4) single-source, universal, first-dollar publicly financed insurance with no parallel private insurance sector (for example, as is the case for physician and hospital services in Canada).

Insurance, Insurance Markets, and Financing Health Care

[13] Unpredictability in the need for health care and the high costs of health care (which can exceed an amount that even many forward-looking, prudent members of society could afford) generate an important role for insurance in health care financing. Insurance pools individuals' financial risks associated with health care, reducing the total amount of risk in society and allowing those who fall ill to obtain the care they need. From an ethical perspective, it is interesting to note that, unlike most goods and services, the production of insurance is by definition a collective activity: it is literally impossible for a single individual to "produce" insurance (except in the very limited sense of pooling risk over time through saving). One can produce insurance only by joining together with others (even if through market-based, voluntary transactions) to form a risk pool.

[14] A system of private insurance markets alone (even one that is well-functioning by economic criteria discussed below) could not provide the broad access called for by the analysis in the previous section. Markets allocate goods and services on the basis of a person's ability and willingness to pay. Low-income members of society would be unable to afford health care insurance policies. This is particularly so given the well-established inverse relationship between socioeconomic status and health status, which would make premiums in a private market highest on average for those with the fewest economic resources (and the most need). From

an economic perspective, however, this is simply a problem of the distribution of income. If health care insurance markets are otherwise well-functioning, all that may be required to address this problem is a system of public subsidies to allow the purchase of health care insurance by all members of society.

[15] A role for public financing beyond a system of subsidies for private insurance depends on how well a system of private health care insurance markets functions, or, in economic language, the extent to which markets fail to allocate resources efficiently. Economics defines a situation to be efficient if one beneficial activity cannot be increased without decreasing some other beneficial activity.[31] The ethical force of this concept of efficiency within a consequentialist line of reasoning is clear: to tolerate an inefficient allocation of resources is to forgo an opportunity to provide benefit (however one wants to measure this) to one person or group without decreasing benefit to anyone else.

[16] Within this broad concept, economists distinguish three types of efficiency. Technical efficiency requires that we not waste physical or human resources when producing goods and services. Cost-effectiveness efficiency integrates the relative costs of resources, and requires that we use the least-cost combination of inputs to produce goods and services. And allocative efficiency integrates a consideration of the value of goods and services to members of society. It asks whether society is producing the "right" amount of each good and service and distributing those goods and services in accord with the "value" individuals place on them. The "right" mix and distribution of goods depends, of course, on how value to an individual is assessed (utility, health, other notions of wellbeing) and on the decision-criterion by which different allocations are ranked, (for example, a maximisation criterion, a Pareto criterion, a Rawlsian maxmin criterion).

Economies of Scale

[17] Private health care insurance markets suffer from two sources of technical inefficiency that can be mitigated or avoided through public financing. The fixed costs to a private insurer of providing insurance (for example, the cost of determining risk-rated premiums), which are the same whether the insurer sells 100 policies or 100 million policies, generate economies of scale in insurance provision that make it impossible in many settings to sustain competitive markets for insurance if firms are to operate at technically efficient sizes.[32] In addition, systems of private insurance with multiple insurance organisations are technically inefficient because they require a host of administrative costs absent from public insurance programmes (for example, rate-setting, marketing, claims administration). Estimates suggest, for example, that administrative costs within the private, multipayer US system account for 19–24% of health care spending while they account for only 8–11% in Canada's publicly financed system.[33]

[18] Allocative inefficiency in private insurance markets that arises from informational asymmetries between sellers and purchasers of insurance further supports the argument that public financing is necessary to achieve broad access to health care. In private insurance markets that form risk pools by voluntary enrolment, informational asymmetries between insurance providers and insurance purchasers can cause risk selection. Risk selection arises when insurers selectively enroll low-risk individuals (cream-skimming) or when high-risk individuals selectively seek out more generous insurance (adverse selection). Risk selection, and adverse selection in particular, can make it impossible to sustain private insurance markets. As a consequence, even people who are willing and able to purchase insurance at a price that reflects their risk

status are unable to do so because the dynamic of adverse selection makes it impossible to sustain an insurance market. Although risk-adjusted premiums can reduce such risk selection, it is not possible to risk-adjust premiums accurately enough to eliminate risk selection. Universal, publicly financed insurance that covers all residents of a jurisdiction completely avoids risk selection.

[19] Asymmetry of information between patients and health care providers furnishes an additional rationale for public financing and for first-dollar coverage with no patient cost-sharing. Individuals are frequently unable to identify what is wrong with them and, once diagnosed, what health care services they need to resolve their health problem. A primary reason for seeing a health professional is precisely to obtain such information. This informational asymmetry gives health care providers tremendous market power and can generate inefficiency-inducing supply-side moral hazard (higher prices, increased use of marginally beneficial services). Moral hazard plagues both privately and publicly financed insurance systems, but public insurers within single-payer systems of finance may have more effective policy levers and the countervailing power required to control better the various forms of supply-side moral hazard.[32, 34]

[20] Patient-provider informational asymmetry also suggests that patient cost-sharing will be inefficient by leading to non-optimal health care consumption. The fact that patients often cannot distinguish between necessary and unnecessary care, that cost-sharing discriminates on the basis of ability to pay, and that those with low income, on average, have greater needs for care, means that cost-sharing leads to a reduction in both necessary and unnecessary care, with potentially important adverse health effects.[35]

Key Messages

[21] The key messages of such efficiency analyses are that: (1) it will likely be more costly to produce insurance through private markets than through a public, single-payer system; (2) a system of private insurance markets will be incomplete, leaving members of society with either no insurance or less-than-complete insurance (for reasons other than ability to pay) while public insurance can provide universal coverage; (3) the usual prescription of cost-sharing within insurance systems is not supported in the health care sector. Taken together, they imply that a system of publicly financed insurance is more likely to provide the broad access to and utilisation of health financing demanded by the utilitarian, extra-welfarist and Rawlsian frameworks than is a system of private insurance markets. Indeed, these efficiency arguments, when combined with equity considerations provide a strong rationale for universal, mandatory, first-dollar public insurance for health care. A few qualifications to this general conclusion are required.

[22] Within the utilitarian calculus, the benefits of such a programme of public financing, which provides the same amount of insurance to all members of society, would have to be weighed against a welfare cost that arises in a world of heterogeneous risk attitudes and preferences for insurance. A system of public financing that provides everyone with the same level of insurance forces some to consume more insurance than they desire and others less insurance than they desire. The size of this welfare loss depends on the extent of heterogeneity relative to the welfare cost of imperfect market arrangements. The universal programme may still be justified, but technically it becomes an empirical matter.

[23] Secondly, given the correlation between health and other markers of socioeconomic status (for

example, income, education, control, etc), the "least advantaged" member of society is likely to be one of those most disadvantaged under private insurance markets and most helped by a system of public financing. Hence, the rationale for public financing is likely to be quite strong within a Rawlsian framework. Similarly, given that within the extra-welfarist framework health can only be equalised by improving the health of those with low health status (recall the side constraint on not lowering the health of anyone), the rationale for public financing is again likely to be quite strong within health-oriented extra-welfarism.

[24] Thirdly, although significant public financing may be a necessary condition for achieving the access and utilisation sought by the different frameworks, the funding, organisation and delivery of services will have an important impact on realising the full vision.

[25] Lastly, the patterns of income redistribution associated with public finance through progressive systems of taxation advance broader social objectives, an aspect not considered above.[32, 34] Private insurance with risk-rated premiums does not embody any *ex ante* redistribution of income (though of course, *ex post*, it redistributes from the well to the sick in the insurance pool). In contrast, public financing embodies both *ex ante* redistribution from the wealthy (and generally healthy) to the poor (who generally have lower health status) as well as *ex post* redistribution from the healthy to the sick.

Public Financing with No Parallel Private Finance

[26] The vast majority of countries with universal publicly financed systems of health care insurance allow a parallel private insurance sector in which individuals can purchase private insurance for publicly insured services. The benefits of such insurance to its beneficiaries may include a wider range of treatment choices, the ability to jump a public queue, and so forth. Advocates also argue that such private insurance helps improve access to the public sector by lessening the demands placed on it. Is there an ethical rationale, however, for going beyond the provision of universal public finance by prohibiting such parallel private insurance, as is done in Canada for medically necessary physician and hospital services?

[27] Restricting private insurance this way might follow directly from certain ethical approaches that demand equal access to health care or equal maximum possible consumption of health care by all members of society (for example, perhaps some solidarity-based approaches). It would not, however, follow directly from any of the three ethical frameworks considered in this paper or many other approaches framed within the four propositions identified above. But within a wide range of consequentialist approaches, such a restriction might derive indirectly from the operation of parallel systems of finance. That is, it is an empirical question whether a system of financing that prohibits private insurance for publicly insured services better advances the access and utilisation patterns ethically demanded. Evidence suggests that this is at least plausible.

[28] Parallel systems of private finance can drain resources from the public system, erode public support for the public system, lead to longer waiting times in the public sector, and make it harder to provide all members with timely access to high quality services.[36] Parallel private insurance is in general associated with an expansion of resources devoted to health care, though these additional resources are often used for services that generate smaller health gains (otherwise, they would have been given greater priority within the public system).

[29] These dynamics imply that a parallel private insurance sector is not, as is commonly suggested, simply an add-on to a publicly financed system. Rather, complex interaction occurs that affects the viability of the publicly financed system, which leads to cross-subsidies (most often from public to private), and which may draw scarce resources into the health sector that are allocated in ways not consistent with the ethically justified patterns of access and utilisation.

[30] Once again, this potential empirical justification is perhaps most tentative within a utilitarian framework, as the benefits of such a restriction on parallel private insurance must be weighed against its cost in the form of frustrated preferences among those who would prefer to purchase such insurance. The rationale is perhaps strongest within the extra-welfarist approach that calls for an equal distribution of health and which strongly de-emphasises utility effects in the valuation process. Given that on average it is those who are of low income and poor health status who are hurt most by the dynamics of parallel systems of finance, such a restriction may well also be supported within a Rawlsian framework.

Conclusions

[31] My hope is that this short paper has documented at least two contributions of economic reasoning to the development of ethical arguments regarding public financing of health care. First, that economic methods have helped to clarify concepts such as access and need, which are central to discussions of ethically justified allocations of health care resources. And second, that economic analysis, which has demonstrated both analytically and empirically that private insurance markets suffer a number of both equity- and efficiency-relevant deficiencies, has a central role to play within a wide range of ethical approaches in identifying the ethically justified institutional arrangements for financing health care. Both of these points exemplify a broader cross-fertilisation between ethics and economics that has emerged in recent years (see, for example, Sen, Hausman and McPherson, and Broome[6, 37–39] among others) which promises to advance both disciplines.

References and Notes

1. Health care financing refers to the raising of revenue from individuals in society to support the provision of health care services. *Public* financing refers to raising the revenues through the public tax system. Financing should be distinguished from delivery. Delivery refers to the actual provision of health care services. There is no logical relationship between the nature (ie, public or private) of financing and the nature (ie, public or private) of the delivery system: public financing can be (and often is) combined with the delivery of health care services by private organisations (not-for-profit, not-only-for-profit and for-profit organisations).
2. Culyer AJ. The normative economics of health care finance and provision. *Oxford Review of Economic Policy* 1989;5:34–58.
3. Culyer AJ. Commodities, characteristics of commodities, characteristics of people, utilities and quality of life. In: Baldwin S, Godfrey C, Propper C, eds. *Quality of life: perspectives and policies*. London: Routledge, 1990: 9–27.
4. Rawls J. *A theory of justice*. Oxford: Oxford University Press, 1971.
5. Wolff RP. *Understanding Rawls*. Princeton: Princeton University Press, 1977.
6. Sen A. *On ethics and economics*. Oxford: Blackwell, 1987.
7. Sen A. *The standard of living*. Cambridge: Cambridge University Press, 1987.
8. Sen A. *Commodities and capabilities*. Oxford: Oxford University Press, 1999.
9. See reference 4: 92.

10. Culyer AJ, Wagstaff A. Equity and equality in health and health care. *Journal of Health Economics 1993; 2:431–57.*
11. Culyer AJ. *Equality of what in health policy? Conflicts between the contenders.* York: University of York Centre for Health Economics, 1995. Discussion paper 142.
12. Rawls J. *Political liberalism.* New York: Columbia University Press, 1993.
13. Williams A, Cookson R. Equity in health. In: Culyer AJ, Newhouse JP, eds. *Handbook of health economics.* Amsterdam: North-Holland, 2000: 1863–910.
14. Health care is sometimes consumed for reasons other than improving health, such as a diagnostic test that provides information valued by the patient even if it will not alter treatment decisions or health. This definition holds true for a large portion of health care consumption.
15. Evans RG, Barer M, Marmor T. *Why are some people healthy and others not?* New York: DeGrutyer, 1994.
16. Mooney G. Equity in health care: confronting the confusion. *Effective Health Care 1983;1:179–85.*
17. Mooney G. *Key issues in health economics.* New York: Harvester Wheatsheaf, 1994.
18. LeGrand J. *Equity and choice.* London: HarperCollins Academic, 1991.
19. Pereira J. What does equity in health mean? *Journal of Social Policy 1993;21:19–48.*
20. Wagstaff A, Van Doorslaer E. Equity in health care finance and delivery. In: Culyer AJ, Newhouse JP, eds. *Handbook of health economics.* Amsterdam: North-Holland, 2000: 1803–62.
21. Williams A. Need—an economic exegesis. In: Culyer AJ, Wright KG, eds. *Economic aspects of health.* London: Martin Robertson, 1978: 32–45.
22. Olsen EO, Rogers DL. The welfare economics of equal access. *Journal of Public Economics 1991;45:91–105.*
23. Culyer AJ. Need—is a consensus possible? *Journal of Medical Ethics 1998;24:77–80.*
24. Robertson A. Critical reflections on the politics of need: implications for public health. *Social Science and Medicine 1998;47:1419–30.*
25. Braybrooke D. *Meeting needs.* Princeton: Princeton University Press, 1987.
26. Barry B. *Political argument.* London: Routledge, 1965.
27. Thomson G. *Needs.* London: Routledge and Kegan Paul, 1987.
28. Springborg P. *The problem of human needs and the critique of civilization.* London: George Allen and Unwin, 1991.
29. Culyer AJ, Simpson H. Externality models and health: a Rückblick over the last twenty years. *Economic Record 1980;56:222–30.*
30. Evans RG, Wolfson AD. *Faith, hope and charity: health care in the utility function.* Vancouver, BC: University of British Columbia, 1980. Discussion paper 20–46.
31. Nicholson W. Efficiency and welfare. *Intermediate microeconomics and its application.* New York: Dryden Press, 1983: 541–69, at 542.
32. Evans RG. *Strained mercy: the economics of Canadian health care.* Toronto: Butterworths, 1984.
33. Woolhandler S, Himmelstein D. The deteriorating efficiency of the US health care system. *New England Journal of Medicine 1991;324:1253–8.*
34. Evans RG. The welfare economics of public health insurance: theory and Canadian practice. In: Soderstrom L, ed. *Social insurance.* Amsterdam: North-Holland, 1983: 71–103.
35. Stoddart GL, Barer M, Evans RG. *User charges, snares and delusions: another look at the literature.* Toronto: Premier's Council on Health, Well-being and Social Justice, 1994.
36. MacDonald P, Shortt S, Sanmartin C, Barer M, Lewis S, Sheps S. *Waiting lists and waiting times for heatlh care in Canada: more management!! More money??* Ottawa: Health Canada, 1998.
37. Hausman D, McPherson MS. *Economic analysis and moral philosophy.* New York: Cambridge University Press, 1996.
38. Broome J. *Weighing goods.* Oxford: Basil Blackwell, 1991.
39. Broome J. *Ethics out of economics.* Cambridge: Cambridge University Press, 1999.

Questions

1. Why does Hurley believe it's necessary to consider economics when arguing for publicly financed health care/insurance?
2. Articulate the relationship between the purpose of life, health, access to health care, and public financing. (If you're having trouble with the last link in the chain, read carefully para 11: "What is noteworthy....")
3. What do you think of the definition of "need" provided (and seemingly endorsed) by Hurley?
4. Why does Hurley say that private insurance alone cannot provide the broad access to health care that is ethically required?
5. What arguments does Hurley provide for the necessity of public financing?
6. Outline and evaluate the arguments for and against prohibiting private insurance when there is universal publicly funded health care.

Ethics, Pricing and the Pharmaceutical Industry[*]

Richard A. Spinello

ABSTRACT. This paper explores the ethical obligations of pharmaceutical companies to charge fair prices for essential medicines. The moral issue at stake here is distributive justice. Rawls's framework is especially germane since it underlines the material benefits everyone deserves as Kantian persons and the need for an egalitarian approach for the distribution of society's essential commodities such as health care. This concern for distributive justice should be a critical factor in the equation of variables used to set prices for pharmaceuticals.

Introduction

A perennial ethical question for the pharmaceutical [1] industry has been the aggressive pricing policies pursued by most large drug companies. Criticism has intensified in recent years over the high cost of new conventional ethical drugs and the steep rise in prices for many drugs already on the market. One result of this public clamor is that the pricing structure of this industry has once again come

[*] *Journal of Business Ethics* 11.8 (August 1992): 617–26. © 1992 by Kluwer Academic Publishers. Reprinted with permission of the publisher and the author.

under intense scrutiny by government agencies, Congress, and the media.

[2] The claim is often advanced that these high prices and the resultant profits are unethical and unreasonable. It is alleged that pharmaceutical companies could easily deliver less expensive products without sacrificing research and development. It is quite difficult to assess, however, what constitutes an unethical price or an unreasonable profit. Where does one draw the line in these nebulous areas? We will consider these questions as they relate to the pharmaceutical industry with the understanding that the normative conclusions reached in this analysis might be applicable to other industries which market *essential* consumer products. Our primary axis of discussion, however, will be the pharmaceutical industry where the issue of pricing is especially complex and controversial.

The Problem

[3] Beyond any doubt, instances of questionable and excessive drug prices abound. Azidothymide or AZT is one of the most prominent and widely cited examples. This effective medicine is used for treating complications from AIDS. The Burroughs-Wellcome Company has been at the center of a spirited controversy over this drug for establishing such a high price—AZT treatment often costs as much as $6,500 a year, which is prohibitively expensive for many AIDS patients, particularly those with inadequate insurance coverage. The company has steadfastly refused to explicate how it arrived at this premium pricing level, but industry observers suggest that this important drug was priced to be about the same as expensive cancer therapy.[1] In dealing with its various constituencies, Burroughs has relied on two key arguments to justify this price: high research and development cost and the threat of obsolescence. Burroughs maintains that in order to recoup its oppressively high research and development costs for this medication, it has no choice but to charge a price in the range of $6,500 per year. The company also defends its pricing policy by noting that proceeds from the sale of AZT will be used to finance other drugs for AIDS which are more effective than present treatments. Of course, if there is a superior second generation of the AZT medication, the drug will soon become obsolete. Moreover, once the patent expires, generic competition could erode the drug's current market share. Hence the need to generate substantial profits very quickly.

[4] The lack of more reasonable prices for drugs such as AZT can be attributed to the functioning of the American free market and the oligopolistic nature of the drug industry. Prices in other countries are often much lower since they are the result of a negotiation process between drug companies and their host governments. For example, the average price of Roche Products' valium is $9.70 in the United States but $3.60 elsewhere. Most European governments determine pricing levels by bargaining with pharmaceutical companies. The end result is that these prices cover companies' manufacturing and distribution costs and, to a much lesser extent, research and development costs. But since these companies pass on such costs to their customers in the United States, they can still make a reasonable profit at these lower price levels.[2]

[5] Thus, there are many inequities in the distribution of pharmaceutical products. Within the United States, certain medicines are simply inaccessible for many people due to the industry's pricing scheme. High drug prices have the most negative impact on the elderly and the chronically ill. The elderly, for example, are usually forced to pay for their prescription drugs, since Medicare does not cover their drug costs unless they are in a hospital. In addition, the American consumer ends up subsidizing lower drug prices for other countries

in which medicine is often available at much lower prices. As a result, many of the industry's most vocal critics contend that the only solution to this injustice is government regulation, perhaps in the form of the European model.

[6] But the major pharmaceutical companies strongly resist any form of regulation as a serious threat to the stability of their powerful industry. This industry has consistently put forward the same arguments for high prices as those advanced by Burroughs. These focus on the premise that premium prices are justified due to the excessive costs of developing new drugs. This rationale is based on the most fundamental principle of free market economics: high risk deserves high rewards. Beyond question, there *are* great risks involved in researching and developing new drugs, especially since such a small percentage make it through the long and costly process. Moreover, even if a drug is a commercial success, there is always the impending threat of product liability problems and expensive law suits. Finally, the industry maintains that earnings received from breakthrough drugs such as AZT are necessary to stimulate future research and compensate for many commercially unsuccessful drugs.

[7] Regardless of the merit of these arguments, the superior financial performance of the pharmaceutical industry in recent years is beyond dispute. In studies which compare the performance of various U.S. industries, the pharmaceutical industry has consistently been the leader in several important categories such as return on sales, return on assets, and return on common equity. For example, the drug industry currently boasts a return on sales of 20%. Also, its return on common equity of 31.9% compares quite favorably with the average return of 11.7% and is the highest of all the industry groups tracked by *Business Week*.[3] These figures reveal that at least according to some criteria drug companies and their stockholders are receiving substantial returns for the risks they take.

Ethical Questions

[8] The behavior of Burroughs and the tendency of most drug companies to charge premium prices for breakthrough medicines raises serious moral issues which defy easy answers and simple solutions. As Clarence Walton observed, "no other area of managerial activity is more difficult to depict accurately, assess fairly, and prescribe realistically in terms of morality than the domain of price" (1969, p. 209). This difficulty is compounded in the pharmaceutical industry due to the complications involved in ascertaining the true cost of production.

[9] To be sure, every business is certainly entitled to a *reasonable profit* as a reward to its investors and a guarantee of long-term stability. But the difficulty is judging a reasonable profit level. When, if ever, do profits become "unreasonable?" It is even more problematic to determine if that profit is "unethical," especially if it is the result of premium prices.

[10] Obviously, the issue of ethical or fair pricing assumes much greater significance when the product or service in question is not a luxury item but an essential one such as medicine. Few are concerned about the ethics of pricing a BMW or a waterfront condo in Florida. But the matter is quite different when dealing with vital commodities like food, medicine, clothing, housing, and education. Each of these goods has a major impact on our basic well-being and our ability to achieve any genuine self-fulfillment. Given the importance of these products in the lives of all human beings, one must consider how equitably they are priced since pricing will determine their general availability. Along these lines several key questions must be raised. Should free market, competitive forces determine the price of "essential" goods such as pharmaceuticals? Is it morally wrong to charge exceptionally high prices even if the market is willing to pay that price? Is it ethical to profit excessively at the expense of human

suffering? Finally, how can we even begin to define what constitutes reasonable profits?

[11] Also, the issue of pricing must be considered in the context of the pharmaceutical industry's lofty performance guidelines for return on assets, return on common equity, and so forth. On what authority are such targets chosen over other goals such as the widest possible distribution of some breakthrough pharmaceutical that can save lives or improve the quality of life? Pharmaceutical companies would undoubtedly contend that this authority emanates from the expectations of shareholders and other key stakeholders such as members of the financial community. In addition, these targets are a result of careful strategic planning that focuses on long-term goals.

[12] But a key question persistently intrudes here. Should *other* viewpoints be considered? Should the concerns and needs of the sick be taken into account, especially in light of the fact that they have such an enormous stake in these issues? In other words, as with many business decisions, there appear to be stark tradeoffs between superior financial performance versus humane empathy and fairness. Should corporations consider the "human cost" of their objectives for excellent performance? And what role, if any, should fairness or justice play in pricing decisions? It is only by probing these difficult and complex questions that we can make progress in establishing reasonable norms for the pricing of pharmaceuticals.

Free Market vs. Regulation

[13] Of course, many would question the validity of basing drug prices on anything other than pure economic factors. Milton Friedman and his followers have argued persuasively that the only social responsibility of business is to increase profits. According to this "free market" philosophy, the responsible course of action is to charge whatever price the market will accept. Thus, if the market will support an annual price of $8,000 a year for a drug such as AZT, that should be the end of the matter. Managers who fail to price in a fashion that will maximize profits are shirking their primary fiduciary duty to stockholders. Therefore if executives in the pharmaceutical industry refrained from raising prices for a social objective, they would be unfairly imposing a tax on shareholders. When managers go beyond economic and financial data in their decisions, they become political agents with a social agenda. This is regarded by Friedman as a pernicious state of affairs which "will undermine the very foundations of our free society," since managers lack the wisdom and ability to resolve complex social problems such as the equitable distribution of pharmaceutical products (1979, p. 90).

[14] One problem with this narrow view of corporate responsibility is that it fails to appreciate that corporate decisions often have a powerful social impact. The strategic decisions of large organizations "inevitably involve social as well as economic consequences, inextricably intertwined" (Mintzberg, 1989, p. 173). Thus such firms are social agents whether they like it or not. It is virtually impossible to maintain neutrality on these issues and aspire to some sort of apolitical status. The point for the pharmaceutical industry and the matter of pricing seems clear enough. The refusal to take "non-economic" criteria into account when setting prices is itself a moral and social decision which inevitably affects society. Companies have a choice—either they can explicitly consider the social consequences of their decisions or they can be blind to those consequences, deliberately ignoring them until the damage is perceived and an angry public raises its voice in protest.

[15] If companies do choose, however, to be attentive and *responsible* social agents they must begin to

cultivate a broader view of their environment and their obligations. To begin with, they must treat those affected by their decisions as people with an important stake in those decisions. This stakeholder model, which has become quite popular with many executives, allows corporations to link strategic decisions such as pricing with social and ethical concerns. By recognizing the legitimacy of its stakeholders such as consumers and employees, managers will better appreciate all the negative as well as positive consequences of their decisions. Moreover, an honest stakeholder analysis will compel them to explore the financial and human implications of those decisions. This will enable corporations to become more responsible social agents, since explicit attention will be given to the social dimension of their various strategic decisions.

[16] Quite simply, then, the assumption that corporations are pure economic agents represents a facile approach to this issue. Hence the free market philosophy of Friedman offers little guidance for reaching a solution to the dilemma of fair pricing in the pharmaceutical industry. At the other extreme, we find the solution offered by a framework of government regulations, but this too seems to be fraught with difficulties. Obviously, there would be severe practical and procedural problems if an attempt were made to directly regulate drug prices through a government agency such as the FDA. To begin with, there is the problem of exclusive trademark and patent rights. If the investment supporting these patented drugs is treated as a cost, firms would be able to raise prices by increasing these costs, and this would open the door for all sorts of abuses. Similar problems would arise with the regulated pricing of generic drugs. If, for example, generic drug prices were based on an industry wide basis, the price would most likely be determined by calculating the industry's average cost. Inefficient firms with above average costs, however, would fail to make a profit at this price and would be forced to withdraw from the market. As these firms exit, competition is diminished, and in the long run fewer players will probably mean higher costs and higher prices. Indeed, the problem with any regulatory solution is that it provides no real incentives for efficiency and cost controls. Hence relying exclusively on cumbersome government regulations to solve the problem of high drug prices seems completely unfeasible.

[17] Given the inadequacy of regulating prices or letting them be determined by the marketplace, the only viable means of realizing fair pricing appears to be some form of self-regulation. According to Goodpaster and Matthews, the most effective solution to this and most other moral dilemmas is one "that permits or encourages corporations to exercise independent, non-economic judgment over matters that face them in their short- and long-term plans and operations" (1989, p. 161). In other words, the burden of morality and social responsibility does not lie in the marketplace or in the hand of government regulation but falls directly on the corporation and its managers.

[18] Companies that do aspire to such moral and social responsibility will adopt *the moral point of view*, which commits one to view positively the interest of others, including various stakeholder groups. Moreover, the moral point of view assigns primacy to virtues such as justice, integrity, and respect. Thus, the virtuous corporation is analogous to the virtuous person. Each exhibits these moral qualities and acts according to the principle that the single-minded pursuit of one's own selfish interests is a violation of moral standards and an offense to the community. The moral point of view also assumes that both the corporation and the individual thrive in an environment of cooperative interaction which can only be realized when one turns from a narrow self-interest to a wider interest in others.

Pricing Policies and Justice

[19] This brings us back to the specific moral question of fair pricing policies for the pharmaceutical industry. The moral issue at stake here concerns justice and more precisely distributive justice. As we have remarked, justice has always been considered a primary virtue and thus it is an indispensable component of the moral point of view. According to Aristotle, justice "is not a part of virtue but the whole of excellence or virtue" (1962, p. 114). Thus, there can be no virtue without justice. This implies that if corporations are serious about assimilating the moral point of view and exercising their capacity for responsible behavior, they must strive to be just in their dealings with both their internal and external constituencies. Moreover, traditional discussions on justice in the works of philosophers such as Aristotle, Hume, Mill, and Rawls have emphasized distributive justice, which is concerned with the fair distribution of society's benefits and burdens. This seems especially relevant to the matter of ethical pricing policies.

[20] Corporations which control the distribution of essential products such as ethical drugs like AZT can be just or unjust in the way they distribute these products. When premium prices are charged for such goods an artificial scarcity is created, and this gives rise to the question of how equitably this scarce resource is being allocated. The consequence of a premium pricing strategy whose objective is to garner high profits would appear to be an inequitable distribution pattern. As we have seen, due to the expensiveness of AZT and similar drugs they are often not available to the poor and lower middle class unless their insurance plans cover this expense or they can somehow secure government assistance which has not been readily forthcoming. However, if this distribution pattern can be considered unjust, what determines a just distribution policy?

[21] There are, of course, many conceptions of distributive justice which would enable us to answer this question. Some stress individual merit (each according to his ability) while others are more egalitarian and stress an equal distribution of society's goods and services. Given a wide array of different theories on justice, where does the manager turn for some guidance and straightforward insights?

[22] One of the most popular and plausible conceptions of justice is advanced by John Rawls in his well known work, *A Theory of Justice*. A thorough treatment of this complex and prolix work is beyond the scope of this essay. However, a concise summary of Rawls's work should reveal its applicability to the problem of fair pricing. Rawls's conception of justice, which is predicated on the Kantian idea of personhood, properly emphasizes the equal worth and universal dignity of all persons. All rational persons have a dual capacity: they possess the ability to develop a rational plan to pursue their own conception of the good life along with the ability to respect this same capacity of self-determination in others. This Kantian ideal underlies the choice of the two principles of justice in the original position. Furthermore, this choice is based on the assumption that the "protection of Kantian self-determination for all persons depends on certain formal guarantees—the equal rights and liberties of democratic citizenship—plus guaranteed access to certain material resources" (Doppelt, p. 278). In short, the essence of justice as fairness means that persons are entitled to an extensive system of liberties *and* basic material goods.

[23] Unlike pure egalitarian theories, however, Rawls stipulates that inequities are consistent with his conception of justice so long as they are compatible with universal respect for Kantian personhood. This implies that such inequities should not be tolerated if they interfere with the basic rights, liberties, and material benefits all deserve as

Kantian persons capable of rational self-determination. In other words, Rawls espouses the detachment of the distribution of primary social goods from one's merit and ability because these goods are absolutely essential for our self-determination and self-fulfillment as rational persons. These primary goods include "rights and liberties, opportunities and power, income and wealth" (Rawls, 1971, p. 92). Whatever one's plan or conception of the good life, these goods are the necessary means to realize that plan, and hence everyone would prefer more rather than less primary goods. Their unequal distribution in a just society should only be allowed if such a distribution would benefit directly the least advantaged of that society (the difference principle).

[24] The key element in Rawls's theory for our purposes is the notion that there are material benefits everyone deserves as Kantian persons. The exercise of one's capacity for free self-determination requires a certain level of material well-being and not just the guarantee of abstract and formal rights such as freedom of expression and equal opportunity. Thus the primary social goods involve some material goods, like income and wealth. To a certain extent health care (including medicine) should be considered as one of the primary social goods since it is obviously necessary for the pursuit of one's rational life plan. Therefore, the distribution of health care should not be contingent upon ability and merit. Also it would be untenable to justify an inequitable distribution of this good by means of Rawls's difference principle. It is difficult to imagine a scenario in which the unequal distribution of health care in our society would be more beneficial to the least advantaged than a more equal distribution which would assure all consumers access to hospital care, medical treatment, medicines, and so forth. If we assume that the least advantaged (a group which Rawls never clearly defines) are the indigent who are also suffering from certain ailments, there is no advantage to any inequity in the distribution of health care. Unlike other primary goods such as income and wealth, it cannot be distributed in such a way that a greater share for certain groups will benefit the least advantaged. In short, this is a zero sum game—if a person is deprived of medical treatment or pharmaceutical products due to premium pricing policies, that person has lost a critical opportunity to save his life, cure a disease, reduce suffering, and so on.

[25] Thus, at least according to this Rawlsian view of justice with its Kantian underpinnings, there seems to be little room for the unequal distribution of a vital commodity such as health care in a just society. It follows, then, that the just pharmaceutical corporation must be far more diligent and consider very carefully the implications of pricing policies for an equitable distribution of its products. The alternative is government intervention in this process, and as we have seen, this has the potential to yield gross inefficiencies and ultimately be self-defeating. If these corporations charge premium prices and garner excessive profits from their pharmaceutical products, the end result will be the deprivation of these goods for certain classes of people. Such a pricing pattern systematically worsens the situation of the least advantaged in society, violates the respect due them as Kantian persons, and seriously impairs their capacity for free self-determination.

[26] It should be emphasized, however, that this concern for justice does not imply that pharmaceutical companies should become charities by distributing these drugs free of charge or at prices so low they must sustain meager profits or even losses. To be sure, their survival, long-term stability, and ongoing research are also vital to society and can only be guaranteed through substantial profits. Thus, the demand for justice which we have articulated must be balanced with the need to realize key eco-

nomic objectives which guarantee the long-term stability of this industry. As Kenneth Goodpaster notes, "the responsible organization aims at congruence between its moral and nonmoral aspirations" (1984, p. 309). In other words, it does not see goals of justice and economic viability as mutually exclusive, but will attempt to manage the joint achievement of both objectives.

[27] We are arguing, then, that pharmaceutical companies should seek to balance their legitimate concern for profit and return on investment with an equal consideration of the crucial importance of distributive justice. There must be an explicit recognition that for the afflicted certain pharmaceutical products are critical for one's well-being; hence they are as important as any primary social good and are deserved by every member of society. As a result these products should be distributed on the widest possible basis, but in a way that permits companies to realize a realistic and reasonable level of profitability.

[28] It is, of course, quite difficult to define a "reasonable level of profitability." In many respects the definition of "reasonable" is the crux of the matter here. Unfortunately, as outsiders to the operations of drug companies we are ill prepared to judge whether development costs for certain drugs are inflated or truly necessary. As a result, these corporations must be trusted to arrive at their own definition of a reasonable profit, given the level of legitimate costs involved in researching and developing the drug in question. But we can look to some case histories for meaningful examples that would serve as a guide to a more general definition. One of the most famous controversies over drug prices concerned the Hoffman-LaRoche corporation and the United Kingdom in which the government's Monopoly Commission alleged that Hoffman-LaRoche was charging excessive prices for valium and librium in order to subsidize its research and preserve its monopoly position. In the course of the prolonged deliberations between the British government and the company reasonable profits were defined as "profits no higher than is necessary to obtain the 'desired' performance of industry from the point of view of the economy as a whole."[4] In general, then, under normal circumstances reasonable profits for a particular product should be consistent with the average return for the industry. Exceptions might be made to this rule of average returns if the risks and costs of development are inordinately and unavoidably high.

[29] Thus, based on this Rawlsian ideal of justice I propose the following thesis regarding ethical pricing for pharmaceutical companies: for those drugs which are truly essential, the just corporation will aim to charge prices that will assure the widest possible distribution of these products consistent with a reasonable level of profitability. In other words, these companies will seek to minimize the deprivation of material benefits which are needed by all persons for their self-realization by imposing restraints on their egocentric interests in premium prices and excessive profits. Since only some pharmaceutical products can be considered as truly "essential," it remains to be seen which of those products should be subject to the imperative of justice. Moreover, we must present some sort of methodology for reaching this determination.

A Tentative Model for Evaluating the Role of Justice in Pricing Decisions

[30] As we have observed, for companies producing essential goods such as pharmaceuticals, the moral imperative of justice is one element in a complex equation that includes the need for profit, a respectable return on investment, and many other factors. Obviously some drugs are far more important than others and hence the issue of their just distribution must be weighted much more heavily than it would be for other medicines. The weight given to

the concern for distributive justice in this equation will be directly proportionate to some measurement of how critical this drug is to patients. For pharmaceutical products, this can be determined by considering the nature of the illness, the efficacy of the particular product, the availability of low-price substitutes, and so forth. The framework in Table 1 includes the key questions for determining the importance of a pharmaceutical product for society. The way in which these questions are answered will determine the role which should be played by the demands of distributive justice in the pricing equation.

- What is the nature of the malady? Is it life threatening or physically and/or mentally disruptive? Does it deprive the afflicted of their physical or mental well-being (e.g., schizophrenia) or is it more of an inconvenience (e.g., baldness)?
- Do patients have other options? Is there any other therapeutic recourse? Is this medication a last resort for the illness in question?
- Are there other drugs available for similar effectiveness and if so how affordable are these drugs?
- At the planned pricing level will people likely be deprived of treatment?
- How "experimental" is this drug considered to be? What is the likelihood that government agencies and insurance companies will offer assistance so that it can be afforded by everyone who needs it?
- Who is the likely end-user of the drug? The chronically ill? The elderly? Special consideration should be given to these groups who bear the biggest burden of high drug prices.

Table 1 Questions for Considering the Relative Importance of a Pharmaceutical Product

[31] This brief framework serves as a general guide for pharmaceutical managers, which will enable them to discern how essential the product is, the likelihood of its affordability, and the probability of government assistance for the indigent. The more critical the product and the less likely it will be affordable to certain segments of society, the more prominent should be the consideration given to distributive justice in pricing policy deliberations. Justice cannot be the exclusive concern in these deliberations, but must be given its proportionate weight depending upon the way in which the questions in this framework are addressed. Thus, as pricing decisions duly consider factors such as production and promotion costs, etc., they should also take into account the element of distributive justice. Clearly, however, drugs that are less important for society because they deal with less serious ailments should not be subject to the same demands of justice as those for diseases which are truly life threatening or debilitating. Hence drug companies should have much more flexibility in pricing medicines for these less critical ailments.

A Collaborative Approach

[32] There is no doubt that pharmaceutical executives would raise many objections to the proposal on fair pricing which we are advocating. Thus, despite their concern about these issues, the likelihood of any significant change is probably quite slim. Unfortunately, the premium pricing policy of these companies is perpetuated by industry-wide peer pressure for above average returns and the quasi-monopoly status of certain brand name drugs. Also, if a company unilaterally sought to distribute some of its products more equitably, it would probably find itself in an anomalous position in the drug industry with no followers. In the face of this threat, it is difficult to envision one of the pharmaceutical companies taking the initiative and complying with Rawls's distribution criterion, even if there is some concession that in principle this is

the right thing to do. Hence the current impasse which many argue can only be overcome by decisive intervention and regulation, perhaps in the form of "European style" controls of drug prices.

[33] Although these arguments have some merit, they should not interfere with a proper ethical resolution to the intractable dilemma of high returns versus accessibility and a reasonable pricing scheme. Of course the apprehension that following the right course of action will jeopardize one's competitive position is quite common and is frequently brought forth to justify all sorts of corporate inaction and indifference on ethical matters. It is a variation of the traditional but jaded claim that ethics cannot be reconciled with economics.

[34] As we have been at pains to insist here, however, ethical values can be integrated with economic success. But in order to accomplish this, it is necessary to transcend traditional thinking which posits a sharp dichotomy between morality and the economic criteria of success. As Laura Nash and others have argued, this "bottom line" mentality erects many barriers between managers and the marketplace. An exclusive and relentless focus on profit, continued growth, and increased market share tends to shut off much of the legitimate feedback from customers. For example, the demise of the automobile industry in the 1970s and '80s can partially be attributed to Detroit's narrow focus on these criteria and its unwillingness to listen to its customers.

[35] On the other hand, when the focus shifts from pure economic measures of success to the relationship between corporations and their customers, the prevailing concerns become value creation and mutual benefit (Nash, 1990, pp. 91–94). In other words, mutual benefit is the essence of a sound business relationship, and this is achieved by delivering created value. When we consider the problem of pricing from this perspective, it becomes clear that an essential part of value creation in the pharmaceutical industry is the provision of medicines to those who need them at a fair and reasonable price. Moreover, listening to the concerns of its customers and various other constituencies on this matter is also an important aspect of value creation and a key to long-term success. Thus, by adopting a framework that centers on mutually beneficial *relationships* and value creation, pharmaceutical executives will come to realize that pricing is not a remote ethical problem that can be dismissed by invoking the principle of free market economics. Rather, it is a grave business problem which impedes these corporations from delivering value and impairs the critical relationship with their customers.

[36] But even if the companies in question accept this line of reasoning, how should they proceed? A unilateral action might be well intentioned but it will probably not settle this acute industry-wide problem. Instead, the optimal solution must follow a more complicated path that entails a collaborative effort in which the major firms work with government agencies such as the FDA to develop a tenable pricing framework that addresses the social costs of high prices. Both the industry and government share responsibility for dealing with this problem given the community's need for reasonably priced medicine. Also, as we have argued previously, if government regulators act independently they will not have access to the information, and specialized competence necessary to make the most effective decisions. A collaborative approach, on the other hand, will ensure that the community will be well-served and it will also preserve the level playing field for all the firms involved. It will also allow these companies to retain control of the pricing process and avoid the intricate problems associated with explicit price controls of any sort.

Final Observations

[37] Let us now summarize and conclude. Our aim has been to attempt an ethical analysis of pricing in the pharmaceutical industry in order to make some normative recommendations. This analysis might also be applied to other industries which are in the business of supplying essential commodities. We have argued that if these pharmaceutical companies seek to be responsible and adopt the moral point of view, they must practice the primary virtue of justice. No person can be considered virtuous and moral if he or she is unjust, and the same can be said for the corporation. Although there are several conflicting notions of distributive justice, the conception delineated by John Rawls seems both compelling and practically feasible. It is grounded in a Kantian view of the person which stresses the need for both abstract rights and concrete material resources for one's rational self-determination.

[38] We have argued with some insistence that an essential commodity such as health care is analogous to the primary social goods considered by Rawls since it is so crucial for one's self-determination. Hence its distribution should not be contingent on one's abilities and standing in the community. Thus pharmaceutical firms must be prepared to impose some restraints on profits for the sake of distributive justice. The alternative is a more comprehensive involvement of government in this process which will lead to cumbersome pricing regulations that are likely to be ineffectual in the long run.

[39] Given the importance of profitability and the long-term stability of these companies, however, justice cannot be their exclusive concern. Rather, the imperative of justice must be balanced with the need to realize key financial objectives. We are simply arguing that these objectives should not be pursued to the exclusion of justice, which must be responsibly and fairly factored into the pricing equation. Moreover, the weight given to justice in that equation will depend on how critical the product is, and this depends on the nature of the illness, the availability of substitutes, and so forth.

[40] We have also pointed out that since this is such an entrenched and complex industry-wide problem, it cannot be resolved by any unilateral policy changes by a particular firm. Rather, the major producers must act in concert in collaboration with the government in order to ensure a fair pricing scheme.

[41] This analysis does not by any means eliminate the frustrations regarding ethical pricing which were cited earlier by Walton. We can offer no definitive, quantitative formulae or comprehensive criteria to assure that pricing in this industry will always be fair and just. As with most moral decisions, much will depend on the individual judgment and moral sensitivity of the managers making those decisions. But if managers are sincere in their quest for the primary virtue of justice, the general guidelines proposed here will offer some modest assistance for this foray into the uncharted territory of fair pricing. It seems beyond doubt that responsible and fair pricing in the pharmaceutical industry is a serious moral imperative, since for so many consumers it is a matter of well-being or infirmity and perhaps even life or death.

[42] We might consider once again the wisdom of Aristotle on this topic of justice. In the *Nicomachean Ethics* he writes that "we call those things 'just' which produce and preserve happiness for the social and political community" (1962, p. 113). If corporations respond to the demands of justice for the sake of the common good, it will help promote the elusive goal of a just community and a greater harmony between the corporation and its many concerned stakeholders.

Notes

1. Holzman, D. 1988. "New Wonder Drugs at What Price?," *Insight* (March 21), pp. 54–55. For more recent data on drug prices, see "Maker of Schizophrenia Drug Bows to Pressure to Cut Costs," *The New York Times* (Dec. 6, 1990), pp. Al and D3.
2. Kolata, G. 1991. "Why Drugs Cost More in U.S.," *The New York Times* (May 24), p. D3.
3. "Corporate Scorecard," *Business Week* (March 18, 1991), pp. 52ff.
4. "F. Hoffman-LaRoche and Company A.G.," Harvard Business School Case Study, in Matthews, Goodpaster, Nash (eds.), *Policies and Persons* (New York: McGraw Hill Book Company, 1985).

References

Aristotle. 1962. *Nicomachean Ethics*, trans. by M. Oswald. Indianapolis: Library of Liberal Arts, Bobbs Merrill Company, Inc.

Doppelt, G. 1989. "Beyond Liberalism and Communitarianism: Towards a Critical Theory of Social Justice." *Philosophy and Social Criticism* 14 (No. 3/4).

Friedman, M. 1979. "The Social Responsibility of Business Is to Increase Profit." In T. Beauchamp and N. Bowie (eds.), *Ethical Theory and Business*. Englewood Cliffs, NJ: Prentice Hall.

Goodpaster, K. 1984. "The Concept of Corporate Responsibility." In T. Regan (ed.), *Just Business: New introductory Essays in Business Ethics*. New York: Random House.

Goodpaster, K. and Matthews, J. 1989. "Can a Corporation Have a Conscience?" In K. Andrews (ed.), *Ethics in Practice*. Boston: Harvard Business School Press.

Mintzberg, H. 1989. "The Case for Corporate Social Responsibility." In A. Iannone (ed.), *Contemporary Moral Controversies in Business*. New York: Oxford University Press.

Nash, L. 1990. *Good Intentions Aside: A Manager's Guide to Resolving Ethical Problems*. Cambridge: Harvard Business School Press.

Rawls, J. 1971. *A Theory of Justice*. Cambridge, MA: Harvard University Press.

Walton, C. 1969. *Ethos and the Executive*. Englewood Cliffs, NJ: Prentice Hall, Inc.

Questions

1. "The refusal to take 'non-economic' criteria into account when setting prices is itself a moral...decision" (para 14)—explain.
2. How does Spinello reconcile justice theory with virtue ethics?
3. How do health care and medicine fit into the Kantian/Rawlsian theory, according to Spinello?
4. What do you think of the definition of "reasonable profit" given (para 28)?
5. How does distinguishing between essential and nonessential medicines when pricing increase the potential for justice?
6. Does it make any difference to Spinello's arguments whether the price is paid by the consumer or a private or government medical insurance program?

Case Study: The St. Michael's-Wellesley Hospital Merger

Should a Catholic hospital be compelled to offer services that conflict with Catholic beliefs?

This issue came to the fore in the spring of 1998 when the Ontario government merged Wellesley Hospital in Toronto with St. Michael's, a few blocks away. The two buildings would be operated and administered by St. Michael's, but much of the former Wellesley would be closed. This was one of a number of hospital mergers in 1997–98 recommended by the Ontario Hospital Restructuring Commission, which was established to examine and find ways to make the hospital system in Ontario more effective and efficient.

As soon as the merger was proposed, opponents expressed concern. "Why close Wellesley?" asked many, including its doctors and nurses. It was apparently busy and served people who were low-income or had so-called "alternate lifestyles." What was particularly worrisome for many of the Wellesley patients was the absence of services such as abortion, contraception, and AIDS treatment at the Catholic hospital: prior to closing, doctors at Wellesley did up to 1,500 abortions a year; they also had an extensive HIV/AIDS program including treatment and prevention. Many patients expressed a real fear that they would have to seek treatment further afield if the "new" St. Michael's followed its traditional policy of refusing to offer services the hospital administration found morally unacceptable.

Michele Landsberg, a *Toronto Star* columnist, wrote about these concerns in May 1998. She objected to a statement by Jim O'Neill, Director of Services at St. Michael's, who was quoted as stating, "Our core values have served us well for over 100 years and those values are not going to change." Landsberg pointed out that although St. Michael's was a Catholic hospital, it was also a public hospital built with public money. They have an obligation, according to Landsberg, to serve all of the public and not deny services that people need because of their religious beliefs; the services in question were especially needed in that neighbourhood of Toronto. Landsberg argued that it would be immoral for any public hospital to limit women's choices and infringe on their reproductive rights. She concluded by stating, "How can this hospital justify taking over the assets of another public hospital and promptly cancelling services the public needs, wants, and is entitled to?"

By mid-1998, the province of Ontario had 220 publicly funded hospitals, including 28 under Catholic governance. According to an *Ottawa Citizen* article by April Lindgren, "Hospitals under Catholic governance adhere to the *Catholic Health Care Ethics Guide*, which says contraception is 'morally unacceptable,' bans sterilization as a means of birth control, and says that abortion of an embryo or fetus is 'immoral.'" Physicians at Catholic hospitals are asked to "sign on" to the Catholic ethics guide. Many, of course, do so quite willingly; as Peter Lauwers pointed out, why should people have to perform procedures (such as abortion) which violate their beliefs and values?

References

Landsberg, Michele. "St. Mike's Religious Rules Undemocratic." *Toronto Star* 30 May 1999: L1.

Lauwers, Peter D. "Wellesley's Sore Losers Need to Move On Now." *Toronto Star* 6 Jun. 1998: C3.

Lindgren, April. "Hospital Closings Spark New Debates: Catholic Integration Cuts Abortion, Birth Control." *The Ottawa Citizen* 14 June 1998: A5.

Questions

1. Should patients who need and want services such as abortion and contraception be forced to go beyond their neighbourhood to find these services? Beyond their town/city? Beyond their province? (Should any consumers be forced to do so? Are "consumers" of medical services different from other "consumers"?)
2. Is the hospital administration justified in asking its physicians to sign onto a particular ethics guide? (Is the administration of any *other* business justified in doing so?)
3. Is there a way that both the rights of the hospital workers (not to violate their beliefs/values) and the rights of the hospital users (to have access to needed services) can be respected?
4. Why are publicly funded hospitals run by religious organizations, in any case? Should that be permitted? (For hospitals or any other business?)
5. (a) Should privately funded hospitals be allowed to restrict their services in this way? Maria Cosillo (quoted in the Lindgren article) says that "the purpose of hospitals is to serve patients, not to promote certain values"—to what extent, if any, do you agree?
(b) Should any other privately funded businesses be allowed to restrict their services according to their beliefs and values? Do you think Cosillo's comment can be said of every business or just some, like the medical business?

CHAPTER NINE

Information and Communications Technology (ICT) Issues

What to Do?—The IC

You work at the company that has just developed the IC: the Internet Chip. It's designed to be implanted directly into the human body to provide a seamless connection with...well, everything. The interface (at the moment) is a voice-controlled holographic screen that appears in front of the person's eyes.

No doubt it will become illegal very quickly to drive while IC-connected, just as it's illegal now (finally) to talk and text while driving. But people do it anyway. And even when they're not driving—you can picture IC-connected people so oblivious to their surroundings that they walk across the street on a red light. Remember when GPS first came out? People drove over cliffs when their GPS told them to "Turn right."

Eventually the voice control may be replaced with something else, but in the meantime, you anticipate that "outside" will become cacophonous. Good thing there's no signal in Algonquin Park.

Another concern is privacy. Not only will the conglomerates know where you are, but they'll also have a pretty good idea about what you're doing. Of course, there's an upside to that. The IC could tell you when your blood pressure is too high, your blood sugar too low—it could even zap you when you start to take that second drink.

You're not trying to decide whether to proceed or not; that decision has already been made. Your job is to set up the defaults. And that's where the real control is: most people accept the defaults. The company wants the power default mode to be ON. You want it to be OFF. As for all the other settings? The list itself is long enough—providing explanations so consent is truly informed would fill a book. So you have to prioritize. At best, you figure, people will make decisions about ten settings, and then leave the rest at default. So you have to decide what to put at the top of the list, and what the defaults will be for the rest.

For example, should the user's physical location be pre-set to "share"? What about their physical condition? Their browsing? Their downloads? Their banking? Their conversations? What about all the notification bells and whistles? And the "automatic" subscriptions to various apps? And what about the facial recognition program that provides all sorts of detail—age, marital status, address, employment history, criminal record, etc.—about people in their field of view? Should that be ON (and "share"?) or OFF?

What do you decide to do?

Introduction

The Internet, whether accessed via workplace computers, personal laptops, tablets, or smartphones, has changed and continues to change the way we live. E-mail, the Web, search engines like Google, social networks like Facebook and Twitter (both likely to be passé by the time you read this book, given how quickly everything about ICT develops), knowledge databases like Wikipedia, online banking, online shopping, online gaming.... No doubt there are ethical issues in this area that business must consider.

Some people point to how the various information and communications technologies (ICTs) are affecting us. They claim that reading books via e-readers is making us lose the ability to process extended arguments because we can see only a hundred words or so at a time; reading on the Web further reduces our ability to pay attention to one thing for a long period of time because we are constantly interrupted and distracted by pop-ups and all the extra bits that appear on the page. "Once I was a scuba diver in the sea of words. Now I zip along the surface like a guy on a Jet Ski," writes Carr, who references several studies as well as Wolf's *Proust and the Squid*. (Speaking of those pop-ups, we're devolving in to frogs: if it doesn't move, we don't see it.) Communicating by e-mail and Twitter is making us lose the ability to write with any depth; our use of acronyms and emoticons suggests that we're regressing—back to pictograms. Calling strangers we've just met "friends" is making us socially inept. We have become addicted to our phones, answering them whenever they ring, like Pavlovian dogs, without making any judgement about relative importance (of answering the phone versus whatever else we're doing at the time). For an analogy, imagine what life was like before people started wearing watches on their wrists. It's another example of the effect of an ever-present technology on the way we live.

But first, I don't think that's really a business ethics issue. No one is forcing us to use these new technologies. (Though not getting "on board" does come at a cost.) Second, on balance, I suspect the new technologies come with more benefits than detriments. (The development of the printing press ruined our capacity to remember stuff. But look at all the positive changes!) With the Internet, secondary research has never been easier; hyperlinks are way better than footnotes. I myself can now do in 20 hours what used to take 40, though I'm appalled that Google ranks by popularity, not relevance, thus reinforcing the herd mentality. The ability to communicate easily with people anytime, anywhere (via e-mail and programs like Skype) has increased opportunities not only for social interaction, but also for work interaction. The virtual office is here.

What *is* certainly a business ethics issue is privacy. But what exactly is privacy? Let's say you have privacy when your biographical and current activity information is *not* broadcast all over the internet. On what basis do we have a right to it? Some argue that it's actually an indirect right, in that it is required for *other* rights, such as the right to dignity, the right to autonomy (self-determination), and/or the right to enjoyment. Others appeal to the importance of anonymity as a way of securing the right to be free from harm or threat. Still others simply extend ownership of our bodies to ownership of information about our bodies. However conceived, is the right to privacy absolute? That is, can it *never* be justifiably violated? More to the point, when can *business* violate it? And *does* business violate it when they access information we have voluntarily posted on social networking sites in order to make hiring decisions? What about accessing our blogs or just doing a Google search for that purpose? What if information they find online leads to a firing decision? (See the article by Clark and Roberts in this chapter.)

Sites like Google and Facebook are becoming notorious for their "big brother" powers, their ability to know everything about us (not only because of their upfront data acquisition, but also because of their tracking activities): our name, age, sex, physical address, e-mail address, phone number, the particular device from which we access the Internet, our religious and political affiliation, relationship status, what we look like, where we are at any given time, who our friends and family members are, as well as our favourite foods, books, movies, hobbies, Web sites, restaurants, stores, clothes, vacation destinations, travel history, past experiences, and so on (Markkula Center). And that's not all: "Increasingly, you may also be allowing some entities to collect a lot of personal information about all of your online 'friends' (by simply clicking 'allow' when downloading applications that siphon your friends' information through your account). On the flip side, your "friends" can similarly allow third parties to collect key information about you, even if you never gave that third party permission to do so" (Markkula Center). ('Allow' 'Follow' 'Share' 'Like'—such innocuous words. Coincidence or manipulation?)

In some cases, this can be beneficial: as an advertiser, I love GoogleAds because they're so targeted—my ads appear (only) to interested people (even better, I pay only when someone clicks on them, which means I'm not wasting my money); as a potential customer/client, I also love GoogleAds because I see only ads that are most likely to interest me. (Except that I keep seeing ads for hotels even after I've booked a room.) So imagine the woman who keeps seeing ads for baby things even after her baby dies. So why couldn't Google just *ask us* what ads we want to see, instead of making that decision for us based on our browsing activity? And scanning our gmail messages? Their terms of service do explicitly say that automated systems analyze e-mail content when it is sent, received, and stored, in order to provide "customized search results, tailored advertising, and spam and malware detection"—but is that enough to make it morally acceptable?

Furthermore, some sites make the provision of information a prerequisite for even *using* the site. ("All boxes must be completed.") On what grounds? For example, why does a shopping site need to know whether I'm male or female before it allows me to buy something? Obviously, the site owners intend to make assumptions based on my sex, so they're maintaining the sexist status quo by simply asking that question. Of course, I could just enter incorrect information in order to gain access (some sites seem happy to simply have the boxes filled in; others are more discriminating), but why should I have to lie?

And on this note of entering incorrect information, clearly any data mining can't possibly be scientifically rigorous. Does that change businesses' rights and responsibilities with regard to data mining?

Of course, if people have a right to control information about themselves, they should know exactly how the information they provide will be used. But do they have such a right? On what grounds? *All* information or just some? What would be exempt? Will the information be used only to improve the site (though even that should require our permission), or will it be sold to other sites and/or companies and/or agencies? And what will *those* people use it for? Some sites are very upfront (transparent) about this; others are not. So even though providing personal information *seems* voluntary, it's not—full consent to something involves full knowledge of the consequences of that consent to that something. (Is full consent always morally required? When is implied consent sufficient?)

And it's not just the information provided in the boxes that we should be concerned about. The Electronic Frontier Foundation points out that AT&T (and, no doubt, others) is collecting (and giving to government agencies) copies of *everything* that is carried along major domestic fibre-optic cable networks (e-mail messages, financial transfers—everything). I suspect they've justified it on utilitarian grounds: privacy of the individual (person, company) can be sacrificed for the good of the group (nation, society). Charters argues that "electronic monitoring is almost always an invasion of the right to privacy regardless of how the right to privacy is conceived. However, it can still be ethically justified on a Utilitarian basis provided its benefits exceed realizable harm" (244). But is such sacrifice justified on principle- or value-based grounds? Charters goes on to argue that yes, "[i]f Internet advertisers gave users the option of permitting or rejecting electronic monitoring, they could ethically justify the invasion of privacy on a Kantian basis" (244), but he goes on to qualify that the option shouldn't be "in the fine print," so to speak.

Tene and Polonetsky describe several instances in which "big data" has been very beneficial. For example, "Google Flu Trends...predicts and locates outbreaks of the flu by making use of information—aggregate search queries—not originally collected with this innovative application in mind." They argue that "[t]he principles of privacy and data protection must be balanced against additional societal values such as public health, national security and law enforcement, environmental protection, and economic efficiency" and note that "an increasing focus on express consent and data minimization, with little appreciation for the value of uses for data, could jeopardize innovation and beneficial societal advances."

Privacy becomes even more important when people not only provide personal information to various sites but also store their documents on the Internet via cloud computing. And when they are stored on a cloud provided by someone other than themselves, who owns those documents?

So business has important decisions to make. On the one hand, you're urged to be transparent and accountable. On the other, you're urged to respect people's rights to privacy. You can't have your cake and eat it too. Or can you? Do some people count more than others? Do some bits of information count more than others?[1]

And if someone hacks into your website or network and steals your data, what policies and procedures do you have in place? Do you notify your users immediately? Do you compensate your users for their losses? What's fair? Consider the 2011 Sony PlayStation breach, considered "one of the largest-ever Internet security break-ins" (Baker and Finkle), which resulted in the theft of names, addresses, and possibly credit card data of 77 million users.

Another issue involving business and ethics concerns intellectual property rights.[2] It's not a new issue: debates about whether people (artists, authors, academics) have copyright to their work are longstanding. The question is whether the ephemeral (digital) nature of that work and its easy access, due to the Internet, changes the debates. For example, does it make a difference whether music exists on a vinyl disc or in digital code? In both cases, the artist worked to create the music; should she or he not be paid for that labour? And paid a fair amount: under current rates, "The Barenaked Ladies would need 9,216 plays of their classic song, 'If I Had $1,000,000' to earn enough royalties *to buy one box of Kraft Dinner*" (Burgess, my emphasis).[3] And in both cases, unless you access the musician's website, several different people (marketers, distributors, retailers) work to make the music available to you; should they also not be paid?

But then once you buy a piece of music, whether it's on a vinyl disc or in digital code, shouldn't you be able to share it with your friends if you want? So when your friends make and keep a copy of it, they're not stealing, are they? You gave it to them. It's the same as photocopying a few pages from a book, isn't it? But since that's now considered stealing—if it's more than "a few pages"—isn't it stealing if you copy a whole piece of music? A whole movie? A whole e-book? So are we saying that for work that can be replicated people *can't* give it to anyone? If my friend wants to buy a sculpture and give it to me as a gift, where's the moral wrong in that? (Well, wait until 3D printing becomes generally affordable.) Does it matter how many copies they give

---

1 See TekSavvy's dilemma, in the case study.
2 "Imagine a world without free knowledge," says Wikipedia. I do. And it's one in which those who "make" knowledge actually get paid for their work. (And it *is* work—we don't just wake up one day *knowing* something: we have to do months of background research required to understand what's known at the time, then formulate a hypothesis, then design and carry out an experiment, and then analyze the data, and then maybe go back and do another experiment…and if we're not working in fields that require experimentation per se, the 'creation' of knowledge likely involves a lot of tedious observation and recording, followed by analysis after a lot of thought…).
3 Incidentally, Canada is one of the top countries for unpaid-for music downloads (Tencer)!

away? Gayle MacDonald notes that the RCMP "has found a clear link between organized crime and film piracy, [which is] often more profitable than drug trafficking."

On the other hand, many artists and authors believe the practice of downloading from file-sharing sites is good for business; it's like free promotion. It doesn't necessarily mean lost sales; in fact, it can mean *increased* sales. But shouldn't it be *their* call not that of the ISP, publisher, or device manufacturer? Read Sobol for an engaging explanation of the disconnect between those who think accessing intellectual property is okay and those who don't.

This issue of unauthorized file sharing leads us to another issue that business must consider: who's responsible for policing the internet? Let's start with another argument by analogy: when you own a bricks-and-mortar business, isn't it your responsibility to make sure that no moral wrongdoing occurs there? Isn't that why you monitor your employees' behaviour, in addition to ensuring that they are being productive and not engaging in anything illegal? So does that mean you're responsible for making sure no immoral behaviour occurs at your website? (And *with* your website?) Or is there something significantly different about a virtual business location that weakens that argument by analogy?

Or does responsibility extend further up the chain? In 2004, Music Canada went to court to force five Canadian internet service providers (ISPs) to provide the names of 29 people accused of copyright infringement by file sharing. Should Music Canada have gone after the owners of Pirate Bay or BitTorrent (or whatever) instead? Or the people who *use* Pirate Bay and BitTorrent? If I make a crime possible by leaving my door unlocked, am *I* the one responsible for the subsequent theft? And then, as mentioned above, if you're the ISP or website owner, do you comply with the law or do you protect the privacy of your users? Does it depend on whether your users are accused of stealing songs or engaging in human-rights activism? Or teaching people how to make bioweapons? And does it matter whether it's a huge conglomerate that is going after your users' names, or the starving artists themselves?

And how far does your responsibility (assuming you have some) go? The Children's Online Privacy Protection Act (COPPA) is US legislation, but the US Federal Trade Commission has said that its requirements apply to foreign-operated websites if they are directed to children in the US. (See my comment in Chapter 6 about how globalization has made all business essentially international business.) So it is your legal responsibility to prevent children from revealing personal information on your website. Is it also your *moral* responsibility?

Speaking of legal responsibilities (despite my comments about legal moralism, one can certainly argue that legal responsibilities *are* moral responsibilities), and coming back to the policing question, the intellectual property copyright section of the TPP (Trans Pacific Partnership), to which Canada will likely be party, will give ISPs the power (or the responsibility) to censor people's use of the internet: it will enable them to prohibit access to individuals and to shut down entire websites. Is that censorship or CSR? Or both? That is, can censorship be considered a form of corporate social responsibility?

On the flip side, can *undoing* censorship be a form of CSR? According to Smith, Google could end China's censorship of its citizens' access to the internet. Is Google morally permitted to do so? Is it morally *obligated* to do so? (It would be a reversal of their earlier complicity in China's censorship. Much like Microsoft's and Yahoo's complicity.[1])

An issue that might appeal especially to economists is the virtual economy of online games or worlds (see the Grimes reading below). People (mostly in "developing" countries) play multi-player online games to acquire in-game currency (via virtual objects), which they then exchange for real-world currency (by selling it on eBay or whatever). Although figures are hard to obtain and confirm, sources estimate that 150,000 people are such "gold farmers," and sales could amount to US$3 billion. Game developers have tried to ban gold farming. They're concerned about in-game inflation, and about attracting hackers. Perhaps, also, "they don't want to undercut or short-circuit the whole reason for playing…which is to demonstrate some kind of skill or prowess in front of other real human beings," as Kaydee notes. "And there is a kind of pretense or implied fraud committed by a person who has purchased a new spaceship or sexy avatar or what have you with real money instead of earning it in the 'proper' way" (Kaydee).

Despite these concerns, the World Bank has actually discussed gold farming as a tool for socioeconomic development. Referencing an InfoDev.Org report, Stokes notes that gold farming sends proportionately more money to the developing countries than does coffee production.[2] Doesn't that consequence have greater moral value than the concerns mentioned in the preceding paragraph? Maybe there's a huge opportunity here for doing good, or for changing the world. Of course, if someone is being *forced* to be a gold farmer[3] or if the gold farmer him- or herself doesn't get that real-world money, we might have something like online sweatshops (see RPG Site Staff).

And is gold farming—*acquiring* virtual goods for sale—really any different from *creating* them for sale?[4] So if the latter is morally acceptable, shouldn't the former also be? And if creating virtual goods for sale in virtual worlds isn't morally acceptable, how is it that creating real goods for sale in real worlds is?

Another issue one might consider is free-to-play gaming. Are companies that offer free-to-play games exactly like drug dealers who offer free samples? The intent is the same: hook the user (with bright, colourful, and moving imagery), get them addicted (tap into the pleasure centres of the brain), then start charging big time (to continue, to continue with cool extras, to continue on uncongested servers, and so on). It's psychological (and perhaps biochemical) manipulation designed to bypass or usurp the person's autonomy. The consequence is also the same, isn't it? And so it's morally wrong?

---

1 See Barboza and Zeller. And see Martin, who has prepared a detailed case study of Google and China.
2 See also Heeks.
3 See Vincent.
4 Check out the marketplace for Second Life (https://marketplace.secondlife.com/). The virtual goods are for sale in virtual worlds, instead of the real-world (via ebay), but participation in these virtual worlds requires in-game currency that is purchased with real-world money. (See their pricelist for participation: https://secondlife.com/corporate/pricing.php.)

Further Reading and References

Baker, Liana B., and Jim Finkle. "Sony PlayStation suffers massive data breach." Reuters. 26 Apr. 2011. http://www.reuters.com/article/article/us-sony-stoldendata-idUSTRE73P6WB20110426

Barboza, David, and Tom Zeller, Jr. "Microsoft Shuts Blog's Site after Complaints by Beijing." *New York Times* 6 Jan. 2006. http://www.nytimes.com/2006/01/06/technology/06blog.html?th&emc=th&_r=0

Burgess, Quentin. "Under Tariff 8, Barenaked Ladies would need 9,216 plays of 'If I Had $1,000,000' to earn enough royalties to buy one box of Kraft Dinner." *Music Canada*. 9 July 2014. http://musiccanada.com/news/under-tariff-8-barenaked-ladies-would-need-9216-plays-of-if-i-had-100000-to-earn-enough-royalties-to-buy-one-box-of-kraft-dinner/

Carr, Nicholas. "Is Google Making Us Stupid?" *The Atlantic* July/Aug. 2008. http://www.theatlantic.com/magazine/archive/2008/07/is-google-making-us-stupid/306868/

Charters, Darren. "Electronic Monitoring and Privacy Issues in Business-Marketing: The Ethics of the DoubleClick Experience." *Journal of Business Ethics* 35 (2002): 243–54.

Clark, Leigh A., and Sherry J. Roberts. "Employer's Use of Social Networking Sites: A Socially Irresponsible Practice." *Journal of Business Ethics* 95 (2010): 507–25.

Electronic Frontier Foundation. "NSA Spying on Americans." https://www.eff.org/nsa-spying

Geist, Michael. "Why the Vertically Integrated TV Giants Are the CRTC's Hidden Target in Pick-and-pay Decision." Michael Geist. 23 Mar. 2015. http://www.michaelgeist.ca/2015/03/why-the-vertically-integrated-tv-giants-are-the-crtcs-hidden-target-in-pick-and-pay-decision/

Heeks, Richard. "Current Analysis and Future Research Agenda on 'Gold Farming': Real-World Production in Developing Countries for the Virtual Economies of Online Games." Development Informatics Group. http://www.sed.manchester.ac.uk/idpm/research/publications/wp/di/documents/di_wp32.pdf

Kaydee. "Gold Farming: Not Just a Game." Engineering Ethics Blog. 21 Dec. 2009. http://engineeringethicsblog.blogspot.com/2009/12/gold-farming-not-just-game.html

MacDonald, Chris. "Microsoft & Yahoo: Complicit in Repression?" *The Business Blog*. 6 Jan. 2006. http://businessethicsblog.com/2006/01/06/microsoft-yahoo-complicit-in-repression/

MacDonald, Gayle. "Pirates of the Canadians." *Globe and Mail* 17 Jan. 2007. http://www.theglobeandmail.com/arts/pirates-of-the-canadians/article1068784/?page=all

Markkula Center for Applied Ethics. "Your Privacy Online." Santa Clara University. http://www.scu.edu/ethics-center/privacy/

Martin, Kirsten E. "Google, Inc. in China." Institute for Corporate Ethics, Business Roundtable. Case BRI-1004. http://www.corporate-ethics.org/pdf/Case_BRI-1005_Google_in_China_condensed.pdf

RPG Site Staff. "The Ethics of Gold Farming." RPG Site. 7 Oct. 2006. http://www.rpgsite.net/news/2808-the-ethics-of-gold-farming

Smith, Charlie. "Google could end China's web censorship in 10 days—why doesn't it?" *The Guardian* 22 Nov. 2013. http://www.theguardian.com/commentisfree/2013/nov/22/google-end-china-web-censorship-10-days

Sobol, John. "The Copyright Wars of 2017: how cut-and-paste culture turns kids into the enemy." *This Magazine* May–June 2006: 28+.

Stokes, Jon. "WoW players could one day buy 'Fair Trade' gold from Chinese Farms." arstechnica.com. 7 Apr. 2011 http://arstechnica.com/gaming/2011/04/wow-players-could-one-day-buy-fair-trade-gold-from-chinese-farms/

Tencer, Daniel. "Music Piracy: Canada among Top Countries for Unauthorized Downloading of Music." *The Huffington Post* 20 Sept. 2012 http://www.huffingtonpost.ca/2012/09/20/music-piracy-canada-top-countries_n_1899752.html

Tene, Omer, and Polonetsky, Jules. "Privacy in the Age of Big Data: A Time for Big Decisions." *Stanford Law Review* 64 (2 Feb. 2012). http://www.stanfordlawreview.org/online/privacy-paradox/big-data

Vincent, Danny. "China used prisoners in lucrative internet gaming work." *The Guardian*.25 May 2011. http://www.theguardian.com/world/2011/may/25/china-prisoners-internet-gaming-scam

Wolf, Maryanne. *Proust and the Squid.* New York: Harper, 2007.

Employer's Use of Social Networking Sites: A Socially Irresponsible Practice*

Leigh A. Clark and Sherry J. Roberts

Abstract

The Internet has drastically changed how people interact, communicate, conduct business, seek jobs, find partners, and shop. Millions of people are using social networking sites to connect with others, and employers are using these sites as a source of background information on job applicants. Employers report making decisions not to hire people based on the information posted on social networking sites. Few employers have policies in place to govern when and how these online character checks should be used and how to ensure that the information viewed is accurate. In this article, we explore how these inexpensive, informal online character checks are harmful to society. Guidance is provided to employers on when and how to use these sites in a socially responsible manner.

---

* *Journal of Business Ethics* 95 (2010):507–25.

Introduction

[1] Advances in technology have once again shifted how people communicate with each other. Not only has wireless communication made it possible for us to talk to one another when thousands of miles apart, but now we can instantly receive e-mails, send text messages, and "twitter." Older generations recall how people mainly talked face to face, while members of the newest generation often prefer texting to talking face to face (Reid and Reid, 2004). New communication tools are available such as blogs, wikis, and chat rooms, as well as entire virtual communities such as Second Life. There are 1.6 billion Internet users worldwide (Internetworldstats.com, 2009).

[2] Many people use social networking sites (SNSs) to stay in touch with each other. SNSs such as Facebook and MySpace initially began as forums for young people to connect and have evolved into a new type of community for social and commercial exchange. Through a variety of tools (e-mail, chat, blogging, instant messaging, photo sharing, news feeds), SNSs are used for job networking, targeted marketing, and entertainment. The impact of SNSs for communication is just now being understood. Following the 2009 elections in Iran, SNSs were credited with keeping communication open with people within and outside of Iran when traditional means of communication were limited by the Iranian government (Labott, 2009).

[3] Many SNSs require the user to create a webpage that contains information about the user that he or she wants to share with others. Some members use these pages as billboards about themselves while others use them as personal diary pages. Most SNSs allow the user to limit access to posted online material to a designated group of people while sharing a public portion with all fellow users. However, users are learning that information posted on the SNS often becomes available to people beyond the intended audience. For example, Facebook allows its advertisers to use members' posted photos in their advertisements without requiring further consent or compensation to members. Few users are aware of this policy or the steps required to prevent their posted photos from being used in this manner (Harrington, 2009). Depending on how the SNS works and the privacy restrictions selected, friends of friends, including employers, may have access to their full profiles (Brandenburg, 2008; Facebook, 2008).

[4] SNSs are also serving as an inexpensive and quick source of background information on job applicants and current employees for employers. We are at the crest of a major shift in practice by employers. Employers have always been able to request background and reference information on job applicants but have been self-restrained in doing so because of the cost and legal requirements. Typically, background checks were reserved for serious candidates and for jobs which had a business necessity for the background information. This norm is now shifting, as employers are routinely conducting informal online background checks on people and without applicants' knowledge. Based on the information they find, employers are making decisions.

[5] In a study of students and current human-resources professionals about their attitudes toward online background checks, we found that future employees expect employers to check online for information available about them. Many employers also believe that this is an acceptable practice.[1] Other studies support this conclusion that employers are carrying out these checks and that employees understand that they are doing so (Brandenburg, 2008; Zeidner, 2007).

[6] In this article, we argue that, even though employers may have a legal right to use SNSs in this way and future employees expect them to do

so, it is wrong for employers to do this unless the information obtained in this manner is essential to the job. To support our position, we explore how social responsibility theory directs employers to conduct online background checks only when there is a business necessity because of the negative impact such checks have on society. We conclude by providing guidance to employers on when and how to conduct online checks responsibly.

Technology and Interaction

[7] Advances in technology have greatly impacted on how people communicate. Prior to the existence of the postal service, people depended on messengers to deliver messages verbally. Then, people depended on word to come from others via handwritten letters (Bellis, 2009). The telegraph made communication possible over great distances and within a shorter time. The telephone greatly changed how people communicated, becoming a main mode of communication for more than 100 years (Bellis, 2009).

[8] During the past 20 years, technology has evolved rapidly. The creation of the fax machine allowed people to send documents instantly to people elsewhere, to be followed by the Internet and e-mail, which has provided a new way for people to communicate. Now, people use sophisticated cellular telephones to access the Internet, send instant messages, text, shop online, determine their location, and document their lives in small "tech bytes" by "twittering" or posting comments to their SNS's "walls" (New Media Consortium, 2007).

[9] Clemmitt (2006) noted that advances in technology have an impact on how people interact socially. This is evident with the growth in the use of SNSs. Facebook, a popular SNS, began in 2004 as a way for college students to interact with each other (Brandenburg, 2008; Facebook, 2009a). In 2006, Facebook expanded membership to the corporate sector in the hope of retaining college alumni as members (Peluchette and Karl, 2008). In 2009, Facebook reported over 200 million users (2009b), Friendster had more than 100 million (Friendster, 2009), MySpace declined to 100 million users (Arrington, 2009), and hi5 had more than 80 million users (hi5, 2009). hi5 states that it is the most globally diverse SNS, with 80% of its users outside of the USA (hi5, 2009). When ranking sites based on the number of unique monthly visits, the top three in 2009 were Facebook, MySpace, and Twitter (Kazeniac, 2009). Wikipedia (2009) lists more than 100 SNSs.

[10] Facebook describes its purpose as a "social utility that helps people communicate more efficiently with their friends, family and coworkers" (Facebook, 2009a) and explains that it digitally maps users' real-world social connections. A growing site, Bebo, purports to integrate all social networking and Internet sites so a person can go to one place "for Facebook, MySpace, YouTube, Delicious, Twitter, AIM, AOL Mail, Google Mail and Yahoo! Mail updates" (Bebo.com, 2009). Some sites are more targeted to interest areas or time periods. Reunion.com and Classmates.com help people reconnect with people from their past, while Eons.com is for Babyboomers, Epernicus targets research scientists, and Disaboom is an online community for people with disabilities (Wikipedia, 2009).

[11] The online social community is continuing to evolve. Twitter is "a service for friends, family, and co-workers to communicate and stay connected through the exchange of quick, frequent answers to one simple question: 'What are you doing?'" (Twitter, 2009). In 1 year, Twitter moved from the 22nd SNS based on monthly visits to 3rd place in 2009 (Kazeniac, 2009). SNSs are more than a fad. They are the next step in the evolution of interaction between people, in particular among younger generations. They are beginning to be used more and more by older consumers. Facebook noted

significant growth in users with people over the age of 35 years in 2009 (Gaudin, 2009).

Growth in Online Checks

[12] Despite the infancy of SNSs, surveys by various entities over the last few years have found a growing trend of employers conducting online checks using SNSs for information on job applicants. An employer can type an applicant's name into a search engine such as Google to see what he or she finds. Some SNSs allow Internet search engines to search the names of its users and make public profiles available. Some employers have their own Facebook accounts and may be able to see more than the public profiles, depending on the friends-of-friends links and privacy settings. In this way, an employer can get a quick "character" picture of an applicant, depending on what is available online (Campbell, 2008) (Table I).

Consequences of Online Checks

[13] There are two main negative consequences that result when employers view information online that they deem unacceptable: employers do not hire the job applicant, and current employees are fired. We know that the former occurs because employers are telling us that they make decisions based on the information they find online (Careerbuilder.com, 2008; Peacock, 2009). However, most job applicants are not notified by the employer that an adverse decision was made for this reason. Rather, an applicant receives a standard "the position has been filled" letter or the person hears nothing more about the position. An applicant could also have an offer rescinded, as experienced by a law student in the USA. The law firm found that the student was affiliated with a web site that contained negative statements about female law students, even though the law student had not posted any offensive remarks (Samborn, 2007).

[14] Evidence that employees are being fired for online information is discussed in the media and in court documents. For example, a University of Loyola swim-team member was kicked off the swim team for posting disparaging remarks about her coaches on Facebook (Clemmitt, 2006). Joe Gordon is reported to be the first British blogger fired from his job for making rude comments about his boss on his blog (LaFerla, 2006). A US flight attendant lost her job for posting a picture of herself online in her uniform (LaFerla, 2006). A producer for one of CNN's news shows was fired for blogging offwork, even though he did not identify himself as a CNN employee (Wolgemuth, 2008). Sprague (2007) contains additional examples of employees who were fired for information they posted online.

[15] The discussion above demonstrates that, as the use of SNSs is exploding, employers' use of online background checks is increasing rapidly as well. While the practice seems to be taken for granted as acceptable, particularly in the USA, few employers have explored whether the practice is ethical. The authors, in their survey of US human-resources personnel, found that 43% of respondents reported using SNSs to gain information about job applicants, but only 21% had received any training on doing so, and 5% of respondents surveyed had a policy in place governing the practice. In this article, we provide a framework for that discussion, first by examining whether privacy is a right, followed by an exploration of why it is a company's social responsibility to refrain from using SNSs unless there is a strong, legitimate business reason to do so.

Privacy

[16] There is no universal definition of what privacy is or what constitutes workplace privacy (Miller and Weckert, 2000; Rosenblum, 1991). The MerriamWebster Online Dictionary defines privacy as "freedom from unauthorized intrusion" (2009).

Date of study	Study	Percentage of employers performing online checks	Use of information
2006	National Association of Colleges and Employers (Business & Legal Reports, Inc., 2006)	27% of employers report searching SNSs for information on employers	Not reported
2006	Careerbuilder.com (Brandenburg, 2008)	25% of hiring managers have conducted Internet searches (i.e., Google) 12% have looked at SNS profiles	63% (of the 12% who have looked at SNSs) said they did not hire because of information found
2007	Society of Human Resource Management Survey (Zeidner, 2007)	50% of human-resources professionals ran an Internet search (Google, Yahoo!) 15% reported checking SNS, and 40% of those who do not currently check said they were somewhat likely to likely to check within a year	20% of those who ran searches said they have disqualified a candidate based on what they found
2007	University of Dayton Survey (Read, 2007)	40% of employers would look at SNSs for information	Not reported
2008	Vault's Social Networking Web Site Survey (Vault.com, 2009)	44% of employers reported checking SNSs for information	82% reported that they would let something negative on the SNS impact their hiring decision
2008	Careerbuilder.com (2008)	21% of employers reported checking SNSs for information	34% (of the 21% who looked at SNSs) reported finding content which caused them to dismiss the person from consideration
2008	Jackson Lewis LLP Survey (Hrtools.com, 2008)	12% of New York employers had looked at online sites	Not reported
2008	Authors' Human-Resources (HR) Personnel Survey	43% of HR professionals reported they had looked at SNSs to gain additional information	Not reported
2009	Global Interviewing Practices and Perceptions Survey (Peacock, 2009)	25% of global employers 12% of UK employers reported they had looked at SNSs/online for information	52% (of the 25% of the global employers who looked) said the information impacted hiring decisions

TABLE I: Studies reporting employers searching SNSs for background information

We will discuss privacy in terms of a natural or fundamental right to privacy and as a legal right.

Natural or Fundamental Right to Privacy

[17] Discussions of privacy are traced back to Aristotle as he delineated between governmental activity and a private sphere associated with a man's household (DeCew, 1997). In 1690, John Locke also emphasized two distinct domains between public and private spheres in his writings (DeCew, 1997); he espoused that the earth and what was produced by nature belong to all in common, but that "each

person possesses himself (or herself) absolutely and has property rights to that with which he mixes his labor" (p. 11). A person owns that which belongs to and is acquired by himself or herself. Alan Westin provides support that privacy is a natural right, documenting that animals also share a need for individual or smallgroup seclusion (DeCew, 1997). Margaret Mead also observed that different cultures have a universal need to establish realms of privacy: "All societies have techniques for setting distances and avoiding contact with others in order to establish physical boundaries to maintain privacy" (ibid., p. 12).

[18] Although there is a lack of consensus about how privacy should be defined, there is a general belief that there is a natural right to have some information about oneself kept from others. Warren and Brandeis (1890), in an influential paper, The Right to Privacy, argued that humans have a natural right to be left alone. They wrote this paper in response to the press taking photographs of people and publishing the pictures without a person's consent. They built the privacy right on common law that "secures to each individual the right of determining, ordinarily, to what extent his thoughts, sentiments, and emotions shall be communicated to others" (Warren and Brandeis, 1890, p. 198).

[19] Introna and Pouloudi (1999) presented some historical perspectives which describe privacy as a "freedom from the judgements of others" (Introna, 1997, p. 28), as having "control over knowledge about oneself" (Fried 1968 cited by Introna and Pouloudi, 1999, p. 29), or "the exclusive access of a person to a realm of his own" (Van Den Haag, 1971, p. 149).

Legal Right to Privacy

[20] Several countries have created or clarified a right to privacy related to human dignity as a fundamental right in their constitutions or laws. For example, UK enacted the Human Rights Act of 1998 which provides a person with "the right to have one's private life respected" (Jeffery, 2002b, p. 304). France refers to Article 8 of the European Convention on Human Rights for a right to personal privacy (Vigneau, 2002). Historically, courts in the USA have interpreted the existence of a right to privacy stemming from nature and guaranteed from several constitutional amendments (freedom of speech, freedom of religion, and freedom from unreasonable search and seizures) (DeCew, 1997).

[21] Whether there is a legal right to privacy varies greatly depending on the jurisdiction. Each country and smaller jurisdictions within each country have different rules as to what information is deemed private and out of the purview of the employer to consider. We will provide an overview of some of the major differences in these jurisdictions. Some legal systems, such as Spain's, strongly protect a personal realm of privacy that seems to trump an employer's interest in considering personal information when making employment decisions (Arranda, 2002). Other jurisdictions (i.e., Brazil and Italy) guarantee that a person has the right of self-determination, which includes prior notice and consent as to how his or her personal data will be processed by an employer (Faleri, 2002; Filho and Leonel de Rezende Alvim, 2002). Others interpret privacy in terms of a balance between protecting the employee's information and the legitimate needs of an employer to consider the information (Jeffery, 2002a). Some jurisdictions, Germany and UK, hold that it is most important to protect the contractual agreement made between two private individuals (employer and employee), acknowledging that an employee can walk away from the employment relationship if he or she does not want to provide the information (Jeffery, 2002a, b; Reinhard, 2002). The US courts often take this position, citing the doctrine of employment at will (Finkin, 2002). Other jurisdictions take the position that

employees should not lose basic rights of citizenship (rights to privacy) when they walk through an employer's door (Jeffery, 2002a). This latter position is held by France and has been repeated in recent directives by the European Union (Jeffery, 2002a; Vigneau, 2002).

[22] More than 15 years ago, the European Union issued Directive 95/46/EC which specifies minimum standards of data protection that must be granted by all member states and any other state where data may go (Jeffery, 2002a). The directive requires that personal data be processed fairly and lawfully, be obtained for a specific purpose, be accurate, and be stored securely (Jeffery, 2002a). Directive 95/46/EC has led to new legislation and court interpretations which strengthen workplace privacy in France, UK, Spain, Germany, and Italy. Other entities, including the Organization for Economic Cooperation and Development, the Council of Europe, the International Labour Office, and the United Nations, have also passed directives which protect an individual's right to privacy (Jeffery, 2002a). The USA has few legal limitations on the use of personal data by employers when making employment decisions (Finkin, 2002). See Appendix A for a summary of workplace privacy laws in selected countries.

[23] It is unclear how privacy laws will be interpreted when it comes to information an individual posts on a SNS. Key legal questions are whether the individual consented to the information being made available to everyone, whether the information is relevant to the employment decision, and whether the information falls within a protected realm of personal privacy even if a person makes the information available to many people or does not use provided privacy settings.

[24] Legally it is debated where the line is drawn between an employer's right to access information and an employee's right to keep certain information private. Advances in technology make it possible to store lots of information about people and to access that information quickly, cheaply, and without knowledge that such information has been accessed (Miller and Weckert, 2000). For these reasons, many urge that a right to privacy be clearly established (Stross, 2007).

Expectations of Privacy

Even if the information that an individual places on SNSs is personal or protected information, many argue that a job applicant waives an expectation of privacy to that information when he or she places it on a SNS (Introna and Pouloudi, 1999). Warren and Brandeis (1890) were clear that a person's right to privacy ceases once the individual publishes the information or consents to its release. Legally, the critical issue is whether a person "publishes" information about himself or herself when he or she places it on a SNS. [25]

[26] A person's Facebook site often has recent photographs of the person with his or her family and friends, short blogs describing daily activities, and online dialogue by family and friends. For example, as a friend of John's site, one can view the dialogue posted by John and his "friends." When John updates his profile or posts a picture, all of John's friends are notified that an update has been made. Facebook provides users with some options to limit who has access to their full profile. Even by selecting the most restrictive settings, the information displayed may not be hard to access (Brandenburg, 2008). A Facebook user has the ability to search and access profiles more thoroughly. To ensure complete privacy, some SNS users create a public page using their real name and a pseudo site for friends that contains the pictures and dialogue intended for them.

[27] Simms (1994) suggests that there is a difference between self-presentation and self-disclosure. Self-presentation is the "communication of self-data an individual might reveal to most any other person"

(p. 317). Self-disclosure is the "explicit communication of self-data another would not have access to" (p. 317). Self-disclosure strengthens a relational bond and includes sharing of emotional experiences (Simms, 1994). Given this difference, perhaps employers should have access only to self-presentation information and not to self-disclosure information. Young people may also see their profiles as self-presentation tools rather than self-identity tools (Livingstone, 2008). Employers may be basing decisions on information that shows poor judgment in what a young person decides to present to others but may not represent whether the individual is of good character or not.

[28] Some argue that young people have a different expectation of privacy than older employees. Livingstone (2008) disagrees, noting his research that teenagers want control over who has access to the information they post online (see also Thibodeau, 2008). They want their friends to read their profiles but do not want their parents or employers snooping through their private space. Currently, social networking privacy settings are too limited to allow users to designate who is able to receive what type of information beyond allowing a "friend" into the site (Livingstone, 2008). Facebook is tweaking its privacy settings to allow users to control who can view each post (Noyes, 2009). Privacy advocates urge Facebook to default to the highest privacy settings rather than defaulting to the lowest as it currently does (Noyes, 2009).

[29] There appears to be a disconnect between how members use their SNSs to communicate daily on a personal level with friends, and employers' practice to judge job applicants based on what is posted. The online sites serve as a local gathering place where people run into each other, make plans, and share news. Unlike a traditional bricks-and-mortar gathering place, now conversations are immortalized, and it is very easy for others to be voyeurs and make judgments based on social interactions. The purpose and activity taking place in the gathering places are the same as those that would occur in a bricks-and-mortar gathering place. The difference is that the digital information becomes permanent and employers are being the voyeurs. Employers are taking in all kinds of personal information, and making decisions based upon that information, without job applicants being aware. Employers are doing so because it is easy and cheap to do so. We contend that an employer would not ask a human-resources staff member to follow a job candidate to a local restaurant or bar and sit in the booth beside him or her for the purpose of overhearing conversations and witnessing behavior for a character check. As long as the job candidate is in a public place, the employer could legally do so, but for most this action would seem extreme and inappropriate. Why do we not have a similar reaction when the same behavior occurs online?

Next, we discuss how this change in practice is [30] damaging to society and why employers need to curb this practice.

Corporate Social Responsibility

The traditional view of a company is that the com- [31] pany has a responsibility to make as much profit as it can for its shareholders (Friedman, 1962; Grossman, 2005; Jensen and Wygant, 1990). An alternative view of the firm was suggested by Edward Freeman in 1984 and termed the stakeholder approach. The stakeholder approach directs organizations to manage the interests of and acknowledge a duty of care to a range of stakeholders (Jamali, 2008). A stakeholder is "any group or individual who can affect or is affected by the achievement of the firm's objectives" (Freeman, 1984, p. 25). Stakeholders include the traditional ones—shareholders, customers, employees, and suppliers—but are expanded to include such groups as competitors, governmental entities, special interest groups, media, and local community organizations (Freeman, 1984).

[32] A stakeholder perspective of social responsibility has been developed and is categorized as descriptive or normative. The descriptive stakeholder theory examines how well an organization attends to the needs and interests of various stakeholders. An organization is viewed as being socially responsible using this approach if it attends to the needs and interests of at least half of its stakeholders (Jamali, 2008). The normative stakeholder approach focuses "on the ethical requirements that cement the relationship between business and society" (Jamali, 2008, p. 219).

[33] Using the traditional view of the firm or a limited stakeholder view of the firm, one can understand why an organization would conclude that online character checks are an acceptable business practice. From the employer's position, there are many reasons why conducting an online background check is in the interest of its shareholders. It provides an easy way to gain a "character" assessment of candidates without much hassle and allows the employer to learn more about a candidate than is possible any other way. Employers argue that they have a right and need to protect themselves (i.e., shareholders) from negligent hiring (Blackwell, 2004). Negligent hiring may occur if a company "fails to uncover an applicant's incompetence or unfitness by a diligent search of references, criminal background or even general background" (Edwards and Kleiner, 2002, p. 137). Employers also state that using SNSs gives them a sense of the type of decisions job applicants will make (Brandenburg, 2008).

[34] In the USA, many job applicants, having been warned of the practice, believe it is acceptable for employers to check up on them by conducting Google searches or reviewing their SNS pages. In a University of Dayton study, 68% of students surveyed did not believe it was unethical for employers to look at their SNSs (Read, 2007) despite many students reporting that they believed there is a strong line between personal and work life (Read, 2007). In the authors' study of students about their perceptions of an employer's use of SNSs in the hiring process, only 33% of students thought that viewing SNSs was unethical. Thirty-six percent thought the practice was ethical, while 32% were undecided about the practice. In follow-up interviews, some students expressed a view that what is online is public. They argue that a job applicant should know by now not to post anything that the applicant does not want a potential employer to see. Employers also share the view that job applicants need to clean up their sites and remove anything that could be viewed negatively, stating that nothing is safe online. Some employees are willing to give up some privacy to ensure that they are safe in the workplace, which they believe is more likely if employers conduct thorough background checks (Blackwell, 2004).

[35] We believe that these views of the firm ignore the impact that online character background checks have on stakeholders not considered in this reasoning and on society at large. There are users of SNSs who are not yet of an age to apply for jobs. There are older stakeholders who have a different view of privacy and are not willing to concede that an employer can look. Also not considered are the stronger views of privacy held by global partners and employees. Some stakeholders are in a better position to articulate their interests (Introna and Pouloudi, 1999) and others are in a position of power imbalance and cannot honestly represent their concerns.

[36] Blanket acceptance of this practice destroys the utility and positive impact of this new communication medium. The practice sends a message to SNSs users that you cannot communicate honestly online for fear that your views will be judged and prevent you from getting a job. Currently, people use SNSs as they would a telephone or restaurant table. If a

realm of personal privacy is not provided to this type of communication, society will forever lose the benefits that online communication provides. For these reasons, a return to more conventional social responsibility focused on what is in the best interest of society is warranted.

[37] A broader view of the purpose of a company gained momentum in the 1960s with the discussion of corporate social responsibility (Wines, 2008). Corporate social responsibility includes the claim that organizations should be not only concerned about making a profit but also engaged in "actions that appear to further some good, beyond the interests of the firm and that which is required by law" (McWilliams et al., 2006, p. 1).

[38] Proponents of social responsibility justify this approach, explaining that businesses do not exist in isolation, they receive benefits from society to exist, and they have an obligation to give back to society. Some use a marketing approach to justify social responsibility, arguing that it is sound business practice for a business to appear socially responsible (Shaw, 2009). Grossman (2005) explains that there is an interconnectedness between social and financial performance and true corporate social responsibility which is focused on the long term. Grossman (2005) defines true corporate social responsibility as "the implementation of sound management structures aimed at minimizing risk in areas such as governance, environmental impact, social impact and workplace practices" (p. 582). Stated simply, companies should "earn money in a moral and ethical way" (McClenahen, 2005, p. 64). For the purposes of this paper, corporate social responsibility is defined as "a business obligation to pursue policies, make decisions, and take actions that benefit society" (Williams, 2010, p. 71).

[39] Currently, the virtual door is wide open and companies are racing through. With the click of the mouse, employers are conducting unfettered online character checks, creating a global norm that this intrusion into one's personal realm is acceptable. There is no time to wait for laws to be passed to curb this practice. We believe that companies must act out of a higher responsibility to society, a global society, to preserve a natural right to personal privacy. Bloustein (cited by Manning, 1997) stated that invasions of privacy are wrong because "they are invasions of liberty as individuals to do as we will," and "they undercut individuality and create a society of conventional, mediocre persons" (p. 818).

Online Character Checks Harm Society

In the following section, we explore in greater detail [40] why conducting online character checks is damaging to society in the following ways:

- Online communities are a new way for people to interact, and this evolution of communication should be protected;
- Areas of privacy should be shielded from employer use;
- Online communication is permanent, and consideration of decisions years later may be harmful;
- It is good for society for there to remain boundaries between one's work and personal life.

Online Communities

Advances in technology have always changed how [41] society communicates and interacts. With the creation of the Internet in the 1970s, "online socializing has helped people worldwide link to others with common interests for conversation and support" (Colin, 2006, p. 625). A generation ago, people were more likely to remain in the same place and develop long-term friendships based on face-to-face contact. Now, many of us live in a city different from where we grew up, and the number of traditional friendships is down (Clemmitt, 2006).

[42] The use of the Internet is largely social (Clemmitt, 2006). A survey by the Pew Internet and American Life Project found that 34% of respondents said that the Internet played an important role in a major decision they had made, meaning they sought advice and support from other people online (Clemmitt, 2006). In the same survey, 84% of Internet users reported joining a group or organization with an online presence. "Members of online groups also say the Internet brings them into more contact with people outside their social class or their racial or age group" (Clemmitt, 2006, p. 627). The Internet allows people to stay in touch with old friends and make new ones (Clemmitt, 2006).

[43] Others argue that web-based socializing strengthens online and offline relationships because it is facilitating a shift to new communication modes rather than causing a decrease in communication altogether (Clemmitt, 2006). A report by the Pew Internet and American Life Project and the University of Toronto discusses "a shift from neighborhood and village based groups to communities oriented around geographically dispersed social networks" (Clemmitt, 2006, p. 634). The Pew Internet study found that people were in more contact with members of their communities and social networks than before, and those who e-mailed closest friends/family often were more likely to speak to them on the phone as well. A University of Toronto study found that people who had high-speed Internet access knew more names of neighbors than those who were not wired (Clemmitt, 2006).

[44] Online socializing is very important for teenagers because they need to have their own space, and social networking provides them with their own space online (Clemmitt, 2006). Online communities also provide previous outcasts with a way to connect with friends who have similar interests from around the world (Clemmitt, 2006). Socializing online may occur without initial judgments based on physical appearance, disabilities or other stereotypes (Clemmitt, 2006).

[45] Despite these benefits, critics of online socializing argue that online communication cannot "support human bonding the way real-world communities do" (Clemmitt, 2006, quoting Clifford Stoll, p. 633). Stanford University's Institute for the Quantitative Study of Society found that Internet use was directly related to social isolation (Clemmitt, 2006). This study found that, for every hour spent online, a person spends 23.5 min less face to face with family and friends (Clemmitt, 2006). Online socializing does not allow physical contact.

[46] In contrast, some argue that online communication makes people more connected. "Tele-cocooning" is described as "carrying your friends around with you, using technology to be literally in contact with them all the time" (Clemmitt, 2006, p. 634, quoting Mimi Ito). For example, Sam posts comments throughout the day on his Facebook wall such as: "Leaving for kids' soccer games. Dawson made a goal. Mom's surgery went well." An e-mail alert is sent to each of Sam's Facebook friends letting them know that Sam has updated his wall. Friends can immediately read and post a return comment on Sam's wall.

[47] The invention of the telephone changed the interaction between people drastically from face-to-face meetings and letter-writing to verbal communication. Likewise, the Internet and wireless communication is quickly modifying how humans interact. There is no stopping this process, and there is a global interest in protecting some realm of privacy within this communication medium. If employers continue to conduct online character checks, we believe there will be a chilling effect on this type of communication. People will modify what they post and write to conform to the expectations of employers, resulting in what Bloustein predicted: Invasions of privacy will lead to a society

of "conventional, mediocre persons" (cited by Manning, 1997, p. 818). The chilling effect will render this form of communication inferior, as people will be less honest and self-censor interactions.

Privacy

[48] As a Facebook user, a person is able to search the profiles and invite acquaintances to become friends. Facebook will search for potential friends based on people a new user has e-mailed in the past. When a new user reviews a suggested person to invite as a friend, he or she can review the list of that person's friends. When reviewing a friend of a friend's list of friends, a user is able to access portions of the friend of a friend's profile and the online communications that are posted on that person's wall. A person is a voyeur to various conversations to which he or she has no prior relationship. Friends can post pictures that may include other people without obtaining the consent of the people in the picture. Quickly, a user loses control over the content that is posted online and made available to other people.

[49] If we do not recognize a realm of privacy to protect these conversations, we are opening Pandora's box to a different world with very little privacy. It would be similar to allowing public restaurants to place bugs under each table and broadcast the hundreds of conversations that occur daily on a public feed for employers to view. In online communities, people are having conversations using a different technology that is easier for them to use. This new technology is also archived, leaving a permanent digital trail. Our traditional conversations are rarely archived unless someone is taping them, a practice often prohibited by law (Clemmitt, 2006).

[50] Many users of SNSs communicate with a false sense that these online communities are safe (Clemmitt, 2006). Others have a belief that the communication one conducts on the Internet is private since it is often done in one's own home (New York Times, 2006). People use the Internet to check their financial records, research sensitive medical issues, and seek advice on topics about which they would be ashamed to ask a friend. Many teenagers post with a belief that no-one is watching. While teenage girls would be horrified if someone read their diary, they are posting so much more personal information online (Clemmitt, 2006).

[51] In the future, online communications and social networking will become even more deeply rooted in our lives. Social networking addresses may be the most consistent way to reach someone (Clemmitt, 2006). As the flood gates are open, for the good of society, we need to ensure that technology does not strip away our privacy.

[52] Edwards and Kleiner (2002), who wrote an article about conducting traditional reference checks in 2002, cautioned employers to realize "a social responsibility not to invade the privacy of an applicant more than necessary" (p. 146). They argued that employers have access to so much information, that job applicants do not know how much information is being considered, and that employers need to limit their consideration to only job-related information. Miller and Weckert (2000) agree, stating that an employer is buying labor not things outside of work, and privacy is a moral right. Recently, some countries have passed laws to limit the information that may be considered by an employer about a job applicant (Jeffery, 2002a).

Permanency of Online Communication

[53] A major difference of online communication is that it is a permanent type of communication. Even when a user deletes the information, it remains the property of the SNS and can be recalled at a later time. Sometimes a user's deleted profile is still retrievable upon an Internet search because it exists somewhere online. In contrast, many laws protect the interception of a telephone conversation by a

third party or government entity (Jeffrey, 2002a). It is also a violation of most laws for a written letter to be opened by someone other than the intended receiver. Online communication is not afforded similar protection. Because of this permanency, a person's mistakes or misjudgments cannot be retracted and may come back to haunt him or her. This permanency has a greater impact on minors, who are known for making errors of judgment.

[54] Most countries protect minors from the decisions they make when it is believed they lack full mental capacity to assess the risks and consequences of their actions. In some jurisdictions, minors who commit crimes are prosecuted and punished in a separate juvenile system, and their records are sealed and purged when they reach the age of majority (Junger-Tas and Decker, 2006).

[55] New technologies are developing all the time and are creating a generational divide. Young adults and teenagers have grown up with technology and have done most of their communication through computers. They have learned to multitask while communicating with several people at the same time (Sherman, 2008). Teenagers are quick to jump onboard with the new technology, making it hard for legislators, parents, and others to stay on top of it (Clemmitt, 2006). Most cyber social network users are aged between 12 and 25 years (Clemmitt, 2006). Although SNSs may restrict accounts to users of certain ages, often teenagers are allowed on the sites legitimately; thirteen-year-olds are allowed an account on MySpace. Since there is no good way to verify a user's identify or age, much younger users are online.

[56] Eighty-three percent of teenagers surveyed about MySpace said they believe it is safe (Clemmitt, 2006). College students also perceive SNSs, especially Facebook, to be private (Peluchette and Karl, 2008). However, a proposed Facebook change in 2006 made users more aware that whatever they put online remains saved forever (Clemmitt, 2006). Online information cannot be deleted permanently and may remain accessible for years due to caching (Oblinger and Hawkins, 2006). The information one posts online is only as safe as your friends keep it (Clemmitt, 2006).

Teenagers and younger users sometimes use [57] SNSs in a risky manner. However, it is important to remember that a lot of online behavior was happening anyway in teen hangouts but parents and employers did not have access to it (Clemmitt, 2006). In 2006 a survey of US students explored what kind of information they post on their SNS profiles (Peluchette and Karl, 2008). Results indicated that males were more likely to post self-promoting and risqué pictures or comments while females were more likely to post cute or romantic material. Teenagers expressed comfort with family, friends, and classmates seeing their sites, but one in five did not want employers seeing their sites. The study confirmed that students did not realize the consequences of posting such information online (Oblinger and Hawkins, 2006; Peluchette and Karl, 2008).

It is in the public interest to protect the privacy [58] and actions of people in their social interactions. It is also not in society's interest for employers to have access to the missteps, questionable decisions, or nonmainstream ideologies of job candidates when making employment decisions. Allowing employers access to this personal information may forever impact a person's ability to get a job. It has yet to be established that judgments made based on information from SNSs is related to job performance.

Boundaries between Work and Private Life

Currently, there is a debate about whether there still [59] exists a boundary between work and an employee's private life (Charlesworth, 2003). Such a boundary has not always existed. Conway (2003) notes that it was only with the Industrial Revolution and a change in where work was conducted that such a wall formed. Prior to the Industrial Revolution, it was common for work to be conducted within a person's home. The Industrial Revolution led to people working within factories in cities, and the separation between work and one's home life developed. Now, with the advancement of technology and the desire for flexibility (Cowan and Hoffman, 2007), there seems to be a blurring of the line, as people return to working more at home (Duxbury and Higgins, 2001; Johnson and Chadwick, 2009).

[60] Manning (1997) argues that an employee has a right to liberty, and flowing from liberty is a right to lead one's life separate from work. This freedom is required for private thoughts and development of one's self apart from his or her work identity (Manning, 1997). Others strongly counter that work is not a right but a privilege, and argue that an employer has a right to know whatever it can about a person to protect its property right in the business (Myatt, 2009; Sugarman, 2003). Myatt explains that an employee is a direct representative of the company at all times, on and off work. Manning (1997) makes the point that a person does not have to work for an employer if he or she does not agree with the employer's hiring practices. Often a job applicant or employee is unaware that the employer is conducting an online background check and has made an adverse decision based on that information. Manning's view of employment ignores an employee's unique contribution and value to the organization and seems to treat employees as a means to an end.

[61] Maintaining a separation between work and life is something that brings value to the organization, the employee, and therefore society. For example, organizations that offer flexibility and work–life balance options provide a mechanism to reduce stress resulting from high work–life conflict (Eos Life Work, 2007; Van Steenbergen and Ellemers, 2009). It also makes employers more competitive in attracting and retaining employees (Gregory and Milner, 2009; Hakala, 2008).

[62] If the boundary between work and an employee's private life is destroyed, it becomes more likely that employees will modify their behavior for fear of being judged by their employer. Employees may then express religious, political, and other views they believe the employer deems acceptable, resulting in masses of people who act in a cult-like fashion. This type of groupthink can have dire consequences and eliminate originality and creativity (Dvorak, 2001; Whyte, 1989).

[63] While it is true that working for a particular employer is not a right, having the opportunity to work is an economic necessity (Eos Life Work, 2007). If the boundary between work and family is eroded in part based on this rapidly developing social norm, then some may not be able to work because of the judgment of others ("she is too conservative or too liberal"; "she is a sinner for sexual preference"; etc.). It is important that the line between work and one's private life be clearly marked and preserved (Stross, 2007).

Summary of the Potential Harm to Society

[64] The current practice of employers conducting online character checks that include reviewing information posted on job applicants' SNSs is harmful to society because it allows employers to be undetectable voyeurs to very personal information and make employment decisions based on that information. The acceptance of this practice would have a chilling effect and permanently render a promising communication medium inferior and dangerous for people to use. We believe that society needs SNSs because they are the next step in human social interaction. Currently, within these sites, people are reconnecting and maintaining daily contact with others across geographical distances. Society needs this communication medium but along with it realms of personal privacy must be protected.

[65] In addition to the potential of damaging an evolving communication medium, the current practice of unfettered checks further destroys a line between what is appropriate for the work realm and what should exist in one's private realm. The current practice attacks a natural right of humans to have a personal space. The practice also has a greater impact on younger generations, as they are the most dominant users of SNSs and are more likely as teenagers to use the sites for boasting, which may haunt them later when they seek employment. These issues are amplified because currently our digital communications remain permanently in digital storage for people to judge years later. For these reasons, we call upon employers to make a practice change that will benefit society by protecting this virtual communication space from their judgment.

Guidance for Socially Responsible Use of Online Background Checks

[66] Employers should cease the practice of informal, online background checks of job applicants and take the necessary time to discuss and establish a policy to guide when and how an employer will use information obtained from online sources in the future (Rifkin, 1991). The first step in developing a policy is for an employer to establish that there is a link between what is contained on applicants' SNSs and on-the-job behavior (Peluchette and Karl, 2008). If this link exists, then an employer should determine for which jobs the employer has a legitimate business interest in gathering this information (Bahls, 1990). Sugarman (2003) provides a more detailed discussion of what a legitimate business interest may include. For those jobs for which there is a legitimate business interest, employers should determine what impact online background checks have on the trust formation between the employer and the future employee. The employer should also weigh the benefits gained against the potential negative consequences from further erosion of the boundary between a person's private and work life.

For those jobs for which there is a legitimate [67] interest to consider the information found on a SNS that outweighs the negative consequences to society at large, the employer should establish guidelines to be sure that the employer is not seeking or using information based on protected class membership (Greenwald, 2008) or in violation of a law or regulation. The employer should weigh whether it is better not to look in order to prevent the inference that a protected characteristic was illegally considered (Greenwald, 2008).

Guidance provided to employers on how to con- [68] duct and use information from traditional background checks applies as well to informal online background checks. For example, Bahls (1990, pp. 30–31) provides the following guidance:

- Do not conduct a check unless the information is job related and the employer can justify a legitimate reason in court;
- Provide fair notice to the employee prior to the background check;
- Make sure the information obtained is accurate, complete, and relevant;
- Keep promises of confidentiality;
- Restrict in-house access to information to those with legitimate interest in the information;
- Discard outdated information;
- Avoid intrusive data collection.

Charlesworth (2003, p. 222) provides similar [69] guidance to employers who are considering a measure that intrudes on an employee's privacy:

- Have a legitimate purpose for the intrusion;
- Ensure that the intrusion is offset by a greater utility to the employer or society;

- Use the least intrusive measure possible that achieves the desired outcome;
- Ensure that the measure is fair and lawful;
- Apply the measure equally to similarly situated job applicants or employees;
- Be transparent in your use of the measure and the process the employer used to develop the measure.

Conclusions

[70] There appears to be a disconnect between how users of SNSs view the purpose and utility of SNSs and how employers view the sites. Users of SNSs use them mainly for social interaction, whereas employers use a site to gather character information about job candidates without the applicants ever knowing what information was considered. SNSs serve as a local gathering place, albeit online, where people run into each other, make plans, and share news. Unlike a traditional bricks-and-mortar gathering place, online conversations are immortalized in the online gathering place, and others (friends and strangers) can be voyeurs and listen in. The purpose of and activity taking place in these gathering places are the same, but the permanency and judgment of the activities by employers are something very different.

[71] We call upon employers to take a moment to consider the impact these easy, informal background checks have on society. The greatest impact is the chilling effect this practice will have on the quality of human interaction that will occur online. Rather than expecting users of SNSs to change their behavior by not posting anything they do not want an employer to view, we argue that it is better for society for employers not to enter an employee's virtual front door.

Appendix A

TABLE II: Workplace privacy orientation and laws

Country	Workplace privacy orientation and laws
Brazil (Filho and Leonel de Rezende Alvim, 2002)	An employee sells his work time to the employer. The legal system tries to balance the employee's private life and private correspondence with an employer's private property rights and a manager's right to manage. Courts have recognized that employees have a private sphere that is protected from employer intrusion. Employers are required to provide notice before any workplace surveillance occurs. When it comes to personal data, an employee should be able to decide what happens to it (self-determination orientation). In 1998, a provision was added to the Constitution which protects workers from automation. It called for the development of tools to achieve a balance between workers' productivity and the automation of work. Courts have found that e-mails, even when sent from a company's computer, are private correspondence. Courts have made decisions based on an employer's "(a) respect for the worker's dignity, and (b) consistency between surveillance procedures and their stated purpose" (p. 290).
UK (Jeffery, 2002b)	There are several recent laws in UK that address the surveillance of workers and the processing of personal data. The Data Protection Act 1998 was passed to implement European Council directive 95/46/EC. The Human Rights Act 1998 includes "the right to have one's private life respected" (p. 304). The Regulation of Investigatory Powers Act 2000 provides a legal framework for all interceptions of communications on both public and private telecommunications systems (p. 305) and requires that both parties to the communication consent to the communication being intercepted by another party. Laws have required an employee's notice, consent, and fair treatment when specifying what *(continued)*

UK (Jeffery, 2002b)	behavior is legal. In summary, these laws required an employee's notice, consent, and fair treatment prior to processing of personal data. These laws are just now being implemented and interpreted by the courts. It is likely that, when in doubt, the courts will interpret the law to provide for individual privacy. Common law has also recognized a right to personal privacy. Initially the laws seemed to weigh in favor of employees and protect personal data from employee surveillance. Recently, laws seem to have been in favor of employers.
Germany (Reinhard, 2002)	Germany has a mixture of laws that provide some workplace privacy and are in compliance with Directive 95/46/EC. Employers have the right to collect some personal data on employees. Surveillance without an employee being given notice can only occur in rare circumstances. Courts have ruled that "the protection of personal data is a fundamental right under the Constitution" (p. 393). The collection of personal data must be authorized by law or when a person consents.
Spain (Arranda, 2002)	A 1980s law established a right of the employer to monitor the employee regardless of the methods used. Judicial interpretations of this law have limited the degree to which an employer may monitor. The monitoring must relate to employment. The employee must be informed of the monitoring before it occurs. The courts look to company rules for guidance on whether the monitoring is appropriate. Monitoring must be justifiable and related to its purpose. The Spanish Constitution of 1978 included Article 18.4, which states that "the law shall limit the use of computers in order to safeguard the honour and privacy of all its citizens, whether related to the individual or the family, and ensure that they may fully exercise their rights" (p. 449). In 1999, a new law (Ley Orgánica de Protección de Datos de Carácter Personal, referred to as LOPDCP) provided protection of personal data and implemented Directive 95/46/EC. The LOPDCP has two main requirements. First, personal data sought by an employer must have a legitimate purpose. Second, the data sought must be relevant, appropriate, and not excessive with regards to that purpose. In determining whether the purpose is legitimate, the consideration of the personal data cannot lead to unlawful discrimination based on sex, race, ideology, or union membership. Sensitive personal data requires the consent of the data subject prior to its processing.
USA (Finkin, 2002)	In the USA, the employment-at-will doctrine is strong. Unless there is a contract stating otherwise, the employment-at-will doctrine states that an employer or employee may end the employment relationship for any reason at any time. Very little employee privacy protection exists in federal and state legal codes. Likewise, there is very little workplace privacy protection afforded in common law. The Electronic Communications Privacy Act (1968) provides some protection against wire taps and the release of stored communications, but what is protected is interpreted narrowly. Common law protection against wrongful invasion of privacy requires that a person has a reasonable expectation of privacy and that the nature of the invasion of privacy to a reasonable person is "highly offensive." In contrast to laws in other countries, recent state legislation has afforded more protection to employers when providing reference information about a former employee rather than limiting what information an employer may consider.
France (Vigneau, 2002)	Law and culture in France recognize a sphere of personal privacy. In French law, there are three principles that guide workplace privacy. The principle of transparency requires that prior notice be provided to an employee before workplace surveillance or personal data is processed. The principle of proportionality requires that the means used to gather the information is balanced to the depth or type of information needed. The third principle of relevance requires the employer to justify the need for the information. An employer must notify an employee that personal data will be collected. The employee can challenge its use. Article L.121-6 of the French Labor Code requires that "information sought from job applicants and employees must aim exclusively at evaluating their professional abilities" (p. 354). Recent decision by the highest appeal court in France found that an employer *(continued)*

France (Vigneau, 2002)	did not have the right to open an employee's private e-mail even though it was retrieved using the employer's computer during work hours. An employer can monitor work activities of employees only to the extent that such surveillance does not interfere with the employee's right to privacy. Article 9 of the French Civil Code and Article 8 of the European Convention on Human Rights clarify that an individual has a right to personal privacy. French law also follows European Community Directive 95/46/EC.
Italy (Faleri, 2002)	Italian law seems to ensure a balance between the employer and the employee in contrast to recognizing an employee's right to privacy. The law recognizes an employee's "right to data self-determination" (p. 426). Changes were made to Italian law to comply with Directive 95/46/EC. Sensitive data requires a data subject's consent before it can be processed, and the processing must be authorized by the Guarantor. The Guarantor has provided authorization for many types of data processing through the issuance of a list. Ordinary data does not require the consent of the data subject. An employee's right to privacy is "limited by the Freedom of Economic Initiative, as established by Article 41 of the Italian Constitution" (p. 414). This constitutional provision specifies that any law cannot impose excessive bureaucracy that would impact an employer's ability to run the business efficiently.

Note

1. The aforementioned authors' study was approved by the authors' university's Office of Compliance in accordance with the ethical standards laid down in the 1964 Declaration of Helsinki. All respondents in the study provided their informed consent prior to beginning the survey and identifying information was not collected.

References

Arranda, J.T. 2002. "Information Technology and Workers' Privacy: The Spanish Law." *Comparative Labor Law and Policy Journal* 23(4), 431–470.

Arrington, M. 2009. "Facebook Now Nearly Twice the Size of MySpace Worldwide." http://www.techcrunch.com/2009/01/22/facebook-now-nearly-twice-the-size-of-myspace-worldwide/. Accessed 20 June 2009.

Bahls, J.E. 1990. "Checking Up on Workers." *Nation's Business* 77(12), 29.

Bebo.com. 2009. "Bebo." http://www.bebo.com/c/site/index. Accessed 4 June 2009.

Bellis, M. 2009. "The History of Communication." http://inventors.about.com/library/inventors/bl_history_of_communication.htm. Accessed 20 June 2009.

Blackwell, C.W. 2004. "Current Employee Privacy Issues." *The Journal of Applied Management and Entrepreneurship* 9(1), 113–118.

Brandenburg, C. 2008. "The Newest Way to Screen Job Applicants: A Social Networker's Nightmare." *Federal Communications Law Journal* 60(3), 597–626.

Business & Legal Reports, Inc. 2006. "Employers Check Social Networking Sites." http://hr.blr.com/news.aspx?id=18685. Accessed 8 June 2009.

Campbell, B.A. 2008. "Choose Your Online Friends Wisely." http://www.law.com/jsp/legaltechnology/pubArticleLT.jsp?id=1202426779555. Accessed 11 Aug 2009.

Careerbuilder.com. 2008. "One-in-Five Employers Use Social Networking Sites to Research Job Candidates, CareerBuilder.com Survey Finds." http://www.careerbuilder.com/share/aboutus/pressreleasesdetail.aspx?id=pr459&sd=9%2F10%2F2008&ed=12%2F31%2F2008&cbRecursionCnt=1&cbsid=2e371ebfbdf845fb985c1303f725badf-297778093-JT-5. Accessed 8 June 2009.

Charlesworth, A.J. 2003. "Opinion. Privacy, Personal Information and Employment." *Surveillance & Society* 1(2), 217–222.

Clemmitt, M. 2006. "Cyber Socializing." *CQ Researcher* 16(27), 627–648.

Colin, T.J. 2006. "Cyber Socializing." *CQ Researcher* 16(27), 625.

Conway, J.F. 2003. *The Canadian Family in Crisis*, 5th Edition. Toronto: James Lorimer.

Cowan, R. and M.F. Hoffman. 2007. "The Flexible

Organization: How Contemporary Employees Construct the Work/Life Border." *Qualitative Research Reports in Communication* 8(1), 37–44.

DeCew, J.W. 1997. *In Pursuit of Privacy: Law, Ethics, and the Rise of Technology.* Ithaca, NY: Cornell University Press.

Duxbury, L. and C. Higgins. 2001. "Work-Life Balance in the New Millennium: Where Are We? Where Do We Need to Go?" *Canadian Policy Research Networks Discussion Paper* W 12, http://www.cprn.org. Accessed 22 June 2009.

Dvorak, J.C. 2001. "The Group-Think Phenomenon." *PC Magazine* 20(12), 75.

Edwards, R.M. and B.H. Kleiner. 2002. "Conducting Effective and Legally Safe Background and Reference Checks." *Managerial Law* 44(1/2), 136–150.

Eos Life Work. 2007. "Managing the Life Work Boundary." http://www.eoslifework.co.uk/boundaries.htm. Accessed 23 June 2009.

Facebook. 2008. "More Privacy Options." http://blog.facebook.com/blog.php?post+11519877130. Accessed 11 Aug 2009.

Facebook. 2009a. "Facebook Factsheet." http://www.facebook.com/press/info.php?factsheet. Accessed 4 June 2009.

Facebook. 2009b. "Facebook Statistics." http://www.facebook.com/press/info.php?statistics. Accessed 4 June 2009.

Faleri, C. 2002. "Information Technology and Workers' Privacy: The Italian Law." *Comparative Labor Law and Policy Journal* 23(4), 399–430.

Filho, R.F. and J. Leonel de Rezende Alvim. 2002. "Information Technology and Workers' Privacy: The Brazilian Law." *Comparative Labor Law and Policy Journal* 23(4), 281–300.

Finkin, M.W. 2002. "Information Technology and Workers' Privacy: The United States Law." *Comparative Labor Law and Policy Journal* 23(4), 471–506.

Freeman, R.E. 1984. *Strategic Management: A Stakeholder Approach.* Marshfield, MA: Pitman Publishing Inc.

Friedman, M. 1962. *Capitalism and Freedom.* Chicago: University of Chicago Press.

Friendster. 2009. "About Friendster." http://www.friendster.com/info/index.php. Accessed 4 June 2009.

Gaudin, S. 2009. "Facebook Use Jumps—Thanks to Older Users." *Computerworld: Networking & Internet,* http://www.computerworld.com/action/article.do?command=viewArticleBasic&articleId=9129652. Accessed 20 June 2009.

Greenwald, J. 2008. "Web-Based Screening May Lead to Bias Suits." *Business Insurance* 42(1), 1–2.

Gregory, A. and S. Milner. 2009. "Trade Unions and Work-Life Balance: Changing Times in France and the UK?" *British Journal of Industrial Relations* 47(1), 122–146.

Grossman, H.A. 2005. "Refining the Role of the Corporation: The Impact of Corporate Social Responsibility on Shareholder Primacy Theory." *Deakin Law Review* 10(2), 572–596.

Hakala, D. 2008. "16 Ways to Encourage Work/Life Balance in Employees." http://www.hrworld.com/features/encourage-work-life-balance-041608/. Accessed 23 June 2009.

Harrington, J. 2009. July 24, "Facebook Ads with Your Photos—Steps to Stop." http://photobusinessforum.blogspot.com/2009/07/facebook-ads-with-your-photos-steps-to.html. Accessed 2 Aug 2009, from Photo Business News & Forum.

hi5.com. 2009. "About Us." http://www.hi5networks.com/aboutus.html. Accessed 20 June 2009.

Hrtools.com. 2008. "Social Networking Survey Results by One of Nation's Largest Employment Law Firms." http://www.hrtools.com/staffing/social_networking_survey_results_released_by_one_of_nations_largest_employment_law_firms.aspx. Accessed 8 June 2009.

Internetworldstats.com. 2009. "Internet Usage Statistics: The Internet Big Picture." http://www.internetworldstats.com/stats.htm. Accessed 20 June 2009.

Introna, L.D. 1997. "Privacy and the Computer: Why We Need Privacy in the Information Society." *Metaphilosophy* 28(3), 259–275.

Introna, L.D. and A. Pouloudi. 1999. "Privacy in the Information Age: Stakeholders, Interests and Values." *Journal of Business Ethics* 22(1), 27–38.

Jamali, D. 2008. "A Stakeholder Approach to Corporate Social Responsibility." *A Fresh Perspective into Theory and Practice* 82(1), 213–231.

Jeffery, M. 2002a. "Information Technology and Workers' Privacy: Introduction." *Comparative Labor Law and Policy Journal* 23(4), 251–280.

Jeffery, M. 2002b. "Information Technology and Workers' Privacy: The English Law." *Comparative Labor Law and Policy Journal* 23(4), 301–350.

Jensen, L.C. and S.A. Wygant. 1990. "The Developmental Self-Valuing Theory: A Practical Approach for Business Ethics." *Journal of Business Ethics* 9(3), 215–225.

Johnson, M. and A. Chadwick. 2009. "Today's Workplace Is About Flexibility." *Financial Executive* 25(3), 34–39.

Junger-Tas, J. and S.H. Decker. 2006. *International Handbook of Juvenile Justice* (Springer, Netherlands).

Kazeniac, A. 2009. "Social Networks: Facebook Takes Over Top Spot, Twitter Climbs." http://blog.compete.com/2009/02/09/facebook-myspace-twitter-social-network/. Accessed 4 June 2009.

Labott, E. 2009. "Officials: Social Networking Providing Crucial Info from Iran." http://www.cnn.com/2009/TECH/06/16/iran.twitter.facebook/index.html. Accessed 20 June 2009, from CNN.com/technology.

LaFerla, B. 2006. "Don't Tell Me to Shut Up." *IEE Engineering Management* December/January 2005/06, 1.

Livingstone, S. 2008. "Taking Risky Opportunities in Youthful Content Creation: Teenagers' Use of Social Networking Sites for Intimacy, Privacy and Self-Expression." *New Media & Society* 10(3), 393–411.

Manning, R.C. 1997. "Liberal and Communitarian Defenses of Workplace Privacy." *Journal of Business Ethics* 16(8), 817–823.

McClenahen, J.S. 2005. "Defining Social Responsibility: It's Much More than Good Works and Charities." www.industryweek.com. Accessed 19 Mar 2005.

McWilliams, A., D.S. Siegel and P.M. Wright. 2006. "Corporate Social Responsibility: Strategic Implications." *Journal of Management Studies* 43(1), 1–18.

Miller, S. and J. Weckert. 2000. "Privacy, the Workplace and the Internet." *Journal of Business Ethics* 28(3), 255–265.

Myatt, M. 2009. "Employer's Rights vs. Employee's Privacy." http://EzineArticles.com/?expert=Mike_Myatt. Accessed 23 June 2009.

New Media Consortium. 2007. "Social Networking, the "Third Place" and the Evolution of Communication." White Paper, http://www.nmc.org/pdf/Evolution-of-Communication.pdf. Accessed 4 June 2009.

New York Times. 2006. "Online Party Crashers." *The New York Times*, June 18, 2006 (Late Edition—Final), Section 4, Column 1, p. 11.

Noyes, K. 2009. "Facebook Hones Privacy Settings, Scraps Regional Networks." *TechNewsWorld*, http://www.technewsworld.com/story/68795.html. December 2, 2009. Accessed 15 Dec 2009.

Oblinger, D.G. and B.L. Hawkins. 2006. "The Myth about Putting Information Online." *Educause Review* September/October, 14–15.

Peacock, L. 2009, March 17. "Social Networking Sites Used to Check Out Job Applicants." http://www.personneltoday.com/articles/2009/03/17/49844/social-networking-sites-used-to-check-out-job-applicants.html. Accessed 8 June 2009, from Personneltoday.com.

Peluchette, J. and K. Karl. 2008. "Social Networking Profiles: An Examination of Student Attitudes Regarding Use and Appropriateness of Content." *CyberPsychology & Behavior* 11(1), 95–97.

Privacy. 2009. Merriam-Webster Online Dictionary. http://www.merriam-webster.com/dictionary/privacy, Accessed 30 Dec 2009.

Read, B. 2007. "Online." *Chronicle of Higher Education* 53(19), A31.

Reid, F.J.M. and D.J. Reid. 2004. "Text Appeal: The Psychology of SMS Texting and Its Implications for the Design of Mobile Phone Interfaces." *Campus-Wide Information Systems* 21(5), 196–200.

Reinhard, H.-J. 2002. "Information Technology and Workers' Privacy: The German Law." *Comparative Labor Law and Policy Journal* 23(4), 377–398.

Rifkin, G. 1991. "Do Employees Have a Right to Electronic Privacy?" *The New York Times*, December 8, 1991, Column 1, p. 8.

Rosenblum, M.F. 1991. "Security vs. Privacy: An Emerging Employment Dilemma." *Employee Relations Law Journal* 17(1), 81–101.

Samborn, H.V. 2007. "Go Google Yourself!" *ABA Journal* 93(8), 56–57.

Shaw, W.H. 2009. "Marxism, Business Ethics, and Corporate Social Responsibility." *Journal of Business Ethics* 84(4), 565–576.

Sherman, R. 2008. "Gen Y v. Boomers: Generational Differences in Communication." http://www.

fastcompany.com/blog/ruth-sherman/lip-service/gen-y-v-boomers-generational-differences-communication. Accessed 27 Feb 2009, from FastCompany.com.

Simms, M. 1994. "Defining Privacy in Employee Health Screening Cases: Ethical Ramifications Concerning the Employee/Employer Relationship." *Journal of Business Ethics* 13(5), 315–325.

Sprague, R. 2007. "Fired for Blogging: Are There Legal Protections for Employees Who Blog?" *University of Pennsylvania Journal of Labor and Employment Law* 9(2), 355–387.

Stross, R. 2007. "How to Lose Your Job on Your Own Time." *The New York Times*, December 20, 2007, http://www.nytimes.com/2007/12/30/business/30digi.html. Accessed 23 June 2009.

Sugarman, S.D. 2003. "Lifestyle Discrimination in Employment." *Berkeley Journal of Employment and Labor Law* 24(2), 377–438.

Thibodeau, P. 2008. "The Grill: Marc Rotenberg." *Computerworld*, Feb 18, 2008, 19–20.

Twitter.com. 2009. "About Twitter." https://twitter.com/about#about. Accessed 12 Aug 2009.

Van Den Haag, E. 1971. "On Privacy." *Nomos* 13, 147–153.

Van Steenbergen, E.F. and N. Ellemers. 2009. "Is Managing the Work-Family Interface Worthwhile?" *Journal of Organizational Behavior* 30(5), 617–642.

Vault.com. 2009. "Social Networking Web Site Survey." http://www.vault.com/surveys/social-networking/index.jsp. Accessed 8 June 2009.

Vigneau, C. 2002. "Information Technology and Workers' Privacy: The French Law." *Comparative Labor Law and Policy Journal* 23(4), 351–376.

Warren, S.D. and L.D. Brandeis. 1890. "The Right to Privacy." *Harvard Law Review* 4(5), 193–220.

Whyte, G. 1989. "Groupthink Reconsidered." *Academy of Management Review* 14(1), 40–56.

Wikipedia, 2009. "List of Social Networking Websites." http://wn.wikipedia.org/wiki/List_of_socialnetworking_websites. Accessed 4 June 2009.

Williams, C. 2010. *MGMT* 2009–2010 Edition (South-Western Cengage Learning, Mason, OH).

Wines, W.A. 2008. "Seven Pillars of Business Ethics: Toward a Comprehensive Framework." *Journal of Business Ethics* 79(4), 483–499.

Wolgemuth, L. 2008. "Stupid Computer Tricks." *U.S. News & World Report* 144(16), 67.

Zeidner, R. 2007. "How Deep Can You Probe?" *HR Magazine* 52(10), 57–60.

Questions

1. On what grounds do we have a right to privacy about information about us?
2. Does an expectation of privacy matter to whether it is morally acceptable for employers to access online sources of information about potential employees? Current employees?
3. Do you think the difference between self-presentation and self-disclosure is relevant to the moral issue?
4. "We contend that an employer would not ask a human-resources staff member to follow a job candidate to a local restaurant or bar and sit in the booth beside him or her for the purpose of overhearing conversations and witnessing behavior for a character check. As long as the job candidate is in a public place, the employer could legally do so, but for most this action would seem extreme and inappropriate. Why do we not have a similar reaction when the same behavior occurs online?" (para 29). What answers can you come up with to that question?
5. (a) What arguments do Clark and Roberts present to justify online character checks?
(b) Which argument do you consider to be the weakest (least convincing)? Why? (Be sure to consider any counterarguments presented.)

(c) Which argument do you consider to be the strongest (most convincing)? Why? (Be sure to consider any counterarguments presented.)
6. (a) What arguments do Clark and Roberts present to reject online character checks? (Consider each of the harms to society as a separate argument.)
(b) Which argument do you consider to be the weakest (least convincing)? Why? (Be sure to consider any counterarguments presented.)
(c) Which argument do you consider to be the strongest (most convincing)? Why? (Be sure to consider any counterarguments presented.)
7. What problems can you foresee with Bahls's and Charlesworth's recommendations? (Can you refine them to avoid those problems?)

Online Multiplayer Games: A Virtual Space for Intellectual Property Debates?[*]

Sara M. Grimes

Introduction

[1] With the continued proliferation of information and communication technologies (ICTs) and the increasing primacy of information in social systems as diverse as economics, health and even culture, the question of how the newly-digitized society will address and incorporate human rights has become a matter of global urgency. The emergent "internet culture" (Castells, 2001) has presented us with an opportunity to express and share a plural and extensive array of cultural products and artifacts. As long as the digital cultural landscape continues to escape the commodifying reach of the transnational corporate giants, the emergent world information society will retain its potential to include the voices of innumerable cultures, independent filmmakers, amateur animators, local musicians, artists and grassroots organizations. In stark contrast to previous media and technological innovations, the internet and other new ICTs provide users with access to both the means of cultural production (through software and programs that are easy to use and are relatively affordable or even free) and potential mass distribution (primarily through the world wide web). This enables new media users to partic-

---
[*] *New Media Society* 2006; 8; 969.

ipate—albeit in varying degrees—in the construction and evolution of online culture, through both the creation of content (such as websites or digital video clips) and their contributions to multi-user online environments (such as games or social networking sites).

[2] The fact remains, however, that the most popular websites, online environments and games are commercially owned and operated (Lastowka and Hunter, 2004; Nielson/Netratings, 2004), responding primarily (if not solely) to corporate and shareholder interests. Since the advent of the internet, a number of factors and developments have contributed to its encroachment by the growing online presence of transnational cultural industries and accompanying consumer discourses. As the rest of the globe slowly gains access to the technologies, conventions and interactions of the digitized society, corporate entities strive to establish themselves as the primary gatekeepers of cyberspace. Corporate fervor to dominate the internet is motivated by the very nature of digitization which, as Hamelink suggests,

> reinforces a social process in which the production and distribution of information evolves into the most important economic activity in a society, in which information technology begins to function as the key infrastructure for all industrial production and service provision and in which information itself becomes a commodity tradable on a global scale. (1995: 73)

At the center of this process lies the contentious issue of intellectual property and the expansionary forces of copyright laws—both in terms of their application and enforcement. In his comprehensive analysis of the growing influence of copyright on cultural production and distribution, Bettig (1996) argues that copyright and patent laws provide the legal grounding and support for the appropriation and commodification of an ever-expanding breadth of intellectual and artistic products. This is particularly true in the USA, for example, where the tendency for copyright laws to be monopolistic is amplified further by the oligopolistic nature of American cultural industries. Within global commercial culture, the US Government also plays an important role in the enactment and enforcement of copyright laws both nationally and abroad, resulting in the legitimization of 'the concentration of ownership of inventions, art and literature in the hands of the expanding capitalist class' (Bettig, 1996: 17).

The ideological foundations of existing copy- [3] right laws have been the topic of significant debate, as it is often argued that contemporary copyright systems are not operating according to the underlying principles or ideals of intellectual property—namely, to serve as a way of rewarding creators and inventors and encouraging them to share their works with the rest of society (Boyle, 1996). A number of crucial problems have been identified with the way in which copyright law is interpreted and enforced, many of which stem from the fact that its basic premises were formulated in the early stages of the Industrial Revolution. At that time, creative production was a far simpler process, often involving a single author and a single publishing house. However, in the early 21st century, many creative works involve the contribution and participation of a number of creators, sub-contractors and offshore production studios working in a post-Fordist system that has alienated many creators from "authorship" of the final product. As a result, Bettig argues, "Ownership of copyrights increasingly rests with the capitalists who have the machinery and capital to manufacture and distribute them" (1996: 7–8). Furthermore, as the international cultural environment becomes increasingly entangled within restrictive copyright systems, new ICTs are increasingly conceived and defined within the confines of the commercial framework.

[4] In conjunction with the broad commercialization of new media formats, increasing debate and controversy has arisen over the encroachment of corporate interests on the online activities of internet users. The fundamental conflict of interest that exists between the culture industries and internet users was first brought to public awareness in the late 1990s. An example of this is the music industry's highly publicized pursuit of legal actions to obstruct online file-sharing activities through popular programs such as Napster and KaZaa!, which led to widespread public debate and a number of important corporate and legal developments. More recently, media (Dibbell, 2003; Thompson, 2004) and academic (Lastowka and Hunter, 2004; Taylor, 2002) attention has shifted to the realm of online multiplayer games, a massively popular internet activity (Entertainment Software Association (ESA), 2004; Jones, 2003) at the center of numerous legal, economic and ethical debates that have the potential to impact significantly upon the future of the global information society.

[5] This article seeks to examine how online digital game players and creators are contributing to a shift in both contemporary notions about the nature and limits of intellectual property rights, as well as the growing relationship between virtual leisure activities and real-world economics. A brief overview of the debate as it has been portrayed in both academic literature and the popular press will provide the context for this analysis. The focus will then shift to an examination of the ways in which existing laws and widely accepted understandings about intellectual property are transforming to accommodate and incorporate the changing characteristics of new media technologies. The argumentation and theoretical perspective applied to this analysis draws from the political economy of communication framework formulated by Mosco (1996), and seeks to incorporate a Marxian analysis to the issues surrounding intellectual property within online games.

A Viable Market for Magic Wands?

[6] The concept of intellectual property—what it means, what it should include and how it should be articulated in legal documents and trade agreements—has remained an important point of contestation and debate since its first appearance in pre-Industrial England. Historically, "ideas" in themselves were considered beyond the scope of copyright and intellectual property law—at the turn of the 20th century, it was widely understood that ideas and facts were decisively part of the public domain (Boyle, 2002). In recent years, however, these "Long-standing limits on the reach of intellectual property—the anti-erosion walls around the public domain—[have been] eaten away" (Boyle, 2002: 15–16). Copyright and patent laws are continuously expanding to include "ideas" and "concepts" which, only 20 years ago, would have been considered outside the realm of intellectual property ownership, including recent campaigns in the USA to apply copyright to raw compilations of facts and data (through database rights, for example).

[7] With the continued global proliferation of digital ICTs, intellectual property debates have become increasingly heated. Much controversy has stemmed from the fact that digitization has drastically altered the nature of information, which now can be reproduced infinitely and distributed to "countless people simultaneously without mutual interference or destruction of the shared resource works" (Boyle, 2002: 17). The digital "commons" and intellectual properties of the 21st century are vastly different from the plots of land and printed texts that the

original definitions of property and copyright were intended to protect. As Vaidhyanathan (2001) argues, since copyright was fundamentally designed to regulate unauthorized "copying" of a work (not the audience's right to read or share works), new technologies have presented copyright policymakers with a difficult challenge. In essence, digitization has caused a collapse or merger between previously distinct activities, such as accessing, using and copying (Vaidhyanathan, 2001).

[8] Furthermore, ICTs and online cultural environments are highly interactive, calling for a level of participation and contribution from users and audiences that is much more active and involved than previously thought possible. Boyle (2004) highlights that one of the key challenges that ICTs present to the World Intellectual Property Organization (WIPO) is that intellectual property laws now have a much more direct impact upon individual citizens than they previously did. Whereas intellectual property rights were once primarily the "preserve of major industrial concerns," Boyle argues, the WIPO is now called upon to implement a "set of laws that regulate the citizen-publishers of cyberspace as well as protecting traditional publishers from competitors in the same industry" (2004: 4). However, while these two groups may be subject to the same laws, they do not always have access to the same legal knowledge and resources, nor do they benefit from the same level of representation within domestic and international councils (Boyle, 2004). Nonetheless, individuals are increasingly confronted with intellectual property issues and laws relating to personal privacy, freedom of expression and access to information and culture.

[9] It is, therefore, not surprising that users of new technologies are becoming concurrently entangled in legal disputes and ethical conflicts, in terms of the extent and nature of their participation in commercially-owned and operated programs, games and sites. Nowhere have the tensions between user and corporate interests more clearly manifested than within the realm of online gaming. Unlike the ongoing conflicts surrounding music file-sharing software (including Napster and KaZaa!), cases involving online multiplayer games (most often involving Massively Multiplayer Online Games [MMOGs] such as *EverQuest, SimsOnline* and *World of Warcraft*) illustrate how the interactive and collaborative nature of many internet applications problematizes traditional notions of authorship. Online multiplayer games consist of ongoing cultural productions, the result of the combined efforts and participation of both corporate employees (designers, programmers, customer support agents, etc.) and the games' players. The collaborative and often symbiotic aspects of these shared production processes are presenting new challenges to legal concepts such as intellectual property and ownership. The emerging debates have the potential both to significantly alter the structure of the internet and to redefine future articulations and treatments of intellectual property issues worldwide. Thus, while file-sharing cases may effectively demonstrate the conflict between corporate interests and the notion of a cultural commons, online multiplayer games present a unique venue for a critical investigation of how online environments and communities are redefining social conceptualizations of cultural work, digital copyright and intellectual property.

[10] Lastowka and Hunter (2004: 50) identify *Blacksnow Interactive v. Mythic Interactive* as the "first dispute over virtual property to make it to the real-world court system." The owners of Blacksnow Interactive had set up a "point-and-click sweatshop" in Tijuana, Mexico, where employees were paid a substandard hourly wage (under $3.74 per hour) to play the online multiplayer game *Dark*

Age of Camelot in order to build up characters and acquire rare (in-game) items to then sell to other players over the internet (Dibbell, 2003). When the game's developers, Mythic Interactive, found out about the outfit, they demanded that operations cease on the grounds that Blacksnow was infringing upon Mythic's intellectual property. Blacksnow responded with a countersuit, claiming that Mythic was engaging in "unfair business practices" and had their lawyer publicly state, "What it comes down to is, does a ... player have rights to his time, or does Mythic own that player's time?" ("Blacksnow Sues Mythic for Online Property Rights," 2002). Although the *Blacksnow Interactive v. Mythic Interactive* lawsuit was eventually dropped, early legal actions of this kind mark an important shift in both legal and public perceptions of the nature of virtual copyright and the problems spawned by the commercialization of online interaction and play.

[11] The conflict over virtual assets and intellectual property in the context of online games has not been limited to inter-corporation disputes. As Taylor (2002) describes, in 2000 Sony Entertainment secured the cooperation of popular online auction sites including eBay and Yahoo! in order to prevent *EverQuest* players from selling game characters and other in-game items for real-world profit. She explains, "Up until that time a sort of 'cottage industry' had sprung up in which users were turning their online labor into offline cash" (2002: 231). The online auction market for *EverQuest* goods, such as virtual armor, weapons, magic wands and even entire characters, had developed into a $5 million industry. Although Sony succeeded more or less in putting an end to *EverQuest* commerce on eBay and Yahoo!, the prohibition has been largely ineffective, as auctions and sales continue to flourish on less compliant, less traceable websites (Lastowka and Hunter, 2004), generating somewhere between US$200 and US$400 million a year in sales (Dibbell, 2003; Leupold, 2005).

[12] The reasons behind the heavy-handedness of the corporation's reaction to these activities are twofold, the most obvious being the real economic repercussions that unsanctioned trade can have on corporate profits. As Taylor argues, the main problem that companies have with allowing players to buy and sell their accounts and items is that "it short-circuits the economic model that is the lifeblood of many commercial virtual environments—subscriptions" (2002: 231). In order to participate effectively and "succeed" in these games, players must gain substantial "experience" through participation in quests and battles, each of which require a considerable amount of time and effort to complete. This process is bypassed significantly when items and "pre-leveled" characters (previously-played avatars with high levels of experience) can be simply bought in an auction, as the time usually required to attain the more desirable features of gameplay—as well as the accompanying subscription fees a player would pay while working towards those features—is removed from the equation. Since some items and "experience" levels can take months to acquire, the accumulative loss accrued can be substantial (Taylor, 2002). If players are able to bypass the amount of play-time typically required to earn an especially rare sword, for example, the incentive to dedicate extraneous subscription time toward the attainment of such a sword may be lost. If this practice becomes sufficiently widespread, the subscription-based economic model of many online games could be threatened—an outcome that some game developers are attempting to avoid by authorizing a more limited, company-run version of the player-auctions within the official game site, such as *Ultima Online*'s "Advanced Character Service" or *EverQuest* II's "Station Exchange," although players

are encouraged to use this service to purchase an "additional character on an existing account [or if the player is] already familiar with the development process" ("Support," 2004).

[13] The later part of *Ultima Online*'s recommendation highlights another important aspect of offline trade, namely the impact that "pre-leveling" or "by-passing" can have on the content and context of the game. In the case of *EverQuest*, for the implementation of a ban on offline auctioning to be effective, the game developers were required to commence regulating certain in-game practices which, when left to the discretion of the players, were used to conduct unsanctioned trade. The game owner's interest in preserving the game's structure also relates to issues of authorship, such as respecting the artistic expressions of the scriptwriters and programmers who developed the game software, or ensuring that control of the corporate image is maximized. The fact that offline sales of items bypass the rules of the game also has a potentially negative effect on other players, who may consider these practices unfair or disruptive and see their enjoyment of the game diminished as a result.

[14] The vested interests of the players and the corporate owners of games have provided sufficient justification for some states to intervene in cases of "unjust" game or play practices. In South Korea, for example, the police "actively prosecute people who hack into games and they give more weight to cases in which valuable game items are destroyed or transferred" (Castronova, 2003: 4). State involvement is rationalized by the fact that in-game assets take time to acquire or build, can be observably bought and sold on real-world markets and that players are manifestly distressed by the "unfair" loss or theft of their game items (Castronova, 2003). In a country where an online game, *Lineage*, was recently reported to be more popular than television (King, 2002), the growing influence of online gaming on social, economic and political life is unmistakable.

[15] However, it is argued that many of these disputes and developments can be traced to the fact that most online multiplayer games revolve around a common central theme—property-based economics. Lastowka and Hunter (2004) have identified a number of commonalities within online game structures that relate directly to commercial discourse, including exclusive ownership, the transfer of goods and a currency system to support (or even necessitate) trade. Even in those games set in the most fantastical of settings, such as the medieval, Tolkienesque worlds of *EverQuest* or among the anthropomorphized creatures of Neopia, the world of *Neopets* (www.neopets.com), gameplay incorporates a virtual economy that faithfully reproduces the western capitalist system (Lastowka and Hunter, 2004). Furthermore, the very design and layout of many online games often emphasizes or privileges commercial and economic features above other, extra-economic activities. In *Neopets*, for example, the primary activity of caring for a cyberpet (a virtual, online version of the Tamagotchi) necessitates a near-daily purchase of "food" and other goods in order to maintain the cyberpet's health and well-being. Without continuous participation in the commerce and trade systems of Neopets, players see their cyberpets wither away, starving from malnourishment and neglect.

[16] That online worlds conform to western capitalism and consumer ideology is not all that remarkable when one considers their place and function within predominantly American culture industries. As Lastowka and Hunter (2004) describe, the most popular online games are often those produced, owned and operated by private US-based corporations. However, what is surprising is the sheer volume of trade and commerce that takes place within virtual worlds through the actions

and interactions of the players themselves. The economies of some online games are so massive and refined that economists such as Castronova (2002) are able to analyze them using the same methods applied to the analysis of real national economies. Castronova calculates that the average hourly income of a character in *EverQuest* is $3.42, while the gross national product (GNP) of Norrath is estimated at around $135 million (Dibbell, 2003). Even in cases where virtual worlds start off with no property-based market system, it can be argued that the players themselves actively reproduce and impose capitalist economies onto the game environment through both their in-game and offline trade practices. Thus the question becomes whether these transactions are legitimate—are virtual assets truly equivalent to real-world commodities?

[17] Lastowka and Hunter (2004) suggest that by both descriptive and normative accounts, virtual property is the legal equivalent of real-world property. They argue that because the "development of Western property law and property systems over the last 200 years has been characterized by a shift from tangible to the intangible" (2004: 40), any objection to the legitimacy of virtual property based on its intangibility is unfounded. Furthermore, they conclude that virtual property is justified by three of the major accounts of property that have informed legal decision-making in the western world since the industrial era—Bentham's utilitarian theory, Locke's labor-desert theory and Hegel's personality theories. Their analysis shows that, in principle, all three theories support with qualification the claim that virtual entities and assets count as legitimate and real property. However, as Castronova points out, the results of this analysis do not confirm that virtual items must be treated as equivalent to real-world items—they simply show that "there are no prima facie grounds for dismissing the putative property rights of people who believe they own magic wands" (2003: 4).

[18] Yet the intellectual property debates taking place within the context of online gaming are resolved only partially by the conclusion that, theoretically, virtual assets can be understood as legitimate property. The more complex issue is that of ownership—the players' and industry's conflicting claims over who actually "owns" these assets and who should benefit from their real-world exchange value. Is the owner and operator of an online game also the owner of the characters and objects that the players spend months (perhaps even years) creating within the space of the game environment? Even among US legal experts, the world's leaders in stringent, corporate-driven copyright and intellectual property laws, opinions are divided when it comes to determining which party can rightfully claim ownership of avatars. On the one hand, players argue that their in-game characters and other virtual assets become their property through the amount of time, effort and creativity that they are required to put into them. On the other hand, the owners and authors of the games claim that because they own the software, as well as maintain and operate the sites and game designs, any activities that occur within the confines of the game fall under their legitimate copyright. Their claims are supported further by the existence of End-User License Agreements (EULAs; also called Terms of Service [TOS] and Terms of Use [TOU] contracts), which explicitly warn players that by agreeing to the terms of the site, they are in essence forfeiting their rights and any future claims of ownership or authorship. Both sides of this compelling conflict will now be examined, as the arguments presented by each represent important challenges to contemporary legal and social conceptualizations of intellectual property.

Player Interests versus Industry Interests

[19] While the subject of these conflicts, namely games and gameplay, may appear to be a somewhat playful and perhaps even trivial topic for such a heated dispute, Taylor (2002) maintains that with the advent of multiplayer capabilities, online games have become much more than "just a game." She argues that online games are also spaces in which individuals invest a significant amount of time congregating, occupying the virtual space, creating avatars, producing cultures and communities, sharing in leisure activities and reproducing economies. In terms of the characters and items that players acquire and create through the process of gameplay, Taylor writes that players are at the very least the collaborative authors (and hence partial owners) of any cultural artifacts that result from their efforts:

> It takes a player to create a character and it takes the time of the player to develop the character. Through their labor they imbue it with qualities, status, accomplishments. Indeed, while the owners of a game provide the raw materials through which users can participate in a space, it is in large part only through the labor of the players that dynamic identities and characters are created, that culture and community come to grow. (2002: 232)

The focus of this line of argument is on the meaning of culture and community, which require *collective* participation and formulation in order to produce shared and cohesive social meanings. If the average *EverQuest* or *World of Warcraft* player is dedicating 20 hours a week to the construction of a character and participation in the game community (Castronova, 2002), are they not entitled to some level of recognition for their roles as game "citizens" and productive members of the game society? Players contribute to various features of the gameplay not only through the creation of characters or avatars but also through the customization of items such as costumes, houses and weaponry. Part of what makes a game attractive to other players (and potential subscribers) is its ability to offer a well-developed social dynamic, a feature that would not exist without the continued efforts and participation of regular players. On the one hand, games such as *EverQuest* often use their large user-base (or population) as a key selling point in advertisements and press releases. On the other hand, online games that do not attract a minimum number of players often fail miserably, as the design and gameplay are dependent to a certain degree upon player interactions and contributions to make the game worthwhile.

A further, more explicit, way in which players [20] contribute to the construction of online game environments is through participatory design and market research. Kline et al. (2003) describe how the makers of the first-person shooter game *Doom* are able to exploit players' ideas and programming skills directly by releasing parts of the game's source code on the internet for players to modify and refine. In so doing, the company "turned every player into a potential programmer who could create his or her own levels of the game... opening an ever-expanding vista of worlds created by other players" (Kline et al., 2003: 204). As Postigo (2003) explains, the practice of modifying game code (also called "modding") operates essentially as a "gift economy" among hobbyist game programmers and hackers (known as "modders"). However, in appropriating the works of modders ("mods"), game companies convert these gifts into commodities, resulting in "the circumvention of the initial investment risk for the commercial developers as the development work is transferred to the fan base where costs are negligible" (Postigo, 2003: 597). From a labor theory approach, Postigo argues, modders add

> a considerable amount of value to commercial games, [contributing] six to twenty-four months of additional time, developing additions to the original code that can range from thousands to millions of lines of code and earn no salary for their work. (2003: 602)

While the exceptional case of "modders" lies somewhat beyond the scope of the current discussion of common player practices, the special role of "mods" within game development highlights how the game industry does recognize certain forms of unpaid labor put forth by players.

[21] Players' activities and interactions, both within and outside of the game world, have also provided inspiration for new product development and informed marketing strategies. The online game/community *There.com* (www.there.com) for example, used the organic commerce that cropped up from the *EverQuest* eBay auctions as a model for their own commercialized game design (Lastowka and Hunter, 2004). Children's game website *Neopets*, on the other hand, compiles and sells detailed youth market studies based on data collected from surveys, gameplay and the interactions that players contribute while participating in the site (Grimes and Shade, 2005). Although these types of practice are by no means limited to the world of online gaming, they remain highly relevant to the intellectual property debate, as the determination of authorship is crucial to any claim of ownership of intellectual or cultural products.

[22] In addition, digital games have attracted a significant online fan community, wherein fans (presumably players) of particular games create websites, form discussion groups and exchange game-related information and add-ons (Nutt and Railton, 2003). As with traditional media fan subcultures, the industry has tapped into this fan base for ideas and fostered further community development by hosting fan-generated websites and maintaining discussion forums. As Postigo explains, these fans add value to the games by contributing "large amounts of the content for these sites making them valuable resources for gamers, which serve as, amongst other things, a ready-made 'tech-support' group for other gamers" (2003: 595). In the case of *The Sims*, Nutt and Railton describe how the online fan community is encouraged by Electronic Arts (the game's production company) to produce "detailed and complex artworks and fictional narratives" (2003: 578) about their avatars and gameplay experiences. Rehak (2003) notes that the massive online fan base dedicated to video game heroine Lara Croft has played a significant role in the character's elevation from pixilated avatar to full-fledged virtual celebrity. Rehak also suggests that while a great deal of the online content dedicated to Lara Croft is "generated *by* fans, *for* fans," the majority is surprisingly "always in line with the interests of Eidos and Core Design" (2003: 489; emphasis in original).

[23] A similar set of producer–creator relationships is found within recent studies of online science fiction fan communities, such as Consalvo's (2003) examination of fan websites dedicated to the *Buffy the Vampire Slayer* and *Star Trek* television series. Traditionally, studies of fan subcultures and communities have tended to emphasize the "*interpretative* tension between popular culture's producers and consumers, who vie for authority over textual meanings" (Rehak, 2003: 482; emphasis in original). Fans of science fiction and fantasy television, for example, have continuously negotiated and reappropriated copyrighted media texts, characters and images in their production

of 'fan fiction," zines and artwork, often coming into direct conflict with television networks and producers (Bacon-Smith, 1992; Radway, 1984) in a practice that De Certeau (1984) and Jenkins (1992) term "textual poaching." As Consalvo (2003: 74) describes, within the context of the internet, fan communities have discovered a "preeminent publishing opportunity" to reach a potentially international audience, as well as greater access to media texts and materials for creative appropriation. In response, television networks and producers have threatened many fan-sites with lawsuits, often resulting in the removal of unauthorized materials and the closure of a number of offending sites. In the case of *Buffy the Vampire Slayer*, the Warner Brothers network attempted to incorporate fan activities by offering fans a space for their sites on the network server and granting them access to a limited selection of officially sanctioned images and content (Consalvo, 2003). Consalvo (2003: 76) suggests, however, that while fans' online activities challenge the centrality of corporate ownership, the "corporate-produced media product" remains the focal point or nexus of most fan activities. Thus, while fan communities may be engaged in a type of conflict or negotiation with media producers, the producers have the distinct advantage based on their greater level of control over the content and availability of the media texts.

[24] The discussion of authorship and intellectual property within online games is compounded by the "peculiar characteristics" of virtual assets and game environments (Lastowka and Hunter, 2004). After all, no matter how vividly players identify with their avatars or treasure their special, customized swords, the swords, chairs, princesses and dungeons of *EverQuest* are first and foremost the manifestations of strings and strings of code. As Stephens (2002) argues, virtual "assets" are entries in a database which resides on a server, which transmits data to the player's computer monitor, which then displays one of a finite number of possible images already programmed into the software. Although opportunities for user-customization are becoming increasingly intricate and frequent, many of the current "player creations" are simply an amalgamation of choices made from a limited selection of possible characteristics. In fact, the decisions about what options are included, how many and where these selections and other set features of the gameplay appear, are made and implemented by the game designers and developers.

[25] The Entertainment Software Association (ESA), a digital game trade association, reports that the digital games industry directly employs 90,000 workers, many of which are in highly skilled positions (Kline et al., 2003). Game development is "a synthesis of narrative, aesthetic and technological skills to conceive, plot and program virtual worlds, deploying the combined expertise of digital coders, graphics designers, software testers, scriptwriters, animators, sound technicians and musicians" (Kline et al., 2003: 199). Production, which is often done in studios by teams of six to 50, can take up to two years to complete, with many projects cancelled or thrown out before completion (Kline et al., 2003). Although players may claim that their actions and interactions are what make a game enjoyable, it is apparent that the game parameters and the structure of the content are both imagined and realized through the work, knowledge and artistry of its creators. The collaborative nature of the authorship of games is also hard to dispute, although player contributions may be quite minimal when compared to the combined, highly skilled labor of the design and development teams.

[26] At the center of the industry's claim to intellectual property ownership is the controversial issue of EULAs. EULAs are virtual contracts that players must agree to before entering a game environment,

by clicking an affirmation that they have read and accepted the terms and conditions outlined in the EULA. By clicking, the user agrees to waive a number of significant rights, such as the "rights to own the fruits of labor, rights to assemble, rights to free speech" (Castronova, 2003: 8). For example, Blizzard Entertainment Inc.'s Terms of Use (2003–2006) agreement for *World of Warcraft* includes the following stipulations:

> All title, ownership rights and intellectual property rights in and to World of Warcraft (including without limitation any user accounts, titles, computer code, themes, objects, characters, character names, stories, dialogue, catch phrases, locations, concepts, artwork, animations, sounds, musical compositions, audio-visual effects, methods of operation, moral rights, any related documentation, "applets" incorporated into World of Warcraft, transcripts of the chat rooms, character profile information, recordings of games played on World of Warcraft, and the World of Warcraft client and server software) are owned by Blizzard Entertainment or its licensors.

Miller (2003) supports the legitimacy of these claims to complete ownership and suggests that the eventual allocation of property rights will depend largely on EULAs, as per the terms demarcated within them. Furthermore, the fact remains that online game spaces are not only private and explicitly profit-driven, but users willingly accept these terms and conditions when they voluntarily agree to the EULA (Taylor, 2002).

[27] However, other scholars and economists argue that it remains unclear whether the EULAs in their current form will prove strong enough to survive the growing challenge posed by players and other opposing parties (Castronova, 2003; Lastowka and Hunter, 2004). Castronova argues that game owners cannot prevent fair and equal treatment of individuals and virtual property just because they have a EULA that says so. He writes: "Synthetic worlds are being treated as special cases, but no law has defined when and how this special treatment should apply" (2003: 9). Lastowka and Hunter also conclude that as more people come to inhabit "virtual worlds," users will seek to protect the fundamental rights that EULAs currently contract away. Furthermore, it is likely that a large number of suits will be filed as users attempt to circumvent or attack EULA restrictions in pursuit of profit and other economic incentives (Lastowka and Hunter, 2004). On the other hand, game owners and producers might anticipate an eventual shift in players' acceptance of EULA terms and modify their approach. For example, during a 2003 conference on legal issues in online gaming (called "State of Play," held by the New York Law School), Linden Lab announced that it was changing the TOS for its online multiplayer game *Second Life*, and granting players full intellectual property ownership of any in-game content that they created, "including characters, clothing, scripts, textures and objects" (Calvert, 2003: 1). As the debate over EULAs and intellectual property in online multiplayer gaming gains prominence within public discourse, it is possible that other companies will either follow Linden Lab's example, or devise alternative strategies for accommodating player demands.

Play versus Labor

While players' claims to intellectual property necessarily imply a concurrent claim of (at least partial) authorship, the exact extent and nature of the "work" that they contribute remains ambiguous and largely undocumented. Although participation in online multiplayer games is voluntary and presumably motivated by the pursuit of leisure [28] and fun, the intellectual property debates seem to have resulted in a confusion or loss of distinction between the concepts of *labor* and *play*. For example, Taylor (2002) argues for the development of broader social conceptualizations of cultural production and ownership, as well as the recognition of collective authorship that includes the contributions of the players. This perspective is supported in part by Terranova, who contends that the "acknowledgement of the collective aspect of labor implies a rejection of the equivalence between labor and employment.... Labor is not equivalent to waged labor" (2000: 14). This confusion of play with work is a reversal of McRobbie's (2002) notion of the "cultural turn," wherein both society and the economy are seen as increasingly assuming a cultural dimension. Here, it is culture that is seen to be assuming additional social and especially economic characteristics.

[29] By equating play activities with work (and all the rights and claims that accompany the role of worker), the real labor of the programmers who create the software and the factory workers who assemble the hardware becomes lost in translation. As Willis suggests, "the abstraction of labor... is not something we as consumers can directly grasp, rather it enters our daily life experience as the inability to apprehend fully or even imagine non-fetishized use values" (2001: 338). Within the context of online gaming, the resulting confusion may be caused at least partially by the digital game industry's own attempts to blur the boundaries between work and play within media and public relations campaigns. Within media discourse, as Kline et al. describe,

> making games is itself shown as play—work as fun... so that not only consuming games but also producing them is represented as a continuum of endless fun [which] is a part of the interactive game industry's hip self-image. (2003: 197)

[30] In reality, the labor that goes into digital game production spans across many years and several continents. In addition to the intense work ethic of predominantly male game development companies and the immense creativity essential to high-quality software development, digital games are also the product of the painstaking efforts of a primarily female labor force that constructs game consoles and cartridges within the enterprise zones of the developing world. Underpaid and working in arduous conditions, the young women who assemble semiconductors and other components of game hardware are often "subjected to ferocious work discipline under conditions that destroy health within a matter of years" (Kline et al., 2003: 205). While players often associate their contributions and participation in online multiplayer games with the labor performed by game designers and programmers, little mention is made of the more explicitly laborious, manual work that goes into manufacturing game hardware. Although the crux of the players' argument lies in demonstrating how gameplay can be experienced and understood as a form of cultural work, this oversight is relevant in that it demonstrates a fairly limited and highly particular interpretation of labor and labor processes. The position that voluntary, leisure-driven activities should be seen as a type of labor—while crucial elements of game and information communication technology (ICT) production remain ignored and unrecognized—thus jeopardizes our ability to comprehend fully the multifaceted and often abstracted labor processes involved in the global digital game industry.

[31] However, it is not only our understanding of "labor" that is at risk here but also our notion of play. A number of the leading theorists in this area (Castronova, 2003; Lastowka and Hunter, 2004; Taylor, 2002) argue that ultimately, the possibility of an economic valuation of play will depend

on whether online multiplayer games are granted the legal status of either a "game" or "not game." In a widely-cited definition of the term "game," Huizinga (1950[1938]) suggests that the key criteria that an activity must meet in order to be considered as a game is that it has no moral consequence. As Castronova explains, "Whatever is happening, if it really matters in an ethical or moral sense, it cannot be a game. Rather, games are place [sic] where we only *act* as if something matters" (2003: 2; emphasis in original). Taylor suggests that within the context of games such as *EverQuest* and *SimsOnline,* where the game has certainly come to matter a great deal for members involved in intellectual property disputes, the environments are described more accurately as "dynamic communities" than simple games. For Taylor, the unique characteristics of multiplayer online games have transformed gameplay itself into just "one of many activities users engage in and play is in turn made up of a complicated mix of social and instrumental actions" (2002: 228). There are numerous examples of "offline" games that are viewed in a similar manner and accepted as important social and political events, including the Olympic Games and a number of large-scale spectator sports. Castronova observes that games produce real moral and tangible consequences as the result of a "self-confirming social consensus: if all society says that the World Series matters, then it does" (2003: 3). It is through society's shared agreement that certain games (such as the Olympics or the Stanley Cup) are important and meaningful that the consequences of these games come to be understood as serious and relevant.

[32] On the one hand, if it is decided that online games are not merely "games," then these online spaces are not only important sites of social and cultural activity but must also answer to real-world laws and state intervention. On the other hand, if online games are defined legally as "games," while they may remain important sites of social and cultural activity, they will operate outside the confines of the law and real-world economics (Castronova, 2003). Castronova further warns that the more real-world meaning permeates online play spaces, the more likely it is that their status as games will erode and that they will be opened to the laws, expectations and norms of capitalist society. He calls instead for the preservation of play spaces as a fundamental human right. The right to play, to a cultural life and leisure activities, he argues, is addressed implicitly within two separate articles of the Universal Declaration of Human Rights, Article 27 ("Everyone has the right freely to participate in the cultural life of the community, to enjoy the arts and to share in scientific advancement and its benefits") and Article 24 ("Everyone has the right to rest and leisure"). By allowing economic imperatives to encroach upon the newly-formed play spaces of online multiplayer games, we risk our greater—and arguably more important—rights to enjoyment, leisure and escape from the broad commercialization of the outside world.

[33] Although the right to play may be recognized as fundamental by scholars such as Castronova, its articulation remains absent from the various trade agreements and laws that currently regulate global commerce and ICTs. Although EULAs may be interpreted as "contracts that restrict the ability of individuals to erode the play-ness of the space" (Castronova, 2003: 10), in order for a declaration of "play space" to be effective and just, first it must be formulated and regulated by government. In addition, for a play space to retain its special status as a "game," it would have to "maintain strict separation of its economy from the economy of the outside world" (Castronova, 2003: 12). Although Castronova's "call to action" may be both idealistic and naive given the current political and eco-

nomic climate that pervades the western world, it is useful nonetheless in considering how play might be defined and preserved, as well as envisioning a viable (although perhaps unlikely) alternative to the current commercial model.

Use Value versus Exchange Value

[34] The online gaming debates can also be understood in terms of Marx's theory of the use-value–exchange-value relationship. As Jhally (1987: 27) suggests, "The relation between use value and exchange value is central to Marx's concept of the fetishism of commodities." Mosco (1996) defines the process of commodification as follows: use-value is determined by a product's ability to meet individual and social needs, whereas exchange-value is determined by what a product can bring to the marketplace. Commodification occurs when use-value is transformed into exchange-value. In Marx's discussion of this relationship, he describes use-value as ultimately subordinate to exchange-value—that the true disjuncture of "commodity flows" is how the exchange-values of commodities seem to "have value inherent in them when in fact value is produced by humans" (Jhally, 1987: 29). For Marx, commodities are the "embodiment of human labor in the abstract" (Willis, 2001: 338) and therefore the only way to undermine the fetishism of commodities is to understand the process of exchange-value and reclaim human labor. In discussing the intellectual property in online gaming debates within a Marxian context, it becomes clear that both players and industry are contributing to the same commodifying process and that the resulting confusion between play and labor is understood better as a confusion of use-value and exchange-value.

[35] Although this line of argumentation may seem to support the players' claims to collaborative authorship and limited ownership, Willis (2001) emphasizes the dialectical role of use-value which—although it often goes unnoticed and unidentified—is recovered in "daily-life social practices" and the individual ways that we appropriate, use and understand commodities and goods. In the context of online games, use-value might be seen as the value which players derive from experiencing the many facets of the game environment, from the enjoyment and effort put into acquiring a new item, even from finding ways to cheat or break the rules of the game. However, the arguments supporting the players' claim of ownership over their in-game contributions position use-value as a justification for (as opposed to resistance to) further commodification. For example, in her study of *EverQuest* players, Taylor (2002) describes how one respondent perceives her game avatar as a personal "creation" or "product"—imbued with the meanings and personality traits that she has bestowed upon it. By interpreting gameplay and in-game interaction (use-value) as a form of cultural *labor* and by claiming ownership over the fetishized cultural artifact (exchange-value), the players commodify their own gaming experience. While the players have become aware of the exchange-value of their participation, however, it seems that use-value has remained unaccounted for within the intellectual property debates of online games.

[36] Of course, the players' use-value is also commodified by the game owners, who use the players' pleasure, personal investment and social gratification to compel them to continue to purchase monthly subscriptions and software upgrades. The possibility for players to participate in the creation of a gaming experience and storyline is also a key selling point of online multiplayer games. This trait is reflective of a greater trend that pervades the cultural economy, particularly in

relation to digital media formats such as the internet. As Terranova argues, "the internet is about the extraction of value out of continuous, updateable work and it is extremely labor intensive. It is not enough to produce a good Web site, you need to update it continuously" (2000: 16). Thus, it would seem that the very aspects that allow players to reclaim the use-value of online games, such as high levels of interactivity and the opportunity to play and communicate with other players, are often the same features that make online games a profitable market commodity.

[37] In many ways, this discussion is reminiscent of Smythe's (1981) treatise on the television audience-as-commodity proposed 25 years ago. Smythe describes the audience's relationship and interaction with the media as a continuum, which departs from the audience's entertainment and eventually becomes an advertiser's commodity. He writes:

> In economic terms, the audience commodity is a non-durable producers' good which is bought and used in the marketing of the advertiser's product. The work which audience members perform for the advertiser to whom they have been sold is learning to buy goods and to spend their income accordingly.... In short, they work to create the demand for advertised goods which is the purpose of the monopoly-capitalist advertisers. (1981: 222)

Perhaps the relationship between players and the game industry can be described in similar terms. The players' participation in online gaming is commodified and marketed as both a paid-for leisure experience (through gameplay) and as a key selling point of the games themselves (as a community of other players). Through these processes, the "audience" and "audience commodity" are created. Thus within the narrative and aesthetic frameworks of the game designs, as well as the commercial frameworks constructed by the presence of EULAs, the players' gameplay (or unpaid labor) is channeled through a commodifying economic lens. Through their shared interpretation of the gameplay experience and the products of gameplay as potential intellectual property, both the players and the game owners engaged in the current debate legitimate and contribute to the commodification of the players' participation.

Conclusion

[38] In seeking to explore online gaming as a potential space for the evolution of concepts of intellectual property and cultural ownership, this article has attempted to include the arguments and perspectives of two main perspectives that seem to predominate in the conflict and surrounding debates. The recent developments examined herein, in conjunction with the growing visibility of this topic throughout academic and legal discourse, are evidence of its significance to changing social and legal conceptualizations of intellectual property and virtual assets. However, although players may eventually contribute in meaningful ways to new formulations of intellectual property, they remain highly disadvantaged in their fight for ownership rights. The corporate game owners have access to a plethora of resources that individual players do not, including the financial means to delay legal proceedings and settle disputes out of court, or simply ban the player from the game altogether. As Taylor suggests, "The battle over user autonomy would not be nearly as worrisome if users were operating on a level playing field with the corporate owners they are wrangling with" (2002: 233). Although the outcome of this conflict remains to be seen, it is important to remember the superior vantage

point from which the corporations are operating and their subsequent role in a decision-making process which, ultimately, could affect all current and future users of ICTs. However, the more significant threat to players' rights and enjoyment of online gaming activities is the lack of a truly oppositional perspective within this debate. While the players and game owners compete for the right to claim ownership over game content, an alternative to the continued expansion of intellectual property laws across cultural forms and forums has yet to be adequately articulated. While Castronova's (2003) "right to play" argument offers an interesting starting point for thinking about this issue from a human rights perspective, the proposition that games could exist beyond the scope of law or commerce is problematic at best. Meanwhile, player resistance to the corporate appropriation of online game culture has consisted of little other than the internalization and legitimization of the processes of commodification. It thus seems that there is only limited space within capitalist discourse to seriously consider extra-economic, non-commodified use-value as an important and valid aspect of daily social life. Taking a Marxian perspective, which argues that use-value is made subordinate to exchange-value within the capitalist system, it is likely that as long as no other recourse is available to them, players will continue to participate in their own commodification. While online games may present an interesting and compelling forum for discussions on the future of intellectual property and virtual assets, as well as how ownership and authorship are to be determined, the debate thus far has been limited severely by the commercial context from which it stems. As the current discourse operates primarily within the confines of this framework of commodification, both the players and the online gaming industry can be seen as promoting the extension of intellectual property to emerging forms of virtual leisure, as well as confirming the pre-eminence of exchange-value in online play.

Acknowledgements

The study was funded by the Social Sciences and Humanities Research Council of Canada (SSHRC). The author would like to thank Yuezhi Zhao, Andrew Feenberg, Anil Narine and the anonymous reviewers for the valuable comments and feedback.

References

Bacon-Smith, C. (1992) *Enterprising Women: Television Fandom and the Creation of Popular Myth*. Philadelphia, PA: University of Pennsylvania Press.

Bettig, R.V. (1996) *Copyrighting Culture: The Political Economy of Intellectual Property*. Boulder, CO: Westview Press.

'Blacksnow Sues Mythic for Online Property Rights' (2002) Kanga.Nu: MUD Development Thread. 6 February–2 March, URL (consulted January 2004): http://www.kanga.nu/archives/MUD-Dev-L/2002Q1/msg00362.php

Boyle, J. (1996) *Shamans, Software, and Spleens. Law and the Construction of the Information Society*. Cambridge, MA: Harvard University Press.

Boyle, J. (2002) 'Fencing Off Ideas: Enclosure and the Disappearance of the Public Domain', *Daedalus* (spring): 13–25.

Boyle, J. (2004) 'A Manifesto on WIPO and the Future of Intellectual Property', *Duke Law & Technology Review* 9, 8 September, URL (consulted October 2004): http://www.law.duke.edu/journals/dltr/articles/PDF/2004DLTR0009.pdf

Calvert, J. (2003) 'Second Lifers Get Intellectual Property Rights', *GameSpot*, 14 November, URL (consulted March 2004): http://www.gamespot.com/pc/rpg/secondlife/news_6083556.html

Castells, M. (2001) *Internet Galaxy*. Oxford: Oxford University Press.

Castronova, E. (2002) 'Virtual Worlds: A First-hand Account of Market and Society on the Cyberian Frontier', CESIfo Working Paper No. 618, URL (consulted December 2003): http://papers.ssrn.com/abstract = 294828

Castronova, E. (2003) 'The Right to Play', paper presented at the State of Play Conference, New York Law School, 13–14 November, URL (consulted January 2004): http://www.nyls.edu/docs/castronova.pdf

Consalvo M. (2003) 'Cyber-slaying Media Fans: Code, Digital Poaching and Corporate Control of the Internet', *Journal of Communication Inquiry* 27(1): 67–86.

Dibbell, J. (2003) 'The Unreal Estate Boom', *Wired* 11(1), URL (consulted January 2004): http://www.wired.com/wired/archive/11.01/gaming.html

Entertainment Software Association (ESA) (2004) 'Americans Playing More Games, Watching Less Movies and Television', press release, 12 May, URL (consulted October 2004): http://www.theesa.com/5_12_2004.html

Grimes, S.M. and L.R. Shade (2005) 'Neopian Economics of Play: Children's Cyberpets and Online Communities as Immersive Advertising in Neopets.com', *International Journal of Media and Cultural Politics* 1(2): 181–98.

Hamelink, C. (1995) *World Communication: Disempowerment and Self-Empowerment*. London: Zed Books.

Huizinga, J. (1938/1950) *Homo Ludens*. Boston, MA: Beacon Press.

Jenkins, H. (1992) *Textual Poachers: Television Fans and Participatory Culture*. New York: Routledge.

Jhally, S. (1987) *The Codes of Advertising: Fetishism and the Political Economy of Meaning in the Consumer Society*. London: Routledge.

Jones, S. (2003) 'Let the Games Begin: Gaming Technology and Entertainment Among College Students', Report, Pew Internet & American Life Project, 6 July, URL (consulted June 2004): http://www.pewInternet.org/pdfs/PIP_College_Gaming_Reporta.pdf

King, B. (2002) 'Online Games Go Multicultural', *Wired*, 30 January, URL (January 2004): http://www.wired.com/news/games/0,2101,50000,00.html

Kline, S., N. Dyer-Witheford and G. de Peuter (2003) *Digital Play: The Interaction of Technology, Culture and Marketing*. Montreal: McGill-Queen's University Press.

Lastowka, F.G. and D. Hunter (2004) 'The Laws of the Virtual Worlds', *California Law Review* 92(1): 3–73.

Leupold, T. (2005) 'Spot On: Virtual Economies Break Out of Cyberspace', *Gamespot News*, 6 May. URL (consulted May 2005): http://www.gamespot.com/news/2005/05/06/news_6123701.html

McRobbie, A. (2002) 'From Holloway to Hollywood: Happiness at Work in the New Cultural Economy?', in P. Du Gay and M. Pryke (eds) *Cultural Economy: Cultural Analysis and Commercial Life*, pp. 97–114. Thousand Oaks, CA: Sage.

Miller, D.C. (2003) 'Determining Ownership in Virtual Worlds: Copyright and License Agreements', *Review of Litigation* 22(2): 435.

Mosco, V. (1996) *The Political Economy of Communication: Rethinking and Renewal*. London: Sage.

Nielsen/Netratings (2004) 'Online Games Claim Stickiest Web Sites', press release, 16 June, URL (consulted September 2004): http://direct.www.nielsen-netratings.com/pr/pr_040616.pdf

Nutt, D. and D. Railton (2003) 'The Sims: Real Life as Genre', *Information, Communication & Society* 6(4): 577–92.

Postigo, J. (2003) 'From Pong to Planet Quake: Post-industrial Transitions from Leisure to Work', *Information, Communication & Society* 6(4): 593–607.

Radway, J. (1984) *Reading the Romance: Women, Patriarchy and Popular Literature*. Chapel Hill, NC: University of North Carolina Press.

Rehak, B. (2003) 'Mapping the Bit Girl: Lara Croft and New Media Fandom', *Information, Communication & Society* 6(4): 477–96.

Smythe, D.W. (1981) *Dependency Road: Communications, Capitalism, Consciousness and Canada*. Norwood, NJ: Ablex.

Stephens, M. (2002) 'Sales of In-game Assets: An Illustration of the Continuing Failure of Intellectual Property Law to Protect Digital-content Creators', *Texas Law Review* 80(6): 1513–15.

'Support' (2004) *Ultima Online*, Entertainment Arts (EA), URL (consulted October 2004): http://support.uo.com/advancedcharacter.html

Taylor, T.L. (2002) 'Whose Game Is This Anyway? Negotiating Corporate Ownership in a Virtual World', in F. Mäyrä (ed.) *Proceedings of Computer Games and Digital Cultures Conference*, URL (consulted May 2003): http://social.chass.ncsu.edu/~ttaylor/papers/Taylor-CGDC.pdf

Terranova, T. (2000) 'Free Labor: Producing Culture for the Digital Economy', *Social Text* 18(2): 33–58.

Thompson, C. (2004) 'Game Theories', *Walrus* 1(5): 38–47.

Vaidhyanathan, S. (2001) *Copyrights and Copywrongs: The Rise of Intellectual Property and How it Threatens Creativity.* New York: New York University Press.

Willis, S. (2001) 'Unwrapping Use Value', in M.G. Durham and D.M. Kellner (eds) *Media and Cultural Studies: Key Works*, pp. 334–50. Malden, MA: Blackwell Publishing.

'World of Warcraft® Terms of Use Agreement' (2003–2006) Blizzard Entertainment Inc. URL (consulted September 2006): http://www.worldofwarcraft.com/legal/termsofuse.html

Questions

1. According to Grimes, what makes intellectual property debates regarding online multi-player gaming different from those regarding file sharing?
2. Should (ethically speaking) eBay and the others have agreed to Sony's request that they prevent the sale of *EverQuest* goods? Why/why not? (Is it different from buying a CD of piano pieces to listen to instead of spending the time, and paying for lessons, to learn to play them yourself?)
3. After reading and carefully considering the arguments presented, who do you think owns the virtual property of online gaming—the players and/or the game owners/authors?
4. If you're a game player, do an ethical assessment of the End-user License Agreement you signed. That is, do you think the terms to which you agreed are *ethically* acceptable? For the terms you consider ethically *un*acceptable, can you justify them from the point of view of the game's owners/authors? Are those justifications on ethical grounds or some other grounds?
5. Is there an ethically significant difference between work and play?

Case Study: Canipre: Hero or Villain?

Montreal-based Canipre (Canadian Intellectual Property Rights Enforcement) is a private anti-piracy firm that uses online technologies to "identify, monitor, collect, validate, and manage data harvested from across file sharing portals and traditional web based platforms" (Canipre website). Then, "Working on behalf of rights holders, Canipre provides 'Notice' programs, a robust content take-down service, and forensic data arising from unauthorized file sharing" which can then "support legal remedy on behalf of [their] clients."

The firm markets to film studios and distributors, independent film producers, software publishers, music composers or publishers, television content producers, entertainment and intellectual property lawyers, specialty software developers, Canadian rights holders, brand-protection executives, and specialty content broadcasters, including live-stream sporting events. And it currently has files on over a million Canadians who have been illegally downloading copyrighted material and/or engaging in peer-to-peer file-sharing (see Huffington Post Canada).

The International Intellectual Property Alliance (IIPA) refers to Canada's "reputation as a haven for technologically sophisticated international piracy operations" (report available via the Canipre site) and recommends we stay on their watch list. Estimates of losses due to music file sharing in Canada are $250 million (2003–06, estimate by CIRPA, the Canadian Recording Industry Association, per CBC News), $1.4 billion due to PC software theft (2011, report available at Canipre site), and $1.8 billion due to movie piracy (2009–10, report available at Canipre site). The last-mentioned figure is reported to be the equivalent to the loss of 12,600 full-time jobs and $294 million in taxes. (But see the Geist article.) Barry Logan, Canipre's Director, "wants piracy to become a taboo, much like drinking-and-driving is now.... That's (not) the attitude here in Canada: it's a pervasive sense of entitlement" (The Canadian Press).

Canipre's evidence was the basis of a recent (February 2014) groundbreaking decision by the Federal Court of Canada: TekSavvy Solutions, Inc., a Toronto-based ISP, was ordered to release to Voltage Pictures the names and addresses of over 2,000 subscribers suspected of pirating Voltage movies. Voicing opposition to the court proceedings, the Canadian Internet Policy and Public Interest Clinic (CIPPIC) argued that "privacy considerations and broader interests of justice should prevail" (Shaw); the CIPPIC also referred to Canipre as a "copyright troll," deriding their methods.

What are Canipre's methods? Their "Notice" program involves "speculative invoicing"—sending letters to people suspected of making illegal downloads (a single IP address may have several users, hence the "suspected" part), asking them to pay a specified amount in restitution or risk a lawsuit. CIPPIC accused Canipre of intimidation and threat: "[T]he cost and the uncertainty or stigma of litigation coerces most individuals into making payments, whether or not they were involved in the unauthorized copying and distribution of films on the Internet" (Shaw).

References

The Canadian Press. "Effort afoot in court to sue Canadians for illegal downloads." The Canadian Press. 12 May 2013. http://www.macleans.ca/news/effort-afoot-in-court-to-sue-canadians-for-illegal-downloads-2/

Canipre website. http://canipre.com

CBC News. "Downloading Music." 1 May 2006. http://www.cbc.ca/news2/background/internet/downloading_music.html

Geist, Michael. "Piercing the peer-to-peer myths: An examination of the Canadian Experience." Michael Geist. 1 May 2005. http://www.michael-geist.ca/2005/05/piercing-the-peer-to-peer-myths-an-examination-of-the-canadian-experience/

Huffington Post Canada. "File-Sharing Lawsuits Canada: Canipre, Copyright Group, Accused of Stealing Photos." 15 May 2013. http://www.huffingtonpost.ca/2013/05/15/canipre-file-sharing-copyright-_n_3280523.html

Shaw, Gillian. "Illegal downloaders in federal court's crosshairs." *Vancouver Sun* 20 Feb. 2014. http://www.vancouversun.com/technology/personal-tech/Illegal+downloaders+federal+court+crosshairs/9533007/story.html

Questions

1. Wikipedia defines a copyright troll as "a party that enforces copyrights it owns for purposes of making money through litigation, in a manner considered unduly aggressive or opportunistic, generally without producing or licensing the works it owns for paid distribution" (http://en.wikipedia.org/wiki/Copyright_troll). So was the CIPPIC claim accurate?
2. Is Canipre's "speculative invoicing" the best way to go about copyright enforcement? The most ethical way? Would it be better to first send notice of copyright infringement, simply asking the person to cease and desist? Is it plausible that the person is unaware or mistaken about what they're doing? And *then* one could follow up with what is essentially an offer to settle out of court, making the settlement less than $5,000, the maximum fine, as set by Canada's Bill C-11 for non-commercial copyright infringement.
3. Is Canipre doing the right thing in enforcing copyright law? That is, (a) is it a good law? (Must people *pay* for everything?) And (b) should private firms get into the business of law enforcement?

CHAPTER TEN

Business and Our Environment

What to Do?—Canadian Natural Resources, Inc.

It is 2025. And as the International Water Management Institute projected back in 1999, a billion people are living in countries facing absolute water scarcity. Water tables have fallen on every continent; major rivers run dry for part of every year, a longer part each year. (Once a train flies off a cliff, which happened in 2017—Big Oil was at the wheel—there's not much you can do to reverse its course.)

You are the CEO of Canadian Natural Resources, Inc. (True to form, Canada has neither completely privatized nor completely nationalized its businesses.) The country finds itself in a unique, but not surprising, position: it is the largest nation on the planet (the former Russia and the former USA have since subdivided into smaller nations because of various ethnic, racial, and religious conflicts; and China split in two, one half capitalist, the other socialist). More importantly, the natural resources and the population density of Canada are enviable, to say the least.

Several countries want to buy fresh water from Canada. Due to a combination of overpopulation (whether because of sociocultural/religious, educational, or health-care reasons, you don't know), environmental changes, and less-than-democratic governance, these countries are desperate for water, not only for agricultural purposes (industrial purposes have long ceased to be a consideration), but also for drinking. Simply put, people will die if they don't get water. (Then again, you realize, they may die anyway.)

You have two major concerns. One, whether it is achieved by truck convoys, pipelines, or iceberg tows, getting the water from here to there will surely involve the re-routing of rivers and the lowering of lake levels—which is sure to worsen things, environmentally speaking.

Two, if you don't sell the water to them, they threaten to explode their entire nuclear arms arsenals (of which, no surprise, there is no shortage, thanks to Canadian sales a few decades ago) as well as their nuclear power reactors, creating worldwide radiation hazards.

Although it's not as if we're swimming in the stuff (that was made illegal several years ago), unless there's a dramatic change in immigration policies, Canada has enough fresh water for its current, and probably its future, population (pesticide use continues to cause male sperm counts to plummet). You *could* sell the excess.

But why just the excess? Why should you look after Canadians first? Is a Canadian life worth more than, say, an African life?

And at what price? Is it right to let the free market call the shots? People are dying—what about compassion and generosity? But what about justice—whose fault is the overpopulation? Okay, but we're one of the industrialized nations; surely the climate changes leading to the desertification are partly our fault. But what about the government? It could have legislated to meet Kyoto.... In any case, you suspect it'll be a while before customer countries can pay, whatever the price.

What do you decide to do?

Introduction

Why should you be concerned about our environment? Broadly speaking, there are two approaches to this question, depending on whether you think our environment has intrinsic or instrumental value. (Of course, it could have both. Did you catch that almost false dichotomy mistake?) If our environment has intrinsic value, then even if we didn't need to breathe and drink, even if we didn't find starry night skies stunningly beautiful, we should refrain from damaging it.[1] In a sense, our environment can be considered a stakeholder: it can be affected by business decisions.[2]

More common, however, is to consider our environment's instrumental value: what's in it for us? (See Baxter for a good articulation of this view.) As long as the "us" is human beings, it's a rather speciesist view: after all, we're as much a part of the beaver's or tree's environment as the beaver or tree is part of ours.

So on what ethical basis can one justify concern for our environment, given this instrumental view? Egoism probably comes to mind first. As a person, you need the environment to live (for food, water, and so on) and you need it pretty much the way it is in order to live the way you do. But as a *business* person, you'll need the environment to maintain your supply: if your

---

[1] See Rolston for this view; see Stone too, who argues not only for value, but also for rights.
[2] See Starik, as well as Hoch and Giacalone.

source material runs out, you're out of business. The same applies if you run out of dumping grounds or they become scarce and disposal costs increase—there goes your profit. (Can you develop a fully recyclable product, eliminating the disposal problem? Consider the ice cream cone.) Quite simply, our environment has economic value to business.

That is, if *you're* the one who has to pay for disposal. Recall the discussion in Chapter 7 about externalities. Traditionally, the impact of business operations on the environment has been considered an externality, which may account for the shape it's in. But is that morally right? Why should others bear the consequences (by way of environmental damage) of your profit making? Justice theories come in handy here.

You may say, "Well, it's not my fault, or not only my fault; after all, you *bought* X, *you* wanted it!" See Bowie, who argues that if consumers aren't willing to pay more for environmentally friendly products, it's not the responsibility of business to "correct" that "market failure." But that argument depends on consumers *knowing* the environmental cost of the products they buy. And if you've externalized it, if you haven't included it in your price, how *could* they know? If the cost to the environment *were* included, people might well decide *not* to buy it; they might not want it *that* badly. And what about the people who *don't* buy it, at *any* cost? Why should *I* have to pay to clean up the mess you made, or, if you're a consumer, the mess you paid to have made, because you had to make/have your wedding rings and steak?[1]

If you're running your business according to the stakeholder model, however, egoism won't cut it. You'll be concerned about the effects of your business on your customers, your employees, the community, perhaps even society-at-large, if you have that much influence or power, and all of them depend on the environment as much as you do. In that case, utilitarianism would be more appropriate.

However, assessing the consequences, as utilitarianism requires, is particularly complicated when it comes to the environment, for a number of reasons. First, everything is connected. For that reason, it's difficult to *identify* the consequences. Furthermore—and this applies to determining moral responsibility rather than determining consequences—it's impossible to keep the consequences of what you do on (or with) your own property *on* your own property. If I burn tires or even leaves on my so-called private property, chances are good the smoke will drift over onto your so-called private property and give you a headache or, if you have your windows open, require you to clean (or have cleaned) your drapes and carpets. Less easy to see, but hopefully just as easy to understand, if I send carbon molecules (or CFCs or PCBs) into my air, or if I dump toxins (including fertilizers, pesticides, herbicides, fungicides, BGH) onto my ground (or even straight into my stream, bypassing the groundwater system), they will, maybe not today, maybe not tomorrow, but eventually, show up somewhere else. Earth is a closed system; what goes around comes around.

---

1 Gold mining means deforestation and mercury poisoning; beef production releases five times the greenhouse-gas emissions as other meat production, and requires 28 times more land and 11 times more water [Boehrer]—one study goes so far as to say that eating meat is worse for our environment than driving a car.

Which is why, as far as the environment is concerned, every business issue will be a global business issue; environmental issues are international issues. (So if you're doing business in other countries *because* they have lower environmental standards—should you do that? just because you can? This interconnectedness may be a good reason *against* private ownership of natural resources.[1] *Can* water, earth, and air be owned? Because if they cannot, that would radically change the way we do business.

The question applies, of course, not only to water, earth, and air *per se*: "One drug company extracted the multimillion-dollar cancer drug, vincristine, from Madagascar rosy periwinkle, paying just a few dollars for the plant. The company made millions, and Madagascar received nothing" (De George 573). Was that morally right? Why? Why not? Did they pay too little? Or did they pay too much? That is, should the periwinkle have even *been* for sale? Should *vincristine* be for sale? Can the company claim ownership of—can it patent—vincristine? Can it patent the periwinkle?

So, similarly, what about the fish that swim in the ocean—who owns them? Everyone? No one? Whoever catches them? Without regulation or joint consent, overfishing can (will?) occur. This is the "tragedy of the commons" (so named and perhaps best articulated by Garrett Hardin). But see the piece by Angus, the accompanying comments, and his reply. Private ownership is suggested as the solution to this overuse (and contamination): if someone owned the lake, the argument goes, it would be in their best interest to look after it, so they wouldn't allow overfishing (or pollution). Of course, if privatization of our water, for example, meant cleaner water, then we should go for it.[2] Though it must be said that there's a difference between owning the water and owning the treatment plants that deliver and keep the water clean. (Or is there? So the rich can afford *clean* water, but the poor can't...?)

But *would* private ownership mean cleaner water? Yes, in theory, it would, or should: Roark argues that Locke's Proviso concerning the duty of appropriators of natural resources to leave enough and as good for others should apply to appropriation *and* use; he considers the destructive use, degrading use, overuse, and restricting-access use of unappropriated natural resources. But in practice? People, private owners, can be short-sighted or reckless or ignorant. So just because it's privately owned, that doesn't mean it'll be taken care of.

But the same is true when it's *not* privately owned. Many people consider Crown land and water not as something that is *jointly* owned and so requiring the consent of others before doing something, but as land and water that is *un*owned, which they understand to mean they can do whatever they want on it. For example, ATVs and snowmobiles have the (legal) right to go wherever they want on Crown land. But that means that others' enjoyment of that Crown land is lost. I haven't been able to go for a walk in the forest for over five years—unless I want to hear constant engine noise (a two-stroke engine can be heard for about five miles in every direction) and breathe neurotoxic fumes (whether I turn around or keep going, I'll have to walk in the fume

---

1 See the "Property and Ownership" entry in the *Stanford Encyclopedia of Philosophy* for a good introduction to this topic, and Lefevre and many others have written entire books on the matter.
2 See Carty, Clarke and Barlow, and Brubaker on this issue.

trail). Compared to drinkable water and breathable air, that's a relatively trivial example, but I hope it makes the point: as a result of others' freedom and/or rights to basically do whatever they want, my freedom and/or rights have been severely constrained.

Another reason against private ownership is that water is a basic need, like, presumably, health care and education, neither of which (for the most part) is privatized in Canada for that reason. (But then, isn't warmth also a basic need? And yet we pay private companies for oil, propane, electricity, and wood to heat our homes.) But if we treat water like a commodity.... Consider the comments by Barlow and Clarke (especially relevant given the fact that our water consumption doubles every twenty years):

> Water is listed as a "good" in the WTO and NAFTA, and as an "investment" in NAFTA.
>
> ...
>
> NAFTA contains a provision that requires "proportional sharing" of energy resources now being traded between the signatory countries. This means that the oil and gas resources no longer belong to the country of extraction, but are a shared resource of the continent. For example, under NAFTA, Canada now exports 57 percent of its natural gas to the United States and is not allowed to cut back on these supplies... Under this same provision, if Canada started selling its water to the United States... the State Department would consider it to be a trade violation if Canada tried to turn off the tap.
>
> ...
>
> The commodification of water is wrong—ethically, environmentally and socially. It insures that decisions regarding the allocation of water would center on commercial, not environmental or social justice considerations. Privatization means that the management of water resources is based on principles of scarcity and profit maximization rather than long-term sustainability. Corporations are dependent on increased consumption to generate profits and are much more likely to invest in the use of chemical technology, desalination, marketing and water trading than in conservation. (Barlow and Clarke, "Who Owns Water?")

They also note that "In England and France, where water has already been privatized, rates have soared, and water shortages have been severe. The major bottled-water producers... are part of one of the fastest-growing and least regulated industries, buying up freshwater rights and drying up crucial supplies."[1]

The second factor, after interconnectedness, that complicates assessing the consequences of our actions on our environment is that the consequences are far-reaching in terms of space. PCBs emitted in the US, Russia, and Asia (and quite possibly other countries) are now in breast milk in the Arctic. For another example, consider the 2011 legal case about whether Monsanto has the right to sue farmers for patent infringement if their seed should end up on their property. Did they really not consider this possibility beforehand? Did they not know that creatures fly

---

1 See https://www.amazon.com/Blue-Gold-Fight-Corporate-Worlds-ebook/dp/B005OCJC3K/ref=sr_1_1?ie=UTF8&qid=1470017471&sr=8-1&keywords=blue+gold+barlow#nav-subnav

and walk from one field to another? That pollen drifts with the wind? And do they really think they can hold the *farmers* responsible? You *have* to be suspicious of a company that inserts into a contract a clause that absolves them of all responsibility (see Organic Alberta). No wonder people are protesting, trying to keep Monsanto out of Canada.

The third factor is that the consequences are also far-reaching in terms of time. The use of CFCs in the 1970s led to a more than 70-per-cent increase in skin cancer in the 1990s. Consider the following, which illustrates both previous points:

> Since its massive use in the 1940s, the footsteps of DDT can be followed from wheat, to insects, to rodents, to larger animals and birds, and to man [sic]. In its wake it left whole species of animals more or less extinct or with serious reproductive problems. To illustrate the degree of interaction involved and the insignificance of time and distance, traces of DDT can now be found in the flesh of polar bears. (Law Reform Commission of Canada, 22)

And the effects are persistent; they won't, they don't, they can't, just "go away." For example, carbon stays in the atmosphere for over a hundred years, as do CFCs, PCBs, and DDT.

Relevant to the third factor is the practice of discounting: "Economists generally value future goods less than present ones: they discount future goods. Furthermore, the more distant the future in which goods become available, the more the goods are discounted" (Broome 2008, 71). Is that morally acceptable? The rationale is that a dollar to a poor person means more than a dollar to a rich person, and future people will be richer than current people. How do they figure that, exactly? Won't a litre of drinkable water be *more* precious in 2030 than now?[1]

Yet another factor, but one that should make assessment simple, rather than complicated, is that environmental consequences are now pretty much life-threatening. So, the question that applies to business is the same one that applies to the drunk driver: What right do you have to put me, my life, at risk? Ever.

Now surely the developers among you are sputtering that our environment doesn't sustain us *just as is*. Mining? Agriculture? Paper doesn't grow on trees, you know! If we didn't develop the environment, we'd still be hunters and gatherers. And every development, even agriculture, causes some environmental destruction. It's a trade-off.

And therein lies an important ethical question: Is X worth Y? For example, are cars worth smog? Is a cheap burger worth the loss of rainforests?[2]

Before you answer, consider your alternatives: crop rotation "costs" less than other agricultural methods that wreak havoc on the topsoil; solar and wind power cost less than nuclear or hydroelectric power (*and* provide six to eight times as many jobs), and so on. So maybe you *can* have your cake and clean air too. But it's not easy to figure this out: producing plastic bags requires 20–40 per cent less energy than producing paper bags (Fredericksen and Jones), but

---

1 See Broome (a moral philosopher trained in economics) for further discussion about the discount rate used by economists when they consider whether and what to do about climate change.
2 See Baxter's *People or Penguins* on this.

paper bags decompose in the dump while plastic bags don't—so which should you go with? With any luck, environmental scientists, *independent* environmental scientists, can tell us.

But let's back up a step: Who decides? Who decides whether the trade-off is a good one? Utilitarianism and justice theories probably lead you to "whoever would be affected"—which is, given the interconnectedness, pretty much everyone, right? So am I saying you have to get everyone's permission before you open your business? Well, if your business creates by-product A, which does B, which affects C, which makes a hundred lakes toxic for half a century, yes. Even if it makes one lake toxic for ten years, yes.

This may be where government plays a part: by setting regulations (e.g., don't change the climate), isn't it granting or withholding permission on behalf of "everyone"? So as long as you conform to the regulations, you're okay? How is the government doing on this regulation thing anyway? And what might people say who have skin cancer from ultraviolet exposure?

> **BOX 10.1   Canada's Export Development Corp.**
>
> "Since its inception in the 1940s, EDC has acted as a trade facilitator for Canadian businesses doing deals abroad. It provides financing to exporters and their customers, and insures investments abroad against political risks.... But in recent years, EDC has pushed deeper into banking territory, doing deals with foreign companies that offer no certainty they will benefit Canadian exporters" (Kirby).
>
> Among projects backed by the EDC (and so, taxpayer money) are the following (McKay):
>
> - the Omai gold mine in Guyana, site of a massive cyanide spill that poisoned an ocean-flowing river (EDC financing: $163 million, all figures US)
> - the Ok Tedi copper mine in Papua New Guinea, site of a major tailings dam break and poisoning of river (EDC financing: $88 million)
> - the Lihir gold mine in Papua New Guinea, which dumps toxic mine wastes directly into the Pacific Ocean (EDC loan guarantee: $29.6 million)
> - the Idah Kiat pulp and paper mill in Indonesia, which has chronic air- and water-pollution emissions, and depends on clearcut rainforest wood (EDC financing: $285 million)
> - the Musi Pulp mill in Indonesia, supplied by clearcut rainforest wood (EDC financing: $50 million)
> - the Kumptor gold mine in Kyrgystan, site of a deadly cyanide spill (EDC financing: $50 million)
> - the Marcopper gold mine in the Philippines, site of direct dumping of toxic tailing in river and ocean estuary (EDC financing: $1.6 million.)

> And that's just up to 2000. Since then, the EDC has funded Barrick Gold Corp. ($200–250 million) for its operations in the Dominican Republic; SNC-Lavalin Inc. ($200–250 million) for its aluminum smelter in the United Arab Emirates, on one of the last coastal white sand habitats; and more.
>
> *Sources*
> Export Development Canada Project List. *Probe International*.http://journal.probeinternational.org/export-credit/export-development-canada-project-list/
> Kirby, Jason. "Export Development Canada: A Crown corp. that thinks it's a bank." *Maclean's* 22 Apr. 2014. http://www.macleans.ca/economy/economicanalysis/a-crown-corp-that-thinks-its-a-bank/
> McKay, Paul. "'This is a race to the bottom.'" *Ottawa Citizen* 19 Mar. 2000.

But what if your by-product A isn't the only cause (of B which does C)? One smokestack may be okay; it may be within the coping threshold of the natural environment. But two may not be. So are you in the wrong only if your smokestack is the second one? That doesn't seem quite right. Or if another factory wants to set up, and you're the first one, should you cut your exhaust in half and share responsibility? Think of China as the second smokestack. Can we defensibly deny them the benefits of the industrialization we've had—just because, due to that industrialization, the planet is now maxed out in terms of emissions? Does it matter what the alternatives are? (Can the second factory set up somewhere else? The Moon, maybe? Is there a way to manufacture your product with less exhaust?) Does it matter what you're making? (Do we need it? badly?)

And, of course, after "who," the next big question is "how"—How do we decide if X is worth Y? Unless we can use some common measure (like money?), we're measuring apples against oranges. We can put a monetary price on paper, cars, and burgers. But should we—could we—put a dollar value on the starry sky, the quiet, the loon's call, drinkable water, breathable air—life itself? If we say we can't, because we say they're "priceless," then they're certainly worth more than what's on the other side of the equation.[1]

But of course it's not so black and white. Surely a few cars—police cars and ambulances, at least—are worth a little air pollution and noise. And, well, the freight trucks that get food to my local stores are worth a little pollution. Where do we draw the line? Two-car households? Single-occupant trips? Bananas from the tropics?

The utilitarian approach, weighing the consequences on both sides, is not the only way to approach this decision. Perhaps a principle-based approach can be enlightening. Do no harm.

---

[1] In addition to Barlow and Clarke mentioned above, and Kelman (and a great many more), Sagoff questions whether we should put a price on our environment, whether we should figure in how much people would be willing to pay for environmental qualities: "What is wrong with that?" he asks, and answers, "Not all of us think of ourselves simply as *consumers*." See Shrader-Frechette for a response to his critique.

Period. So find yourself a non-toxic way to make money. Is that really too much to ask? And is it really that simple?

We could also, or instead, as suggested above, look at the issue as a conflict of rights: my right to a certain quality of life against your right to profit (i.e., a certain quality of life?)—my clean air or your idling BMW?[1] The right to private property is also invoked in this context. But are rights ever absolute? Does the right to private property include the right to do anything you want to your property, on your property, regardless of harm to others?[2] Is the right to a liveable environment a *human* right? If so, then any company that contaminates the air, water, or earth is guilty of human-rights violations. Why isn't it that simple? And if that right extends to future generations....

Speaking of rights, I keep coming back to "Why does business have the right of way?"[3] Even for something as simple as turning out the lights. People were asked to reduce their electricity use long ago: don't stand in front of the fridge with the door open; turn out the light when you leave a room. But most businesses keep at least some of their lights on all night, especially their advertising sign lights. (What is so important about your business that we need to know about it 24/7?)

One might object to all these complicating factors, and the difficulty of weighing X against Y, with "I can only mind my *own* business, here and now; the rest is really none of my business." Really? On what basis, on what *moral* basis, could you make *that* claim? Besides which, that's what your predecessors thought. And now look: bluntly put, business as usual is killing us. The way we've been doing business is leading us to an almost-certain planet-wide death. *Planet-wide*. And I'm not exaggerating or speaking metaphorically.

> **BOX 10.2 Climate Change 101**
>
> An increase of one degree, two, three, four... Ambient air temperature doesn't have much of a direct effect on humans—the difference between 15 degrees and 18 degrees on any given day isn't that big of a deal. But when we talk about climate change and global warming, we're talking about *average global* temperature.
>
> Many species thrive in a much narrower temperature range than we do; with such temperature change they will not survive. Other species could adapt if they had enough time, but the warming is happening too fast for that to happen. This will have a number of food-chain reactions that will eventually affect us; the lower on the chain, the more effect their extinction will have. Also, if species we depend on to pollinate food crops become extinct (bees, for example, though they're dying

---

1 See Blackstone for an analysis of this right to a liveable environment.
2 See Harbrecht for an interesting angle on this issue.
3 Running a business is like having kids: they're both seen as some sort of all-purpose legitimizing excuse. You can get away with anything if you're doing it for your kids. Similarly, you can get away with anything if you have a business to run. ("I've got work to do" is similarly legitimizing, an acceptable reason to walk away from something else.) It's as if merely by employing several people, business becomes some sort of social service. And so it's in bad taste, or worse, immoral, to question, to refuse, its right of way. But businesspeople don't contribute their products and services to society; they sell them.

off because of pesticides and fungicides, not warming), that too will have an effect. An increase in global temperature will also affect disease vectors; tropical diseases will increase their range.

However, more to the point is how such an increase affects our climate.

CFCs (chlorofluorocarbons) released into the air (prior to their replacement with HCFCs in the late 1970s), mostly through the use of spray cans and refrigeration, drift up into the ozone layer, where the solar radiation breaks down the CFC, freeing the chlorine molecules, which then eat away at the ozone layer. This means that more of the sun's heat is getting through, which means that the earth's surface is getting warmer.

Carbon dioxide, water vapour, and methane that is released into the air form a blanket that keeps the heat in (normally the earth reflects much of it back out into the atmosphere). The thicker the blanket, the warmer we get. Since the industrialization era, primarily due to the production and consumption of fossil fuels, carbon dioxide emissions into the air have increased significantly, thickening the blanket.

This means that both the permafrost and the polar ice have started melting. As the permafrost melts, the methane currently underground will be released; the more methane, the more melting, the more melting, the more methane.... Since ice reflects the sun's radiation, loss of ice *also* means more warming, and more warming means more loss of ice....

Trees and other vegetation "breathe in" carbon dioxide (and "breathe out" oxygen), so cutting down the forests means even more carbon dioxide in the atmosphere, which means more of a blanket....

When the surface of the earth gets warmer, the air patterns change. This means that storms become more severe. Warming also puts more water vapour in the air which also contributes to more severe storms.

Heat waves will increase and become more severe as well. As will wildfires.

Rainfall patterns will also change, which means availability of drinking water will change.

A warmer surface also means more deserts. This further decreases the amount of arable soil, compounding the effects of urbanization and industry.

Dry earth absorbs water less well, so flooding will increase.

As the polar ice melts and the sun's heat coming through increases, the oceans will get warmer. Warm water is less dense than cold water, so it takes up more space. This means that the ocean levels will rise, flooding islands and coastal areas.

These are facts: cause and effect. They are not matters of opinion. How can the polar ice melt and the ocean levels *not* rise? How can the ocean level rise and the coastal areas *not* flood?

> There is a relationship, then, between the amount of carbon in the atmosphere and warming. There is a broad consensus that anything higher than a 2-degree increase would be disastrous. (Some say 1.5 is dangerous enough.)
>
> And there is a broad consensus that more than 450ppm (parts per million) of carbon dioxide will put us over 2 degrees. (Some say 430, some say 480.) In January 2013, we were at 396ppm and adding 2ppm/year. In January 2015, we were at 400ppm and adding 3ppm/year. This is why many scientists think we're past trying to stay under a 2-degree increase. And economists agree: "The door to reach two degrees is about to close. In 2017 it will be closed forever" (Faith Birol, Chief Economist, International Energy Agency [Klein 23]).

Harris notes, "Only in the United States is there still considerable discussion about whether global warming is happening and whether humans are causing climate change, and only there is uncertainty about the precise consequences used to stifle debate and prevent any real action." I'd add "and in Canada." (You don't think global warming is happening? See if your reasons are among the 117 dealt with on the Skeptical Science website [url in References list]).

> **BOX 10.3   What Is Wrong with This Picture?**
>
> In *This Changes Everything*, Naomi Klein writes, "From the perspective of a fossil fuel company, going after these high-risk carbon deposits [by fracking shale for gas and extracting oil from tar sands, for example] is not a matter of choice—it is its fiduciary responsibility to shareholders, who insist on earning the same kinds of mega-profits next year as they did this year and last year. And yet fulfilling that fiduciary responsibility virtually guarantees that the planet will cook.
>
> "This is not hyperbole. In 2011, a think tank in London called the Carbon Tracker Initiative conducted a breakthrough study that added together the reserves claimed by all the fossil fuel companies, private and state-owned. It found that the oil, gas, and coal to which these players had already laid claim—deposits they have on their books and which were already making money for shareholders—represented 2,795 gigatons of carbon.... That's a very big problem because we know roughly how much carbon can be burned between now and 2050 and still leave us a solid chance (roughly 80%) of keeping warming below 2 degrees Celsius. According to one highly credible study, that amount of carbon is 565 gigatons between 2011 and 2049. And as Bill McKibben points out, 'The thing to notice is [that] 2,795 is *five times* 565 (my emphasis). It's not even close.' He adds: 'What those numbers mean is quite simple. This industry has announced, in filings to the SEC and in

promises to shareholders, that they're determined to burn five times more fossil fuel than the planet's atmosphere can begin to absorb'" (Klein 148).

In other words, Klein goes on to say, "the fossil fuel companies have every intention of pushing the planet beyond the boiling point" (Klein 353–54).

And in *other* other words, "So in order to preserve a roughly habitable planet, we somehow need to convince or coerce the world's most profitable corporations and the nations that partner with them to walk away from $20 trillion of wealth [80% of the carbon they have claims to]" (Hayes, n.p.).

One has to ask, "What is wrong with this picture?"

One has to answer, "Yeah. We need a new business model."

References

Carbon Tracker Initiative. http://www.carbontracker.org/

Hayes, Christopher. "The New Abolitionism." *The Nation* 22 Apr. 2014, https://www.thenation.com/article/new-abolitionism/

Klein, Naomi. *This Changes Everything*. New York: Simon and Schuster, 2014.

McKibben, Bill. "Global Warming's Terrifying New Math." *Rolling Stone* 19 July 2012, http://www.rollingstone.com/politics/news/global-warnings-terrifying-new-math-20120719.

We made the wrong decisions. We used the wrong formulae to calculate the trade-offs. Or something. Because half of the world's wetlands are gone (The EcoAmbassador). Half the world's major rivers are seriously polluted or depleted (The Nature Conservancy). Half of the world's topsoil is gone (World Wildlife Foundation). Half of our forests are gone (World Revolution). We're losing species at 1,000 to 10,000 times the normal rate (Center for Biological Diversity). And there are an estimated 200 million tonnes of uranium tailings in Canada.[1]

So now what? How do we fix things?

Well, first, the more ethically relevant question is "*Who* should fix things?" How do we apportion responsibility? Consider Leahy's description of our current state of affairs:

> The family has just finished up an expensive seven-course restaurant meal, and the late-arriving cousins can only snack on bread sticks. When the bill arrives, the truculent, rich uncles—Canada, Japan and the United States—insist that the cousins, although poor and still very hungry, ought to pay a full share.
>
> And then Uncle Canada suggests that he pay less because he has a big appetite and can't help himself.

---

[1] Tailings are nuclear waste; when ingested through the air, water, or food, they cause cancer and genetic mutations in Canada. See more about our toxic environment at "Our home and toxic land."

With the fate of the planet in the balance, many critics say that is the current state of the negotiations ongoing in Bali at the international climate change talks.

Consider also the comments (made at the UN climate negotiation in Bonn, Germany, in 2009) of Navarro Llanos, chief climate negotiator for Bolivia:

> "Millions of people—in small islands, least-developed countries, landlocked countries as well as vulnerable communities in Brazil, India, and China, and all around the world—are suffering from the effects of a problem to which they did not contribute...." In addition to facing an increasingly hostile climate, she added, countries like Bolivia cannot fuel economic growth with cheap and dirty energy, as the rich countries did, since that would only add to the climate crisis—yet they cannot afford the heavy upfront costs of switching to renewable energies like wind and solar. (as reported by Klein, "Climate Rage")

Klein goes on to say,

> The developing world has always had plenty of reasons to be pissed off with their northern neighbors, with our tendency to overthrow their governments, invade their countries, and pillage their natural resources. But never before has there been an issue so politically inflammatory as the refusal of people living in the rich world to make even small sacrifices to avert a potential climate catastrophe. In Bangladesh, the Maldives, Bolivia, the Arctic, our climate pollution is directly responsible for destroying entire ways of life—yet we keep doing it.

There are a few principles one could use to determine who should pay.[1] The preceding comment implicitly endorses the "polluter pays" principle: the ones who made the mess should be the ones to pay to clean it up. (A quick comparison: "In 2010, Americans emitted about 17.6 tons of carbon dioxide per person; India, by contrast, emitted about 1.7 tons of carbon dioxide per person" [Ezra Klein].) This principle is the one endorsed by Brown and Garver, among many others, who say, "The rules for the developed countries that are responsible for the current financial and ecological crisis should be different from those for developing ones." A standard objection is "But we didn't know!" And a standard reply is "You should've found out!" Another reply is "Even so, you've benefitted."

Harris points out two complicating factors, adds two other dimensions, with his comments about the nature of the emission-generating activities and the effect of refusal to take responsibility:

> No country, however, bears more responsibility than the United States. With about one-twentieth of the world's population, the United States produces about one-quarter of the world's greenhouse gases. Much of that comes from arguably frivolous and certainly nonessential activities, whereas most of the emissions of the world's poor are due to activities necessary for survival or achieving a basic living standard. The United States therefore has a heavy responsibility to act on this problem, and insofar as it fails to do so other industrialized countries—least of all developing countries—are much less likely to take necessary actions.

---

1 See Gardiner, Rosa and Munasinghe, and Wesley and Peterson for further discussion of this matter.

One could use instead an egalitarian principle: everyone should pay equally. There's not much to support this view, however, since both the causes and the effects are not distributed equally.

Yet another principle is "ability to pay": the ones most able to pay should be the ones to pay the most. Peter Singer's analogy of the relative moral obligation to save a drowning child is illustrative: is the child in a wading pool or the ocean? if the latter, can you swim? Singer thus considers whether what you sacrifice by helping is greater than what is gained by doing so. In a sense, the "ability to pay" principle bypasses responsibility and focuses on power. (Or does it just say that with power comes responsibility?) And although in theory it thus differs from the first principle, in practice the results are much the same.

One might point out that all three principles identify *countries*, not businesses. Very true. One can only hope that the country collects from the responsible businesses rather than the taxpayers. (Right?)

Which brings us to the question of how we make the responsible people pay.

Box 10.4 Why Climate Litigation Could Soon Go Global

...Climate change is already causing about $600-billion in damages annually. Here in Canada, the National Roundtable on the Environment and the Economy estimated that climate change will cost Canadians $5-billion annually by 2020.

Canadian oil and gas companies could soon find themselves on the hook for at least part of the damage. For as climate change costs increase, a global debate has begun about who should pay.

Nobel Peace Prize laureate Desmond Tutu recently called on global leaders to hold those responsible for climate damages accountable. "Just 90 corporations—the so-called carbon majors—are responsible for 63 per cent of CO_2 emissions since the industrial revolution," Tutu said. "It is time to change the profit incentive by demanding legal liability for unsustainable environmental practices."

So far, the fossil fuel industry has successfully opposed litigation for climate damages, brought in the United States by victims of hurricanes and sea level rise. But new areas of litigation often fail at first; in the 1980s, tobacco companies were still boasting that they "have never lost a case to a consumer, have never settled, and do not expect that picture to change." As the tobacco industry learned, changes to the interpretation and application of laws sometimes occur quite rapidly.

Nor is litigation in the U.S. or Canada the only thing the fossil fuel industry should worry about. It is becoming increasingly likely that companies could be sued by victims of climate change overseas, in countries with quite different legal systems. There, they might face lawsuits based on constitutional rights to a healthy environment, strict liability for environmental harm, or any number of other legal principles that don't currently exist in Canadian law.

Once a foreign court has ordered a Canadian company to pay for climate damages, that order is a debt—which Canadian courts can be asked to enforce. Chevron is currently fighting court actions in Canada, the United States and Brazil that seek to enforce a $9.5-billion award handed down by the supreme court of Ecuador—for pollution caused by oil spills.

Moreover, new laws could be introduced to facilitate climate litigation. When Canadian provinces encountered impediments to their ability to sue tobacco companies for public health costs, they eliminated those impediments by passing new laws. It's not hard to imagine countries impacted by climate change enacting new laws to clarify the liability of greenhouse gas producers.

Five companies traded on the Toronto Stock Exchange are among the "carbon majors"—Encana, Suncor, Canadian Natural Resources, Talisman, and Husky currently are collectively responsible for about $2.4-billion a year of global climate damages.

Canadians are broadly supportive of the "polluter pays" principle—the idea that those who cause pollution should pay for the harm. But because climate change has seemed far off, there has been relatively little discussion about who should pay. It has been assumed—by industry, politicians, even some environmental activists—that oil and gas companies can continue producing with impunity, at least until a global climate agreement is reached.

But rising climate costs cannot be borne only by taxpayers and by those who suffer the impacts of climate change. We believe that a new global awareness of the moral and legal responsibilities of the carbon majors will lead to a wave of climate litigation. Foreign lawsuits—with damage awards that are potentially enforceable in Canada—will be difficult and expensive to defend.

Source
Gage, Andrew and Michael Byers. "Why climate litigation could soon go global." *The Globe and Mail* 9 Oct. 2014. http://www.theglobeandmail.com/opinion/why-climate-litigation-could-soon-go-global/article21002326/

BOX 10.5   Honouring First Nations Treaties: An Elegant and Brilliant Solution

If the treaties signed by Canada and the US protect the right to traditional ways of living, which include fishing and hunting, then the water and land in the regions covered by those treaties must be able to support fish and animals. So challenges to treaty-right violations have a clear legal leg to stand on (should that suddenly start to matter) when they insist that the water and land be sustainable....

But they could have even more than that...

...the Northern Cheyenne broke legal ground by arguing that *their right to enjoy a traditional way of life included the right to breathe clean air.* In 1977, the EPA agreed and granted the Northern Cheyenne Reservation the highest possible classification for its air quality.... This seemingly bureaucratic technicality allowed the tribe to argue in court that polluting projects as far away as Wyoming were a violation of its treaty rights, since the pollutants could travel to the Northern Cheyenne Reservation and potentially compromise its air and water quality. (Klein 390, my emphasis)

If that sort of thing "takes off"...

Implementing Indigenous rights on the ground, starting with the United Nations Declaration on the Rights of Indigenous Peoples, could tilt the balance of stewardship over a vast geography: giving Indigenous peoples much more control, and corporations much less. Which means that finally *honouring Indigenous rights is not simply about paying off Canada's enormous legal debt to First Nations: it is also our best chance to save entire territories from endless extraction and destruction.* In no small way, the actions of Indigenous peoples—and the decision of Canadians to stand alongside them—will determine the fate of the planet. (Lukacs, my emphasis)

It would require quite a turnaround....

The Oka Crisis in 1990 was essentially about unresolved land claims. Land that was being turned into a golf course by developers was claimed by Mohawk leaders to be theirs; a month-long confrontation (the Quebec government had asked the Canadian army for assistance) near Kanesatake resulted in loss of life.

And yet....

In the mid-1970s, the Lubicon filed a notice under law warning developers that title to the land in question was contested, but the Province of Alberta ignored the notice and dismissed the case (Lubicon Legal Defence Fund). The subsequent development destroyed the hunting that the Cree depended on for food and income; by 1982, there were 400 oil wells within a 15-mile radius of the Lubicon community, and 90 per cent of the community's population was on welfare (compared to 10 per cent prior to the development). Negotiations between the Lubicon and the federal government continued, more or less, but ten years later, Daishowa owned cutting rights to 10,000 square miles of the Lubicon territory. A boycott seemed to succeed in stalling a clear-cut; as a result, the company filed a lawsuit to make the boycott illegal—it lost and agreed not to log until a land settlement has been reached between the Lubicon and the governments. On June 26, 2014, the Supreme Court of Canada (finally) ruled that the Lubicon are the primary title holders of their ancestral lands. This means that First Nations interests are to take precedence to those of the provincial government and resource developers.

So maybe....

References

Klein, Naomi. *This Changes Everything: Capitalism vs. The Climate*. New York: Simon & Schuster, 2014.

Lukacs, Martin. "Indigenous Rights Are the Best Defence against Canada's Resource Rush." *The Guardian* 26 Apr. 2013. http://www.theguardian.com/environment/true-north/2013/apr/26/indigenous-rights-defence-canadas-resource-rush

Perhaps we need to first answer the question, "What exactly would the people responsible pay for?" Which brings us back to "How do we fix it? What do we do?" Some will argue for not doing anything, or at least not anything different. After all, we don't know for sure.... But when the consequences are dire, should you really wait for certainty before taking action? (See the reading by Gardiner below for more on this.)

One idea is to institute pollution taxes. Presumably that would deter pollution.[1] But unless the taxes were retroactive, this wouldn't really address past wrongs.

Another idea is to require licences to pollute. The price of such licences would presumably deter pollution. If these licences could be traded internationally, underdeveloped countries could get rich, or at least debt-free, by selling their hardly necessary pollution licences to the industrialized world. But is that morally right? To *sell* pollution rights? Well, why not—why should this right be *in*alienable? But is it morally right to even *have* pollution rights? Or even pollution taxes—both imply the right to pollute, if you can pay enough to do so. Well, we could set limits—recall the trade-off idea.

Yet another idea is to pay countries to keep their carbon sequestered—that is, *not* to develop resources. That would also shift money from the industrialized countries to the underdeveloped countries. Norway, for instance, pledged $1 billion each to Brazil and Indonesia for forest-preservation efforts, partly to compensate for failing to meet its own greenhouse gas emissions targets. But consider Monbiot's concern that "[i]f a quarry company wants to

---

[1] If only we could *see* carbon dioxide. If the guy idling his pick-up could see clouds of dark purple stuff coming out his exhaust pipe.... If you could see it poof into the air whenever you cut down a tree (?) or drill into the rock.... And it just hung there.... Similarly, if we could *see* the ozone hole above us, a rip in the sky, getting larger every day.... If there were no 'dumps' and we had to keep all our garbage on our own property...

destroy a rare meadow, for example, it can buy absolution by paying someone to create another somewhere else."

In a similar way, in the sense that it also involves paying someone to do the environmentally responsible thing, but without the absolution for an environmentally irresponsible thing, "Vittel-Nestlé Waters recognized a few years ago that its aquifer in northern France was being polluted by nitrate fertilizers and pesticides from nearby farms. It devised a scheme to pay farmers to change their methods and to deliver the ecosystem service of unpolluted water" (Conniff).

This solution addresses Conniff's comments: "Old-style protection of nature for its own sake has badly failed to stop the destruction of habitats and the dwindling of species. It has failed largely because philosophical and scientific arguments rarely trump profits and the promise of jobs. And *conservationists can't usually put enough money on the table to meet commercial interests on their own terms*" (my emphasis). And that's because the "commercial interests" can get a return on their expense when they harvest the wood, for example, but when conservationists buy it, it just sits, untouched. But if, as suggested above, someone (who?) were to pay for just letting it stay untouched—if a tree, for example, was worth $2,000 (per year) as a living carbon dioxide processor and only $1,000 (one time) as lumber—then conservation groups *could* afford to buy and "just let it sit." That's the argument, the theory, behind developing countries asking to be paid for their carbon sinks (their untouched stuff)—asking the rest of the world to pay them to keep their forests uncut and to keep their fossil fuels in the ground (the latter not as carbon dioxide processors but at least not as carbon emitters).

Conniff's comment may imply that the problem is with the economic model we've been using. Certainly MacDonald's comments do this, targeting supply and demand economics: "[I]f the corporate boycott [of Alberta's oil sands] has any impact at all, it will be roughly as follows. The reduction in demand for oil-sands oil will reduce the price it can command. And when you lower the price of something? Yup, you make it easier for other people to buy it. So, more—not less—will end up being used" (MacDonald).

Others argue that the current economic model isn't the problem and can actually provide us with solutions:

> Free market environmentalism can correct these problems. Short of privatizing the national forests, timber leases could be put up for competitive bid with no requirement that timber be harvested; environmentalists could then bid with timber companies. Environmental groups could lease the most critical owl habitat and allow no logging there. On other tracts, they might allow some logging, thus partially offsetting lease costs, but require that logging be done with minimal impact on the owls. Because it owns its timberlands, International Paper has successfully minimized impacts on endangered species such as the red-cockaded woodpecker, and the Audubon Society has demonstrated that oil development can occur on its private preserves without significant damage to bird habitat. (Anderson and Leal)[1]

---

1 See also Taylor for a defence of free-market environmentalism. Then see Tokar for a criticism of such a view, one that turns environmental protection into a profit-making commodity, and Smith for succinct replies to four arguments sup-

Many advocate, instead, increased government regulations. For a comparison of the market-based approach and the "command-and-control" (government regulation) approach, see Stavins and Whitehead. Freeman explains that of the two remedies for market failure, the government regulation approach suits environmental concerns better than the property rights approach because the environment is not easily divisible.

That last point underlines the necessity for coordinated effort. Yet Poff makes the argument that the global economy, with its increasing weakening of national boundaries (through privatization, deregulation, and liberalization of national economies) makes environmental sustainability impossible: any country strengthening its environmental protection laws unilaterally will be at a competitive disadvantage. Hence the need for nations to negotiate internationally.

Unfortunately, the past implies that such planet-wide coordination is unlikely. Governments have been trying to reach agreements for decades… and failing. So even if we recognized that a *radical* solution is required—such as earth, water, and air can't be privately owned anymore, anywhere, and there can be no non-sustainable development anymore, anywhere—it's unlikely it would be implemented.

So in the meantime? What new business model should we adopt? What should business look like *from this point on?* Well, we know what doesn't work. And only an insane person does the same thing over and over, expecting a different outcome.

To the extent that environmental destruction has resulted from the "bigger/more is better" view of development, a view that might just have been excusable back when natural resources seemed infinite and causal connections were not understood, one would argue (as many have, for decades) that sustainable growth (rather than unlimited growth) should be our standard.[1] Such a model, according to DesJardins, proposes three things:

1. Businesses should not use renewable resources at rates that exceed their ability to replenish themselves….
2. Businesses should use nonrenewable resources only at the rate at which alternatives are developed or loss of opportunities compensated….
3. Businesses cannot produce wastes and emissions that exceed the capacity of the ecosystem to assimilate them. (455)[2]

Some argue for zero-growth, which doesn't necessarily mean no development. What would that look like? (And would full-cycle costing help?)

Rocha, Searcy, and Karapetrovich believe that sustainable development can be integrated into business as is. But others disagree. Korhonen asks this question: "Is there something that is fundamentally wrong in the dominant business paradigm in the light of sustainability?" As a

---

porting free-market environmentalism. See also Simon and Partridge for another version of the Palmer and Peacock debate in this chapter. Lastly, see Bromley for an analysis of the ethical problems with basing environmental policy on economic analysis (and, as a bonus, ways to overcome these problems).

1 See Hawkens, for example, and Brown.
2 See Beckerman for a counter to DesJardins.

result of his search for "upstream principle mechanisms of current known and future unknown negative environmental impacts downstream," he identifies growth without limits (suggesting instead creativity within limits), competition (suggesting instead symbiosis), specialization (suggesting instead diversity), and globalization (suggesting instead locality), concluding with "a new, alternative theory of corporate environmental management."

Considering the matter from the Canadian perspective, one of the characteristic features of Canada is our plentiful natural resources, which give rise to many very serious ethical questions. First is whether or not to develop them. According to a recent paper published in *Nature* (one of the pre-eminent scientific journals), and echoing the box above, Canada's tar sands and the 100 billion barrels of oil estimated to exist in the Arctic have to stay in the ground, undeveloped, if we are to keep under a two degree temperature increase (McGlade and Elkins). Though I haven't found a similar fact for the fresh water that's locked in our ice, I suspect it's the same, since the melting of the polar ice is a significant factor in the warming chain.

Then, if you *do* decide to develop them, you'll have to decide what to do with them. Sell them to rich countries like the US? Sell them to poor countries like those in parts of Africa? Sell them to countries hell-bent on following our lead over the cliff, like China?

And, of course, in the process, you have to consider the process. Do you access the oil through deep-sea oil drilling? Do you get to the natural gas by fracking?

And then, once you've got it, you have to consider your delivery method. Do you run a pipeline through thousands of miles of sensitive habitat? (XL Keystone.) (And keep in mind that by the time you're in business, *all* habitat is going to be sensitive.) Run roughshod over private land? (Texas.) Do you send it halfway around the world in tankers that may hit an iceberg? (Exxon.) Or trains that have a tendency to derail? (Lac Mégantic, Quebec.) Seriously, is it worth all that risk?

Take a minute to define exactly that "it." *What are you doing it for?* Wouldn't most people prefer renewable energy if it were cheaper? (And if you included the damage you cause it *would* be cheaper. Considerably cheaper. Put a price on the planet. Go ahead. I want to see your number.)

So are you doing it just because you have to finish what you started? Because you've got all that money committed, you can't stop now? Why not? Because you yourself need more money? Because your shareholders need more money? Will the world fall apart if we have to shift to solar, wind, and tidal power? (It will if we don't.)

And if you do take responsibility for disposal, should you go ahead and, for example, ship 1600 tonnes of nuclear waste through the Great Lakes and on to Sweden without conducting an environmental assessment? Even if your government allows you to? (Bruce Power Inc.)

We *have* solutions. Technological solutions. Windmills. Solar panels. Tidal power. Electric cars, with battery-swapping stations instead of gas stations. Fuel cells. We just need business to make them work, and we need to figure out a way to make them work, to make business and technology work together.[1] Denmark switched more than 40 per cent of its electricity consump-

---

[1] See Quartz on Better Place; see Ballard on fuel cells. For a detailed list of companies that have made great progress in the area of environmental and corporate social responsibility, see the *Maclean's* articles on Canada's top 50 socially

tion to renewables; Germany has achieved a 25-per-cent switch. How did *they* do it? (Canada's at 17 per cent.) Being in business is not incompatible with being environmentally responsible. (Despite beliefs to the contrary: very few Canadian corporate codes even discuss environmental affairs; a mere 6.7 per cent of 75 respondents, from 461 queried, of the top 500 corporations in Canada, do so [Lefebvre and Singh]. Shame on us.)

Note, though, that all of the forementioned solutions, from pollution taxes on, do nothing to fix the current problems. They all address simply not adding to the problems. And maybe that's because so many of the current problems are unfixable. We can't retrieve the CFCs. We can't retrieve all the carbon we've set into the atmosphere. We can't retrieve the PCBs, the DDT, and all the other toxins that caused genetic mutations. Can we do something with all the garbage floating in the oceans? Can we neutralize nuclear waste? Can we purify our polluted water? Can we make soil out of thin air? I don't know.

But the bottom line is that the decisions being made by business are critical, and they become more critical with every passing day. Even if you're not in the fossil-fuel business, your business decisions have more consequence than the decisions of any individual person; your business probably uses more natural resources than any individual person. "This is where multinational corporations come in," Patchell and Hayter say. "Their global reach and tremendous capacity for the research, development, demonstration, and diffusion of new technologies offer the best chance of addressing climate change." They also claim that "[f]ocusing on multinational corporations is also a more equitable approach to dealing with climate change."

Governments have failed; look at all the climate negotiations, the summits, the conferences. Maybe it's time for business to try. Why don't those 85 richest people in the world (see Chapter 7) or the Global 500 get together and work out a *global business accord* that *takes the planet—the very possibility of future business—into consideration*. I say we need a revolution. Who better to lead it than business? You're already in the driver's seat.

Kevin Anderson, deputy director of the Tyndall Centre for Climate Change Research, one of the UK's premier climate research institutions, and Alice Bows-Larkin, an atmospheric physicist and climate change mitigation expert at the Tyndall Centre, say that a 4-degree Celsius increase (an increase of 2 degrees is considered the "safe" limit) is "incompatible with any reasonable characterization of an organized, equitable, and civilized global community" (Klein 2014, 13)—the World Bank says we're on track for such an increase by the end of this century, and provides a more detailed description of what will happen: "extreme heat waves, declining global food stocks, loss of ecosystems and biodiversity, and life-threatening sea level rise" (13). Given that, Klein says "[we] are going to have to quickly figure out how to turn 'managed degrowth' into something that looks a lot less like the Great Depression and a lot more like what some innovative economic thinkers have taken to calling 'The Great Transition'" (89).

Yvo de Boer, who held UN's top climate position until 2009, says that "the only way that a 2015 agreement [referring to the upcoming Paris conference in December 2015] can achieve a

---

responsible corporations: http://www.macleans.ca/work/bestcompanies/top-50-socially-responsible-corporations-2014/; http://www.macleans.ca/economy/business/canadas-top-50-most-socially-responsible-companies/.

two-degree goal is to shut down the whole global economy" (Morales), which is perhaps why applied physicist Graham Turner says "preparing for a collapsing global system could be even more important than trying to avoid collapse" (16). Klein takes the same message from Anderson and Bows-Larkin: "[W]hat [they're] really saying is that there is still time to avoid catastrophic warming, but not within the rules of capitalism as they are currently constructed.... Rather than pretending that we can solve the climate crisis without rocking the economic boat, Anderson and Bow-Larkin argue, the time has come to tell the truth...'we need to have the audacity to think differently and conceive of alternative futures'" (2014, 88–89).

Please. I'm begging you. Have that audacity. Be imaginative about the companies you start. Be vocal with the companies you join. Change the way we do business. (But do it quickly.)

(And save the world.)

References and Further Reading

Anderson, Terry L., and Donald R. Leal. "Free Market versus Political Environmentalism." *Harvard Journal of Law and Public Policy* 15.2 (Spring 1992): 297–310.

Angus, Ian. "The Myth of the Tragedy of the Commons." *Climate and Capitalism* 25 Aug. 2008. http://climateandcapitalism.com/2008/08/25/debunking-the-tragedy-of-the-commons/

Barlow, Maude. "Human race needs new water ethic." The Council of Canadians. *Globe Gazette* 27 Feb. 2014. http://canadians.org/blog/human-race-needs-new-water-ethic

Barlow, Maude, and Tony Clarke. *Blue Future: Protecting Water for People and the Planet Forever.* New York: The New Press, 2013.

———. *Blue Gold: The Fight to Stop the Corporate Theft of the World's Water.* New York: The New Press, 2005

———. "Who Owns Water." *The Nation* 2 Sept. 2002. https://www.thenation.com/article/who-owns-water/

Baxter, William F. *People or Penguins: The Case for Optimal Pollution.* New York: Columbia University Press, 1974.

Beckerman, Wilfred. *Two Cheers for the Affluent Society: A Spirited Defense of Economic Growth.* New York: St. Martin's Press, 1974.

Blackstone, William T. "Ethics and Ecology." In *Philosophy and Environmental Crisis.* Ed. William T. Blackstone. Athens: University of Georgia Press, 1973. 55–71.

Boehrer, Kathrine. "Study: To Cut Down on Environmental Impact, Eat Less Beef." *The Huffington Post* 21 July 2014. http://www.huffingtonpost.com/2014/07/21/beef-environmental-impact_n_5599370.html

Bourdeau, Annette. "Northern Exposure." *This Magazine* Nov.–Dec. 2003.

Bowie, Norman. "Morality, Money, and Motor Cars." In *Business, Ethics, and the Environment: The Public Policy Debate.* Ed. W. Michael Hoffman, Robert Frederick, and Edward Petry, Jr. New York: Quorum Books, 1990. 89–97.

Bromley, Daniel W. and Jouni Paavola (eds.). *Economics, Ethics, and Environmental Policy: Contested Choices.* New York: Wiley-Blackwell, 2002.

Broome, John. *Climate Matters: Ethics in a Warming World*. New York: Norton, 2012.

———. "The Ethics of Climate Change." *Scientific American* 298.6 (2008): 69–73.

———. *Weighing Goods*. New York: Wiley-Blackwell, 1995.

———. *Weighing Lives*. New York: Oxford University Press, 2006.

Brown, Peter. *Ethics, Economics, and International Relations: Transparent Sovereignty in the Commonwealth of Life*. Edinburgh: Edinburgh University Press, 2008.

Brown, Peter G., and Geoffrey Garver. "How to save the planet? It's the economy, stupid." *The National* 16 Dec. 2008. http://www.thenational.ae/article/20081216/OPINION/804770548/1080

———. *Right Relationship: Building A Whole Earth Economy*. San Francisco: Berrett-Koehler, 2009.

Brown, Peter G., and Jeremy J. Schmidt. *Water Ethics*. Washington, DC: Island Press, 2010.

Brubaker, Elizabeth. *Liquid Assets—Privatizing and Regulating Canada's Water Utilities*. Toronto: University of Toronto Press, 2002.

Carty, Bob. "Hard Water: The Uphill Campaign to Privatize Canada's Waterworks." The International Consortium of Investigative Journalists. 13 Feb. 2003. http://www.icij.org/projects/waterbarons/hard-water-uphill-campaign-privatize-canadas-waterworks

Conniff, Richard. "What's Wrong with Putting a Price on Nature?" *environment 360: opinion, analysis, reporting & debate* 18 Oct. 2012. http://e360.yale.edu/feature/ecosystem_services_whats_wrong_with_putting_a_price_on_nature/2583/

Coward, Harold, and Thomas Hurka (eds.). *Ethics and Climate Change: The Greenhouse Effect*. Waterloo: Wilfrid Laurier University Press, 2012.

Cragg, Wesley. "Sustainable Development and Mining: Opportunity or Threat to the Industry?" Canadian Institute of Mining, Metallurgy, and Petroleum Conference, Montreal, May, 1998.

Cragg, Wesley, David Pearson, and James Cooney. "Ethics, Surface Mining and the Environment." *Resource Policy* 21.4 (1995): 229–35.

De George, Richard T. *Business Ethics*. 5th ed. Englewood Cliffs, NJ: Prentice Hall, 1999.

DesJardins, Joseph R. "Sustainable Development and Corporate Social Responsibility." In *Contemporary Issues in Business Ethics*. Ed. Joseph R. DesJardins and John J. McCall. 3rd ed. Belmont, CA: Wadsworth, 1996. 452–56.

Dietz, Simon, Cameron Hepburn, and Nicholas Stern. "Economics, ethics and climate change." Presented at Climate Change and Global Justice Conference at the Department of Politics and International Relations, University of Oxford, 2007.

Di Norcia, Vincent. "Environmental and Social Performance." *Journal of Business Ethics* 15.7 (1996): 773–84.

———. *Hard Like Water: Ethics in Business*. Toronto: Oxford University Press, 1998.

The EcoAmbassador. http://www.theecoambassador.com/WaterPollutionFacts.html.

The Ethics of Fracking. Green Planet Films. http://www.greenplanetfilms.org/product/the-ethics-of-fracking/

Frankel, Carl. *In Earth's Company: Business, Environment, and the Challenge of Sustainability*. Branford, CT: New Society Publishers, 1998.

Fredricksen, Liv, and Laura Jones. "The Green Team." http://www.fraserinstitute.ca/forum/1998/june/environment.html

Freeman, A. Myrick, III. "The Ethical Basis of the Economic View of the Environment." In *The Environmental Ethics and Policy Book: Philosophy, Ecology, Economics*. Ed. Donald VanDeVeer and Christine Pierce. Belmont, CA: Wadsworth, 1994. 307–15.

Frosch, Robert, and Nicholas Gallapoulos. "Strategies for Manufacturing." *Scientific American* 261.3 (1989): 144–52.

Gardiner, Steve M. "Ethics and Climate Change: An Introduction." *WIRES Climate Change* 1 (Jan/Feb 2010): 54–66.

Gardiner, Stephen M., Simon Caney, Dale Jamieson, Henry Shue, and Rajendra Kumar Pachauri. *Climate Ethics: Essential Readings*. New York: Oxford University Press, 2010.

Garvey, James. *The Ethics of Climate Change: Right and Wrong in a Warming World*. London: Continuum, 2008.

Hamilton, Clive. *Requiem for a Species: Why We Resist the Truth about Climate Change*. New York: Routledge, 2010.

Harbrecht, Doug. "A Question of Property Rights and Wrongs." *National Wildlife* 32.6 (1994): 4–11.

Harris, Paul G. "Fairness, Responsibility, and Climate Change." *Ethics & International Affairs* 17.1 (2003): 149–56.

Hawken, Paul. "A Declaration of Sustainability." *Utne Reader* 59 (Sep/Oct 1993).

Hoch, David, and Robert A. Giacalone. "On the Lumber Industry: Ethical Concerns as the Other Side of Profits." *Journal of Business Ethics* 13.5 (1994): 357–67.

Hoffman, W. Michael. "Business and Environmental Ethics." *Business Ethics Quarterly* 1.2 (1991): 169–84.

Kelman, Steven. "Cost-Benefit Analysis: An Ethical Critique." *Regulation* (Jan.–Feb. 1981): 74–82.

———. "Economists and the Environmental Muddle." *The Public Interest* 641 (Summer 1981): 106–23.

Klein, Naomi. "Climate Rage." *Rolling Stone* 12 Nov. 2009. http://www.rollingstone.com/politics/news/climate-rage-20091112

———. *This Changes Everything*. New York: Simon & Schuster, 2014.

Korhonen, Jouni. "On the paradox of corporate social responsibility: how can we use social science and natural science for a new vision?" *Business Ethics: A European Review* 15.2 (April 2006) 200–14.

Law Reform Commission of Canada. *Crimes Against the Environment* (Working Paper 44, Protection of Life Series). Ottawa: Ministry of Supply and Services Canada, 1985.

Leahy, Stephen. "Climate Change: Who Should Pay the Carbon Bill?" Inter Press Service. 10 Dec. 2007. http://ipsnorthamerica.net/print.php?idnews=1206

Lefebvre, Maurica, and Jang B. Singh. "The Content and Focus of Canadian Corporate Codes of Ethics." *Journal of Business Ethics* 11.10 (Oct. 1992): 799–808.

Lefevre, Robert. *The Philosophy of Ownership*. Auburn, AL: Ludwig von Mises Institute, 1971.

Lertzman, David A., and Harrie Vredenburg. "Indigenous Peoples, Resource Extraction and

Sustainable Development: An Ethical Approach." *Journal of Business Ethics* 56 (2005): 239–54.

Levant, Ezra. "A Gap in Credibility for Companies." *Daily Herald Tribune* Aug31/10. http://www.dailyheraldtribune.com/2010/08/31/column-a-gap-in-credibility-for-companies

MacDonald, Chris. "The Oil Sands, and the Battle of the Boycotts." *The Business Ethics Blog* 6 Sept. 2010. http://businessethicsblog.com/2010/09/06/ethics-oil-sands-boycott/

McGlade, Christopher, and Paul Elkins. "The Geographical Distribution of Fossil Fuels Unused When Limiting Global Warming to 2C." *Nature* 517 (8 Jan. 2015): 187–90.

Northcott, Michael S. *A Moral Climate: The Ethics of Global Warming*. New York: Orbis Books, 2007.

Organic Alberta. "Monsanto Shifts ALL Liability onto Farmers." 4 Mar. 2011. http://organicalberta.org/news/monsanto-shifts-all-liability-to-farmers

"Our home and toxic land." *This Magazine* Mar./Apr. 2001: 2–3.

Partridge, Ernest. "Holes in the Cornucopia." In *Ethical Issues in Business: A Philosophical Approach*. Ed. Thomas Donaldson and Patricia H. Werhane. 6th ed. New York: Prentice Hall, 1999. 574–91.

Patchell, Jerry, and Roger Hayter. "How Big Business Can Save the Climate: Multinational Corporations Can Succeed Where Governments Have Failed." *Foreign Affairs* Sept./Oct. 2013. http://www.foreignaffairs.com/articles/139642/jerry-patchell-and-roger-hayter/how-big-business-can-save-the-climate

Peacock, Kent A. "The Economics of Extinction." In *Living with the Earth: An Introduction to Environmental Philosophy*. Ed. Kent Peacock. Toronto: Harcourt Brace, 1996. 338–41.

Poff, Deborah. "Reconciling the Irreconcilable: The Global Economy and the Environment." *Journal of Business Ethics* 13.6 (1998): 439–45.

Property and Ownership. *Stanford Encyclopedia of Philosophy*. http://plato.stanford.edu/entries/property/

Public Citizen. "Top 10 Reasons to Oppose Water Privatization." www.citizen.org/documents/Top_10_(PDF).pdf

Quartz. "Why Better Place failed with swappable batteries—and your cars might just use them one day." N.d. http://qz.com/88871/better-place-shai-agassi-swappable-electric-car-batteries/

Roark, Eric. "Applying Locke's Proviso to Unappropriated Natural Resources." *Political Studies* 60.3 (2012): 687–702.

Rocha, Miguel, Cory Searcy, and Stanislav Karapetrovic. "Integrating Sustainable Development into Existing Management Systems." *Total Quality Management* 18.1–2 (2007): 83–92.

Rolston, Holmes, III. "Are Values in Nature Subjective or Objective?" *Environmental Ethics* 4 (Summer 1982): 125–51.

Rosa, Luiz Pinguelli, and Mohan Munasinghe. *Ethics, Equity and International Negotiations on Climate Change*. Cheltenham, UK: Edward Elgar, 2003.

Sagoff, Mark. "At the Shrine of Our Lady of Fatima *or* Why Political Questions Are Not All Economic." *Arizona Law Review* 23 (1981): 1283–98.

———. *Economy of the Earth*. New York: Cambridge University Press, 1990.

Shrader-Frechette, Kristin. "A Defense of Risk-Cost-Benefit Analysis." In *Environmental Ethics:*

Readings in Theory and Application. Ed. Louis P. Pojman. 2nd ed. Belmont, CA: Wadsworth, 1998. 507–14.

Sierra Club. "Bill C-38 inflicts first significant blow to environmental justice in Canada." http://www.sierraclub.ca/en/save-canadas-environment-laws/bill-c-38-inflicts-first-significant-blow-environmental-justice-canada

Simon, Julian. "Scarcity or Abundance?" In *Ethical Issues in Business: A Philosophical Approach*. Ed. Thomas Donaldson and Patricia H. Werhane. 6th ed. Englewood Cliffs, NJ: Prentice Hall, 1999. 565–73.

Singer, Peter. *One World: The Ethics of Globalization*. New Haven, CT: Yale University Press, 2002.

Singh, Jang B., and V.C. Lakhan, "Business Ethics and the International Trade in Hazardous Wastes" *Journal of Business Ethics* 8.11 (1989): 889–99.

Skeptical Science. "Global Warming & Climate Change Myths." http://www.skepticalscience.com/argument.php

Smith, Tony. "Free Market Environmentalism: Against." *The Ag Bioethics Forum* 6.2 (1994): 2, 5–7.

Starik, Mark. "Should Trees Have Managerial Standing? Toward Stakeholder Status for Non-Human Nature." *Journal of Business Ethics* 14.3 (1995): 207–17.

Stavins, Robert N., and Bradley W. Whitehead. "Market-Based Incentives for Environmental Protection." *Environment* 34.7 (1992): 7–11, 29–42.

Stone, Christopher. *Should Trees Have Standing? Toward Legal Rights for Natural Objects*. Los Altos, CA: W. Kaufmann, 1974.

Taylor, Robert. "Economics, Ecology and Exchange: Free Market Environmentalism." *Humane Studies Review* 8.1 (1992): 2–8.

Tokar, Brian. "Trading Away the Earth: Pollution Credits and the Perils of 'Free Market Environmentalism.'" In *Taking Sides: Clashing Views on Controversial Environmental Issues*. Ed. Theodore D. Goldfarb. 7th ed. Guilford, CT: Dushkin, 1997. 15–21.

Wesley, E., and F. Peterson. "The Ethics of Burden-Sharing in the Global Greenhouse." *Journal of Agricultural and Environmental Economics* 11 (1999): 167–96.

World Commission on the Ethics of Scientific Knowledge and Technology (COMEST). *The Ethical Implications of Global Climate Change*. Paris: UNESCO, 2010.

BOX 10.6   Feel Like Watching a Movie?

I highly recommend *H2O* ("a cautionary thriller about Canada's destiny" featuring Paul Gross as Prime Minister).

And several documentaries: *The Ethics of Fracking, Waste Land, Gasland, Chasing Ice, An Inconvenient Truth, Waterlife, The 11th Hour*

Business Ethics and the International Trade in Hazardous Wastes

Jang B. Singh and V.C. Lakhan

ABSTRACT. The annual production of hazardous wastes which was less than 10 million metric tonnes in the 1940s is now in excess of 320 million metric tonnes.[†] These wastes are, in the main, by-products of industrial processes that have contributed significantly to the economic development of many countries which, in turn, has led to lifestyles that also generate hazardous wastes. The phenomenal increase in the generation of hazardous wastes coupled with various barriers to local disposal has led to the thriving international trade in these environmentally hazardous substances. This paper examines the nature of the international trade in hazardous wastes and the ethical issues associated with such business activity.

[1] The export of hazardous wastes by the more developed countries to the lesser developed nations is escalating beyond control. The ethical implications and environmental consequences of this trade in hazardous wastes highlight the need for international controls and regulations in the conduct of business by corporations in the more developed countries. In the late 1970s, the Love Canal environmental tragedy awakened the world to the effects of ill conceived and irresponsible disposal of hazardous by-products of industries. Today, the media focuses its attention on the alleged illegal dumping of hazardous wastes in the lesser developed countries (see Barthos, 1988, and Harden, 1988). The most recent dramatic case so far is that of Koko, Nigeria where more than eight thousand drums of hazardous wastes were dumped, some of which contained polychlorinated biphenyl (PCB), a highly carcinogenic compound and one of the world's most toxic wastes (Tifft, 1988). The government of Nigeria has detained a number of Nigerians in connection with the incident and President Babangida has indicated that they may face a firing squad if found guilty of illegal dumping. Previous to this was the media documentation in the spring of 1987 of an American barge laden with 3,000 tonnes of garbage being turned back to the United States by the Mexican navy. The barge had already tried, unsuccessfully, to dump its noxious cargo in North Carolina, Alabama, Mississippi and Louisiana. The Mexican navy action was aimed at preventing the barge from dumping its cargo in Mexico.

The three cases cited above serve as disturbing [2] examples of the international trade in hazardous

---

† Note that since this article was first published, the figure is over 400 million tonnes. See http://www.theworldcounts.com/counters/waste_pollution_facts/hazardous_waste_statistics.

* Jang B. Singh and V.C. Lakhan, "Business Ethics and the International Trade in Hazardous Wastes" *Journal of Business Ethics* 8.11 (1989): 889–99.

wastes. Not all of the activities involved in this trade are illegal. In fact, governments are often directly involved in the business of hazardous wastes. This paper examines various characteristics of the international trade in hazardous waste and discusses the ethical implications of such business activity.

The International Trade in Hazardous Wastes and Attendant Problems

[3] Miller (1988) defined hazardous waste as any material that may pose a substantial threat or potential hazard to human health or the environment when managed improperly. These wastes may be in solid, liquid, or gaseous form and include a variety of toxic, ignitable, corrosive, or dangerously reactive substances. Examples include acids, cyanides, pesticides, solvents, compounds of lead, mercury, arsenic, cadmium, and zinc, PCB's and dioxins, fly ash from power plants, infectious waste from hospitals, and research laboratories, obsolete explosives, herbicides, nerve gas, radioactive materials, sewage sludge, and other materials which contain toxic and carcinogenic organic compounds.

[4] Since World War II, the amount of toxic by-products created by the manufacturers of pharmaceuticals, petroleum, nuclear devices, pesticides, chemicals, and other allied products has increased almost exponentially. From an annual production of less than 10 million metric tonnes in the 1940's, the world now produces more than 320 million metric tonnes of extremely hazardous wastes per year. The United States is by far the biggest producer, with "over 275 million metric tonnes of hazardous waste produced each year" (Goldfarb, 1987). The total is well over one tonne per person. But the United States is not alone. European countries also produce millions of tonnes of hazardous wastes each year (Chiras, 1988). Recent figures reported by Tifft (1988) indicate that the twelve countries of the European Community produce about 35 million tonnes of hazardous wastes annually.

[5] The problems associated with hazardous wastes started to gain world-wide attention after 1977 when it was discovered that hazardous chemicals leaking from an abandoned waste dump had contaminated homes in a suburban development known as Love Canal, located in Niagara Falls, New York. This event triggered a frantic search for new ways and places to store hazardous wastes, and an introduction of new environmental regulations to store, handle, and dispose of hazardous wastes. With the "not in my backyard" (NIMBY) syndrome in the developed societies, the manufacturers and creators of hazardous wastes began to escalate the practice of dumping their wastes in the lesser developed countries.

[6] Table 1 mainly provides an extensive list of companies which are exporting various toxic wastes to the lesser developed countries. [...] It is seen that the United States and certain European countries are now turning to areas in Africa, Latin America, and the Caribbean to dump their wastes. Historically, the trade in wastes has been conducted among the industrialized nations. A major route involving industrialized nations is that between Canada and the United States. The movement of wastes from the United States into Canada is governed by the Canada-U.S.A. Agreement on the Transboundary Movement of Hazardous Waste which came into effect on November 8, 1986 (Environment Canada). In 1988, the United States exported 145,000 tonnes. Of this amount, only one third was recyclable, leaving approximately 96,667 tonnes of hazardous organic and inorganic wastes such as petroleum by-products, pesticides, heavy metals, and organic solvents and residues for disposal in the Canadian environment. Of interest is the fact that Canada restricts the import of nuclear waste, but not toxic, flammable, corrosive, reactive, and medical wastes from the United States.

Table 1 Identification of Actual Waste Shipments and Active Proposals

	Importing Country	Name of Firm	Point of Export	Type of Waste
1	Argentina	American Security International	Florida, USA	Solvents/ Chemical Sludge
2	Benin	Sesco Ltd.	Gibraltar	Non-Nuclear Toxic Waste
3	Benin	Government of France	France	Radioactive Wastes
4	Brazil	Applied Technologies	USA	Unspecified Toxic Waste
5	Brazil	Ashland Metal Co.	Pennsylvania, USA	N/A
6	Brazil	Delarre Metals Inc.	California, USA	N/A
7	Brazil	Astur Metals Inc.	Puerto Rico, USA	N/A
8	Canada	Over 400 Firms	Mainly points in New England, New York and Michigan	Petroleum By-products, Pesticides, Heavy Metals and Organic Solvents and Residues
9	Dominican Rep.	Arbuckle Machinery	Texas, USA	PCB Wastes
10	Dominican Rep.	Franklin Energy Res.	New York, USA	Refuse
11	Dominican Rep.	World Technology Co.	Italy	Toxic Liquid Wastes
12	Equatorial Guinea	Unspecified British	UK	Chemical Wastes
13	Gabon	Denison Mining	Colorado, USA	Uranium Tailing Wastes
14	Guinea	Bulkhandling Inc.	Philadelphia, USA	Toxic Incinerator Ash
15	Guinea-Bissau	Hamilton Resources	UK	N/A
16	Guinea-Bissau	B/S Import-Export Ltd.	UK	Pharmaceutical Industrial Waste
17	Guinea-Bissau	Hobday Ltd.	UK	Pharmaceutical Industrial Waste
18	Guinea-Bissau	Intercontrat SA	Switzerland	Pharmaceutical Industrial Waste
19	Guinea-Bissau	Lindaco Ltd.	Michigan, USA	Pharmaceutical Industrial Waste
20	Guyana	Pott Industries	California, USA	Industrial Oil Wastes
21	Guyana	Teixeria Farms International	California, USA	Paint Sludge
22	Haiti	Palino and Sons	Philadelphia, USA	Toxic Incinerator Ash
23	India	Jack & Charles Colbert	USA	Lead Tainted Hazardous Waste
24	Mexico	Arm Co. Steel	Missouri, USA	N/A
25	Mexico	Border Steel Mills	Texas, USA	N/A
26	Mexico	Chapparral Steel	Texas, USA	N/A
27	Mexico	Nucor Steel, Nebraska	Nebraska, USA	N/A

28	Mexico	Nucor Steel, Texas	Texas, USA	Furnace Dust
29	Mexico	Nucor Steel, Utah	Utah, USA	Furnace Dust
30	Mexico	Razorback Steel	Arkansas, USA	N/A
31	Mexico	Sheffield Steel Corp.	Oklahoma, USA	N/A
32	Mexico	Federated Metal	New Jersey, USA	Lead Wastes
33	Mexico	B.F. Goodrich	Texas, USA	PCB's, Mercury Cinders
34	Mexico	Diamond Shamrock	Texas, USA	PCB Wastes
35	Mexico	Bayou Steel Corp.	Louisiana, USA	Furnace Dust
36	Nigeria	Jack & Charles Colbert	USA	Lead Tainted Hazardous Waste
37	Paraguay	American Securities Int	Florida, USA	Solvents/Chemical Sludge
38	Peru	American Securities Int	Florida, USA	Solvents/Chemical Sludge
39	Senegal	Intercontrat, S.A.	Switzerland	N/A
40	South Africa	American Cyanimid	New Jersey, USA	Mercury-Laced Sludge
41	South Africa	Quanex	Texas, USA	PCB Wastes
42	South Korea	Jack & Charles Colbert	USA	Lead Tainted Hazardous Waste
43	Surinam	Mine Tech Intl.	Netherlands	PCB Wastes
44	Tonga	Omega Recovery	California, USA	Hazardous Wastes
45	Uruguay	American Security Int.	Florida, USA	Solvents/Chemical Sludge
46	Zimbabwe	Jack & Charles Colbert	USA	Lead Tainted Hazardous Waste

This table includes information mainly on actual waste shipments and active proposals for shipments from Europe and the United States to less developed countries. *Source:* Klatte *et al.*, 1988.

[7] Most of the United States hazardous wastes are shipped from the New England states, New York and Michigan and enter Ontario and Quebec which in 1988 received approximately 81,899 and 62,200 tonnes respectively. The neutralization and disposal of the imported hazardous wastes are done by several Canadian companies, with the two largest being Tricil and Stablex Canada Inc. Tricil, with several locations in Ontario, imports wastes from more than 85 known American companies, which it incinerates and treats in lagoons and landfill sites. Stablex Canada imports a wide variety of hazardous wastes from more than 300 U.S. companies. It uses various disposal methods, including landfills and cement kilns which burn not only the components needed for cement but also hazardous waste products. With the established Canada-U.S. Agreement on the Transboundary Movement of Hazardous Waste, companies like Tricil and Stablex may increase their importation of hazardous wastes generated in the United States. As it stands, the United States Environmental Protection Agency estimates that over 75% of the wastes exported from the U.S. is disposed of in Canada (Vallette, 1989). This esti-

mate will likely have to be raised in the near future. Canada-United States trade in hazardous wastes is not a one-way route. It is believed that all of the hazardous wastes imported by the United States (estimated at 65,000 tonnes in 1988) is generated in Canada (*Ibid.*).

[8] An especially controversial trend in the international trade in hazardous wastes is the development of routes between industrialized and "lesser developed countries". For example, according to the United States Environmental Protection Agency, there have been more proposals to ship hazardous wastes from the United States to Africa during 1988, than in the previous four years (Klatte *et al.*, 1988).

[9] African nations have recently joined together to try to completely ban the dumping of toxic wastes on their continent. They have referred to the practice as "toxic terrorism" performed by Western "merchants of death". Some African government officials are so disturbed by the newly exposed practices that they have threatened to execute guilty individuals by firing squad. Recently, Lagos officials, seized an Italian and a Danish ship along with fifteen people who were associated with transporting toxic wastes in the swampy Niger River delta, into Nigeria. This occurred shortly after the discovery of 3,800 tonnes of hazardous toxic wastes, which had originated in Italy. Local residents immediately became ill from inhaling the fumes from the leaking drums and containers which were filled with the highly carcinogenic compound PCB, and also radioactive material.

[10] Companies in the United States have been responsible for sending large quantities of hazardous wastes to Mexico. Although Mexico only accepts hazardous wastes for recycling, which is referred to as "sham re-cycling", there are numerous reports of illegal dumping incidents. Two Californian companies have proposed the shipping of 62,000 tonnes of hazardous wastes each year to Guyana for incineration. They are also close to concluding a deal with the Guyana Government "to build a giant toxic waste incinerator in that country". The companies have suggested that "the incinerator ash be sold as fertilizer and building materials" (Morrison, 1988, p. 8). Guyana is one of a large number of developing countries whose economic plight makes it willing to accept proposals such as this, despite the long term human and environmental costs (*Ibid.*, p. 9).

[11] Given the fact that hazardous wastes are:

(1) toxic;
(2) highly reactive when exposed to air, water, or other substances that they can cause explosions and generate toxic fumes;
(3) ignitable that they can undergo spontaneous combustion at relatively low temperatures;
(4) highly corrosive that they can eat away materials and living tissues;
(5) infectious, and
(6) radioactive;

Miller (1988) has, therefore, emphasized correctly that the proper transportation, disposal, deactivation, or storage of hazardous wastes is a grave environmental problem which is second only to nuclear war.

[12] The practice of transporting and dumping hazardous wastes in lesser developed nations, where knowledge of environmental issues is limited is causing, and will pose, major problems to both human health and the environment. Several comprehensive studies have outlined the detrimental impacts which hazardous waste can have on humans and natural ecosystems. Epstein *et al.* (1982) have provided a thorough and dramatic coverage of the impacts of hazardous wastes, while Regenstein (1982), in his book *America the Poisoned*, gives a good overview of the implications

of hazardous wastes. Essentially, hazardous wastes not only contaminate ground water, destroy habitats, cause human disease, contaminate the soil, but also enter the food chain at all levels, and eventually damage genetic material of all living things. For instance, when hazardous wastes enter water bodies, they are taken up by Zoo plankton, which single cell fish ingest while feeding. Other higher-level organisms also accumulate these substances, so that tissue concentrations become higher at higher levels of the food chain. The accumulation and biological magnification which occurs exposes organisms high on the food chain to highly dangerous levels of many chemicals. Understanding toxic chemical repercussions is still barely out of the dark ages, but it is known that metals present in water are toxic for fish. The metals irritate their gills and cause a mucus to build up on them, which eventually causes the fish to suffocate (Chiras, 1988). When hazardous wastes are deposited in the soil it is taken up by food crops, which eventually affect livestock as well as humans. When the ash enters the air, it also has the ability to cause pollution. Even though air is a finite resource capable of cleansing itself, it cannot entirely get rid of all pollutants. Besides causing respiratory problems in the local inhabitants, air pollution will damage the crops and reduce the yields. The rate of photosynthesis will be decreased with harmful effects on animal respiratory and central nervous systems (Miller, 1988).

[13] The hazardous wastes can also directly threaten human health through seeping into the ground and causing the direct pollution of aquifers, which supply "pure" drinking water. Today, in the United States, a long list of health related problems are caused by hazardous chemicals from "leaking underground storage tanks" (LUST). Investigations now show that human exposure to hazardous wastes from dumpsites, water bodies, and processing and storage areas can cause the disposed synthetic compounds to interact with particular enzymes or other chemicals in the body, and result in altered functions. Altered functions have been shown to include mutagenic (mutation-causing), carcinogenic (cancer-causing), and teratogenic (birth-defect causing) effects. In addition, they may cause serious liver and kidney dysfunction, sterility and numerous lesser physiological and neurological problems (see Nebel, 1987).

The Ethical Implications

The very notion of dumping one's wastes in someone else's territory is repulsive. When the Mexican navy turned back an American barge laden with garbage, one Mexican newspaper columnist commented that "the incident serves to illustrate once again the scorn that certain sectors of U.S. society feel toward Mexico in particular and Latin America in general" ("Mexico Sends Back", April 27, 1987, p. F9). Others have pointed to the export of wastes as an example of neo-colonialist behaviour. An official of an environmental organization expressed this view in the following manner: "I am concerned that if U.S. people think of us as their backyard, they can also think of us as their outhouse" (Porterfield and Weir, 1987, p. 343). In addition to arousing emotions such as those described above, the international trade in hazardous wastes raises a number of ethical issues. The rest of this paper examines some of these. [14]

The Right to a Livable Environment

The desire for a clean, safe and ecologically balanced environment is an often expressed sentiment. This is especially so in industrialized countries where an awareness of environmental issues is relatively high—a fact that is gaining recognition in political campaigns. However, expression of the desire for a clean, safe environment is not the same as stat- [15]

ing that a clean, safe environment is the right of every human being. But the right of an individual to a livable environment is easily established at the theoretical level. Blackstone (1983) examines the right to a livable environment from two angles—as a human right and as a legal right. The right to a clean, safe environment is seen as a human right since the absence of such a condition would prevent one from fulfilling one's human capacities.

> Each person has this right qua being human and because a livable environment is essential for one to fulfill his human capacities. And given the danger to our environment today and hence the danger to the very possibility of human existence, access to a livable environment must be conceived as a right which imposes upon everyone a correlative moral obligation to respect. (Blackstone, 1983, p. 413)

Guerrette (1986) illustrates this argument by reference to the Constitution of the United States. He proposes that people cannot live in a chemically toxic area, they cannot experience freedom in an industrially polluted environment, and they cannot be happy worrying about the quality of air they breathe or the carcinogenic effects of the water they drink (Guerrette, 1986, p. 409). Some even argue (e.g., Feinberg, 1983) that the right to a livable environment extends to future generations and that it is the duty of the present generation to pass on a clean, safe environment to them.

[16] Establishing the right to a livable environment as a human right is not the same as establishing it as a legal right. This requires the passing of appropriate legislation and the provision of a legal framework that may be used to seek a remedy if necessary. Such provisions are more prevalent in the industrialized countries and this is one of the push factors in the export of hazardous wastes to the lesser developed countries. This points to the need for a provision in international law of the right to a decent environment which with accompanying policies to save and preserve our environmental resources would be an even more effective tool than such a framework at the national level (Blackstone, 1983, p. 414). As ecologists suggest, serious harm done to one element in an ecosystem will invariably lead to the damage or even destruction of other elements in that and other ecosystems (Law Reform Commission of Canada, 1987, p. 262) and ecosystems transcend national boundaries. The need for international law in this area has not led to the formulation of the same. However, there have been campaigns to stop the flow of hazardous wastes across national boundaries. In a current campaign, the international environmental group, Greenpeace, is calling for a global ban on the transboundary movement of wastes. Greenpeace is basing its appeal on Principle 21 of the 1972 Declaration of the United Nations Conference on the Human Environment which declares that each state is responsible for ensuring that activities within their jurisdiction or control do not cause damage to the environment of other states or of areas beyond the limits of their own national jurisdiction (Klatte *et al.*, 1988, p. 3).

[17] A more direct harmful effect of the international trade in hazardous wastes is the damage to the health of workers involved in the transportation and disposal of these toxic substances. For example, prolonged exposure to wastes originating in Italy and transported by a ship called *Zanoobia* is suspected of causing the death of a crew person and the hospitalization of nine others (Klatte *et al.* 1983, p. 12). Whereas worker rights in work-place health and safety are gaining wider recognition in many industrialized nations this is not so in the "less developed" countries which are increasingly becoming the recipients of hazardous wastes. Widespread violation of workers' right to a clean, safe work environment

should therefore be expected to be a feature of the international trade in hazardous wastes.

Racist Implications

[18] The recent trend of sending more shipments of hazardous wastes to Third World countries has led to charges of racism. *West Africa*, a weekly magazine, referred to the dumping of toxic wastes as the latest in a series of historical traumas for Africa. The other traumas cited by the magazine were slavery, colonialism and unpayable foreign debts. An article in another African magazine viewed the dumping of wastes in Koko, Nigeria as follows:

> That Italy did not contemplate Australia or South Africa or some other place for industrial waste re-echoes what Europe has always thought of Africa: A wasteland. And the people who are there, waste beings. (Brooke, 1988, p. A10)

Charges of racism in the disposal of wastes have been made before at the national level in the United States. A study of waste disposal sites found that race was the most significant among variables tested in association with the location of commercial hazardous wastes facilities. The findings of this national study which were found to be statistically significant at the 0.0001 level showed that communities with the greatest number of commercial hazardous wastes facilities had the highest concentration of racial minorities (Lee, 1987, pp. 45–46). The study found that although socio-economic status appeared to play a role in the location of commercial hazardous wastes facilities, race was a more significant factor.

[19] In the United States, one of the arguments often advanced for locating commercial waste facilities in lower income areas is that these facilities create jobs. This is also one of the arguments being advanced for sending wastes to poor lesser developed countries. An examination of Table 1 would reveal that nearly all the countries receiving hazardous wastes have predominantly coloured populations. This is the reason why charges of racism are being made against exporters of wastes. However, it must be noted that even though the trend of sending wastes to countries such as those listed in Table 1 has recently gained strength, the bulk of the international trade in hazardous wastes is still within industrialized Europe and North America which have predominantly non-coloured populations.

[20] For example, the United States Environmental Protection Agency estimates that as much as 75% of the wastes exported from the U.S. is disposed of in Canada (Klatte *et al.*, 1988, p. 9). Another striking example is that a dump outside Schonberg, East Germany, is the home of well over 500,000 tonnes of waste a year from Western Europe ("Rubbish Between Germans", March 1, 1986, p. 46). Thus, while charges of racism in the export of hazardous wastes are being made by some Third World leaders, figures on the international trade in such substances do not substantiate these claims.

Corporate Responsibility

[21] The international trade in hazardous wastes basically involves three types of corporations—the generators of wastes, the exporters of wastes, and the importers of wastes. These entities, if they are to act in a responsible manner, should be accountable to the public for their behaviour.

> Having a corporate conscience means that a company takes responsibility for its actions, just as any conscientious individual would be expected to do. In corporate terms, this means that a company is accountable to the public for its behaviour not only in the complex organizational environment but in the natural physical environment as well. A company is thus responsible for its prod-

uct and for its effects on the public. (Guerrette, 1986, p. 410)

Using Guerrette's definition of corporate responsibility, it seems clear that a corporation involved in the international trade in hazardous wastes is not likely to be a responsible firm. The importer of hazardous wastes is clearly engaged in activities that will damage the environment while the exporter being aware that this is a possibility, nevertheless, sends these wastes to the importer. However, it is the generator of hazardous wastes that is the most culpable in this matter. If the wastes are not produced then obviously their disposal would not be necessary. Therefore, in view of the fact that virtually no safe method of disposing hazardous wastes exists, a case of corporate irresponsibility could easily be formulated against any corporation involved in the international trade in these substances.

Government Responsibility

[22] Why do countries export wastes? A major reason is that many of them are finding it difficult to build disposal facilities in their own countries because of the NIMBY syndrome mentioned earlier. Other reasons are that better technologies may be available in another country, facilities of a neighboring country may be closer to a generator of waste than a site on national territory and economies of scale may also be a factor. However, to these reasons must be added the fact that corporations may be motivated to dispose of waste in another country where less stringent regulations apply ("Transfrontier Movements", March 1984, p. 40). It is the responsibility of governments to establish regulations governing the disposal of wastes. In some countries, these regulations are stringent while in others they are lax or non-existent. Moreover, some countries have regulations governing disposal of wastes within national boundaries as well as regulations relating to the export of hazardous wastes. For example, companies in the United States that intend to export hazardous wastes are requested to submit notices to the Environmental Protection Agency (EPA) and to demonstrate that they have the permission of the receiving country (Porterfield and Weir, 1987, p. 341). However, the effectiveness of these controls is in question. The General Accounting Office has found that "the E.P.A. does not know whether it is controlling 90 percent of the existing waste or 10 percent. Likewise it does not know if it is controlling the wastes that are most hazardous" (*Ibid.*). Moreover, there is evidence indicating that other U.S. government agencies are encouraging the export of hazardous wastes. The Navy, the Army, the Defence Department, the Agriculture Department and the Treasury Department are some government agencies that have provided hazardous wastes to known exporters. Also, major U.S. cities, sometimes with the approval of the State Department, have been suppliers to the international trade in hazardous wastes (Porterfield and Weir, 1987, p. 342).

[23] While more stringent regulations, higher disposal costs, and heightened environmental awareness are pushing many companies in industrial countries to export hazardous wastes, it must be, nevertheless, realized that the governments of lesser developed countries are allowing such imports into their countries because of the need for foreign exchange. These governments are willing to damage the environment in return for hard currency or the creation of jobs. One must assume that on the basis of cost-benefit analysis these governments foresee more benefits than harm resulting from the importation of hazardous wastes. However, these benefits go mainly to a few waste brokers while the health of large numbers of people is put at risk. In some cases, decisions to import wastes are made by governments which hold power by force and fraud.

For example, Haiti which has imported wastes (see Table 1) is ruled by a military dictatorship and Guyana which is actively considering the importation of industrial oil wastes and paint sludge is ruled by a minority party which has rigged all elections held in that country since 1964. The ethical dilemma posed by this situation is that of whether or not an unrepresentative government of a country could be trusted to make decisions affecting the life and health of its citizens. In fact, a larger question is whether or not any government has the right to permit business activity that poses a high risk to human life and health.

[24]   Generally, governments of waste generating countries, in reaction to political pressure, have imposed stringent regulations on domestic disposal and some restrictions on the export of hazardous wastes; however, as the examples above illustrate, the latter restrictions are not strictly enforced, hence, indicating a duplicitous stance on the part of the generating countries. The governments of importing countries, in allowing into their countries, wastes that will disrupt ecosystems and damage human health, deny their citizens the right to a livable environment.

Conclusion

[25] Hazardous wastes are, in the main, by-products of industrial processes that have contributed significantly to the economic development of many countries. Economic development, in turn, has led to lifestyles which also generate hazardous wastes. To export these wastes to countries which do not benefit from waste generating industrial processes or whose citizens do not have lifestyles that generate such wastes is unethical. It is especially unjust to send hazardous wastes to lesser developed countries which lack the technology to minimize the deleterious effects of these substances. Nevertheless, these countries are increasingly becoming recipients of such cargoes. The need for stringent international regulation to govern the trade in hazardous wastes is now stronger than ever before. However, this alone will not significantly curb the international trade in hazardous wastes. International regulation must be coupled with a revolutionary reorganization of waste-generating processes and change in consumption patterns. Until this is achieved the international trade in hazardous wastes will continue and with it a plethora of unethical activities.

Bibliography

Barthos, G. 1988. "Third World Outraged at Receiving Toxic Trash." *The Toronto Star* June 26, pp. 1, 4.

Blackstone, W.T. 1983. "Ethics and Ecology.' In Beauchamp, T.L., and Bowie, N.E. (Eds), *Ethical Theory and Business* 2nd. edition. Englewood Cliffs, NJ: Prentice-Hall, Inc., pp.411–424.

Brooke, J. 1988. "Africa Fights Tide of Western Wastes." *The Globe and Mail* July 18, p. A10.

Chiras, D.D. 1988. *Environmental Science.* Denver: Benjamin Commings Publishing Co. Inc.

Environment Canada. 1986. *Canada-U.S.A. Agreement on the Transboundary Movement of Hazardous Waste.* Ottawa: Environment Canada.

Epstein. S.S., Brown. L.O., and Pope, C. 1982, *Hazardous Waste in America.* San Francisco: Sierra Club Books.

Feinberg, J. 1983. "The Rights of Animals and Unborn Generations." In Beauchamp, T.L. and Bowie, N.E., (Eds), *Ethical Theory and Business* 2nd. edition. Englewood Cliffs, NJ: Prentice-Hall Inc., pp. 428–436.

Goldfarb, T.D. 1987. *Taking Sides: Clashing Views on Controversial Environmental Issues.* Connecticut: Dushkin Publishing Co. Inc.

Guerrette, R.H. 1986. "Environmental Integrity and Corporate Responsibility." *Journal of Business Ethics* Vol. 5, pp. 409–415.

Harden, B. 1988. "Africa Refuses to Become Waste Dump for the West." *The Windsor Star,* July 9, p. A6.

Klatte, E., Palacio, F., Rapaport, D., and Vallette, J. 1988. *International Trade in Toxic Wastes: Policy and Data Analysis.* Washington, DC: Greenpeace International.

Law Reform Commission of Canada. 1987. "Crimes Against the Environment." In Poff, D., and Waluchow, W., *Business Ethics in Canada.* Scarborough, ON: Prentice-Hall Canada Inc., pp. 261–264.

Lee, C. 1987. "The Racist Disposal of Toxic Wastes." *Business and Society Review* Vol. 62, pp. 43–46.

Miller, T. 1988. *Living in the Environment.* Belmont, CA: Wadsworth.

Montreal Gazette. April 27, 1987. "Mexico Sends Back U.S. Barge Filled With Tonnes of Garbage." p. F9.

Morrison, A. 1988. "Dead Flowers to U.S. Firms that Plan to Send Waste to Guyana." *Catholic Standard*, Sunday, May 8.

Nebel, B.J. 1987. *Environmental Science.* Englewood Cliffs, NJ: Prentice-Hall, Inc.

OEGD Observer. March 1984. "Transfrontier Movements of Hazardous Wastes: Getting to Grips with the Problem." pp. 39–41.

Porterfield, A., and Weir, D. 1987. "The Export of U.S. Toxic Wastes." *The Nation*, Vol. 245, Iss. 10 (Oct. 3), pp. 341–344.

Regenstein, L. 1982. *America the Poisoned.* Washington, DC: Acropolis Books.

The Economist. March 1, 1986. "Rubbish Between Germans." p. 46.

Tifft, S. 1988. "Who Gets the Garbage." *Time* July 4, pp. 42–43.

Vallette, J. 1989. *The International Trade in Wastes: A Greenpeace Inventory* 4th edition. Luxembourg: Greenpeace International.

Questions

1. What happens when hazardous waste is not properly transported, deactivated, and disposed of or stored?
2. How could you argue that the right to a liveable environment extends to future generations?
3. What fact weakens the claim of racism (with respect to the international trade in hazardous wastes)?
4. Which of the three types of corporations found responsible by Singh and Lakhan do you think bears most responsibility—why?
5. If it's fair for developed countries to share their wealth, why isn't it fair for them to share their waste?
6. What conditions do you think must be met if trade in hazardous waste is to be morally acceptable? (Consider the rights- and consequence-based arguments presented by Singh and Lakhan, but consider other ethical approaches to decision making as well.)
7. Do any of Singh and Lakhan's arguments about the trade in hazardous wastes apply to trade in carbon emissions?

If a Tree Falls...

John Palmer, Eugene Tan, and Kent A. Peacock

[The first letter below, by Palmer, appeared in the *UWO Gazette* in 1992. Tan, a student there at the time, responded, with the second letter. Then Peacock spoke up (the third piece).

When the three pieces were published in the first edition of this text, I contacted Palmer to ask if he wanted to respond to Peacock. He did so (the fourth piece).

As I was preparing the second edition, I thought I'd contact Tan to see if he wanted to add anything to his initial comments; he did (the fifth piece).]

John Palmer, Letter to the Editor

"We can continue to log our brains out, and we probably won't run out of wood for another 50 years. But we will run out, because current management is not sustainable."

[1] The above quotation from a touchy-feely tree-hugger is pure and simple hogwash. Why?—Because the writer has an incomplete understanding of economics.

[2] Will we run out of timber for logging? Not likely. As current supplies are harvested, the decline in supply will cause prices to rise. Furthermore, as population and wealth increase, so will the demand for timber, also putting upward pressure on prices.

[3] But these higher prices provide important signals. They encourage people who would like to earn some profits to plant more trees. And they encourage potential buyers to look for substitutes for timber and to cut down on their use of lumber.

[4] We will not run out of timber, because, despite the warnings of naive tree-huggers, prices will rise, eliciting responses that promote conservation and more production.

[5] If the tree-huggers really believe we will run out of timber, they should buy up lots of land and plant lots of trees. And they and their progeny will be rich beyond their wildest dreams, if their predictions of doom and gloom are correct.

[6] But if they *do* plant more trees now, there will be more trees in the future, and their predictions will be wrong. And even if the doom-sayers don't plant the trees, some people will; the anticipation of future profits will keep us from running out of timber.

---

* University of Western Ontario *Gazette*, March 13, 1992. © 1992 by John Palmer. Reprinted with permission of the author. University of Western Ontario *Gazette*, March 19, 1992. © 1992 by Eugene Tan. Reprinted with permission of the author. Kent A. Peacock, "The Economics of Extinction" in Kent A. Peacock, Ed., *Living with the Earth: An Introduction to Environmental Philosophy*, pp. 338–341. © 1996 by Harcourt Brace & Company, Canada, Ltd. All rights reserved. Reprinted with permission of the publisher and the author.

[7] There is a heavy shadow of doubt clouding this rosy picture, though. It comes from the spectre of government intervention in the timber market in two ways.

[8] First, as the government gets involved in tree-planting and the leasing of timber lands, the incentive for lumber companies to practice conservation is diminished. "Why conserve," they reasonably ask themselves, "if the government is going to undercut our actions with their own programs?"

[9] Second, government intervention designed to keep prices low will further deter private conservation efforts. "Why plant more trees," people will reasonably ask, "if we can't sell them for a price high enough to cover all our costs?"

[10] And so the more the government tries to keep future prices down, the more it deters private conservation efforts.

[11] Will we run out of timber? Only if we implement really stupid government policies that discourage private conservation.

Eugene Tan, Letter to the Editor

[1] On March 13, an article by John Palmer, a professor of economics, appeared in *The Gazette*. He accused environmentalists (tree-huggers) of having an incomplete understanding of economics and of naivety. He pleaded for unencumbered markets to control forestry practices. Palmer's article affirmed that corporate North America is leading us down the path towards environmental degradation. The road to hell is paved with sickening rationalizations.

[2] The Greek roots of economy and ecology are inextricably linked. Economy, from *oikonomic*, means the management of the household, whereas ecology, from the root *oikos* plus *logos*, means household.

[3] But Palmer suggests that the free market will provide all that we need when it becomes profitable.

[4] Palmer maintains that an incomplete understanding of economics has led to the naive view that trees are becoming endangered. The market will provide all that we need. Scientific reality maintains:

- The widespread destruction of trees for timber or farmland has contributed to global warming;
- Logging practices practically ensure soil destruction, harming future growth;
- Planting trees for short-term economic gain is an asinine proposition because trees take substantial time to grow;
- So much is wasted that demand-side economics just makes sense;
- One of the leading causes of animal species extinction is loss of habitat.

[5] Has simple economics accounted for these factors or are they the 'externalities' evoked by many economists when a model goes wrong? The presence of externalities means that economists don't understand all factors involved. I fail to see how Dr. Palmer's 'complete' understanding of economics would preserve vital resources.

[6] Palmer's article is guilty of the heinous crime of which he accuses environmentalists. Economists simply have an incomplete understanding of ecology and cannot begin to account for the infinite number of variables and nuances in an ecosystem. Physician, heal thyself.

Kent A. Peacock, The Economics of Extinction

[1] Professor John Palmer condemns "tree-huggers" for failing to understand economics. Don't worry about running out of trees, he tell us, market forces will guarantee that timber producers will do the right thing and make sure that there are lots of trees for the future. The only thing, he says, that could

cause us to run out of timber would be government intervention in environmental management, since that would remove the incentive for private conservation.

[2] I wish I could agree with this rosy picture of the magic of market economics; life would be so much simpler. But the relationships between market forces and ecological necessities are far more complex and problematic than Palmer is apparently aware. Of course there is an incentive to conserve a resource, or renew it if one knows how; that is elementary. However, the free-market boosters forget that all too often there are also enormous short-term *disincentives* to conservation and renewal. Sometimes it is highly economically advantageous to *wipe out* a resource rather than conserve it. This dismal process is known as the *economics of extinction*, and it is worthwhile, although unpleasant, to remind ourselves how it works.

[3] As a resource (say timber, whales, cod, rhino horns) becomes more and more scarce, its market value approaches infinity. Market value often has little to do with the actual value of the resource for human welfare; we do need timber, but no one has any real need for pulverized rhino horns. Nevertheless, they command such a fabulous price on certain markets that poachers will risk death to hunt down the few remaining rhinos. No incentive to conserve can override the immediate gain to be made from cashing in the resource. Furthermore, any measure which could increase the supply (say, establishing a rhino ranch) would tend to lower its market value; the more effective the renewal method, the more it would tend to cancel out the scarcity value of the resource. Add to all this the fact that measures to renew and conserve a resource can be economically risky and have costs, often large, which may not be recoverable in the short term at all. Hence, when a resource is scarce there are positive *disincentives*

to renew it. The scarcer the resource, the more it is in demand, and the harder it is to renew, the more these disincentives tend to operate. If nothing but pure market forces govern, the result (and this has happened time and again in history) is very often the extinction or commercial exhaustion of the resource, not its preservation.

Another practice that contributes to extinction [4] is *discounting the future* when carrying out an economic cost-benefit analysis. This means that we often apply a discount to the value of a resource that we will not be able to profit from right away; the longer we will have to wait to use it, the more we discount it. This is just an academic way of saying that we often grab all of something for ourselves now, and let the future take care of itself. Sometimes people have even deliberately destroyed remaining stocks of a resource so that no one else can profit from it; butterfly collectors used to burn out the hillsides that were home to rare species so that they would have the only remaining specimens to sell (see Rolston 1989.) The grab-it-all-now factor is especially likely to operate if the resource is very expensive or impossible to renew, if there is a very high immediate demand for it, or if its renewal is so slow that the money invested in the harvesting technology cannot be recovered if one waits for the resource to renew itself. (The latter is the case for whales; see Dobra 1978.) We need something like the *seventh-generation rule* of many Native North American peoples—before you act, consider the effect on the seventh generation to follow!

Nothing I have said here should be news to any- [5] one familiar with economics or the long and tragic history of resource depletion. Let's talk about forestry, for instance, since Palmer brought the subject up; the eroded, desiccated area of the world now known as Lebanon is a very good example of what can happen if the needs of commerce are allowed to determine the fate of a resource. (To be sure, commercial exploitation is not the only reason for the deforestation of the Levant—but it was one of the major reasons.) Three thousand years ago, Lebanon had at least two million acres in timber, the famous cedars of Lebanon. (See the selection in *Living with the Earth* by Carter and Dale, Chapter 4.) In fact, the topography, climate, and tree types were remarkably similar to those of British Columbia today. For several centuries, while the trees held out, forestry was the basis for the thriving Phoenician commercial empire. Eventually, though, the ecology collapsed, and with it the prosperity of the society it supported. Billions of tons of topsoil washed into the sea and the forests disappeared completely except for a few guarded sacred groves. The country today has only the remotest resemblance to its lush and fertile condition in biblical times.

[6] And this is just a typical example; there is very little historical evidence to support the faith that market forces by themselves can guarantee adequate renewal and conservation of resources, and much evidence against it. What almost always seems to happen is that the immediate demand for a resource outweighs the perceived advantage to be gained by long-term measures. Many societies in the past have desperately attempted to reforest, to replenish topsoil or conserve stocks of fish or game; only a few have succeeded, because the short-term pressure to exploit the resource was always too great.

[7] Still speaking of forestry, Palmer also shows no sensitivity to the really tough biological and technical problems posed by reforestation. In fact, it is very unclear that we really know how to replace the forests that we are harvesting so rapaciously. Foresters would have us believe that they are competent to replace them with "managed" forests as good as or better than those that they clear-cut away. This, like the belief in the power of the "invisible hand" itself, is mostly an article of faith; there is insufficient evidence that present methods work, and some evidence that they do not (in the sense that they may lead to a long-term but inevitable decline in the vitality of the ecology). I am certainly not saying that sustainable harvesting of forest products is impossible, but I am saying that we have not yet found a completely reliable method, especially if we insist on continuing to be able to harvest at the rate and scale that we now find necessary.

[8] The biggest problem we face right now is just the problem that Aldo Leopold identified many years ago: there is very little correspondence between the market value of a "resource" such as a plant or animal species and its real value to the health and functioning of the ecology. We must figure out how to devise an economic system that reflects ecological reality, or our hi-tech culture will go the way of all the other failed cultures whose ruins lie weathering in the deserts they created.

References

Clark, C. 1973. "The Economics of Overexploitation," *Science* 181, 630–634.

Dobra, Peter M. 1978. "Cetaceans: A Litany of Cain," *Boston College Environmental Affairs Law Review* 7(1), 165–183.

Invited Response, John Palmer[*]

[1] On a recent trip to Alberta, I was subjected to a lengthy lecture from a retired gentleman about all the trains passing his house, carrying lumber from British Columbia to the east. He was quite

---

[*] © 1999 by John Palmer. Reprinted with permission of the author.

concerned about all the trees being cut down in British Columbia. I suggested that if his concerns have merit, he could do his grandchildren a great service by buying up a bunch of land and planting trees on it—he'd be able to leave them an extremely valuable resource.

[2] The point of this story, and of my original brief editorial, is simply this: people respond to incentives. When people expect prices to rise in the future, some will respond by trying to make sure they have more to sell then, when prices are higher. The second point of the editorial was that government programs which keep timber prices low will inhibit both the incentives (prices) and the response (private reforestation), thus creating more future deforestation than we would have with an unfettered market.

[3] The key to having the market work effectively is that there be well-defined and well-enforced property rights. Only if people can rely on being able to capture future gains will they make decisions to conserve now and plant more for the future. We don't have persistent shortages of wheat, eggs, or cattle for this very reason: people know they can reap what they have sown. We do have persistent shortages, however, of things for which property rights cannot be well-defined or well-enforced, such as whales, even though whales, like cattle, are replenishable resources.

[4] The difference in sustainability between whales and cows is not the fault of the market economy. Non-market economies have the same problems of over-exploitation of resources. Rather, the difference between whales and cows is that property rights to cows are relatively easily defined and enforced. Property rights to whales aren't, and so whales have been seriously over-hunted to the brink of extinction.

[5] The same thing can happen to our forests. We have a myriad of government programs that continue to erode property rights and the expectations that people will be able to reap what they have sown. For example, stumpage fees on government lands are set so low that in many instances private reforestation doesn't pay.

[6] Note that nowhere have I discussed other values of having forests. The only point I wished to make initially was that we won't run out of wood (see the initial quotation on which I based the original editorial) if market forces are allowed to work. I was very disappointed that those commenting on my original piece chose to ignore this simple point and raise other issues I did not have the space to address in that editorial. I do, however, discuss the concepts of externalities and other market failures at length in my book, *The Economic Way of Thinking* (Paul Heyne and John Palmer, 1st Canadian edition, Prentice Hall, 1999).

Invited Response, Eugene Tan

[1] It's been twenty-three years since I, a young idealistic science student at the University of Western Ontario, filled with the bravado of youth, felt qualified to take on a Professor of Economics on the subject of economic theory. Much has passed since my exuberant outburst, and time may have tempered my confidence, but not my conviction. At this point, I would like to offer to Professor Palmer two messages: first, I do apologize for the indiscretion of my *ad hominem* attacks; and, second, respectfully, I still disagree.

[2] I had the good fortune to attend law school the year following these exchanges. My bravado had not subsided in that short time, and in response to my professor's query, "What is property?", I responded, "Property is theft." The clarity of that moment has subsided, but, I must admit, it is a position that still

informs much of my view of the market approach to the environment.

[3] The free, unregulated market approach to the preservation of the environment relies upon the fundamental principle that a growing demand in relation to supply will naturally drive prices of the scarce resource. A related principle is that people respond to incentives, and as prices rise, the incentive to plant more, preserve more, or conserve more increases based on the motivation of wealth. In his invited response, Professor Palmer proposes that the key to this approach is the enforcement of (personal) property rights, free from the erosion by ill-conceived government regulation.

[4] I think that we can agree that such society does not currently exist anywhere. I have been party to numerous major undertakings where the findings of environmental impact assessments have given way to speculative assertions of economic stimulation or suggestions that the projects in question were necessary to sustain unsustainable local economies. There are almost always external considerations that form part of the equation, interfering with the theoretical ideal. I would further suggest that we have the common ground that half way is no way at all when striving for lofty goals.

[5] I recognize now that Professor Palmer's point was to demonstrate that people, acting in their own self-interest, will tend to preserve what is valuable, and, in this example forests (and, perhaps as a by-product, our environment) would benefit. My initial, visceral reaction years ago was that the economic theory clearly ignored scientific and historical reality. My second reaction was disbelief: we are as far removed from that pure, free market society as we are from a society that adequately protects the environment through consensus or regulation.

[6] Upon further reflection, I believe that a further fundamental flaw in the "environmental capital" theory is that it just doesn't seem to ring true. Some people may have the discipline and foresight to invest wisely, extract responsibly, conserve, preserve, and grow this environmental wealth. However, observationally, the opposite seems to be true far more often: the self-interest upon which this theory relies is not the self-interest that many of us demonstrate.

[7] The other single, perhaps most important criticism that I have of Professor Palmer's approach is that it relies exclusively on reactionary forces. In other words, scarcity drives up prices, which *then* leads to conservation because people are motivated by wealth. Given the extremely long history demonstrating our imperfect understanding of ecosystems, I believe that the point of scarcity may often be past the point of protection. Lost along the way may be biodiversity, habitat, soil health, and other unknown contributors to a thriving forest ecosystem in which we all have a stake.

[8] Is this then advocacy for collective rights rather than individual rights in relation to the environment? I believe that acknowledgement of a collective right informs much of my philosophy on this subject, but I must admit that the clarity of any philosophy has been clouded over time. Do I still believe that (personal) property is theft? That conviction has been dulled, but I suggest we must know that each of us have a stake in our resources. Forests are a product on one hand, one that can be extracted and refined for the production of (personal) wealth. However, forests are much more: they are places for all of us to enjoy, they are means of providing us with clear air, and they are habitats for diverse species, many of which have been, or may be, important to all of us. I no longer have easy answers, so, for now, my approach is to strive to live simply, use responsibly, and always recognize that everything I do has an impact on others.

Questions

1. (a) What assumption about human behaviour does Palmer's free-market environmentalism, and indeed all free-market theory, rest on?
   (b) What evidence do we have that that assumption is correct?
2. (a) Is there an element of the paper tiger fallacy in Tan's first response to Palmer?
   (b) Which of the scientific facts that Tan lists does most damage to Palmer's argument?
3. (a) Explain "the economics of extinction."
   (b) What ethical approach(es) would support the poacher's actions as morally right?
   (c) Both Palmer's tree-planters and Peacock's poachers seem to be acting out of self-interest, so why does the one renew resources and the other wipe them out?
   (d) Even if Palmer is right, there are problems, Peacock says and Tan implies, with the solution of just planting more trees. What are they?
4. (a) (i) Explain Palmer's point about the danger of government regulation, to which neither Tan nor Peacock responded.
   (ii) Assess Smith's response: "Citizens have a right to a livable environment, and enforcing rights is part of the legitimate function of government. The thesis that responsibility for the environment should be left entirely in the hands of private economic agents is as ludicrous as the idea that rights to freedom of speech or freedom of religion should be left entirely to the market" (see this chapter's "References and Further Reading" list for citation).
   (b) (i) Find out what "the tragedy of the commons" refers to (if you don't already know) and explain how it supports Palmer's view.
   (ii) What relevance does Peacock's telling of "the tragedy of the Lebanon forests" have here?
   (c) How can we make sure whales don't become extinct, given Palmer's comment that both market and non-market economies fail in this regard? (And is this something we should do? Why/not?)
5. What sort of thing do you think Tan is talking about when he says, in his second response, "I have been party to numerous major undertakings where the findings of environmental impact assessments have given way to speculative assertions of economic stimulation or suggestions that the projects in question were necessary to sustain unsustainable local economies"?

Ethics and Climate Change: An Introduction*

Stephen M. Gardiner

[1] Significant values are incorporated into the foundations of international climate policy, and necessarily so. As the leading scientific authority on climate change, the United Nations' Intergovernmental Panel on Climate Change (IPCC), recognized at the outset of one of its recent reports, while 'natural, technical, and social sciences can provide essential information and evidence needed for decisions... at the same time, *such decisions are value judgments...*' [[1], p. 2, emphasis added]. With this in mind, it is no surprise that ethical concepts play a leading role in the way the issue is set out in the foundational legal document, the United Nations framework convention on climate change of 1992.[2] This treaty states as its motivation the 'protection of current and future generations of mankind', declares as its major objective the prevention of 'dangerous anthropogenic interference' with the climate system, and announces that this objective must be achieved while also protecting ecological, subsistence, and economic values. In addition, the text goes on to list a number of principles to guide the fulfillment of these objectives, and these make heavy use of value-laden concepts. For example, appeals are made to 'equity', 'common but differentiated responsibilities' (Article 3.1), the 'special needs' of developing countries (Article 3.2), the 'right' to development (Article 3.4), and the aim of promoting a supportive, open, sustainable, and nondiscriminatory international economic system (Article 3.5). There is no doubt then that ethical concerns are central to climate policy. Still, important questions arise concerning how to interpret, reconcile, and implement the relevant values, and whether the legal account of them should be challenged or extended. This brings us squarely into the realm of moral and political philosophy, broadly construed.

In this brief introduction to the subject, I will [2] not attempt the large project of assessing the values of the framework convention. Instead, my aim is to indicate how ethical analysis can make a contribution to five central concerns of climate policy: the treatment of scientific uncertainty, responsibility for past emissions, the setting of mitigation targets, and the places of adaptation and geoengineering in the policy portfolio. Inevitably, the account I offer here will be too simplistic and selective. Still, I hope that it provides a useful gateway into the emerging literature (see also[3]).

---

* *WIREs Climate Change* 1.1 (2010): 54–66.

Skepticisms

[3] On the face of it, the claim that climate change poses a real threat that justifies serious action is supported by a broad scientific consensus.[4,5] Still, in the public realm this claim has been subject to three prominent challenges.

[4] The first asserts that the science remains uncertain, so that current action is unjustified. This claim raises important epistemic and normative questions about what constitutes relevant uncertainty, and what amounts to appropriate action under it. We can make some progress on the first question if we begin with a distinction. In economics, situations involving uncertainty are distinguished from those involving risk. Suppose one can identify a possible negative outcome of some action. That outcome is a risk if one can also identify, or reliably estimate, the probability of its occurrence; it is uncertain if one cannot.[6] On this account, it is unclear whether the science is uncertain in the technical sense. On the one hand, the IPCC does assign probabilities to many of its projections, making the situation one of risk. Moreover, many of these assignments are both high, and associated with substantial negative damages; hence, they do seem sufficient to justify significant action.

[5] On the other hand, most of the IPCC's probability assignments are based on expert judgment, rather than direct appeals to causal mechanisms. Hence, these are 'subjective', rather than objective probabilities. Appeal to subjective probabilities is common in many approaches to risk. Indeed, some claim that all probabilities are ultimately subjective (e.g.,[7]). But if one is suspicious of subjective probabilities in general, or has particular reasons to be skeptical in this case, one might reject the IPCC assignments and continue to regard climate change as genuinely uncertain in the technical sense.

[6] Still, granting this concession is not enough by itself to make the skeptic's case. Suppose that we do lack robust probability information about climate change. Still, there is something troubling about the claim that one should refuse to act just because of this. We do not get to pick and choose the problems we face, and ignoring those whose shapes we do not like seems both a bizarre strategy, and also out of step with how we behave elsewhere. Many important life decisions come without good probability information attached (e.g., who to marry, what career path to follow, where to live). But this does not paralyze us there.

[7] This brings us to the issue of precaution. The framework convention makes the claim that 'where there are threats of serious or irreversible damage, lack of full scientific certainty should not be used as a reason for postponing (precautionary) measures (to anticipate, prevent, or minimize the causes of climate change and mitigate its adverse effects)' (Article 3.3). Hence, the treaty explicitly rules out some kinds of appeal to uncertainty as justifications for inaction.

[8] Stated as it is in the convention, this appeal to precaution is extremely minimal and underdeveloped. However, some have tried to generate a more general precautionary principle. According to one standard statement, this asserts 'when an activity raises threats of harm to human health or the environment, precautionary measures should be taken even if some cause and effect relationship are not fully established scientifically'.[8] However, such claims have frequently been dismissed as extreme, myopic, and ultimately vacuous. Could not a precautionary principle be invoked to stop *any* activity, however beneficial, on the basis of any kind of worry, however fanciful? If so, the critics charge, surely it is irrational, and ought to be neglected. This is the second challenge to action on climate change.

[9] Understood in a completely open-ended way, the precautionary principle may be vulnerable to such objections. However, it is plausible to try to restrict its application by introducing criteria to guide when the principle ought to be applied.[9] In previous work, I have tried to illustrate this using John Rawls's criteria for the application of a maximin principle: that the situation is uncertain, in the sense that the parties lack reliable probability information; that they care little for potential gains above the minimum they can secure by acting in a precautionary manner; and that they face outcomes that are unacceptable [[10], p. 134]. This approach not only diffuses the original objections, but suggests that many disputes about precaution ultimately do not rest on a rejection of the principle, but rather on disagreement about whether the relevant criteria are met. This significantly reframes the theoretical debate.

[10] At a more practical level, a reasonable case can be made that the Rawlsian precautionary principle applies to climate change. First, presumably some of the projected impacts, being severe or catastrophic, are morally unacceptable. Second, we have already seen that there may be uncertainty in the technical sense. However, third, the claim that we care little for the gains that can be made beyond those secured by precautionary action is more contentious. On the one hand, Cass Sunstein has argued that this condition threatens to confine the Rawlsian version of the principle to trivial cases, and moreover undermines the application to global warming because the costs of mitigation amount to hundreds of millions of dollars [[11], p. 112]. (Because of this, he tries to 'build on' the Rawlsian version to develop an alternative catastrophic harm precautionary principle [[12], p. 168].) On the other hand, though Sunstein is surely right that more work needs to be done in fleshing out the precautionary principle, it is not clear that the problem is that the Rawlsian version is 'trivial'. Remember that Rawls is speaking of gains that can be made *above some minimum we can guarantee* through eliminating the worst case scenario. Hence, much depends on how one understands the alternative options. Suppose, e.g., that we could avoid the possibility of catastrophic climate change and guarantee a decent quality of life for everyone, all at the cost of slowing down our rate of accumulation of purely *luxury* goods by two years (*cf.* [13]). This might satisfy the 'care little for gains' condition even if the cost of those luxury goods in dollar terms were very large. For example, the importance of averting catastrophic climate change might simply make such a loss relatively unimportant. Given this point, the real issue seems to revolve around the interpretation and elaboration of the 'care little for gains' condition, rather than whether it is 'too stringent' (pace. [12], p. 156). In my view, resolving this issue is likely to involve a substantive project in normative ethics.

[11] The issue of how to understand the costs of climate change brings us to the third challenge. Many economists maintain that only modest steps should be taken, since (they say) the costs of substantial action outweigh the benefits.[14-16] This result, however, is hardly robust, and other prominent economists argue for the contrary conclusion, that substantial action is strongly justified.[17,18] There are many reasons for this disagreement. One concerns the integrity of the relevant calculations. Some distinguished economists argue that economic costs and benefits simply cannot be projected with any precision over the relevant timeframes (of a century or more), so that fine-grained calculations amount to 'self-deception'.[19,20] But it is also true that long-range economic models must implicitly make many important ethical judgments, about which there is substantial disagreement. These include issues such as the distribution of benefits and burdens across individuals, countries, and time, and the correct

way to deal with noneconomic (e.g., interpersonal, aesthetic, and natural) values.

[12] Most prominently, conventional economics adopts the practice of discounting future costs and benefits at a uniform rate of 2–10% per year. This has the effect of sharply reducing the impact of high values in the future, especially when the rates are high.[21] Some argue that this practice is unethical, since it discriminates against future generations. Moreover, its theoretical foundations appear to be weak. Several distinct rationales are offered for discounting, and these often seem to pull in different directions.[22,23] More importantly, many of the rationales are essentially ethical: they claim that future people will be better off and so should pay more, or that the current generation ought to be able to protect itself from excessive demands by the future, or that political institutions ought to respect the pure time preference of the present generation (if it has one). Given this, what might initially appear to be merely a 'technical issue' within economics turns on substantive (and controversial) claims in ethical theory.

Past Emissions

[13] If action is warranted, who should take it, and what should be done? One proposal is that responsibility should be assigned in light of past emissions. Two kinds of argument are prominent. The first invokes historical principles of responsibility, along the lines of the commonsense ideals of 'you broke it, you fix it' and 'clean up your own mess'.[24,25] Such principles are already familiar in environmental law and regulation, appearing, e.g., in various versions of the 'polluter pays' principle (PPP). They imply that those who cause a problem have an obligation to rectify it, and also assume additional liabilities, such as for compensation, if the problem imposes costs or harms on others. The second kind of argument appeals to fair access. The thought is that the atmosphere's capacity to absorb greenhouse gases without adverse effects is a limited resource that is, or ought to be, held in common. If some have used up the resource, and in doing so denied others access to it, then compensation may be owed. The latecomers have been deprived of their fair share.

[14] Such rationales for considering past emissions seem straightforward and readily applicable to climate change. However, this application has been subject to four prominent objections.

[15] The first objection asserts that past polluters were ignorant of the adverse effects of their emissions, and so ought not to be blamed. They neither intended nor foresaw the effects of their behavior, and so should not be held responsible. This objection initially seems compelling, but turns out to be more complicated when pressed. First, it is worth distinguishing blame as such from responsibility. Though it is true that we do not usually blame those ignorant of what they do, still we often hold them responsible. Hence, showing that blame is inappropriate is insufficient to dismiss past emissions.[24] Second, there are reasons for holding the ignorant responsible in this case. On the one hand, consider the 'you broke it, you fix it' rationale. If I accidentally break something of yours, we usually think that I have some obligation to fix it, even if I was ignorant that my behavior was dangerous, and perhaps even if I could not have known. It remains true that I broke it, and in many contexts that is sufficient. After all, if I am not to fix it, who will? Even if it is not completely fair that I bear the burden, is it not at least less unfair than leaving you to bear it alone?[24,26] On the other hand, consider the fair access rationale. Suppose that I unwittingly deprive you of your share of something and benefit from doing so. Is it not natural to think that I should step in to help when the problem is discovered? For example, suppose that everyone in the office chips

in to order pizza for lunch. You have to dash out for a meeting, and so leave your slices in the refrigerator. I (having already eaten my slices) discover and eat yours because I assume that they must be going spare. You return to find that you now do not have any lunch. Is this simply your problem? We do not usually think so. Even though I did not realize at the time that I was taking your pizza, this does not mean that I have no special obligations. The fact that I ate your lunch remains morally relevant.

[16] The second objection emerges from the claim that there is a disanalogy between the pizza case and that of past emissions. In the pizza case, you have a clear right to the eaten slices, because you have already paid for them. But in the case of emissions, where the shares of the latecomers are used up by those who come earlier, it might be maintained that the latecomers have no such claim. Perhaps it is simply 'first-come, first-served', and hard luck to the tardy.

[17] In my view, this response is too quick. We must ask what justifies a policy like 'first-come, first-served' in the first place. To see why, consider one natural explanation. If a resource initially appears to be unlimited, then those who want to consume it might simply assume at the outset that no issues of allocation arise. Everyone can take whatever they want, with no adverse consequences for others. In this case, the principle is not really 'first-come, first-served' (which implies that the resource is limited, so that some may lose out), but rather 'free for all' (which does not). Since it is assumed that there is more than enough for everyone, no principle of allocation is needed.

[18] But what if the assumption that the resource is unlimited turns out to be mistaken, so that 'free for all' is untenable? Do those who have already consumed large shares have no special responsibility to those who have not, and now cannot? Does the original argument for 'free for all' justify ignoring the past? Arguably not. After all, if the parties had considered at the outset the possibility that the resource might turn out to be limited, which allocation principle would have seemed more reasonable and fair: 'free for all, with no special responsibility for the early users if the resource turns out to be unlimited', or 'free for all, but with early users liable to extra responsibilities if the assumption of unlimitedness turns out to be mistaken'? Offhand, it is difficult to see why ignoring the past would be favored. Indeed, there seem to be clear reasons to reject it: it makes later users vulnerable in an unnecessary way, and provides a potentially costly incentive to consume early if possible. Given this, 'first-come, first-served' looks unmotivated. Why adopt an allocation rule that so thoroughly exempts early users from responsibility? Clearly, more needs to be said.

[19] The third objection to considering past emissions emphasizes that, since significant anthropogenic emissions have been occurring since 1750, many past polluters are now dead. Given this, it is said that 'polluter pays' principles no longer really apply to a substantial proportion of past emissions; instead, what is really being proposed under the banner 'polluter pays' is that the descendants of the original polluters should pay for those emissions, because they have benefited from the past pollution (because of industrialization in their countries). However, the argument continues, this 'beneficiary pays principle' (BPP) is unjust because it holds current individuals responsible for emissions that they did not cause (and could not have prevented), and in ways which diminish their own opportunities.[27,28]

[20] Much could be said about this objection (see also [29] and [30]), but here let me make just two comments. First, the claim that polluter pays does not apply is more complex than it first seems. For example, it does apply if it refers not to individuals as such but to some entity to which they are connected, such

as a country, people or corporation. Moreover, this is the case in climate change, where polluter pays is usually invoked to suggest that countries should be held responsible for their past emissions, and these typically have persisted over the time period envisioned.

[21] Many proponents of the objection recognize this complication. To meet it, they typically reject the moral relevance of states, and instead invoke a strong individualism that claims that only individuals should matter ultimately from the moral point of view. Still (second) it should be noted that this move makes the argument more controversial than it initially appears. On the one hand, even many individualists would argue that states often play the role of representing individuals and discharging many of their moral responsibilities. Given this, more needs to be said about why the fact of membership is irrelevant for assigning responsibility. On the other hand, the argument ignores the issue that a very strong individualism would also call into question many other practices surrounding inherited rights and responsibility. Put most baldly, if we are not responsible for at least some of the debts incurred by our ancestors, why are we entitled to inherit all of the benefits of their activities? Hence, if we disavow their emissions, must we also relinquish the territory and infrastructure they left to us? The worry here is that, if successful, the attempt to undermine the PPP and BPP is liable to prove too much, or at least to presuppose a radical rethinking of global politics.

[22] The fourth objection to taking past emissions seriously claims that doing so would be impractical. Instead, it is said, if agreement is to be politically feasible, we should be forward-looking in our approach. The most prominent response to this objection is that it makes a rash claim about political reality. On the contrary, it might be said, since a genuinely global agreement is needed to tackle climate change, and since many nations of the world would not accept an agreement that did not explicitly or implicitly recognize past disparities, any attempt to exclude the past from consideration is itself seriously unrealistic.

Future Emissions

Whatever we say about the past, most people accept [23] that something should be done to limit future emissions. Such a limit would transform an open access resource into one that must be distributed. This raises profound ethical questions, and especially ones of procedural and distributive justice.

Procedurally, the main issue is how to get an [24] agreement that pays due respect to all of the parties involved. In practice, international discussion has treated emissions reductions as a matter for political horse-trading. Individual nations offer cuts in terms of their own emissions in exchange for cuts from the others, and other non-climate-related benefits. However, in an international system characterized by historical injustice and large imbalances of power, the prospect that such bargaining will be fair to all parties seems dim. Moreover, as Henry Shue argues, there is a threat of compound injustice.[31] Those treated unfairly in the past are likely to be more vulnerable to current injustices because of their past treatment. Finally, there are worries that the interests of those most affected by future climate change—future generations, the very poor, animals and nature—are not adequately represented. Why expect an agreement driven by representatives of the world's most affluent people to produce justice in this context?

The question of how to arrange a climate regime [25] that is procedurally fair is an important one. But some of the concerns might be met if we had a good idea of what a fair distributive outcome might look like. At the theoretical level, this issue is complex.

But one natural way to frame it is in terms of two questions.

[26] The first question is what the appropriate trajectory of global carbon emissions should be over the long term. To answer this question, we need technical information about what kinds of emissions scenarios produce what kinds of impacts over time, and what kinds of technological and social changes—especially away from a carbon economy—we can expect, or bring about, and on what time scale. Still, as the IPCC recognizes above, we also need to make value judgments. For example, importantly, we need to know how to reconcile the concerns of present and future generations. Presumably, other things being equal, it would be better for the future if we reduced our emissions faster, and so diminished the risks of severe climate change; but, on the other hand, it would be better for the present if we minimized the impacts on our own social infrastructure, and so proceeded more slowly. So what balance should we strike between these concerns? Similarly, presumably there would remain something wrong if we succeeded in protecting future and current people, but allowed the natural world to be devastated. So deciding what trajectory to aim for raises issues about our responsibilities with respect to animals and nature.

[27] Interestingly, there has been very little explicit discussion of the ethical dimension of the trajectory question. Instead, policy has been framed in terms of quantitative targets (such as avoiding a temperature rise of 2°C, or limiting atmospheric concentration of carbon dioxide to 450 or 550 ppm) without much attention to what justifies such targets, or how we might choose between them. This approach tends to hide the relevant value judgments. For example, if limiting climate change to 2.3 rather than 2°C makes a significant difference to specific populations or industries, how is the lower benchmark to be justified? As time goes on, such issues will no doubt become increasingly important.

[28] The second theoretical question about distribution is how emissions allowed under the overall trajectory at a particular time should be allocated. This question has received much more attention than the first, in politics and academia. Here I shall review just three basic proposals, to get a sense of the terrain. [Of course, more complex proposals exist (cf. [32] and [33]). But my remarks here should provide an entry point into thinking about those too.]

[29] The first proposal is that of equal per capita entitlements (e.g., [25,34-37]). The intuitive idea is that, other things being equal, permissible carbon emissions should be distributed equally across the world population, because no individual has a presumptive right to more than an equal share. Such a position has significant initial appeal. However, it also faces a number of prominent obstacles.

[30] First, people in different parts of the world have different energy needs. For example, those in northern Canada require fuel for heating whereas those in more temperate zones do not. Hence, there is a question about whether equal entitlements really do treat people as equals. This resonates with a deep issue in political philosophy about what the appropriate aim of equality should be: equality of resources, welfare, capabilities, or something else.[38-40]

[31] Second, a shift to per capita entitlements is likely to have radically different implications for different nations. Recent figures show that in 2005, global per capita emissions were at 1.23 metric tons of carbon. But national averages show wide discrepancies. In the United States, e.g., the average in 2005 was 5.32; in the United Kingdom it was 2.47; in China 1.16; in India 0.35; and in Bangladesh 0.08.[41] This raises serious issues. Suppose, e.g., that we were to call for roughly a 20% cut in global emissions in the next decade, and distribute the remaining emissions on

a per capita basis, at roughly 1 metric ton each. This would imply that citizens of the United States would have to cut their emissions by more than 80%, those of the UK by nearly 60%, and those of China by around 14%, while the Indians could increase their emissions by around 285% and the Bangladeshis by 1250%. In short, on the face of it, the burden of the shift to equal per capita entitlements seems very different in different countries. In particular, it is often said that it would be more dislocating for those who emit the most to make such drastic cuts, since much of their infrastructure depends on much higher rates of emission.

[32] In practice, most proponents of the equal per capita approach suggest that this problem can be dealt with by making the right to pollute tradable once allocated. Hence, on this version of the proposal, those for whom the costs of reduction are high can buy unused allocations from others whose costs are low. Moreover, for administrative simplicity, it is usually thought that allocations will actually be made to states on the basis of their populations, rather than directly to individuals. In practice, then, the thought is that the effect of the per capita proposal is that developed nations will end up buying large amounts of currently unused capacity from the developing world in order to make their own cuts more manageable.

[33] This more complex proposal raises many new issues. On the one hand, there are concerns about feasibility. For one thing, on the face of it, trading seems to involve a massive transfer of wealth from the rich to the poor nations. For another, the proposal of giving the allowances to states may lead far away from the initial intuition toward equality. In many countries, the thought goes, such allowances are likely to become just another resource for the elite to plunder, perhaps in collusion with, and on behalf of, outside forces. What then of individuals in poor countries to whom the right is nominally given? Does the appeal to individualism turn out merely to be a convenient illusion? On the other hand, concerns about fairness remain. Do tradable allowances simply allow the rich countries to continue their polluting habits by 'buying off' the poor? Perhaps they are morally akin to environmental indulgences, simply a fancy way for the rich to spend their way out of the implications of their bad behavior;[42] and perhaps they also undermine a sense of collective moral endeavor.[43,44]

[34] More generally, it may be that in practice the main appeal of the 'equal per capita plus trading' proposal lies not in equal division, but elsewhere, in the way it appears to reconcile concern for the future with recognition of the past, and with global justice more generally. After all, the trading mechanism provides a mechanism for the rich nations to provide some compensation to the developing world (and without clearly appearing to do so). If the numbers had worked out differently (if, i.e., the poor countries turned out to be the big current polluters per capita), then it may be that the modified per capita approach would have little support.

[35] The second proposal for allocating emissions initially appears to overcome some of the worries about the modified per capita approach by putting concern for the poor and for individuals right at the heart of its approach. Henry Shue maintains that individuals have an inalienable right to the emissions necessary for their survival or some minimum level of quality of life. He proposes that such emissions should be open neither to trading, nor appropriation by governments, and that they ought to be sharply distinguished from other emissions, especially those associated with luxury goods.[13] At first glance, this proposal has a sharply different logic than that of tradable per capita rights. On the one hand, subsistence emissions rights are inalienable, suggesting not only that they cannot be exchanged but also that they should be guaran-

teed even if this would predictably lead to serious harm to others, such as future generations. On the other hand, subsistence emissions are subject to a strict threshold, suggesting that emissions above that threshold might be distributed according to principles other than equality.

[36] Of course, the subsistence emissions proposal also raises new difficulties. Most obviously, what counts as a 'subsistence emission'? After all, former US President George H. Bush infamously stated at the Rio Earth Summit in 1992 that 'the American way of life is not up for negotiation'. Does that mean that we should regard an emissions rate of 5.32 metric tons per capita as the subsistence level for Americans? Surely not. Yet even subsistence at a minimal level of quality of life presumably does include some social and cultural factors,[45] and these may involve different levels of absolute emissions. So how do we decide what is necessary and what is not? Again, some moral and political philosophy seems needed.

[37] Less obviously, in practice it is not clear that the proposal has real advantages over the equal per capita approach. On the one hand, the two may not be easily separable. Given the fungibility of the notion of 'subsistence', it seems likely that the task of determining an adequate minimum may turn out to be very close to that of deciding on an appropriate trajectory and then assigning equal per capita rights. On the other hand, if the two approaches do diverge, it is not clear that the subsistence approach does a better job of protecting vulnerable individuals. For example, if culturally sensitive subsistence emissions overshoot the equal per capita allocation, then they justify an increase in the burdens on future generations. Alternatively, if they undershoot that allocation, then the 'excess' emissions need to be distributed in some other way. If this is equal per capita, then (again) the two approaches may amount to much the same thing. But if it is not—in particular if they are to be distributed by market forces—then the subsistence approach may end up being less favorable to the poor than equal per capita.

[38] The third allocation proposal is that nations should share the costs of mitigation fairly among themselves by trying to equalize their marginal costs in reducing emissions. This is presumably part of the appeal of nations declaring percentage reduction targets. The thought is that if each reduces their own emissions by, say, 20% in a given period, then all take on equal burdens. Martino Traxler suggests that this approach has major political advantages. No nation has any stronger reason to defect than any other, and each experiences the maximum moral pressure to participate.[45]

[39] I am not so sure. First, the proposal is entirely future-oriented. Not only does it ignore past emissions but also has it the effect of embedding recent emissions levels. For example, a cut of 20% reduces per capital levels in the United States to 4.26 and in India to 0.28. Is this fair, given that the United States is so much richer? Even more starkly, if ultimately the global cut needs to be 80%, is it fair that the equal percentage cut approach reduces the United States to 1.64 per capita, when this is still significantly higher than current Chinese and Indian levels, and when Bangladesh is pushed down to a miniscule 0.1 per capita?

[40] Second, as the first point already suggests, the correct measure of 'equal burdens' is morally contentious. Consider just three proposals. The first aims to equalize the marginal economic cost of reduction in each country. Say that this turns out to be $50 per metric ton. Does it matter that this amounts to the cost of a nice evening out for the average American, but more than a month's income for the average Bangladeshi? Presumably, it does. Given this, a second proposal might aim at equalizing marginal welfare instead. But what if the

worst-off are in so wretched a condition that taking more from them will make little difference to their misery, but the very well-off are so accustomed to luxury that even small losses hit their subjective states very hard? Does this justify taking more from the poor? Again, presumably not. Finally, as a third proposal, suppose that we adopt a more substantive account of goods, distinguishing (for example) between luxuries and subsistence goods, and differentiating their importance to welfare. Then we could protect the poor from additional deprivation by insisting that the rich should give up all their luxuries before the poor give up anything.[31,45] However, even if this is morally correct, it seems highly politically controversial, and so undermines many of the (alleged) practical advantages of the 'equal burdens' approach.

Impacts

[41] Efforts to reach agreement on mitigation are complicated by the further issue of adaptation. Clearly, at this point, adaptation measures must be part of any sensible climate policy, because we are already committed to some warming due to past emissions, and because almost all of the proposed abatement strategies envisage that overall global emissions will continue at a high level for at least the next few decades, committing us to even more. However, it is also sometimes maintained that adaptation should be our predominant or even sole strategy. Some maintain that the key problems are human vulnerability to weather and the social conditions that lead to environmental degradation, and that these are strongly influenced by poverty and global population. Given this, the argument continues, these issues should be our focus rather than emissions reductions.[46]

[42] In this vein, Bjorn Lomborg has argued that the climate change problem ultimately reduces to the question of whether to help poor inhabitants of the poor countries now or their richer descendants later, and that the right answer is to help the current poor now, because they are poorer than their descendants will be, because they are more easily (i.e., cheaply) helped, and since in helping them, one also helps their descendants. For example, Lomborg claims that a mitigation project like Kyoto 'will likely cost at least $150 billion a year, and possibly much more,' whereas 'just $70–80 billion a year could give all third world inhabitants access to the basics like health, education, water, and sanitation'.[15,16]

[43] Lomborg's approach incorporates two main ideas. The first is a straightforward appeal to opportunity costs: the resources used for climate change mitigation could produce greater net benefits if employed elsewhere.[15] Mitigation efforts like Kyoto are, Lomborg says, a 'bad deal'.[16]

[44] In some contexts, opportunity cost arguments are compelling. But we should be careful about their import for climate change. The first worry concerns Lomborg's framing of the issue. The claim that the choice is between current and future generations of the world's poor assumes that climate change poses no serious threats to (say) current or future inhabitants of richer countries, to animals, or to the rest of nature. This seems either false, or highly optimistic. In addition, the choice seems to represent a false dichotomy. Helping the poor does not foreclose the option of mitigating climate change. Perhaps we can do both. Moreover, plausibly, the two are inextricably linked. Perhaps digging new wells in Africa would not make much difference if climate change induces severe drought (perhaps it will even be simply a waste of resources), and perhaps some mitigation projects also help the poor (e.g., by reducing air pollution).

[45] A second worry concerns the compensation rationale. It turns out that 'even hard-nosed benefit-

cost analysts' agree that the claim that future people could be compensated by an alternative policy loses relevance if we know that the compensation would not actually be paid, or would not suffice [[47], p. 6-7]. This may be so if catastrophic climate change undercuts our efforts to grow the global economy,[17] or if an otherwise rich future beset by severe climate change is not better off than a poorer one without such problems, perhaps because throwing money at the problem does not help that much.

[46] The third worry about the opportunity cost argument is that, because it assumes that we can compensate the future for failure to act on climate change with a larger economy, the argument overlooks the possibility that future people may be entitled to both. If we owe it to our successors both that we refrain from climate disruption and that we try to improve their material conditions, then we cannot simply substitute one for the other and say that we are even. This would be a morally mischievous sleight of hand. It would be like arguing that we should not save for our own retirements but invest in our kids' education instead, because then they will be able to look after us (better) in our old age. On a standard view of things, we owe our children freedom from the burdens of supporting us when we are older, and also some help in securing a good education. The one obligation cannot simply be silenced by the other.

[47] This brings us to Lomborg's second main idea, that future people will be better off and so should pay more. This position is also open to challenge in the case of climate change. First, the approach ignores all issues of responsibility. If our generation causes the climate problem, it is far from clear that the future victims should pay to fix it (or pay disproportionately). This is so even if they happen to have more resources. We do not *always* think that those who have a greater ability to pay should pay (or pay more). Sometimes we think that those who caused the problem should pay instead. Second, future people may not be richer. For one thing, many of the world's poorer people in 2050 or 2100 may be better off than the poor are today, but still much worse off than the current global rich. So there is no reason to make them pay more. For another, if climate change has severe effects on matters such as food, water, disease, and the regional economies, then many people in the future may be worse off than people now.

Even if adaptation ought not to be our sole [48] concern, it is clearly a crucial component of any defensible climate policy. Unfortunately, very little philosophical work has been done on this topic to date (exceptions include[48] and [49]), although some of the discussion about past emissions and mitigation remains relevant, as does development ethics more generally (e.g., [50,51]). Still, it may be worth noting two initial points.

First, much resistance to mitigation seems [49] implicitly bound up with the idea that it will be difficult for existing economic systems to 'adapt' to emissions restrictions, but not to climate impacts. This is a surprising assumption. Other things being equal, one might think that it would be easier for economic institutions to cope with sensibly managed regulation than with specific climate impacts, since the former could be designed to be gradual, predictable, and incremental, whereas the latter are likely to be sudden, unpredictable, and potentially large-scale. But whatever we say about this, it seems clear that at least some of the existing climate debate turns on background assumptions about the relative resilience of different kinds of social and natural systems. This complicated the ethics of adaptation.

Second, the natural world interacts in complex [50] ways with the social so that it will often be very difficult to separate climate impacts from other factors. Hence, the harms and costs of failures to adapt will often be hidden—as Dale Jamieson puts it, no one's death certificate will ever read 'climate change'.[49] Given this, it is difficult to address adaptation without engaging with issues of global poverty and injustice more generally.

Direct Intervention

[51] A different approach to climate policy would have us try to make the planet 'adapt' to us. Perhaps, the thought goes, we should try a 'techno-fix'. Why not directly intervene in the climate system in order to prevent emissions from having negative effects? Such 'geoengineering' solutions to climate change have been proposed for decades, but have recently gained some prominence. Proposals include deploying space mirrors to reflect incoming sunlight, 'fertilizing' the ocean with iron in order to suck carbon dioxide from the atmosphere, and pumping emissions from coal-burning power plants deep underground into sedimentary rock.

[52] Philosophically, it is not clear that all such interventions are best grouped together, in part, because they seem to raise different ethical issues. However, here I shall not try to develop a general definition of geoengineering. Instead, I shall merely gesture at the idea that geoengineering involves something 'global, intentional, and unnatural'.[52] Wherever it makes a difference, the reader should assume that I am taking, as my model, the proposal that is currently the most popular—that of trying to manage the earth's albedo through injecting sulfur into the stratosphere.[53] I take this to be a paradigm case of geoengineering.[54]

[53] Different arguments can be (and often are) offered in favor of various interventions. For example, some advocate a given approach because they think it much more cost-effective than mitigation (cf.[52] and [55]), others say that it will 'buy time' while mitigation measures are implemented,[56] and still others claim that geoengineering should only be implemented as a last resort, to stave off a catastrophe.[53,57] Differences in rationale are important because they often have divergent implications for research, governance, and policy, affecting what kinds of geoengineering should be pursued, to what extent, and with what safeguards. Given this, it is good to be clear about *why* an intervention is proposed.

[54] Consider a few prominent arguments.[54] The first claims that geoengineering is relatively cheap and administratively simple.[53] Thus far, this argument has not proven very persuasive. The claim that geoengineering is cheap focuses on the costs of implementation, but appears to ignore the risk of dangerous side effects, and the fact that many geoengineering options leave some aspects of the carbon dioxide problem (such as ocean acidification) unaffected. The claim that it is administratively simple relies on the idea that it would be technically feasible for one country or corporation to undertake a serious geoengineering project. This ignores the moral and political implications of unilateral geoengineering, and the real possibility of geopolitical conflict.[58] More widely, some worry that this argument fails to take seriously the wider context of global environmental problems and the problematic human relationship to nature that they reflect.

[55] A second argument for geoengineering suggests that we can adopt a 'research-only' approach. For example, Ralph Cicerone, the President of the National Academy of Sciences, maintains that we should do further research in order to eliminate bad geoengineering options and discover if there are good ones, because there is a presumption in favor of freedom of enquiry since it promotes the acquisition of knowledge. While this is happening, he adds, there should be a moratorium on deployment and field testing. If promising proposals emerge, scientists can then bring these to the wider

community so that political and ethical considerations may be brought to bear.[59]

[56] There is something attractive about this proposal, and about the model it implies of science and its role in society. However, there are concerns about how good that model really is, and in particular how it holds up in the real social and political world in which we live. One concern is that it is not obvious that any particular research project should be supported just because it enhances knowledge. After all, there are limited resources for research. If we prioritize geoengineering, other knowledge-enhancing projects will be displaced. Some rationale is needed for this displacement. In addition, some kinds of knowledge enhancement seem trivial. This is relevant because some experts claim that geoengineering research is highly unlikely to yield the kind of results needed to justify action on the timescale envisioned,[60] and that the rate of technological progress is so fast that it may make little sense even to try.[52]

[57] A second concern about the research-only approach is that there is a crucial ambiguity in the notion of 'supporting research'. There are major differences between, e.g., individual scientists and journals being willing to review and publish papers, major funding agencies encouraging geoengineering proposals, and governments providing massive resources for a geoengineering 'Manhattan Project'. Importantly, giving preeminence to the cause of geoengineering research cannot be justified merely by appealing to the value of knowledge for its own sake. Instead, a much more robust argument is needed.

[58] The final concern is that it is not clear that geoengineering activities can really be limited to research. First, there is such a thing as institutional momentum. In our culture, big projects that are started tend to get done.[61] Second, there are real worries about the idea of a moratorium. After all, if the results of research are to be published in mainstream journals that are freely available online or in libraries across the world, what is to stop a rogue scientist, engineer, or government deciding to use that research? Third, there are issues about who gets to make such decisions and why, and about how they are enforced. If the future of the planet is at stake, why is it that the rest of humanity should cede the floor to a 'gentleman's agreement' among a specific set of scientists? Fourth, there are issues about conducting geoengineering research in isolation from public input, and in particular divorced from discussions about the ethics of deployment. The background assumption that is being made seems to be that such input and discussion has *nothing to tell us* about the goals of geoengineering research or how it should be conducted. But it is not clear why we should accept this assumption (*cf.*[61]).

[59] A third argument for pursuing geoengineering argues that 'arming the future' with geoengineering is the lesser of two evils. The argument begins with the thought that if the current failure to act aggressively on mitigation continues, then at some point (probably 40 years or more into the future) we may end up facing a choice between allowing catastrophic impacts to occur, or engaging in geoengineering. Both, it is conceded, are bad options. But engaging in geoengineering is less bad than allowing catastrophic climate change. Therefore, if it comes to it, we should choose geoengineering. However, if we do not start doing serious research now, then we will not be in a position to choose geoengineering should the nightmare scenario arise. Therefore, we should start doing the research.[53]

[60] This argument initially seems both straightforward and irresistible. However, it is subject to a number of important challenges.[54] First, it is not clear that the nightmare choice scenario it describes is the one we should prepare for. Perhaps other nightmares are more likely, such as having to cope with catastrophic change that is already upon us,

or with a geopolitical catastrophe caused by unilateral or predatory geoengineering. Second, there may be other ways to prepare. Perhaps a Manhattan Project for alternative energy, or a massive climate assistance and refugee program, or a Strategic Solar Panel Reserve, would be better than geoengineering. Such alternatives should at least be considered. Third, if the nightmare scenario comes about because of our inaction on mitigation, then this seems to be a moral failure on our part, for which we may owe the future compensation beyond that of geoengineering research. The 'arm the future' argument is thus too limited in describing our obligations. Fourth, similarly, the argument is silent on the issue of how to make geoengineering intervention politically legitimate and broadly in keeping with norms of global justice and community (e.g., not seriously unfair or parochial in its concerns). For example, a basic principle of modern political thought is that political institutions are legitimate only if they are justifiable to those governed by them. How then are geoengineering institutions to be justified, and what does this imply for global ethics and political philosophy? The final challenge concerns how we are to understand such issues in a context where the need to geoengineer is to be brought on by our failure to mitigate and adapt. Are just and effective geoengineering policies any more likely than just and effective mitigation policies? And if not, what can we say about the ethics of any likely decision to geoengineering?

[61] In addition to the major arguments for pursuing geoengineering, there are also significant arguments against it. One prominent argument concerns how risky it is likely to be, and whether we are morally entitled to take this risk, especially in a context where ethical norms are not in place to protect the victims of side effects (for a first step toward such norms, see [61]). A second argument concerns what kind of people we aim to be. Many people, including a number of climate scientists, appear to believe that the attempt to geoengineer is not only risky, but also both an attempt to divert attention from the obligation to reduce emissions, and ultimately a sign of hubris. This argument sees the decision to pursue geoengineering in a wider context, raising questions that go beyond consideration of what the narrow consequences of this or that intervention are likely to be. If the decision to pursue geoengineering is made in the context of serious inertia on mitigation and adaptation for climate change, and a more general indifference to global environmental problems, the claim is that this reflects badly on the particular societies and generations who make that decision and perhaps on humanity as such. On one way of looking at things, having created a problem, we are obstinately refusing to face it in a serious way, but instead doing whatever we can to defer action, impose the burden on others, and obfuscate matters by arguing that we must hold out for a less demanding solution (however unrealistic that may be). What kind of people would do such a thing?[54,62-64]

Conclusion

In this introduction to ethics and climate change, [62] I have tried to illustrate how ethical analysis contributes to our understanding of five central areas of climate policy: the treatment of scientific uncertainty, responsibility for past emissions, the setting of mitigation targets, and the places of adaptation and geoengineering in the policy portfolio. Much more can (and should) be said about these topics, and many other important ethical issues that I have not discussed. Of special interest is the place of climate policy within wider approaches to global justice, environmental ethics, and the ethics of human well-being. In particular, much of the current discussion (including those aspects I have emphasized above) tends to assume that we must work more-or-less within the constraints of the current geopolitical system. But, of course, climate change might be thought to pose a practical and philosophical challenge to that system.[65] If so, then much current writing is at best work on what one might call the 'ethics of the transition', helping us to bridge the gap between what is and what should be. Vitally important though that project is, presumably we also need help in working out what we should ultimately be aiming for, in terms of better institutions and ways of life. Ethics should be a central part of this 'ideal' project too.

Notes

Earlier versions of this paper were presented at the University of Oslo and at a National Academies of Science workshop on America's Climate Choices. I thank those audiences, two anonymous referees, and Dale Jamieson for their comments. Some sections of the paper rely on and update material from Ref. [66]; the section Direct Intervention draws on Ref. [54].

References

1. Intergovernmental Panel on Climate Change (IPCC). *Climate Change 2001: The Synthesis Report.* Cambridge, UK: Cambridge University Press.
2. United Nations Framework Convention on Climate Change. *Framework Convention on Climate Change.* 1992. Available at: http://unfccc.int/essential background/convention/background/items/1349.php.
3. Gardiner S, Caney S, Jamieson D, Shue H eds. *Climate Ethics: Essential Readings.* Oxford: Oxford University Press; 2010. In press.
4. Intergovernmental Panel on Climate Change (IPCC). *Climate Change 2007: The Physical Science Basis.* Cambridge: Cambridge University Press; 2007.
5. Oreskes N. The scientific consensus on climate change. *Science* 2004, 306:1686.
6. Knight F. *Risk, Uncertainty, and Profit.* Boston, MA: Houghton Mifflin Company; 1921.
7. Friedman M. *Price Theory.* Chicago, IL: Aldine; 1976.
8. *Wingspread Statement.* 1998. Available at http://www.gdrc.org/u-gov/precaution-3.html.
9. Gardiner S. A core precautionary principle. *J Polit Philos* 2006, 14:33–60.
10. Rawls J. *A Theory of Justice.* Revised ed. Cambridge, MA: Harvard University Press; 1999.
11. Sunstein C. *The Laws of Fear.* Cambridge: Cambridge University Press; 2005.
12. Sunstein C. Irreversible and catastrophic. *Cornell Law Rev* 2006, 91:841.
13. Shue H. Subsistence emissions and luxury emissions. *Law and Policy* 1993, 15:39–59.
14. Nordhaus WD, Boyer JG. *Warming the World: Economic Models of Global Warming.* Cambridge, MA: MIT Press; 2000.
15. Lomborg B. *The Sceptical Environmentalist.* Cambridge: Cambridge University Press; 2001.
16. Lomborg B. *Cool It: The Skeptical Environmentalist's Guide to Global Warming.* London: Marshall Cavendish; 2007.
17. Stern N. *The Economics of Climate Change: The Stern Review.* Cambridge: Cambridge University Press; 2007.
18. Stern N. The economics of climate change. *Am Econ Rev* 2008, 98:1–37.
19. Broome J. *Counting the Cost of Global Warming.* Isle of Harris, UK: White Horse Press; 1992.
20. Spash C. The economics of climate change impacts a la Stern: novel and nuanced or rhetorically restricted? *Ecol Econ* 2007, 63:706–713.
21. Broome J. The ethics of climate change. *Sci Am* 2008, 298(6):97–102.
22. Cowen T, Derek P. Against the social discount rate. In: Laslett P, Fishkin J, eds. *Justice Between Age Groups and Generations.* New Haven, CT: Yale University Press; 2001, 144–161.
23. Caney S. Human rights, climate change and discounting. *Env Polit* 2008, 17:536–555.
24. Shue H. Global environment and international inequality. *Int Aff* 1999, 75:531–545.

25. Singer P. *One World: The Ethics of Globalization.* New Haven, CT: Yale University Press; 2002.
26. Shue H. *Historical Responsibility. Technical Briefing for Ad Hoc Working Group on Long-term Cooperative Action under the Convention [AWG-LCA], SBSTA, UNFCC, Bonn, 4 June 2009.* 2009. Available at: http://unfccc.int/files/meetings/ad_hoc_working_groups/lca/application/pdf/1_shue_rev.pdf.
27. Caney S. Cosmopolitan justice, responsibility and global climate change. *Leiden J Int Law* 2005, 18:747–775.
28. Posner E, Sunstein C. Climate change justice. *Georgetown Law J* 2008, 96:1565–1612.
29. Gosseries A. Historical emissions and free riding. In: Meyer L, ed. *Justice in Time: Responding to Historical Injustice.* Baden-Baden, Germany: Nomos; 2003, 355–382.
30. Meyer L, Roser D. Distributive justice and climate change: the allocation of emission rights. *Analyse Kritik* 2006, 28:223–249.
31. Shue H. The unavoidability of justice. In: Hurrell A, Kingsbury B, eds. *The International Politics of the Environment.* Oxford: Oxford University Press; 1992, 373–397.
32. Baer P, Athanasiou T, Kartha S. *The Right to Development in a Climate Constrained World: The Greenhouse Development Rights Framework.* London: Christian Aid; 2007.
33. Chakravarty S, Chikkatur A, de Coninck H, Pacala S, Socolow R, et al. Sharing global CO2 emission reductions among one billion high emitters. *Proc Natl Acad Sci USA.* 106(29):11884–11888, DOI:10.1073 pnas.0905232106.
34. Agarwal A, Narain S. *Global Warming in an Unequal World: A Case of Environmental Colonialism.* New Dehli: Centre for Science and Environment; 1991.
35. Meyer A. *Contraction and Convergence.* Dartington, UK: Green Books; 2000.
36. Jamieson D. Climate change and global environmental justice. In: Edwards P, Miller C, eds. *Changing the Atmosphere: Expert Knowledge and Global Environmental Governance.* Cambridge, MA: MIT Press; 2001, 287–307.
37. Athanasiou T, Baer P. *Dead Heat: Global Justice and Global Warming.* New York: Seven Stories Press; 2002.
38. Sen A. Equality of what? In: McMurrin S, ed. *Tanner Lectures on Human Values.* Cambridge: Cambridge University Press; 1980.
39. Dworkin R. *Sovereign Virtue: The Theory and Practice of Equality.* Cambridge, MA: Harvard University Press; 2002.
40. Page E. *Climate Change, Justice and Future Generations.* Cheltenham: Elgar; 2007.
41. Marland G, Boden T, Andreas RJ. *Global CO2 Emissions from Fossil-Fuel Burning, Cement Manufacture, and Gas Flaring.* Dept of Energy, United States: Carbon Dioxide Information Center. 2008, 1751–2005. Available at: http://cdiac.oml.gov/trends/emiss/em_cont.html.
42. Goodin R. Selling environmental indulgences. *Kyklos* 1994, 47:573–596.
43. Sandel M. Should we buy the right to pollute? In: Sandel M, ed. *Public Philosophy: Essays on Morality in Politics*: Cambridge, MA: Harvard University Press; 2005.
44. Sagoff M. Controlling global climate: the debate over pollution trading. *Rep Inst Philos Publ Pol* 1999, 19:1–6.
45. Traxler M. Fair chore division for climate change. *Soc Theory Pract* 2002, 28:101–134.
46. Sarewitz D, Roger P Jr. Breaking the global warming gridlock. *Atl Mon* 2000, July. Available at:http://www.theatlantic.com/doc/200007/global-warming/5.
47. Portney PR, Weylant JP. Introduction. In: Portney, PR, Weylant JP, eds. *Discounting and Intergenerational Equity.* Washington, DC: Resources for the Future; 1999.
48. Adger N, Huq S, Mace M, Paavola J, eds. *Fairness in Adapting to Climate Change.* Cambridge, MA: MIT Press; 2005.
49. Jamieson D. Adaptation, mitigation, and justice. In: Sinnott-Armstrong W, Howarth R, eds. *Perspectives on Climate Change*: Elsevier; 2005, 221–253.
50. Nussbaum M. *Women and Human Development.* Cambridge: Cambridge University Press; 2001.
51. Crocker D. *Ethics of Global Development: Agency, Capability and Deliberative Democracy.* Cambridge: Cambridge University Press; 2008.

52. Schelling T. The economic diplomacy of geoengineering. *Clim Change* 1996, 33:303–307.
53. Crutzen P. Albedo enhancement by stratospheric sulphur injections: a contribution to resolve a policy dilemma? *Clim Change* 2006, 77:211–219.
54. Gardiner S. Is "arming the future" with geoengineering really the lesser evil? Some doubts about the ethics of intentionally manipulating the climate system. In: Gardiner S, Caney S, Jamieson D, Shue H eds. *Climate Ethics: Essential Readings*. Oxford: Oxford University Press; 2010. In press.
55. Barrett S. The incredible economics of geoengineering. *Environ Res Econ* 2008, 39:45–54.
56. Wigley TML. A combined mitigation/geoengineering approach to climate stabilization. *Science* 2006, 314:452–454.
57. Victor D, Morgan MG, Apt J, Steinbruner J, Ricke K. The geoengineering option: a last resort against global warming? *Foreign Aff* 2009, 88(2):64–72.
58. Bodansky D. May we engineer the climate? *Clim Change* 1996, 33:309–321.
59. Cicerone R. Geoengineering: encouraging research and overseeing implementation. *Clim Change* 2006, 77:221–226.
60. Bengtsson L. Geoengineering to confine climate change: is it at all feasible? *Clim Change* 2006, 77:229–234.
61. Jamieson D. Intentional climate change. *Clim Change* 2006, 33:323–336.
62. Kiehl J. Geoengineering climate change: treating the symptom over the cause? *Clim Change* 2006, 77:227–228.
63. Schneider S. Geoengineering: could we or should we make it work? *Philos Trans R Soc A* 2008, 366:3843–3862.
64. Schmidt G. Geoengineering in vogue. *Real Clim* 2006, 28 June. Available at: http://www.realclimate.org.
65. Gardiner S. Climate change as a global test for contemporary political institutions and theories. In: O'Brien K, Clair AL St, Kristoffersen B, eds. *Climate Change, Ethics and Human Security*. Cambridge, UK: Cambridge University Press. In press.
66. Gardiner S. Ethics and global climate change. *Ethics* 2004, 114:555–600.

Further Reading

Gardiner S, Caney S, Jamieson D, Shue H eds. *Climate Ethics: Essential Readings*. Oxford: Oxford University Press; 2010. In press.

Garvey J. *The Ethics of Climate Change: Right and Wrong in a Warming World*. London: Continuum; 2008.

Page E. *Climate Change, Justice and Future Generations*. Cheltenham: Elgar; 2007.

Vanderheiden, S. *Atmospheric Justice: A Political Theory of Climate Change*. Oxford: Oxford University Press; 2008.

Questions

1. Despite "uncertainty" about climate change, action can be justified on what two grounds?
2. (a) How is it that economists disagree about whether the costs of substantial action outweigh the benefits?
   (b) Gardiner mentions one ethical argument against discounting and three in favour. Which do you find more persuasive?
3. (a) With respect to whose responsibility it is to "fix" the climate, Gardiner presents two arguments that appeal to past emissions. What are they?
   (b) Explain Gardiner's two responses to the first objection to these arguments.
   (c) Can you think of another problem with the "first-come, first-served" objection? (Think opportunity...)

(d) Explain the similarity between the third objection and a common objection to affirmative action programs. Does the similarity extend to a consideration of beneficiary-ness?

4. (a) With respect to arranging a climate regime that is fair, Gardiner presents several proposals. What is the first one? What are two objections to it? What solution does Gardiner describe?

(b) What is the second proposal? What definition problem does it have?

(c) In what way does the third proposal penalize those who have been responsible to date?

5. With respect to Lomborg's argument, Gardiner identifies a questionable assumption and a false dichotomy. Explain.

6. Suppose you decided to invest in one of the geoengineering solutions. How would you decide which one to back? Which, if any, of the arguments mentioned by Gardiner would figure in your decision?

....

Case Study: Neil Young's Tour

In January 2014, Neil Young embarked on a four-city concert tour (Toronto, Winnipeg, Regina, and Calgary) in order to raise funds for the Athabasca Chipewyan First Nation (ACFN) Legal Defense Fund. The ACFN maintains that Shell's development of the oil sands in Northern Alberta (what has been described as "perhaps the largest-scale industrial development in human history" [Nasca]) violates their treaty rights, specifically that a proposed expansion of the oil sands mine was approved (despite findings that it would have a long list of environmental impacts on wetlands and old growth forests) without proper consultation with the ACFN. Their "multi-prong legal strategy [challenges] public policy, individual tar sands projects and inadequate environmental protection in Alberta's Athabasca tar sands region in order to preserve and protect what is left of their homelands... [It focuses on] defending culture, the lands required to exercise Treaty and Aboriginal Rights, and the resources associated with those rights" (Nasca).

The Nation "has eight reserves around the southern shores of Lake Athabasca, with a combined area of 34,767 hectares, but considers its traditional territory to encompass all of Treaty 8," which was signed in 1899 at Fort Chipewyan (Walker)—which means the oil sands development is on their land.

According to the Oil Sands Reality Check website, among the detrimental impacts of the oil sands development are the following:

- Oil sands production emits 3 to 4 times more greenhouse gases than producing conventional crude oil. This makes it one of the world's dirtiest forms of fuel.

- More than 600 million cubic feet of natural gas are used per day to extract and upgrade the oil from the tar sands. That's enough to heat more than 3 million Canadian homes every day—almost every house in Western Canada.
- 95% of the water used in tar sands surface mining is so polluted it has to be stored in toxic sludge pits. That's 206,000 litres of toxic waste discharged every day.
- 11 million litres of toxic wastewater seep out of the tailing pits into the boreal forest and Athabasca river every day. That's 4 billion litres a year.
- Air pollutant guidelines in Alberta are less stringent than international standards. Despite that, air quality objectives were exceeded 1,556 times in 2009, up from 47 times in 2004.
- Over 30 million birds will be lost over the next 20 years due to tar sands development.
- Under current oil sands expansion plans, woodland caribou populations are expected to disappear.
- A higher than normal incidence of rare and deadly cancers has been documented in First Nations communities downstream of the oil sands by doctors, the Alberta Health Department, and First Nations since 2007.[1]
- 71% of oil sands production is owned by foreign shareholders.
- In 46 years of development, only 0.15% of the environment disturbed is certified as "reclaimed."

And yet the industry and government plan to triple tar sands production (Honour the Treaties website).

"Our issue is with the government breaking treaties with the First Nation and plundering the natural resources the First Nation has rights to under the treaties," said Young. The tour surpassed its goal of raising $75,000, eventually raising $600,000.

References

Atkins, Emily. "Plagued With High Cancer Rates, One Tar Sands Community's Eight Year Quest For Answers." *Climate Progress* 2 Apr. 2014 http://thinkprogress.org/climate/2014/04/02/3345311/tar-sands-cancer/

Christian, Carol. "Doc's claims 'hurtful': O'Connor." *FortMcMurrayToday.com* 15 Apr. 2009. http://www.fortmcmurraytoday.com/2009/04/14/docs-claims-hurtful-oconnor

Honour the Treaties website. http://www.honourtheacfn.ca/

Nasca, Tessa. "Case Study: Neil Young's Honour the Treaties Tour. *Transforming Relations*. 8 May 2014 https://transformingrelations.wordpress.com/2014/05/08/case-study-neil-youngs-honour-the-treaties-tour/

Oil Sands Reality Check website. http://oilsandsrealitycheck.org

Walker, Connie. "Neil Young Tour: 5 Facts about the First Nation He's Singing For." *CBCnews*. CBC/Radio Canada. 16 Jan. 2014.

---

1 When, in 2006, Dr. John O'Connor went public with his claims of unprecedented cancer rates in Fort Chipewyan, and his suspicion that the tar sands just 150 miles upstream and/or the uranium mines in the area were the cause, he was "questioned, threatened, falsely accused, and forced to move" (Atkins); Health Canada filed four complaints of misconduct against O'Connor accusing him of causing "undue alarm" and "engendering a sense of mistrust" in the Canadian government.

Three years later, the Alberta Cancer Board confirmed O'Connor's reports: "Cancer rates in Fort Chip were 30 percent higher than expected. There were elevated rates of blood cancer, lymphatic cancer, and soft tissue cancers" (Atkins). But that could just be coincidence, the Board said. Or maybe O'Connor was just really good at detecting cancer. Never mind that fish from Lake Athabasca, which had developed a surface sheen subsequent to the tar sands development, showed deformities (pushed in faces, bulging eyes, two lower jaws).

Health Canada said the fish deformities were "not necessarily related to water pollution or toxic discharges." And yet Health Canada told residents to stay away from the water anyway because it has "higher-than-expected levels of mercury, aluminum, and selenium" (Atkins).

Question

1. Was the tour just another useless celebrity awareness-raising thing? A marketing ploy by an aging musician? Or an example of an ethically motivated "CEO" of a successful music business using its brand equity to make a difference in the form of a $600,000 contribution to a legal fund?

PART IV

INSTITUTIONALIZING ETHICS

Introductory Note

An ethically good workplace depends, to a large extent, on having people who understand and engage in ethically good decision making. However, some companies institutionalize or formalize their ethics as well (and hopefully it is "as well" rather than "instead"), adding a sort of organizational behaviour to individual behaviour.

Ethics Offices/Officers/Committees

First, companies can create an ethics office and appoint or hire an ethics officer; often an ethics committee is also formed. Ethics officers, note Ferrell and Fraedrich, are responsible for the following:

> coordinating the ethical compliance program with top management, the board of directors, and senior management; developing, revising, and disseminating a code of ethics; developing effective communication of ethical standards; establishing audit and control systems to determine the effectiveness of the program; developing consistent means of enforcing codes and standards; reviewing and modifying the ethics program to improve its effectiveness. (178)

In addition (or as part of the ethics program), the ethics officer or committee may act as a support system for people trying to do the right thing. At the very least, ethics officers are usually available for consultations to help resolve ethical dilemmas. A good template for use in such consultations might be as follows:

1. Identify the ethical issue, the question to be answered.
2. Identify the relevant facts, consulting all involved.

3. (a) Identify the relevant moral principles and values.
   (b) Rank them.
4. (a) List all the decision options.
   (b) Identify the consequences for each option.
5. Align the options with the values and principles—which are upheld, which are violated?
6. Decide on the "rightest" thing to do.
7. Repeat the process for deciding about the "rightest" way of doing it.

Unfortunately, it seems to me, ethics officers are usually high-ranking people in the company: Kelley notes that "in many cases, the job is reserved for longtime company loyalists" (20). I say this is unfortunate because I'm not convinced that "the cream rises to the top" with regard to how one *becomes* high-ranking; nor am I convinced that company loyalty is a good thing for ethics officers to have, as ethical analysis requires a degree of impartiality.

Perhaps even more unfortunately, such employees hardly ever have any ethics training or expertise: sometimes they're from the legal department (and we now understand the questionable relationship between legality and morality); often they're from the human resources department. This is especially unfortunate because we have people across the country who are specially trained in applied ethics; to our collective shame, business people often don't have much use for philosophers, and nor do philosophers often have much use for business people.[1]

But perhaps that doesn't matter if, as Kelley notes, quoting Michael Josephson, president of the Joseph and Edna Josephson Institute of Ethics, "most ethics officers don't even have the clout to come close to over-riding the bottom-line-ism that governs most business goals" (20).

Ethics Consultants

A company can also, or instead, hire an ethics consultant. Although external consultants often perform the same tasks as in-house officers, especially those of providing training programs and developing codes of ethics, there can be differences. For one thing, companies will often hire out-of-house for their audits, whether financial or social or ethical—for obvious reasons (increased impartiality, increased disclosure by employees, etc.).

Ethics consultants may also provide a number of other services. Ethicscan, based in Toronto, publishes a newsletter (*The Corporate Ethics Monitor*) and provides information for ethical investors and shoppers. They have a database of corporate social performance for 1500 companies, and they publish *The Ethical Shoppers' Guide to Canadian Supermarket Prices* and *Shopping with a Conscience: The Informed Shoppers' Guide to Retailers, Suppliers, and Service Providers in Canada.*

---

1 The profession of philosophy is especially known for its critical inquiry skills: "[philosophers] ask sequenced questions to reveal presuppositions or inconsistencies, [they] give focused examples to clarify ideas or evoke intuitions, [they] pose counter-examples to refine or, if necessary, refute a view, [and they] lay out connected reasons to show how a view can be grounded or why it should be accepted" (Audi 144). All of this is *essential* for ethical decision making. And yet it's been my experience that many business people think philosophers are of little practical use to them.

Many consultants belong to the Ethics Practitioners' Association of Canada (Toronto), a professional organization that provides a directory of members and their services. Other resources for ethics consultants, as well as ethics officers, include the Canadian Centre for Ethics and Corporate Policy (Toronto), the Clarkson Centre for Business Ethics (Toronto), and the Centre for Professional and Applied Ethics (Vancouver). Most of these organizations have websites—you may want to check them out.

Ethics Programs

An ethics program can include a number of things. Certainly a code of ethics is a typical component (see below). The development of ethical policies and procedures is also part of the ethics program, insofar as this is not covered by the code.

An educational component is also typically part of the program, and, if it is good, it will attend not only to *what* the ethical policies are, but also to *how* they are to be applied; as you have (I hope) discovered, putting ethical theory into practice is not always straightforward.

Various educational strategies are used: guest speakers and presentations (especially by ethics consultants—see above), study groups, videos, workshops involving role-playing or ethics games, brochures, newsletters, orientation packages and sessions, and seminars. But I have to wonder how many of these do more than scratch the surface. Rigorous ethical thinking is critical thinking, and this is not likely to be achieved with a brochure or a morning workshop; I suspect even the "study groups" fail to be more than discussion groups.

This apparent irrelevance could explain why it was reported that some RBC employees cheated on their ethics tests. (The irony!) The Royal Bank of Canada implemented a web-based training program with a testing component, and at least once every two years, employees had to "electronically role-play their way through scenarios that test their decision-making mettle, allowing higher-ups to evaluate whether they truly understand the policies and principles outlined in the RBC code" (Bogomolny). A (former) RBC employee said that he routinely did other people's tests for them. "I would just knock these things out," he said. "People were annoyed that they had to do them. A lot of the account managers thought it was stupid" (Bogomolny).

Some ethics programs include a whistle-blowing system that encourages (or at least enables) and protects those who disclose wrongdoing. Some companies have 24-hour ethics "hot lines." Among the mechanisms listed by Lindsay, Lindsay, and Irvine, in addition to those already mentioned, are a reward system and a judiciary board. (See their study for more about how companies manage their ethics.) In-house surveys may be conducted to determine just what is needed in the company (such a survey could determine current levels of ethical awareness as well as current practices), and ongoing assessment tools are often put in place to monitor the program.

According to Paine, many ethics programs focus on compliance ("to prevent, detect, and punish" [527]); she criticizes such programs, suggesting instead an "integrity strategy" approach ("to define and give life to an organization's guiding values, to create an environment that supports ethically sound behaviour, and to instill a sense of shared accountability among employees" [531]). Murphy (1989) notes two other problems with ethics programs: they can be too issue-centred and too narrow in scope.

Nevertheless, ethics programs are especially valuable, Murphy (1989) notes, when the company conducts business in many different locations; an ethics program can increase consistency in decision making. Perhaps simply increasing awareness levels is sufficient justification for ethics programs: identifying an issue as ethical is a necessary prerequisite to handling it well.

Codes of Ethics

Along with education, often prior to it, but sometimes in tandem with it, the development of a code of ethics is a primary responsibility of the ethics office or officer. However in order to be successful, Newton notes, there must be input from all levels of the company during its development, the code must be defensible by reasoned argument, and people at all levels must be bound by it.

After its initial development, updating and enforcing the code are also important. Murphy (1988) recommends that the code be blunt and realistic about violations. Shaw states that the ethics committee should have

> full authority and responsibility to communicate the code and decisions based on it to all corporate members, clarify and interpret the code when the need arises, facilitate the code's use, investigate grievances and violations of the code, discipline violators and reward compliance, and review, update, and upgrade the code. (180)

Some codes are implicit and are therefore more appropriately called corporate culture than corporate code, and some are explicit. Of the explicit codes, some are mere mission statements or corporate credos; others are extensive statements of policy and procedure.

One of the common criticisms of company codes of ethics is that they're just for show; no one really takes them seriously, let alone actually abides by them.[1] Another criticism, and this one may explain the previous one, is that codes are bound to be too simplistic to be effective. Often, the terms—typically values—aren't defined. For example, what exactly is meant by "integrity"? Worse, as you now know, a list of values or principles can only go so far. Unless those values or principles are ordered by importance, the code won't be very helpful. For example, one code I looked at says that employees "shall act in a manner that is in the best interests of their clients and employer consistent with the public interest." That one item alone is fraught with internal conflicts: it doesn't take a genius to imagine an instance in which the best interests of the client *collide with* the best interests of the employer. (And what exactly is in the best interests of the public?) Whose interests are to take precedence? The code didn't say. I've seen *no* code of ethics provide a means of ranking values, a means of resolving such conflicts. Also, unless all the relevant extenuating circumstances are covered, the code won't be very helpful.[2]

---

1 After all, Enron had a code of ethics.
2 See Hosmer for more on this point.

Furthermore, a code of ethics might actually do more harm than good because it suggests that the morality we're to use at work is somehow different from the one we should use in the rest of our lives. If they're the same, why do we need a separate code?[1]

So why bother? In fact, don't we already *have* a code of ethics to follow? The Canadian Criminal Code and all the other legislation that forms our justice system—isn't that enough? Apparently not. Consider all the businesses that have done wrong even though they did nothing illegal. They found loopholes. Well, then, a code of ethics won't be enough either; people will find loopholes in it too. Exactly. So it comes down to you personally. "The Corporation" doesn't make decisions—you do.

Consider the Walmart class action suit in which 1.6 million female employees went to court with evidence that, in 3,400 stores since 1998, female employees had been paid less than male employees in equivalent positions and had been promoted less than male employees with similar qualifications and experience. And Walmart *had* an anti-discrimination policy. So what happened? Decisions were left to the local managers who were not, apparently, supervised in any way to ensure they were following the policy. One manager reportedly paid women less than men because the latter supported a wife and kids. And the justice system just mentioned? It wasn't any more effective: in 2011, after a decade, the US Supreme Court ruled in favour of Walmart, saying that women didn't have enough in common to constitute a class. (Being female in an apparently sexist society isn't enough?)

Even so, a code of ethics might also be a reminder to be ethically involved, to *do* the right thing. It might at least partly counteract all the pressures on us *not* to do the right thing.

And here's an encouraging sign: Stohl, Stohl, and Popova say that unlike first- and second-generation ethics, which focus, respectively, on the legal context of corporate behaviour and groups directly associated with the corporation, third-generation ethics "transcend both the profit motive and the immediate corporate environment [and] are grounded in responsibilities to the larger interconnected environment" (abstract). Based on a study of 157 codes from corporations on the Global 500 and/or Fortune 500 lists, they say that "there is some evidence that third generation ethics and thinking are becoming part of the corporate landscape" (abstract).

In addition to company codes of ethics, one should also consider industry-wide codes:[2] they may be quite valuable if adhered to,[3] because the risk of losing competitiveness by being morally right is reduced if everyone does the same morally right thing. For example, if every business in your field is required to be environmentally responsible, then your environmentally responsible choices won't "cost" you. However, such industry self-regulation may be insufficient; some argue that government regulation is necessary.

---

1 See Ladd on this point.
2 See, for example, the Canadian Marketing Association's Code of Ethics and Standards of Practice.
3 See Arrow, and Maitland.

> **BOX IV.1 Do Businesspeople Need to Be Professionals?**
>
> Licensed members of the so-called "learned professions" such as engineering and medicine are legally required to order their ethical priorities in a completely unambiguous fashion and to bear a high level of personal accountability for the outcomes of their decisions. Engineers, for example, are given certain legal privileges and powers in return for the understanding that they will put public safety (which includes environmental safety) above all other considerations. The interests of their clients or employers come second, the reputation of their profession comes third, and their own personal interests come a distant fourth. A structural engineer cannot overlook a dangerous defect in a commercial building (such as a shopping centre) just because his client does not want to pay to remedy the defect. Engineers are required *by law* to "blow the whistle" if their client or employer is doing something that threatens public safety and if all other reasonable channels of professional communication have failed, *even if* they thereby risk losing their jobs. Similar principles apply to most licensed professions in Canada and the U.S. No one is saying that engineers cannot earn a living from their work; in fact, generally they are well paid. And yet their ethical obligations must come first.
>
> Prepared by Kent A. Peacock, University of Lethbridge

Ethics Audits

Financial audits can have an ethical audit role, to the extent that they could expose and/or prevent fraud. Legal reviews can also have an ethical audit role, to the extent that they prevent illegal behaviour that is also considered immoral behaviour. Social audits, which measure the social impact of a business, can also have an ethical role, insofar as social impact is part of morally good behaviour. (Reports of social audits are available through Ethicscan, as mentioned above, and published in books such as *Rating America's Corporate Conscience* put out by the Council on Economic Priorities.)

An ethical audit, however, is a little different, in that it measures how well the company is doing with respect to ethical policies and practices. "An ethical audit," according to Murphy (1988), "would pose questions about manufacturing practices, personnel policies, dealings with suppliers, financial reporting and sales techniques to find out if ethical abuses may be occurring" (109). Ferrell and Fraedrich say that an ethics audit "would provide a systematic and objective survey of the ethical condition of the organization" (185) and list over twenty questions that might be asked. Treviño and Nelson also provide questions to ask, based on Wilkins, divided into those for auditing the formal system and those for auditing the informal system. I doubt many companies engage in ethics audits. Why do you think this might be the case?

Closing Note

"A glossy code of conduct, a high-ranking ethics officer, a training program, an annual ethics audit—these trappings of an ethics program do not necessarily add up to a responsible, law-abiding organization," says Paine (537). Nor, say I, do they necessarily add up to a responsible, *morals-abiding* organization. What more is needed? I hope that you now know the answer to that question.

References and Further Reading

Arrow, Kenneth J. "Business Codes and Economic Efficiency." *Public Policy* 21 (1973). Rpt. in *Ethical Theory and Business*. Ed. Tom L. Beauchamp and Norman E. Bowie. 5th ed. Englewood Cliffs, NJ: Prentice Hall, 1997. 124–26.

Audi, Robert. "Philosophy in American Life: The Profession, The Public, and The American Philosophical Association." *Proceedings and Addresses of The American Philosophical Association* 72.5 (1999): 139–48.

Bogomolny, Laura. "Good Housekeeping." *Canadian Business* 77.5 (2004). 87–88

Brooks, Leonard J. "Business Ethics in Canada: Distinctiveness and Directions." *Journal of Business Ethics* 16: 591–604. Rpt. in *Business Ethics in Canada*. Ed. Deborah C. Poff and Wilfrid J. Waluchow. 3rd ed. Scarborough, ON: Prentice Hall Allyn and Bacon, 1999. 70–84.

Cava, Anita, Jonathan West, and Evan Berman. "Ethical Decision-making in Business and Government: An Analysis of Formal and Informal Strategies." *Spectrum: The Journal of State Government* (Spring 1995): 28–36.

Ferrell, O.C., and John Fraedrich. *Business Ethics: Ethical Decision Making and Cases*. 3rd ed. Boston: Houghton Mifflin, 1997.

Flynn, Gillian. "Make Employee Ethics Your Business." *Personnel Journal* (June 1995): 30–32, 34, 36, 38–39, 41.

Hosmer, LaRue Tone. *The Ethics of Management*. Burr Ridge, IL: Irwin Press, 1987.

JournalStar.com "Graduate business students more likely to cheat, study shows." JournalStar.com. 19 Sept. 2006. http://journalstar.com/business/graduate-business-students-more-likely-to-cheat-study-shows/article_8dfffe75-a7de-5ed0-9aa3-8bc858255dfd.html

Kelley, Tina. "Charting a Course to Ethical Profits." *The New York Times* 8 Feb. 1998: 1, 12. Rpt. in *Annual Editions: Business Ethics 99/00*. Ed. John E. Richardson. Guilford, CT: Dushkin, 1999. 20–24.

Ladd, John. "The Quest for a Code of Professional Ethics: An Intellectual and Moral Confusion." In *Ethical Issues in Engineering*. Ed. Deborah G. Johnson. Englewood Cliffs, NJ: Prentice-Hall, 1991. 130–36.

Lefebvre, Maurica, and Jang B. Singh. "The Content and Focus of Canadian Corporate Codes of Ethics." *Journal of Business Ethics* 11.10 (1992): 799–808.

Lindsay, R. Murray, Linda M. Lindsay, and V. Bruce Irvine. "Instilling Ethical Behaviour in Organizations: A Survey of Canadian Companies." *Journal of Business Ethics* 15 (1996):

393–407. Rpt. in *Business Ethics in Canada*. Ed. Deborah C. Poff and Wilfrid J. Waluchow. 3rd ed. Scarborough, ON: Prentice Hall Allyn and Bacon, 1999. 91–106.

Maitland, Ian. "The Limits of Business Self-Regulation." *California Management Review* 27.3 (1985). Rpt. in *Ethical Theory and Business*. Ed. Tom L. Beauchamp and Norman E. Bowie. 5th ed. Englewood Cliffs, NJ: Prentice Hall, 1997. 126–35.

Martin, Andrew. "Female Wal-Mart Employees File New Bias Case." *The New York Times* 27 Oct. 2011. http://www.nytimes.com/2011/10/28/business/women-file-new-class-action-bias-case-against-wal-mart.html?_r=1&

McNamara, Carter. *Complete Guide to Ethics Management: An Ethics Toolkit for Managers*. http://www.mapnp.org/library/ethics/ethxgde.htm

Murphy, Patrick E. "Creating Ethical Corporate Structures." *Sloan Management Review* (Winter 1989): 81–87. Rpt. in *Annual Editions: Business Ethics 97/98*. Ed. John E. Richardson. Guilford, CT: Dushkin, 1999. 212–18.

———. "Implementing Business Ethics." *Journal of Business Ethics* 7 (1988): 907–15. Rpt. in *Annual Editions: Business Ethics 97/98*. Ed. John E. Richardson. Guilford, CT: Dushkin, 1999. 107–15.

Newton, Lisa H. "The Many Faces of the Corporate Code." *Institutionalizing Corporate Ethics Programs*. Proceedings of the Conference "Corporate Visions and Values." Fairfield University, November 1991. Rpt. in *Ethical Issues in Business: A Philosophical Approach*. Ed. Thomas Donaldson and Patricia H. Werhane. 6th ed. Englewood Cliffs, NJ: Prentice Hall, 1999. 519–26.

Paine, Lynn Sharp. "Managing for Organization Integrity." *Harvard Business Review* (March/April 1994): 106–17. Rpt. in *Ethical Issues in Business: A Philosophical Approach*. Ed. Thomas Donaldson and Patricia H. Werhane. 6th ed. Englewood Cliffs, NJ: Prentice Hall, 1999. 526–38.

Shapiro, Lila. "What's at Stake in the Massive Walmart Anti-Discrimination Case Before the Supreme Court." *Huffington Post* 29 Mar. 2011. http://www.huffingtonpost.com/2011/03/29/walmart-supreme-court-antidiscrimination_n_841919.html

Shaw, William. H. *Business Ethics*. 2nd ed. Belmont, CA: Wadsworth, 1996.

Singh, Jang B. "Ethics Programs in Canada's Largest Corporations." *Business and Society Review* 111:2 (2006): 119–36.

Stohl, Cynthia, Michael Stohl, and Lucy Popova. "A New Generation of Corporate Codes of Ethics." *Journal of Business Ethics* 90 (2009): 607–22.

Treviño, Linda K., and Katherine A. Nelson. *Managing Business Ethics: Straight Talk about How to Do It Right*. New York: John Wiley & Sons, 1995.

Wilkins, A.L. "The Culture Audit: A Tool for Understanding Organizations." *Organizational Dynamics* (Autumn 1983): 24–38.

Willis, Alan. "International Sustainability Reporting Guidelines Released for Comment." *Management Ethics* (April 1999): 3–4.

Permissions Acknowledgements

Clark, Leigh A., and Sherry J. Roberts. "Employer's Use of Social Networking Sites: A Socially Irresponsible Practice," from *Journal of Business Ethics* 95, 2010: 507–25. Copyright © Springer 2010. Reprinted with the permission of Springer.

CoopZone. "The Co-operative Advantage," as seen at http://www.coopzone.coop/about-co-operatives/the-co-operative-advantage/?. Reprinted with the permission of CoopZone.

Dimock, Susan, and Christopher Tucker. "Affirmative Action and Employment Equity in Canada," copyright © 1999 by Susan Dimock and Christopher Tucker. Reprinted with the permission of Susan Dimock and Christopher Tucker.

Duska, Ronald. "Whistleblowing and Employee Loyalty," copyright © 1983 by Ronald Duska. Reprinted with the permission of Ronald Duska.

Gage, Andrew, and Michael Byers. "Why Climate Litigation Could Soon Go Global," from *The Globe and Mail*, October 9, 2014. Reprinted with the permission Andrew Gage and Michael Byers.

Gardiner, Steve M. "Ethics and Climate Change: An Introduction," from *WIREs Climate Change* 1, Jan/Feb 2010: 54–66. Reprinted with the permission of John Wiley & Sons via Copyright Clearance Center, Inc.

PERMISSIONS ACKNOWLEDGEMENTS

Grant, Colin. "Whistle Blowers: Saints of Secular Culture," from *Journal of Business Ethics* 39 (4) 2002: 391–99. Republished with permission of Springer-Verlag Dordrecht via Copyright Clearance Center, Inc.

Grimes, Sara M. "Online Multiplayer Games: A Virtual Space for Intellectual Property Debates?" from *New Media & Society* 8, December 2006: 969–90. Copyright © 2006 by Sage Publications. Reprinted with the permission of Sage Publications, Ltd., via Copyright Clearance Center, Inc.

Guiltinan, J. "Creative Destruction and Destructive Creations: Environmental Ethics and Planned Obsolescence," from *Journal of Business Ethics* 89, 2009: 19–28. Copyright © Springer 2008. Reprinted with the permission of Springer.

Hurley, Jeremiah. "Ethics, Economics, and Public Financing of Health Care," from *Journal of Medical Ethics* 27 (4), August 2001: 234–39. Reprinted with the permission of BMJ Publishing Group Ltd., via Copyright Clearance Center.

Jacobsen, Rockney. "Economic Efficiency and the Quality of Life," from *Journal of Business Ethics* 10 (3) March 1991: 201–09. Copyright © 1991 by Kluwer Academic Publishers. Reprinted with the permission of Springer.

Jamieson, Dale, and Tom Regan. "On the Ethics of the Use of Animals in Science," from *And Justice for All: New Introductory Essays in Ethics and Public Policy*, edited by Tom Regan and Donald Van De Veer. Rowman and Littlefield, 1982. Republished with permission of Rowman and Littlefield via Copyright Clearance Center, Inc.

Klein, Naomi. Excerpts from *This Changes Everything: Capitalism vs. The Climate*, copyright © 2014 by Naomi Klein. Reprinted in the United States with the permission of Simon & Schuster, Inc. All rights reserved. Reprinted in Canada with the permission of Alfred A. Knopf Canada, a division of Penguin Random House Canada Ltd.

Livesey, Bruce. Excerpt from "Gildan Workers in Haiti, Honduras Complain of Harassment, Pay Too Meagre to Live On," from *The Globe and Mail*, November 27, 2014. Reprinted with the permission of Bruce Livesey.

MacDonald, Chris, and Bryn Williams-Jones. "Ethics and Genetics: Susceptibility Testing in the Workplace," from *Journal of Business Ethics* 35, 2002: 235–41. Copyright © 2002 Kluwer Academic Publishers. Reprinted with the permission of Springer.

Maguire, Stephen. "The Discourse of Control," from *Journal of Business Ethics* 19 (3), March 1999: 109–14. Copyright © 1999 by Kluwer Academic Publishers. Reprinted with the permission of Springer.

PERMISSIONS ACKNOWLEDGEMENTS

McMurtry, J.J. "Ethical Value-Added: Fair Trade and the Case of Café Femenino," from *Journal of Business Ethics* 86, 2009: 27–49. Copyright © Springer 2008. Reprinted with the permission of Springer.

MEC. Excerpts from "Our Roots," as seen at the MEC website: https://www.mec.ca/en/explore/our-roots/. Reprinted with the permission of MEC.

Palmer, D.E. "Pop-Ups, Cookies, and Spam: Toward a Deeper Analysis of the Ethical Significance of Internet Marketing," from *Journal of Business Ethics* 58, 2005: 271–80. Copyright © Springer 2005. Reprinted with the permission of Springer.

Palmer, John. Letter to the Editor, *University of Western Ontario Gazette*, March 13, 1992, and invited response. Copyright © 1992 by John Palmer. Reprinted with the permission of John Palmer.

Parker, Martin, and Gordon Pearson. "Capitalism and Its Regulation: A Dialogue on Business and Ethics," from *Journal of Business Ethics* 60, 2005: 91–101. Copyright © Springer 2005. Reprinted with the permission of Springer.

Pava, Moses L. "Why Corporations Should Not Abandon Social Responsibility," from *Journal of Business Ethics* 83, 2008: 805–12. Copyright © Springer 2008. Reprinted with the permission of Springer.

Peacock, Kent A. "The Economics of Extinction," from *Living With the Earth: An Introduction to Environmental Philosophy*, First Edition. Copyright © 1996 Nelson Education Ltd. Reproduced with permission. www.cengage.com/permissions.

Phillips, Michael J. "The Inconclusive Ethical Case Against Manipulative Advertising," from *Business and Professional Ethics Journal* 13 (4), Winter 1994: 31-64. Copyright © 1994 by Michael J. Phillips. Reprinted with the permission of the Philosophy Documentation Center.

Reitz, H. Joseph, James A. Wall, Jr., and Mary Sue Love. Figure 1 from "Ethics in Negotiation: Oil and Water or Good Lubrication?" in *Business Horizons* 41 (3), May/June 1998: 5–15. Copyright © 1998 by Indiana University Kelley School of Business. Reprinted with the permission of Elsevier, via Copyright Clearance Center, Inc.

Resnik, David. "Trans Fat Bans and Human Freedom," from *The American Journal of Bioethics* 10 (3) 2010: 27–32. Reprinted with the permission of Taylor & Francis Ltd., http://www.tandfonline.com.

PERMISSIONS ACKNOWLEDGEMENTS

Simpson, James R. "Ethics and Multinational Corporations vis-à-vis Developing Nations," from *Journal of Business Ethics* 1, 1982: 227–37. Copyright © 1982 by D. Reidel Publishing Co., Dordrecht, Holland and Boston, USA. Reprinted with the permission of Springer.

Singh, Jang B., and V.C. Lakhan. "Business Ethics and the International Trade in Hazardous Wastes," from *Journal of Business Ethics* 8 (11), November 1989: 889–99. Copyright © 1989 Kluwer Academic Publishers. Reprinted with the permission of Springer.

Spinello, Richard A. "Ethics, Pricing, and the Pharmaceutical Industry," from *Journal of Business Ethics* 11 (8), August 1992: 617–26. Copyright © 1992 Kluwer Academic Publishers. Reprinted with the permission of Springer.

Stewart, Wayne, and Peter Dickey. "Corporate Responsibility," from *Ethics and Climate Change: The Greenhouse Effect*, edited by Harold Coward and Thomas Hurka. Waterloo: Wilfrid Laurier University Press, 1993. Reprinted with the permission of Wilfrid Laurier University Press.

Tan, Eugene. Letter to the Editor, *University of Western Ontario Gazette*, March 19, 1992. Reprinted with the permission of Eugene Tan.

Wible, Andy. "It's All on Sale: Marketing Ethics and the Perpetually Fooled," from *Journal of Business Ethics* 99, 2011: 17–21. Copyright © Springer Science+Business Media B.V. 2012. Reprinted with the permission of Springer.

Yates, Charlotte A.B. "In Defense of the Right to Strike," from *University of New Brunswick Law Journal* 59, 2009: 128–37. Reprinted with the permission of Charlotte Yates.

The publisher has endeavoured to contact rights holders for all copyrighted material, and would appreciate receiving any information as to errors or omissions.

From the Publisher

A name never says it all, but the word "Broadview" expresses a good deal of the philosophy behind our company. We are open to a broad range of academic approaches and political viewpoints. We pay attention to the broad impact book publishing and book printing has in the wider world; we began using recycled stock more than a decade ago, and for some years now we have used 100% recycled paper for most titles. Our publishing program is internationally oriented and broad-ranging. Our individual titles often appeal to a broad readership too; many are of interest as much to general readers as to academics and students.

Founded in 1985, Broadview remains a fully independent company owned by its shareholders—not an imprint or subsidiary of a larger multinational.

For the most accurate information on our books (including information on pricing, editions, and formats) please visit our website at www.broadviewpress.com. Our print books and ebooks are also available for sale on our site.

On the Broadview website we also offer several goods that are not books—among them the Broadview coffee mug, the Broadview beer stein (inscribed with a line from Geoffrey Chaucer's *Canterbury Tales*), the Broadview fridge magnets (your choice of philosophical or literary), and a range of T-shirts (made from combinations of hemp, bamboo, and/or high-quality pima cotton, with no child labor, sweatshop labor, or environmental degradation involved in their manufacture).

All these goods are available through the "merchandise" section of the Broadview website. When you buy Broadview goods you can support other goods too.

broadview press
www.broadviewpress.com

The interior of this book is printed on 100% recycled paper